The Complete Guide to Hedge Funds and
Hedge Fund Strategies

Global Financial Markets

Global Financial Markets is a series of practical guides to the latest financial market tools, techniques and strategies. Written for practitioners across a range of disciplines it provides comprehensive but practical coverage of key topics in finance covering strategy, markets, financial products, tools and techniques and their implementation. This series will appeal to a broad readership, from new entrants to experienced practitioners across the financial services industry, including areas such as institutional investment, financial derivatives, investment strategy, private banking, risk management, corporate finance and M&A, financial accounting and governance, and many more.

Titles include:

Daniel Capocci
THE COMPLETE GUIDE TO HEDGE FUNDS AND HEDGE FUND STRATEGIES

Guy Fraser-Sampson
INTELLIGENT INVESTING
A Guide to the Practical and Behavioural Aspects of Investment Strategy

Michael Hünseler
CREDIT PORTFOLIO MANAGEMENT
A Practitioner's Guide to the Active Management of Credit Risks

Gianluca Oricchio
PRIVATE COMPANY VALUATION
How Credit Risk Reshaped Equity Markets and Corporate Finance Valuation Tools

Michael C. S. Wong and Wilson F. C. Chan (*editors*)
INVESTING IN ASIAN OFFSHORE CURRENCY MARKETS
The Shift from Dollars to Renminbi

Global Financial Markets series
Series Standing Order ISBN: 978–1137–32734–5

You can receive future titles in this series as they are published by placing a standing order. Please contact your bookseller or, in case of difficulty, write to us at the address below with your name and address, the title of the series and the ISBN quoted above.

Customer Services Department, Macmillan Distribution Ltd, Houndmills, Basingstoke, Hampshire RG21 6XS, England

The Complete Guide to Hedge Funds and Hedge Fund Strategies

Daniel Capocci

First published 2013 by
PALGRAVE MACMILLAN

Palgrave Macmillan in the UK is an imprint of Macmillan Publishers Limited,
registered in England, company number 785998, of Houndmills, Basingstoke,
Hampshire RG21 6XS.

Palgrave Macmillan in the US is a division of St Martin's Press LLC,
175 Fifth Avenue, New York, NY 10010.

Palgrave Macmillan is the global academic imprint of the above companies
and has companies and representatives throughout the world.

Palgrave® and Macmillan® are registered trademarks in the United States,
the United Kingdom, Europe and other countries

ISBN: 978–1–137–26443–5

This book is printed on paper suitable for recycling and made from fully
managed and sustained forest sources. Logging, pulping and manufacturing
processes are expected to conform to the environmental regulations of the
country of origin.

A catalogue record for this book is available from the British Library.

A catalog record for this book is available from the Library of Congress.

To my son Mateo

Contents

List of Figures

List of Tables

Foreword

Since the middle of the 20th century, wealthy individuals have invested their capital alongside talented traders in opaque, lightly regulated investment vehicles designed to safeguard investor anonymity and to allow capital accumulation in relative privacy, in contrast to publicly available regulated vehicles such as mutual funds. These exclusive, opaque investment vehicles, managed by eclectic investment professionals, have come to be referred to as hedge funds.

Since the turn of the century, anecdotal evidence has revealed a steady increase in the allocations of institutional investors in hedge funds. Institutional investors, in contrast to private investors, prefer transparency, emphasize corporate governance, and demand regulatory compliance from their third-party managers. In addition, they generally prefer moderate risk-adjusted returns, and stress persistency rather than periodic out-sized returns and their attendant volatility. This is a significant change in the clientele of the hedge fund industry – a change that affects both the return and risk profile of hedge funds as well as hedge fund managers' business models.

Despite these changes and the 2008 financial crisis, the hedge fund industry has flourished, accumulating substantial amounts of capital from these diverse investors. What is it about hedge funds that attracts investors and continues to do so consistently over decades? Daniel Capocci's book gives us important clues to answering this question. It provides valuable insights into hedge fund strategies and a framework for assessing hedge fund products.

Chapter 1 offers some illuminating vignettes of a number of legendary hedge fund managers, beginning with Alfred Winslow Jones's fund in 1949. The brief history of these hedge fund legends hints at how successful hedge fund managers not only have to navigate through dynamic, and at times stormy, investment environments, but must also evolve their business models to adapt to changing investor demands and regulations. Daniel's balanced approach, illustrating difficult concepts by way of well-chosen examples and statistical evidence, sets the framework for an effective, comprehensive description of complex hedge fund investment strategies in the subsequent chapters.

The second and fourth chapters of the book take the investors' perspective and ask the questions: How have hedge funds performed? And what should I be wary of? Anecdotal evidence suggests that institutional investors prefer large, well-capitalized hedge fund firms. For investors considering investing in a hedge fund, Daniel provides a helpful check-list of risks they should be aware of – risk factors cover both strategy risk as well as operational risk.

Chapter 3 tackles the core subject of this book: How do hedge fund managers make their money? Or, What is inside their investment tool-box? If coming up with a definition for hedge funds is difficult, describing hedge fund managers' investment strategies in a succinct fashion without undue reference to quantitative models is, to say the least, even more challenging. Here Daniel artfully applies the same balanced approach of insightful examples interlaced with empirical data on how different strat-egy performs, taking the reader on an insightful tour into the type of investment opportunities that attract hedge fund managers, how portfo-lio positions are crafted, and how the investments are managed over time. Through the first decade of the 21st century there has been a continuing trend for the industry's assets to be concentrated in the hands of a few mega large hedge fund firms. Hedge fund managers are the quintessence of active management, and are certainly no strangers to applying lever-age to enhance their bets. This rising trend of risk capital being concen-trated in the hands of a small number of leveraged speculators operating in opaque and lightly-regulated investment vehicles inevitably catches the attention of, and at times creates discomfort for, the regulators. In Chapter 5, Daniel takes the reader through some of that decade's stress-ful events in global capital markets. The chapter examines how hedge funds performed during crisis conditions and their market impact. The last chapter rounds off the text with a discussion on the issues relating to hedge fund regulations.

Overall, this is an excellent 'go to' text for answers to many key ques-tions on the hedge fund industry – answers that are presented with a fine balance between rigorous analysis and intuitive, practical examples.

William Fung, Visiting Research Professor of Finance,
London Business School, and
Vice chairman, CFA Research Foundation

Acknowledgements

I would like to express my gratitude to my wife Renata Vitórica for her constant support, and to Peter Baker from Palgrave Macmillan for his trust in me.

I would like to thank Jean Bensadoun (York Asset Management Limited), Martin Blum (Ithuba Capital), Andrew Bonita (Bonita Capital Management), David Capocci (Deloitte Luxembourg), Guilherme Carvalho (York Asset Management Limited), Gabriel Catherin (KBL European Private Bankers), Deborah Ceo, Gregory Gregoriou, Maria Dermes (Borsa Italia), Scott Eser (Hedge Fund Research), Fredrik Huhtamäki (Estlander & Partners), Guillaume Jamet (Lyxor Asset Management), Jamie Handwerker (CRM, Llc), Todd Harman (Hedge Fund Research), Marc Mediratta, John Paulson (Paulson), Andrej Rojek (Lydian Asset Management), Joshua Rosenberg (Hedge Fund Research), Bruno Sanglé-Ferrière (Carrousel Capital), Michael Schueller (HVB Alternatives), Patrick Vander Eecken (Pure Capital), Nick Walker (York Asset Management Limited), Diego Wauters (Coriolis Asset Management), and Mark Swickle (Professional Traders Management).

Preface

When I published the first edition of my French book on hedge funds in 2004, I started it with the following sentence:

> Today, hedge funds are part of the investment universe of more and more investors, whether they are institutional or private. Not a single week goes by without this term being found in the financial press, either to introduce the concept, to present one or a few of their particularities, to define a strategy, to analyse the regulation in one or a few countries, to present a bankruptcy of a fund or to comment on the performance of the industry or a fund.

The situation has continued to evolve since 2004, and the industry has come of age, with its functioning rules, its events, leaders, successes and failures. The strong equity markets of the 2003–2007 period and the increased level of sophistication of financial products available have enabled the industry to continue its development, and new strategies to emerge or consolidate. The liquidity crisis that affected the entire financial system including hedge funds slowed the industry's growth, but 2009 performance numbers indicate that the situation has stabilized and that the best managers have been able to reposition themselves and come back to the previous highs in less than a year. At the outset, the interest in these funds – almost unknown until the 1990s – comes from the impressive track record of the funds of Soros, Steinhart or Robertson during the 1970s or the 1980s that were reported in financial publications such as *Fortune* or *The Wall Street Journal*. From that point onwards, more and more potential investors started to show an interest in hedge funds. But then the failure of Long-Term Capital Management in 1998 damaged the reputation of the whole industry. Since then, hedge funds have often been reported in the press because of a particular positioning (for example the short subprime position taken by some funds), a fraud (such as Madoff) or liquidity or leverage issues.

There were several reasons for the media secrecy that for a long time shrouded this type of fund. The first was that the hedge fund industry was small compared to other types of investment products, and it was only at the start of the 1990s that the number of hedge funds increased significantly. Second, hedge funds historically took a private form in order to profit from maximum freedom in their management, and that private structure precluded any kind of advertising.[1] Finally, in most jurisdictions there were constraints not only regarding the kind of investors that could invest in the fund but also regarding minimum investments.

More recently, hedge funds have gained much interest because, after a few years of sustained strong performance, the world market faced an almost unlimited fall between April 2000 and December 2002. From that time, many investors looked for new investment opportunities and, in parallel, the academic and financial press started to be more and more interested in hedge funds that globally performed correctly over this difficult period. This phase included an important educational element. Unlike mutual funds, the performance of hedge funds should be measured by definition in absolute terms and not relative to an index. The original aim of the industry was to offer positive returns despite the evolution of the market as a whole. At that time, several academic studies maintained that hedge funds were able to offer returns superior to those offered by classical markets, thanks mainly to their ability to protect the portfolio during financial crisis. This explains why the industry profited from a rapid growth phase over that period of uncertainty and over the years that followed.

Hedge funds as an industry performed strongly until 2007 when the subprime crisis happened. This was an issue for a few funds, but the vast majority were not exposed – and several actually profited from it. The issues started in 2008. The equity strategies were the first to be hit, on the performance side early in the year, as equity markets became volatile. Then the markets became tighter when Bear Stern went bankrupt. Liquidity disappeared from the market once Lehman Brothers failed in September. The liquidity squeeze and the ban on short selling of financials were enough to directly hurt the industry in September but even more in October; this was when the bad press on hedge funds reached its peak. Most funds investing in less liquid strategies had to gate (that is, suspend redemptions) and so investors remained stuck in funds or funds of funds without any possibility of exiting for some time. All in all, the cost was considerable – but the industry came out much stronger, and the majority of the funds that survived this difficult period recovered within a year or two. In parallel, the industry continued its development through onshore vehicles like UCITS funds or private regulated European onshore funds. The largest players became stronger, and they continue to attract assets while the hedge funds consisting of two guys in a room have vanished. The industry has matured; numbers have been correct since then and growth is back to positive terms.

The academic world started to look at hedge funds in 1997; the first important studies on the subject were published at that time. The pioneers were William Fung and David Hsieh (1997) with their paper called 'Empirical Characteristics of Dynamic Trading Strategies: The Case of Hedge Funds' and Brown, Goetzmann and Ibbotson (1997) with the paper titled 'Offshore Hedge Funds: Survival and Performance 1989–1995'. The first authors found that the strategies applied by hedge funds are fundamentally different from those applied by mutual funds. The second team concluded that the majority of hedge fund managers are unable to outperform classical indices. Today, the literature on the subject is important, and several academic journals now specialize in alternative investments; these include the *Journal of Alternative Investments* and the *Quarterly Hedge Fund Journal*. The majority of the studies have been possible thanks to the creation of private hedge fund databases; these were started early in the 1990s with the primary objective of providing information to potential investors.

This book aims to cover hedge funds and the hedge fund industry in detail. I will start the process from scratch by answering the question 'What is a hedge fund?' In Chapter 1, I approach the subject with a broad scope. Chapter 2 goes into more detail by focusing on the characteristics of hedge funds; this chapter discusses the tools required to understand the particularities that can appear in the hedge fund world. Chapter 3, the heart of the book, presents every hedge fund strategy and illustrates each of them, first with many figures and tables to convert words into visual concepts, and, then more importantly, with one or more practical examples. Chapter 4 focuses on the performance of hedge funds over time. I report a series of statistics, and cover various time periods to give you a good sense of how the industry functions as a whole and also how strategies tend to perform over time. Chapter 5 covers hedge funds in difficult times. We start with the failure and bailout of Long-Term Capital Management in 1998, before analysing the role and potential impact of hedge funds on the financial markets during the financial crises of the last 20 years. Finally, Chapter 6 has two main objectives. First, the regulation of hedge funds and its evolution. This aspect is of particular importance because regulation is what enables the industry to continue its growth. Second, the differences between hedge funds and mutual funds; these differences cover not only legal niceties but, more importantly, structure and many other points. All in all, the many aspects of the hedge fund world are covered. Once you reach the last page of this book, I trust that your knowledge of this industry will have broadened significantly.

1
What Is a Hedge Fund?

This chapter aims to define hedge funds in a broad sense, listing and defining elements common to all such funds that explain why these investment products are grouped within what is called the hedge fund industry. The first section of this chapter gives a general definition of hedge funds. The second section describes the birth of the industry and its development over the years. The third focuses on the geographical development of hedge funds, and the fourth presents the big names of the industry. We end this chapter with a description of the future perspective of the industry, and we present a theory on its state of maturity.

1 General definition of hedge funds

In the financial semantic field, the verb "to hedge" means to cover or spread risks. In contrast to what we might think, not all hedge funds have the objective of neutralizing one or several sources of risk; today this term includes a variety of funds that use non-traditional management strategies. There is no legal definition of these funds, but practically every author or specialist has a definition that ranges from the general to the very precise. So, many definitions of hedge funds exist; we report on a few of these below.

According to the Alternative Investment Management Association (AIMA), hedge funds are difficult to define. The association does nevertheless include a definition in its glossary:

> There is no standard international/legal definition though they may have all or some of the following characteristics: May use some form of short asset exposure; may use derivatives and/or more diverse risks or complex underlying products are involved; may use some form of leverage, measured by gross exposure of underlying assets exceeding the amount of capital in the fund; Funds charge a fee based on the

performance of the fund relative to an absolute return benchmark as well as a management fee; investors are typically permitted to redeem their interest only periodically, e.g. quarterly or semi-annually; often, the manager is a significant investor alongside other fund investors.

The Hedge Fund Association (HFA), an international not-for-profit industry trade and non-partisan lobbying organization devoted to advancing transparency, development and trust in alternative investments, gives the following definition on its website:[1]

> Hedge funds refer to funds that can use one or more alternative investment strategies, including hedging against market downturns, investing in asset classes such as currencies or distressed securities, and utilizing return-enhancing tools such as leverage, derivatives, and arbitrage. At a time when world stock markets appear to have reached excessive valuations and may be due for further correction, hedge funds provide a viable alternative to investors seeking capital appreciation as well as capital preservation in bear markets. The vast majority of hedge funds make consistency of return, rather than magnitude, their primary goal.

Hedge Fund Research, Inc. (HFR), a hedge fund database provider specializing in alternative investments, states:[2]

> [A] structure that usually takes a limited partnership or an offshore legal form. This structure is paid by a performance fee that is based on the fund profits. Exemptions exist and include a limit in the number of participants that should all be accredited or institutional. All hedge funds are not the same; managers are usually specialized in one of the investment strategies that are applied using a hedge fund structure.

Investopedia.com provides the following definition:[3]

> An aggressively managed portfolio of investments that uses advanced investment strategies such as leveraged, long, short and derivative positions in both domestic and international markets with the goal of generating high returns (either in an absolute sense or over a specified market benchmark). Legally, hedge funds are most often set up as private investment partnerships that are open to a limited number of investors and require a very large initial minimum investment. Investments in hedge funds are illiquid as they often require investors keep their money in the fund for at least one year.

The Securities and Exchange Commission recently defined hedge funds as:[4]

Any private fund (other than a securitized asset fund):

(a) with respect to which one or more investment advisers (or related persons of investment advisers) may be paid a performance fee or allocation calculated by taking into account unrealized gains (other than a fee or allocation the calculation of which may take into account unrealized gains solely for the purpose of reducing such fee or allocation to reflect net unrealized losses);

(b) that may borrow an amount in excess of one-half of its net asset value (including any committed capital) or may have gross notional exposure in excess of twice its net asset value (including any committed capital); or

(c) that may sell securities or other assets short or enter into similar transactions (other than for the purpose of hedging currency exposure or managing duration).

On the basis of the definitions given above and many others, and arising from my own experience, please see below a general definition of hedge funds that is in accordance with the industry:

A Hedge Fund is an investment limited partnership (private) that uses a broad range of instruments like short selling, derivatives, leverage or arbitrage on different markets. Generally, the managers of the fund invest some of their own money in the fund and are paid by performance-related commissions. These funds require high minimum investments and their access is limited. These funds apply particularly to individual investors or to institutions with high financial resources.

This definition specifies many characteristics from the hedge fund industry, although not all of these will always be present at the level of individual funds. This definition does not give any information on the investment strategy applied by the investment team. This is in line with what we can find for mutual funds. The term "investment fund" does not give the investor information about what the fund is doing and/or if it is invested in shares, bonds or in derivatives. It does not confirm whether or not the fund has a geographical focus. But as we will see in the section relative to the origin of the industry, the situation was very different at the dawn of the industry. Every term in this definition has its importance; we will briefly cover these one by one, then explore each of them individually in detail later.

Hedge funds generally take the legal form of a private investment vehicle. Historically, the private structure arose from the fact that in the United States hedge fund managers had to comply with certain specific rules in order to limit the number of constraints on their management. Such constraints include, for example, restrictions regarding advertising or access being limited to high net worth individuals or professional investors. Such limitations tend to be standard even if some hedge fund strategies have been made available in a regulated onshore UCITS format in Europe. This means that the private structure is no longer an exclusive rule by which to define hedge funds, at least in Europe; however, in the US hedge funds are still proposed as private investments.

Hedge funds tend to invest in classic financial instruments such as equities and bonds, but their investment range is not always restricted to such securities. The use of more sophisticated instruments, including derivatives such as options (including exotic ones), futures, swaps, credit default swaps (CDS), warrants or convertible bonds, are common. Typically, they also use original and more complex investment techniques such as short selling[5] or arbitrage. Depending on the investment strategy and their investment styles, managers may also tend to take the opportunity of using leverage.[6] This part of the definition illustrates the level of freedom that managers tend to retain; the scope here is very broad, as some managers may only invest in equities by combining long and short positions in a market-neutral portfolio, while others will consider a wide range of different asset classes, including stocks, bonds and derivatives, and short-sell equities, take short positions in credit through CDS and combine naked, long, short, and some arbitrage or relative value positions.

Another characteristic of the definition is that hedge fund managers are paid mainly through performance-related fees, and that they invest a – usually significant – part of their personal cash holdings in their fund. This has been the case historically, and has become standard. Investors see that as an alignment of interest; when managers have their own money invested alongside that of investors, they are more involved and incentivized to deliver. The risk is that managers that have not co-invested with their clients could focus more on the management fee and on raising the asset rather than on delivering. While originally hedge funds involved only a 20 per cent performance-related commission, today management fees are also imposed, ranging between one and two per cent.

The last part of the definition stresses that hedge funds have been created for high net worth individuals and institutional investors. This arises from the fact that in most countries investments in individual hedge funds are limited to high net worth individuals, complying with strict rules. This constraint comes from the rules governing public funds that can be sold to any customer, but are restricted regarding the investment securities used, and cannot have sophisticated investment techniques applied to them. This rule protects the smaller investors; richer investors are likely to be more sophisticated, or they can pay for advice if needed; they can also afford a greater level of risk in their investments. Investment in hedge funds via funds of hedge funds is, however, usually allowed thanks to the diversification of individual fund risks.

At the outset, those general characteristics were the only constraints defining hedge funds. As the industry grew, however, and as managers tended to start applying comparable investment techniques and offering a similar profile, funds became grouped by investment strategy.[7] The world of hedge funds is highly diversified in terms of strategies, and the differences between (and sometimes within) the strategies are usually important. Hedge fund investment strategies are defined by the instruments used and on the basis of the markets on which the corresponding funds are active. The funds' risk profile will be very variable, based on the markets in which the strategy is implemented, the level of leverage allowed, the concentration and the instruments used. The range of strategies available has broadened over the last two to three decades, and certain strategies have had their moments of glory: in the 1980s and 1990s, macro funds aroused most interest not only from investors but also from the press; during the bear market of 2000 to 2002, long/short equity funds attracted attention; and between 2005 and 2008 event driven funds gained attention from numerous investors.

The main concept to bear in mind from this introductory definition of hedge funds is freedom. Hedge fund managers create private structures in order to apply original investment strategies with the greatest level of freedom possible.

The term "offshore hedge funds" is often seen in the literature. While we will present these structures in more detail in the last chapter we will briefly mention here that they were originally created to enable American tax-exempt investors such as pension funds to invest in hedge funds without having to pay American taxes. They also enable European, Asian and other non-US hedge fund investors to invest in offshore versions of American hedge funds without being taxed.

2 Hedge funds over time

Hedge funds have existed for more than 60 years. It is not easy to determine who first created a fund structure that later became the first hedge fund, but the literature usually attributes this to Alfred Winslow Jones, and we accord with this here. In the first part of this section we describe the origin of hedge funds accompanied by the reasons for their inception. In the second part of the section we study the evolution of hedge funds from their origin until today. Finally, we present the breakdown of the industry by investment strategy.

2.1   The origin of hedge funds

The first hedge fund was created in the United States in 1949 by an Australian sociologist and journalist called Alfred Winslow Jones. Born in 1901, he graduated from Harvard in 1923 before getting a PhD in sociology from the University of Columbia. He worked for *Fortune* magazine until 1946, then worked independently. He wrote papers on a number of non-financial subjects, then in 1949 discovered finance while working on a paper on financial market techniques. He became passionate about the subject, and in 1949 he created A.W. Jones & Co with four friends and US$100,000 in assets (including US$40,000 of his own funds).

The innovation in Jones' fund was the combination for the first time of three existing tools: a private company (under a general partnership structure converted into a limited partnership in 1952), short selling and leverage. Jones used the structure of a private company for his fund in order to profit from as much freedom as possible in the construction of his portfolio. The brilliance of Alfred Winslow Jones was his understanding that he could establish a fund that fitted into the 3(c)1 and 3(c)7 exemptions of the Investment Company Act of 1940. Such a fund would not have to register with the Securities and Exchange Commission. Section 3(c)1 was designed for family offices originally and permits the exclusion of investment companies from standard registration requirements if they have fewer than 100 US investors. Section 3(c)7 permits companies to avoid registration if all US investors are considered to be either "accredited investors" or "qualified purchasers." The idea was to combine long and short positions in order to maximize returns and reduce the level of market risk of the portfolio. The three basic principles in Jones' fund were:

1. Always use leverage
2. Always sell short
3. Give 20 per cent of the profits to the manager.

These principles are still some of the most important in the industry today. According to Jones, there were two main sources of risks in the case of an investment in shares: the risk arising from the choice of individual securities, and the market risk. His objective, by having a portfolio of short positions, was to protect the portfolio against a fall in the market. He used leverage in order to maximize returns and to increase the impact of security selection. In this case, once the market risk was covered the manager's sole task was to pick the good securities, buying undervalued securities and selling overvalued ones, in order to make profits regardless of the market direction.

In reality, managers were taking a net long position when they were anticipating an increase in prices (buying more securities than selling) and a net short position (selling more securities than buying) when they were cautious and anticipating a fall in prices. Jones never managed his own fund. Although he had originated the concept, he never selected any stocks; instead, he developed the business, hired managers, attracted capital and ran the business side.

According to some authors the concept of performance-related fees was invented by Benjamin Graham, the father of securities analysis; Jones had met him at the University of Columbia during his studies.

The term "hedge fund" appeared for the first time in a 1966 article in *Fortune*[8] by Carol J. Loomis. In this article, Loomis compared the net performance of Jones' fund with the best-performing mutual funds – the Fidelity Trend Fund and the Dreyfus Fund – over five and ten years; the concept developed by Jones outperformed these funds by 44 per cent and 87 per cent respectively. In this article, Loomis used the wording "hedged fund" because it was a good way to illustrate the investment strategy implemented by Jones. Hedge funds were practically created by this article.

A second paper by Loomis on the subject[9] described the strategy of the fund in more detail. This second paper is still considered as one of the main papers on the subject, and a pillar of the industry. In 1970 a hedge fund was defined as a limited partnership structured in such a way as to enable the general partner to share the profits made using his money alongside external investors' money. At the outset, hedge funds always used leverage, and also short stocks. The profit distribution method was defined in the structure of the fees; in the case of Jones, the manager received 20 per cent of the profits and this performance fee was his only source of revenue. This was a clear incentive to offer strong returns. Jones' fund never charged management fees; he wanted managers to be fully committed to focusing on returns.

At the outset, Jones' objective was not to create a complex product but he hoped that this risk-reduction strategy would be understood and then applied by a large number of investors. He expected such a strategy to become standard over time. The problems were firstly that the financial press did not cover the topic for long time – and secondly that when hedge funds started to be more widely covered this was almost exclusively negatively. There are numerous examples of papers covering the Quantum or Tiger funds in the 1990s and more recently Harbinger or Paulson.

Jones started his fund with US$100,000, and for the first 20 years of its existence, the strategy performed without a hitch. The fund continued to perform well in both rising and falling markets; but then, like many other funds, it faced its first losses at the end of the 1960s and early 1970s when markets fell drastically. This showed that the strategy is not infallible. According to the *New York Times* the fund had gained almost 1000 per cent during the 10 years preceding 1968. The fund had around US$200 million in assets at that time. The situation became more complicated later, and following a more turbulent period over the next few years the Securities and Exchange Commission estimated that the fund had only US$30 million under management a few years later. The company had lost around US$170 million as a result of market losses and unhappy investors redeeming their investment. The fund, however, survived and became a fund of hedge funds in 1984. Jones retired from the management of the company and died in 1989.

It is important to stress that even if the definition of hedge fund as conceived by Jones has broadened over time, the main characteristics defined at the origin of the fund are still applied today. Hedge funds are defined by their private structure, but now also by the markets on which they operate as well as by the products in which they invest. The definition has expanded because other funds started to apply the same strategies in other sectors such as convertible bonds or mergers and acquisitions. In addition, a high number of funds started to use derivatives when they were created. The investment community also called them "hedge funds" even when the strategies applied became more and more complex and were no longer limited to the three original principles of private company, leverage and performance-related commissions. Nowadays, numerous different strategies are grouped under the term "hedge funds."

The first fund of hedge funds was created in 1969, after the rapid development of the industry in the 1960s. It is called *Leveraged Capital Holdings* and is still in operation today.

2.2   The growth of the industry from 1949 until today

The success of the first hedge fund reported in the article of Carol J. Loomis in 1966 led to an increase in the number of funds in the 1960s. A study by the Securities and Exchange Commission identified 140 funds managing around US$2 billion at the end of 1968;[10] the majority of these funds had been created that year. The rapid growth in the number of funds took place in a growing equity market. This led many managers to consider the short book as expensive. In addition, shorting was time consuming, and it was sometimes difficult to implement. Furthermore, in up markets short positions represent a cost. A large number of funds started to increase the use of leverage to amplify their long book while keeping the same short positions or even reducing them.

The successive falls in the markets of 1969 and 1970, however, seriously weakened this new industry. Another study by the Securities and Exchange Commission, in 1971, indicated that the assets invested in the industry fell by almost half and that aggregated assets were around US$1 billion. Caldwell (1995) indicated that the 28 largest hedge funds of the study of the Securities and Exchange Commission of 1969 lost 70 per cent of their assets, between market losses and investors' redemptions. Five of the funds closed down. He stressed that funds with the smallest asset base suffered less than their larger counterparts. Then the market fall of 1973–74 led to a second contraction in the industry. This period of difficulty for the industry can probably be put in parallel with 2007–08 period when hedge funds tend to increased their long bias before facing very difficult market conditions.

In the decade that followed 1974, hedge funds continued to operate relatively discreetly until an increasing interest from the financial press put them under the spotlight again. In 1984, the industry was at rock bottom with only 68 hedge funds around.[11]

The second cycle of development of the industry started at the end of the 1980s. It was particularly focused on macro funds; the largest hedge funds in the world were applying this investment strategy. (Macro funds are different from more traditional hedge fund strategies because they do not aim to determine what shares or bonds they want to buy. Macro managers are global or international managers who use an opportunistic approach and focus on macroeconomic variables. They anticipate change in the global economic environment as reflected in stock prices, interest rates, currencies, inflation and/or fiscal politics, and take positions accordingly.) Macro funds represented the bulk of hedge fund money at that time. In 1990, around 70 per cent of the assets of the industry were invested in macro funds according to Hedge Fund Research, Inc. In the 1990 the main macro funds (for example Soros Quantum Fund or Robertson Jaguar fund) each managed several billions in assets under management. Since the end of the 1980s, the growth of the industry came however not only from macro funds. The percentage of macro funds as a part of the industry has diminished significantly since then, and currently (in early 2013) the strategy represents only a few per cent of the industry in number of funds.

Over the 1990s the number of hedge funds increased at a rapid pace. According to Van Hedge there were around 1000 funds in 1988. The total number of funds increased by a multiple of ten over 20 years before going down in 2008 and coming back to the same kind of level more recently. These numbers include funds of hedge funds investing in other hedge funds.

Figure 1.1 shows the evolution of the number of hedge funds and of the assets under management from 1988 until December 2012. Unlike with mutual funds, there are no official sources that count the number of hedge funds, so the number reported is an approximation based on an aggregation of various sources, including database providers, consultants and other participants. While this graph is based on estimation it should be close to reality.

We estimate that at the end of 2012 there were around 10,000 funds managing close to US$2 trillion in assets. These levels are close to those of 2007, just before the liquidity crisis. This leads to an average size of US$200 million per fund. But as a few huge players manage tens of billions of US dollars, the median size is actually much lower – probably around US$75–100 million.

Table 1.1 reports the average size of hedge funds on the basis of analysis of the largest ones. We estimate that there are approximately 10 funds with US$20 billion in assets on average, 30 funds with US10 billion, 60 funds with US$5 billion and around 100 funds with US$1 billion. These large funds represent 47 per cent of the industry in assets but only 2 per cent in the number of funds; the other 9800 funds share the remaining 53 per cent of the assets. This means that on average when we exclude the 200 biggest funds, hedge funds have around US$100 million in assets;

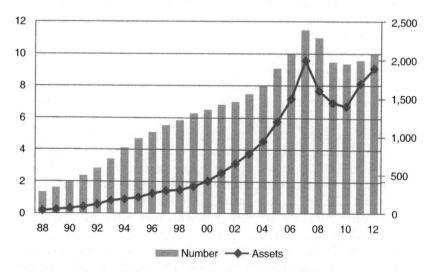

Figure 1.1 Evolution of the number of hedge funds and their assets under management (1988–2012)

Table 1.1 Breakdown of the hedge fund industry by assets under management

Assets (billions of US dollars)	Number of funds	Assets (billions of US dollars)	% of the industry
20	10	200	11
10	30	300	16
5	60	300	16
1	100	100	5
ND	200	900	47
Assets (millions of US dollars)	**Number of funds**	**Assets (billions of US dollars)**	**% of the industry**
102	9800	1000	53

Source: The author.

20 funds with US$50 million in assets are required to counterbalance a single fund with US$1 billion in assets.

The annual growth rate in number of funds has been strong, averaging 9 per cent per year between 1988 and 2009 and 4 per cent per year over the last 10 years. The growth in assets has been stronger, at 18.2 per cent over the whole period and 12.7 per cent over the last 10 years. The growth in assets has been directly linked to the performance of the industry; it peaked just before the liquidity crisis in 2007 at between 25 and 34 per cent. Since the start of the crisis in 2008 the number of funds decreased marginally, by 2.5 per cent, while the assets returned to the same level. Over the whole period covered, the number of funds increased by 630 per cent. Starting from a lower base, assets were multiplied 44 times. This rapid growth can be explained by several reasons:

- **New markets**: in many countries, direct investments into hedge funds have been limited to high net worth individuals. The exact definition of these investors, called accredited investors in the United States, depends on the country under consideration. The rapid development of funds of hedge funds in the mid-2000s, enabling retail investors to access the industry, sustained its growth. In addition, an increasing interest from institutional investors sustained the growth in assets after the liquidity crisis in 2008.
- **New structures**: hedge fund strategies are available not only through investment funds structure but also through structured products, closed-ended funds and capital-guaranteed products. More recently, the emergence of alternative UCITS since 2008 has also opened a new door for liquid hedge fund strategies. Finally the European AIFM Directive on Alternative Investment Fund Management coming into force in 2013 will probably support future development.

- **Investors**: today's investors are much better informed than they were 15 or 20 years ago, and they look to invest in products that match their needs. So hedge funds, thanks to their specific features, profiles and diversity, are being considered by an increasing number of investors.
- **Literature**: the literature on hedge funds has expanded significantly over the years; today not a week goes by without a paper on the industry in the financial press. The industry started to grow after articles by Loomis in 1966 and 1970. The second part of the development started in the 1990s, with papers on the exceptional performance of Julian Robertson's Tiger fund and Soros' Quantum fund. More recently, press coverage of Paulson and his range of funds that profited strongly from the subprime crisis continued to attract interest not only for this manager but for the industry as a whole.
- **Correlation aspects**: several academic and professional studies stressed the interest of hedge funds as a diversifier in a portfolio context. Not only can hedge funds offer attractive absolute returns over time, but also they do it with a limited correlation with traditional assets. While this was true for a long time and supported the industry growth, the 2008 liquidity crisis balanced this argument.[12]
- **Market volatility**: most hedge funds take balanced long and short positions, enabling them to limit the volatility of returns over time. This argument led more and more investors to allocate a part of their portfolio to hedge funds in order to manage the global volatility of their portfolio.
- **Relative performance**: several academic papers stress the ability of hedge funds to offer a better performance over the long run than their long only counterparts. This is particularly true in periods of higher volatility.[13]

2.3   Breakdown of the industry into investment strategies

Several features should be stressed regarding the breakdown of the industry into investment strategies. Firstly, the breakdown is different if we base the analysis on the number of funds or on the assets under management. Some strategies have been designed to manage large assets while others more rapidly face capacity issues. In addition, in certain strategies, such as macro, just a few large players manage the bulk of the assets, while in others, such as long/short equity, the number of players tends to be much higher.

Figure 1.2 shows the breakdown of the industry per investment strategy.[14] We start with the event driven type of strategies (event driven, distressed securities and risk arbitrage), then macro and Commodity Trading Advisers (CTA) followed by equity strategies (long/short equity, equity market neutral and assimilated and equity non-hedge). Equity strategies that may be balanced with bonds (emerging market and sector) follow, with fixed-income strategies and convertible arbitrage.

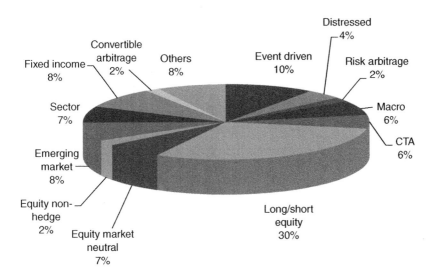

Figure 1.2   Breakdown of the hedge fund industry by investment strategy (based on the number of funds) as of 31 December 2012

The *long/short equity* strategy is the highest represented, probably because it is the easiest to implement and because a large number of hedge fund managers come from the long only world where they were managing long only portfolios. Event driven funds, equity market neutral funds and fixed-income specialists are also well represented.

Figure 1.3 shows the same information, but based on the assets under management. In this context the strategies with large players are over-represented. These are mainly event driven funds going from 10 per cent to 16 per cent on an asset base, distressed securities going from 4 per cent to 7 per cent, and macro funds going from 6 per cent to 10 per cent. On the other hand, long/short equity funds range from 30 per cent in number of funds to 20 per cent in assets, and emerging markets from 8 per cent in number to 6 per cent in assets.

Single funds do not always implement a single strategy. Some fund managers will adapt their strategy to market conditions and/or combine two or more strategies. In this case a perfect match is impossible and they will usually be classified in the strategy closest to theirs.

It is also worth mentioning that there are some niche strategies that are not represented in the breakdown of the industry per investment strategy. Such relatively rare strategies will usually be integrated within others that are more broadly defined, such as "event driven". Examples include Private Investments in Public Entities (PIPE) funds, asset-based lending funds, closed-end fund arbitrage, funds dealing in electricity trading, and funds investing in wine or other commodities, as well as funds invested in Master Limited Partnership (MLP). We illustrate this development in Figure 1.4,

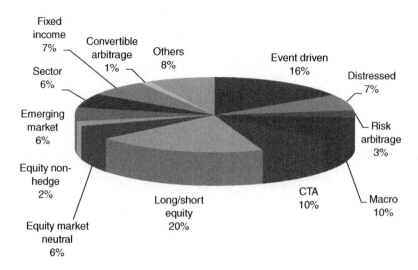

Figure 1.3 Breakdown of the hedge fund industry by investment strategy (based on assets under management) as of 31 December 2012

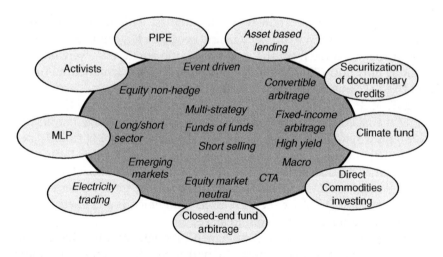

Figure 1.4 Broadening of the ranges of hedge fund strategies

showing the main classic hedge fund strategies in the centre circle and the emerging ones around it getting closer to the hedge fund industry.

3 Hedge funds around the world

There are today around 10,000 hedge funds in the world. There are funds in most countries, and new laws and regulations are continually being written somewhere in the world to enable or facilitate the establishment or the sale of hedge funds. Some countries have adapted their regulation to enable individual funds to be sold while others have allowed investment into hedge funds via funds of funds only.[15]

Table 1.2 shows in which countries hedge funds can be implemented or sold (sometimes under certain conditions). As regulation constantly evolves and as hedge funds were originally designed to be private, we may not cover all the countries where hedge funds can be bought. It is, however, clear that there certainly is a way to buy them in the countries listed. With the arrival of alternative UCITS, and if we integrate these into our analysis, the list of countries will grow even longer, as these structures

Table 1.2 Countries in which hedge funds can be created and/or sold

Hedge fund presence in the world					
Developed markets		Emerging markets		Offshore places	
NORTH AMERICA	Canada				
	United States	ASIA	China		Netherlands Antilles
	Germany		South Korea		Bahamas
	Austria		Hong Kong		
			Malaysia		
	Belgium		Thailand		Bermuda
	Spain				
	France				Curacao
	United Kingdom	EASTERN EUROPE	Russia		Guernsey
	Ireland		Poland		
	Italy		Czech Republic		
	Luxembourg				Isle of Man
EUROPE	Malta	AFRICA	South Africa	OFFSHORE	
	Monaco				Caymans Island
	Norway		Brazil		
	The Netherlands	SOUTH AMERICA	Argentina		Channel Island
	Switzerland		Colombia		
	Sweden				British West Indies
	Australia	MIDDLE EAST	Dubai		Turks et Caicos
ASIA PACIFIC	Japan				And so on
	Singapore				

enable the promoter to sell the fund not only across Europe but also out of Europe, including in Latin America and Asia.

Hedge funds are present in most countries of Europe and in North America. There are also hedge funds in the developed markets of Asia Pacific, such as Australia, Japan and Singapore, as well as in emerging Asia, with a relatively high number of funds based in Hong Kong. In Eastern Europe, Russia, Poland and the Czech Republic remain exceptions. Africa remains under-represented, as its capital markets are still undeveloped. South Africa is the only exception, having a legal framework for the creation of hedge funds; in 2004 there were already more than 50 hedge funds, with a few fund of funds managers with more than US$1 billion.[16] South America, led by Brazil, has experienced relatively rapid growth in the number of funds. In the Middle East, the recent and rapid development of Dubai and an attractive regulation and tax treatment has led to the arrival of hedge funds. Finally hedge funds can be created and sold offshore; we list the main offshore jurisdictions, but the list is non-exhaustive. As we will note later in the book, the Cayman Islands, the Bermuda and the Bahamas remain the preferred places to domicile hedge funds.

We emphasize that we have listed the countries in which funds can be sold or domiciled; this is different from areas where the funds are invested. These funds are usually invested in various parts of the world, but should not be domiciled in these regions. A fund can be invested exclusively in emerging markets while being domiciled in the United States, in Europe or in offshore jurisdictions.

Figure 1.5 shows the geographical breakdown of hedge funds around the world. Based on our estimations, around 42 per cent of the hedge funds are based in offshore jurisdictions. The United States follow, with 33 per cent of the industry. Europe follows with 13 per cent, followed by Asia Pacific at 9 per cent (where Japan and Australia remain predominant) and finally Latin America, Eastern Europe and a few funds in Africa. Offshore funds are usually managed by asset managers based in Europe and United States; such jurisdictions have certain advantages, the main one being tax-related. This is true not only for European investors but also for tax-exempt American pension funds.

Figure 1.6 shows the same information based on the breakdown of the assets under management. The concentration is more important in the main markets, namely the United States and offshore jurisdictions where funds exist for a longer period of time. The impact is even bigger for offshore funds that usually have a larger asset base than their American counterparts thanks to the investment of tax-exempt American institutional investors.[17]

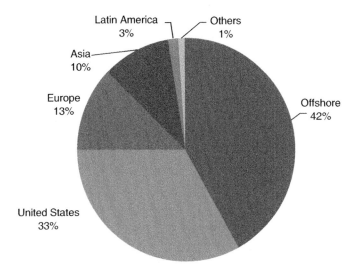

Figure 1.5 Geographical breakdown of hedge funds domicile based on the number of funds as of 31 December 2012

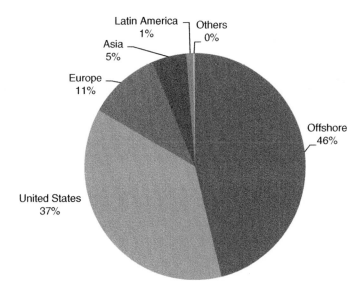

Figure 1.6 Geographical breakdown of hedge funds domicile based on the assets under management as of 31 December 2012

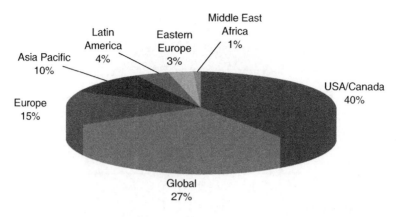

Figure 1.7   Geographical breakdown of hedge funds on the basis of their investment zone as of 31 December 2012

The first hedge fund was created in 1949 in the United States. When the industry started to grow, the partners usually created a US version of the fund for American investors and an offshore version for other potential investors. Until 15 years ago there were few funds domiciled outside the United States or offshore jurisdictions. The situation, however, evolved rapidly. The next sub-sections focus on the development of hedge funds in the United States then in Europe, Asia, Latin America and Eastern Europe.

Figure 1.7 shows the breakdown of the hedge fund industry by investment zone. North America, the most liquid market in the world, is the main market for hedge fund investments, with 40 per cent of the funds focused on that market. Global diversified funds follow, well ahead of European and Asia Pacific markets. Finally, Latin America, Eastern Europe and Africa and Middle East each represent less than 5 per cent.

For years, hedge fund management companies were almost exclusively based in recognized financial centres such as New York or London. Today the situation has evolved, and management companies can be found all around the world. The geographical breakdown of hedge fund management companies is given in Figure 1.8.

3.1   Hedge funds in the United States and Canada

Until the 1990s, when a few European and Asian-based hedge fund managers started their business, the hedge fund market was almost exclusively North American and offshore. Nowadays the American hedge fund market remains the main one, as around one third of the hedge funds are still

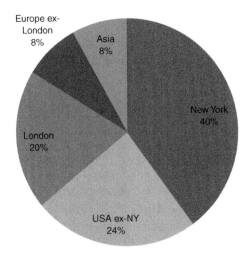

Figure 1.8   Geographical breakdown of hedge fund management companies
Source: The author based on Harcourt and the AIMA.

American. But this market is the most mature, and so the growth of this market has slowed.

3.1.1   American hedge fund development

The development of American hedge funds is to some extent contradictory. While a decent percentage of funds exist for several years many new funds are created every year; this growth is counterbalanced with a relatively high percentage of dissolutions. All in all, this leads to a limited growth in the American industry. The United States has been the main market for hedge funds for years, and investors are more demanding there than anywhere else. Hedge funds suffered outflows and redemptions in and post 2008, as shown in Figure 1.9.

The high attrition rate[18] of the industry has led to a size bias within it. Most funds have a small asset base; 40 per cent of American hedge funds have less than US$20 million in assets, and 50 per cent of the funds have less than US$50 million (see Figure 1.10). Such an amount is usually seen as the breakeven point, where all the costs of running a fund are covered. In all, 70 per cent of the American hedge funds have less than US$100 million in assets. Only 10 per cent of American hedge funds have more than US$500 million in assets and fewer than 5 per cent of them more than US$1 billion.

The average fund size has increased over the last decade. While in 2000 it was around US$50–100 million, it is currently US$150–200 million.

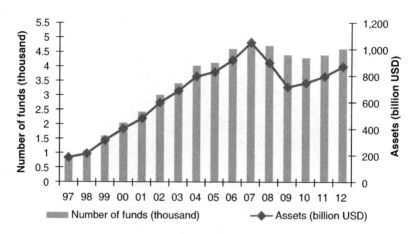

Figure 1.9   Development of American hedge funds
Source: Adapted from Capocci (2008).

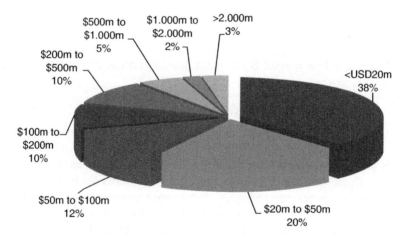

Figure 1.10   Breakdown of American hedge fund assets
Source: Adapted from Capocci (2008).

This trend is illustrated in Figure 1.11; it shows the evolution of number of funds by assets under management between 2002 and 2007.

3.1.2   American hedge fund investment strategy

One way to classify investment strategies[19] is to use three investment categories: directional funds, non-directional funds and balanced strategies. Directional strategies aim to profit from large market movements. Non-directional strategies, also called market-neutral strategies, include

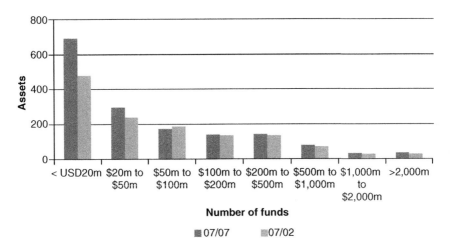

Figure 1.11 Number of funds by assets under management
Source: Adapted from Capocci (2008).

the strategies that have a low correlation to traditional markets such as bonds and equities; these strategies aim to neutralize, or at least to reduce, market risk by combining long and short positions. Balanced strategies may be either lightly directional or very actively managed and difficult to classify in either of the first two.

Figure 1.12 indicates that most American hedge funds apply directional strategies including long/short equity, macro, CTA and directional fixed-income strategies, against 17 per cent of purely non-directional strategies such as relative value or arbitrage. The rest is in balanced strategies, such as event driven or distressed securities. Figure 1.13 shows the breakdown per strategy on the basis of assets under management. Long/short equity is the most highly represented, followed by event driven, which has gained much interest over recent times. Distressed, fixed-income strategies and macro have around 20 per cent together, almost evenly split, and the remaining 40 per cent is divided between the other strategies. This figure confirms our statement that the industry has matured and that the macro funds that represented the bulk of the assets early in the 1990s have lost their pre-eminence. In addition, the convertible arbitrage fashion of the early 2000s has faded, and many convertible arbitrage players have adapted their strategy.

3.1.3 American hedge fund mandate

Any fund can invest in any open market, regardless of its domicile. There is however a trend in the fund industry; many managers base their team

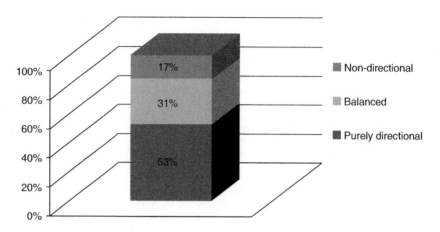

Figure 1.12 Breakdown of American hedge fund strategies by investment categories
Source: Adapted from Capocci (2008).

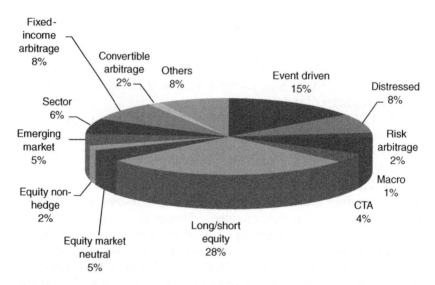

Figure 1.13 Breakdown of the American hedge fund industry by investment strategy
Source: Adapted from Capocci (2008).

in the geographical zone in which they invest. In terms of mandate, American hedge funds remain focused on their home market. Figure 1.14 shows that 45 per cent of the funds invest only in the United States and Canada. However, although the vast majority of these could invest

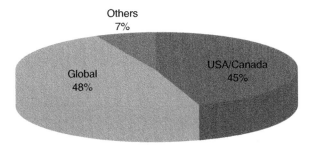

Figure 1.14   Breakdown of the investments of American hedge funds
Source: Adapted from Capocci (2008).

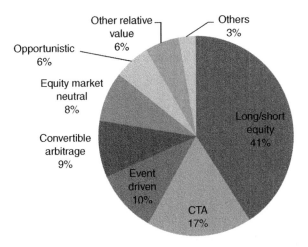

Figure 1.15   The breakdown of Canadian hedge funds by investment strategy
Source: AIMA Canada.

globally, only 7 per cent of the funds domiciled in the United States invest exclusively outside North America. This number has grown over time, but remains marginal.

3.1.4   Canada

In 1999 the Canadian hedge fund market was made up of less than 50 funds managing approximately US$2.5 billion in assets. By June 2004, the industry had more than US$20 billion in assets, and 190 funds including 55 per cent of individual funds. In 2009, there were 350 funds managing more than US$50 billion. As shown in Figure 1.15, the breakdown of the industry by investment strategy indicates the predominance of long/short equity funds followed by CTA, event driven funds, convertible arbitrage funds and equity market neutral funds.

3.2   Hedge funds in Europe

The European hedge fund market underwent rapid growth in the 2000s. This can be explained by several elements including regulatory changes and investor interest.

3.2.1   Development

The European hedge fund industry has faced the most rapid growth rate of the markets presented. Early in the 2000s, the difficult equity markets and the low bond yield environment led financial institutions to look closely at alternative investments, and more specifically at hedge funds. The development of the local European hedge fund market started from there. While 10 years ago European hedge funds were managing less than US$100 billion, by 2008 their assets had increased to more than US$250 billion in 2007. Today, European hedge funds manage close to US$ 200 billion.

3.2.2   European hedge fund development

The European hedge fund market has grown rapidly since the late 1990s. Figure 1.16 illustrates this; the growth rate of the industry both in number of funds and in assets grew rapidly until 2007. Then it suffered from the liquidity crisis before returning to positive growth.[20]

The European hedge fund market remains small in comparison to the American market, which is three times bigger. Its potential for growth is, however, real as many institutional investors have not looked at it and have not yet invested in it. One of the main issues with the European hedge fund market is that there are important differences in mentality from one country to another. While German banks have started to propose funds of hedge funds for some time, the market is more biased

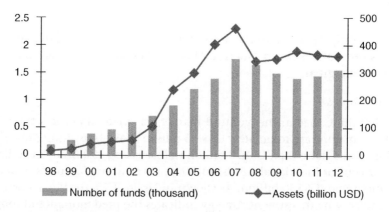

Figure 1.16   Development of European hedge funds
Source: Adapted from Capocci (2008).

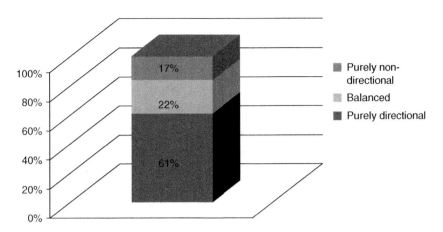

Figure 1.17 Breakdown of European hedge fund strategies by investment category

Source: Adapted from Capocci (2008).

towards guaranteed products. In France and Belgium, insurance wrappers are preferred. In most cases, advertising is limited. All in all, local features do not help the European hedge fund industry. This also explains why alternative UCITS are gaining a lot of interest, as they enable the promoter to sell funds throughout Europe.

3.2.3 European hedge fund investment strategies

The breakdown of European hedge funds in investment categories is similar to that reported for the United States. More than half of the managers implement directional strategies, against roughly one in five being purely non-directional and another one applying a balanced strategy (Figure 1.17).

The breakdown by strategy is reported in Figure 1.18. Approximately 33 per cent of the European hedge funds apply a long/short equity strategy. This is an improvement compared to a few years ago when two-thirds of the European managers were applying the same long/short equity strategy. On the other hand, the number of strategies available has increased, and even driven and fixed-income strategies became more important.

3.2.4 European hedge fund mandate

As in the United States, the majority of the funds retain their freedom to invest globally; only one fund in four focuses exclusively on Europe. The remaining 20 per cent are split between global emerging markets, North America, Emerging Asia and Eastern Europe and Japan. Figure 1.19 illustrates this.

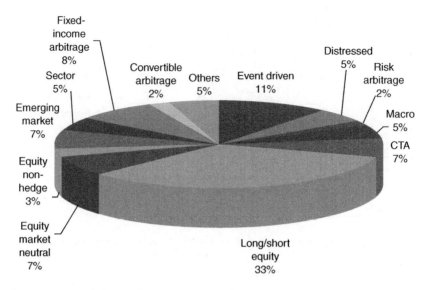

Figure 1.18   Breakdown of European hedge funds by investment strategy
Source: Adapted from Capocci (2008).

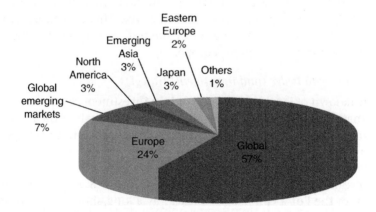

Figure 1.19   European hedge fund investment zone
Source: Adapted from Capocci (2008).

3.2.5   *European hedge fund localization*

As shown in Figure 1.20 London remains the preferred domicile for European hedge fund managers. Based on the assets under management, more than three out of four funds are located in London; and based on the number of funds around 65 per cent are located there.

Figure 1.21 reports the evolution of hedge funds and funds of hedge funds domiciled and administrated in Luxembourg. As at the end of June

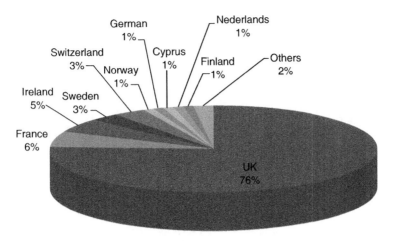

Figure 1.20 European hedge fund manager domicile
Source: Adapted from Capocci (2008).

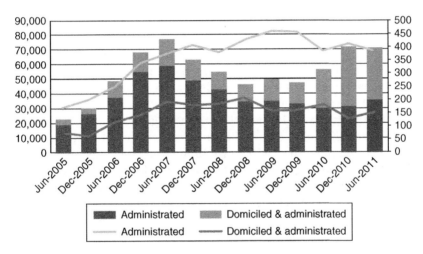

Figure 1.21 Evolution of the assets under management of hedge funds and funds of hedge funds domiciled and administrated in Luxembourg (based on the assets)
Source: Association Luxembourgeoise des Fonds d'Investissement (ALFI).

2011, there were more than €35.5 billion in assets under management in the 148 funds domiciled and administrated in Luxembourg and almost the same amount in addition in the 380 funds administrated only in Luxembourg. Regarding funds of hedge funds, there were €25.4 billion in the 731 funds both domiciled and administered there, and €46.7 billion in the 557 funds only administered there.

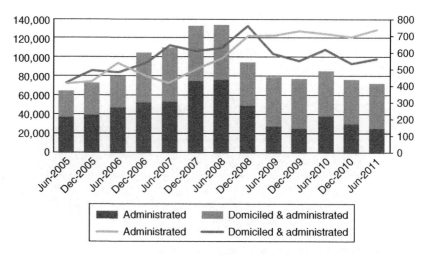

Figure 1.22 Evolution in the number of hedge fund and fund of hedge funds domiciled and administrated in Luxembourg (based on the number of funds)

Source: Association Luxembourgeoise des Fonds d'Investissement (ALFI).

Figure 1.22 shows the same information based on the number of funds. The numbers show only a slight increase in the number of funds of funds, but a stronger one for individual funds, mainly since the creation of the Specialized Investment Funds (SIF) structure.

Italy and Malta have also benefited from a significant increase in their local hedge fund market. The Malta Financial Service Authority indicated early 2013 that more than 400 hedge funds were domiciled in Malta. In Italy, 242 funds managing over €34 billion were identified early in 2008, according to MondoAlternative (previously known as MondoHedge).[21] Unfortunately, as of the end of March 2013, there were only 19 individual funds and 69 fund of funds remaining with respectively €965 million and 4.16 billion in assets according to the same source.

3.2.6 Characteristics of the industry

The European hedge fund industry is different from its American counterpart for various reasons. The first difference relates to the size of the funds; European hedge funds are smaller than American ones. In both markets, however, a significant proportion of the funds have less than US$25 million in assets under management. A smaller asset base may lead to several risks: firstly, the manager may not be able to diversify the portfolio efficiently. Secondly, transaction costs have a higher impact on performance. Thirdly, as the team is paid from the fees, it may become difficult for an investment management company to keep the best talents if they cannot pay them at the same level as competitors do. In addition, to gain interest from potential investors, managers will have to spend a significant part of their time marketing the fund at the start, giving them less time to focus on the management of the fund. Finally, for smaller funds there is usually a client concentration risk, just a few clients tending to represent the bulk of the assets.

The second main difference between the European hedge fund industry and its American counterpart is that European markets are less crowded than American ones, giving more opportunities to European managers. However, European markets are less liquid, and in Europe the transaction costs are higher and the range of liquid derivatives available is smaller.

3.2.7 Perspectives

The development and the depth of the European hedge fund market create new opportunities for investors. Investors can now have access to a range of investment strategies in Europe. The presence of new participants specialized in alternative strategies will bring liquidity and efficiency to local markets. This will contribute to the further development of local markets. As in any market, the difficult element for investors is to avoid the funds that will fail and those that will attract a lot of early interest and will rapidly close to new investments or lose their advantage.

3.3 Hedge funds in Asia

This section focuses on the Asian hedge fund industry. This part of the industry grew very rapidly during the bull market of 2005 to 2007, but then faced difficulties in the volatile times that followed.

3.3.1 The development of Asian hedge funds

The Asian hedge fund market is younger than the American and European ones. This can be explained by the facts that many Asian markets did not allow the implementation of short positions, and because these markets were not as developed as the European and American ones. The main and notable exception has been Japan. The limitations to implement hedging strategies led the industry to start with funds sold as hedge funds but that were practically long only equity funds with no or very limited hedges in place. Numbers have been strong in some cases but usually almost as volatile as the markets. The situation started to evolve after 1999 when Asian markets fell sharply; most funds that performed strongly in 1999 fell significantly the year after. The bulk of the funds were unable to outperform the indices and to offer uncorrelated returns.

The consequence of this situation is that the Asian hedge fund industry stayed on hold for several years. Then markets started to perform again and the industry evolved in two ways. On the one hand, long-biased hedge funds attracted interest in a portfolio diversification context. In addition, long-term investors were looking to play the development of Asia while investing with managers that could mitigate the downside risk. On the other hand, diversified funds emerged. Such funds invested in a combination of bonds, equities, convertibles and potentially derivative products. Such funds were the next step of development of the local industry. Globally, many funds started to implement a stricter risk management process as another form of development.

Asian hedge funds are paradoxical. On the one hand, many established funds were closed to new investors for years (at least until the crisis of 2008), while on the other side the vast majority offunds faced difficulties in raising assets. As liquidity is limited in Asia, managers tend to close their funds to new investments earlier than in Europe or North America. The growth of the Asian hedge fund market was strong over that period: the number of funds increased by 116 per cent over 10 years, while assets increased by 330 per cent. The 2008 crisis period has been particularly difficult and the number of funds fell, rapidly (Figure 1.23). In Asia, Hong Kong and Singapore are competing to develop a local industry, as are (at the time of writing) Ireland and Luxembourg in Europe.

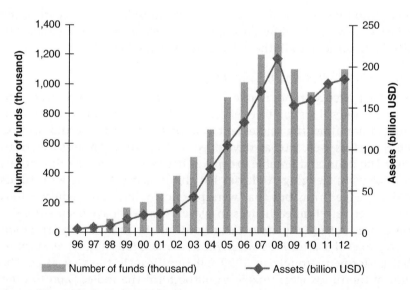

Figure 1.23   Asian hedge funds development
Source: Adapted from Capocci (2008).

We estimate that there are around 1100 Asian hedge funds managing around US$185 billion. Several factors explain the growth of the Asian hedge fund industry:[22]

- *Favourable regulations*: short selling is now permitted in most markets. In addition local regulations are favourable to the creation of local hedge funds in several markets.
- *Increased diversification in the strategies proposed*: while long/short funds represented the vast majority of the funds available for a long time, the offer broadened and this trend is continuing to increase with the development of local markets.
- *Fundamentally attractive local markets*: Asia is one of the fastest growing regions on earth. Many investors are attracted by these markets, but their high volatility can be scary. The hedge fund approach to investing is attractive to many investors as the aim is to profit from the growth while mitigating the risk during market turmoil.
- *Attractive long-term historical performance*: emerging markets largely outperformed developed markets over the last decade and the historical performance of the Asian hedge funds has been strong.

3.3.2 Asian hedge fund investment strategy

Figure 1.24 reports the breakdown of the Asian local industry by investment category. The figure shows that the breakdown of the industry is in line with the fundamentally attractive elements mentioned in the previous section. The vast majority of Asian hedge funds are purely directional or balanced; only 6 per cent of the funds apply purely non-directional

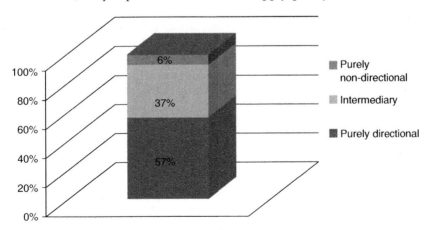

Figure 1.24   Breakdown of Asian hedge fund by investment category
Source: Adapted from Eurekahedge (2012).

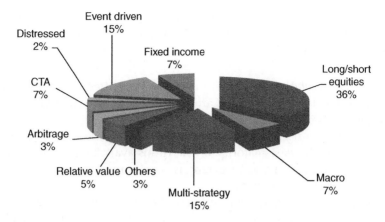

Figure 1.25   Asian hedge funds breakdown by investment strategy based on assets under management

Source: Eurekahedge (2012).

strategies. There has been somewhat of a move over the last few years from purely directional to balanced, but not much to purely non-directional.

As the industry matures, the number of strategies available increases. While long/short equity managers still represent 36 per cent of the Asian hedge fund industry, the range of strategies available has broadened.[23] Multi-strategy, event driven and fixed-income funds were the main beneficiaries of this development. In addition within the long/short equity offer, specialized strategies such as sector or country funds including China, Thailand and South Korea emerged (Figure 1.25).

3.3.3   Asian hedge fund mandate

The geographical breakdown of Asian hedge fund investments is more diversified than that of American and European hedge funds. Asia represents 60 per cent of the total, but it can be split by country and regional investments. Japan is the country where global funds remain predominant (Figure 1.26).

3.3.4   Asian hedge fund localization

The localization of Asian hedge fund managers is interesting. A relatively large portion of Asian hedge fund managers are based in the United Kingdom and the United States. However, those markets have recently been overtaken by Hong Kong, which represents 20 per cent of Asian hedge fund domiciles. Singapore now represents 15 per cent, and Australia is also relatively important, at around 10 per cent (Figure 1.27). The Japanese hedge fund market has lost some share, as only 5 per cent of the funds are based there, as against 20 per cent in 2004.

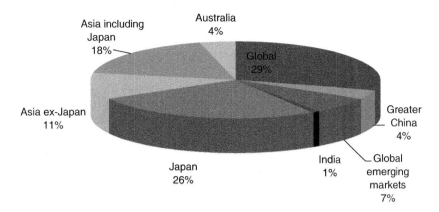

Figure 1.26 Asian hedge funds investment zone
Source: Capocci (2008).

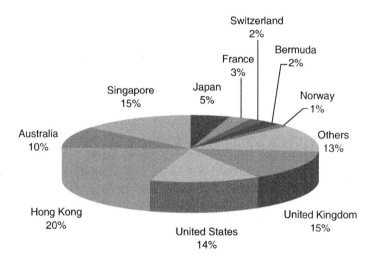

Figure 1.27 Asian hedge funds domicile
Source: Eurekahedge (2012).

3.3.5 Hedge funds in Australia: an exception

Australia can be seen as an exception in Asia, as the Australian market is not a developing market, unlike most countries in the region. According to numbers from AsiaHedge used by the Australian government[24], the country is the second largest Asian market in the Asia Pacific Region in terms of assets just over $33 billion just after Hong Kong with just over $38 billion in assets. The numbers are reported in Table 1.3.[25] As of the end of 2010, there were 85 Australian hedge fund investment managers.

Table 1.3   Breakdown of the Asia Pacific hedge fund industry

	Assets (US$ million)	Market share
Hong Kong	38.28	25.1%
Australia	33.16	21.8%
Japan	11.03	7.2%
Singapore	21.55	14.1%
China	3.8	2.5%
Other	4.39	2.9%
Sub-total	112.21	74%
United Kingdom	12.31	8.1%
United States	27.88	18.3%
Total	152.4	100%

Source: Australian Trade Commission (2011).

The top 10 manages more than 85 per cent of the assets managed out of Australia.

Australian funds of hedge funds represent approximately an additional A$ 14 billion and all in all, the Australian industry has over US$47 billion in assets.[26] The development of the industry on the continent over time was strong from 2000 until 2007. Then, it slowed down and catch back more recently, as indicated in Figure 1.28.

The breakdown of funds by investment strategy is reported in Table 1.4. It indicates that around 14 per cent of Australian hedge fund assets are focused on Australia and that 84 per cent of the assets of the industry is invested at least partially outside of Australia. The majority of Australian hedge funds are global equity players and close to 24 per cent of the assets are invested in Asia broadly define (regional and country funds investing in equity or fixed-income markets).

Investors in Australian hedge funds and fund of hedge funds can be categorised into retail and high net worth individuals, Australian institutional, and offshore institutional investors. The majority of investor funds have come from retail and high net worth individuals. The Australian Trade Commission (2011) estimates that retail and high net worth represents around 64 per cent of the assets invested in the industry followed by Australian institutional investors at 19 per cent and international institutional investors at 17 per cent.

3.4   Hedge fund development in Eastern Europe

Hedge funds have started investing in Eastern Europe since, roughly, the Russian crisis of 1998. Most of the positions taken since then have been almost exclusively long, and over the years their role has mainly been to

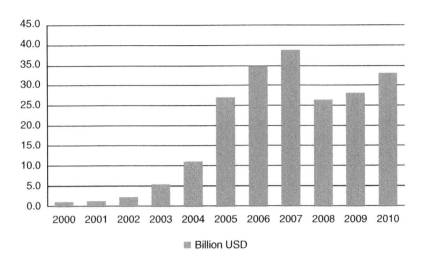

Figure 1.28 Australian hedge fund industry assets evolution
Source: Australian Trade Commission (2011).

Table 1.4 Australian hedge fund assets breakdown by investment strategy

	Assets under management ($ million)	Market share (%)
Global equity	13.552	40.9
Asian equity excluding Japan	4.610	13.9
Macro	2.699	8.1
Managed futures	2.261	6.8
Asian equity including Japan	1.209	3.6
Japanese equity	781	2.4
Global fixed income	725	2.2
Multi-strategy	622	1.9
Chinese equity	441	1.3
Asian market-neutral	419	1.3
Asian fixed income	407	1.2
Commodity	345	1.0
Currency	78	0.2
Total investment strategies in global markets	**28.149**	**84.9**
Australian equity	4.860	14.7
Event driven	120	0.4
Distressed securities	12	0.0
Specialist	5	0.0
Other	10	0.0
Total investment strategies in Australian markets	**5.007**	**15.1**

Source: Australian Trade Commission (2011).

give liquidity to the market. Since then things have evolved – but have evolved slowly.

3.4.1 Eastern European hedge fund localization

The Eastern European hedge fund industry is unique for various reasons:

- *Volatility*: Eastern European markets in general, and Russia in particular, have been very volatile historically.
- *Performance*: market performance was strong for a long time after the Russian crisis.
- *Natural resources*: Russia has attracted interest from many investors, as natural resources are a significant part of the Russian economy, and Russia is a large player in natural resources worldwide.
- *Political risk*: Eastern European political systems in general, and the Russian system in particular, have not always been stable, and there is a real political risk that may be more or less present at any specific moment in time.
- *European Union*: a number of Eastern European countries have joined the European Union over the last decade.
- *Growth*: growth has been strong in the region.

These elements suggest that Eastern European markets have specific characteristics that may be attractive to some investors and to some hedge fund managers. There are, broadly speaking, two kinds of funds available: first, long-biased long/short equity funds, which will be part of the same family of the long/short equity funds that can be found in other emerging markets. Secondly, there are funds that invest in less liquid and potentially smaller companies where the edge of the manager is more to pick the good companies in a market where management understanding and business relations are of particular importance. They also play an important role of liquidity provider. Whilst the second category of funds increased significantly between 2005 and 2007, it has decreased and almost disappeared during the 2008 liquidity crisis. Currently there are between 70 and 100 hedge funds invested in Eastern/Emerging Europe and Russia.[27] The most liquid markets in the region are Russia and Turkey. The vast majority of the funds have the ability to invest in several markets in the region, and in some cases they even consider the Middle East and/or Africa.

3.4.2 Eastern European hedge fund investment strategies

Four investment strategies have emerged over the years:

- *long/short equity* funds
- *event driven* funds

- *fixed-income/currency* funds
- *multi-strategy* funds

The long/short equity strategy is relatively young in Russia. Until recently funds were exclusively longs, and the absolute return objective was based exclusively on the manager's ability to manage volatility during market difficulties. More recently the increase in the number of companies that can be shortened enabled more managers to implement real long/short equity strategies even if they tended to have a long bias. In addition, the only stocks that can be shortened are those of very large companies. Another possibility is to hedge the portfolio by shortening indices. The event driven strategy emerged in parallel with the important changes that the region has faced since 1998 and that are still taking place now. Fixed-income/currency funds aim to take advantage of the local bond market and local currencies. Multi-strategy funds combine other strategies even if they tend to have some long/short equity exposure.

3.5 Hedge funds in Latin America

The Latin American hedge fund market is still in its infancy, but it has become a reality for a few years and the speed of its development leads us to spend some time on it and to present its development and its current profile.

3.5.1 Hedge fund development in Latin America

The first fund was created around the middle of the 1990s and the industry really started to grow from 1999 on. There are three main reasons for this:

- The lowering of hyperinflation and the stabilization of most local markets.
- The opportunities that emerged after the local crisis that the region faced in the 1990s (Mexican crisis of 1994 or Argentinian default of 2001 for example).
- The increase in quality and experience of local managers.

We estimate that the Latin American hedge fund market has around 330 funds managing around US\$60 billion. Note that the AIMA estimates that there are close to 500 individual funds managing approximately \$60 billion in assets as of the end of 2012. The majority of these funds focus on Brazil, by far the most important market on the continent. As a point of comparison, Brazil also represents around 80 per cent of the

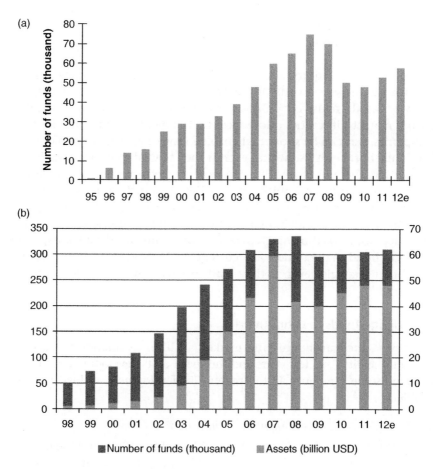

Figure 1.29   Latin American hedge fund industry development
Source: The author.

local mutual fund market. A few funds have focused on Argentina since the country's default in 2001. We show in Figure 1.29 the evolution of the number of funds and of their assets under management since 1998; assets fell significantly in 2008, but the number of funds fell only a little, as the number of closing funds approximately matched new fund launches.

The Latin American hedge fund industry underwent two phases during its development. The first was the creation of multi-strategy funds, which were proposed to local high net worth investors looking to limit the risk of loss during market turmoil. The second phase of development of this market arose from offshore funds that decided to enter the market after the crisis that the region faced in 2002. Such players were more oppor-tunistic, and were usually global players increasing their allocation to incorporate Latin America. Onshore Latin American funds tend to have a limited equity exposure that usually stays at around 35 per cent. Such positioning tends to be balanced, with a fixed-income book, whereas offshore funds are usually more heavily exposed to equities and are more opportunistic. Figure 1.30 reports the repartition of the domicile of offshore hedge funds investing in Latin America.

The split between onshore and offshore funds per geographical mandate is reported in Figures 1.31 and 1.32. The main difference between

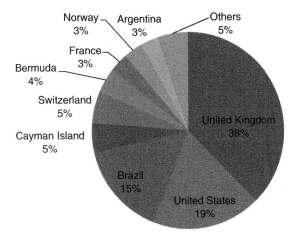

Figure 1.30 Domicile of the hedge fund managers investing in Latin America

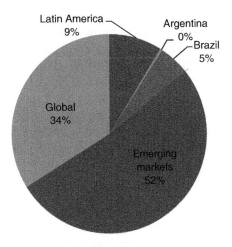

Figure 1.31 Breakdown of South American offshore hedge funds by geographical mandate

Source: Adapted from Capocci (2008).

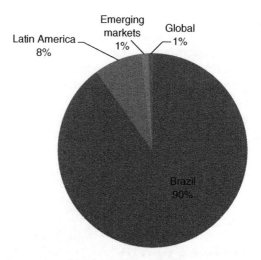

Figure 1.32   Breakdown of South American onshore hedge funds by geographical mandate

Source: Adapted from Capocci (2008).

offshore and onshore funds is that onshore funds tend to be focused on Brazil while offshore funds tend to have a broader mandate.

3.5.2   Latin American hedge fund investment strategies

The breakdown per investment strategy is different if we consider local/onshore funds or offshore funds sold to international investors. On the local market, multi-strategy funds represent half of the regional industry, followed by macro funds, long/short equity funds, fixed-income arbitrage funds and, to a lesser extent, relative value funds and distressed securities funds. On the offshore side, fixed-income funds, distressed securities funds and event driven funds represent a large portion of the offering. Note also that long/short equity funds have gained much interest recently. This can be easily explained by the strong rally that Latin American markets, and Brazil in particular, experienced from 2003 until 2007. Figure 1.33 and Figure 1.34 illustrate the breakdown per investment strategy.

3.6   Future perspective of the industry

Figure 1.35 shows the size of the hedge fund industry relative to other asset classes. The interest of Figure 1.35 is not so much in the figures in absolute terms but the relatively small size of hedge funds compared to the other asset classes. The numbers reported are based on several studies made in 2006 and 2007. Hedge funds remain marginal in comparison to

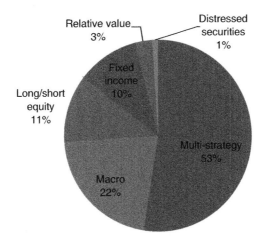

Figure 1.33 Breakdown of onshore Latin American hedge funds by strategy
Source: Adapted from Capocci (2008).

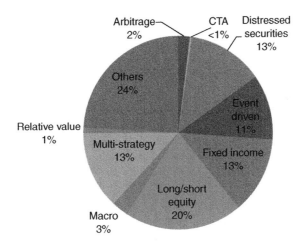

Figure 1.34 Breakdown of offshore Latin American hedge funds by strategy
Source: Adapted from Capocci (2008).

global assets, compared to global long only assets that include pension funds, mutual funds and insurance companies. Interestingly it is also smaller than these three categories considered individually.

I wrote a few years back that at its current state of development the hedge fund industry was comparable to the mutual fund industry a few years back, and that the growth of the mutual fund industry was a good indicator of the growth potential of the hedge fund industry. This was

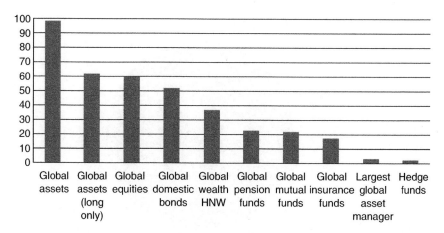

Figure 1.35   Estimation of the size of various asset classes (thousands of billions)
Sources: Alternative Investment Solutions, International Financial Services London based on Watson Wyatt, Merrill Lynch/Capgemini, BCG, World Federation of Exchanges, BIS.

correct at the time of writing, but things have changed. Firstly, hedge funds became more standard in the year 2000, and they became more and more important in investors' portfolios. The industry doubled in size over a few years. Then 2008 happened. The industry was directly hit by the liquidity crisis, and many investors lost confidence in it. Since then, institutional investors have continued to look at the industry and to invest in it, as their investment horizon is a long term one. The industry is back to life but the prospects are not at the same level as they were a few years back. Arguments in favour of the industry are the development of alternative UCITS funds that give hedge funds access to retail investors. Another helpful factor is the Alternative Fund Investment Management Directive that aims to regulate alternative funds including hedge funds and to bring them onshore into Europe. It is difficult to anticipate the evolution of an industry, but a deep analysis of the development of the American hedge fund industry and the current state of development of the other regional industries enabled us to build Figure 1.36 in 2008.

According to our theory, the evolution of the industry comprises four steps:

1. **Childhood**: the birth of financial markets leads to the emergence of investment opportunities in which the most dynamic managers will invest. In current markets, this phase lasts between three and seven years; at the start of the industry it was much longer.

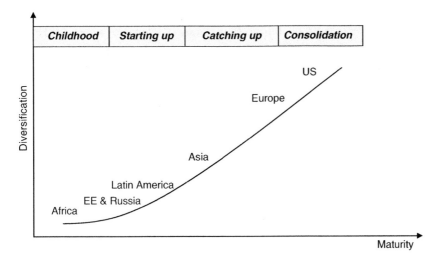

Figure 1.36 Hedge fund industry evolution
Source: Capocci (2008).

2. **Starting up**: this is a key phase in the development of an industry (or one of its components) because it shows the first signs of rapid future growth. It is no more a few managers trying to make money differently from usual in a specific market, but it is the start of a progression to the next level. Pioneers are still there, but only as a part of something bigger. The growth starts to be significant. This phase lasts between three and five years.
3. **Catching up**: this phase of rapid growth and adjustments is the heart of the growth of an industry. Over this period, the industry becomes significantly bigger. It is also at the end of this phase that the industry starts get diversified. This relatively rapid period lasts between five and seven years.
4. **Consolidation**: after growing rapidly and diversifying, and after catching up, a consolidation phase is entered, in which evolution is slower but still present. This phase lasts between five and ten years at least.

As shown in Figure 1.37, the US leads the evolution of the industry followed by the European industry and then emerging markets. Within emerging markets, Asia is the one that offers the largest opportunity set in terms of strategies, and the one where growth is the most important, whereas in Latin American and East European markets, the industry is still in its infancy.

It was difficult for us to foresee what the next step in the development of the industry would be, but various potential scenarios emerged (Figure 1.37):

1. **Rapid growth**: the consolidation phase might be followed by rapid growth. This phase can be seen as a second stage of growth; global attraction for investors in the industry might result in renewed growth at a relatively high rate.
2. **Persistent consolidation**: the consolidation phase may continue. In this case the industry is slowly continuing along the diversification route before going up at the end of the persistent consolidation phase.
3. **No interest**: interest from investors in the industry can decrease significantly. This would lead to a relatively important decrease in the diversification of the industry even if the strongest players were able to survive. This is what we saw, at a sub-industry level, with convertible arbitrage players in 2004 and 2005.

In 2008, we concluded that the most probable phase would probably be somewhere between phases one and two; we expected the industry to continue its development and to continue to consolidate. The 2008 crisis, however led us to mitigate this conclusion, and the reality turns out to probably be somewhere between persistent consolidation and no interest, as the difficulties encountered by most of the funds during the crisis led many investors to lose interest in the industry. We do, however,

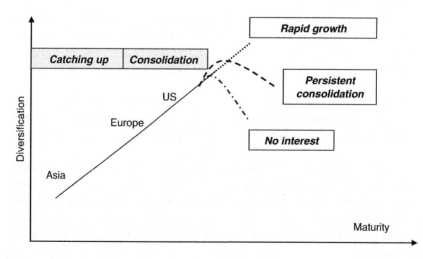

Figure 1.37   The future of the hedge fund industry
Source: Capocci (2008).

believe that once the acute phase of the crisis had passed, a consolidation phase appeared as larger, institutionalized funds became more and more interested, and acquired an increasing share of the assets of the industry. Everybody involved in the industry will agree that the industry is not currently at a start of a rapid growth phase; the situation will, however, continue to evolve.

4 A few big names from the hedge fund industry

While A.W. Jones is renowned as the founder of the industry, there have been a few hedge fund managers that have been key in its development. Most of them are famous and have interesting stories. In this section we briefly present a few of the big names of the hedge fund industry. We have started with the three kings of the industry, the stars of the 1980s and 1990s: George Soros, Michael Steinhardt and Julian Robertson. Then we have picked a few more recent well-known players.

4.1 George Soros

George Soros was born in 1930 in Budapest in Hungary. He has been called the biggest investor in the world. In 1968 he created a series of hedge funds, managed by Soros Fund Management, with US$4 million in assets, and over the years, his Quantum and Quota funds became the flagships of the company. Soros was the main shareholder and the manager of the funds. Assets under management increased relatively rapidly and reached US$100 million in 1979. In 1989, by which time the Quantum fund had no less than US$7 billion in assets, Stanley Druckenmiller became its new manager. The funds were managed using a macro strategy, investing opportunistically in bonds, equities, currencies and commodities. They offered an average return over 30 per cent over their existence, the manager's strengths being international vision and fabulous intuition. The famous move that made Soros front page news was the short position he took in 1992 against the British pound, pushing it out of the pre-defined bands against the other European currencies; Soros became known as "the man who broke the Bank of England". Early in 1998, Soros funds reached a total of US$28 billion. But then on 28 April 2000, Soros Fund Management announced in a letter to investors that the managers of the US$8 billion Quantum and Quota funds, Stanley Druckenmiller and Nicholas Roditi, had decided to retire from the management of their funds, having lost 22 per cent and 33 per cent respectively over the last 12 months. This was a significant change in the industry. Soros reorganized his offer, as shown in a section of the letter sent to the investors. It interestingly illustrates what happened:

We have come to realize that a large hedge fund like Quantum Fund is no longer the best way to manage money. Markets have become extremely unstable and historical measures of value at risk no longer apply. Quantum Fund is far too big and its activities too closely watched by the market to be able to operate successfully in this environment. ... We shall convert Quantum Fund into a lower risk/ lower reward operation. We shall engage in a variety of less volatile macro and arbitrage strategies, with a smaller portion of the assets devoted to stock picking on the long and short side. The allocation of funds between the various strategies may vary from time to time depending on market conditions and other considerations. To reflect the changed character of the fund, it will be renamed Quantum Endowment Fund.[28]

So the Quantum Fund was merged with the Quantum Emerging Growth Fund, and was renamed the Quantum Endowment Fund; investors were given the choice of either retaining their investment in the new entity, being paid back or having their assets transferred into another newly created specialized fund (set up specifically for the Quantum Fund investors).

Investors withdrew close to US$6 billion. It is worth pointing out that despite the losses over the original Quantum Fund's last year of existence, an investment of US$100,000 in it at the start of its 31.5 years would have netted the investor U$400 million by the end of the period, an average annual return of over 30 per cent.

4.2   Julian Robertson

Julian Robertson was born in 1933 in Salisbury, northern California, in the US. In 1980, after a long career at the well established securities firm Kidder he created Tiger Management Corporation with Thorpe McKenzie. They started with US$8.8 million in assets, and their underlying philosophy was to focus on individual stock selection to build a long/short equity portfolio. The assets grew rapidly and they broadened the range of the fund. By the time they decided to dissolve the company, at the end of March 2000, they were managing a total of six funds, including the famous Tiger Fund, Jaguar, Panther and Puma. Julian was very well known and highly respected in the industry. According to him, his investment strategy could be summarized as follows:

Find the best 200 companies in the world and invest in them, and find the 200 less attractive companies in the world and short them.

By applying this investment strategy, independently of market movement, the return was based purely on the capabilities of the fund manager to identify the best companies and to differentiate them from the weaker ones. Of the managers presented in this section Julian Robertson follows most closely the strategy implemented by Alfred W. Jones.

In order to select the companies, Robertson was helped by a team of 35 analysts and consultants. Their role was to find the best investment opportunities in their field by performing a very deep analysis and by getting a long-term target price for every single security. Once the decision was taken they became very dynamic and tended to take large positions. An investment was of interest when the fundamentals of the industry were favourable, when the management was stable and competent and when the security was cheap. The fee structure included a 1 per cent management fee and a 20 per cent performance fee with a high-water mark.[29]

The Tiger Fund, flagship of the Tiger Management Corporation, became a titan of the industry. It was one of the first to ask for a minimum investment of up to US$5 million per investor. Robertson's funds offered the most attractive returns of the industry in the 1980s and early in the 1990s; the compounded net return of the fund over its life was close to 32 per cent net. In 1997 the fund even offered 56 per cent net; by the end of the 1990s a US$100,000 investment with Robertson in 1980 would have become US$8 million. Over time the strategy of the long/short equity fund became more macro-oriented.

The performance of the fund became problematic in 1998, 1999 and early 2000. After being only slightly positive in 1998, it lost close to 20 per cent in 1999, and it was already slightly down for the year when its closure was announced in March 2000. The assets of the Tiger Fund dropped from US$22 billion in 1998 to close to US$6 billion in 2000. The two main reasons were performance and withdrawals by investors. At the end of March 2000, Robertson closed the six funds managed by Tiger Management Corporation and gave 80 per cent of the investments back to investors.

In his letter to his investors Robertson blamed the irrationality of the markets:

> As you have heard me say on many occasions, the key to Tiger's success over the years has been a steady commitment to buying the best stocks and shorting the worst. ... In a rational environment, this strategy functions well. But in an irrational market, where earnings and price considerations take a back seat to mouse clicks and momentum, such logic, as we have learned, does not count for much.[30]

4.3   Michael Steinhardt

Steinhardt is the youngest of the three kings of the industry. Born in 1941, he founded Steinhardt Partners, managing four funds at its peak. He created his first hedge fund in 1967 with two partners, Howard Berkowitz and Jerold Fine. His fund gained 139 per cent over its first 14 months of existence, and by 1970 it was the biggest American hedge fund, with over US$150 million in assets under management, according to the Securities and Exchange Commission. Their report, published over the first half of 1971, stated that this fund was the only one that had seen its assets grow over the period analysed; markets were difficult during that period and the industry suffered greatly. But the fund started to lose money in 1994 because of a losing bet on the European debt market; it lost around 24 per cent over that year. In 1995 Michael Steinhardt closed down his fund, then worth US$2.6 billion. He said:

> I realized large gains on the same positions in 1993. However the pain of 1994 was much more important that the pleasure of 1993.[31]

When the fund closure was announced, Stephanie Strom, journalist at the *New York Times*, wrote that a significant part of the losses had already been recovered;[32] a US$100,000 investment with Steinhardt in 1967 would have reached the value of US$46 million at fund closure in 1995, so the average annual return of the fund over its life was around 24 per cent.

4.4   John Paulson

John Paulson started his career at Boston Consulting Group before joining Odyssey Partners. He discovered the world of mergers and acquisitions when he worked at Bear Stern and Gruss Partners a few years later. He created his hedge fund in 1994 with US$2 million and one administrative assistant. John managed his merger arbitrage fund for a few years and it started to outperform its peers not only during up markets but also during more challenging years. Early in the 2000s, the company faced an important evolution; the first event driven fund was created. The underlying idea of this fund was not only to focus on mergers and acquisitions but to combine this strategy with other positions in companies that were facing important changes and/or events. The first fund was called Paulson Advantage, and a leveraged version called Paulson Advantage Plus was created a few months after. While performance was average for some time the situation changed in 2006 when Paulson and his team decided to allocate a part of their assets to protect the portfolio against the risk of default of subprime debt in some parts of the United States. The level of allocation depended on the profile of the fund, but every fund had some exposure. At that time they also created a new fund dedicated to this position, Paulson Credit Opportunities. In 2007 the whole range of funds offered a very attractive performance, that of the riskiest reaching 300 per cent. In 2008 the positioning was reviewed and the funds were moved to profit from difficulties in the financial sector. This enabled the range to continue to offer attractive returns in a very difficult market environment where most hedge funds lost money and when confidence was being lost in the industry as a whole. In 2009, the funds moved then to become long credit and distressed, and continued to offer good returns; assets under management peaked at around US$35 billion. More recently, they decided to go long on the equity market and to bet on the recovery of the financial sector. This, however, came at a cost to investors and in 2011 the funds lost – up to 40 per cent for the leveraged version.

4.5 Louis Bacon

Louis Bacon, who became known as one of the few traders who accurately foresaw the 1987 crash, is the founder of Moore Capital Management, LP, an asset management company founded in 1989. Bacon is a macro trader, taking global directional views on financial markets. He takes positions in equities, bonds, currencies and commodities. Louis Bacon has created his own way of applying the strategy. He launched his fund a few years later with US$100 million in assets under management, offering 31 per cent net, annualized between 1990 and 2005. His key strength was the management of the volatility of the returns. To put it into context, between 1995 and 1999 he offered between 23 per cent and 32 per cent while Soros' Quantum fund offered from −1.5 per cent to +39 per cent and Robertson's Jaguar fund offered from −18 per cent and +57 per cent over the same period. A few key positions in the life of the fund includes the anticipation of the fall of the Japanese market in 1990 or a short position of oil companies before Saddam Hussein invaded Kuwait. At the end of 1990, the fund had US$200 million in assets.

The Moore Global Fixed-Income Fund was launched in 1993. This fund was managed by a series of management teams. Until 2002, Bacon himself had been very much involved in the management of the fund but later it became a macro fund and the name was revised accordingly. Between 2002 through 2005, assets under management grew to US$4 billion. The fund has not had any down years and has compounded at 15 per cent annually through 2010, though despite decent performance during the liquidity crisis, the fund lost US$5 billion in assets. In 2009 the company launched two new funds: an emerging long/short equity fund and an emerging fixed-income and currency fund. In 2010, British regulators entered Moore Capital Management's London offices and arrested trader Julian Rifat for allegedly participating in illegal insider trading in concert with other traders. In April of that year, Moore Capital Management paid US$25 million to settle the charges brought against it by the Commodity Futures Trading Commission (CFTC) which accused the company of manipulating settlement prices for NYMEX platinum and palladium futures contracts. In September 2010, the firm had over US$4 billion in assets under management,and it is estimated that Louis Bacon has a personal fortune over US$2 billion.

4.6   Paul Tudor Jones II

Paul Tudor Jones II is the founder and president of Tudor Investment Corporation, a hedge fund based in Connecticut close to New York. He started his career early in the 1970s as a cotton trader with Eli Tullis, known to be one of the best cotton traders of all times. Paul differentiates himself from its peers by a real risk aversion. This is probably one of the reasons why he invested in futures, which can be traded rapidly in case of need.

Paul Tudor Jones created the Tudor Investment Corporation in 1983 with US$300,000; by 2006 he was managing more than US$6 billion and had close to 300 employees. His investment strategy is based on a very large set of information that will help him to anticipate buyer and seller behaviour. As he said, the importance lies not in whether you are considering pork bellies or Yahoo! but in understanding the tools available in order to decide whether or not to invest. Risk management is also fundamental in this process; according to Paul, 90 per cent of the quality of any good trader is risk management. His risk management techniques combine technical and fundamental analysis. One of the main trademarks of Paul Tudor Jones remains his anticipation of the 1987 crash; he predicted the fall based on an analysis of derivative products. According to him, this market would amplify any significant down pressure because many investors who were selling hedges would have to pay for the losses while realizing other positions, leading to more losses. He gained close to 200 per cent in 1987, and he did the same in Japan in 1990.

4.7   Bruce Kovner

Bruce Kovner is the son of a Russian immigrant. He studied in Harvard and did a lot of odd jobs before discovering the futures market in the

1970s. The story goes that Bruce borrowed US$3000 from somebody in exchange for his MasterCard; he then invested this money in soya futures, increasing it to a high of US$40,000 before it fell to US$23,000. This was how he discovered risk management and futures trading. He founded Caxton Corporation in New York in 1983. At the peak Caxton was managing more than US$11 billion in assets and had approximately 350 employees. In 2010 it was reported that since 1983 Caxton Associates had returned US$12.8 billion to clients whilst continuing to manage US$6 billion; it ranked second amongst managers who have returned more than they currently manage.[33] By the end of 2012, the company and its affiliates were managing approximately US$7.3 billion in assets.

Sometimes called Soros' twin, Bruce is a pure macro trader. He has been known since the early 1990s, having offered more than 80 per cent annualized to his customer in the 1980s. His investment strategy is based on risk management, with the underlying idea that you should not play in markets where you may lose heavily for reasons you don't understand. He also advocates listening to markets to ensure you do not go against them. He uses his interpretation of the evolution of politics in order to take positions in currencies, bonds and commodities.

4.8   Steve Cohen

Steve Cohen, founder of SAC Capital Advisors, started his career in option trading in 1978 having graduated at Wharton. The story says that on his first day at work he realized a US$8000 profit, and that he peaked at US$100,000 during the day. He created SAC Capital Advisors in 1992 with US$25 million, and the company currently manages around US$12 billion.

Called the Prince of Wall Street by the *New York Times* or the King of Hedge Funds by *The Wall Street Journal*, Steve is a pure trader. According to *BusinessWeek* he spends up to US$150 million per year in transaction costs. Assets are split into a number of portfolios (close to 40), each managed by a set of 10 to 15 traders. Rapidity is key in the investment process, which was developed by Steve, who trains his traders himself. He teaches them how to identify trends from various sources like capital flows, and to pay particular attention to cutting losses. According to Jack Schwager, author of *Stock Market Wizard*, a book that presents the best traders, his main strengths lie in being able to integrate a large set of elements, in rapidly determining which of these are essential, and in staying calm under any circumstances. Steve's success also comes from the pressure he puts on his employees; traders are paid on their personal performance, and any position in portfolio for longer than a few weeks will be cut by Steve. A position cut by Steve is a bad sign.

His story is pretty interesting. When he was a child, he was fanatical about numbers, closely following sports results in the *New York Post*. This was how he discovered the financial pages, full of numbers. He found those interesting, and became passionate about them when he understood that the numbers were in fact prices that changed every day.

Three illustrations can enlighten us on Steve's investment strategy.

1. **Inverse transaction**: Steve takes hidden positions in order to protect his portfolio from competitors that would like to follow his investment strategy. The idea is the following: it happens that a trader decides to sell a position that Steve might want to buy. As he discovered early on, the price of the security often falls when the trader is selling, so it then becomes even more interesting to buy; this is how a reversed position works. SAC buys a number of small positions in such a stock, that it then sells through various brokers. When the market identifies the sales, larger transactions often take place – and this is the point at which Steve decides to buy the security.
2. **Take the street**: SAC takes large block positions through a few important brokers; in order to retain a stock of the security, those brokers have to buy more of them, leading to a rebound in the price. SAC can then swiftly sell the securities at a small gain.
3. **Short squeeze**: when a lot of market players short a security, SAC sometimes buys it. This leads a lot of investors that have stop-loss systems to close down their positions, and SAC can then sell at a profit.

It is also worth mentioning that Steve and his traders do not hesitate to put pressure on well-known brokers' analysts to persuade them to share their views. *BusinessWeek* mentioned an analyst giving an example of getting more than 15 messages from SAC traders regarding one of his recommendations on a single day.

Finally every trader signs a very strict confidentiality and non-compete agreement. On the other hand, Steve Cohen is known for sharing more profits with his team than do others. To finish it is worth noting that SAC Capital Advisors has been the focus of a federal insider trading probe regarding two stocks that could have been improperly traded. A settlement has been found earlier in 2013. This settlement removes a major distraction that had prompted some investors to pull their money out of the hedge fund.

4.9   Alan Howard

Alan Howard founded Brevan Howard in 2002; today it is one of the most important European hedge funds. Before that, Alan was in charge of the derivative and interest rate team at Credit Suisse; the story goes that he left because of a decrease in his salary. The investment strategy applied by Brevan Howard is purely macro. He takes positions mainly in currencies and government bonds of developed countries. Each of his traders has a risk budget, which they use to invest and maximize gains; the traders making money then see their allocation increase while others lose part of the assets they manage. Every trader has a clear objective. The limits, capital allocation and the instruments that can be used are also set. Finally, they have liquidity constraints and stop-losses per trader as well as portfolio stop-losses.

As of the end of March 2013, Brevan Howard was managing US$40 billion, and had 348 employees split between Geneva, London, New York, Jersey, Hong Kong, Washington, Dublin and Tel Aviv.

4.10   Stephen Feinberg

Stephen Feinberg is the manager of Cerberus Capital, run by Cerberus Capital Management LP. Based in Manhattan, New York, the company has offices all around the world. Cerberus Capital is an investment fund that has existed since 1992, starting with approximately US$10 million under management. This fund has always been invested in distressed securities. The first objective has always been to make money directly but also to straighten out the companies; while the asset base was not sufficient at the start to become activist, the rapid growth in its assets enabled Stephen to start to do so. The fund had approximately US$8 billion in assets in 2003, and touched US$20 billion early in 2008.

The investment process is unique. It starts with the search of potentially interesting companies on the basis of fundamental research. Then Cerberus takes a first position in a friendly way before contacting the management and/or large shareholders to propose working with them in order to help the company grow. In this context, Cerberus Capital Management uses the service of a team of experts as a direct link with the companies. The idea is to find the good business and the right person to help these businesses expand. By the end of 2007 Cerberus Capital had taken interest in 28 companies, and owned more than a 15 per cent stake in 15 more. According to a *BusinessWeek* estimation, Cerberus Capital held important positions in companies representing total sales of close to US$30 billion and more than 100,000 employees. Well-known companies with which Cerberus has worked include the car manufacturer Chrysler, the car rental companies National and Alamo, Warner Hollywood Studios and the global electronics company Delphi.

5   Summary

In this first chapter we introduced the notion of hedge funds. We started by defining the term in a broad sense before proceeding to a historical and a geographical analysis of the industry. This enabled us to understand not only where the industry stands now, but how the industry may evolve. In this context, we presented a theory of the evolution of the hedge fund industry before anticipating its future development. In the last section we focused on the big names of the hedge fund industry, giving information on each of these star managers, thus providing an introduction to some investment strategies and illustrating the temporal and geographical evolution described earlier.

2
Hedge Fund Characteristics

In Chapter 1, we introduced the concept of hedge fund. We described their evolution over time and geographically before analysing their future development and the big names in the industry. In this second chapter, we focus on the characteristics of hedge funds – including investment strategies, fund structure, risks, investors and the fee structure – that will enable us to identify and individualize every single one of them. Then we describe specific asset management techniques such as short selling and leverage, before presenting some global statistics of the industry. We will devote a section to the link between hedge funds and other alternative products before presenting the strengths and weaknesses of hedge funds. We end this chapter with a comparison between hedge funds and managed accounts, the presentation of hedge fund replication and the introduction of the structures available to gain exposure to such strategies.

1 Database providers[1]

The definition of "hedge fund" given in the first chapter is general, providing no information on the investment strategies adopted by the fund managers. There is, indeed, no official definition of "hedge fund strategies"; the large number of strategies implemented has made it necessary to group funds on the basis of similarities in the strategies applied, in the tools used, in the markets covered or in the management processes. These strategies can use totally different tools in order to reach the same objective, or they can use the same tools but with completely different objectives.

As hedge funds are private vehicles, information relative to the investment strategy has to be collected on a case-by-case basis. This task is performed by database providers, in this case private companies that have usually existed for more than two decades. Each of these has its own characteristics, and they do not all classify funds in the same way. The

Table 2.1   Characteristic of the main hedge fund database providers

Company	Creation	Number of funds	Number of hedge fund indices*	Fund of funds strategies	Website
Morningstar CISDM	1979	5,000	14	2	www.cisdm.org
Hedge Fund Research	1992	6,800	39	4	www.hedgefund research.com
Dow Jones Credit Suisse	1994	8,000[a]	11	NA	www.hedgeindex. com
EurekaHedge	2000	7,000[b]	10	10	www.eurekahedge. com
Greenwich Alternative	1995	7,000	22	NA	www.greenwichai. com
eVestment[c]	1997	7000+[d]	29	4	www.evestment.com
BarclayHedge	1985	6000+[e]	19[f]	1	www.barclayhedge. com

*These estimations include strategy and aggregate indices only.
[a]Note that while the database has more than 8,000 funds, only 900 are included in the global index.
[b]The number of funds comes from a 2009 study.
[c]Previously known as hedgeFund.net
[d]This number includes over 5,000 individual hedge funds.
[e]This number includes hedge funds, funds of funds and managed futures.
[f]This number includes a category called "Others" that includes unclassified funds as well as seven sub-sector funds.
NA = not applicable

main database providers are shown in order in Table 2.1.[2] Let me present them briefly one by one.[3]

The Morningstar CISDM Database (formerly the MAR Database) is the oldest Hedge Fund and CTA database in the market. Tracking qualitative and quantitative information for more than 5000 hedge funds, funds of funds and CTAs since 1994. In addition to 5000+ surviving funds, the Morningstar CISDM Database also includes a graveyard database which contains qualitative and quantitative information for over 11,000 inactive hedge funds, funds of funds and CTAs. Hedge Fund Research, Inc. (HFR) was established in 1992. HFR specializes in the indexation and analysis of hedge funds. HFR database gathers information on more than 6,800 funds. It produces over 100 indices of hedge fund performance ranging from industry-aggregate levels down to specific, niche areas of sub-strategy and regional investment focus. With performance dating back to 1990, the HFRI Fund Weighted Composite Index is probably the industry's most widely used standard benchmark of hedge fund performance globally.

The Dow Jones Credit Suisse Hedge Fund Index (formerly known as the Credit Suisse/Tremont Hedge Fund Index) is based on a spread of more than 8,000 funds. It is an asset-weighted index, and its range encompasses only funds with a minimum of US$50 million in assets under management, a minimum one-year track record, and current audited financial statements. The index in all cases represents at least 85 per cent of the assets under management (AUM) in each category of the index's range, which currently contains more than 900 funds. The index is calculated and rebalanced monthly.

In addition to the three database providers recognized worldwide and active for more than 20 years, other players have entered the field more recently. Such databases include EurekaHedge, Greenwich Alternative, eVestment and BarclayHedge. We did not report the Morningstar MSCI classification because it is the most granular one and it cannot be easily compared to the others.[4]

1.1 The indices – classifications

There is a real need to classify funds, and to be able to compare funds with common characteristics in their investment strategies in terms of both performance and profile. It is not, however, always easy to classify hedge funds by investment strategy as each manager develops its own unique form of strategy. Nevertheless, it is possible to identify some characteristics in common.

Each main player in the industry defines a set of investment strategies in order to group funds and to give global trends, and also to create subsets to enable comparison, to help potential investors. Each database provider has its own classification. This means that some of them will define a dozen strategies while others will apply a much more precise break-up of the opportunity set.[5]

Our classification has its own specific features, but most strategies will be similar, or can be seen as a mix of those developed by the main database providers. We report the classification of the six main database providers in Table 2.2. To make the comparison as easy as possible we report the investment strategy category on the left (*event driven, long/short equity, sector* and so on). Next to that we list the investment strategies as defined by each database provider. When the database provider also defines categories (for example *event driven* by Dow Jones Credit Suisse) we report this category on the first line of the corresponding family in bold and we list the strategies included below it.

The objective of these classifications is to enable potential investors to find the funds that correspond to their needs and expectations, and to differentiate them. The number and definition of strategies are not fixed forever, and it is conceivable or even probable that the evolution of the markets and of financial products may lead to the evolution of certain strategies or to the creation of new strategies that will respond to a demand from the market.

1.1.1 Morningstar CISDM

The Morningstar CISDM Hedge Fund indices are median performance indices of strategies in the Morningstar CISDM Hedge Fund/CTA[6] Database. There are 16 hedge fund strategy indices, as well as a broad-based equal-weighted hedge fund index that reflects the performance of all hedge funds reporting to the database. The CTA indices represent a series of both asset-weighted and equal-weighted performance indices of commodity trading advisors in the database. There are 20 CTA indices.

The Morningstar CISDM Hedge Fund Database (formerly MAR) is the oldest CTA and hedge fund database in the market, and is the source of data for the Morningstar CISDM indices. The database began tracking CTAs in 1979 and hedge funds in 1992, and currently contains qualitative and quantitative information for approximately 5,000 hedge funds, funds of funds and CTAs. A "graveyard database" is also available that contains qualitative and quantitative information on over 9,000 defunct hedge funds, funds of funds and CTAs.

Morningstar CISDM hedge fund strategies can be grouped into eight families, and most of them can be split into strategies. The families are event driven, equity long/short, sector, market neutral/relative value, macro/CTA, emerging markets, fixed-income directional funds of funds and the global index. This classification is coherent except for the fact that some sub-strategies are grouped by means of a global index (equity long/short and equity long/short Asia for example) while some others are not. In addition there is no directional fixed-income strategy outside of mortgage-backed securities, and no multi-strategy funds.

1.1.2 Hedge Fund Research

The licensed HFR Database currently has over 6,800 funds, including about 1,700 funds of funds. Information on their hedge fund range is collected directly from the fund managers and/or their administrators, while other pertinent information is culled from memoranda, visits, and due diligence interviews. The HFR Database is the foundation for the HFRI indices that are usually used as benchmarks of hedge fund performance information. The HFRI Fund Weighted Composite alone is comprised of over 2,000 funds from the database range. The database has also a dataset of over 10,000 dead funds.

HFR has changed its way of classifying hedge funds a few times over the last decade. Until recently seven families sub-divided by strategy were used, but nowadays HFR defines four families of strategies: equity hedge, event driven, macro and relative value. We report the HFR in its original format in Figure 2.1 and reclassify it to be able to compare it with the others in Table 2.2.

This method of classifying makes sense, as they group pure equity strategies, event driven strategies, macro/CTAs and relative value. On the negative side, long-biased sector funds are grouped with equity market neutral funds. To the same extent, long-biased high-yield funds are in the same category as fixed-income arbitrage and pure volatility funds. We appreciate this classification but prefer to delve deeper in the splitting of families.

1.1.3 Dow Jones Credit Suisse

The Dow Jones Credit Suisse indices are made up of ten core indices with an addition of three strategy indices and the global index. The families include convertible arbitrage, dedicated short bias, emerging markets,

Equity Hedge	Event Driven	Macro	Relative Value
Equity market neutral	Activist	Active trading	Fixed Income – Asset Backed
Fundamental growth	Credit arbitrage	Commodity: Agriculture	Fixed Income – Convertible Arbitrage
Fundamental value	Distressed/ Restructuring	Commodity: Energy	Fixed Income – Corporate
Quantitative directional	Merger arbitrage	Commodity: Metals	Fixed Income – Sovereign
Sector: Energy/ Basic materials	Private Issue/ Regulation D	Commodity: Multi	Volatility
Sector: Technology/ Healthcare	Special situations	Currency: Discretionary	Yields alternatives: Energy infrastructure
Short bias	Multi-Strategy	Currency: Systematic	Yields Alternatives: Real estate
Multi-Strategy		Discretionary Thematic	Multi-Strategy
		Systematic	
		Diversified	
		Multi-Strategy	

Figure 2.1 Hedge Fund Research hedge fund strategies classification
Source: www.hedgefundresearch.com

Table 2.2 Classification of hedge funds by investment strategy

	Morningstar CISDM	DOW JONES CREDIT SUISSE[a]	EUREKAHEDGE[b]	GREENWICH ALTERNATIVE	EVESTMENT	HEDGE FUND RESEARCH	BARCLAYHEDGE
EVENT DRIVEN	ND Event driven multi-strategy Merger Arbitrage Distressed securities	**Event driven** Distressed securities Multi-strategy Risk arbitrage	ND Distressed securities Event driven	**Event driven** Distressed securities Merger arbitrage Special situations	ND Event driven Merger/Risk arbitrage Distressed regulation D Special situations	**Event driven** Activist Distressed/Restructuring Merger arbitrage Private issue/Reg D Special situations Multi-strategy	Distressed securities Event driven Merger arbitrage
LONG/SHORT EQUITY	**Equity long/short** Equity long/short Asia Equity long/short Europe Equity long/short	ND Long/short equity Dedicated short bias	**Long/short equity**	**Long/short equity** Aggressive growth Opportunistic Short selling Value	**Equity hedge agg.** Long/short equity Small/Micro cap Value Long only short bias	**Equity hedge** Fundamental growth Fundamental value Quantitative directional Short bias Multi-strategy	ND Equity long bias Equity long/Short Equity long-only
SECTOR	ND	ND	ND	ND	ND Energy sector Finance sector Healthcare sector Technology sector	ND Sector – Energy/Basic materials Sector – Technology/Healthcare	**Sector** Technology Finance Energy Real estate Bio-Tech Metals & mining Miscellaneous

	ND	ND	ND	Market neutral	Relative value agg.	Relative value[d]	NA
MARKET NEUTRAL/ RELATIVE VALUE	Fixed-income arbitrage Convertible arbitrage Equity Market Neutral	Equity market neutral Convertible arbitrage Fixed-income arbitrage	Arbitrage Relative value	Equity market neutral Market-Ntl – Convertible Arbitrage Market-Ntl – Fixed income arbitrage Market-Ntl – Other arbitrage Market Ntl – Statistical arbitrage	Market neutral equity Convertible arbitrage Fixed-income arbitrage Statistical arbitrage Asset-based lending Option strategy	Equity market-neutral Fixed income – Convertible Arbitrage Fixed income – corporate Fixed income – Sovereign Yield alternatives: Energy infrastructure Yield alternatives: Real Estate Multi-strategy Credit arbitrage	Convertible arbitrage Equity market neutral Fixed income
MACRO/CTA	ND Global macro Various CTA Indices	ND Global macro Managed futures	ND Macro CTA/Managed Futures	**Directional trading** Futures Macro Market timing	ND CTA/Managed futures Macro	Macro Active trading Various CTA indices Multi-strategy	**Macro** Active trading
EMERGING MARKETS	Emerging markets ND	**Emerging markets** ND	ND	**Specialty strategies** Emerging markets	**Emerging markets**	ND	**Emerging markets**
FIXED INCOME DIRECTIONAL	ND Mortgage-backed Sec.	ND	ND Fixed income	NA	ND Fixed income non-arb. Mortgage	ND[e] Fixed income – Asset-backed Volatility	ND Fixed income
MULTI-STRATEGY	ND	**Multi-strategy**	**Multi-strategy**	**Multi-strategy** **Specialty – Income**	**Multi-strategy**	**Multi-strategy[f]**	**Multi-strategy[f]**
OTHER	ND	ND	ND		ND	ND	**Others[g]** ND

Continued

Table 2.2 Continued

	Morningstar CISDM	DOW JONES CREDIT SUISSE[a]	EUREKAHEDGE[b]	GREENWICH ALTERNATIVE	EVESTMENT[c]	HEDGE FUND RESEARCH	BARCLAYHEDGE
FUND OF FUNDS	ND	ND	Fund of funds	ND	Fund of funds aggr.	FoF composite	Fund of funds
	Fund of funds				Market neutral	FoF: Conservative	
	Fund of funds diversified				Multi-strategy	FoF: Diversified	
					Single strategy	FoF: Market defensive	
						FoF: Strategic	
GLOBAL	Equal-weighted hedge fund index	DJ CS hedge fund index	EurekaHedge hedge fund index	Greenwich global hedge fund index	HFN hedge fund aggregate index	HFRI fund weighted composite index	Barclay hedge fund index

[a] The DJ CS indices are asset-weighted.
[b] EurekaHedge also proposes this strategy classification per geographical region, by assets and for funds of funds.
[c] eVestment does not define any family of strategy but only individual strategies that may or may not be linked.
[d] Credit arbitrage funds are grouped in the event driven family in HFR.
[e] Fixed income directional and volatility funds are grouped into the relative value family at HFR.
[f] The strategy multi-strategy is split between the four families of strategies at HFR.
[g] Other: Include funds categorized as Regulation D, Equity Short Bias, Option Strategies, Mutual Fund Timing, Statistical Arbitrage, Closed-End Funds, Balanced, Equity Dedicated Short and without a category.

equity market neutral, event driven, fixed-income arbitrage, global macro, long/short equity, managed futures and multi-strategy funds. The classification is similar to that of the others, but only one of these families is sub-divided. This means that under broad categories such as long/short equity may be grouped funds with very different profiles. In addition the classification does not include directional fixed-income strategies and sector funds. They do, however, publish some specialist emerging market indices.

1.1.4   EurekaHedge

EurekaHedge is the world's largest alternative investment funds research house, specializing in hedge fund databases. On their website (www.eurekahedge.com) they mention that they maintain a hedge fund list of 27,704 funds (as of the end of April 2013) inclusive of specialist funds covering Islamic, real estate, enhanced equity (130/30), fund of private equity, SRI, CTA/managed futures, fund of funds and absolute return, across all strategies and asset classes. Although we do not have the exact number of real individual hedge funds followed, in a study performed in 2009 we reported 7,000 hedge funds.[7]

This database has been created more recently than most of the other databases, but they have been very active in gathering information on a very high number of funds. This provider uses a different classification from its peers; it defines nine strategies (arbitrage, CTA/managed funds, distressed debt, event driven, fixed-income, long/short equity, macro, multi-strategy, relative value) and each of these strategies has a global version as well as regional versions including Asia Pacific, Asia ex-Japan, United States, Europe, Japan and emerging markets). In addition, there are also indices built on the basis of the value of the assets under management (funds with less than US$100 million, US$100–500 million and more than US$500 million). A lot of indices; but on the negative side, these classifications are fairly broad particularly on the fixed income, and the sector families are missing.

1.1.5   Greenwich Alternative

The Greenwich Global Hedge Fund Indices (previously known as Van Hedge Fund advisors indices) have been published since 1995. The database includes a sample of approximately 7,000 hedge funds. Eighteen individual hedge fund strategies and four major strategy group indices are provided, in addition to the broad Greenwich Global Hedge Fund index, for further insight into the composition and performance of the hedge fund asset class. The four families of strategies include market neutral funds (equity market neutral, event driven and market neutral arbitrage), long/short equity funds (aggressive growth, opportunistic, short selling and value), directional trading funds (futures, macro and market timing) and special strategies (emerging markets, income and multi-strategy). Then market neutral funds and event driven funds are sub-divided into sub-strategies.

While interesting, this classification is substantially different from the other ones, and some strategies, such as aggressive growth and opportunities long/short equity funds, are difficult to understand conceptually. In addition there are in most cases only two levels of detail – as in the other cases – while in a few there are three levels. In addition, there is no classification for sector funds, meaning that they will be somewhere within the long/short equity family of funds. Finally, there is no directional fixed-income strategy, meaning that these funds are going to be grouped in a strategy that should differ from their fundamental concept.

1.1.6   eVestment

eVestment (previously known as HedgeFund.Net) defines a large number of strategies but does not group them by category. The classification is interesting because it includes strategies that are not specifically represented in other classifications, and because it creates a precise split between sector funds and market neutral/relative value funds. There are four aggregate indices (HFN Hedge Fund Aggregate Index, HFN Fund of Funds Aggregate Index, HFN Equity Hedge Aggregate Index and HFN Relative Value Aggregate Index) as well as 29 strategies, including asset-based lending, convertible arbitrage, CTA/managed futures, distressed, emerging markets, and various equity-based strategies including sector funds, a few fixed-income ones, event driven, macro, and market neutral equity as well as a few specialized ones. eVestment groups information from 7,000+ hedge funds, funds of funds and commodity products.

1.1.7   BarclayHedge

BarclayHedge, formerly known as The Barclay Group, was founded in 1985, and consists of a team of research specialists, programmers, and data administration staff. The BarclayHedge Alternative Investment Database tracks and analyses the performance of 6,000+ hedge fund and managed futures investment programmes worldwide, including approximately 3,600+ individual hedge funds and 1200+ funds of hedge funds as at the end of April 2013.

The BarclayHedge classification is interesting. All the main strategies are represented, while sector funds are split. In addition it is the only classification with a formal extra family of strategies that includes the less well represented ones. With this methodology, the other strategies remain cleaner. On the other hand, the fixed income classification remains too basic, with only one category for directional and non-directional strategies.

1.2   The indices – daily indices

A few database providers publish weekly or even daily indices. These aim to give an idea of the evolution of the performance of the corresponding strategies. Such indices are more interesting for liquid strategies than for less liquid strategies, where daily or even weekly movements are limited.

2   Constitution of a hedge fund

The constitution of a fund is a long and demanding process. Barham and Bonnett (2005) estimate in *Starting a Hedge Fund: A European Perspective* that a minimum of six months is necessary to launch a fund in the United Kingdom. The main elements include:

1. define the legal constraints
2. look for service provider (prime broker, legal advice and administrator)
3. prepare the marketing documents
4. look for offices
5. implement the infrastructure necessary to implement the investment strategy
6. integrate other operational elements like personal and procedures.

The definition of the investment strategy is probably the most important part of the process for the manager. In this section we focus on the aspects linked to asset management when a fund is launched.[8] We present this process in seven stages. The analysis of these stages is interesting because it reveals the complexity of the structure of a fund. Even if every fund is not created in exactly the same way, the main stages shown here remain identical in most cases; starting with the choice of the investment strategy, the determining of the level of accepted risk, the selection of alternative risks, the choice of manager, the management methodology, the fund domicile and the distribution of interest.

2.1   Definition of the fund objective

When a fund is created, the objective of the company at the origin of the project is not always the same. It may be to offer attractive risk-adjusted returns or to offer exposure to complex investment products or strategies. It can also be to attract new investors or to offer a new product to existing investors. This means that there are important differences in terms of objectives within the industry. It is important to keep that in mind when you compare a fund created by a long-only boutique trader looking to create his own business by applying alternative strategies, against a fund launched by a larger institution aiming to meet a specific need identified within its clientele.

The objective of the fund has an important impact on several factors. It should also be stated in juxtaposition to the liquidity terms. In the hedge fund world the objective is usually derived from the chosen investment strategy and the market within which the fund will operate. It is important also because in the end it should correspond to what most potential investors are looking for, and be balanced between the return objectives and the risks taken to offer them.

Examples of objectives for a long/short long-biased equity fund will be to catch half to 75 per cent of the upside and to protect the downside by limiting the losses to one-third of the market drawdown. In the case of a large distressed fund it tends to be to offer low double-digit returns net of fees to investors, with a volatility around 4–6 per cent. An actively managed long-biased volatility fund may try to offer 7–8 per cent per year over a three to five-year cycle, but with a relatively high volatility as the returns will be concentrated around the volatile period for equity markets.

2.2   Investment strategy

The investment strategy is usually the most important element, and the objective of the fund derives from the fund manager profile and the strategy implemented. To perform this choice the partners look at the strategies available, their risk–return characteristics and the expertise of the management team. They start by deciding whether the strategy will be directional, non-directional or carried out via the selection of external fund managers through a fund of funds.

Figure 2.2 illustrates some of the strategies available in the range; the one finally chosen may be more precise or specific than those shown in the figure.

The choice of investment strategy is fundamental. In practice, it is usually made before the start of the process as funds tend to be launched because a manager or a team has already successfully developed and applied a specific investment process.

2.3   Risk profile

In tandem with the choice of the investment strategy, the risk profile of the fund has to be defined. Each investment strategy presents specific

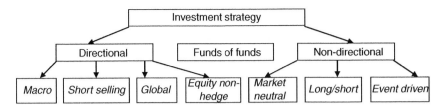

Figure 2.2 Hedge fund constitution (choice of investment strategy)

risk characteristics; it is clear that an emerging market equity fund will be riskier than an equity market neutral fund. In addition, the implementation of the strategy and the concomitant constraints will impact the risk profile of the final product. Not all emerging market equity funds or equity market neutral funds have the same risk profile.

Figure 2.3 illustrates the idea of risk profiling. When a manager wants to propose a product with a low level of risk he or she will usually invest in liquid securities and the use of leverage will be limited, and the portfolio will be diversified and focused on liquid markets. For a balanced risk profile, traditional investment securities may be used, leverage may be used to some extent and the manager will be active on markets that have a good liquidity in normal market conditions. A more dynamic fund will be able to invest in complex securities, and it may be leveraged to a larger extent (directly or through derivative products). The portfolio will be more concentrated, and less liquid markets may be considered. In practice, funds will generally combine several of these characteristics, and the risks will be close to balanced, not because of the individual characteristics but because of the combination of defensive and dynamic aspects. As an example, an emerging market fund will be invested in less liquid markets, and the portfolio will be relatively concentrated. Leverage will, however, be hardly used at all, and such funds tend to be focused on the most liquid part of the market.

2.4 Risk selection techniques

Alternative strategies lead to several discrete type of risk. These can be volatility risk (convertible arbitrage), convexity risk (fixed-income arbitrage specializing in government bonds), spread risk (fixed-income arbitrage specializing in high yield), default/bankruptcy risk (distressed securities), transaction risk (risk arbitrage), model risk (statistical arbitrage), emerging market risk (emerging markets) or stock-specific risk (long/short equity). Each of these risks should contribute to the performance of the portfolio, but the overall risk of the portfolio should stay in line with its predefined volatility budget; the partners will want to be exposed to some risks but

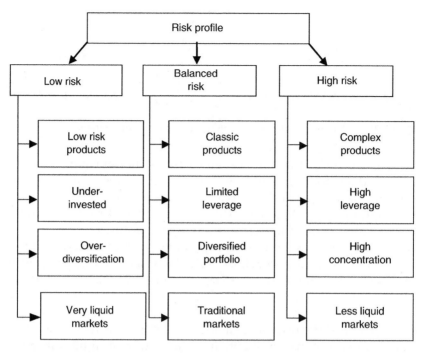

Figure 2.3   Constitution of a fund (determining the profile or risk accepted)

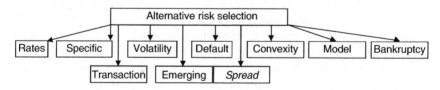

Figure 2.4   Constitution of a fund (alternative risk selection)

to limit the impact of others by combining positions. This choice is usually made in tandem with the level of risk taken. An optimal portfolio will employ a risk selection technique that will combine assets or at least positions whose returns are not correlated to each other while staying within the predefined investment strategy. Figure 2.4 illustrates the alternative risk selection process.

2.5 Manager

The next step is to decide how the fund will be managed: centralized, multiple (in-house or external) or automated.

Management is centralized when the expertise necessary to the implementation of the investment strategy is present within the asset management company or when it is decided to hire one or several managers specializing in the investment strategy.

The multiple management style of investing is specific to funds of funds or to multi-strategy funds.

The management is automated when the objective is to create a quantitatively managed strategy, whether directional or not. The model aims to automatically detect price gaps, and the role of the manager is secondary in the day-to-day running of the fund but important in the development of the algorithm.

The various types of management are illustrated in Figure 2.5a.

2.6 Management methodology

The next step consists of defining the management methodology: systematic, discretionary, trend-follower based on individual security selection, pure trading or fundamental security selection. Systematic management consists of considering security prices and information specific to the market in order to take investment decisions. This kind of management usually consists of integrating the buy and sell recommendation identified thanks to the use of a quantitative program or a series of programs developed by specialized quantitative programmers. These are based on repeatable patterns, but will usually evolve over time. Several strategies are applicable, the most common being based on technical analysis. In this context, a first program is looking to identify buy/sell signals on the market, while a second follows the evolution of the risk.

Discretionary management is the most common way to manage funds. It uses the intuitive judgment of the management team. The personal anticipation of the team is at the basis of the reasoning, without relying on any model. The team may and usually will use some quantitative and qualitative tools in order to confirm or refine their decision, but in this case these are only aids. Discretionary management can be based on market analysis, on individual security selection or on trading capabilities. The objective is not necessarily to get a neutral global position in terms

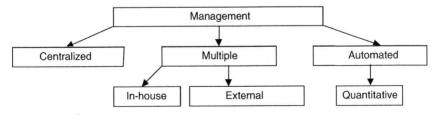

Figure 2.5a Constitution of a fund (choice of manager)

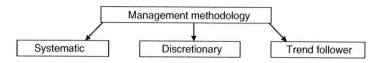

Figure 2.5b Constitution of a fund (management methodology)

of risk, but to change the positioning on the basis of market conditions, not only on the basis of individual security analysis. Managers can go from net long to net short positions, arbitrate between values and so on. Investments can, by being focused on regions, be regional or global, but they can also be focused on certain sectors or themes. Fundamental stock picking means that the manager uses fundamental pricing methodologies to determine if a stock is under- or over-priced. Figure 2.5b illustrates management methodology.

Trend-followers define an area within which they will develop a mathematical model that aims to identify short-, medium- or long-term trends in the market. The objective is to identify trends and to close the wrong signals or the trades whose risk–return trade-offs are not in line with the objective or the volatility budget. Whenever the management methodology is systematic, discretionary or trend-following, the security selection process can be based on individual security selection, pure trading capabilities or fundamental security selection. Individual security selection should be seen in a broader sense and it is not in contradiction with trading or fundamental security selection processes. The other ones can be applied on a stand-alone or considered as a part of it. Security selection can however be broader as there are some managers that do not limit themselves to a specific security selection style. This also includes applying less consensual ways of selecting securities including for example behavioural finance, macro based analysis or a combination of any of them or others. Pure trading is based on market flows and news. This usually includes managers using technical analysis where managers take positions using technical analysis which is a methodology based on historical data including price, volume or open interest to predict future market trends. This way to manage tends to be short term, of higher risk and very active. Fundamental security selection is about estimating the intrinsic value of security by examining economic and financial quantitative and qualitative factors of the corresponding company. In this process, the manager analyzes everything that affects the security's value including overall and industry specific macro factors as well as company specific factors. The end goal being to determine if the company is attractively priced or not.

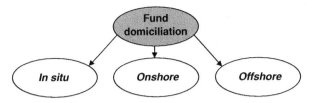

Figure 2.6   Fund constitution (domiciliation)

2.7   Fund domicile

A crucial step in the creation of a fund relates to where the fund will be domiciled. This choice will determine the freedom of the management team in their day-to-day work as well as the potential level of tax. The choice will generally be either in the same country as the fund manager (in situ), onshore (regulated) or offshore. These possibilities are illustrated in Figure 2.6. In situ domiciliation is rarely the best choice, as the number of countries that allow the implementation of alternative strategies is limited. An onshore domicile means setting up a fund in a regulated jurisdiction, for example in Europe, leading to potential constraints on the manager and to higher costs and, potentially, taxes. Offshore centres offer many advantages, but are losing interest from more and more investors mainly since the 2008 liquidity crisis. These advantages increase with the rapid increase in the number of strategies that can be implemented in UCITS structures.

There are many elements to consider at this stage. The most important are the following:

– experience of the jurisdiction relating to alternative investments: there is little interest in domiciling a fund within a jurisdiction that has no or very little experience with alternative strategies; this may slow the process down and can lead to higher costs. Good examples in Europe are Ireland and Luxembourg that are much more familiar with hedge fund strategies than most other European countries are likely to be.
– target investors: the target investors should also be considered when choosing where the fund will be implemented. Some categories of investor may not be able to invest in funds domiciled within certain jurisdictions or contained within certain legal structures such as closed-ended funds.
– degree of local regulation: local laws and regulation may impact the fund and its investors directly or indirectly.
– tax aspects: it is fundamental to take into account tax aspects not only at the fund level but also for the asset management company and at investor level.

– anti-money laundering measures: the nature and importance of anti-money laundering measures will have an impact of the reputation and credibility of a fund. The standards relating to this aspect are continuously evolving.
– service providers: the service provider is important not only on the cost side but also on the quality of the service; good services tend to save time and money.
– specific advantages: other elements to consider include the time required for implementation and the reputation of the jurisdiction as well as the political aspects and the stability of the local currency.

2.8 Distribution

The last step in the constitution of a fund consists of choosing the way that the fund will be sold. Investors usually buy fund shares that represent a part of the capital. Other possibilities include more complex structures like performance swaps, notes or options. Figure 2.7 illustrates this step.

The fund will have either an open-ended or a closed-ended structure. In the first case new investors will buy new shares created for them. This structure is the same as mutual funds: assets will evolve over time, and investments and disinvestments will be carried out periodically and regularly. Closed-ended funds are created for a specific period of time, and investors invest for that period; there are no regular exit dates. Assets are stable and the management team keeps these assets over the life of the fund to implement the investment strategy. Such funds tend, like equities, to be listed on exchanges, but their liquidity tends to be relatively limited. The fund will have a net asset value and the market price will depend on the demand and the offer.

Note that a fund can be closed to new investors even if it has an open-ended structure. This happen when the team believes that the total amount in assets under management is high for the market in which the fund operates and that more assets would make it difficult for them to apply the strategy efficiently.

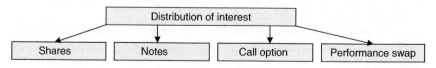

Figure 2.7 Constitution of a fund (distribution of interest)

3 The structure of a hedge fund

The hedge fund is the entity in which investors will invest. It is different from the asset management company, which is legally the manager of the fund that will earn the fees charged by the fund.

The partners at the outset of the project will generally be the manager(s) and a few close partners. External investors will invest in the investment fund. Every fund has its own structure. A typical structure is shown in Figure 2.8; it shows that the hedge fund is the central element. It needs assets under management, coming from investors (partners, management team and/or external investors). It is managed by a management team that may use external consultants for advice. This management team is part of the asset management company that is owned by the partners.

On the right-hand side of Figure 2.8 we list the activities that support the structure, that may or may not meet legal obligations. It includes the administrator, the auditor, the legal adviser, the custodian and the distributor that helps the asset management company to raise its assets. The management team will usually include partners who manage the fund on a day-to-day basis and who take operational decisions. In some cases or circumstances this team may be helped by one or several investment advisors or consultants.

The prime broker is a service provider that puts in place the infrastructure required to enable the manager to implement his investment strategy. This includes financing transactions though daily funding, and the

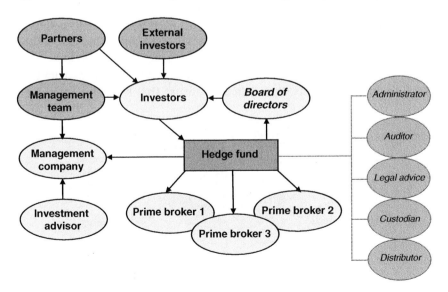

Figure 2.8 Typical hedge fund structure

implementation of leverage and security lending necessary to the implementation of short positions; the scope of the services provided by a prime broker has widened over the last few years. Other services include research, real time reports (execution and risk management reports for example), consulting services to support new funds, intermediary services for the secondary market in some cases, or support in operational risk management.

We illustrate the important role of prime brokers in Figure 2.9. In addition, they can provide capital introduction services, which include the introduction of new products to potential investors. The underlying idea is that these brokers will get more business with the corresponding funds as their assets grow.

The board of directors plays a fundamental role in the context of investment funds because it has the final power and responsibility in case of liquidity or pricing issues (fraud excluded). Directors have evolved their responsibility to take all the decisions necessary in the interest of the shareholders in case of disagreement with the management company, and they are the last resort in case of problems. Directors have for example the power to take special resolutions, and to block capital outflows in case of unexpected liquidity issues. There are usually at least three directors. It is important that the majority of the directors remain independent of the asset management company and the management team.

The administrator is a company that has the legal responsibility for everything relating to the financial aspects of a fund. It is for example in charge of the calculation of the net asset value (usually called NAV) of a fund and dispatches the estimation to interested parties including investors, exchanges and data providers. In addition the administrator receives the investments, and pays the investors back if they redeem, estimates the commissions and is in charge of preparing and distributing the financial statements. It should also ensure that the rules defined in

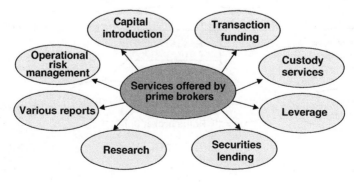

Figure 2.9 Prime broker services

the memorandum are respected. These rules include minimum investments, limits on leverage and any other investment restrictions including potential limits per position, sector or country exposures as well as any specific pricing rule specified in the contract between the administrator and its client. In some cases it will propose additional services like being the contact for the quotation of a fund or liquidity management, and it can propose one or several independent directors for the board (see Figure 2.10).

The auditor is a company that proceeds to the independent inspection of operations and documents of a company and that checks the conformity of these documents with regulatory standards and/or accounting standards.

The legal adviser gives all the legal advice needed in the day-to-day management of the asset management company, the fund or, in case of conflict, with an external entity. It plays an important role at the time when the fund is created.

The custodian is an entity that keeps the assets or cash for other entities. It is only in charge of keeping the assets. The custodian does not own the assets for a third party. It improves the protection for the investors, as securities are kept by a third party independent of the management company. It can be the same entity as the administrator.

In order to distribute their fund as widely as possible, many asset managers work with distributors that can be brokers, banks, independent marketers or asset managers. Their role is to find new investors. Usually they are also investors in the fund themselves.

4 Hedge funds and risk

It is not easy to analyse the risks present in hedge funds, as they will depend on the strategy under consideration and they will be different

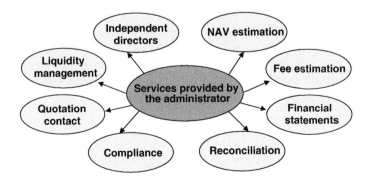

Figure 2.10 Role of the administrator

from one strategy to another. Risks important for some strategies may be completely hedged in other cases and vice versa. In this section we focus on the main risks present for one or several strategies. They will not, however, all be present for every strategy.

4.1 Investment risk

The investment risk is the risk an investor is prepared to take when he invests in a fund. It is may not be a risk that the investor wants to take, but the risk he accepts taking in order to get the expected returns. The investment risk covers several aspects. Firstly, it includes portfolio diversification . A fund can be directional (high level of market risk) or being balanced (low to medium market risk exposure). It can be concentrated in certain types of securities, like equities, or diversified across asset classes. It can be specialized within a sector or largely diversified in terms of sector exposure. Finally a fund can be managed by a single manager or by a team; this will lead to different sources of risk.

The second aspect of investment risk regards the risks specific to a manager. These include the uncertainty regarding his or her abilities to manage the portfolio during market turmoil. In some cases managers that strongly outperform during bull markets are not able to perform in line with expectations during turbulence. At the same time, it is not easy to determine which part of the performance of a fund is due to luck and which part of the returns is pure alpha[9] that cannot be explained by specific biases like small caps, value or an emerging market exposures. Another specific risk is that a manager that has a certain competitive advantage may lose this advantage. As an illustration, consider a manager that manages his fund using a quantitative model that works well. If a similar model is published in an academic study or if a competitor develops a similar model it is likely that the manager will lose his advantage. Another risk linked to the competitive advantage that some funds have is that some strategies work well in certain market conditions only. Convertible arbitrage in 2004 and 2005 is a good example, as well as PIPE funds in 2008 or asset-based lending funds in 2009.[10] Figure 2.11 illustrates the importance of specific risk in the case of hedge funds compared to mutual funds; market risk is key for mutual funds while specific risk is the most important type in the case of hedge funds.

4.2 Model risk

Several investment strategies are based on complex quantitative models that rely on large datasets or relations between series of numbers in order

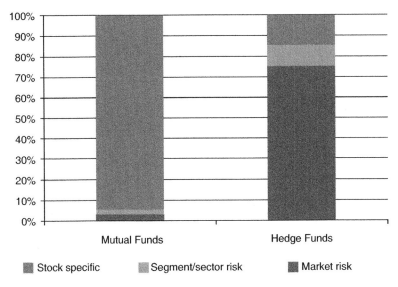

Figure 2.11   Market vs. stock-specific risk for hedge funds and mutual funds

to estimate the risk price of a security or in order to anticipate the evolution of some relations.

Model risk can take two forms. On one side the model based on the series of returns and their interactions may be wrong. On another side in some cases portfolio managers have over-passed the recommendations of the models and this decision can also lead to risk and to important potential losses.[11]

4.3   Manager and industry risk

Managers tend to be discreet regarding their investment strategy and on portfolio construction. Because of that it is of particular importance that managers have integrity. It is key that managers admit their mistakes and explain them to their investors. This enables investors to stay or not in the fund if the investment strategy does not correspond to what they had been anticipating. Finally, it is important that the management team takes decisions in favour of existing investors. This includes limiting the assets under management to a level defined at the start, and the fact the investment team will not increase a lot the number of funds they are managing, to remain focused. The breakdown of the personal investment of the management team across the funds they manage is also important to avoid any potential conflict of interest.

These three aspects illustrate the manager risk. This risk is higher in the case of hedge funds than it is for mutual funds, as funds are usually domiciled in offshore centres where investor protection is limited. In addition, hedge funds tend to be relatively illiquid, meaning that it takes time to realize an investment. Finally, hedge fund management companies tend to be small and owned by a few partners with a concentration of risk. It is very risky to make a choice to invest in funds domiciled offshore by hearsay or on the basis of the memorandum only; it is important to know the manager and the partners involved in order to check their integrity.

The industry risks arise from the fact that the growth of the industry may lead to industry issues like the one we had in 2008 when the industry as a whole faced liquidity issues and significant redemptions.

4.4 Portfolio construction risk

The construction of a portfolio is not only about securities being grouped in order to limit the risk. A portfolio with more than a hundred or so positions is not necessarily less risky than another with only a few lines, as long as the construction process used to build the latter is based on a strict method that aims to diversify the portfolio. This could for example be the automatic closure of positions with stop-loss limits.

Consider a manager that combines long and short positions in equities from car manufacturer A with a corresponding short in the equity of auto manufacturer B. The global position will be lightly exposed to market and sector risk and the global position seems limited. If, on the one hand, company A gains market shares of company B and its stock price appreciates while that of B falls, the position pays. If, on the other hand, company B gains market shares on company A the manager may lose on both counts; losses will be made on the long positions in company A, which is falling, and further losses will be made on company B, which is appreciating. This illustrates the importance of taking the correlation of securities into account when building a portfolio – but it is also important to remember that markets evolve and that correlation may not remain stable over time. A diversified portfolio is not always correctly diversified; it is important to check that opposing long and short positions are strongly correlated. This theory is almost identical with the modern portfolio theory that maintains that a low correlation helps to diversify, the difference being that a combination of long and short positions add to the complexity of the analysis.

In this context it is interesting to mention a study published by Deloitte[12] that stresses a few alarming elements in terms of the construction of portfolio risk (Figure 2.3). The study mentions that half of the funds use assets that contain implicit leverage without explicitly integrating it, and that 26 per cent of the managers would be using Value at Risk and equivalents without performing stress test and correlation tests. A subset of these elements is shown in Table 2.3. While the study was performed in 2007, it does, however stress the importance of the due diligence process that enable investors to see that the funds under consideration are managed by respecting risk management rules that have been defined.

4.5 Pricing risk

Several hedge fund strategies are invested in less liquid securities, in private securities or in over-the-counter tailor-made securities. These securities are difficult to price, leading to a pricing risk as the price used in the portfolio may not be valid if the position is sold in the market. We report a few examples and the strategy that may use them in Table 2.4.

Pricing risk is present when it is not possible to obtain an independent price for a security or not possible to get a price close to the value that would be paid by a potential buyer on the market. Strategies like private investments in public entities, usually called PIPE, and asset-based lending, usually called ABL, are almost textbook cases. PIPE managers do private deals that are not transferable while ABL managers lend money using as collateral an asset that has no recognized market value. We illustrate the case of PIPE funds in Figure 2.12. In this case the pricing risk lies at the level of the unregistered convertibles, at the equity level (as the corresponding shares tend to be illiquid), at the level of the notes and

Table 2.3 Questioning elements on risk management for hedge funds

	Percentage of funds in default
No limit per position	14
Liquidity management without stress test and correlation analysis	21
Measure of off-balance sheet leverage without stress test and without correlation analysis	26
No concentration limit per industry	30
No liquidity management	33
Use of VaR without back-testing	36
Use of VaR without stress and without correlation analysis	40
Positions in assets with implicit leverage (forwards, futures, swaps and so on) without estimating global leverage	50

Source: Deloitte (2007).

Table 2.4 Investment strategies and securities exposed to a high pricing risk

High-yield/ distressed securities	Fixed income arbitrage	Convertible arbitrage	Macro	Emerging markets
Collateralized debt	Bonds with complex option features	Convertible bonds	Inflation-linked bonds	Equities
Loans	Forwards on interest rates	Credit derivatives	Swaps and swaptions	Warrants
Bank debt	Options on bonds	Warrants	Exotic commodities	Options
Senior debt	Exotic options on interest rates	Options on bonds		Futures
Mezzanine debt	Mortgage bond			Forwards
Subordinated debt	Credit derivatives			Swaps
Letter of credit	Swaps and swaptions			Government bonds
High-yield bonds	Collateralized debt obligations (CDO)			Convertibles
Convertibles	Convertibles			Certificates of deposit
Distressed bonds				Bank loans

debentures, and on the short side when the manager hedges the risk. In a nutshell, it is present everywhere.

The importance of pricing risk in a hedge fund is so important that the Technical Committee of the International Organization of Securities Commissions wrote a report on the topic at the end of 2007.[13] This committee stressed the importance of developing common valuation principles for the following reasons:

– hedge funds are becoming more important in global capital markets;
– some strategies are particularly difficult to understand;
– financial instruments play a central role in the pricing of hedge funds;
– conflict of interest can potentially reinforce pricing difficulties.

It proposes nine principles that should help to reduce the pricing risk:

1. pricing policies and securities pricing procedures should be understandable and documented

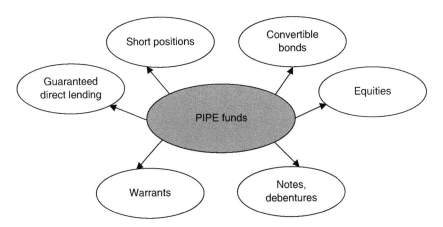

Figure 2.12   Main sources of pricing risk for PIPE funds

2. pricing policies should identify the methodologies to be used to value each kind of security held or used by hedge funds
3. financial instruments held or employed by hedge funds should be valued constantly over time using predefined procedures and policies
4. pricing policies and procedures should be examined periodically in order to ensure their continuity
5. the controlling authority should try to ensure that a sufficient level of independence is applied, and check the frequency of the control mechanism
6. pricing policies and procedures should aim to ensure an appropriate level of independent check for each valuation and particularly for any pricing influenced by the manager
7. policies and procedures should describe the procedure to apply to manage and document price changes, even in the case of intervention by a third party
8. the controlling authority should perform an initial and periodic due diligence on third parties that intervene in the pricing process of securities and portfolios
9. the rules implemented for the valuation of investment portfolios invested in hedge funds should be transparent to investors.

4.6   Infrastructure and legal risk

American hedge funds cannot be considered for investment by European investors who want to avoid tax issues. This means that European investors can consider only European and offshore funds. This situation is evolving with the UCITS regulation, and will continue to evolve with the

Alternative Investment Fund Management Directive (AIFMD). Offshore funds do not provide proper protection for investors in case of conflict or problems, directors always having the final word. A risk like this is a good illustration of the risk of infrastructure.

The legal risk comes from the fact that changes in laws or regulations can always happen. They can be favourable to the fund manager (lower taxes or less stringent rules) or not (more taxes, more binding rules). The best illustration of such risk is provided by offshore locations undergoing ever-increasing pressure from regulated countries to align their regulation. The risk is also present in regulated locations and for regulated structures, and it should not be underestimated, particularly in periods of crisis. As an practical illustration of this risk on 19 September 2008, just as the failure of Lehman Brothers had shaken investor confidence in bank solvency and pushed stocks down drastically, the US Securities and Exchange Commission (SEC) prohibited short selling of financial companies' stocks. The hope was that this would stem the tide of sales and help support bank stock prices. Europe followed suit later. This is a real example of legal risk that can directly impact the industry.

4.7 Counterparty risk

Some hedge funds invest in less liquid securities, in structured products or in tailor-made securities, which are often specific to the desired positioning. This inevitably leads to an exposure to a counterparty risk. Funds usually enter into this kind of transaction with well-known counterparties, but a risk is always present, particularly for funds with a larger asset base.[14] A second aspect to counterparty risk arises from the fact that until recently the assets of hedge funds were not always clearly separated from that of their brokers, although in normal market conditions this is not a major issue. September 2008 illustrates this risk, however, when Lehman Brothers went bankrupt, and when the assets of funds whose assets were not clearly dissociated from Lehman's remained blocked. Several changes followed this event. Firstly, more and more contracts specified that the assets of the funds be dissociated from the assets of the broker. Secondly, a vast majority of the funds started to diversify their counterparty risk and to work with a few different brokers. In the case of UCITS funds, the rule is even stricter as exposure to any counterparty must be limited to 10 per cent of the assets.

4.8 The risk of default

The risk of default classically relate to the risk of default by a debt issuer, and it can concern the non-payment of interest on and/or principal of a bond. Another way to present this risk is the default of a counterparty not to deliver or pay for a security in the case of a transaction. This second way to present this risk is close to the concept of counterparty risk presented in the previous section.

4.9   The liquidity risk

Hedge funds are not very liquid, or at least they offer less liquidity than traditional mutual funds.[15] They usually have lockup periods of one year, or an early redemption fee. Then redemptions are usually allowed on a monthly or quarterly basis with a one to three-month notice. Investing in hedge funds directly has a real opportunity cost, as the money is locked up for months or years, leading to a liquidity risk for investors. Funds of hedge funds offer usually more attractive liquidity features.

Depending on the strategy and structure of the corresponding fund, the liquidity risk will be more or less important. Figure 2.13 shows a liquidity scale; it shows securities that are more liquid on the left-hand side, and less liquid on the right. Liquid markets include interest rate markets, currency markets, developed markets, equities and commodities. On the less liquid side we show markets that have a valuation risk and where the impact of managers on price may be more important; such markets include high yield bonds and smaller companies or emerging market equities as well as over-the-counter securities. The securities of bankrupt companies and private securities bear the highest degree of risk. The more a fund is invested in less liquid securities, the higher the risk of it not being able to meet its obligations in periods of stress.

4.10   Operational risk

The Basel Committee defines operational risk as *the risk of loss resulting from inadequate or failed internal processes, people and systems, or from external events.* This risk has become a hot topic in the financial world and

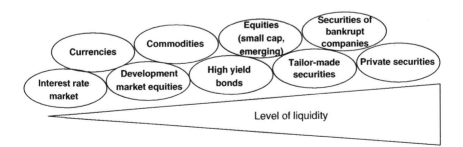

Figure 2.13   Illustration of liquidity risk

particularly in the hedge fund industry, and some will define it as the risk for which investors are not paid.[16] We start this section by presenting the results of a study focused on hedge fund failure performed by CAPCO.[17] While this study was carried out a few years ago, it has probably worked as a catalyst for the industry, having led many players to pay particular attention to operational risk (Figure 2.14). According to this study 50 per cent of hedge fund failures arise from operational issues (including fraud as shown in Figure 2.14). We complete the analysis by presenting the results of selected academic studies on the subject.

A deeper analysis of the failures due to operational risk indicates that errors in reporting and bad performance reporting, the misappropriation of funds and deliberate frauds are the main sources of operational risk. Figure 2.15a reports the exact figures.

A closer look at the definition of operational risk indicates that there are four aspects to it in the Basel Committee definition:

Internal processes: This means that operational risk includes errors in execution and valuation.

People: The main risks directly linked to humans include fraud, market abuse and non-respect of rules or limits, as well as the definition of responsibility and the ability of a company to retain good staff.

Systems (including the technological aspects around fund management and the management company): Issues with programs or a computer may block a manager from trading, may allow only a limited access to information, or stop a fund manager from being in touch with clients.

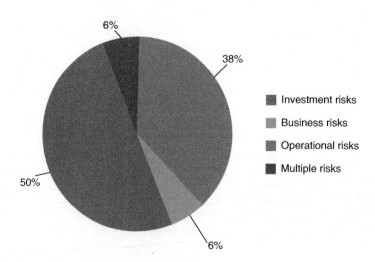

Figure 2.14   Analysis of hedge fund failure
Source: Capco (2003).

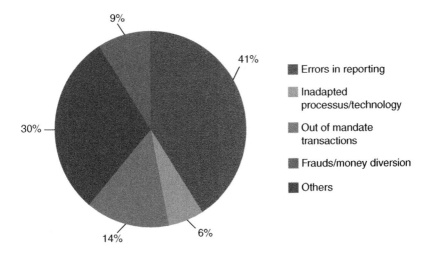

Figure 2.15a Decomposition of hedge fund failure due to operational risk
Source: Capco (2003).

Figure 2.15b Operational risk illustration

External events: These problems may come from service providers such as the administrator or the broker. Terrorism, vandalism, and robbery, and natural disasters such as fires and earthquakes, must also be taken into account.

We illustrate this concept by summarizing some of the main sources of operational risk in Figure 2.15b.

In order to mitigate this risk, more and more investors perform an operational due diligence, focusing on the elements only lightly covered, or not covered at all, by the standard due diligence process:

– *Experience of the people in charge of operational aspects*: is there a chief
operating officer in charge of operational aspects? If yes, what has been
improved?

– *Compliance*: is there a compliance officer? If yes, what is his/her role
and his/her experience? What does he/she add in the day-to-day management of the fund? What are the controls in place? In this context,
Deloitte (2007) mentions in its study on the hedge fund industry that
in close to 90 per cent of the funds had a written compliance policy and
a compliance officer.

– *Internal control procedures*: internal procedures have to be developed in
order to avoid any risk of mistakes in day-to-day operations. These procedures should be adapted to the fund strategy (a quantitative fund
invested only in equities does not have the same requirements as a concentrated macro fund).

– *Portfolio valuation*: the valuation procedure of a portfolio should be
written and shared with investors. Any change should be notified to
interested parties. It is important that the valuation process remain
consistent over time and that it is realized by an independent entity.
Table 2.5 reports the results of a study performed by Deloitte (2007); it
indicates that three funds out of four had a net asset value estimated by
an independent third party, and that close to half of these funds had
another check carried out by a third party. In addition, 86 per cent of
the funds have a written valuation policy, and two-thirds of the funds
share this policy with their investors.

– *Service providers*: it is important to check the reputation of service providers such as prime broker, administrator, custodian and other parties
directly involved with the fund.

Figure 2.16 shows that managers intervene directly in the valuation
process in less than 10 per cent of the cases.

Brown et al. (2011) performed an interesting academic study on operational risk based on a large set of due diligence provided by a due diligence
service provider. They found that despite the fundamental importance
of integrity in the delegated asset management business, incomplete
and inaccurate disclosure of important information is not uncommon.
Reporting issues are significantly associated with measures of operational
risk and that three main elements are associated with operational risk:
failure to use a well-known accounting firm, reliance on internal pricing,
and inadequate signature controls. Finally, they find evidence that exposure to operational risk does not appear to be a major factor influencing
investor decisions. This result confirms Brown et al. (2008).

Other studies have tried to price the cost of operational risk. Brown et
al. (2007) show that operational risk associated with conflicts of interest

Table 2.5 Analysis of hedge fund valuation process

	Funds respecting the rule (%)
NAV estimated by the administrator or a third party	78
Independent valuation by a third party	47
Written valuation policy	86
Written valuation policy reviewed on an annual basis minimum	38
Valuation policy shared with investors	68
Valuation policy shared with investors on an annual basis minimum (and if there is any change)	50

Source: Deloitte (2007).

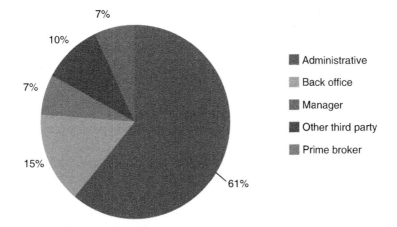

Figure 2.16 Official net asset value calculator
Source: Deloitte (2007).

(both withtin the fund and external to the fund) can lead to a reduction in return of 1.68 per cent average on an annualized basis. Brown et al. (2008a) on the cost of operational due diligence for fund of funds found that operational due diligence can add up to 260 basis points of return in a well diversified hedge fund strategy. They also conclude that the value of die diligence lies more in avoiding hedge funds that underperform or go out of business than it does in selecting top performing hedge funds. This justify why hedge fund investors should emphasize their due diligence process on operational risk. These results confirm that while the importance of analyzing operational risk and operational due diligence in the broadly defined due diligence process has become a fact for most hedge fund investors, many of them still do not see this part of the process as key. This is contradictory to the fact that operational issues represent the bulk of the failures.

5   Hedge fund investors

Through their complex characteristics, their relative opacity and their limited liquidity, hedge funds are not designed for just any kind of investor. This section focuses on the typical investors in hedge funds before focusing more precisely on the evolution of the investment of institutional investors in hedge funds over time.

5.1   Typical investors

The first hedge fund was implemented in the United States. This market has always been the most important for hedge funds and it still is, as shown in Figure 2.17.

Until the middle of the nineties, typical investors in hedge funds were high net worth individuals. Then other types of investor started to express an interest in the industry, and today the investor base includes pension funds, private bankers, foundations and other financial institutions. Figure 2.18 shows the breakdown of the American hedge fund industry by type of investor. Figure 2.19 gives the same information, for non-American investors.

Private investors represent just over 17 per cent of the assets of the industry. The other principal sources of capital that grew significantly over the last few years are institutional investors, currently representing the vast majority of the assets at 69 per cent of the assets, and funds of funds lost of importance since the liquidity issues in 208 at, 10 per cent. The remaining

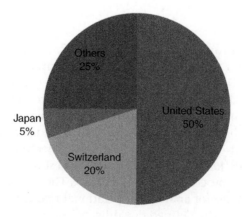

Figure 2.17   The origin of assets invested in hedge funds

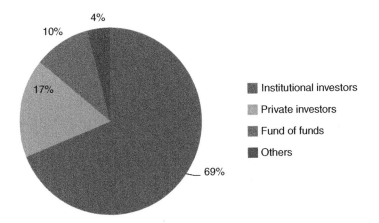

Figure 2.18 Breakdown of American investors into hedge funds (excluding funds of funds)

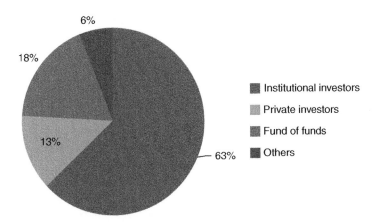

Figure 2.19 Breakdown of non-American investors into hedge funds

4 per cent is divided between financial institutions and non-financial institutions (excluding funds of funds and institutional investors).

Around the rest of the world, the breakdown is slightly different. In Europe, funds of funds have historically been the main source of assets but lost importance now at 18 percent. Institutional investors took the lead at 63 per cent. High net worth individuals represent 6 per cent of the asset base. The remainder is taken by non-financial institutions excluding funds of funds and institutional investors. It is worth insisting on the fact that the situation has evolved over the last few years, and particularly since the liquidity crisis of 2008. Funds of funds directly affected by the crisis lost the interest of many investors and their share of the asset base decreased significantly. On the other hand, institutional investors have continued to invest; we can estimate that institutional investors today represent close to two thirds of the assets of the industry and funds of funds slightly more than 15 per cent (dropping from close to 35 per cent a few years ago).

The Australian government provides interesting numbers on this topic in its annual report on the hedge fund industry. According to their statistics, private investors represent the vast majority of the assets invested in the Australian hedge fund industry; local pension funds follow with approximately 20 per cent of the assets, and then foreign institutions. These numbers are given in Figure 2.20.

5.2 Institutional investors

Institutional investors are particularly important in financial markets. They collect savings from private investors to invest in financial securities, that is: pension funds, endowments, insurance companies, foundations and other management companies. They play a fundamental role in financial markets because they control the volume of very important assets.

Institutional investors are particularly demanding in terms of reporting and communication. Most of them did not invest in hedge funds for a long time, but now they have taken the plunge and their minimum requirements include: regular and complete reporting, frequent contact with the management team, audited financial statements, a compliance officer and/or a risk manager, and independent valuation by an administrator as well as a precise description of the investment strategies and

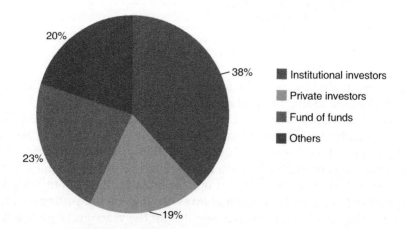

Figure 2.20 Breakdown of assets of Australian hedge funds and funds of funds
Source: Australian Government (2010).

details on the people involved. The main reasons for institutional investors not to consider investment hedge funds in the past included:

- *Lack of transparency*: the majority of managers wanted to keep quiet about their investment processes to avoid other people replicating their methods of managing and/or positioning. With institutional investors this risk is low as those are professional investors. In addition it has become standard to use non-disclosure agreements.
- *Lack of risk control*: the bankruptcy or advertised dissolution of funds such as Long-Term Capital Management that were not fraud cases but where the level of risk control was insufficient kept institutional investors away. Many funds have implemented risk management processes in order to be clear on the potential risk of the strategy and to show potential investors that unwanted risks are hedged.
- *Under-developed risk management tools*: the industry has for a long time remained underequipped in terms of risk management for management or operational risks. The industry standards have evolved significantly over the last few years.
- *Fraud cases and reputational issues*: Fraud cases, including Madoff or Bayou, negatively impressed many investors To manage this issue, more and more controls have been implemented through the hiring of Chief Operation Officers (COOs) and compliance.
- *Lack of regulation*: a large part of the funds are domiciled in offshore centres. This can be perceived as negative by some investors. To balance this risk more and more investment management companies registered with their national regulatory body even if it is not mandatory, increasing investor confidence. In addition, the emergence of regulated structures such as UCITS, enabling implementation of hedge fund strategies within regulated centres, is continuously improving this aspect. The AIFMD will be the next move.
- *Niche industry*: until recently the hedge fund industry was not well known by many institutional investors. This arose, between other things, from difficulties encountered in understanding complex and unknown investment strategies.
- *High fees and commissions*: the level of fees paid by hedge fund investors has always been high, and the estimation of these fees complex. The addition of management and performance fees has not been accepted by all players in the market. However, the strong outperformance of hedge funds in difficult times changed the perception of many investors.
- *Lack of liquidity*: hedge funds are relatively illiquid investment products with only monthly or quarterly liquidity, lockup periods and notice

periods. This lack of liquidity has also contributed to keeping institutional investors away.

This situation has evolved over the last few years. Institutional investors in general and pension funds in particular were significantly exposed to the fall in equity markets at the start of the century, and the hedge fund industry was the only asset class to perform correctly and positively during that period. In this context the interest of institutional investors for this kind of product, hardly surprisingly, increased.

Fund managers have accepted that they must give more transparency to investors, they have developed risk control systems and many have registered the asset management companies with regulatory bodies. In addition, in the case of important investments they have accepted that they must offer attractive liquidity structures and competitive fees. In sum, the small industry has grown up, and it has become more professional; it has evolved from a limited group of private investors to an institutionalized industry with much higher standards regarding reporting and the flow of information.

In terms of institutional investments a very interesting study is performed on a bi-annual basis by Russell Investment Group. This study analyses the perception, the use and the expectations of institutional investors in relation to alternative investments including hedge funds. It separates American institutional investors from the European, Australian and Japanese. Figure 2.21 reports the use of hedge funds as percentages; the

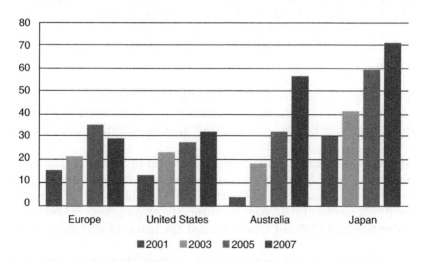

Figure 2.21   The use of hedge funds by institutional investors
Source: Russell Research (2007).

first number indicates that in 2001 approximately 15 per cent of European institutional investors were using hedge funds within their asset allocation. This number increased to 35 per cent in 2005 before decreasing slightly. Russell Research (2012) concludes that all in all, 59 per cent of the respondents globally (without splitting them by geographical zone were) using hedge funds.

The numbers reported in Figure 2.20 include a few interesting elements. Firstly the percentage of institutional investors using hedge funds was low in 2001, particularly in Australia and to a lesser extent in the United States and in Europe. Numbers increased significantly over the following years, even with a slight setback in Europe between 2005 and 2007, when the allocation decreased from 35 to 29 per cent. They also indicate a break between the duo made up of Australia and Japan on one side and Europe and the United States on the other; growth has been much more rapid in the Asia Pacific region, and in Australia and Japan more than 50 per cent and 70 per cent of institutions invested in hedge funds in 2007, against 30 per cent in Europe and the United States. Russell Research (2012) concludes that as of the end of March 2012, 59 per cent of the respondents worldwide were holding hedge funds in their portfolio.

Figure 2.22 completes this information. It shows the strategic allocations in percentage of assets between 2001 and 2007 with an estimation for 2009. The average allocation for European institutional investors rose from 2 per cent to 7.4 per cent in 2007. In the United States the reaction was quicker and the allocation stayed stable at around 7.5 per cent. In

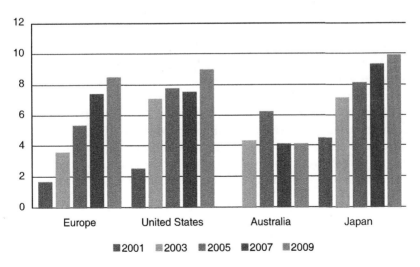

Figure 2.22 Strategic allocation in percentage of assets by institutional investors
Source: Russell Research (2007).

Australia it has, however, remained lower. This, combined with the previous figure, indicates that in Australia a higher number of institutional players are investing in hedge funds but that existing players are not increasing their allocation significantly; Japanese growth is stronger and more consistent. Russell Research (2010) estimated that 4.2 per cent of the global portfolios were allocated to hedge funds. More recently, Russell Research (2012) estimated that 6.6 per cent of total portfolio assets, on average, are allocated to hedge funds. Deutsche Bank (2013) estimated this allocation to be at 5 per cent for pension funds on a stand-alone basis. This study also found that almost 70% of pension funds increased their allocations over the preceding 12 months and that almost half of pension funds expect to increase allocations by $100 million or more in 2013.

6   The constraints

There are many constraints with respect to investing in hedge funds. This section analyses the investment constraints that have to be respected.[18]

6.1   Minimum investment

Hedge funds are complex investment products that cannot in most countries be sold to retail investors. They are usually available only to high net worth or accredited investors.[19] Minimum investments for individual funds usually range between US$100,000 and US$5 million, with the mean at US$500,000 and the median at US$1 million. The legal minimum investment for funds sold in the United States is US$1 million; this rule aims to prohibit smaller investors from investing in such strategies; the underlying idea is to limit access to hedge funds to the high net worth investors that can afford to invest in sophisticated investment strategies and have sufficient knowledge or can afford to pay for advisors. In addition, they can support higher potential losses. In the United States, the maximum number of investors is limited by law; this explains why some funds ask for a minimum investment well in excess of US$1 million. In Europe and offshore the trend is to offer funds with a lower minimum investment; in funds of funds this can even be as low as a few thousand dollars.

6.2   Liquidity constraints

The lockup period is the time during which the invested assets are locked in the fund; during that time the investor cannot withdraw the money invested. The traditional rule is to set a one-year lockup.[20] Lockup periods have two origins. Firstly, by accepting a one-year lockup the investors give the management team enough time to show its capabilities. Secondly, a one-year lockup means that the inflows and the outflows are spread over time, giving the management team time to focus on investments and to limit the flows, at least for some time. In addition, many alternative investment strategies invest in less liquid investment products. Such securities are difficult to evaluate and to sell; a sale or an early exit from this kind of security can have a direct impact on performance. So smoother assets flows help the manager and the remaining investors.

Soft lockups have appeared more recently. The idea is to replace the lockup period with an exit fee. These fees usually represent a few per cent and they decrease over time. A classic example would be 5 per cent over the first year, 2 per cent between years 1 and 2, and zero thereafter, the fee usually being paid back into the fund. This is normal and necessary, as the cost of withdrawal impacts the remaining investors.

The term "liquidity date" refers to the moment when a withdrawal from a fund can be carried out. Money can be removed from a fund only at certain predefined moments; these are normally set up on a monthly basis but may also be quarterly, semi-annual or even annual. These dates may be calendar-based or relative to the date of the investment.

The notice period stipulates how long before the liquidity date the investor should notify the manager or the administrator that he/she wants to be paid back. This notice period is usually 30 to 90 days, but it can be longer for less liquid strategies. The gate, which exists only for less liquid strategies, represents the maximum percentage of assets, usually between 10 and 25 per cent, that can be paid back on a liquidity date. The underlying idea is to protect the remaining shareholders from panic selling, and to give the manager time to create enough liquidity to repay investors. There is also a holdback, a small percentage of the investment that is not paid back on the liquidity date following the notice period. It is not invested, and it will be repaid to the investor only after the next annual audit, which confirms the final net asset value on the date of the redemption.

The set of liquidity constraints presented in this section means that it is possible to redeem an investment in a fund on only a few specific dates per year, and that the process may take time, usually a few months. Note that the investors remain invested in the fund until the next liquidity date takes place. If the gate is activated the proportion of assets gated (that is, not paid back at the first liquidity date), will be paid later, and in this case too the investor remains invested.

We illustrate the liquidity constraints in Table 2.6. The client invested US$10 million in a fund on 1 November 2011. The assets of the fund were

Table 2.6   Liquidity constraints, a practical case

Data:	Investment date:	1 November 2011		
	Investment:	US$10m		
	Asset of the fund:	US$110m		
	Lockup:	12 months		
	Liquidity date:	Quarterly calendar (March, June, September and December)		
	Notice:	60 calendar days		
	Gate:	10%		
	Holdback:	5%		
Liquidity analysis:				
Date of sale:	**12 June 2012**	**29 August 2012**	**31 October 2012**	**10 November 2012**
Investment value at liquidity date:	US$9m	US$9m	US$9m	US$10m
Fund assets at liquidity date:	US$80m	US$80m	US$80m	US$110m
Lockup ends:	1 November 2012	1 November 2012	1 November 2012	1 November 2012
Liquidity date:	31 December 2012	31 December 2012	31 December 2012	31 March 2013
Notice:	1 November 2012	1 November 2012	1 November 2012	1 February 2013
Gate:	Activated	Activated	Activated	Not Activated
First payment:	US$7.6m at the NAV of 31 December 2012	US$7.6m at the NAV of 31 December 2012	US$7.6m at the NAV of 31 December 2012	US$9.5m as at 31 March 2013
Second payment:	The rest at the NAV of 31 March*	The rest at the NAV of 31 March*	The rest at the NAV of 31 March*	/
Payment of the holdback:	US$400,000 for June 2013, the rest in 2014	US$400,000 for June 2013, the rest in 2014	US$400,000 for June 2013, the rest in 2014	US$500,000 for June 2014

*The rest remains invested, and the final amount will be known only after the publication of March net asset value.

US$110 million, the lockup period was one year and the fund offered quarterly liquidity with a 60-day notice period. The memorandum also stipulates that the fund could be gated on receiving redemption requests of more than 10 per cent of the assets on a single liquidity date, and the holdback is 5 per cent.

A few months later, disappointed by the performance, the investor decides to redeem his investment. We consider four distinct cases in order to illustrate the impact on liquidity constraints on the flow of cash for our investor. The dates considered are:

1. 12 June 2012
2. 29 August 2012
3. 31 October 2012
4. 10 November 2012

Consider, in the first three cases, that the value of the investment in 2011 stays at US$9 million and that the total assets of the funds stay at US$80 million. In 2013, the value of the investment rises to US$10 million within a fund worth a total of US$110 million (so it is stable over time).

If the investor notifies their decision to sell their position in early June 2012 he/she must first wait for the lockup to expire; then he/she can claim to be repaid at the next liquidity date. The lockup ends in November. With quarterly redemptions the next liquidity date is at the end of December. In a US$80 million fund, however, the investor has US$9 million invested, representing more than the 10 per cent gate.[21] So the manager activates the gate, meaning that this time the investor will get only US$8 million of his/her US$9 million; their remaining US$1 million remains invested until the next liquidity date. In addition, there is the 5 per cent holdback, meaning that the investor will not get US$8 million but only US$7.6 million – their remaining US$400,000 will be repaid after the final audit, but will not stay invested.

The next two cases give exactly the same answer. Whether the investor redeems his/her investment at the end of August or at the end of October they will go out at the end of December for the bulk of the investment, the remainder being repaid to them at the end of March, and the holdback after the audit.

In the last case, the investor decides to put in a sale order early in November 2012. The next liquidity date is 31 March 2012. At that time the asset base happens to be larger, and our redeeming investor represents less than 10 per cent of the assets of the fund. So he/she receives 95 per cent of his/her investment in cash based on the net asset value at the end of March. The 5 per cent holdback is paid in June 2013, after final audit.

Our example is of interest because it shows that liquidity conditions may have a significant impact on the value of an investment and on the timing of redemption payments. It also reconfirms that it is very important to think twice before investing in a hedge fund, and to diversify in terms of not only strategy but also liquidity.

6.3   The limit of total assets under management

The rapid development of the industry means that it became more and more difficult for the less experienced managers to raise assets, whereas well-known managers usually achieved a larger asset base and as a result usually had to limit the flow of assets. This constraint – surprising as it may seem at first sight – has two main consequences. Firstly, it will incentivize potential investors to move quickly; investors, not unnaturally, tend to do this when they know that the fund will be closed to new investors once a certain asset size has been reached. Secondly this limit represents security for investors; they can be sure that the fund will be contained at a manageable size even if performance continues to be attractive. The reason for the underlying fear of oversize became apparent a few years ago when the hedge fund industry was led by a few very large macro hedge funds representing almost 50 per cent of the industry in terms of assets. The size per se was not a serious issue, but the positions taken by these funds were followed by the market and this became problematic.

The closure of a fund to new assets has usually two steps. First, the funds are closed to new investors; this process is called "soft close." Once a fund is soft closed, only existing investors may add to their position in it. Then, once full capacity has been reached the fund gets hard closed and no new money can be invested into the fund. Investors in a soft closed fund can be seen as holders of what would in America be known as a call option.[22] This option has a value that we will not try to estimate but that should be considered for any investment decision as it has some value.

7   The fees

In our definition of hedge funds presented in the first chapter we stated that hedge fund managers tend to be co-investors in the funds and that they are paid on the basis of their performance. The fee structure of hedge funds is very specific. When A.W. Jones created his first hedge fund created in 1949, he wanted the best managers and he wanted them to be well paid if they were performing well, so he created the performance fee system. Performance fees were the only way for managers to make money but through it they were able to make a fortune if their performance was strong. The logic is the same today; hedge fund managers receive a performance fee so that the managers that offer strong absolute performance numbers receive competitive pay – but as performance fees are not always sufficient to cover the complete set of costs of a management company, hedge funds also charge management fees. However the performance reported by managers should always be net of all fees, for comparison with other investment products.

7.1 The classic fee model

The majority of hedge funds charge a standard fee that includes a management fee and a performance fee. For decades the classic fee structure was 1 and 20 (1 per cent management fee and 20 per cent performance fee). In the early 2000s the management fees increased, and many managers now charge 2 and 20, but since the crisis the management fee has decreased again in many cases.

Management fees vary between 1 and 2 per cent of assets, while performance fees vary between 15 and 25 per cent of the profits. A study performed in 2008[23] concluded that the average management fee (respectively median) for hedge funds is at 1.52 per cent (respectively 1.5 per cent). These results confirm a trend from a few years ago that indicated that an increasing portion of the industry charges a 1.5 per cent management fee, against 1 per cent before. A study performed in 2013[24] reports numbers similar to those in Figure 2.23.

The 2008 study also indicates that the average performance fee (respectively median) was at 19.34 per cent (respectively 20 per cent). The 2013 results are similar, and are shown in Figure 2.24.

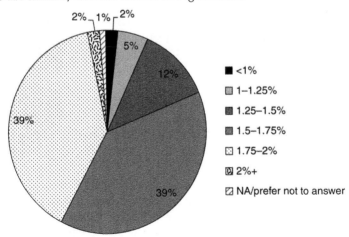

Figure 2.23 Breakdown of hedge fund management fees
Source: Deutsche Bank (2013).

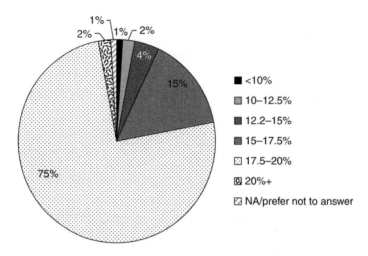

Figure 2.24   Hedge fund performance fee breakdown
Source: Deutsche Bank (2013).

The level of commission depends on many factors. The most important is the investment strategy, where the manager is based, and the success of the funds, measured by its AUM. This is illustrated in Table 2.7. Some strategies have a comparatively high implementation cost – for example, the CTA fund, which is based on research carried out by a large team of trained researchers and very powerful computers. The next factor is the geographical location of the fund.[25] Other costs, including any legal fees, need to be taken into account. Depending on the fund's policy, these costs may or may not be included in the management fee.

(Incidentally, the fees charged by European funds are higher than those of American-based managers, which are in turn higher than those charged by Asian managers. It is difficult to understand the rationale behind this gradation, even taking into account the fact that the American market is more mature and that Asian funds should be competitive to attract assets.)

The last element that can impact on the level of fees is the success of the fund. Successful managers that attract a lot of interest tend to created a new share class as the assets grow, offering less liquid, and usually more expensive, shares to new investors.

In some cases management companies set up several share classes for the same product, charging lower management fees for the less liquid classes and higher fees for the more liquid, for example, a fund may charge a 1 per cent management fee for a share class A whose assets remain blocked for three years minimum, and 2 per cent for a class B whose assets remain blocked for just one year.

Table 2.7 Average management and performance fee by investment strategy

	Management fee (%)	Performance fee (%)
CTA	2.2	18.9
Event driven	1.7	20.0
Special situations	1.7	20.0
Distressed securities	1.7	19.3
Credit	1.7	18.1
Relative value	1.7	16.7
Macro	1.7	16.3
Others	1.6	18.2
Multi-strategy	1.6	16.6
Market neutral	1.5	18.9
Long/short equity	1.5	18.6
Fixed income arbitrage	1.4	18.3
Funds of funds	1.3	10.6

Source: Preqin (2009).

A study by Dresdner Kleinwort Equities reports interesting results on the impact of costs on hedge fund performance; the results are illustrated in Figure 2.25. This study shows that on a gross performance of 22.5 per cent, 4.3 per cent disappears in execution costs, and that on the remaining 18.2 per cent gross performance, 5.3 per cent covers all the commissions charged; the client ends up with just under 13 per cent.

7.2   High-water mark and the hurdle rate

Fees are high in the hedge fund industry. There are, however, two forms of protection for investors regarding performance fees. The first is called the "high-water mark"; it prevents investors that gain, then lose, then regain money from paying performance fees twice over. The second is called the "hurdle rate"; it is the minimum return that has to be provided before a performance fee is received.

The underlying idea of the high-water mark is that if the fund drops, no performance fee can be charged on any subsequent profit until the net asset value reaches its previous high. This rule is a must across the industry; investors should never have to pay a performance fee twice on the same profits. We illustrate the floors in Figure 2.26. In this case an investor invested in a new share class at US$100 in January 2012. As the fund has a high-water mark, a performance fee will be charged only if the net asset value of the fund is over US$100. Figure 2.26 indicates that the fund posted a loss over the first month. This means that the client will not pay any performance fee before the net asset value goes back to US$100 (light grey line). So in practice, every time that the net asset value drops below its peak, the investor does not pay any performance fee.

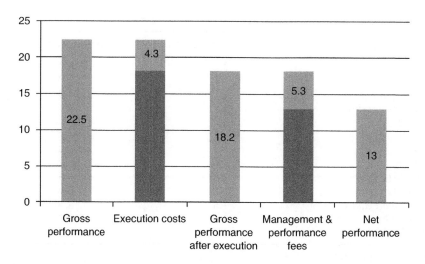

Figure 2.25   Breakdown of the gross performance of a fund
Source: Dresdner Kleinwort Equities.

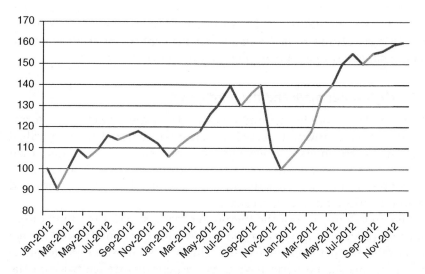

Figure 2.26   High-water mark illustration

   The hurdle rate, also called preferred return or benchmark, means that
the fund will not charge any performance fee until a certain minimum
return is achieved. This level can be fixed (at 5 or 10 per cent for example)
or floating (usually LIBOR or EONIA plus a few per cent). Any fund with
a hurdle rate will automatically have a high-water mark in place. A study
by Deutsche Bank (2013) interestingly stressed the fact that in 2013 83

per cent of the investors think that managers should have a hurdle rate against 17 per cent in 2003.

7.3   Fee illustration

We illustrate the impact of performance fees in Table 2.8: an investor who takes a position in a hedge fund charging a 1.5 per cent management fee and a 20 per cent performance fee on profits of over 5 per cent per year. The fund has a high-water mark. We consider four different scenarios after one year:

1. The fund ends the year with a gross profit of 10 per cent after execution costs, so the profit, net of management fee, is 8.5 per cent. After performance fee, this drops to 7.8 per cent, while the management company makes 2.2 per cent; so in the end 22 per cent of the profits will be paid to the manager.
2. The fund finishes down by 10 per cent. The management fee is still charged, but no performance fee. The client loses 11.5 per cent, while the manager makes 1.5 per cent.
3. Should the fund finish the year up by 20 per cent, investors get 15.8 per cent net on assets and the manager 4.2 per cent. The proportion of the profits paid to the manager is 21 per cent. Without the hurdle rate, the manager would have taken 5.8 per cent on the assets and investors only 14.2 per cent, so the proportion of the profits going to the manager would then have been 29 per cent.
4. Should the fund finish the year up by just 2 per cent, the management fee would be charged, but no performance fee. The manager would

Table 2.8   The impact of commission on performance

Data:	Management fee:	1.50%		
	Performance fee:	20%		
	Hurdle rate:	5%		
	High-water mark:	Yes		
Commission analysis:				
Profits made:	**+10%**	**–10%**	**+20%**	**+2%**
Management fee:	1.50%	1.50%	1.50%	1.50%
Performance, net of management fee:	8.5%	–11.5%	18.5%	0.5%
Hurdle rate:	5%	5%	5%	5%
Performance fee:	20% of 3.5%	None	20% of 13.5%	None
Net performance:	7.80%	–11.5%	15.8%	0.50%
Return to the manager:	2.20%	1.50%	4.2%	1.50%
Percentage of the profits paid to the manager:	22%	ND	21%	75%

earn 1.5 per cent and investors 0.5, so the manager would take 75 per cent of the profits. Without the hurdle rate the manager would have taken 80 per cent of the profits.

This example illustrates the important role played by fees in the context of investments in hedge funds.

When funds offer attractive returns, this aspect is seen as not particularly important; in periods of turmoil, however, investors tend to have more difficulties in accepting that they must pay more than half of their profits to the manager for the work done.

Figure 2.27 shows the gross performance and its breakdown between investors and the management company for various levels of profit between –30 per cent and +50 per cent gross, with a hurdle rate at two per cent. The figure shows the impact of the performance fee for global returns over the high-water mark. This situation is normal in the industry. Note that a manager that gets performance fees and that subsequently loses money does not have to pay the fees back even if investors lose money throughout the period overall.

7.4 Equalization or series of shares

The existence of a performance fee in hedge funds significantly complicates the estimation of the net asset value. Let's consider a simple example to illustrate the problems. An investor called Renata V. decides to invest US$100,000 in a hedge fund that takes positions in a fund investing in mergers and acquisitions; she buys 100,000 shares at US$1 each. Over

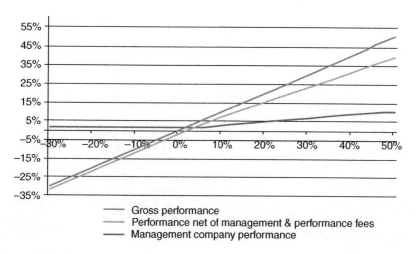

Figure 2.27   Gross vs. net performance

the first six months of its existence the fund loses 20 per cent, so it is valued at only US$80,000. At that point, another investor, Louis C., buys 100,000 shares in the fund, for US$80,000. This means that the fund has now total assets of US$160,000 and that the number of shares stands at 200,000. Over the next six months the fund performs strongly and the value of the assets increases to US$200,000 for 200,000 shares meaning a return to the original value of US$1 per share. This number is net of management fee but gross of performance fees.

At the end of the year a performance fee is paid on any profits. The assets had stood at US$180,000 and their final value is US$200,000. The performance fee is 20 per cent of the profit; so that is 20 per cent of US$200,000 less US$180,000, a total of US$4000. This means that the assets of the funds after performance fees are US$196,000. If nothing is adjusted relative to their buying price, the two investors each end the year with an investment value of US$98,000 for 100,000 shares. But this is not correct as the first investor, Renata V., had invested US$100,000 initially while Louis C. had invested only US$80,000; Renata V. should not have to pay a performance fee as she has lost money.

There are several ways to solve this issue. The two main ways are the use of an equalization factor or a series of shares. The first tends to be used more in Europe, while the multi-series or series of shares tends to be used more in the United States.

Equalization is based on the principle that the fund has a same net asset value for all investors. An equalization credit is added when necessary. Three elements are essential:

- The final net asset value of the fund, which is the value on which the performance fee is estimated – or the issuing share price if the fund has not provided a profit over the period.
- The gross value of the assets of the fund: the value of all active and passive assets of the fund, excluding the performance fee, divided by the number of shares available.
- The net asset value of the fund when each investor invested.

When each investor enters the fund and receives shares, he or she can either have an equalization credit or pay an additional performance fee.

If an investor invests in a fund when the gross assets are higher than the last maximum net asset value of the fund, they will pay an additional amount to the net asset value, commonly called the equalization credit. This credit will be equal to the performance fee multiplied by the difference between the value of the current gross assets and the last maximum net asset value of the fund. For example, where the maximum net asset value of a fund is US$100, the gross value of the assets is US$120, the performance fee is at 20 per cent and the net asset value per share at the subscription is US$116, the equalization credit will be US$120 less US$100, times 20 per cent. This equals US$4. This credit is at risk should the value of the fund decrease, but its value could go back to US$4 if the fund recovers. When the performance fee is estimated, this money is converted into shares.

If an investor invests in a fund when the value of gross assets is below the last maximum net asset value, the situation is the opposite. The additional performance fee due will be received by reducing the number of shares to the net asset value when the performance fee is calculated. The additional performance fee will be calculated as the difference between the highest net asset value of the fund less the gross value of the assets multiplied by the performance fee level.

The multi-series approach consists of creating a new series of shares for every liquidity date. This methodology has the advantage of simplicity but in practice investors will have to run several lines for the same investment.

8 Short selling

We already used the term "short selling" several times without defining it precisely. This term is not common in the mutual fund industry, as mutual funds cannot – or at least tend not – to short sell securities. The principle of short selling is to sell a security that the manager does not actually own. In order to do that, the manager borrows the security and sells it. Then, at a future point in time, the manager buys the security via the market, to return it to the lender.

Short selling is of interest in two main cases:

– To profit from a drop in an asset price: the manager, privately predicting the drop, borrows the security and sells it at the current market price. Then he or she buys it back at a future point in time, and returns it to the lender. He or she makes a profit if the price of the security drops between sale and purchase so that he or she will have bought the security at a lower price than he or she sells it at.
– To cover the risk of a long position: managers may wish to hedge a long position temporarily, but without selling it. In this case he or she can short sell a security linked to the one he or she wants to hedge.

In the process of short selling, the cost of borrowing the security and the return obtained from the sale of that security on the market also need to be taken into account. The lender of the security must be paid for

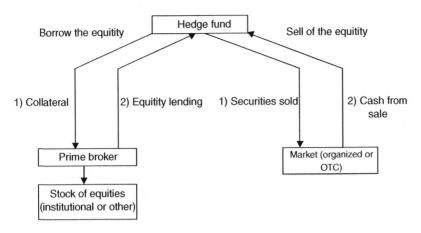

Figure 2.28 Implementation of a short sell

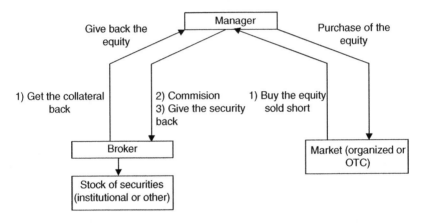

Figure 2.29 Closure of a short sell

the service provided, but the borrower will receive cash immediately on selling the securities; the manager will generally invest that liquidity in risk-free accounts, and will receive a return at cash plus. It is worth noting that when a security is sold short the seller should pay those dividends to the counterparty lending the security.

Figures 2.28 and 2.29 illustrate the concept of short selling. Figure 2.28 shows the implementation of short selling and Figure 2.29 reports the outcome. On the left-hand side of Figure 2.28 the manager borrows the security through its prime broker. In exchange for the security, the borrower should post a collateral – usually a percentage of the value of the security in cash or very liquid government debt – in order to be able to perform the daily adjustment to the value of the securities sold short. The lender either provides a security from stock, or borrows it from another institution.

The other side of the transaction is about the sale of the security. The manager who has borrowed the security sells it. The buyer pays for the security as usual, and does not know that the securities he or she is buying have been short sold. The money received is placed at the risk-free rate. The fact that we are in presence of a short sale has no direct impact on the second part of the transaction.

The close of the position follows an opposing process, also with two steps. First, (right-hand side of Figure 2.29) the manager buys the security that has been short sold on the market, using the funds earned from the sale and the interest on them.[26] Then he/she pays a commission to the institution that has lent them the security; the size of the commission depends on the liquidity of the security. They he/she returns the securities to the lender, closing the position. Finally he/she receives the cash posted as collateral for the short position.

In practice, funds have global agreements with their prime brokers, and short positions are opened and closed constantly. The whole process is carried out rapidly in most cases; only for the less liquid securities is there not always a price available, and the number of securities available for shorting may be limited.

9 Leverage

Leverage is another tool widely used in the hedge fund industry while its use in the mutual fund industry is very limited. Leverage allows hedge fund managers to amplify their return on a security, a sector or a market (and as a consequence the level of risk) for a same level of initial capital. In most cases there is no legal limit on the level of leverage that can be implemented. This does not mean that there is no formal or informal limit, as the manager usually gives a limit in the prospectus, and prime brokers define the maximum level of leverage that can be given to any single manager based on the strategy implemented.

There are various ways to create leverage, the easiest being to borrow additional assets from a financial institution. If a US$200 million fund borrows US$100 million, the fund is leveraged 1.5 times. In other words, the fund is invested at 150 per cent for 100 per cent of the initial capital.

Other ways to create leverage include buying derivative products like futures where the margin required to take a position only represents a fraction of the global exposure short selling positions or a repurchase agreement.[27] Leverage can be defined in terms of the balance sheet (when it is shown as the ratio of assets on net value) or in terms of risk (shown as the economic risk compared to the capital).

Managers use leverage in two main cases. The first is when they calculate that the additional investment they are considering will, with the additional liquidity, pay more than the cost incurred in building the position. The second is when they apply arbitrage strategies and try to scale up the realized profits. But leverage leads to a higher level of risk. Let's compare an equity mutual fund with a hedge fund that applies a long/short equity strategy. They both have US$10 million AUM. The classic fund is invested at 95 per cent in equities and retains 5 per cent of its assets in cash. The hedge fund is leveraged twice. The manager can invest in up to US$20 million. At a specific point in time the hedge fund has US$12 million in long positions that are partially hedged with US$8 million invested in short positions. The exposure to the market is US$4 million, which represents 40 per cent of the initial capital, against 95 per cent for the mutual fund. In this case the hedge fund is in the end less exposed to direct market risk than the mutual fund, even if it is leveraged. If the hedge fund borrows US$30 million more to go to a leverage of 5:1, and combines US$30 million long positions with US$15 million short positions, the total exposure is US$15 million. This gives a total long exposure of 150 per cent of the initial capital. Such positioning would be more aggressive than the long only mutual fund.

10 Gross and net exposition

Hedge funds combine long and short positions. The concepts of net and gross exposures have been defined to integrate combined positions in single numbers or ratios that can be used to compare funds. The gross exposure measures the total investment of the fund; it is calculated by adding the long and short positions and viewing the total as a percentage of total assets. This measure gives an estimation of the global risk of the product. The level of risk can be totally different for the same gross exposure, as positions may be taken to balance the risk of other positions. This measure gives an idea of the capital invested relative to the AUM. It does not give a measure of the market exposure, as long and short positions are added – but it does give an estimation of the assets at risk. This can be estimated with the following formula:

$$EB_t = L_t + C_t \tag{2.1}$$

where:
EB_t = the gross exposure at time t
L_t = the sum of long positions at time t
C_t = the sum of short positions at time t.

Consider the following (theoretical and simplified) case of an equity manager who combines 35 long positions (representing 75.5 per cent of the assets) with 12 individual short positions and a short position in an index (together representing 39 per cent of the asset) at time t. His/her gross exposure is 114.5 per cent.

The net exposure measures the exposure of the fund to the underlying market by differentiating long and short positions. This measure is closer to the idea of market exposure; it is worth remembering that long positions can drop while short positions can rise in value meaning potentially doubling the losses. The net exposure, EN_t, can be calculated as follows:

$$EN_t = L_t - C_t \tag{2.2}$$

Our manager would thus have a net exposure of 36.5 per cent. Table 2.9 illustrates the principle of gross and net exposure in our theoretical case, with 35 long positions in individual equities, 12 short positions in individual stocks and one in an index.

Table 2.10 reports the evolution of long positions, short positions and the net and gross exposures of a hedge fund over a 16-week period. This case is of interest because it illustrates four positions typically taken by managers under various market conditions:

1. **High long exposure combined with important short exposure**: in this context the management team has a relatively important long book (usually 50–100 per cent) balanced with a portfolio of short positions that is relatively important (likely to be 40–80 per cent). The combination of the two gives high gross exposure with a positive but limited market exposure. The management team accepts the risk of being heavily invested but keeps their exposure to market direction low; the idea is to make money using relative value positions (the relative performance of the long positions against the short) rather than by being directional. The net positioning of the portfolio is low or even market neutral. Such a positioning is of interest when the direction of the market is uncertain and its volatility is limited; such high gross exposure could lead to high volatility under volatile market conditions.

2. **Reduced long positions combined with important short positions**: the manager has a relatively small long portfolio (usually 10–50 per cent), counterbalanced by a relatively important portfolio of short positions (20–70 per cent). The combination of the two gives a high gross exposure and a net positioning that is generally negative. Such a positioning is of interest under difficult market conditions; high vola-

Table 2.9 Illustration of gross and net exposure

Long positions		Short positions	
Equity 1	6.0%	Equity 1'	1.5%
Equity 2	5.0%	Equity 2'	1.5%
Equity 3	5.0%	Equity 3'	1.5%
Equity 4	4.0%	Equity 4'	1.5%
Equity 5	4.0%	Equity 5'	1.5%
Equity 6	4.0%	Equity 6'	1.0%
Equity 7	4.0%	Equity 7'	1.0%
Equity 8	3.0%	Equity 8'	1.0%
Equity 9	3.0%	Equity 9'	1.0%
Equity 10	3.0%	Equity 10'	1.0%
Equity 11	3.0%	Equity 11'	0.5%
Equity 12	2.0%	Equity 12'	0.5%
Equity 13	2.0%	Index 1'	25.0%
Equity 14	2.0%		
Equity 15	2.0%		
Equity 16	2.0%		
Equity 17	2.0%		
Equity 18	2.0%		
Equity 19	2.0%		
Equity 20	2.0%		
Equity 21	2.0%		
Equity 22	1.0%		
Equity 23	1.0%		
Equity 24	1.0%		
Equity 25	1.0%		
Equity 26	1.0%		
Equity 27	1.0%		
Equity 28	1.0%		
Equity 29	1.0%		
Equity 30	1.0%		
Equity 31	0.5%		
Equity 32	0.5%		
Equity 33	0.5%		
Equity 34	0.5%		
Equity 35	0.5%		
Long positions	75.5%	Short positions	39%
Gross exposure	= 75.5+39	114.5%	
Net exposure	= 75.5−39	36.5%	

tility may be dangerous because the risk of signficant losses in case of rebound is important. Managers will be positioned like this when they are highly confident in their security selection but also when negative on the market as a whole.[28]

3. **Reduced long positions combined with reduced short positions**: a manager has a portfolio of relatively limited long positions (generally

Table 2.10 Illustration of the positioning of an equity portfolio over time

Positioning	Time	Long positions	Short positions	Gross exposure	Net exposure	Objective
High longs/high shorts	Week 1	85	65	150	20	To be at risk by being invested but to limit the exposure to the market
	Week 2	83	70	153	13	
	Week 3	80	72	152	8	
	Week 4	78	80	158	-2	
Reduced longs/high shorts	Week 5	60	75	135	-15	To be at risk by being invested but limit the market exposure and even play a fall in the market
	Week 6	50	70	120	-20	
	Week 7	47	60	107	-13	
	Week 8	40	54	94	-14	
Reduced longs/reduced shorts	Week 9	42	40	82	2	To limit the capital at risk by being under-invested with no exposure to the market
	Week 10	44	30	74	14	
	Week 11	38	26	64	12	
	Week 12	33	20	53	13	
High longs/reduced shorts	Week 13	50	18	68	32	Play the rebound in the market but limit the capital at risk by being under-invested
	Week 14	65	15	80	50	
	Week 15	82	16	98	66	
	Week 16	95	9	104	86	

10– 50 per cent) balanced by a small portfolio of short positions (also 10–50 per cent). The addition of the two gives a gross exposure of less than 100 per cent with a positive but limited market exposure. The manager aims to limit the risk of the portfolio by being under-invested, but he/she takes relative bets. The net exposure is small or even market neutral. Such a positioning is of interest in case of uncertainty in the markets combined with high volatility; a counterbalanced limited exposure limits the total amount of risk taken. Many managers implemented such a positioning in 2008.

4. **High long exposure combined with reduced short positions:** the manager has an important book of long positions (generally 50–100 per cent) balanced with a small portfolio of short positions (0–50 per cent). The combination of the two gives a gross exposure close to 100 per cent and a long bias (50–100 per cent). The manager aims to limit the capital at risk but is clearly exposed to the market. Such positioning is taken during bull market conditions, or in an emerging market portfolio where the managers want to profit from the long-term positive trend while protecting the assets from any market turmoil. During positive market conditions managers reduce the hedge, and many of them also replace individual shorts by indices whose function is more to hedge the global level of risk of the portfolio rather than create alpha.

The evolutions of the gross and net exposures are given in Figure 2.30, illustrating our practical case, first with a positioning made up of important long and short positions with a limited net exposure. The second part of the graph illustrates a more defensive positioning with a low to negative net exposure. Over the third part of the period the team takes limited gross and net exposures during volatile market conditions. Finally, the fund has a high long exposure partially balanced with a high net exposure.

11 Active trading

Active trading is a management style in which positions are changed very frequently. This tool is used by many hedge funds; it can be implemented either to retain a low-risk profile when prices move rapidly or in order to profit from short-term price changes. This practice means that the turnover of a typical hedge fund will tend to be higher than that of a mutual fund. It will depend on the manager's style and the strategy implemented, but it is usually part of arbitrage strategies and those based on quantitative models that suggest that positions be taken quickly and frequently, aiming to profit from price variations over time.

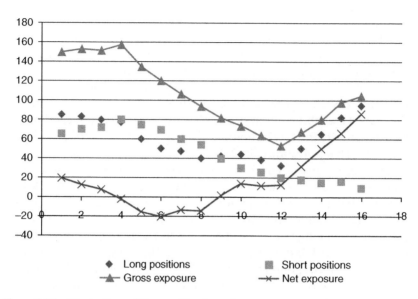

Figure 2.30   Illustration of the positioning of a manager over time

12   Other characteristics of the hedge fund industry

The hedge fund industry is made up of individual funds with specific characteristics at the level of the investment process and relating to their structure. We have grouped funds per investment strategy, but every fund will have its own unique characteristics; practically every characteristic of a fund will be different from those of the others, and we have already presented their specific features in terms of fees and liquidity. As an example it is worth remembering that the classification of funds into investment strategies comes from the need to group funds whose strategies are relatively similar; this classification comes from existing funds applying their own strategies and not from managers looking at the lists of existing investment strategies in order to create their own product. In this section we start with size of funds, other common characteristics and the use of leverage. We then present a typical hedge fund, then focus on the use of investment products, before discussing the dissolution rate in the industry.

12.1   The size of the funds

One of the first characteristics of the industry to bear in mind is that the majority of the funds have a small asset base. The industry has grown rapidly over the last decade (except during 2008 and 2009) and the number of funds has increased significantly. The majority of the funds have less than US$100 million AUM. Figures 2.31 and 2.32 report the percentage of funds by AUM in the US and in Europe; both figures show that 75 per cent of the funds have up to US$100 million and that only 2 per cent of the funds have more than US$1 billion. The hedge fund industry remains highly fragmented.

Just 25 per cent of the managers manage more than US$100 million, thus between them managing the vast majority of the assets of the

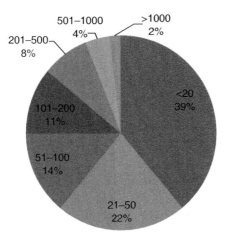

Figure 2.31   Breakdown of the American hedge fund industry by assets under management

Source: Eurekahedge (2012a).

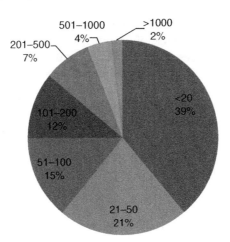

Figure 2.32   Breakdown of the European hedge fund industry by assets under management

Source: Eurekahedge (2012c).

industry – at least five category 1 funds (below US$20 million) are needed to balance one category 3 fund (between US$100 million and US$500 million), and, in practice, more like 10 to 20 of them.

12.2   Common characteristics

Every hedge fund has specific characteristics, but we can identify several commonalities in the existing literature. For example, 90 per cent of the funds have a high-water mark; less than half of the funds have a lockup period. Almost 100 per cent of the funds use external auditors and perform an annual independent audit. In addition more than 75 per cent of the managers invest in their own fund, 80 per cent take short positions and more than 70 per cent can use leverage. These common characteristics are also minimum standards.

12.3   The use of leverage

A study published in 2007[29] focuses on the use of leverage in the hedge fund industry. Although the actual numbers are based partially on prospectus limits that may be much broader than practical limits, the trend identified is still of interest. The numbers reported on Table 2.11 are per strategy, meaning that the use of leverage at individual fund level may deviate significantly from those shown. We recommend to focus our attention to the the simple average leverage within each strategy. The maximum leverage tends to give interesting information too even if in some cases (long/short equity), the maximum leverage possible is excessively high and probably only theoretical.

The strategies where the use of leverage is the most common are fixed income related strategies where leverage tends to be between 2 and 5 on average. Convertible arbitrage, macro funds and equity non-hedge strtategies follow. On the other side we find less liquid or higher risk strategies like short sellers or distressed securities investors. All in all, the maximum level of leverage reported tends to stay at or below 10 times and below 3 in several occasions. These results are in line with the perception of risk of the corresponding strategies and their typical performance objectives; all in all, three funds out of four use leverage to some extent.

12.4   A typical hedge fund

We give the main characteristics of a typical hedge fund in Table 2.12. Such a fund has on average close to US$150 million in AUM (the median

Table 2.11 Use of leverage

	Simple average leverage within each strategy	Asset-weighted average leverage within each strategy	Leverage	
			Minimum	Maximum
Equity market neutral	1.7	1.8	1	3
Long/short equity	1.4	1.4	0.7	20
Sector composite	1.2	1.2	1	2
Equity non-hedge	2.2	2.9	1	12
Short selling	1.2	1.1	1	2
Emerging markets	1.3	1.4	1	3
Convertible arbitrage	2.5	3	1	7
Event driven multi-strategy	1.5	1.4	1	10
Risk arbitrage	1.4	1.6	1	10
Distressed securities	1.3	1.2	1	3
Fixed income: diversified	5.4	8.3	1	18
Fixed income: mortgage-backed	3.9	4.3	1	10
Fixed income: high yield	3	3.3	1.3	5.2
Fixed income arbitrage	2	2.1	1	12
Global macro	2	2.4	1	5

Source: Bertelli (2007).

Table 2.12 Characteristics of a typical hedge fund

	Average	Median
Fund size	US$150m	US$50m
Age of the fund	5 years	4 years
Minimum investment	US$1m	US$750,000
Age (in months)	36	24
Management fees	2%	1.5%
Performance fees	20%	15.0%
Manager experience in asset management	15 years	10 years

is US$50 million) and it has a five-year track record (the median is four years). Its minimum investment is around US$1 million. The management and performance fees average 2 and 20 per cent respectively. The manager has an average experience of 12–15 years in asset management (10 years is the median).

12.5   Hedge funds and investment products

Hedge funds use many investment products; we can group these into three categories:

– **Cash instruments**: including ordinary shares, fixed income securities such as bonds, convertible bonds, high-yield bonds or mortgage-backed bonds as well as spot exchanges. These investment products are traditional, and their risk can be estimated relatively easily. This does not mean that the risk is negligible, but that it can be estimated accurately with relatively simple tools.
– **Derivative products other than options** (on indices, interest rates, currencies, weather and commodities): this category includes futures, forward contracts and swaps. The final results of these investment products are similar to those of cash instruments, as their value increases or decreases in tandem with the value of the underlying product. The use of such products is very common. Futures and forwards are probably the more widely used, as they enable a position to be taken on the value of the underlying product without involving ownership of the security itself – funds have no interest in owning the underlying security, which can be a commodity such as oil, soybean or live cattle. The most widely used contracts are forward contracts on currencies, interest rate swaps and products linked to individual equities or indices.
– **Options and other non-linear investment products** (on indices, interest rates, currencies, weather and commodities): this category is very different from the previous one. Such securities offer either a positive return, or a limited loss, or a limited profit with an unlimited loss potential. As an option gives a right and not an obligation to execute the contract, the total return of an investment in such a security is convex and non-linear. This has various implications, the main one being the need for much more complicated risk management tools.

In practice, most hedge funds managers focus on certain type of securities but retain the ability to use financial securities in the memorandum. This situation is mainly true for event driven funds or funds applying the distressed securities strategy.

12.6   The dissolution rate

The growth in the hedge fund industry has a characteristic weakness: its high attrition rate. Several academic studies have analysed this feature, and our estimation is that the median lifetime of a fund is between three and five and a half years.[30] The main factors that have to be taken into consideration are the AUM, the monthly performance, the liquidity, the leverage and the minimum investment.

The results indicate that any given fund has an approximately 7 per cent probability of disappearing during its first year of existence, 20 per cent over its first two years, and 60 per cent within five years or so of its launch. Such a result is in line with the concept that managers of a new fund will tend to take more risks during its first years of existence in order to offer tempting returns and thus attract capital.

13 Hedge funds and other alternative investment products

The hedge fund industry is part of the bigger family of alternative investments as defined by the Alternative Investment Management Association (AIMA); these alternative products include hedge funds, private equity, real estate, future funds, timber, antiques, art, fine wine, cars and so on.

Hedge funds are getting closer to other alternative investments, and nowadays there are hedge funds invested in private companies, real estate, art and even fine wines.

Hedge funds and private equity funds became particularly close over the few years preceding the 2008 financial crisis. This happened mainly at two levels. On the one hand private equity managers have created funds that use typical hedge fund structures. The differences between these products and private equity funds are in the type of investment realized and the liquidity offered. When they take such a structure, funds have to publish a net asset value at least quarterly, while typical private equity funds tend to publish them less regularly. In addition they should also offer a certain level of liquidity whether through a quoted equity or through liquidity terms that are more advantageous than typical of private equity funds. Such funds often request longer lockup periods than hedge funds, of two to three years, and they offer semi-annual or annual liquidity thereafter. Such terms are very restrictive, but are nevertheless more attractive than those typical of the private equity industry.

The second aspect of the connection relates to the managers that are between the two industries. While hedge funds generally invest in listed securities, some will invest in companies just before they are listed; this leads to an additional liquidity risk, but the expected return is naturally superior. Figure 2.33 illustrates the borderline between private equity and investments in listed companies as well as the intermediary situation of these new managers. It shows three phases in the evolution of a company. The first, when the founder launches its company on the basis of a product, service or another concept. Second, an investor discovers the company

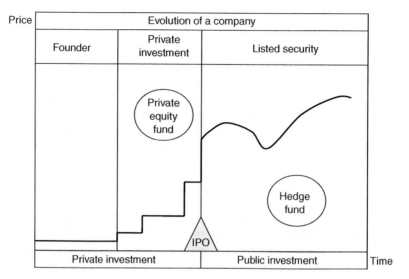

Figure 2.33　Link between hedge funds and private equity

and decides to co-invest with the founder. During this second phase the investments and securities remain private. Private equity funds tend to intervene during this phase; their role is to provide capital and to work with the founder on the development of its company. During this phase the securities are revalued, depending on the development of the company and the issuing price of the new shares. The third phase starts after the initial public offering. It is at this moment that the security is listed, and it is usually after this phase that hedge funds become involved.

The connection between hedge funds and private equity funds arises from the fact that some hedge funds invest during the private investment phase. They do not usually become involved at the start of the private investment phase, but a few months before the initial public offering. Then these managers typically exit on the initial public offering.

14　The strengths and weaknesses of hedge funds

Hedge funds as we have described them in the current chapter have some attractive characteristics but also weaknesses. In this section, we summarize the main advantages and weaknesses of hedge fund investing.

14.1　The strengths

We have grouped the main advantages of hedge funds within five categories: flexibility of techniques, co-investment by the manager, managers' capabilities, absolute return objective, and limited correlation with classic investment products.

14.1.1 Flexibility of techniques

As early as 1996, Beckier (1996) stressed that according to studies carried out with institutional investors it had been concluded that the main advantage of hedge funds relative to other investment products was the flexibility of the investment techniques. This flexibility includes a wide variety of instruments and their presence on various markets as well as the possibility of hedging the risks through short selling and the potential use of leverage.

More than 15 years after this study, the flexibility of the investment techniques remains key in the hedge fund industry. The main difference comes from the fact that more and more classic mutual funds can now use some of the techniques that were until recently specific to hedge funds.[31] This flexibility of techniques explains why 90 per cent of the investors in alternative investments use them as diversification tools.[32]

14.1.2 Co-investment by the fund manager

Hedge fund managers are almost always co-invested with their investors, and this investment tends to always represent a significant part of their wealth. This element is specific to the industry and one of its strengths, as the interests of the managers and/or the team are completely aligned with those of the final investors.

14.1.3 Managers' capabilities

The typical profile of a hedge fund manager has for a long time been to have studied for a long time in a business school and to have worked as an equity analyst for a few years then to have managed a mutual fund. Over the last decade, however, the situation has changed; more and more managers start their career in the hedge fund industry as analysts and move into fund management. Hedge fund managers should also have not only a clear and understandable investment process, but also be able to manage a company or to be associated with somebody that can do so. This last element has increased in importance over the last few years as the industry has become more institutionalized; institutional investors require not only a fund manager but somebody to manage the company itself, as well as a chief operating officer, compliance and/or a risk manager.

14.1.4 Absolute return objective

The vast majority of hedge funds aim to offer absolute returns. In consequence they aim to offer positive performance under any market conditions. This profile is completely different from that of traditional mutual funds, whose objective is to beat a reference index called a benchmark. In practice, the industry as a whole has been able to attain this objective almost every year; 2008 remains an exception as the industry lost more than 20 per cent in a particularly difficult environment – where equities lost more than 40 per cent. This absolute return is one of the most appealing features of the industry.

14.1.5   Low correlation with classic investment products

Hedge funds aim to offer absolute returns and they may use a large set of securities and tools to achieve it. These elements explain the fact that hedge funds tend to have a relatively low correlation with classic investment products such as bonds and equities. As a matter of fact many investors tend to use hedge funds as a diversification tool in their portfolio. This limited correlation has been mentioned by several academic authors and is analysed in Chapter 4.[33]

14.2   The weaknesses

The hedge fund industry also presents specific weaknesses: high attrition rate, lack of information, limited liquidity, a complex fee structure with high fees, specific risks and legal constraints.

14.2.1   High attrition rate

One of the main weaknesses of hedge funds is the high attrition rate of the industry. The number of funds that disappears is high relative to the size of the industry, particularly if compared to the mutual fund industry. Many funds are dissolved in their first few years of existence. This means that the results obtained for the whole industry are of interest only if investors select a fund that will survive. Table 2.13 gives an analysis of the attrition rate for single hedge funds; it indicates that the liquidation rate of the industry has stayed around 10 per cent per year until 2006. From there, the number increased significantly during the financial crisis before coming down just below 16 per cent in 2010.

Table 2.14 shows the attrition rate for the year 2008, the most difficult year for the industry since its inception. The numbers based on another data source indicate a significant increase in the attrition rate, with an average of over 30 per cent for the strategies analysed. This number falls to 22 per cent when for funds of over US$50 million.

14.2.2   Lack of information

The sources of information on hedge funds are limited; there is no official information or widely accepted source that can be considered as a reference. Private database providers are an interesting source of information

Table 2.13   Attrition rate of single hedge funds

	Equity hedge (%)	Event driven (%)	Relative value (%)	Tactical treading (%)	Total universe (%)
2002	10.07	8.47	7.64	7.29	8.71
2003	8.10	6.73	9.40	7.61	8.01
2004	9.26	5.65	12.87	8.54	9.04
2005	10.44	5.46	16.81	13.12	11.20
2006	10.52	13.49	12.16	13.48	11.62
2007	14.40	14.31	19.24	14.50	14.85
2008	24.23	25.83	31.45	19.96	24.11
2009	18.28	24.13	24.29	14.22	18.70
2010	15.46	16.07	17.09	15.02	15.87
All	13.42	13.35	16.77	12.64	13.57

Source: Kaiser & Haberfelner (2011).

Table 2.14   Estimation of the attrition rate in 2008

	Number of funds on 1 January 2008	Leaving funds	Funds entering	Estimated attrition rate (%)
All HFR funds	3221	894	170	28
Long/short equity	1566	404	74	26
Relative value	702	259	46	37
Credit	215	71	11	33
Directional trading	599	119	30	20
Systematic funds	114	29	8	25
Others	25	12	1	48

but several academic studies indicated their limits.[34] This means that any investor interested in hedge funds should develop their contacts in the industry, use an advisor or invest through a fund of funds. This situation is not ideal, as the final investor does not always have access to a manager or to information related to individual funds. This lack of information is present for individual funds and also at an industry level that tends to remain reticent of its information.

14.2.3   Limited liquidity

There are many liquidity constraints in hedge funds including liquidity dates, notices or gates for example. This is one of the main weaknesses of the industry. Hedge funds are in fact liquidity providers in the financial markets, meaning that they give liquidity to the market but that they do not offer much of it to their clients. The example in Table 2.6 illustrates this weakness and the importance of taking this aspect into consideration before entering into any investment.

14.2.4   A complex and expensive fee structure

We presented hedge fund fee structures in Section 7 of this chapter. High fees are a potential source of problems for investors. Several elements have to be stressed relative to the fee structure. Firstly the management fee amplifies potential losses, as this fee has to be paid in any case. In addition the performance fee reduces any potential profits. Finally clients investing in a fund that performs well for a few months before losing more than the amount gained will have paid performance fees during those first few months, even though the profits are lost in the end.

14.2.5   Specific risks

Investing in hedge funds leads to risks specific to this industry. The investors are exposed to the set of risks presented in Section 4 of this chapter. In addition every strategy will have its own specific risks that should be identified and understood before considering an investment. The specific investment risks of the strategies are covered in Chapter 3. Finally operational risk is a key factor to consider in the case of hedge funds – which in most cases continue to be small business structures relying on a few key individuals.

14.2.6   Legal constraints

In order to profit from maximum freedom in their investment strategies, hedge fund managers should respect certain legal constraints specific to each country where they are based or where they could be sold. These rules do not always concern the implementation of their investment strategy, but they do impact the performance of funds indirectly. In the United States. for example. the number of investors is limited to 99 or 499 investors. depending on their level of wealth. In addition, managers cannot market their product directly to retail investors, and advertising is forbidden.

15   Comparison between funds and managed accounts

While they have been in existence for decades, managed accounts have gained interest since the liquidity crisis of 2008. The industry is attractsing more and more institutional investors, which require more transparency for their larger investments; this explains why managed accountshave become more common. On the other hand, the fund structure has the attraction of low cost, as the implementation and running costs are split between investors. In addition, for a lower minimum investment they give access to a manager. A fund structure is, however, typically less liquid and transparent with a managed account, the investor usually has access to the whole portfolio on a continuous basis. This transparency constitutes a significant advantage for institutional investors using managed accounts, as they can aggregate the positions they have in various funds, enabling them to gain a clear and complete overview of the risk of their overall portfolio.

16 Replication

The hedge fund returns over the 10 years preceding the liquidity crisis of 2008 attracted many investors to see this industry as an investment opportunity. Several teams have in consequence worked on various ways of replicating hedge fund returns. By replication we mean that they have tried to replicate hedge fund returns by combining other investment products that are typically more liquid and cheaper. They have tried to set up portfolios offering a return distribution similar to that of hedge funds, and aiming to be highly correlated with widely used hedge fund indices.

The academic world has analysed replication strategies, and has concluded that hedge fund replicators tend to obtain between 40 and 80 per cent of the average returns of the most common hedge fund strategies.[35] On this basis, several institutions have launched products that aim to do this and they offer them for a lower cost than direct investment into hedge funds. It is worth mentioning a few elements that mitigate the theoretical attraction of these replication strategies:

- All the estimations of these strategies are based on past data, while managers structure their portfolio on the basis of their anticipation of the future.
- Every day, every good, smart choice and every mistake – that is, the manager's experience – is integrated into the management process of funds; but not into a replication strategy.
- Replications are based on a relatively limited amount of data.
- Replications try to replicate global hedge fund indices or strategy indices illustrating the average performance of the industry or the strategy. An experienced investor can aim to select funds that outperform their peers over time. They can also bias their portfolio towards certain strategies or themes under certain market conditions.

On the positive side some of these replicators offer higher liquidity than do hedge funds (usually weekly or daily) and they are cheaper than direct investment into funds. This is, however, not always the case, and it is important to integrate all the fees of a replicator before considering an investment. This can be an interesting way to manage the liquidity of a portfolio.

17   New structures

While hedge funds have existed for more than 60 years and funds of hedge funds were created during the 1960s, new structures have been created more recently. They aim to offer other ways of investing in hedge funds. These evolutions include fund listing, structured products and investable indices. Structured products include, amongst other things, capital guaranteed products, certificate on indices, call options and total return swaps (TRS).

17.1   Listed funds

Fund listing exists for individual funds as well as for funds of funds. It became common in the 2006–2008 period as a way of either offering investors less liquid strategies with daily liquidity (depending on the demand and the offer) or funding successful managers to obtain stable assets. Either way, the funds are closed-ended even though several tranches may have been created.

The creation process is as follows: the management team presents the product to potential investors. Then the fund is offered during the subscription period. At the end of this period the fund is launched under a closed-ended structure; such a fund generally has a predefined life time of between five and ten years. The product is usually listed in an exchange such as the AIM in London, in order to provide some liquidity for investors. The fund publishes a net asset value and there is a market price based on the offer and the demand. In theory there is always a price so that clients can sell their positions, but in practice during a liquidity crisis it is difficult to find a buyer.

This structure has several advantages for issuer and investors:

– Advantage for the issuer:
  • *Asset stability*: the assets under management of the fund remain stable for the life of the fund.
  • *Simplified net asset value estimation*: the net asset value is never impacted by asset flows, meaning that its estimation is simplified.
  • *Potential investors*: a listed fund can be proposed to a higher number of potential investors. Both long-term and shorter-term investors can consider such products.
– Advantages for investors:
  • *Frequency of dealing*: shares in the fund theoretically can be dealt daily or even intraday, whereas classic hedge fund structures tend to be monthly or quarterly.

- *Premium/discount*: listed funds are generally traded at a discount or a premium relative to their net asset value. This can add to the return or lead to a loss. It can be highly advantageous in case of success and strong demand for a product.

Such structures have lost investor interest since the liquidity crisis of 2008, when many closed-ended listed funds suffered from a lack of interest. Discounts increased significantly (up to 90 per cent in some cases) and many investors looking for liquidity made significant losses on certain positions.

17.2 Structured products

Structured products are based on the commitment to offer a minimum return, precise and verifiable. This engagement is called the formula, and the product associated with it is a fund based on this formula. A typical example is shown in Formula 2.3; here, the product aims to offer the performance of a benchmark and to guarantee the capital.

$$NAV_{t+1} = NAV_t(100\% + 100\% \times R_t) \tag{2.3}$$

where:
NAV_t = net asset value of the structured product at time t
R_t = return of the reference index.

Capital protection is not always guaranteed as the offers gets bigger. Figure 2.34, taken from the *Guide to Structured Products* from SG Corporate and Investment Banking, clearly illustrates the positioning of investment products in the investment world. The global universe is subdivided between asset management based on a securities holding (traditional or indexed) and that based on complex products and investment techniques (alternative and with structured products). Alternatively, we can split the range between discretionary management (traditional and alternative) and a more systematic approach (structured products and indexed).

Structured products have existed since the mid-1980s, but have been applied to the world of hedge funds for just a few years. The underlying product can be a fund, a group of fund or an index. There are two types of structured products, the CPPI (constant proportion portfolio insurance) built on insurance portfolio techniques, and the management, based on the use of options. The CPPI were created first; they aim to protect the portfolio from capital losses. The principle is simple: a part of the portfolio is invested in risk-free assets while the rest is invested in riskier ones. The

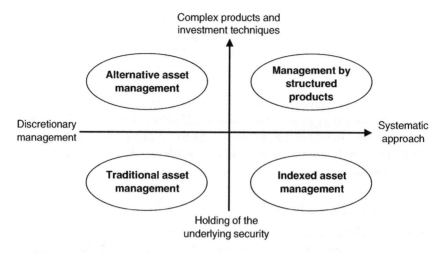

Figure 2.34   Positioning of structure products in the world of investments

weights are re-equilibrated on the basis of the performance of the risky portion. When its performance is superior to historical performance of the product the proportion allocated to the risky asset increases, and it is decreased when recent performance is below historical performance. These products use leverage called the multiple in order to be able to attain the objective. Multiples are usually around three for equities, five for hedge funds and eight for bonds. The multiple is defined by Formula 2.4.

$$A_{Rt} = M(NAV_t - F)/NAV_t \qquad (2.4)$$

where:
A_{Rt} = allocation to the risky asset over period t
M = coefficient multiplier
F = floor, which is the minimum guaranteed return (100 per cent in case of capital protection).

A maximum turnover is generally determined in order to limit transaction costs. Consider the following example:

– length: 10 years
– underlying asset: a fund of funds
– guarantee: 100 per cent capital protection, plus the highest net asset value over the life of the fund
– multiple: three
– risk-free rate : 4 per cent – NAV: 100

To calculate the floor, we can use Formula 2.5:

$$F_t = CPR \times \frac{1}{(1+Rf)^y} \tag{2.5}$$

where:
$y =$ length
$F =$ the floor
$CPR =$ the capital protection rate
$R_f =$ the risk-free rate.

$$F_t = 100\% \times \frac{1}{(1+4\%)^{10}} = 67.5\%$$

In this case the floor comes out at 67.5 per cent.

The cushion is the difference between the net asset value and the floor; so in this case the cushion is 32.5 per cent.

The investment in the risky asset is calculated with Formula 2.4 (see previous page), and the proportion invested in the non-risky asset by can de deducted from there.

$$NAV_{t+1} = A_{Rt}(1+R_{Rt}) + A_{NRt}(1+R_{NRt}) \tag{2.6}$$

where:
$R_{Rt} =$ return on the risky asset over the period t
$R_{NRt} =$ return on the non-risky asset over the period t

Next month, the fund gains 3 per cent. The new guarantee can be estimated using Formula 2.7.

$$NAV_{t+1} = 97.33\% \times 1.03 + 2.67\% \times 1.33\% = 103.8\% \tag{2.7}$$

We can then estimate the floor using the new allocation between the fund of funds and the risk-free asset (see Formula 2.8) and the new allocation between the fund of funds and the risk-free assets (see Formulas 2.9 and 2.10.

$$F_{t+1} = NAV_{t+1} \times \frac{1}{(1+Rf)^{y-1}} \tag{2.8}$$

$$F_{t+1} = 103.8\% \times \frac{1}{(1+4\%)^{10-\frac{1}{12}}} = 70.35\%$$

$$A_{Rt+1} = M(NAV_{t+1} - F_{r+1})/NAV_{t+1} \tag{2.9}$$

$$A_{Rt+1} = 3 * (103.8 - 70.35\%)/103.8 = 96.667\%$$

$$A_{NRt+1} = NAV_{t+1} - A_{Rt+1}$$ (2.10)

$$A_{NRt+1} = 103.8\% - 96.667\% = 7.133\%$$

The following month the fund of funds loses 2 per cent. The guaranteed floor remains at the net asset value of the preceding month at 103.801 per cent. The net asset value, the new floor and the new allocation between the fund of funds and the risk-free assets are shown in Formulas 2.11 to 2.14:

$$NAV_{t+2} = A_{Rt+1}(1 + R_{Rt+1}) + A_{NRt+1}(1 + R_{NRt+1})$$ (2.11)

$$NAV_{t+2} = 96.667\% \times 0.98 + 7.134 \times 1.33\% = 101,797\%$$

$$F_{t+2} = NAV_{t+2} \times \frac{1}{(1 + Rf)^{y-2}}$$ (2.12)

$$F_{t+2} = 103.8\% \times \frac{1}{(1 + 4\%)^{10 - \frac{2}{12}}} = 70.584\%$$

$$A_{Rt+2} = M(NAV_{t+2} - F_{t+2}) / NAV_{t+2}$$ (2.13)

$$A_{Rt+2} = 3 \times (101.797 - 70.584\%) / 101.797 = 91.984\%$$

$$A_{NRt+2} = NAV_{t+2} - A_{Rt+2}$$ (2.14)

$$A_{NRt+2} = 101.797\% - 91.984\% = 9.812\%$$

This process continues throughout the life of the product.

The second type of structured product relies on the use of options. The management of these is based on mathematical models that aim to enable the owner to profit from markets during rises while protecting their capital during difficult market conditions. The main difference between the CPPI and the second type of structure is that in this the capital protection and performance are guaranteed. The underlying idea is, as in the previous case, to invest part of the assets in risk-free assets, the rest being invested in options that aim to offer a return in line with a reference index. This kind of product exists for classic indices but has not been applied to hedge funds as it has not been proved that classic investment products can be used to replicate the performance of alternative strategies.[36]

17.3 Investable indices

While it has become common to take an exposure relative to any equity index through indexed funds of exchange traded funds[37] this is much more complicated in hedge funds. Hedge fund indices are published by database providers that group performance figures from thousands of funds on a monthly basis. This list includes funds still open to investment as well as funds that have reached their maximum capacity and are not accepting any new investment; until recently the only way to gain a diversified exposure to the hedge fund industry has been to invest through a fund of funds or to build a tailor-made portfolio.

The situation has evolved as a result of the emergence of investable indices. Such indices can, thanks to a diversified portfolio of hedge funds, reflect the performance of reference hedge fund indices. This innovation has enabled many investors to build their own diversified portfolio based on various strategies in order to actively manage the strategy allocation.

We show the characteristics of a typical investable index in Table 2.15. An investable index generally includes from 50 to 200 funds, and covers 5 to 15 strategies. The assets are invested through managed accounts and the weight of each fund is based on its AUM. The rebalancing is typically quarterly (with some exceptions, either monthly or semi-annual), and the liquidity of the product tends to be monthly, but can be weekly for liquid strategies.

The theoretical objective of investable indices is to replicate the performance of the publicized hedge fund indices. The reality is more mitigated, for the following reasons:

- A mere sample of funds will be unable to replicate the performance of a few thousand funds
- There is an additional level of fees in an investable index that does not exist in non-investable.
- The funds included in the investable index are funds still open to new investments. By definition, then they cannot include, or will at least under-represent, the best funds, most of which will have been closed to new investors for several years.

Table 2.15 Characteristics of a typical investable index

Number of underlying funds	50–200
Number of strategies	5–15
Type of assets	Managed accounts
Weighting	Assets
Reallocation	Quarterly
Maximum liquidity	Monthly

– There is typically no qualitative overlay either at the selection level of the funds, or at portfolio level. An investable index is a compilation of funds without any qualitative or quantitative logic behind it.
– The liquidity of investable indices is inherently relatively limited; generally monthly, meaning that they are not as liquid as replication strategies. This liquidity constraint also means that the less liquid strategies will not be represented either, leading to a selection bias.
– The construction of investable indices will come either from the funds' AUM or be fixed over time. While the first modus operandi will bias the portfolio towards successful managers, the second one may over-represent less experienced managers.

In other words, first-generation investable indices should be seen as well diversified funds of funds managed without qualitative overlay.

Figure 2.35 illustrates the principle and reports the annual performance of the global Hedge Fund Research index (HFRI) and its investable equivalent index (HFRX). The drawbacks presented earlier explain the under-performance of the HFRX.

The main advantages of the investable indices are that they offer a diversified exposure to each strategy and that they tend to be liquid. The emergence of investable indices is a new step in the development

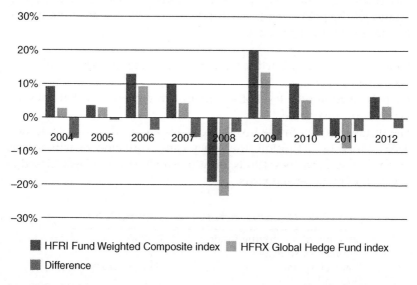

Figure 2.35 Comparison of the performance of a reference index and its investable version

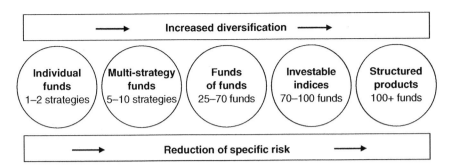

Figure 2.36 Diversification tools for hedge fund exposure

of the offering of hedge fund products. The underlying idea is that a higher level of diversification enables the investor to be exposed to the beta[38]of the hedge fund industry. The principles of the evolution of this offering are shown in Figure 2.36, which shows individual funds (not diversified), multi-strategy funds (partially diversified), funds of funds (diversified but exposure to the manager risk) and investable indices. At the far end there are very diversified structured products that are exposed to over 100 funds, and which are diversified per investment strategy.

18 Summary

In this second chapter we have analysed hedge fund characteristics in detail. We started with the various investment strategy classifications as set up by the main data providers. We then focused on the different phases of the creation of a hedge fund, before presenting the typical structure of a hedge fund. The fourth section focused on hedge funds and risks; we exposed a series of risks linked to the hedge fund industry that enabled us to appreciate its importance.

The fifth section focused on typical hedge fund investors. Then we analysed in detail the investment constraints specific to hedge funds before presenting the fee structure. These two sections have enabled us to separate hedge funds from mutual funds from various aspects without considering the investment process; we presented characteristics specific to the industry such as short selling, leverage, gross and net exposure, and active trading. We then developed other characteristics of the industry, describing the connection between hedge funds and other alternative products before focusing on the advantages and drawbacks of hedge funds.

We continued with a comparison between funds and managed accounts before presenting the principles of replication. Then we ended this chapter by presenting the new investment structures available for investment in hedge funds including structured products and investable indices.

3
Investment Strategies

This chapter forms the heart of the book. Not just because it is the third chapter of a book with six chapters but because it will help you to move from being a generalist who knows about the basics of the hedge fund industry to a specialist familiar with the details about each of the strategies implemented.

It is important to remember that every manager will apply his/her own investment strategy. The industry, led by database providers, has grouped funds with similar strategies into groups but every fund will have some elements of differentiation relative to its peers. Hedge fund managers do not learn how to apply a specific strategy from a book; they tend to have learned the basics through hands-on trading, and then adapt them or invent something new. They make money and attract capital. Then they hire people to help them; these people will first learn the manager's style before discovering their own. In addition things are not set in stone – quite the contrary; hedge funds are the very essence of active management. The strategy and positioning of any fund will evolve over time and will take into account changes in the market as well as the lessons learned. The hedge fund industry evolves more and more quickly than any other industry in financial markets. This characteristic is also probably a core strength.

The need to classify hedge funds into investment strategies comes from the rapid development of the industry and from the diversity of markets covered. As the industry has grown, managers have become more and more specialized and it has rapidly become difficult to compare them even if they might have had the same performance objective. When you invest in a merger arbitrage fund, you are not taking the same risks as in a fixed income arbitrage fund. The increasing use of derivative products as well as the increasingly sophisticated mathematical models have also contributed to that evolution. The final objective of a classification of funds into strategies is to produce investment products closer to the investors' needs and their expectations. Strategy indices have the same objective, that of enabling investors to understand the profile of a strategy over time. This will not be sufficient information for the decisions required to enable investment in funds of the strategy, as many more elements have to be considered, but it is necessary.

There are various ways to classify hedge fund strategies. We start this chapter by presenting our method. From there we present each strategy individually in detail in order to enable you to understand the main principles and the logic behind every alternative investment strategy currently applied in the hedge fund world.

The number and the characteristics of the strategies analysed may change over time. In this context we have covered the main and historical ones in detail before briefly presenting a few niche strategies that may gain importance in the future. We have retained the same structure for every analysis; we start with the main principles of the strategy analysed. Then we precisely describe the methodology before illustrating it with a practical example. Finally we present the main advantages and drawbacks of each strategy before presenting the historical performance of the strategy in comparison to equity and bond markets.[1] We add some sections focused on specific topics like risk management or other principles that are of particular importance or highly specific to any of the strategies presented.

1 General classification

We classify the hedge fund industry in three categories. The first one groups non-directional investment strategies; these do not aim to profit from the direction the markets take. The strategies grouped within this category can be market neutral (when the manager takes deliberately balanced or non-directional positions), event driven (their performance will depend on specific important events occurring at company level) or more specifically based on pure or multi-strategy arbitrage. These are typically absolute return strategies.

Within market neutral strategies we have grouped sub-strategies invested in equities, such as equity market neutral and statistical arbitrage that are based on the mean quantitative models. The fixed income arbitrage strategy focuses on the fixed income market. The convertible arbitrage strategy is a combination of investing in fixed income securities (convertibles) and hedges through equities. The event driven strategy has gained much interest over the last decade; its sub-strategies include risk arbitrage that focuses on mergers and acquisitions, distressed securities that group funds investing in bankrupt companies and special situation funds that invest in companies facing any other important events. A niche strategy called PIPE (private investment in public entities), or Regulation D, follows. Another sub-strategy that gained interest a few years ago is that of activist managers. This strategy comes from the private equity world; activist managers work actively in collaboration with the management of the companies in their portfolio to create a catalyst that will enable them to realize the expected returns. Within other arbitrage strategies we have grouped option arbitrage, volatility arbitrage or closed-ended fund arbitrage. We have also grouped funds that combine specific strategies within the same portfolio as multi-strategy arbitrage funds. Asset-based lending funds make direct loans to companies using real assets as a collateral.

Directional strategies include the original hedge fund strategy – long/short equity – that can be invested in either developed markets or emerging markets. In addition there are sector funds and directional credit funds as well as specific strategies such as short biased funds, long biased leveraged funds and macro funds as well as trend-following strategies. Funds of funds are different from the other categories and need to be considered separately. They can either be diversified, using a broad range of strategies to create a portfolio, or be more focused on certain strategies or on a category of strategies such as market neutral.

Table 3.1 shows how we have classified hedge fund strategies. There are three levels of classification: firstly, the category, secondly the strategy and thirdly the sub-strategy.

2 Equity market neutral

In general, the name of the strategy gives you clear information about what you can expect. In the case of equity market neutral funds we are considering funds investing into equities without, or with only limited, market exposure. Independently of the securities selected, the team aims to keep a neutral exposure to the market by combining long and short positions; the managers protect the portfolio from systemic risk by combining long and short positions. They usually apply the same process on various markets, sectors and industries. A sub-set of the equity market neutral range includes statistical arbitrage funds that use mean reverting quantitative price models to build a diversified market neutral portfolio.

2.1 Methodology

The easiest way to understand the idea behind equity market neutral investing is to consider a theoretical example. Imagine that you decide to buy a new computer. You start to look at the offer and you find a new

Table 3.1 Hedge fund strategy classification

Categories	Strategies	Sub-strategies
Non-directional strategies	Market neutral	Equity market neutral Statistical arbitrage Fixed income arbitrage Mortgage-backed securities Convertible arbitrage
	Event driven	Event driven Risk arbitrage Distressed securities Special situations PIPE/regulation D Activist
	Arbitrage	Relative value arbitrage Option arbitrage Closed-end fund arbitrage Volatility arbitrage
	Multi-strategy arbitrage	Multi-strategy arbitrage
	Others	Asset-based lending Others
Directional strategies	Long/short equity	Developed markets Emerging markets Global
	Sector	Sector
	Credit	High yield
	Short selling	Short selling
	Long only (leveraged)	Long only (leveraged)
	Macro	Macro
	Managed futures	CTA Short-term trader
Fund of funds	Diversified Niche	Diversified Niche

computer made by Apple. This computer has everything you are look-ing for (processor, graphic card, DVD writer) and it is compatible with the programs you tend to use. Your decision is made. To double-check you go to a Microsoft store and you look at their new product, and you discover that it is not as good as Apple's for various reasons. You buy the Apple model. Back at home you think something's up, and you decide to buy US$10,000 of Apple stocks. In our theoretical world you as an individual can also short, and you decide to sell Microsoft short for the same amount. This means that you are long Apple, short Microsoft for the same amount, with no exposure to the market; you have thus built market neutral and even sector neutral positions. Equity market neutral managers do that on a higher scale; positions may be taken using quantitative tools instead of on the basis of a qualitative analysis, but the principles remain the same.

There are various ways to estimate market exposure and to define neutrality. One can for example neutralize the beta of the portfolio by combining a long and a short book with exactly the same beta. This is, however, quite difficult as beta is a very volatile measure. This means that such a positioning should be adjusted frequently.

When the market risk is hedged, or at least partially hedged, specialists have to cover or support other risks, including sector risk or currency risks. It is important to keep them in mind as the sources of alpha and of potential risk in this strategy have to be clear to the client. In practice, managers tend to define neutrality either by investing the same amount long and short, meaning that they are neutral in dollars (or the corresponding currency), or by defining an ex-ante net exposure limit that is usually around plus or minus 10 per cent. A dollar-neutral fund will not always be purely market neutral; short positions are typically higher beta stocks that are more volatile than long positions. It is not unusual to have a long book with a relatively low beta, below one, and a short book with a beta over one meaning a beta-adjusted net short position. A beta-adjusted measure of the exposure of a fund integrates the weights of the exposure and the beta of the underlying stocks. Notional derivatives exposures should also be included.

The basic principles behind the equity market neutral strategy are similar to the long/short equity strategy. The managers take long and short positions in equities. There are, however, a few important differences. Firstly while equity market neutral managers rely exclusively on their stock picking capabilities to offer returns, long/short equity managers will on average keep a long exposure to the market over time. In addition in some cases they will actively manage the exposure to extract more alpha and go from neutral or even net short positions to aggressive long exposure. This is another source of risk and alpha potential. Finally long/short funds tend to be managed by stock pickers that put a strong focus onto fundamental analysis. They tend to have a relatively concentrated portfolio of 50 to 80 stocks, while equity market funds tend to be more diversified.

There are various ways to build a market neutral portfolio. In some cases the team goes long on stocks they estimate to be undervalued (either qualitatively or quantitatively) and short on overvalued securities, without trying to make any link between them. Another way to achieve this is to balance positions in companies that have some links between them; in this case the manager estimates that one is too cheap or expensive relative to the other. A third way to manage a market neutral book is to think of sub-portfolios and/or to combine long positions in some themes or sectors against short positions in some others, while retaining an overall market neutral exposure. The majority of managers active in the field tend to consider linked securities when they build positions, and they look for securities mispriced relative to their peers. Some managers invest in markets that cannot be easily shortened, and combine long positions in stocks with short positions in futures on indices as a partial hedge. In this case their objective is often to identify seriously undervalued securities and to hedge the market risk.

Equity market neutral funds inherently have no, or at least a limited, exposure to the equity markets, and as the short book is as big as the long book the quality of the manager should be measured not only in absolute terms but relative to the risk-free rate – the risk-free rate being paid on the cash received on the short sales.

2.2   Definition of neutrality

Neutrality can be defined in various ways: a fund can be dollar-neutral, beta-neutral and/or sector-neutral: a market neutral fund in dollars has the same amount invested on the long and the short sides; a beta-neutral fund has a net beta of zero; a sector-neutral fund has no significant sector bets within its portfolio. Figure 3.1 illustrates the principle of neutrality.

Many managers define neutrality as a fund with low net exposure. A fund can also be dollar- and sector-neutral. Theoretically it is even possible to build a dollar-neutral, sector-neutral beta-neutral fund with no market exposure. The more neutral a fund, the more difficult it is for the team to create alpha.

The difference between dollar neutrality and beta neutrality can be analysed with the help of portfolio theory. The return of a long/short portfolio or a market neutral portfolio can be seen as the fraction of the portfolio invested in long positions multiplied by its return plus the part

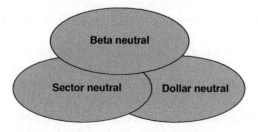

Figure 3.1   The neutrality of equity market neutral funds

of the portfolio invested in short positions multiplied by its return as shown in Formula 3.1.

$$R_P = F_L R_L + F_S R_S \tag{3.1}$$

where:
R_p = return from portfolio P
F_L = fraction of the portfolio invested in long positions
R_L = return from the long part of the portfolio
F_S = fraction of the portfolio invested in short positions
R_S = return from the short part of the portfolio.

This return can also be seen as the sum of two elements. The first one is the fraction of the portfolio invested in long positions multiplied by the product of the beta of long positions and the return of the market, to which we add or subtract the alpha of the long portfolio over the period analysed. The second element is the fraction of the portfolio invested in short positions multiplied by the beta of the short positions times the return of the market plus or minus the alpha of the short portfolio over the period. This is illustrated in Formula 3.2.

$$R_P = F_L (\beta_L R_M + \alpha_L) + F_S (\beta_S R_M + \alpha_S) \tag{3.2}$$

In the dollar-neutral version of the strategy the fractions invested in long and short positions are identical. This means that Formula 3.1 can be simplified and it becomes Formula 3.3. In the theoretical case of 100 per cent long exposure and 100 per cent short exposure we obtain Formula 3.4.

$$R_P = F (R_L + R_S) \tag{3.3}$$

$$R_P = R_L + R_S \tag{3.4}$$

where:
F = fraction of the portfolio invested in long and short positions.

In the case of a beta market neutral strategy it is not the fractions of the portfolio invested in long and short positions that are identical, but the beta of the long and short positions that are the same. Formula 3.2 can be simplified and becomes Formula 3.5. In the theoretical case of 100 per cent long exposure and 100 per cent short exposure, we obtain Formula 3.6.

$$R_P = F_L \alpha_L + F_S \alpha_S \tag{3.5}$$

$$R_P = \alpha_L + \alpha_S \tag{3.6}$$

In the case of a strategy neutral in beta and dollars, Formula 3.2 becomes 3.7. In this case, the fractions of the portfolio invested in long and short positions, as well as the beta of the long and short books, are identical.

$$R_P = F(\alpha_L + \alpha_S) \tag{3.7}$$

Formulas 3.6 and 3.7 illustrate the search for a double alpha in the case of a perfectly neutral portfolio. We have a sum of pure alphas only in the case of a beta-neutral strategy. In the case of a dollar-neutral strategy there is a residual beta. Formula 3.4 can be rewritten by integrating the beta of the long and short positions in Formula 3.8.

$$R_P = F\left[(\beta_L R_M + \alpha_L) + (\beta_S R_M + \alpha_S)\right] \tag{3.8}$$

Consider the practical case of a dollar-neutral fund that is leveraged twice and invests 100 per cent of its assets in long positions and 100 per cent of its assets in short positions. The beta of the long book is at 0.9 while the beta of the short book is 1.1. Consider two market conditions. In the first, the market return over the period is at 8 per cent. In the other case the market drops 8 per cent over the period. On this basis, under a market rise Formula 3.8 becomes 3.9, 3.10 and 3.11, and under a market fall, Formulas 3.12 and 3.13. Meanwhile, Formulas 3.11 and 3.13 clearly indicate that the manager is taking an implicit bet on the market when he or she is taking dollar-neutral positions and not beta-neutral ones. If the beta of the long portfolio is higher than the beta of the short book, the portfolio will profit from a rally. On the other hand, the portfolio will perform better if markets fall and if the beta of the short book is higher than the beta of the long book. In a market rise of 8 per cent over the period we have:

$$R_P = 100\%\left[(0.9 \times 8\% + \alpha_L) + (1.1 \times -8\% + \alpha_S)\right] \tag{3.9}$$

$$R_P = 0.072 + \alpha_L - 0.088 + \alpha_S \tag{3.10}$$

$$R_P = \alpha_L + \alpha_S - 0.016 \tag{3.11}$$

In a market drop of 8 per cent over the period we have:

$$R_P = 100\%\left[(0.9 \times -8\% + \alpha_L) + (1.1 \times 8\% + \alpha_S)\right] \tag{3.12}$$

$$R_P = \alpha_L + \alpha_S + 0.016 \tag{3.13}$$

The case of sector neutrality is similar to dollar neutrality. We can illustrate this by considering a manager who is long in a specific sector and short in another one. We can adapt Formula 3.2 by adding a specific element regarding the sector in which long and short positions are taken. In the basic case, this element is implicitly integrated into the alpha of the long and short positions; see Formula 3.14.

$$R_P = F_L(\beta_L R_M + \alpha_{LxS} + R_{SL}) + F_S(\beta_S R_M + \alpha_{SxS} + R_{SS}) \tag{3.14}$$

with:

$$\alpha_L = \alpha_{LxS} + R_{SL}$$

$$\alpha_S = \alpha_{SxS} + R_{SS}$$

where
α_{LxS} = alpha of long positions excluding the sector impact
R_{SL} = impact of the sector on the performance of long positions
α_{SxS} = alpha of long positions excluding the sector impact
R_{SS} = impact of the sector on the performance of long positions.

The portfolio risk is also different from the risk of a long-only portfolio. The volatility of an equity market neutral portfolio is defined in Formula 3.15; that of a beta-neutral and dollar-neutral portfolio is shown in Formula 3.16.

$$\sigma_P = (F_L^2 \sigma_{RL}^2 + F_S^2 \sigma_{RS}^2 + 2F_L F_S \rho_{R_L R_S})^{1/2} \tag{3.15}$$

$$\sigma_P = (\sigma_{\alpha L}^2 + \sigma_{\alpha S}^2 + 2\sigma_{\alpha L}\sigma_{\alpha S}\rho_{\alpha_L \alpha_S})^{1/2} \tag{3.16}$$

where:
σ_P = volatility of the portfolio
σ_{RL} = volatility of the long book returns
σ_{RS} = volatility of the short book returns
$\rho_{R_L R_S}$ = correlation between the long book and short book returns
$\sigma_{\alpha L}^2$ = volatility of the alpha of long positions
$\sigma_{\alpha L}^2$ = volatility of the alpha of short positions.

Formulas 3.15 and 3.16 illustrate the importance of the correlation between long and short positions. Portfolio theory stipulates that it is interesting to diversify a portfolio with imperfectly correlated securities. In our equity market neutral case, positions have to be counterbalanced, and the correlation between long and short positions will tend to be negative. This significantly reduces the volatility of the portfolio.

2.3   Quantitatively managed funds

Equity market neutral funds can be managed by a manager or an investment team using a fundamental qualitative investment strategy but many funds are managed quantitatively. There are two families of quantitatively managed equity market neutral funds. First, there are the quantitative funds that use mathematical models that integrate fundamental data. Second, statistical arbitrage funds. In both cases the use of quantitative models enables the team to consider a large number of securities, something impossible for a team with just a few analysts. Such a strategy usually implies the construction of a diversified portfolio that can contain over 200 or 300 securities in the case of statistical arbitrage funds.

The investment process starts with the definition of the investment parameters; the team has to determine the markets and sectors covered. Then they define the market capitalizations considered. Once the parameters are defined the managers apply the quantitative models. Funds based on quantitative models have usually two objectives:

1. Identify undervalued and overvalued securities
2. Analyse the risk factors of these securities.

Models enable the manager to be consistent and to analyse every security using certain predetermined indicators integrated into each model. Each manager has their own preferred models, and these will usually evolve with market conditions. Once the companies have been valued using the model, the managers build their global portfolio. Factors used generally integrate various families including growth factors, momentum factors, valuation and quality factors. We give a few examples in Table 3.2.

The statistical arbitrage strategy is based on the quantitative analysis of historical price relation deviations. This strategy is built on the underlying idea of return to the mean. In other words, there are long-term price relations, and any unexplained short-term price deviation will be resorbed.

Table 3.2   Typical factors of a fundamentally based quantitative strategy

Growth	Momentum	Value	Quality
Earnings growth	Short-term momentum	Capitalization rate	Sentiment
Earnings trends	Price trend	Changes in capitalization rate	Quality
Expectations		Various ratios	Analysts' recommendations

Managers use quantitative models to analyse price relation. These models systematically follow many price relations, and positions are taken when prices move outside historical bands. An inherent feature of the strategy is that long and short positions are taken at the same time. Such portfolios tend to be diversified across hundreds of names; it is quite common to have 200 or 300 lines in a statistical arbitrage book.

2.4 Risk management

This strategy is fairly well diversified and it tends to be amongst the lower-risk strategies available. Managers applying this strategy are taking no market risk. Such portfolios tend to be diversified, and are in most cases invested in large companies and developed markets, so the investment risk is limited. In the case of equity market neutral funds, risk management is more in the structure of the portfolio and it is taken into account ex-ante.

2.5 Illustration

Equity market neutral managers combine long and short positions in equities in order to get a neutral position overall. They focus solely on the relative price evolution of the securities considered. The long/short equity strategy is similar to it in principle, the main difference being the final exposure to the market. We give two examples, starting with a theoretical one to help simplify the concept.

2.5.1 Theoretical illustration

Consider a manager that takes a US$100 long position backed by a short position for the same amount. In both cases the money is split in equal portions between two securities; the long side is invested in companies Long A and Long B, and the short side is invested in Short X and Short Y. The companies are all in the same sector. The short positions enable the investor to earn a risk-free return on its investment independently of the evolution of the securities considered. This situation is illustrated in Figure 3.2.

Imagine that the equity market increases by 10 per cent and that the increase in the long positions is 13 per cent (+15 per cent for Long A, +11 per cent for Long B) while the return on the positions shortened is –7 per cent (–9 per cent for Short X and –5 per cent for Short Y). The risk-free rate is 2 per cent. In this context the total return of the portfolio over the period comes to 8 per cent gross of all fees, as shown in Formula 3.17.

$$P_t = \left[15\% * 0.5 + 11\% * 0.5\right] + \left[-9\% * 0.5 - 5\% * 0.5\right] + 2\% = 8\% \qquad (3.17)$$

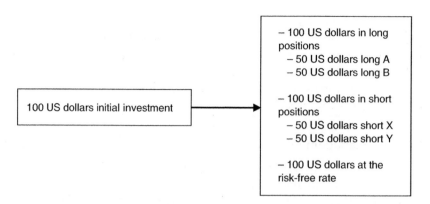

Figure 3.2   Theoretical illustration of the *equity market neutral* strategy

On the other hand, the market could have fallen by 10 per cent over the period. If so, Long A would have lost 5 per cent, and Long B 9 per cent, while Short X would have gained 11 per cent and Short Y 15 per cent. The total return over the period is equal to 8 per cent gross of all fees, as shown in Formula 3.18.

$$P_t = \left[-5\% * 0.5 - 9\% * 0.5\right] + \left[11\% * 0.5 + 15\% * 0.5\right] + 2\% = 8\% \qquad (3.18)$$

Table 3.3 summarizes the two possibilities.

The portfolio is purely market neutral because the return remains the same independently of the market trend. The performance comes from relative outperformance of Long A relative to Short X (outperformance of 6 per cent in both cases) and from the relative outperformance of Long B relative to Short Y (outperformance of 6 per cent in both cases). We also have to add the risk-free rate. This theoretical example correctly illustrates the principles of the strategy but of course in practice, a portfolio will be more diversified, positions will evolve and stocks will not outperform in the same way on the upside and downside.

Table 3.3   Total returns from a theoretical portfolio

	Bull (%)	Bear (%)
Equity market	10	−10
Long A	15	−5
Long B	11	−9
Short X	9	−11
Short Y	5	−15
Risk-free rate	2	2
Total	8	8

2.5.2 Practical example: Career Education Corporation and Apollo Group

Let's go back to December 2002 and consider two companies: first, the Career Education Corporation (CDC), which operated post-graduate courses in the United States and in Canada. It offered various certificates in information technology, communications, cooking. Second, the Apollo Group (Apollo), which operates high-level courses for people in employment; it is based in the United States and Canada and linked with various universities, and offers recognized certificates and diplomas.

Early in December 2002 an equity market neutral manager that had been following the price of these securities for a few months estimated that the CDC share price had become cheap relative to that of Apollo. This perception was based on a fundamental analysis of the companies. The manager decided to take a long position in 1000 CDC shares at US38.95 and to sell 1000 Apollo shares short, at a price of US$41.89. The price ratio of the two securities at that time was 0.93 (38.95/41.89). The manager took an identical position in the number of stocks; if he had wanted to take a dollar-neutral position he should have bought 1000 CDC shares and sold 930 Apollo stocks short.

When a position is taken, the manager usually sets a minimum ratio, meaning a level at which he cuts the position to limit potential losses. In our case the starting ratio was 1.07 and the minimum ratio 0.85. Regardless of direction, any move that would lead the price ratio of the two securities to move outside this limit means the manager would automatically close his/her position. Equity market neutral managers are not so interested in the direction as are other managers, as their positions are balanced; they will make money if their long positions outperform their short ones even if they both go down. Depending on the managers, these levels may be defined on a trade by trade basis or be the same for every trade.

Figure 3.3 gives the evolution of the ratio of Career Education Corporation over Apollo Group. Between January and December it decreased. Then the manager took a position in mid-December, which he closed at the end of April when the ratio hit the 1.07 limit. At that point, the CDC equities were trading at US$57.9 and the Apollo at US$53.74.

This position enabled the manager to earn US$18,950 on the long side and lost US$11,850 on the short side. The total profit was US$7100 on an initial investment of 1000 shares @ US$38.95 – an 18.2 per cent return over a four-month period.

2.5.3 Example: Daimler-Chrysler AG and Ingersoll-Rand Company

In other cases the manager takes shorter-term positions. Consider two other securities: Daimler-Chrysler AG and Ingersoll-Rand Company.

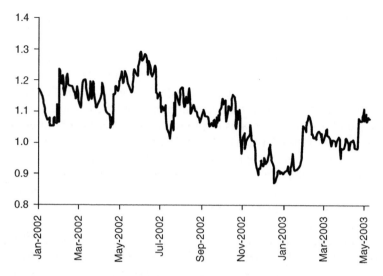

Figure 3.3   Evolution of the ratio of Career Education Corporation to Apollo Group (January 2002–May 2003)

Daimler-Chrysler AG produces cars, small trucks and utility vehicles; its brands include are Mercedes-Benz, Chrysler, Jeep, Dodge and Smart Car. Ingersoll-Rand is an equipment producer that produces amongst other things security systems, compressors, pumps, doors and building equipment. They are both global players. At first sight there is no direct relation between the two companies. The quantitative model used, however, is one that detects trends and correlation patterns. In October 2002 the model detected an opportunity and recommended taking a balanced position; long in Ingersoll-Rand and short in Daimler-Chrysler AG on October 1st. The manager bought 1000 Ingersoll-Rand stocks and sold short the equivalent value in Daimler. The ratio was US$35.64 divided by US$36.35. The model expected an increase in the ratio by 5 per cent, to 1.03. The minimum ratio is 0.93. This corresponds to a 5 per cent decrease in price. On October 18, the ratio reached the predicted 1.03 level, at which point the Ingersoll-Rand share price was at US$38.46 while the Daimler-Chrysler price was at US$36.65. The long position made US$2,820 (US$38.46 –US$35.64) times 1000 shares. The short position cost US$300 (US$36.35– US$36.65) times 1000, so the final position made US$2520 for an initial investment of US$35,640, a 7 per cent return over a few weeks. Figure 3.4 shows the evolution of the ratio over the period covered.

2.5.4   TJX Companies and Whole Foods Market, Inc.

Let's consider a last example, with two other companies: TJX Companies (TJX), a company that produces and sells clothes in the United States,

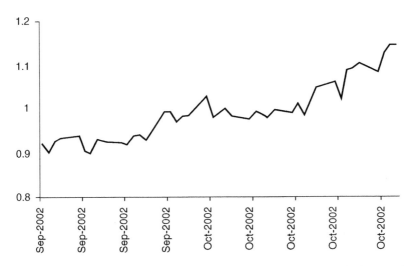

Figure 3.4 Evolution of the ratio of Ingersoll-Rand to Daimler-Chrysler (September 2002–October 2002)

Canada and Europe, and Whole Foods Market Inc. (WFM) which owns a supermarket chain specializing in natural products without any artificial flavours, colourings, flavour enhancers or preservatives. It also produces food supplements. The manager who gave us this example is a fundamental stock picker, who knew the stocks. Early in March 2003 he decided to take a long position in TJX balanced by a short in WFM; this decision was based on an analysis of the sector and strong confidence in the management of TJX. He bought 1000 TJX shares at US$15.93 for a total US$15,930 and sold short 315 WFM shares Food at a price of US$50.7 for a total of US$15,970. The starting ratio was 0.31. The objective was 0.35 with a minimum at 0.27. At the end of the month the respective share prices were at US$17.6 and US$55.64. This meant that the TJX share price had increased which was in line with expectations – but on the other hand the share price of Whole Foods Market had also increased. The ratio stayed at 0.316 and the profit came out at US$114 or 0.7 per cent. This confirm that it is not so much about the overall direction but about the relative performance of securities held. Figure 3.5 shows the evolution of the ratio. Interestingly, the ratio hit the target early in May, and the manager finally closed the position.

2.6 Advantages and drawbacks

The equity market neutral strategy has built into it a limited degree of exposure to the equity market, hence its low volatility. Its objective is to offer positive returns under any market conditions. Its performance will depend on factors that have not been neutralized, as the manager will

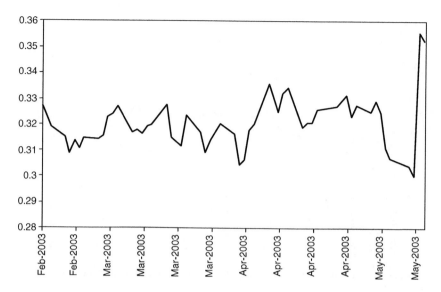

Figure 3.5 Evolution of the ratio of TJX Companies to Whole Foods Market, Inc. (February 2003–May 2003)

not hedge all the risk present in his or her portfolio; some risks have to be taken to offer some returns. The strategy is based on the manager's ability or on the quality of the model used. It is the purest strategy available, as everything depends on the selection of the stocks.

Theoretically this strategy can offer interest returns not only in up market but also in down market conditions; even if the long positions lose value, short positions can offer positive returns. In reality the performance of this kind of fund becomes much less attractive during bull market conditions, as then the numbers reported by market neutral strategies tend to be low compared to the market as a whole.

Quantitatively managed funds have specific advantages including the fact of discounting any emotion whatsoever in the decision-making process. This enables the team to avoid becoming over-attached to positions and thus keeping them despite clear sell signs – or on the other hand, from overreacting to positive news. Quantitative management also usually enables the team to decrease transaction costs.

The limits of the equity market neutral strategy arise mostly from the fact that the transaction costs can be high in the case of high portfolio turnover – this can be high when managers constantly adapt the portfolio in order to stay market neutral. Movements can be quick, and market neutral funds generally have a high turnover. Another limit, however, comes from the short positions themselves; the range of short positions is narrower than that of the long. In addition, if historical price relations move out of their range the manager can make significant losses; they can lose on long positions falling and short positions rising. This situation has happened a few times over the last decade. For quantitatively managed funds, the potential sources of risk include errors in the data used, human intervention, a concentration of risk or an excessive diversification, inconsistent market conditions or non-stationary modelling parameters of non-linear relations.

2.7 Performance

To illustrate hedge fund performance, we use the Hedge Fund Research indices. They are built following the predefined rules described in the appendix to this chapter. The use of indices may lead to potential biases in the performance of the indices, including the fact that the only funds considered are those that report to Hedge Fund Research.[2] In addition, indices are built by aggregating the returns of many funds. In consequence the returns are smoothed; there is thus a diversification effect that is not present at an individual fund level. We report the definition of each Hedge Fund Research index. These definitions come from www.hedgefundresearch.com.

Hedge Fund Research, Inc. defines an equity market neutral index called the HFRI EH: Equity Market Neutral index. Until 2005, this index was sub-divided between an equity market neutral index and an equity market neutral statistical arbitrage index. According to HFR, the difference between the two is the fact that the second is based exclusively on mathematical models. Today these quantitative strategies are grouped with other funds in the HFRI EH: quantitative directional strategies. We are using this index in this section as it includes the statistical arbitrage – but it is worth emphasizing the fact that this directional index will not be focused only on market neutral strategies.

The definition of the two indices is as follows:[3]

- *EH: Equity Market Neutral strategies employ sophisticated quantitative techniques for analysing price data to ascertain information about future price movement and relationships between securities, and select securities for purchase and sale. These can include both Factor-based and Statistical Arbitrage/Trading strategies. Factor-based investment strategies include strategies in which the investment thesis is predicated on the systematic analysis of common relationships between securities. In many but not all cases, portfolios are constructed to be neutral to one or multiple variables, such as broader equity markets in dollar or beta terms, and leverage is frequently employed to enhance the return profile of the positions identified.*
- *Statistical Arbitrage/Trading strategies consist of strategies in which the investment thesis is predicated on exploiting the pricing anomalies which may occur as a function of the expected mean reversion inherent in security*

prices; high-frequency techniques may be employed and trading strategies may also be employed on the basis of technical analysis or opportunistically to exploit new information the investment manager believes has not been fully, completely or accurately discounted into current security prices.

According to Hedge Fund Research, equity market neutral strategies typically maintain a typical net equity market exposure of no more than 10 per cent net long or short. According to HFR, EH: Quantitative Directional strategies employ a sophisticated quantitative analysis of price and other technical and fundamental data to ascertain relationships between securities and to select securities for purchase and sale. These can include both factor-based and statistical arbitrage/trading strategies. Factor-based investment strategies include strategies in which the investment thesis is predicated on the systematic analysis of common relationships between securities, whereas statistical arbitrage/trading strategies consist of strategies in which the investment thesis is predicated on exploiting pricing anomalies which may occur as a function of expected mean reversion inherent in security prices. High-frequency techniques may be employed and trading strategies may also be employed on the basis of technical analysis or opportunistically to exploit new information the investment manager believes has not been fully, completely or accurately discounted into current security prices. Quantitative Directional Strategies typically maintain varying levels of net long or short equity market exposure over various market cycles.

Figure 3.6 shows the evolution of US$100 invested in the strategy since January 1990 compared with other, similar, investments in the HFRI Fund Weighted Composite index, the equity market being represented by the MSCI World and the bond market by the Barclays Aggregate Bond index. An investment of US$100 in the HFRI EH: Equity Market Neutral index would have grown to U$453 by the end of 2012, whereas an investment in the EH: Quantitative Directional index would have become US$1333. The same investment in the equity market, bond market or global hedge fund market would have become US$1105, US$352 or US$472 respectively.

The HFRI EH: Equity Market Neutral index offered an average annual return of 0.9 per cent per year over the whole period, against 7.2 per cent for the equity market and 7.4 per cent for the bond market. The annual performances have been fairly weak, ranging between –2.6 per cent and +3.6 per cent; over the last five years the average annual return has been slightly negative. The performance of the HFRI EH: Quantitative Directional index has been slightly stronger, at 2.6 per cent on average per year over the whole period against 7.2 per cent for the equity market and 7.4 per cent for the bond market. More recently, however, its performance

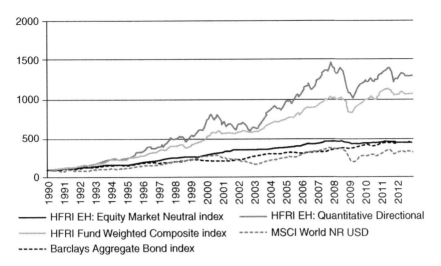

Figure 3.6 Evolution of US$100 invested in the HFRI Equity Market Neutral index or the EH: Quantitative Directional index

Source: Based on numbers obtained from Hedge Fund Research, Inc.

has been lower, at 1.9 per cent on average over ten years and 1.1 per cent per year on average over the last five years.

Its volatility is one of the main strengths of the HFRI EH: Equity Market Neutral index, as it has been very low over the period. Over the whole period it remained at just over 3 per cent and it has not moved significantly during the recent more volatile times. This is significantly lower than equities, that ranged between 15 per cent and 20 per cent depending on the period considered. The strategy has even been significantly less volatile than the bond index with a volatility of close to 6 per cent over the various periods under review. The volatility of the HFRI EH: Quantitative Directional index has been significantly higher and ranges between 10 and 13 per cent. It is interesting to note that the volatility of this index has not increased in the more recent times, as quantitative strategies have performed better than the hedge fund industry as a whole during the liquidity crisis.

Table 3.4 shows the yearly returns, the mean annual return, the standard deviation, the minimum annual return, the maximum annual return and the spread of the strategies relative to the comparative indices. It leads to the following remarks:

– Over the 23 years covered, the HFRI EH: Equity Market Neutral index was negative in only two years: 2003 and 2008. In 2003 its performance was only slightly negative, and 2008 was the most difficult year ever for

Table 3.4 Performance statistics of the HFRI EH: Equity Market Neutral index, the HFRI EH: Quantitative Directional index and comparative indices

	HFRI EH: Equity Market Neutral Index	HFRI EH: Quantitative Directional	HFRI Fund Weighted Composite Index	MSCI World NR USD	Barclays Aggregate Bond Index	Performance vs. HFRI (EMN)	Performance vs. HFRI (quant)	Performance vs. MSCI World (EMN)	Performance vs. MSCI World (quant)	Performance vs. Barclays Aggregate (EMN)	Performance vs. Barclays Aggregate (quant)
1990	2.0%	2.3%	5.8%	-17.0%	12.7%	-3.8%	-3.6%	19.0%	19.3%	-10.7%	-10.5%
1991	2.1%	8.3%	32.2%	18.3%	16.0%	-30.1%	-23.9%	-16.2%	-10.0%	-14.0%	-7.7%
1992	1.5%	3.3%	21.2%	-5.2%	5.8%	-19.7%	-17.9%	6.8%	8.5%	-4.3%	-2.5%
1993	0.8%	3.8%	30.9%	22.5%	11.1%	-30.1%	-27.1%	-21.7%	-18.7%	-10.3%	-7.3%
1994	0.8%	1.0%	4.1%	5.1%	0.2%	-3.3%	-3.1%	-4.3%	-4.0%	0.6%	0.8%
1995	1.0%	1.5%	21.5%	20.7%	19.7%	-20.5%	-20.0%	-19.7%	-19.3%	-18.6%	-18.2%
1996	1.0%	1.7%	21.1%	13.5%	4.9%	-20.2%	-19.4%	-12.5%	-11.8%	-4.0%	-3.2%
1997	0.7%	-0.3%	16.8%	15.8%	3.8%	-16.1%	-17.1%	-15.1%	-16.1%	-3.1%	-4.1%
1998	3.6%	4.8%	2.6%	24.3%	13.7%	1.0%	2.2%	-20.7%	-19.5%	-10.1%	-8.9%
1999	2.4%	10.7%	31.3%	24.9%	-5.2%	-28.9%	-20.6%	-22.5%	-14.2%	7.6%	15.9%
2000	2.6%	1.7%	5.0%	-13.2%	3.2%	-2.4%	-3.3%	15.8%	14.9%	-0.6%	-1.4%
2001	0.5%	3.8%	4.6%	-16.8%	1.6%	-4.2%	-0.8%	17.3%	20.6%	-1.1%	2.2%
2002	0.5%	-2.4%	-1.5%	-19.9%	16.5%	2.0%	-0.9%	20.4%	17.5%	-16.0%	-18.9%
2003	-0.3%	2.5%	19.5%	33.1%	12.5%	-19.8%	-17.1%	-33.4%	-30.6%	-12.8%	-10.0%
2004	0.4%	3.6%	9.0%	14.7%	9.3%	-8.6%	-5.5%	-14.3%	-11.1%	-8.8%	-5.7%
2005	1.5%	5.8%	3.5%	4.5%	1.3%	-2.0%	2.3%	-3.0%	1.3%	0.2%	4.6%
2006	0.8%	1.6%	12.9%	20.1%	6.6%	-12.1%	-11.3%	-19.2%	-18.5%	-5.8%	-5.0%
2007	0.4%	0.4%	10.0%	9.0%	9.5%	-9.5%	-9.6%	-8.6%	-8.7%	-9.0%	-9.1%
2008	-2.6%	0.8%	-19.0%	-40.7%	4.8%	16.5%	19.9%	38.2%	41.5%	-7.3%	-4.0%
2009	0.5%	1.6%	20.0%	30.0%	6.9%	-19.4%	-18.4%	-29.4%	-28.4%	-6.4%	-5.3%
2010	0.9%	2.9%	10.2%	11.8%	5.5%	-9.3%	-7.3%	-10.8%	-8.8%	-4.6%	-2.6%
2011	0.3%	-0.3%	-5.3%	-5.5%	5.6%	5.6%	4.9%	5.9%	5.2%	-5.3%	-6.0%
2012	0.2%	0.4%	6.4%	15.8%	4.3%	-6.2%	-6.0%	-15.6%	-15.5%	-4.1%	-4.0%

Mean annual return (whole period)	0.9%	2.6%	11.4%	7.2%	7.4%	-10.5%	-8.8%	-6.3%	-4.6%	-6.5%	-4.8%
Volatility (whole period)	3.3%	13.0%	7.0%	15.6%	5.5%	NA	NA	NA	NA	NA	NA
Meanannual return 2003-2012	0.2%	1.9%	6.7%	9.3%	6.6%	-6.5%	-4.8%	-9.0%	-7.3%	-6.4%	-4.7%
Volatility 2003-2012	2.8%	10.0%	6.5%	16.2%	6.1%	NA	NA	NA	NA	NA	NA
Meanaverage return 2007-2012	-0.1%	1.1%	2.5%	2.3%	5.4%	-2.6%	-1.4%	-2.4%	-1.2%	-5.6%	-4.4%
Volatility 2007-2012	3.3%	9.9%	7.4%	19.4%	6.4%	NA	NA	NA	NA	NA	NA
Minimum annual return	-2.6%	-2.4%	-19.0%	-40.7%	-5.2%	-30.1%	-27.1%	-33.4%	-30.6%	-18.6%	-18.9%
Maximum annual return	3.6%	10.7%	32.2%	33.1%	19.7%	16.5%	19.9%	38.2%	41.5%	7.6%	15.9%

Source: Based on data from Hedge Fund Research, Inc.

the industry as a whole. The HFRI EH: Quantitative Directional index finished down in just three years, including 1997 and 2011 where it lost only a few per cent, and 2002, which was particularly difficult for equity markets. The equity index finished down in 7 years out of 23, including the 2000–2002 bear market, 2008 and 2011; and the bond index offered negative returns for one year only, in 1999.

– The maximum annual returns of the HFRI EH: Equity Market Neutral index were achieved in 1998 (3.6 per cent), 1999 (2.4 per cent) and 1991 (2.1 per cent), and the best return offered over the last ten years was achieved in 2005 (1.5 per cent). The HFRI EH: Quantitative Directional index achieved its best returns in 1999 (10.7 per cent), 1991 (8.3 per cent) and 2005 (5.8 per cent). This does not mean that all the funds in the category offered low returns, but that the average was low. The low returns of arbitrage strategies can also be explained by the fact that the interest rates have been very low recently, meaning that the managers are not paid as much as previously on their short book.

– The spread in returns between the two indices and the comparative indices varies considerably over time, but tends to be negative, meaning that these strategies tend to underperform against the global hedge fund industry, the equity market and the bond market. The largest outperformance of the HFRI EH: Equity Market Neutral relative to equities was at 38.2 per cent, in 2008, while the largest underperformance was at 33.4 per cent, in 2003. Relative to the bond index the largest outperformance was achieved in 1999 at 7.6 per cent, and the largest underperformance was at 18.6 per cent, in 1995. The largest outperformance of the HFRI EH: Quantitative Directional index relative to the equity index was 41.5 per cent, in 2008, while the largest underperformance was 30.6 per cent, in 2003. Relative to the bond index, the largest outperformance was achieved in 1999 at 15.3 per cent, and the largest underperformance was 18.9 per cent, in 2002.

3   Relative value

Relative value is not really a strategy *per se* but it is a combination of various investment strategies. The main objective is to profit from price disparities for securities whose prices have been historically linked together.

3.1   Methodology

Managers take long and short positions in securities that have been historically or mathematically linked when the price relations move unexpectedly out of their historical range. The manager will then make a profit if the price relation returns to historical levels, or at least when it gets closer to it. The difference between this and the arbitrage strategies described previously is that the relative value strategy is not focused on one particular kind of security, such as convertible or equities; instead, it usually combines a set of other strategies or techniques such as fixed income arbitrage, merger arbitrage, convertible arbitrage, pair trading, capital structure arbitrage or statistical arbitrage. Derivatives such as options or futures may also be considered. In this context, one or a number of sub-strategies will be favoured, depending on the market environment, and the split of the assets will be adapted accordingly.

By definition, the relative value arbitrage strategy implies the combination of several individual strategies. Managers applying only one of the strategies mentioned will be seen as a specialized manager of that strategy. Relative value managers tend to be of two kinds. The first combine relatively similar strategies where they use the same models in areas where they have developed particularly strong experience. For the second category of managers, the portfolio is much more broadly diversified; managers of this kind combine various strategies by taking relative value positions in strategies such as merger arbitrage, equity market neutral, credit or event driven.

It is important to differentiate relative value arbitrage funds from multi-strategy funds and from funds of funds. The relative value arbitrage fund combines relative positions in an arbitrage portfolio of long and short positions with a back-to-the-mean methodology. A multi-strategy fund combines various strategies, which may include, but not be limited to, relative value or arbitrage strategies. Both are managed in-house, unlike funds of funds that involve external managers.

3.1.1 Pair trading

Pair trading is a famous investment technique. As the name suggests, the idea is to combine long and short positions in a pair of securities (usually equities). Its special feature is that it is in two securities from the same sector. The position is market neutral and the idea is to profit from the price relation between the two securities; the position is not taken on the long side because the manager expects the stock to increase and on the short side because they expect the price to decrease – it should instead be seen as a combined position where the relative price evolution is the most important element. It is the price of the long increasing more than, or falling less than, the short that will make the profit. The spread between the two prices should widen. It is a pure non-directional strategy.

Below, we describe two categories of pair trading positions. The first includes direct pair trading; this is based on the theory that the return of a company owning a significant stake in another company will see its stock price linked to it. The stock prices are integrated to some extent, and any significant move in relative prices will create an opportunity for the trader. This kind of positions is also called stub trading. The second, indirect pair trading, relates to companies that are linked by similar fundamentals, but with no cross-shareholding. The manager is looking to identify shares that are exposed to the same markets, factors or industries, and will take positions when significant relative price movements are identified. Such positions are ideally taken in mature industries with weak product differentiation, and with products with relatively long life cycles.

3.1.2   Option trading and warrants

This technique means taking a position in linked equities or options. These positions are based on price movements. Managers buy or sell options or warrants, and they take an equivalent but balanced position in the underlying securities. Such positions can be implemented either at a single name level or using index derivatives balanced with a set of stocks.

3.1.3   Capital structure arbitrage

This technique implies a long position in a part of the capital structure of a company, combined with the short sale of another part of its capital. Such positions can be taken either in equities or in debt instruments. Capital structure arbitrage positions can also be taken in private securities. Opportunities emerge from the fact that the securities of the capital structure of a company do not all reflect the same value for the company at the same time. Managers analyse various scenarios in order to estimate the risk of maximal loss. The aim is to build asymmetric positions that protect the capital to some extent if the positions go against the manager, but that has a greater attraction in case of success. Typical capital structure arbitrage positions include long ordinary shares against short non-voting shares, or a long position in a holding company combined with a short position in a subsidiary. Debt positions could for example be taken in straight bond or in convertibles. Combined positions could be long, for instance a high yield bond balanced with a short in the equity of the same company.

3.2   Fixed income arbitrage

Fixed income arbitrage is a sub-strategy of the relative value category. We are presenting it in detail because this strategy is important even though it is not being currently applied by many managers; it has been predominant in the late 1980s and the world of hedge fund tends to be cyclical. Managers specializing in the strategy take counterbalanced positions in fixed income securities, investing mainly in debt products and currencies, and extensively using derivative products. They mathematically analyse the price relation between the securities of interest to them, and look for a spread relative to an equilibrium situation. They estimate whether or not this spread is justified, and take a position if they expect this spread to disappear. The rule is to balance long positions with short ones.

This strategy attracted much attention in the 1990s, but many fund managers – and more importantly investors – lost interest in it after the 1998 debt crisis.[4] As always, the strategy gained new interest after a few years as new products emerged and as more opportunities appeared in a market with a limited number of players interacting. The development of more complex debt products as well as the emergence of more derivative products enabled managers to implement this strategy more specifically and precisely. These developments created the emergence of arbitrage opportunities.

At the start, the managers identify long-term relations that exist between interest rate products. Then they follow these relations and try to identify when one or several of these relations move outside their historical limits; typical reasons behind such moves include market events, external shocks or changes in investor preference. If a relation moves outside the band, they have to estimate if they expect this relation to go back to the historical standard and to take a position accordingly. Markets on which these funds are present include the interest rate market, the credit market and currencies. On the interest rate market managers will implement trades such as spread trades (taking a position on the price difference in bonds), curve trades (anticipation of flattening or steepening), volatility positions, correlation trades, interest rate spread trades or a directional bets. On the credit side, the strategy usually means relative value or long/short positions. Relative value positions include, for example, a combined position between a bond and the associated credit default swap, curve trades, inter-currency arbitrages or the search for asymmetric returns in new issuances. Long/short positions include balanced long and short positions in credit default swaps, basis trading (arbitrage between bonds and credit default swap), positions on the structure of capital of the company (relative value positions between bonds and equities) or balanced positions with different maturities. These positions can be taken in the securities of a single company or of different companies. They can be taken within a certain industry or outside it. On the currency side, positions are usually directional (long or short) or relative value. We illustrate the main elements of this investment strategy in Figure 3.7.

Managers simultaneously invest long and short positions in various interest rate products that include any kind of debt including government

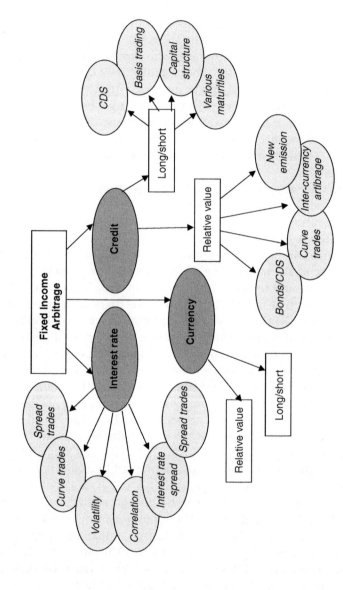

Figure 3.7   Fixed income arbitrage strategy illustration

debt (from developed markets and emerging markets) and corporate debt. Depending on the profile of the fund, it will be concentrated on invest-ment grade or include higher-yielding bonds. In the vast majority of cases it will include derivative products such as swaps or forwards. Arbitragers aim to limit their exposure to changes in the level of interest rates by the use of short positions; they aim to buy cheap securities and sell expensive ones. The principles remain the same as in equity strategies, the differ-ence being the securities used. The effect of a variation in interest rates is controlled if they select instruments that react with the same intensity to changes in interest rates. They realize gains if their expectations are cor-rect and the prices of the securities go back to the original levels. Market exposure is limited, and profits are made thanks to the ability of the team to identify under- or overvalued securities. The spreads in price are gen-erally very small, so this strategy usually implies the use of leverage to amplify the impact of movements. As managers combine long and short positions and play tiny arbitrage opportunities the overall level of risk of the portfolio tends to be lower than the gross exposure suggests. This is, however, not always true during volatile periods during which historical correlation move significantly higher, as in 1998 and 2011–2012.

The main challenges of this strategy lie in defining the equilibrium situation and anticipating future variations relative to this relation. It is difficult to anticipate which relation may deviate in the near future, and whether this change is only temporary or if new factors or company-specific changes will lead to a structural change in the long-term relation. There are no universally recognized rules, and each specialist will have his/her own point of view and pricing methodology. When a relation changes an assessment must be made as to whether this variation is temporary or if there are new fundamental elements justifying the change. Arbitragers generally use very sophisticated models to identify price discrepancies, as fixed income products are complex and rely on factors such as the interest rate curve, the volatility curve, duration, convexity, and company ratings as well as optional characteristics of bonds and derivatives. They ana-lyse various scenarios that may influence the existing relations, and give them a certain probability in order to limit the set of possible outcomes. One of the main difficulties in the strategy is to integrate the complexity of optional characteristics of the securities.

The fixed income arbitrage strategy is one of the most technical strate-gies. Typical examples of such a strategy include combined positions in bonds and interest rate forward, or swap and option arbitrage. Other well publicized positions include curve arbitrage (a three-year government bond versus a four-year government bond for example), convergence play between countries (convergence between Eastern European countries before they join the European Union for example) or combined positions in bonds issued in different currencies (a Japanese yen bond against a US dollar one, for example).

In order to analyse the sensitivity of securities to changes in interest rate levels, managers generally use the concept of duration. This is a statistical measure of the sensitivity of the price of a bond to a change in the level of interest rates. If a bond has a duration of four years, its value will increase by 4 per cent if interest rates fall by 1 per cent and vice versa. Such a bond will be riskier than another with a duration of two years, as the value of that one would increase by only by 2 per cent in case of an interest rate decrease.[5] Duration is a measure of the average life of a bond. Duration of three years means that the bond will react in the same way a three-year zero-coupon bond would.[6] A zero coupon bond is a bond bought at a price lower than its face value. It does not make periodic payments called coupons but the face value is repaid at maturity. In order to take a balanced position, arbitragers usually buy and sell bonds with a similar duration, enabling them to limit the directional bets in their portfolio. In this case, the effect of a rate movement will be identical on the long and the short positions, and the portfolio will be neutral in duration.

3.2.1   Risk management

Fixed income arbitrage fund managers have a special relation with risk. There are many more sources of risk in the fixed income area than in equity. There is a currency risk, whose importance will depend on the geographical focus; this risk is usually managed using forwards. Then there is the credit risk, a counterparty risk an interest rate risk as well as a potential liquidity risk, as bonds tend to be less liquid than equities. In addition, arbitrage opportunities are rare, and they usually require complex investment techniques to be identified. Managers tend to use advanced mathematical models to help them in their decision-making process. This leads to a model risk. Some of these risks will be taken while some others will not be taken and/or be hedged.

The credit risk measures the ability of an issuer to pay the interest due on time and to pay the principal back at maturity. The quality of issuers is rated by specialized agencies, of which the best known are Standard & Poor's (S&P), Moody's, and Fitch. Many arbitragers tend to cover any credit exposure and focus on investment grade securities. Certain risks can be hedged, but there are also some risks that cannot be hedged and for which there are no securities that can be bought to balance the risk; these ones can only be diversified away. A good example is the counterparty risk. A manager that buys or sells a security uses a broker, and there is a risk that the counterparty may undergo difficulties and goes bankrupt. In this case the portfolio is at risk. The only way to limit this risk is to use a number of counterparties and to check their financial stability. This has become standard in the industry, particularly since the Lehman collapse in 2008.

3.3 Illustration

3.3.1 *Relative value – theoretical illustration*

To illustrate operations on direct pairs we consider Company A and Company B, both listed on the New York Stock Exchange. B is owned at 84 per cent by A. On the basis of the securities available and considering historical movements, every US$1 movement in A's stock price corresponds to a US$0.95 move in B's stock price. Based on this historical relation, if the stock price of B decreases or increases significantly while the stock price of A remains relatively stable, or vice versa, the manager takes a position. This movement would lead to the price of B being temporarily cheap or relatively expensive. The position is closed when the price of B relative to A returns to the mean.

Figure 3.8 illustrates this strategy. It shows the evolution of the ratio of the stock price of A divided by the stock price of B; this ratio shows the high price of the one security relative to the other. Imagine that the average ratio of A stocks to B stocks is 2, and that the ratio is around this level at the middle of the price of A is US$20 and the price of B is US$10. A's stock price increases by 25 per cent, to US$25, by the middle of September, whereas B's stock price remains stable; the ratio of A to B has moved to 2.5, and this means that the ratio has moved well away from the historical average. On this basis and if nothing else changes

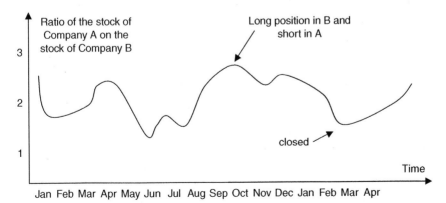

Figure 3.8 Example of operation on direct pairs

the manager takes a position and buys B relatively cheap, and shorts A's relatively expensive stocks, with the objective of making a profit if the ratio decreases. In Figure 3.8 the position is closed by the middle of February at a ratio of close to 1.5, which means that either A's stock price has fallen or B's has increased, or both. Our example is simplified; in practice, variations in ratios tend to be smaller arbitrage deals that need to be scaled up and tend to be closed within a few hours or, at most, a few days.

The underlying idea of taking an indirect pair position is similar. The main difference is that combined positions are taken in companies that have a fundamentally identical profile and that are usually part of the same sector – in this case, securities influenced by the same information relative to their industry. Typical positions would include General Motors against Ford, or Michelin against Bridgestone.

3.3.2   Relative value – Verizon Communications, Inc.

Consider Verizon Communications, Inc. to illustrate our capital structure arbitrage position. Verizon is a global broadband and telecommunications company, and is a component of the Dow Jones Industrial Average. Early in April 2002 and based on historical price relations, the manager anticipated a price gap widening between the bond and the equity. To profit from this he took a long position in the bond combined with a short exposure in the equity – not through direct equities but by buying a put option. There were three possible positive outcomes:

– equities and bonds go up and the bond price increases enough to balance the initial premium cost of the option on which no profit is made
– equities and bonds go down and the loss on the bond is more than compensated for by the profit on the option and its cost
– the stock price falls and the option's value increases while the bond falls only marginally or increases in value

The option enabled the manager to limit the capital required to implement the position as only the premium needed to be paid. In this example, the manager bought US$10 million of the 7.25 per cent Verizon Communications bond with a 2010 maturity at a price of US$102.8. This bond was issued in August 2001 for a nominal value of US$1 billion with a margin of 15 per cent. This position was balanced with a put option on Verizon Communications equities. The share price was at US$46.2 and the exercise price US$25. This option had a September 2005 maturity, a volatility of 60 per cent and a 15 per cent margin. The initial situation is summarized in Table 3.5.

Table 3.5 Example of a capital structure arbitrage position

	Buy	**Sell**
Type of security	Bond 7¼	Put option
Characteristics	Nominal US$1 billion	Volatility 60%
		Margin 15%
Maturity	2010	September 2005
Quantity	US$10 million	US$1.1 million US dollars
		at a 4.2 premium
Bond price/share price	US$102.8	US$46.2

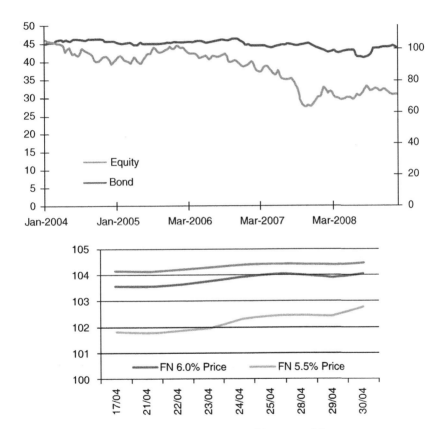

Figure 3.9 Illustration of a capital structure arbitrage position

The manager kept his position for six months. Figure 3.9 shows the evolution of the price of the bond bought as well as the evolution of the stock price underlying the put option. It shows a widening gap between the prices. The money realized positive returns as the stock price fell while the bond one stayed at the same level. The option gained more value than the bond lost. Figure 3.9 indicates that the share price fell from US$46.2 per share to US$30 per share, a fall of more than 30 per cent, whereas the bond price stayed at around US$100. In the end, this movement led the manager to make nearly US$2.3 million profit for an annualized return on capital invested close to 46 per cent.[7]

3.3.3   Fixed income arbitrage – Treasury bond

The following example is a position taken in 10- and 30-year English Treasury bonds. The manager is a fixed income arbitrage manager focusing on government debt. Early in September 2001 he estimated that the spread between the 10- to 30-year UK bonds was too narrow, so he took a long position in the UKT (United Kingdom Treasury) paying a coupon of 5 per cent maturing in July 2012. This position was balanced by a short position in the UKT paying 4 per cent per quarter, maturing in June 2032; his overall position was a bet on the spread widening. The 10-year bond was yielding 4.85 per cent on 17 September while the 30-year bond yielded 4.77 per cent, and at implementation the spread was at 0.083 per cent. The possible outcomes are the following. He would make money:

1. If the two bonds prices increased but if the yield of the 10- year bond fell less than the yield of the 30-year bond
2. If the two bonds prices fell but if the yield of the 10-year bond increased less than that of the 30-year bond, or
3. If the yields moved in opposite directions, and the 10-year bond yield increased while that of the 30-year bond fell.

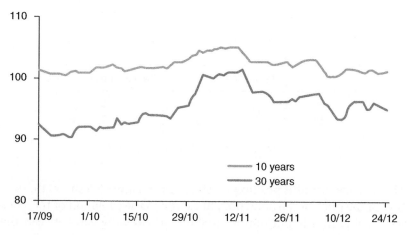

Figure 3.10   Evolution of the price of the 10-year and 30-year UKT bonds

On the other hand the position would cost him money if the spread decreased or, in other words, if the yield on the 10-year bond fell while the yield on the 30-year bond increased.

The position was implemented around the middle of the month. The gap between the yields started to widen by the middle of October; both yields fell, but the drop in the 30-year bond yield was greater than that of the 10-year bond yield. Figure 3.10 shows the evolution of the price of the two bonds over the period.

Figure 3.11 shows the spread between the yields of the two bonds over the period. As with any arbitrage strategy, it is more about relative and not about absolute movements.

3.4 Advantages and drawbacks

The strategy has several advantages. First of all it is market neutral, so good managers should be able to make money under any market conditions. Secondly, the world of investment is large and diversified. Even if a manager focuses only on investment grade securities, the range is broad and it includes more than 50 per cent of emerging market, debt. A few developed countries were downgraded during the financial crisis but globally the average rating tends to improve over time which creates the opportunity on the long side. Thirdly, the bond market became of greater interest during the crisis; for several years, the bond market did not reward investors and the opportunity set was limited, but the European debt crisis changed this situation and over the 2010–12 period there has been enough volatility in the bond markets for good managers to make money.

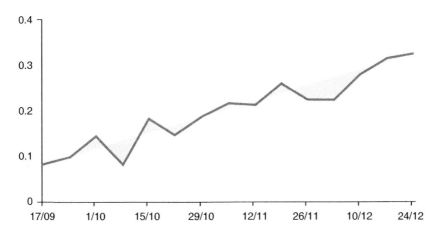

Figure 3.11 Yield spread between the 10-year and 30-year UKT bonds

Fixed income arbitrage managers aim to offer positive returns under all market conditions. Their investment procedure is based on the identification of price relations – more precisely, on their ability to identify abnormal price movements in related securities. In investment, such managers are mainly exposed to macro risks; as important and macro events occur throughout the world, historical price relations change and new standards may prevent price relations from going back to previous levels. This risk may be high in periods of stress. There is also a model risk, which also increases when market are going through phases of significant change. It is also worth emphasizing that arbitrage on the fixed income market requires expert knowledge. The positions taken usually try to profit from very tiny opportunities, and leverage tends to be largely used in the strategy, increasing the level of risk. Finally, as the strategies tend to be implemented using the same basic principles there will be some form of correlation between them even if they may be applied to different securities.

3.5 Performance

Hedge Fund Research, Inc. divides the fixed income relative value (total) strategy into six sub-strategies:

- HFRI RV: Fixed Income – Convertible Arbitrage index (analysed later in the chapter)
- HFRI RV: Fixed Income – Corporate index (analysed later in the chapter)
- HFRI RV: Fixed Income – Asset-backed index (analysed later in the chapter)
- HFRI RV: Fixed Income – Sovereign (no sub-strategy index published)
- HFRI RV: Volatility (no sub-strategy index published)
- HFRI RV: Yield Alternatives.

In this section we focused our analysis on the HFRI Relative Value index. There is no index for fixed income arbitrage funds. Hedge Fund Research, Inc. defines relative value managers as follows:[8]

investment managers who maintain positions in which the investment thesis is predicated on realization of a valuation discrepancy in the relationship between multiple securities'. Managers employ a variety of fundamental and quantitative techniques to establish investment theses, and security types range broadly across equity, fixed income, derivative or other security types. Fixed income strategies are typically quantitatively driven to measure the existing relationship between instruments and, in some cases, identify attractive positions in which the risk adjusted spread between these instruments represents an attractive opportunity for the investment manager. RV position may be involved in corporate transactions also, but as opposed to ED exposures, the investment thesis is predicated on realization of a pricing discrepancy between related securities, as opposed to the outcome of the corporate transaction.

Figure 3.12 shows the evolution of US$100 invested in the strategy since January 1990 compared with other similar investments in the HFRI Fund Weighted Composite index, the equity market, represented by MSCI World, and the bond market, represented by the Barclays Aggregate Bond index. An investment of US$100 in the HFRI Relative Value index would have become US$943 by the end of 2012. The same investment in the equity market, bond market or global hedge fund market would have become US$1105, US$352 or US$472 respectively.

The HFRI Relative Value index offered an average annual return of 11.4 per cent per year over the whole period, as against 7.2 per cent for the equity market and 7.4 per cent for the bond market. More recently, it has offered 6.9 per cent per year on average over the last decade and 6 per cent per year on average over the last five years. The annual performance has been weaker over recent times compared to the 1990s.

Volatility was limited at 4.4 per cent over the whole period, but it has increased to 6.1 per cent over the last five years. This is significantly lower than equities, which ranged between 15 per cent and 20 per cent depending on the period considered. The strategy has even been significantly less volatile than the bond index over the whole period and in line more recently.

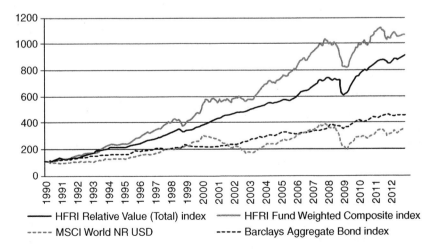

Figure 3.12 Evolution of US$100 invested in the HFRI Relative Value index
Source: Based on numbers obtained from Hedge Fund Research, Inc.

Table 3.6 shows the yearly returns, the mean annual return, the standard deviation, the minimum annual return, the maximum annual return and the spread of the strategies relative to the comparative indices. It leads to the following remarks:

– Over the 23 years covered, the HFRI Relative Value index was negative for one year only, in 2008 (the most difficult year ever for the industry) when it lost 18 per cent. The equity index finished down in 7 years out of 23 including the 2000–2002 bear market, 2008 and 2011. The bond index suffered negative returns for one year only, in 1999.
– The maximum annual returns of the HFRI Relative Value index were achieved in 1993 (27.1 per cent), 2009 (25.8 per cent) and 1997 (15.9 per cent). These numbers are fairly strong.
– The spread in returns between the HFRI Relative Value index and the comparative indices varies considerably over time. The strategy outperformed the global hedge fund index 11 times out of 23, the equity index 10 times and the bond index 14 times. The largest outperformance of the HFRI Relative Value index relative to the equity index was 30.4 per cent in 1990, while the largest underperformance was 23.4 per cent, in 2003. Relative to the bond index, the largest outperformance was achieved in 1999 at 19.9 per cent, and the largest underperformance was 22.8 per cent, in 2008.

4 Mortgage-backed securities

This strategy is usually seen as a sub-strategy of the fixed income arbitrage strategy presented in the previous section. It focuses on mortgage-backed securities that are fixed income products that can be found in the United States and, to a lesser extent, in Denmark, the United Kingdom, Australia and Argentina. They are issued by commercial institutions, such as commercial banks, state agencies or public government-sponsored enterprises, with mortgages as guarantees. The objective is to finance the purchase of houses by the issue of securities representing a debt. Managers take positions in order to profit from the existing price difference between the market price and the price estimated by internal valuation models. One of the main characteristics of this kind of product is that the borrowers have the option of paying their loan back early.

4.1 The securities

Mortgage-backed bonds are securities representing a portion of the grouping of a set of mortgages. They are issued by specialized entities. They can be government-backed or issued by private companies (which are then either the securitization of private mortgages as in the case of securities guaranteed by the government or larger single loans. In the first case a financial institution groups mortgages with similar characteristics within a portfolio, and securitizes them in a debt paper. There are three public refinancing agencies in the US: the Global National Mortgage Association (GNMA, usually called Ginnie Mae), the Federal National Mortgage Association (FNMA, usually called Fannie Mae) and the Federal Home Loan Mortgage Corporation (FHLMC, also called Freddie Mac). Mortgage-backed bonds are not exchanged on a regulated market but are traded over-the-counter. These securities represent a debt, like traditional bonds, and like them they usually pay a regular coupon with the principal being paid at maturity.

The special feature of these bonds is that their maturity is uncertain because each loan has the option of being refinanced or paid back earlier. This characteristic means that the coupons paid by these bonds tend to be higher than the ones paid by traditional bonds. Interest rates have several effects on mortgage bonds. On the one hand, the price of the bond depends on the level of interest rates, as for any bond: when interest rates fall the price increases and inversely when interest rates increase the price of the bond falls. On the other hand, there is a specific element: when interest rates drop, borrowers tend to pay back their loans or to refinance earlier. The average life and expected maturity of these securities is expected to decrease, pushing down the price of the bond. Based on the same logic, the proportion of refinancing or earlier payments is lower when interest rates increase; the average life and expected maturity of these securities, as well as their market value, increases.

The logic behind this phenomenon can be described as follows. When interest rates drop, it becomes more interesting to refinance a mortgage. At the other end of such a transaction the lender of the money will then have to reinvest the money at current market conditions when the mortgage is paid back. The interest rate paid will be lower, justifying the lower value of the bond. The same logic applies when interest rates increase. The ability to pay back the mortgage earlier is an option integrated into the price of the securities. Depending on the interest rate level, the lenders ask for a higher or lower price for that option. When the proportion of earlier payments increases it is higher, while when the proportion decreases it is lower.

Remark: Mortgage-backed securities are part of a larger range of securitized products. This also includes asset-backed securities and commercial mortgage-backed securities that are relatively similar. The main difference is the underlying asset. Asset-backed securities are backed by loans made to finance a new car, credit card loans or leasing for example. However, commercial mortgage-backed securities are not securitized

Table 3.6 Performance statistics of the HFRI Relative Value index and comparative indices

	HFRI Relative Value (Total) Index	HFRI Fund Weighted Composite Index	MSCI World NR USD	Barclays Aggregate Bond Index	Performance vs. HFRI	Performance vs. MSCI World	Performance vs. Barclays Aggregate
1990	13.4%	5.8%	-17.0%	12.7%	7.6%	30.4%	0.7%
1991	14.1%	32.2%	18.3%	16.0%	-18.1%	-4.2%	-2.0%
1992	22.3%	21.2%	-5.2%	5.8%	1.0%	27.5%	16.5%
1993	27.1%	30.9%	22.5%	11.1%	-3.8%	4.6%	16.0%
1994	4.0%	4.1%	5.1%	0.2%	-0.1%	-1.1%	3.8%
1995	15.7%	21.5%	20.7%	19.7%	-5.8%	-5.1%	-4.0%
1996	14.5%	21.1%	13.5%	4.9%	-6.6%	1.0%	9.6%
1997	15.9%	16.8%	15.8%	3.8%	-0.9%	0.2%	12.1%
1998	2.8%	2.6%	24.3%	13.7%	0.2%	-21.5%	-10.9%
1999	14.7%	31.3%	24.9%	-5.2%	-16.6%	-10.2%	19.9%
2000	13.4%	5.0%	-13.2%	3.2%	8.4%	26.6%	10.2%
2001	8.9%	4.6%	-16.8%	1.6%	4.3%	25.7%	7.3%
2002	5.4%	-1.5%	-19.9%	16.5%	6.9%	25.3%	-11.1%
2003	9.7%	19.5%	33.1%	12.5%	-9.8%	-23.4%	-2.8%
2004	5.6%	9.0%	14.7%	9.3%	-3.4%	-9.1%	-3.7%
2005	2.2%	3.5%	4.5%	1.3%	-1.3%	-2.3%	0.9%
2006	12.4%	12.9%	20.1%	6.6%	-0.5%	-7.7%	5.7%
2007	8.9%	10.0%	9.0%	9.5%	-1.0%	-0.1%	-0.5%
2008	-18.0%	-19.0%	-40.7%	4.8%	1.0%	22.7%	-22.8%
2009	25.8%	20.0%	30.0%	6.9%	5.8%	-4.2%	18.9%
2010	11.4%	10.2%	11.8%	5.5%	1.2%	-0.3%	5.9%
2011	0.1%	-5.3%	-5.5%	5.6%	5.4%	5.7%	-5.5%
2012	10.6%	6.4%	15.8%	4.3%	4.2%	-5.2%	6.3%

Mean annual return (whole period)	10.5%	11.4%	7.2%	7.4%	-1.0%	3.3%	3.1%
Volatility (whole period)	4.4%	7.0%	15.6%	5.5%	NA	NA	NA
Meanannual return 2003–2012	6.9%	6.7%	9.3%	6.6%	0.2%	-2.4%	0.2%
Volatility 2003–2012	4.9%	6.5%	16.2%	6.1%	NA	NA	NA
Meanaverage return 2007–2012	6.0%	2.5%	2.3%	5.4%	3.5%	3.7%	0.5%
Volatility 2007–2012	6.1%	7.4%	19.4%	6.4%	NA	NA	NA
Minimum annual return	-18.0%	-19.0%	-40.7%	-5.2%	-18.1%	-23.4%	-22.8%
Maximum annual return	27.1%	32.2%	33.1%	19.7%	8.4%	30.4%	19.9%

Source: Based on data from Hedge Fund Research, Inc.

products; these are direct investments in a debt. Table 3.7 presents their main characteristics.

4.2 Methodology

Mortgage-backed securities managers base their investment decisions on the valuation of the refinancing option. These securities are not easy to price, as it is difficult to estimate the proportion of mortgages that will be paid back before maturity. Managers use internal quantitative models to estimate the value of the option integrated into the securities. Then they buy the securities that they estimate as cheap and sell short those that seem expensive. As they tend to use internal models that rely on their own estimation of anticipated refinancing and on their anticipation regarding interest rate, each manager will take a different position. They estimate the present value of the future cash flows and integrate the value of the refinancing option. The value obtained is called the price-adjusted for the option, and it allows a comparison to be made between mortgage bonds and government bonds of the same maturity. The price-adjusted for the option can be defined as the additional return of the security relative to Treasuries while integrating the volatility of interest rates and their impact into the risk of earlier repayment.

Table 3.7 Characteristics of various asset-backed products

Name	Mortgage-backed securities	Asset-backed securities	Commercial mortgage-backed securities
Underlying asset	Residential mortgages	Other assets	Commercial mortgages
Example	– Mortgages guaranteed by agencies or privately issued	Grouping and asset securitization: – loans to buy a car – credit card loans – leasing	– Financing of shopping mall – Can be a first- or second lien loan with a high interest rate
Main player	– Banks or institutional investors – Loved by hedge fund managers	– Commercial banks – Financial institutions – Only a few hedge funds	– Real estate investors – Only a few distressed securities hedge fund managers invest in these securities

Long positions in mortgage-backed bonds are usually balanced with a short position in government bonds, options on Treasuries, forwards or swaps. The increased sophistication of the American mortgage bond market has led to an increase of the number of derivatives on mortgage-backed bonds (also called collateralized mortgage obligations).

The objective of mortgage-backed securities funds is not to take a bet on the evolution of interest rates but to make money by correctly estimating which security is cheap. Mortgage-backed bonds are well developed in the United States and are also present in a few other countries, although not so well developed in continental Europe. In the United States the demand was very strong before the crisis when the market got strongly hurt by the real estate meltdown in the United States. Leverage tends to be used to a relatively large extent, as we are in the world of fixed income arbitrage. We advise readers interested to read specialized books on the subject.[9]

4.3   Risk management

This investment strategy is complex and exposed to various risks. The main risk arises from the opportunity presented by the strategy: the risk of earlier repayment. It is specific to these securities, as call options are present but not very common amongst traditional bonds. When it becomes interesting for one borrower to refinance their mortgage, it is usually the same for many. More generally, when interest rates fall significantly the whole portfolio is affected. There is also a liquidity risk, particularly for smaller issuers and some derivatives. The bid–ask spread may be wide in some cases and it is not always easy to get a price for every bond in the market. A risk also arises from the leverage that is so commonly used, plus an interest rate risk when the positions taken are not neutral in duration as interest rates have a direct impact on the prices of the bonds.

4.4   Illustration

The mortgage-backed securities strategy typically combines long positions in mortgage-backed bonds and the short sale of a Treasury bond. Inverse positions can also be taken, but this is not common. The main attraction for managers specializing in this strategy comes from the difficulty of valuing the earlier repayment option. Consider the bonds issued by Fannie Mae (FNMA) presented in Table 3.8.[10]

The option-adjusted duration is a measure of the sensitivity of the price to a parallel move in the interest rate curve. In other words it corresponds to the percentage change in price for a 1 per cent move in interest rates. The dollar value of a basis point is the variation of the market value of a security for a one basis point move in interest rates. It is usually calculated

Table 3.8   Mortgage-backed bond example

Description	Price	Option-adjusted duration	Dollar value of a basis point	Position	Quantity (US$ millions)
FNMA 30 YR 6.0% TBA	103–18	1.89	195.73	Buy	100
FNMA 30 YR 5.5% TBA	101–26	3.55	361.43	Sell	38
FNMA 30 YR 6.5% TBA	104–04	0.9	93.71	Sell	62

Source: Bonita Capital Management

for US$100 by multiplying the price by the duration by 100. The position presented in Table 3.8 is neutral in duration, meaning that it is covered for every parallel move in the interest rate curve. The duration of the long side of the portfolio is at 1.89 times US$100 million, which is equivalent to the duration of the short side of the portfolio at 3.55 times US$38 million plus 0.9 times US$62 million, making a total of US$190 million. No initial investment is required, as the values of the long and the short book are the same. The manager will make money if FNMA 6 per cent outperforms the two other bonds. This position is called a butterfly, and it is relatively common. While most positions are neutral in duration, there is an exposure to convexity risk, volatility, repayment risk and liquidity risk. Figure 3.13 shows the evolution of the price of the three bonds presented in Table 3.8. They all moved up during the period analysed, but the price of the FNMA 30-year 6.5 per cent has been more stable than that of the other bonds.

Figure 3.14 shows the evolution of the accumulated performance and the market value of the position. Performance became positive on 23 April and stayed around US$60,000. Then, over the last few days of the month the price of the 5.5 per cent bond increased more rapidly than the other two; the value of the positions went negative on 29 April.

Mortgage-backed bonds offer many opportunities. The butterfly position presented in this section is just one of the ways to profit; other opportunities include mortgage-backed bonds against interest rate swap or government bonds, 30-year mortgage bonds against 15-year mortgage bonds, conventional mortgage bonds against GNMA and mortgage bonds issued by agencies against mortgage bonds issued by other institutions.

4.5   Advantages and drawbacks

The main advantage of this strategy is its low correlation with the market. As managers usually take duration neutral positions, the investor is

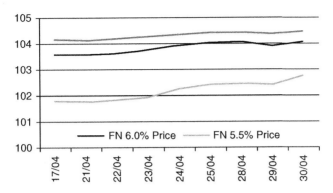

Figure 3.13 Evolution of the price of mortgage-backed bonds (April 2003)

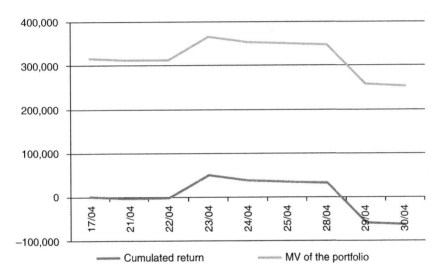

Figure 3.14 Cumulative performance and market value of the portfolio

not exposed to the interest rate risk; performance will depend solely on the ability of the manager to identify under- and overvalued securities. The valuation of the option represents a real opportunity for managers that have developed a performance pricing model. On the other hand, if the markets evolve consistently, a fund performing well may lose its advantage at some point. Another element is that this strategy is based on over-the-counter securities, which amplifies the liquidity risk. If a manager wants to sell some bonds in difficult market conditions they may not be able to sell them at the market price and may have to accept a larger bid–ask spread. This happens in periods of stress, when in the mortgage-backed market the commercial institutions tend to be impacted more than the agencies. Finally there is a strategy risk as the strategy is based on specific securities. While managers can select the securities that will outperform, it will be difficult to offer positive returns in an unfavourable environment, for example when interet rate decrease significantly as repayments increase.

4.6 Performance

Hedge Fund Research follows: *The HFR RV: Fixed Income – Asset Backed index includes strategies in which the investment thesis is predicated on realization of a spread between related instruments in which one or multiple components of the spread is a fixed income instrument backed physical collateral or other financial obligations (loans, credit cards) other than those of a specific corporation. Strategies employ an investment process designed to isolate attractive opportunities between a variety of fixed income instruments specifically securitized by collateral commitments which frequently include loans, pools and portfolios of loans, receivables, real estate, machinery or other tangible financial commitments. Investment thesis may be predicated on an attractive spread given the nature and quality of the collateral, the liquidity characteristics of the underlying instruments and on issuance and trends in collateralized fixed income instruments, broadly speaking. In many cases, investment managers hedge, limit or offset interest rate exposure in the interest of isolating the risk of the position to strictly the yield disparity of the instrument relative to the lower-risk instruments. This means that this index is not a pure mortgage-backed one but that it has a broader scope. It remains however a good proxy for the sector.*

Figure 3.15 shows the evolution of US$100 invested in the strategy since January 1993 compared to other similar investments in the HFRI Fund Weighted Composite index, the equity market, represented by MSCI World, and the bond market, represented by the Barclays Aggregate Bond index. An investment of US$644 in the HFR RV: Fixed Income – Asset Backed index would have become US$590 by the end of 2012. The same investment in the equity market, bond market or global hedge fund market would have become US$652, US$378 or US$341 respectively.

The HFR RV: Fixed Income – Asset Backed index offered an average annual return of 9.7 per cent per year over the whole period, against 8.5 per cent for the equity market and 6.8 per cent for the bond market. More recently, over the last decade, it has offered 8.7 per cent per year on average and over the last five years 11.3 per cent per year on average. Performance has been strong over recent times, with an especially attractive high annual return in 2009.

Volatility has been very low at 4.1 per cent over the whole period, 3.1 per cent over the last decade and 3.8 per cent over the last five years.

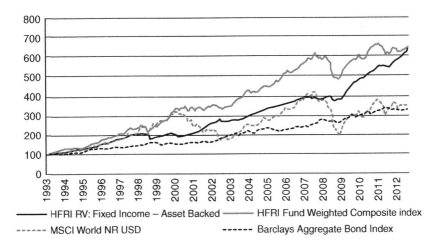

Figure 3.15 Evolution of US$100 invested in the HFR RV: Fixed Income – Asset Backed

Source: Based on numbers obtained from Hedge Fund Research, Inc.

This is significantly lower than equities, which ranged between 15 per cent and 20 per cent depending on the period in question. The strategy was even significantly less volatile than the bond index over the whole period, and this has become even more important in recent times.

Table 3.9 shows the yearly returns, the mean annual return, the standard deviation, the minimum annual return, the maximum annual return and the spread of the strategies relative to the comparative indices. It leads to the following remarks:

– Over the 20 years covered the HFR RV: Fixed Income – Asset Backed index was negative in three years: in 1998 (–9.2 per cent), 2008 (–3.4 per cent) and 2000 (–1.4 per cent). 1998 was a very difficult year in the world of fixed income, 2008 was a weak year for hedge funds and 2000 was a turning year, going from bullish to bearish market conditions. The equity index finished down 7 years out of 20, including in the 2000–2002 bear market, 2008 and 2011. The bond index suffered negative returns for one year only, 1999.
– The maximum annual returns of the HFR RV: Fixed Income – Asset Backed index were achieved in 2009 (23.9 per cent), 2001 (21.2 per cent) and 1997 (17.3 per cent). These numbers are quite strong.
– The spread in returns between the HFR RV: Fixed Income – Asset Backed index and the comparative indices tends to be volatile. The strategy has outperformed the global hedge fund index 8 times out of 23, the equity index 8 times and the bond index 11 times. The largest outperform-

Table 3.9 Performance statistics of the HFR RV: Fixed Income – Asset Backed index and comparative indices

	HFRI RV: Fixed Income – Asset Backed	HFRI Fund Weighted Composite Index	MSCI World NR USD	Barclays Aggregate Bond Index	Performance vs. HFRI	Performance vs. MSCI World	Performance vs. Barclays Aggregate
1993	14.5%	30.9%	22.5%	11.1%	−30.9%	−22.5%	−11.1%
1994	11.6%	4.1%	5.1%	0.2%	−4.1%	−5.1%	−0.2%
1995	16.6%	21.5%	20.7%	19.7%	−7.0%	−6.2%	−5.1%
1996	17.1%	21.1%	13.5%	4.9%	−9.5%	−1.9%	6.7%
1997	17.3%	16.8%	15.8%	3.8%	−0.2%	0.8%	12.8%
1998	−9.2%	2.6%	24.3%	13.7%	14.5%	−7.3%	3.4%
1999	11.3%	31.3%	24.9%	−5.2%	−14.0%	−7.6%	22.5%
2000	−1.4%	5.0%	−13.2%	3.2%	−14.2%	4.0%	−12.4%
2001	21.2%	4.6%	−16.8%	1.6%	6.7%	28.1%	9.7%
2002	8.6%	−1.5%	−19.9%	16.5%	0.1%	18.5%	−17.9%
2003	7.8%	19.5%	33.1%	12.5%	1.6%	−11.9%	8.7%
2004	11.9%	9.0%	14.7%	9.3%	−0.4%	−6.1%	−0.7%
2005	0.6%	3.5%	4.5%	1.3%	4.3%	3.3%	6.5%
2006	8.7%	12.9%	20.1%	6.6%	−1.0%	−8.2%	5.2%
2007	1.1%	10.0%	9.0%	9.5%	−9.4%	−8.4%	−8.9%
2008	−3.4%	−19.0%	−40.7%	4.8%	27.7%	49.4%	3.9%
2009	23.9%	20.0%	30.0%	6.9%	−18.9%	−28.9%	−5.8%
2010	12.9%	10.2%	11.8%	5.5%	−13.7%	−15.2%	−9.0%
2011	6.0%	−5.3%	−5.5%	5.6%	29.2%	29.5%	18.3%
2012	17.1%	6.4%	15.8%	4.3%	10.8%	1.3%	12.8%
Mean annual return (whole period)	9.7%	10.2%	8.5%	6.8%	−1.4%	0.3%	2.0%
Volatility (whole period)	4.1%	7.1%	15.4%	5.5%	NA	NA	NA
Meanannual return 2003–2012	8.7%	6.7%	9.3%	6.6%	3.0%	0.5%	3.1%
Volatility 2003–2012	3.1%	6.5%	16.2%	6.1%	NA	NA	NA
Meanaverage return 2007–2012	11.3%	2.5%	2.3%	5.4%	7.0%	7.2%	4.0%
Volatility 2007–2012	3.8%	7.4%	19.4%	6.4%	NA	NA	NA
Minimum annual return	−9.2%	−19.0%	−40.7%	−5.2%	−30.9%	−28.9%	−17.9%
Maximum annual return	23.9%	31.3%	33.1%	19.7%	29.2%	49.4%	22.5%

Source: Based on data from Hedge Fund Research, Inc.

ance of the HFR RV: Fixed Income – Asset Backed index relative to the equity index was 49.4 per cent in 2008, while the largest underperformance was 28.9 per cent, in 2009. Relative to the bond index, the largest outperformance was achieved in 1999 at 22.5 per cent, and the largest underperformance was 17.9 per cent, in 2002.

5 Convertible arbitrage

Convertible arbitragers aim to profit from the evolution of price relations between a convertible bond and the underlying equity. A convertible bond is a security that gives the holder the right to exchange the security against a predefined number of shares at any point between the issuing date and the maturity of the bond. This bond is convertible into either ordinary shares or preference shares,[11] based on the characteristics specified at issuance.[12] Convertibles are hybrids, with some characteristics specific to equities and others specific to bonds. Their valuation is fairly complex, combining elements and characteristics of both bonds, equities and optionality.

Arbitragers who apply this strategy aim to profit from the complex price relation that exist between convertibles and their underlying equity by combining a long position in the convertible with a short position in the equity. The price of the convertible will generally decrease less that the equity in falling markets, and should perform correctly during up markets. This can be explained by the fact that on the one hand the bond part of the security constitutes a cushion when the price of the underlying security falls. On the other hand the option to convert the bond into equities increases in value when the price of the equity rises. These relations are present but not linear and it is their estimation that is difficult to carry out correctly.

5.1 Principles

Managers aim to identify undervalued convertibles with a favourable risk profile. These are securities whose prices do not fall as rapidly as those of the underlying equity under difficult market conditions, but that follow the stock price increase in bullish market conditions. We illustrate this principle in Table 3.10. Convertible A is more attractive than Convertible B because it loses only 2 per cent when the underlying security loses 10 per cent, as against Convertible B losing 4 per cent. In addition its price increases by 8 per cent against B's 7 per cent when the price of the underlying security increases by 10 per cent.

The two convertibles presented in Table 3.10 are attractive because they capture the majority of the increase while avoiding a significant part of the fall; Convertible A is nevertheless more attractive than Convertible B.

Table 3.10   Convertible bonds

Price variations	Fall	Increase	Flat
Underlying	–10%	10%	0%
Convertible A	–2%	8%	5%
Convertible B	–4%	7%	5%

5.2   Methodology: approach

There are various ways to approach convertibles, but they all derive from the same chronological path, illustrated in Figure 3.16. These steps start with the determination of the type of markets on which the arbitrage is carried out (primary issuance, secondary market or high yield). Secondly, the tools used and the hedging strategy have to be determined. This includes a bullish/bearish or a bearish/bullish position. The last step is to determine whether the strategy will focus on the valuation of the convertibles or on volatility.

5.2.1   Markets

Some funds consider both new issuances and the secondary market while others focus on only one side of the market. Many arbitragers create portfolios based essentially on new issuances for quantitative reasons; it is easier to estimate precisely the assets for new issuances as the risk of default is in most cases excluded from the model. The issiance market is however cyclical in nature.

5.2.2   Tools

When arbitrage opportunities are identified, managers determine what kind of instruments they will use in order to hedge their positions and to neutralize the directional bias implied by the long position. The idea is to limit their exposure to the risk of the underlying security. In most cases the arbitrage consists of building positions into equities and convertibles, and to cancel or at least limit the exposure to the underlying security by implementing a delta-neutral[13] strategy.[14] Depending on market conditions and the experience of the management team, the tools used are not limited to a long position in convertibles and a short position in the underlying security; the managers can also hedge other risks such as the interest rate risk, the currency risk and the credit exposure. The tools used to hedge these exposures – including for example interest rate swaps or interest rate forward for the interest rate risk can help to protect the portfolio against a downgrade in the credit rating of the issuer; these tools can be used singly or in combination.

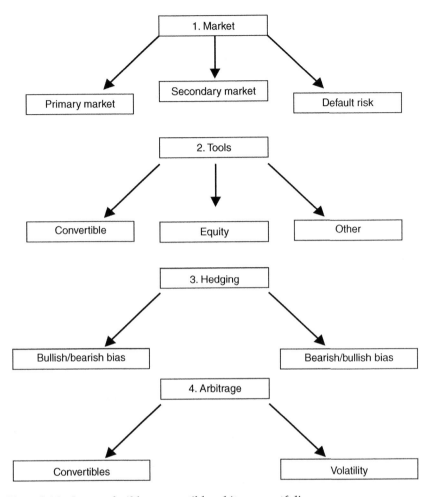

Figure 3.16 Steps to build a convertible arbitrage portfolio

5.2.3 *Hedging*

In parallel to the designation of the tools used for hedging positions, spe-cialists set up the way these tools will be used to hedge the portfolio. Depending on market conditions or prospects regarding companies, the level of hedging will vary over time. It may be partial or full. It is impor-tant for managers to consistently follow the exposure and the evolution of their relation in order to keep the exposure as required; on each price movement of one of the securities in the portfolio, the exposure will be impacted and the hedging will move.

5.2.4   Arbitrage

When they hedge their positions, managers take either a hedge against a potential decrease in value by taking a bearish hedge, or an inverse position against an increase with a bullish hedge. To do this they take a delta-neutral position, and then sell a slightly higher number of equities in the case of bearish hedge, or buy in the case of bullish hedge. There are two kinds of arbitrage:

- Single positions, also called theta-neutral management, defined as being uncorrelated with, and independent of, the passage of time. The managers build a portfolio neutral in theta, that is, proof against the passage of time.
- Multiple positions: in this case, the neutrality is maintained in real time and the portfolio is not neutral in theta but is affected by time.

5.3   Methodology: investment strategy

The managers of convertible arbitrage analyse hundreds or even thousands of convertibles and their relation with the underlying equity in order to identify the securities whose market price does not correspond with their intrinsic value, and which securities are attractive. In order to estimate the potential for companies they use fundamental analysis and perform a deep analysis of the special features of the convertibles. Important features to consider include the ratio of conversion premium to conversion ratio, any optional features attached to the security, the probability of default by the issuer or the coupon and the yield. There is no unanimously accepted model used to determine whether a convertible is under or overvalued, but the Black & Scholes (1970) option model and in the binomial option valuation model:

– price of equity
– level of interest rates
– volatility
– time to maturity
– conversion price.

Managers take a position when they identify an undervalued bond and they sell the underlying equity short. In this way they create a market neutral position or at least a position with a limited exposure to the markets. This will enable them to make profits in many situations, depending on the evolution of the correlation between the convertible bond and the equity.[15] The balanced positions in the equity enable the managers to limit the exposure of the fund to sudden movement on the equity side. The proportion of equities sold short will depend on the views of the team. In bear market conditions, managers tend to sell a proportion of stocks close to the convertible bond conversion ratio. If they anticipate an increase in the underlying equity, however, they will typically sell a lower proportion of shares to keep some exposure to the market and to the stock. The proportion of equities sold short is called the hedging ratio. It is said to be neutral when no directional bets are taken in the portfolio. Managers have to integrate many factors when they decide what market exposure they want to keep; these include the share price of the company, the interest rate curve, the volatility of the underlying equity and the dividend ratio. Managers are looking for bonds that are close to their bond floor, which is the value of the convertible bond without the optionality but that has a high delta, meaning that it would be highly sensitive to increase in the underlying equity. If they find such securities, the overall risk of the portfolio is reduced.

Two factors impact the price of the securities. On the one hand there is the evolution of the market as a whole and on the other side every element that is specific to the issuer. In this context, the market as a whole includes not only the equity market but also the fixed income market. Convertible bonds combine the characteristics of both worlds; their price will vary depending on the volatility of the equity markets, changes in interest rates, significant movements on the currency side and even political events. Another important factor that has a direct impact on the price relation between the convertible and the underlying equity is every news that has a direct relation with the company or its sector. Any announcement regarding the company rating, any shareholder change, any news regarding dividends or the use of an optionality to call a bond will directly impact the price of every convertible bond. Market risk is managed by building a portfolio that remains stable in different scenarios, and liquidity risk is usually managed by having a large number of bonds in the portfolio and by limiting the holding ratio in any bond. Credit risk will be completely hedged by some managers, and it will be part of the source of returns for others.

Positions are closed by selling the convertible and by buying back the equity. Various movements may lead a manager to close a position:

– the price of the securities evolves positively (the convertible price increases or the equity price drops), meaning that the manager realizes the expected returns
– the price of the securities evolves against the manager (the convertible price goes down or the equity price goes up), and the manager decides to realize the loss or to cut the exposure to the equity short positions
– any important news regarding the company or the sector is published

– there is any stress in the market and if the manager sees a potential liquidity risk in the security

– there is any forced conversion called by the issuer.

Figure 3.17 shows the main inputs and outputs of the convertible arbitrage strategy. Inputs include the interest rate curve, credit spreads, equity price, volatility, any currency exposure, the dividend policy (remember that short sellers are at extra risk as they have to pay for any dividend payment made by the company) and the structure of the bond including any special feature. Outputs include the delta, gamma, theta and vega,[16] the duration of the portfolio and its exposure to credit.

5.4   Specific risks

A convertible bond can also be seen as a conventional bond mixed with a call option. The pricing theory of options says that there are five elements to integrate into the pricing of options: the equity price, the strike price, the time until expiration, interest rates and the volatility of the equity.[17] These are also sources of risk. Volatility is of particular importance, as it represents both an opportunity and a major source of risk; a decrease in the implicit volatility of the stock will lead to a fall in the price of the convertible. This confirms that a long position in a convertible bond is equivalent to a long position in the volatility of the corresponding company.

There is also the gamma risk, which is the risk of the delta varying. The only way to hedge this risk is to frequently readjust the exposure and to keep a portfolio that is delta- and gamma-neutral. Interest rate risk is usually hedged using forwards or through a short position in government bonds. The credit exposure can be significant. This risk can be hedged by selling short indices that integrate the risk of default, by the sale of

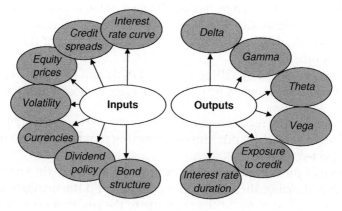

Figure 3.17   Inputs and outputs of the convertible arbitrage strategy

a portfolio of corporate bonds or through credit default swaps. This risk is also mitigated by diversifying the portfolio into various countries and sectors. Another important risk factor in the implementation of the convertible arbitrage strategy is the regulatory risk; short selling on financials was banned for a certain period during the crisis, so that During that time managers could no longer re-hedge their portfolios and become rapidly exposed to unwanted risks.

5.5 Illustration

5.5.1 *Seagate Technology*

Consider a manager who analyses a convertible of Seagate Technology. This convertible has a facial value of US$1 million and offers a coupon of 6.5 per cent. The manager estimates that the convertible is undervalued and decides to take a position in the convertible bond; he invests US$1,244,000. This bond is convertible into 18,360 ordinary shares of the same company, at a price of US$66.75 per share. This means that the market value of the convertible is at US$66.75 times 18,360 shares, a total value of US$1,225,530. The difference between the price of the equities bought through the convertible and the market price of the shares is called the conversion premium. It integrates the fact that the convertible bond pays an annual coupon of 6.5 per cent. The manager hedges the position at 75 per cent, meaning he solds were 13,770 shares short at market price for a value of US$919,148 (US$66.75 times 13,770 shares). The money received from the short sale is kept by the broker as collateral, and invested in short term Treasury bills that pays US$58,200 per year. The manager perceives 75 per cent of this amount, for a total of US$43,650. The rest is paid as commission. Everything else being equal, the coupon of the convertible and the cash resulting from the short sale offer a return of US$65,000 plus US$43,650 for an investment of US$1,244,000, a return just over 8.7 per cent. Next, we must add (subtract) the profit (loss) arising from the movements in the price of the convertible and the underlying equity. If the equity price increases the price of the convertible bond also tends to increase. In this case money would be lost on the equity side but this would be partially covered by the profits on the convertible. The inverse is true if the equity price falls. In this case the profits on the equity would be balanced by losses on the convertible. In our example, the price of the equity fell from US$66.75 to US$56.125 over the two weeks that followed the implementation of the trade, so the manager closed the positions. He made a profit of US$146,036 on the short equity and US$200 on the proceeds from the short sale, and sold the convertible with a loss of US$127,000, for a total profit of US$19,500. All in all, this means a return of 1.6 per cent over two weeks, close to 40 per cent annualized.

5.5.2   BRE Properties[18]

BRE Properties is an American real estate investment trust buying and developing apartment buildings in the western part of the United States. The company was performing well and it had an interesting portfolio of apartments, so in April 2007 our convertible fund manager estimated that the 4.125 per cent 2026 convertible of the company had an implied volatility of 19 per cent while the realized 50 days' volatility was at 23 per cent. At the same time the cost of hedging the credit exposure was 68 basis points. With this information in hand he decided to take a long position in the convertible and to hedge it with a short position in the equity. But over the next few months, the American real estate market started to suffer, and BRE Property's share price fell rapidly yet the convertible held back well. The manager made money on the short side and realized a small loss on the convertible; the credit risk was hedged. In this example the realized volatility had increased significantly while the implicit one increased only marginally. However, the manager made a positive return.

5.5.3   TEVA Pharmaceuticals

Early in 2006, a quantitatively managed program identified the 2024 convertible bond of TEVA Pharmaceuticals with a coupon of 0.25 per cent as being attractively valued. TEVA was liquid and could be easily shortened; the dividend was relatively low and its credit exposure could be hedged for a cost of 55 basis points. The convertible was callable[19] by the issuer, but not until 2010 when it would also become puttable.[20] In April 2006 the bond was trading around 103. The manager took a position and hedged it with a 95 per cent delta. The implicit volatility was around 26 per cent – attractively priced compared to other options on the market that had an implicit volatility of 29 per cent. In May the company announced bad results and the share lost 13 per cent; so the volatility of the share increased – and the manager profited from his gamma management and from the following increase in the implicit volatility of the bond to 30 per cent.

5.6   Advantages and drawbacks

The main advantage of investing in convertible bonds is that these securities have characteristics similar to those of fixed income and equities. This increases the opportunity set. Another advantage is that the strategy has several sources of returns: the coupon, the interest on the cash received from the short sale, and the position in the convertible and in the equity. The hedging through a short position in equities enables the manager to build a strategy that can meet various investment objectives. Some managers will be conservative and focus more on the bond structure of the portfolio and on the credit, while others will use the bonds to implement a more directional strategy where the bond element is there more to manage volatility.

On the negative side, the liquidity of the convertible market is relatively limited, and it tends to get worse during period of stress. September 2008 is a perfect example of this issue. Financial companies have historically represented a significant part of the convertible market. There was a ban on the short sale of financial stocks in September 2008; at that moment in time it was not possible for managers to adjust their exposure any more and to manage the delta and the gamma of their portfolio. As prices continue to evolve, their positioning became more and more unbalanced and the liquidity of the market was not sufficient to close the books; some funds lost more than 20 per cent of their value in that month alone. Finally, convertibles are complex products and it is difficult to fully understand their mechanisms and potential risk.

5.7 Performance

Hedge Fund Research classifies convertible arbitrage funds in the relative value fixed income indices. The HFRI RV: *Fixed Income–Convertible Arbitrage index includes strategies in which the investment thesis is predicated on realization of a spread between related instruments in which one or multiple components of the spread is a convertible fixed income instrument. Strategies employ an investment process designed to isolate attractive opportunities between the price of a convertible security and the price of a non-convertible security, typically of the same issuer. Convertible arbitrage positions maintain characteristic sensitivities to credit quality the issuer, implied and realized volatility of the underlying instruments, levels of interest rates and the valuation of the issuer's equity, among other more general market and idiosyncratic sensitivities.*

Figure 3.18 gives the evolution of US$100 invested in the strategy since January 1990 compared with other similar investments in the HFRI Fund Weighted Composite index, the equity market, represented by the MSCI World, and the bond market, represented by the Barclays Aggregate Bond Index. An investment of US$100 in the HFRI RV: Fixed Income–Convertible Arbitrage index would have become US$669 by the end of 2012. The same investment in the equity market, bond market or global hedge fund market would have become US$1105, US$352 or US$472 respectively.

The HFRI RV: Fixed Income–Convertible Arbitrage index offered an average annual return of 9.7 per cent per year over the whole period,

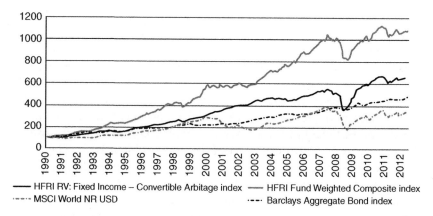

Figure 3.18 Evolution of US$100 invested in the HFRI RV: Fixed Income – Convertible Arbitrage index

Source: Based on numbers obtained from Hedge Fund Research, Inc.

against 7.2 per cent for the equity market and 7.4 per cent for the bond market. More recently, it has offered 9.3 per cent per year on average over the last decade and 11.7 per cent per year on average over the last five years.

Volatility has been relatively limited at 6.7 per cent over the whole period, 9.3 per cent over the last decade and 11.7 per cent over the last five years. The increase in volatility has been significant over recent times, mainly due to the crisis in 2008 and 2009. The volatility nevertheless remains lower than that of equities, which ranged between 15 per cent and 20 per cent depending on the period in question. The strategy has, however, been more volatile than the bond index over the whole period, and this has been even more important over recent times.

Table 3.11 shows the yearly returns, the mean annual return, the standard deviation, the minimum annual return, the maximum annual return and the spread of the strategies relative to the comparative indices. It leads to the following remarks:

– Over the 23 years covered, the HFRI RV: Fixed Income–Convertible Arbitrage index was negative in three years: in 2008 (–33.3 per cent), 2011 (–5.2 per cent) and 1994 (–3.7 per cent). 2008 was the most difficult year for the hedge fund industry as a whole. 2011 was an average year for hedge funds as a whole but the convertible market was weak mainly because of the lack of liquidity in the asset class. The equity index was down 7 years out of 23 including in the 2000–2002 bear

Table 3.11 Performance statistics of the HFRI RV: Fixed Income – Convertible Arbitrage index and comparative indices

	HFRI RV: Fixed Income-Convertible Arb. Index	HFRI Fund Weighted Composite Index	MSCI World NR USD	Barclays Aggregate Bond Index	Performance vs. HFRI	Performance vs. MSCI World	Performance vs. Barclays Aggregate
1990	2.2%	5.8%	-17.0%	12.7%	-3.6%	19.2%	-10.6%
1991	17.6%	32.2%	18.3%	16.0%	-14.6%	-0.7%	1.6%
1992	16.3%	21.2%	-5.2%	5.8%	-4.9%	21.6%	10.6%
1993	15.2%	30.9%	22.5%	11.1%	-15.7%	-7.3%	4.1%
1994	-3.7%	4.1%	5.1%	0.2%	-7.8%	-8.8%	-4.0%
1995	19.9%	21.5%	20.7%	19.7%	-1.7%	-0.9%	0.2%
1996	14.6%	21.1%	13.5%	4.9%	-6.5%	1.1%	9.6%
1997	12.7%	16.8%	15.8%	3.8%	-4.1%	-3.0%	8.9%
1998	7.8%	2.6%	24.3%	13.7%	5.2%	-16.6%	-5.9%
1999	14.4%	31.3%	24.9%	-5.2%	-16.9%	-10.5%	19.6%
2000	14.5%	5.0%	-13.2%	3.2%	9.5%	27.7%	11.3%
2001	13.4%	4.6%	-16.8%	1.6%	8.7%	30.2%	11.8%
2002	9.1%	-1.5%	-19.9%	16.5%	10.5%	28.9%	-7.5%
2003	9.9%	19.5%	33.1%	12.5%	-9.6%	-23.2%	-2.6%
2004	1.2%	9.0%	14.7%	9.3%	-7.9%	-13.5%	-8.1%
2005	2.4%	3.5%	4.5%	1.3%	-1.1%	-2.1%	1.1%
2006	12.2%	12.9%	20.1%	6.6%	-0.7%	-7.9%	5.5%
2007	5.3%	10.0%	9.0%	9.5%	-4.6%	-3.7%	-4.2%
2008	-33.7%	-19.0%	-40.7%	4.8%	-14.7%	7.0%	-38.5%
2009	60.2%	20.0%	30.0%	6.9%	40.2%	30.2%	53.2%
2010	13.3%	10.2%	11.8%	5.5%	3.1%	1.6%	7.8%
2011	-5.2%	-5.3%	-5.5%	5.6%	0.1%	0.4%	-10.8%
2012	8.6%	6.4%	15.8%	4.3%	2.2%	-7.2%	4.3%
Mean annual return (whole period)	9.9%	11.4%	7.2%	7.4%	-1.5%	2.7%	2.5%
Volatility (whole period)	6.7%	7.0%	15.6%	5.5%	NA	NA	NA
Meanannual return 2003–2012	7.4%	6.7%	9.3%	6.6%	0.7%	-1.8%	0.8%
Volatility 2003–2012	9.3%	6.5%	16.2%	6.1%	NA	NA	NA
Meanaverage return 2007–2012	8.6%	2.5%	2.3%	5.4%	6.2%	6.4%	3.2%
Volatility 2007–2012	11.7%	7.4%	19.4%	6.4%	NA	NA	NA
Minimum annual return	-33.7%	-19.0%	-40.7%	-5.2%	-16.9%	-23.2%	-38.5%
Maximum annual return	60.2%	32.2%	33.1%	19.7%	40.2%	30.2%	53.2%

Source: Based on data from Hedge Fund Research, Inc.

market, 2008 and 2011. The bond index suffered negative returns for one year only, in 1999.
- The maximum annual returns of the HFRI RV: Fixed Income–Convertible Arbitrage index were achieved in 2009 (60.2 per cent), 1995 (19.9 per cent) and 1991 (17.6 per cent). These numbers are fairly strong.
- The spread in returns between the HFRI RV: Fixed Income–Convertible Arbitrage index and the comparative indices has been volatile. The strategy has outperformed the global hedge fund index 8 times out of 23, the equity index 10 times and the bond index 14 times. The largest outperformance of the HFRI RV: Fixed Income–Convertible Arbitrage index relative to the equity index was 30.2 per cent, in 2009, while the largest underperformance was 22.3 per cent, in 2003. Relative to the bond index the largest outperformance was achieved in 2009 at 53.2 per cent, and the largest underperformance was 38.5 per cent, in 2008.

5.8   Convertibles in 2004 and synthetic convertibles

The performance of convertibles has been cyclical over the last decade. While it attracted much interest in the early 2000s in general, the 2003–2004 period was difficult. The significant increase in the number of convertible arbitrage funds and the standardization of the valuation tools reduced the opportunity set. Larger assets were chasing a limited amount of opportunities, and the average performance of the strategy started to drop significantly. This problem tends to occur in arbitrage strategies, and it happened to fixed income arbitrage funds in 1998. This led many players to diversify their strategy. Five evolutions occurred, including two significant ones: increased exposure to credit and the implementation of more capital structure arbitrage positions.

1. **Increased exposure to credit**: many managers increased their exposure to credit. More and more managers that tended to use credit default swap to hedge the credit risk of their portfolio decided to play focus on the credit and to take long and short direct credit exposure.
2. **Implementation of capital structure arbitrage strategies**: many managers combined convertible arbitrage positions with arbitrage positions based on other securities. They extended their investment range to subordinated equities, other bonds and in some cases to derivatives. This also includes a particular technique called "stub trading," the taking of a short position in a company combined with a long position in a subsidiary whose price does not reflect its intrinsic value, a well-known example being the long Porsche–short Volkswagen trade.
3. **Inverse position**: some managers took inverse positions, becoming long equity and short in the convertible. Short positions in converti-

bles may be an important potential source of risk. If the share price increases rapidly the convertible may be converted and the holder may be at risk.

4. **Catastrophe bonds**: some managers decided to diversify their portfolio using catastrophe (cat) bonds. Such bonds are linked to extremely rare events that occur only a few times per century, such as natural disasters – earthquakes, hurricanes, eruptions. Cat bonds are made up of a principal and periodic coupon. Both are linked to the occurrence of catastrophic event, and the coupon is defined in advance. Investors have to post the notional amount corresponding to the bond on an account that pays the risk-free rate. Cat bonds are issued with a typical spread of 4 to 7 per cent relative to the risk-free rate, and they tend to be rated.

5. **Synthetic convertibles**: a few funds have created what is known as synthetic convertibles; the underlying idea is to create synthetic convertibles to create new opportunities. As we know, a convertible bond is a combination of a bond, a call option and a credit exposure. Managers replicating convertible arbitrage positions synthetically take the following positions, illustrated in Figure 3.19:
   – long position in a Government or corporate bond
   – long position in a call option that offers the long equity exposure
   – a short position in a put option, enabling the manager to gain the premium of the option. This position is at risk as it exposes the portfolio to a short volatility position; if the equity falls rapidly, the put option will be exercised and the manager will be exposed to potential important losses.

The managers that create such positions can also take the second leg of the convertible arbitrage position by being short directly in the underlying equity.

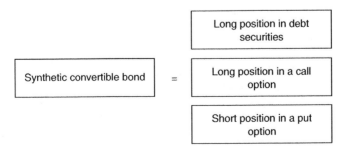

Figure 3.19 Synthetic convertibles

6 Event driven

As the name suggests, event driven funds aim to profit from important events occurring during the life of a company. Such events include recapitalizations, reorganizations, bankruptcies, balance sheet restructuring, mergers and acquisitions, dismantlings, initial public offerings or share buybacks. The uncertainty regarding the outcome of these events creates an opportunity for the specialist able to correctly anticipate it. They generally combine long and short positions, and in contrast to most other strategies will usually use not only equities, preferred shares and bonds, but also any other security that is perceived as mispriced.

Important events are usually classified into three categories. Managers will usually specialize in one of these categories distribute their assets opportunistically between the events that offer the best investment opportunities (Figure 3.20).

– Distressed securities
– Merger and acquisitions, also called risk arbitrage
– Other special situations.

It is worth mentioning two sub-strategies that gained much interest before the crisis called private investments in public entities and activists.[21]

Markets are cyclical and each sub-strategy will perform best at certain points in the cycle. After a recession, many companies face financial difficulties; even good ones may face short-term issues, creating opportunities in distressed securities transactions. During strong market phases many activities are going on, and so the mergers and acquisitions market will tend to be particularly active. The special situations part of the market

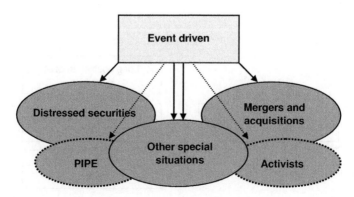

Figure 3.20   The event driven strategy and its sub-strategies

will usually be active at any phase of the cycle, but the opportunity set will evolve. Independently of the cyclical nature of markets, most managers specialize in a particular sub-strategy, so all resorting to single investment strategies.

We will see the term "event driven" more as an investment category that groups several strategies. Out of the three main sub-strategies the special situation is less frequent than the others, so we do not present it in a full section of this chapter but just in a sub-section of the current one. The two others are covered in detail independently of each other.

6.1 Methodology

Event management starts with the announcement of the event, usually in the form of a press release. Once the event has been announced, specialists analyse what is happening and try to anticipate the outcome. The objective is not usually to try to anticipate the occurrence of an event – a highly speculative move – but to determine what the outcome of an announced event will be. The team analyses the event at a fundamental level by combining strategic, financial and operational implications; it should also integrate the legal and regulatory implications of the announcement. The idea is to determine what will happen and to take a position accordingly. The aim is usually to invest in event that should have a favourable outcome and to make money out of it, but inverse positions, betting on the non-realization of the event, can also be taken.

The team should be first convinced that the event will be finalized and will then estimate the investment horizon; it is important to keep a balance between the liquidity of the portfolio and the investment horizon of the portfolio; an investment in a friendly merger will have a much shorter horizon than an investment in a bankrupt distressed company. Once the team has predicted the outcome of the transaction and has determined an investment horizon, they should analyse the securities available and select the best tool to profit from what is happening. They analyse the price of each of the securities considered and their relative evolution over time; at the same time they analyse the potential risks, in terms of volatility, liquidity, market and sector risks. Finally they have to determine how to close the position, and the probability of each of the possible outcomes. If on this basis the team estimate that the event offers an attractive risk–return trade-off and that it will help to diversify the portfolio with a sufficiently high probability, the positions will be taken. Depending on the style of the manager and the strategy, a partial or full position will be taken. Merger arbitrage players tend to take incremental positions as the uncertainty regarding an event decreases and the spread disappears; they will then have to follow the evolution of the situation and to integrate any important news. The typical structure of an event driven investment process is reported in Figure 3.21.

Event driven specialists look for three elements before investing. First, they look for a spread between the market value of an instrument and their estimation of the value of the product. Secondly, they look for a catalyst, which is an event that could lead to a change in the perception of the company by the market and consequently the price of the company in the market. Finally, they estimate the time necessary for the catalyst to be visible and for the market price of the company to change.

There are various sources of profits in such a strategy, but they are all linked to the uncertainty relative to the outcome of the events analysed. The main risks are the inability to predict:

– If the event will be finalized or not
– The final result
– The time required to reach the objective
– The real impact on the price of the securities.

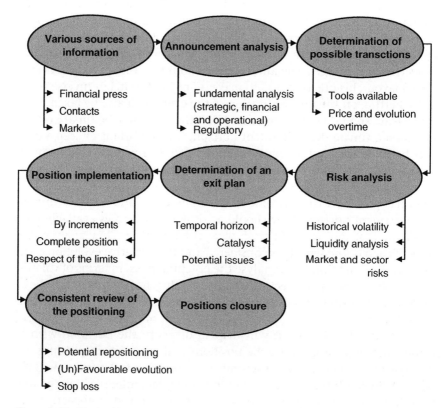

Figure 3.21 Typical investment process of an event driven fund

Managers combine fundamental analysis (when they determine whether they want to take a long position in a specific situation), event analysis (when they estimate the probability of an event) and temporal analysis (as they have to constantly integrate the investment horizon to manage their liquidity). This last element is quite specific to the strategy, as once a company is facing important changes, this may lead to other changes or even potentially to an unexpected acquisition.

Event driven investing has many potential sources of risk, which explains why managers tend to diversify their portfolio. In addition, many managers will combine positions in equities with others in fixed income products and potentially derivatives. Finally, market futures or options can also be bought to hedge a long equity portfolio, in order to limit the exposure and the beta.

6.2 Special situations

This sub-strategy is not defined as a strategy *per se* by all the market participants. It relates to all events other than mergers, acquisitions or bankruptcies – so, it mainly includes balance sheet restructuring, deconsolidation, recapitalization and refinancing, rating change, reorganization, new regulation, government privatization, share buyback, partial sale, public offering and split/LBO. Such positions can be combined with merger or distressed positions (Figure 3.22).

6.3 Activists

Originally coming from the private equity world, activists are more and more present in the hedge fund world. In practice, the success of the hedge

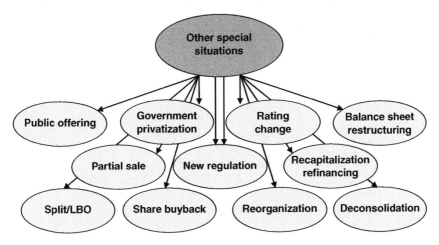

Figure 3.22 Illustration of the *special situations* sub-strategy

fund industry led more and more activists to take hedge fund structures. Activists are managers that aim to be active, meaning that they aim to invest in companies that may perform strongly if a catalyst happens – and they aim to be this catalyst. Activists may or may not be friendly; friendly activists tend to work with the management of the company in order to bring about the necessary changes, while others will to associate with some other large shareholders in order to implement the necessary changes. Activists are managers who analyse the viability of companies in order to identify those that could be improved if some changes were to be implemented. Depending on their asset base, they will focus on smaller or mid-size companies; it is rare that activists invest in large companies as the shareholding of such companies tends to be spread or in the hands of a family.

Figure 3.23 illustrates the management process of a typical activist fund. The first step is the determination of the investment range; the manager identifies the markets of interest. Managers tend to focus on sectors they know well or on sectors that have attractive valuations. It is not unusual, however, for managers to use the help of specialized consultants. At this moment there is also a tendency to be focused on smaller

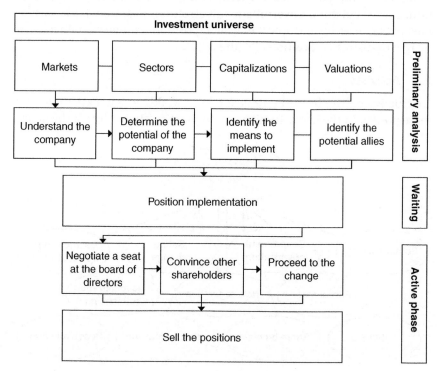

Figure 3.23   Investment process of a typical activist fund

companies. Valuations are naturally an important element to integrate into the process of determination of the investment range; activists will only take positions in securities that have attractive price/earnings ratios not only in absolute terms but also relative to their peers, the underlying idea being to identify companies in which the intervention of the manager can lead to a revaluation.

Typical investments include significantly underpriced companies relative to their tangible valuation, and established companies that have historically profited from stable and foreseeable operational profits in which the manager will typically try to reduce the costs, improve cash management or look for potential mergers or acquisitions. A third family of companies considered by activists are weakly profitable companies where they think they can implement changes to improve the profitability and in consequence the value. In addition there are sector leaders that have diversified their activities and that are undervalued because of the difficulty for market participants to determine their real value. Smaller, rapidly growing, companies looking for assets and/or advice in their growth management constitute another family of companies of potential interest. Figure 3.24 list companies that are typically considered by activist funds. Entering at the second phase, when the manager identifies attractive companies in the sectors and markets of interest. At that point, the objective is to understand how the company is run, and the manager starts to think about the means required to unlock value. At the same time, the managers identify potential allies; typically, these will be other shareholders that may provide support in case of conflict with the management.

The potential of the company is usually based on a single product of particular interest or a management issue to tackle; it is the main element the manager will work on when taking a position in order to create value. The triggers for taking positions vary, from the implementation

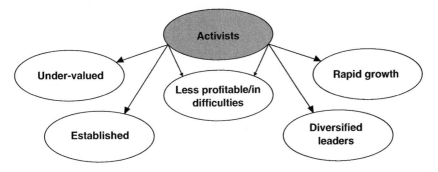

Figure 3.24 Companies typically considered by activist funds

of a marketing campaign about a product or change in procedures and/ or management, to a reorganization of the workflow, to the sale of some securities not directly linked to the main product or service of the company, or to any other action. At the same time, the team consistently determines the potential issues or blocking factors, and what might be done to avoid or manage them.

The early search for allies is particularly important, because without them the manager will have to buy a significant part of the company to implement their actions. These elements justify why managers tend to start with small positions during the first passive investment phase.

Activist managers tend to be active in several positions at the same time. The active phase is time-consuming and may require additional cash to be invested. This is why typical portfolios have a maximum of ten to fifteen positions, including two or three active ones.

From there, the manager takes a position in the company or the position is increased. The whole process can take a long time (from a few weeks to several years). This explains why managers tend to have waiting/sleeping positions in their portfolio that are there as diversifiers and as call options on companies with high potential but usually without catalyst; during the waiting phase, positions rarely go over 5 per cent of the company[22] and a few per cent of the fund's assets. During the active phase, however, positions typically represent more than 10 per cent of the fund's assets and could in some cases go up to 20 per cent. A position will typically represent 5 to 50 per cent of the company, depending on its assets, and the level of conviction and the objectives of the fund manager.

Gaining a seat on the board of directors constitutes the first step of the active part of the process. This will, however, prohibit the manager from dealing in the stocks, particularly around the time of publication of the quarterly, semi-annual and annual results. Any purchase or sale of equities will also be publicized to the market, and they will be advertised by other players. The manager will not usually attend the board personally, in order to keep some distance away from the situation and to limit any feeling of invasion. Yet in parallel to the implementation of the position the manager needs to convince other important shareholders of the added value of his/her presence, as more than 50 per cent of the vote is generally required in order to implement any proposed change; this explains why managers will typically not invest in family-run businesses unless they have achieved a preliminary agreement. Only when the manager has persuaded other shareholders to accept the proposal will the manager announce the proposal to the board.

There are two typical company issues looked at by activists: operational and financial problems. Operational problems can concern management, product distribution, marketing, cost control, size or an over-diversification of activities. Financial problems can arise from real estate assets whose value is not integrated in the equity price, accounting issues that make the analysis of the company more difficult, cash positions not integrated in the price of the equity, or an over-complex capital structure. Typical solutions proposed by activists include a change in management, a strategic reorientation, some work on operational improvement and/or cost management, a strategic reorientation, changes at the distribution level and the sale of non-core activities. Other possibilities include the raising of capital, partial sale of assets, cash investment, balance sheet restructuring or the reorganization of a group of companies, share buybacks and/ or a change in the dividend policy. Figure 3.25 shows issues and typical solutions proposed by activists.

The first phase is generally the longest. The aim is firstly to implement changes. Secondly, the changes have to be communicated to the market. Those are company-specific news, but the global environment will also have an impact on the share. When markets are difficult, liquidity

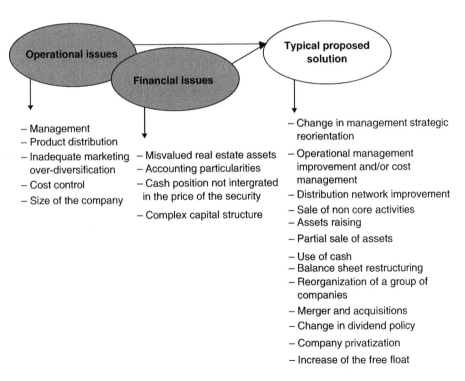

Figure 3.25 Main problems identified by activists and the corresponding solutions proposed

disappears and there is usually a flight to quality, meaning that a strategies such as these is at risk. In addition, managers tend not to hedge their positions, as the positions taken tend to be company-specific and a hedge carried out through an index is of limited interest. Hedging can even increase the overall portfolio risk, as market movements may be opposite to stock-specific performance. During the active phase the fund is at risk; it often happens that the management of a company does not share the view of the activist and so they try to work against them. The situation can rapidly become complicated, and the entire process can be seriously delayed by a non-participatory management. This increases the exposure to liquidity risk. The active phase is very important, as some shareholders may stop supporting the manager, the liquidity of the security may be limited or, even worse, the main product of the company may be less interesting than expected – once the manager has a seat on the board they have access to information that may or may not confirm this. All these elements, in addition to the concentration of activist portfolios, explain the high potential volatility of activist funds.

This strategy has nevertheless existed in the United States and in the United Kingdom for a long time, and in these countries there are a few large activist funds. It has emerged to some extent in Japan since the early 2000s, where activist players tend to be friendly. It also has also emerged in emerging markets such as Brazil and Russia where corporate governance has still to be improved and where the small and mid-cap market is large.

The main source of risk to activist funds comes from the concentration of the portfolio. Not only do activist funds have just a few positions, but they also have large positions relative to the size of the company, usually having more than 5 per cent of a company during the active phase. When they sit on the board, liquidity is even more restricted close to the results publication date. Managers can also face issues with the management of some companies or other shareholders, preventing them from implementing their strategy. In addition while the companies considered are in some cases in good financial situations, it is not always so as companies can be cheap for reasons. Finally, an activist portfolio is a long only portfolio (with some cash to enable a reaction in case of need); while every stock should perform well for specific reasons, the portfolio remains at risk, particularly during volatile periods. On the other hand, it is usually sufficient for just one or two companies to make a good profit over a year. In addition the concept is of interest as a specialized and experienced fund manager should be able to help a company manager improve the performance of their company.

6.4 Illustrations

6.4.1 New Skies Technologies

New Skies Technologies is a satellite operator transporting videos, data and other information between IP addresses. The manager discovered the company at the end of 2002, having performed a quantitative screening. According to his estimations the security became of interest because its price had fallen significantly on low volumes. He performed a fundamental analysis of the company on a stand-alone basis but also on the basis of its positioning in the sector. Share were trading at around €3.50. The manager anticipated four possible outcomes:

1. The company could become a potential takeover target over the next 12 months if the price stayed low or fell further. The manager estimated this probability at 10 per cent and that the price would be around €9.50.
2. The company could be privatized over the year. The probability of this happening was estimated by the manager at 10 per cent – but the potential increase in price was substantial at €8.5.
3. If no outside entity intervened there would be a 50 per cent probability that the company would come back to valuation levels close to its peers, at around €7.
4. Finally, there was a 30 per cent chance that the situation would stay at current level and that the price would not move significantly.

The probabilities are summarized in Table 3.12. All in all, the opportunity seemed attractive and he decided to take a position at an average price of €3.85 in January 2003.

Figure 3.26 shows the evolution of the New Skies stock price over the months that followed the initial position. The manager's analysis was correct; the price finally recovered and he closed his position after one year at a price of €5.85. Interestingly, he could have made a significantly higher return a few years later as SES Global announced the acquisition of New Skies Technologies in cash for a price over US$20 in 2005.

Table 3.12 Analysis of New Skies Technologies

	Exit price	Probability	Horizon	Variation
Takeover target	€9.5	10%	12 months	165%
Privatization	€8.5	10%	12 months	137%
Price recovery	€7.0	50%	24 months	96%
No movement	€3.3	30%	24 months	–8%
Average	€5.6			66%

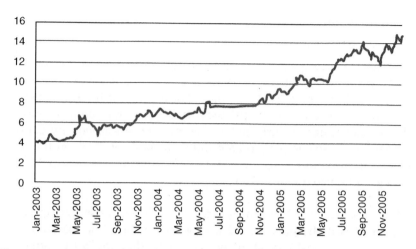

Figure 3.26   Evolution of the price of New Skies Technology

6.4.2   Cumulus Media

Another example relates to Cumulus Media. The manager had been look-ing closely at the media sector for some time, then in spring 2007 the public radio sector suffered as revenues decreased because of the increas-ing competition from alternative media. Valuations lost up to one third of their value, at ten times the EBITDA (earnings before interest, taxes, depreciation and amortization). At the same time, the manager was work-ing with the management of another operator in the industry on the financing of a possible buyback of the company at around 12 times its EBITDA. The manager decided that Cumulus Media was of interest. In addition, as the company was highly levered the management was under more pressure than its peers, confirming that they would be supportive.

The equity was trading at nine times earnings excluding CMP, a radio company that had been bought by Cumulus Media through debt with other partners. The manager estimated that the share of Cumulus Media in CMP was worth around US$80 million. Other elements also contrib-uted to the manager's decision, including firstly that he had followed the company for several years and that he had already been invested in it during the market turmoil of 2001. Secondly, the manager judged that mid-sized media companies would be less exposed to global market trends and internet competition than larger players. Finally, Cumulus Media was one of the only companies in the sector where the founding family did not hold the controlling rights.

The manager took a long position in June 2007 on the basis of his esti-mation of a price/earnings ratio of 7.5 (CMP included). The catalyst came quicker than expected; shortly afterwards, Merrill Lynch financed a leveraged buyout at US$11.75 per share, a price significantly higher than the previous trading price. This price was lower than the fully valued price expected by the manager but he closed the positions as he did not expect any other offer to be made (Figure 3.27).

6.4.3   Eletrobras

Eletrobras, Centrais Elétricas Brasileiras S.A., is a major Brazilian electric company. It is also one of the biggest power utilities companies in the world, and one of the largest clean energy companies in the world. At the end of 2012, Eletrobras held stakes in a number of Brazilian electric companies, so that it generated and transmitted approximately 60 per cent of Brazil's electric supply. The company's generating capacity was about 40,000 MW, mostly in hydroelectric plants. The Brazilian federal government owned 52 per cent of its stock, which was traded on the Bovespa, and is on the Bovespa index, the Ibovespa. It was also traded on the New York Stock Exchange and on the Madrid Stock Exchange.

The manager in this example manages diversified event driven portfolio. He invests widely, including in both developed and emerging markets. Regarding positioning, he combines naked longs and shorts, pair trading, capital structure arbitrage and any other interesting opportunities. He knew Electrobras and he had been following the stock for some time. Everything started with the fact that Brazil's President Dilma Rousseff had promised to cut electricity bills 20 per cent the next year as part of a broader effort to increase economic growth without boosting inflation. The administration would renew power utility licenses that start expiring in 2015, but only if the concessionaires would agree to major revenue cuts; Eletrobras would have no choice as the government was its

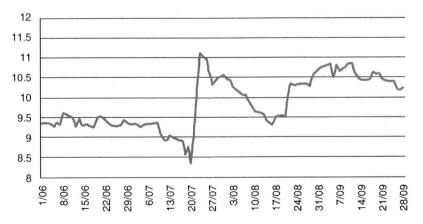

Figure 3.27   Evolution of the equity price of Cumulus Media

major shareholder and the board of directors had recommended renewing concessions. From there, the manager looked at the capital structure of the company and found an opportunity to play between the ordinary and the preference shares; the preference shares had a minimum dividend of around R$1.3 (Brazilian reals), a yield of around a 10 per cent at the historical price of around R$12–13. With this news, the stock fell to R$8, so the minimum dividend thus represented 15 per cent of the share price. This meant that Eletrobras would have to stop paying dividends. The original pair trade was to go long in the preferred and short the ordinary share. When the measure was first announced, the manager shorted the spread and made money. The firm announced that it estimated the new policy would cost close to R$10 billion in annual revenues, and the problems could be exacerbated if a number of utilities did not renew their contracts. Analysts believed the government would force Eletrobras to buy and run those assets at lower prices, further eroding its profitability. In addition, Eletrobras would have to write off several billion Brazilian reals as companies get paid on assets, and as with the new. Its EBITDA was expected to become negative for at least two years.

The manager went short on the spread at the middle of September. The positions paid until the second half of October. Then he went short on the equity without hedges, and closed the position before the end of the month for a solid profit. In November, the stock fell by 50 per cent. It took some time for the market to react because there was a significant amount of passive money in the stock; bonds do not pay, and so high dividend stocks were favoured. Figure 3.28 illustrates the trade.

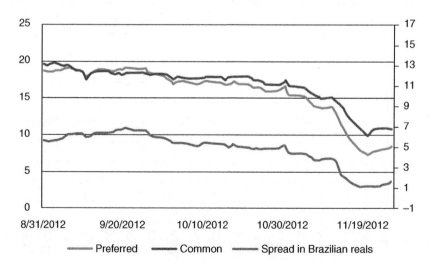

Figure 3.28   Evolution of the price of the shares of Eletrobras

6.5 Advantages and drawbacks

Event driven trading has the first advantage of offering attractive returns over time with a relatively limited market risk. Secondly, the returns from event driven strategies rely more on company-specific events than on broader market movements; as securities evolve in broader markets shorter movements will impact returns, but one can expect event driven managers to be able to offer attractive returns over a cycle independently of the evolution of the market as a whole. In addition, event driven strategies include many opportunities that can be completely different and independent of each other, meaning that a portfolio of a few event driven funds with different profiles invested in various securities should be able to be less correlated with equity markets. Finally, event driven managers tend to invest in an extensive range of securities – and they will consider the entire capital structure of companies before investing; this is singular, even in the hedge fund world.

Investors like event driven strategies because they are relatively easy to understand and because they are concrete. Managers try to profit from an event that is publicized in the press; Company A is acquiring Company B, or Company C has announced a reorganization. This is easier to understand than some quantitative models or strategies invested in derivative products.

On the other hand, some funds may be directional. In addition, they may be concentrated and invested in less liquid securities. In addition, event driven strategies are cyclical to some extent, and market cycles will impact the returns. Finally, the event driven strategy is defined so broadly that much work is required before considering any investment, as the risks underlying any fund will tend to be specific to it.

6.6 Performance

Hedge Fund Research defines event driven managers as:

> *investment managers who maintain positions in companies currently or prospectively involved in corporate transactions of a wide variety including but not limited to mergers, restructurings, financial distress, tender offers, shareholder buybacks, debt exchanges, security issuance or other capital structure adjustments. Security types can range from most senior in the capital structure to most junior or subordinated, and frequently involve additional derivative securities. Event Driven exposure includes a combination of sensitivities to equity markets, credit markets and idiosyncratic, company specific developments. Investment theses are typically predicated on fundamental characteristics (as opposed to quantitative), with the realization of the thesis predicated on a specific development exogenous to the existing capital structure.*

The event driven strategy has seven sub-strategies, including five that have sub-indices. These strategies are:

– ED: Distressed/Restructuring strategies (analysed on a stand-alone basis in Section 8)
– ED: Merger Arbitrage strategies (analysed on a stand-alone basis later)
– ED: Private Issue/Regulation D strategies (analysed on a stand-alone basis in Section 9)
– ED: Activist strategies (no sub-index)
– ED: Credit Arbitrage (no sub-index)
– ED: Special Situations strategies (no sub-index)
– ED: Multi-Strategy managers (no sub-index)

Figure 3.29 shows the evolution of US$100 invested in the HFRI Event Driven (Total) index since January 1990 compared to other similar investments in the HFRI Fund Weighted Composite index, the equity market, represented by MSCI World, and the bond market, represented by the Barclays Aggregate Bond index. An investment of US$100 in the HFRI Event Driven (Total) index would have become US$1237 by the end of 2012. The same investment in the equity market, bond market or global hedge fund market would have become US$1105, US$352 or US$472 respectively.

The HFRI Event Driven (Total) index offered an average annual return of 12.1 per cent per year over the whole period, against 7.2 per cent for the equity market and 7.4 per cent for the bond market. More recently, it has

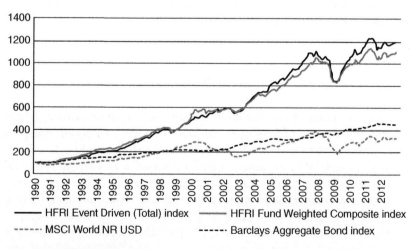

Figure 3.29 Evolution of US$100 invested in the HFRI RV: Event Driven (Total) Index – Convertible Arbitrage index

Source: Based on numbers obtained from Hedge Fund Research, Inc.

offered 8.6 per cent per year on average over the last decade and 4.1 per cent per year on average over the last five years. The fall has been significant.

Volatility has been relatively low and stable, at 6.9 per cent over the whole period, 6.8 per cent over the last decade and 7.7 per cent over the last five years. This remains lower than equities, which ranged between 15 per cent and 20 per cent depending on the period in question. The strategy has however been more slightly volatile than the bond index. The risk–return ratio of the strategy has been very attractive.

Table 3.13 shows the yearly returns, the mean annual return, the standard deviation, the minimum annual return, the maximum annual return and the spread of the strategies relative to the comparative indices. It leads to the following remarks:

– Over the 23 years covered the HFRI Event Driven (Total) index was negative in four years: 2008 (–21.8 per cent), 2002 (–4.3 per cent), 2011 (–3.3 per cent) and 1990 (–0.5 per cent). 2008 was the most difficult year for the hedge fund industry as a whole. 2002 and 2011 were volatile and difficult for equities. The equity index finished down 7 years out of 23 including in the 2000–2002 bear market, 2008 and 2011. The bond index suffered negative returns for one year only, in 1999.
– The maximum annual returns of the HFRI Event Driven (Total) index were achieved in 1993 (28.2 per cent), 1991 (27.4 per cent) and 2003 (25.3 per cent). These numbers are strong.
– The spread in returns between the HFRI Event Driven (Total) index and the comparative indices has been volatile. The strategy has outperformed the global hedge fund index 13 times out of 23, the equity index 15 times and the bond index 17 times. The largest outperformance of the HFRI Event Driven (Total) index relative to the equity index was 29 per cent, in 2001, while the largest underperformance was 22.6 per cent, in 1998. Relative to the bond index, the largest outperformance was achieved in 2009 at 29.9 per cent, and the largest underperformance was 26.6 per cent, in 2008.

7 Merger arbitrage

Merger arbitrage funds aims to invest in companies undergoing mergers and acquisitions. It is also known as risk arbitrage.

7.1 Methodology

Mergers and acquisitions are of interest because the uncertainty surrounding them presents arbitrage opportunities. In addition, traditional

Table 3.13 Performance statistics of the HFRI Event Driven (Total) index and comparative indices

	HFRI Event Driven (Total) Index	HFRI Fund Weighted Composite Index	MSCI World NR USD	Barclays Aggregate Bond Index	Performance vs. HFRI	Performance vs. MSCI World	Performance vs. Barclays Aggregate
1990	-0.5%	5.8%	-17.0%	12.7%	-6.3%	16.5%	-13.2%
1991	27.4%	32.2%	18.3%	16.0%	-4.8%	9.1%	11.4%
1992	19.5%	21.2%	-5.2%	5.8%	-1.8%	24.7%	13.7%
1993	28.2%	30.9%	22.5%	11.1%	-2.7%	5.7%	17.1%
1994	6.0%	4.1%	5.1%	0.2%	1.9%	0.9%	5.8%
1995	25.1%	21.5%	20.7%	19.7%	3.6%	4.4%	5.5%
1996	24.8%	21.1%	13.5%	4.9%	3.7%	11.4%	19.9%
1997	21.2%	16.8%	15.8%	3.8%	4.4%	5.5%	17.4%
1998	1.7%	2.6%	24.3%	13.7%	-0.9%	-22.6%	-12.0%
1999	24.3%	31.3%	24.9%	-5.2%	-7.0%	-0.6%	29.5%
2000	6.7%	5.0%	-13.2%	3.2%	1.8%	19.9%	3.6%
2001	12.2%	4.6%	-16.8%	1.6%	7.6%	29.0%	10.6%
2002	-4.3%	-1.5%	-19.9%	16.5%	-2.8%	15.6%	-20.8%
2003	25.3%	19.5%	33.1%	12.5%	5.8%	-7.8%	12.8%
2004	15.0%	9.0%	14.7%	9.3%	6.0%	0.3%	5.7%
2005	3.3%	3.5%	4.5%	1.3%	-0.2%	-1.1%	2.1%
2006	15.3%	12.9%	20.1%	6.6%	2.4%	-4.7%	8.7%
2007	6.6%	10.0%	9.0%	9.5%	-3.4%	-2.4%	-2.9%
2008	-21.8%	-19.0%	-40.7%	4.8%	-2.8%	18.9%	-26.6%
2009	25.0%	20.0%	30.0%	6.9%	5.1%	-4.9%	18.1%
2010	11.9%	10.2%	11.8%	5.5%	1.6%	0.1%	6.3%
2011	-3.3%	-5.3%	-5.5%	5.6%	2.0%	2.2%	-8.9%
2012	8.9%	6.4%	15.8%	4.3%	2.5%	-6.9%	4.6%
Mean annual return (whole period)	12.1%	11.4%	7.2%	7.4%	0.7%	4.9%	4.7%
Volatility (whole period)	6.9%	7.0%	15.6%	5.5%	NA	NA	NA
Meanannual return 2003-2012	8.6%	6.7%	9.3%	6.6%	1.9%	-0.6%	2.0%
Volatility 2003-2012	6.8%	6.5%	16.2%	6.1%	NA	NA	NA
Meanaverage return 2007-2012	4.1%	2.5%	2.3%	5.4%	1.7%	1.9%	-1.3%
Volatility 2007-2012	7.7%	7.4%	19.4%	6.4%	NA	NA	NA
Minimum annual return	-21.8%	-19.0%	-40.7%	-5.2%	-7.0%	-22.6%	-26.6%
Maximum annual return	28.2%	32.2%	33.1%	19.7%	7.6%	29.0%	29.5%

Source: Based on data from Hedge Fund Research, Inc.

mutual funds and institutional investors usually have constraints preventing them from staying invested or from taking the opportunity. This led specialized managers to be interested in this strategy, some funds having specialized in the sector around for almost 20 years.

A trade usually starts with the announcement of a bid for a company or a merger. The aim of the manager is not to anticipate a merger but to profit from the uncertainty around the event that has been announced. Three main types of transaction are considered: friendly takeover, hostile takeover and partial sales (Figure 3.30).

The first type of transaction includes friendly takeovers and mergers whose purchase price is generally substantially higher than market value. The return is realized by buying shares in the company that is being bought and by shorting shares in the buyer. The second type of risk arbitrage position includes hostile public offerings. In this case, uncertainty is much higher, and the manager tries to estimate the probability of the buyer forcing the target company's shareholders to sell. The third category includes the partial or complete sale of a company that tends to be either below market price or its intrinsic value; in this case the company wants to sell a part of its business, thus creating the opportunity.

When an opportunity is identified the team starts by analysing the companies involved; they first have to check that the potential transaction is in line with rules and regulations. From there the team estimates the probability of the transaction succeeding and the time frame needed. During this first phase evaluation of potential failure is key, as most failures tend to happen early in the process. To do so the team relies on any documents available, not only documents published by the companies involved but anything else relevant, including previous deals done in the same sector, or by comparing companies. Some managers analyse the strategic interest of the transaction. In any case, the managers try to estimate not just the probability of success but also how the transaction would be perceived by the market. Finally, they have to gauge whether any counter-offer may be made, not only for the company being bought

Figure 3.30 Main types of merger arbitrage transactions

but also for the buyer. The potential return is much higher when they are several bidders involved.

Once the analysis of the company is done, the team balances all the arguments to determine whether they will take a position and, if so, its size. Managers take quicker and larger positions when the quantity of information available is more important and when the transaction becomes more certain.

When a company is considering buying another one it usually has to pay a premium over the market price to gain the interest of the current shareholders. The level of the premium depends on many factors, including market conditions, performance of the target company, the financial health of the buyer and the risk of counter-offer. The market usually sees the fact that there is an offer with a premium for a company as positive, meaning that the price of the target tends to increase. At the same time, the uncertainty around the transaction impacts the buyer's price, which tends to decrease. We mentioned that typical merger arbitrage positions combine a long position in the target company bought along with a short position in the buyer. Such a position is implemented when the buyer pays the target company in shares. This arbitrage position combining both legs has a limited market risk, as it is hedged. When an offer is made in cash the manager usually takes a naked long position in the target company without shorting the buyer; in this case it is not really an arbitrage position any more, but a hedge would not help. While it is an arbitrage strategy, leverage tends to be low in this strategy and rarely over two times.

7.2   Illustrations[23]

We present five examples for this strategy. We start with two acquisitions with several counterbids; the third is a cash deal, the fourth a stock-for-stock deal and the last, an unsuccessful deal.

7.2.1   Counterbids: Alcan/Rio Tinto

The Canadian company Alcan was one of the world largest producers of bauxite, alumina and aluminium as well as a leading producer of packaging and machined products. In April 2007 its stock was trading slightly over US$50 per share. At that point, Alcoa, an American aluminium producer, made a public offering for Alcan at US$77 per share. The spread was attractive and our manager decided to take a position; such a deal was very interesting to him because the commodities market was particularly buoyant and the transaction was correctly priced. The manager built a position at US$81 per share. After that, Rio Tinto, the giant Anglo-Australian steel producer, made a counter-offer at US$101 per share, paid cash. The price moved accordingly, and the potential gain for the manager was US$20 per share, close to 20 per cent over two months. The issue was, however, that the markets were particularly difficult at that time. Alcan's share price fell to US$98.45 on July and on down to US$92 in August, in a very difficult credit market. This meant a US$9 spread gross. The manager decided to double his position as he believed that the market movements, while impacting on short term, would in any case not impact the closure of the deal. The transaction was closed in October and the Alcan shareholders received the promised US$101 per share. Figure 3.31 shows the evolution of the Alcan share price over that period; you can clearly see when the first and second bids were made, and the opportunity in August closer to US$90 per share.

7.2.2   Counterbid: Graham Packaging/Reynolds Group

Graham Packaging (Graham) is a US company with a US$1.7 billion market cap early 2011. The company is the number one specialized plastic bottle blow-moulder in the USA, manufacturing plastic bottles for items such as isotonics, ketchups, juices, detergents and lubricants. At the time of the event it had 8,200 employees, with 97 manufacturing facilities in 15 countries. On 13 April 2011 the company received a cash and stock bid from Silgan, the US leader in metal cans for contents such as vegetables and soup, that also manufactures plastic bottles for shampoo, soap and other consumer products manufacturers. It was a friendly deal, offering US$4.75 in cash and 0.4020 Silgan shares for each Graham Packaging share. As well as the owner of Graham Packaging, Blackstone,

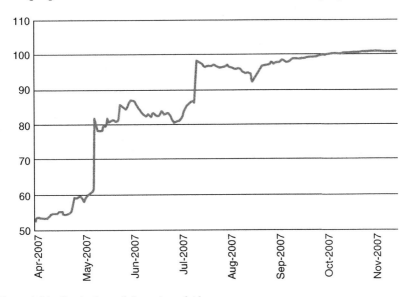

Figure 3.31   Evolution of the price of Alcan

a global investment and advisory firm, was an important holder of Silgan and Graham. On June 14th, Reynolds Group, the maker of the iconic Reynolds aluminium foil, an entity controlled by the wealthiest man in New Zealand, made an unsolicited counterbid cash offer to acquire Graham at US$25.50. There was still an expectation that Silgan would counterbid, since the deal was very synergetic and strategic for them. On 17 June, however, Silgan had not exercised its right to match the offer, and Graham signed a friendly deal with Reynolds, with slightly improved terms. The deal was concluded on 9 September 2011. The manager had started buying at the end of April, over several days. He increased his position considerably after the counterbid was made. His average buying price was US$25 and his selling price was US$25.50, with no currency risk. The fund's annualized return on the transaction was 14 per cent for the 143 days in which it was invested (Figure 3.32).

7.2.3   Cash deal: Redecard/Itaú

Redecard is a Brazilian merchant acquirer company with a US$11.5 billion market cap and 1100 employees as of early 2012. The company operates an extensive network of debit and credit card processing endpoints, extracting a fee from every transaction. It also advances credit to merchants. The company was held at 51 per cent by Brazil's largest private bank, Banco Itaú. The other shareholders, apart from Lazard (holder of close to 10 per cent), were spread out. On 2 February 2012, Banco Itaú made a delisting offer that was not received uniformly by all shareholders. This offer was made at a lower valuation than Cielo, Redecard's main competitor (and

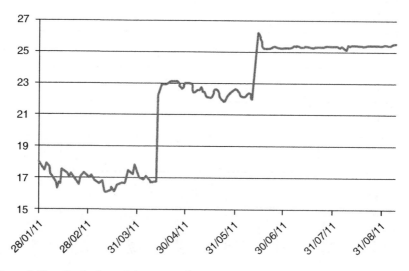

Figure 3.32a   Evolution of the price of Graham Packaging

virtual duopoly partner, this being the heritage of Brazil's previous transaction system, where Cielo dealt exclusively with Visa and Redecard with
Mastercard). Market participants were hopeful of a higher bid, but expectations were demolished by Itaú threatening to sell its controlling stake in
the company and invest in its fully-owned merchant acquirer company,
Hipercard. The manager estimated that this threat not credible, due to
the attractive valuation in which the company was being acquired, the
synergies Itaú would be able to extract, and the cost to invest in Hipercard
compared to the interactions already in place with Redecard. In addition
according to Brazilian law, when there is a squeeze-out offer there has to
be an appraisal by an independent bank. If the price offered is not within
the range of the valuation, the offer cannot go forward.

After the first appraisal, there was resistance from the largest minority
shareholder, Lazard, which demanded a higher price in order to give its
approval. Lazard did not specifically say it would not sell, but called a
meeting where minority shareholder would vote on a second appraisal.
Passing this approval needed just over 10 per cent of votes, which was by
no means certain. At the same time, due to wobbles in the European economy, some Brazilian hedge funds that were minority holders in Redecard
changed their initial assessment, and instead of adding risk by calling
a second appraisal started newspaper campaigns to have the appraisal
voted down and be paid the B\$35 offered. This caused volatility in the
trading price and delays. The need for a second independent valuation,
was approved at an extraordinary general meeting.

The manager analysed the situation and estimated that the transaction
would be finalized. He bought over time, the majority in April and the
remainder in May at an average price of B\$32.06. At its peak, the posi-
tion represented 9 per cent of the portfolio. The currency was hedged.
No counterbid was expected, since Itaú was the controller. A bump was a
possibility, but he did not count on it. From that point, a minority group
pressured shareholders to vote the appraisal down and accept Itaú's offer,
since the bank had threatened to pull out the offer. The second appraisal
was finally approved, but Itaú's original and only offer was within the
range of the independent bank's appraisal, meaning that Itaú could proceed with the offer as planned. The deal was concluded on 24 September;
the company went back to being private, and the fund's annualized return
on the transaction was 17 per cent for the 158 days in which the manager
was invested. Figure 3.32 shows the evolution of the price of Redecard.

7.2.4 Stock-for-stock merger: Giralia Resources/Atlas Iron

Giralia Resources and Atlas Iron were Australian iron ore companies.
Giralia, however, had no mines in operation, just a resource base defined

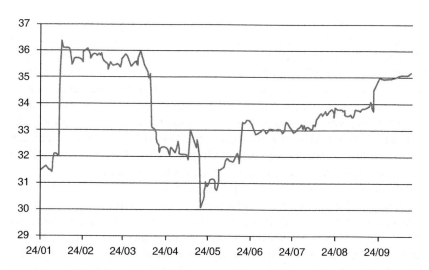

Figure 3.32b   Evolution of the price of Redecard

as ready to be developed as future mines, hence no revenues. At the end of 2010, the company had a market cap of US$850 million and three employees. Meanwhile, Atlas Iron had a market cap of about US$1.7 billion at the time, and 295 employees with operating mines producing 6 million tons per annum of direct shipping ore (DSO), an ore that contains sufficient iron content to be shipped internationally without extra upgrading which cost money. Every iron mine's ore has a different iron content, which can range from as low as 30 per cent to as high as 70 per cent; typically, iron ore traded in global markets has about a 60–63 per cent iron content by weight. It is superior to magnetite, a lower-grade iron ore that needs to be processed before it can be shipped, hence most magnetite resources are not currently mined, but are held as reserves for future use.

On 21 December 2010, Giralia Resources and Atlas Iron announced a friendly stock-for-stock transaction, that would create the fourth largest Australian listed iron ore company. The offer was structured as a tender conditional on achieving a shareholder acceptance level of 90 per cent. The transaction made strategic sense. Atlas had many magnetite resources and very little DSO; it operated two Pilbara iron ore mines producing 6 million tons of iron ore per year, and had secured transportation from giant ore producer BHP plus port capacity in Western Australia's Port Hedland for 35 million tons per year. Atlas owned a reserve base of 54 million tons in its two mines and resource base of another 211 million tons of DSO in mines yet to be constructed. It also owned 2.6 trillion tons of magnetite resources. Giralia, meanwhile, controlled close to 400 million tons of economically viable DSO resources and holdings in areas near Atlas properties; Giralia had resources, but no railway access or port export capacity. The two companies had a combined net cash of US$230 million. Atlas planned to expand its annual production to 12 million tons by 2012, increasing to 20 million by 2015. Giralia was a good fit for Atlas to strengthen its DSO reserves.

The ownership structure was a scattered institutional shareholder base, and no substantial or noteworthy shareholders were clearly identified either in favour of the deal or against it. The consolidation of the two companies made perfect sense from a resource consolidation perspective. From the point of view of cash flow and revenues there was very little difference, as Atlas had 211 million tons of DSO in its mines, enough to continue production for 30 years at the going rate of 6 million tons per year. But Atlas needed Giralia for its long-range plans, when they planned to produce up to 35 million tons DSO per annum. The deal was announced as a friendly, fully negotiated deal and was presented to shareholders as a tender offer. Atlas offered the consideration of 1.5 Atlas shares per 1 Giralia share. There was only one class of shares in each company. No deal improvements were required, and Giralia was not the object of any counterbid. The transaction as such was not amended in any way from the point where it was announced.

The analysis started with the announcement of the deal. Emphasis was laid on the understanding of the Australian iron ore mining industry and its export markets, principally in Asia. Access to ports was also a key issue, as the cost of this is quite substantial, and the large mining companies control railways and ports. This diminished the strategic options of resource plays such as Giralia with no port access capacity and no special access to railways. Atlas used specially constructed highways, an expensive way to ship the ore from mine to port. From the analysis it was understood that Atlas and Giralia would always be minor league players due to their poor access to rail infrastructure and slightly better access to port export capacity. However, neither Atlas nor Giralia owned any interest in ports, but were leasing port space from larger players such as Rio Tinto, BHP Billiton and Fortescue. An analysis of Atlas and Giralia allowed the team to conclude that these companies were not special enough for counterbidders to fight for them. Presentations were made a month later, once the tender documents had been filed and the timeline of the deal and the deadlines were known, thus providing more certainty about the type of return than would be realizable over the time frame. The conclusion was that this deal was not in any way controversial and would, more likely than not, close within the anticipated timeline. The only uncertainty that existed was how fast the company would achieve the 90 per cent tender acceptance from shareholders; they monitored throughout if any shareholder groups were showing resistance to the deal, but this was not the case.

Once they managers had achieved a good comfort level about what the business represented and why this deal was happening strategically, they defined the entry point at which to purchase shares. Since this was a long short trade with a very defined timeline, they defined the entry point in terms of the gross spread that they needed to have at various points in time relative to the closing, to still be able to get an attractive return relative to the capital invested. The gross spread in this situation captured range from A$0.06 to A$0.10 per share. The acquiring company had a share price of around A$3.70, while the target company had a price of around A$5.40. Giralia and Atlas stocks swung widely while the deal was pending, depending on the news that emanated from the global steel industry. The spread itself steadily converged from the 10 cents gross level all the way to 2–3 cents shortly before the deal closed. There was no substantial currency risk, as both the long investment Giralia and the short investment Atlas Iron were Australian listed companies. Residual currency exposure was hedged.

The investment period was relatively short, over an average holding period of 33 days. Some shares were purchased 36 days before the deal closing while the last share lot was purchased 17 days before the deal consideration was received. Any involvement in the trade was based on the existence of an attractive spread. Clearly, in the late stages of the deal, 20 days before closing the spread had substantially disappeared and any share additions were through sporadic and opportunistic trades, catching shares whenever the spread came within reach and satisfying the return requirements. In the end, the deal was announced on 21 December 2010 and was cashed out on 10 March 2011, taking a full 80 days to be completed. Given the volatility of iron ore markets this investment was not bound to be a large exposure of the portfolio, and it was only because of the uncontroversial nature of this deal that the managers decided to get involved to begin with. The manager didn't want to get involved in a stock-for-stock bidding war but in the case of Giralia, however, the assets had seemed reasonably unattractive to bidders; it had no revenues, only three employees and lots of stranded resource, so it was more a concept rather than an actual company worth fighting for – good from the perspective of avoiding counterbids. The fund manager's annualized return for this transaction was 6.9 per cent for the average 33 days of investment.

Figure 3.33 shows the evolution of the price of Giralia Resources and of Atlas Iron. Remember that the deal was 1.5 Atlas stock for 1 Giralia. Over

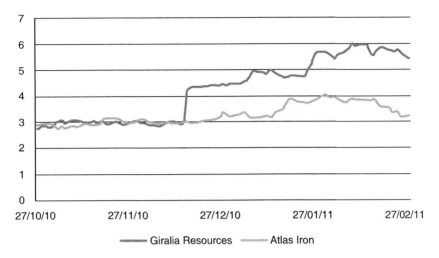

Figure 3.33 Evolution of the price of Giralia Resources and Atlas Iron

the days following the announcement, Atlas stayed around A\$3 per share while Giralia Resources stayed around A\$4.3. At the end of the transaction early in March 2011, Giralia Resources was trading at A\$5.7 against just over A\$3 for Atlas Iron; the long position price increased while the short dropped back to its original level.

7.2.5 Unsuccessful deal: Rhoen-Klinikum/Fresenius

Rhoen-Klinikum is a German company with a €3bn market cap and 38,000 employees as of early 2012. The company was the second largest private hospital operator in Germany, owning 53 hospitals across the country. On 26 April, Rhoen-Klinikum, whose founder was still the majority share-holder, received an unsolicited offer from Fresenius, a global health care group with products and services for dialysis, the hospital and the medical care of patients at home. The offer, a cash offer at €22.50 to acquire the whole company, was conditional on getting 90 per cent of tenders. On 29 May, board approval was gained and the path was cleared for a firm tender offer. However, there was some concern that the 90 per cent shareholder acceptance threshold could be an impediment to the closing of the trans-action. There was a concern among some arbitragers that this threshold would not be met due to the shareholder base being very fragmented. The managers judged differently, believing that awareness of Fresenius' cam-paign would reach all ears; the scattered shareholder base would not rally against the bid and that the market price more than compensated the risk. Unfortunately he was wrong. On the final deal of the offer, Asklepios, a competitor of both companies, announced that it had bought a 5 per cent stake in Rhoen-Klinikum on the open market, with the clear intention of not tendering the shares, and thus to prevent Fresenius from becoming a stronger competitor to Asklepios.

The offer gained 87 per cent acceptance and consequently lapsed. The team had started buying shares on 30 May, and stopped on 22 June, at an average price of €21.56. After the offer failed they spread the sales over 4 weeks, selling the last position on 27 July. The loss on the transaction was 22 per cent on the position which translated into a 1.75 per cent hit to net asset value. Figure 3.34 shows the evolution of the stock price of Rhoen-Klinikum; after a rebound at the end of the month, the share price collapsed early September.

7.3   Advantages and drawbacks

The main advantage of this strategy is that it aims to offer returns with a relatively limited market risk. Merger arbitrage returns rely more on company events than on broader market movements. Secondly, the strategy is easy to understand and based exclusively on broadly available information. In addition, the strategy tends to offer low volatile, stable returns over time. Finally, typical deals are closed within a few months, enabling the manager to turn the portfolio.

On the other hand, mergers and acquisitions work in cycles, so the strategy will not be able to offer the same level of returns every year. This explains why many managers consider merger arbitrage within a broader event driven context. Another drawback of the strategy is that a merger or an acquisition attracts much interest from the market, usually leading

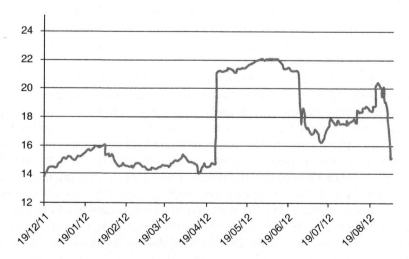

Figure 3.34   Evolution of the price of Rhoen-Klinikum

to a higher volatility in the stock price. In most cases, the managers take long positions in the stock and, as mentioned in the previous section, this long position is not hedged in the case of a cash deal. As illustrated by our Alcan deal, volatility on a deal-by-deal basis may be significant over the short term. While deals tend to be closed in a few months, this may put some pressure on fund managers by investors looking for short-term returns and/or for stable returns over time. This risk is also amplified by the fact that if a deal breaks a fund may lose heavily in a single position, as most players will realize their loss and the spreads will widen. This tail risk is typical of the strategy. FInally, as an arbitrage strategy, the cushion coming from the short positions will depend on the level of interest rates, meaning that the expected level of return will be lower in a low interest rate environment.

7.4 Performance

Hedge Fund Research describes merger arbitrage as:

> *a strategy which employs an investment process primarily focused on opportunities in equity and equity related instruments of companies which are currently engaged in a corporate transaction. Merger Arbitrage involves primarily announced transactions, typically with limited or no exposure to situations which pre-, postdate or situations in which no formal announcement is expected to occur. Opportunities are frequently presented in cross border, collared and international transactions which incorporate multiple geographic regulatory institutions, with typically involve minimal exposure to corporate credits. Merger arbitrage strategies typically have over 75% of positions in announced transactions over a given market cycle.*

Figure 3.35 shows the evolution of US$100 invested in the HFRI ED: Merger Arbitrage index since January 1990 compared with other similar investments in the HFRI Fund Weighted Composite index, the equity market, represented by MSCI World, and the bond market, represented by the Barclays Aggregate Bond index. An investment of US$100 in the HFRI ED: Merger Arbitrage index would have become US$661 at the end of 2012. The same investment in the equity market, bond market or global hedge fund market would have become US$1105, US$352 or US$472 respectively.

The HFRI ED: Merger Arbitrage index offered an average annual return of 8.6 per cent per year over the whole period against 7.2 per cent for the equity market and 7.4 per cent for the bond market. More recently it has offered 5.1 per cent per year on average over the last decade and 3 per cent

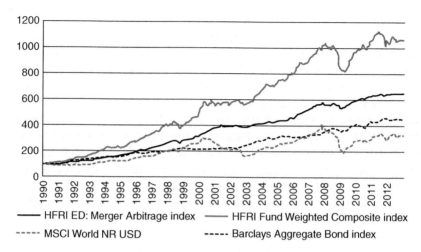

Figure 3.35 Evolution of US$100 invested in the HFRI ED: Merger Arbitrage index

Source: Based on numbers obtained from Hedge Fund Research, Inc.

per year on average over the last five years. The fall has been significant. This can be explained by a few factors including the fact that the spreads have decreased because of an increase in the number of participants. A second element is the fact that interest rates have fallen, meaning that the money paid on the cash generated by the short side has decreased. Finally mergers and acquisitions are cyclical by nature, and recent market conditions have probably not been good for the strategy.

Volatility has been very low, at 4.1 per cent over the whole period, 3.3 per cent over the last decade and 3.3 per cent over the last five years. This is significantly lower than equities, which ranged between 15 per cent and 20 per cent depending on the period in question. The strategy has also offered more stable returns than the bond index; and the risk–return ratio of the strategy has been very attractive.

Table 3.14 shows the yearly returns, the mean annual return, the standard deviation, the minimum annual return, the maximum annual return and the spread of the strategies relative to the comparative indices. It leads to the following remarks:

– Over the 23 years covered, the HFRI ED: Merger Arbitrage index was negative in two years: in 2008 (–5.4 per cent) and in 2002 (–0.9 per cent). 2008 was the most difficult year for the hedge fund industry as a whole. 2002 was particularly volatile and difficult for equities. The equity index finished down in 7 years out of 23, including in the 2000–

2002 bear market, 2008 and 2011. The bond index suffered negative returns for one year only, in 1999.

– The maximum annual returns of the HFRI ED: Merger Arbitrage index were achieved in 1993 (20.2 per cent), 2000 (18 per cent) and 1991 (17.9 per cent). These numbers are strong, especially given the low volatility of the returns.

– The spread in returns between the HFRI ED: Merger Arbitrage index and the comparative indices has been volatile. The strategy has outperformed the global hedge fund index 7 times out of 23, the equity index 10 times and the bond index 13 times. The largest outperformance of the HFRI ED: Merger Arbitrage index relative to the equity index was 35.3 per cent, in 2008, while the largest underperformance was 25.6 per cent, in 2003. Relative to the bond index, the largest outperformance was achieved in 1999 at 19.5 per cent, and the largest underperformance was 17.4 per cent, in 2002.

8 Distressed securities

Distressed securities specialists invest in companies facing financial or operational difficulties, including reorganizations, bankruptcy, recapitalizations and other difficult situations.

8.1 Sources of difficulties

Companies need capital to support their development, whether launching a new product or expanding into new markets for example. They can get access to capital either through the credit market (issuance of debt) or through raising capital (share issuance). The credit market is widely used by companies, and the interest rate paid will depend on the profile of the company and its credit rating. As companies lever themselves to grow, the interest increases; this can become an issue, particularly in a difficult credit environment. When a company cannot pay the interest due, it falls into default.

A company may default on its interest payments for various reasons. Examples include deteriorating capital structure and unexpected external events. Deteriorating capital structures usually arise from a high level of debt while unfavourable external events include operational issues, important changes in the management team or legal proceedings. In any case, the company is in a situation where it cannot meet its payment requirements and where it needs to renegotiate with its creditors or to find new investors. Figure 3.36 shows the main reasons behind most companies in difficulties.

Table 3.14 Performance statistics of the HFRI ED: Merger Arbitrage index and comparative indices

	HFRI ED: Merger Arbitrage Index	HFRI Fund Weighted Composite Index	MSCI World NR USD	Barclays Aggregate Bond Index	Performance vs. HFRI	Performance vs. MSCI World	Performance vs. Barclays Aggregate
1990	0.4%	5.8%	-17.0%	12.7%	-5.4%	17.5%	-12.3%
1991	17.9%	32.2%	18.3%	16.0%	-14.3%	-0.4%	1.8%
1992	7.9%	21.2%	-5.2%	5.8%	-13.3%	13.1%	2.1%
1993	20.2%	30.9%	22.5%	11.1%	-10.6%	-2.3%	9.2%
1994	8.9%	4.1%	5.1%	0.2%	4.8%	3.8%	8.7%
1995	17.9%	21.5%	20.7%	19.7%	-3.6%	-2.9%	-1.8%
1996	16.6%	21.1%	13.5%	4.9%	-4.5%	3.1%	11.7%
1997	16.4%	16.8%	15.8%	3.8%	-0.3%	0.7%	12.7%
1998	7.2%	2.6%	24.3%	13.7%	4.6%	-17.1%	-6.5%
1999	14.3%	31.3%	24.9%	-5.2%	-17.0%	-10.6%	19.5%
2000	18.0%	5.0%	-13.2%	3.2%	13.0%	31.2%	14.8%
2001	2.8%	4.6%	-16.8%	1.6%	-1.9%	19.6%	1.2%
2002	-0.9%	-1.5%	-19.9%	16.5%	0.6%	19.0%	-17.4%
2003	7.5%	19.5%	33.1%	12.5%	-12.1%	-25.6%	-5.0%
2004	4.1%	9.0%	14.7%	9.3%	-5.0%	-10.6%	-5.2%
2005	3.1%	3.5%	4.5%	1.3%	-0.4%	-1.3%	1.9%
2006	14.2%	12.9%	20.1%	6.6%	1.3%	-5.8%	7.6%
2007	7.1%	10.0%	9.0%	9.5%	-2.9%	-2.0%	-2.4%
2008	-5.4%	-19.0%	-40.7%	4.8%	13.7%	35.3%	-10.2%
2009	11.6%	20.0%	30.0%	6.9%	-8.3%	-18.3%	4.7%
2010	4.6%	10.2%	11.8%	5.5%	-5.6%	-7.2%	-0.9%
2011	1.5%	-5.3%	-5.5%	5.6%	6.8%	7.0%	-4.1%
2012	2.8%	6.4%	15.8%	4.3%	-3.6%	-13.1%	-1.6%
Mean annual return (whole period)	8.6%	11.4%	7.2%	7.4%	-2.8%	1.4%	1.2%
Volatility (whole period)	4.1%	7.0%	15.6%	5.5%	NA	NA	NA
Meanannual return 2003–2012	5.1%	6.7%	9.3%	6.6%	-1.6%	-4.2%	-1.5%
Volatility 2003–2012	3.3%	6.5%	16.2%	6.1%	NA	NA	NA
Meanaverage return 2007–2012	3.0%	2.5%	2.3%	5.4%	0.6%	0.8%	-2.4%
Volatility 2007–2012	3.3%	7.4%	19.4%	6.4%	NA	NA	NA
Minimum annual return	-5.4%	-19.0%	-40.7%	-5.2%	-17.0%	-25.6%	-17.4%
Maximum annual return	20.2%	32.2%	33.1%	19.7%	13.7%	35.3%	19.5%

Source: Based on data from Hedge Fund Research, Inc.

Figure 3.36   The main reasons behind most companies being in difficulty

8.2   Methodology

Companies considered for investment by distressed securities managers have a very low rating, generally at CCC[24] or below. Distressed specialists combine a deep knowledge of the bankruptcy and the reorganization code, with fundamental analysis capabilities to determine in what cases it is worth considering an investment in a bankrupt company. Their aim is to isolate the strong businesses with a bad capital structure from the weaker ones. The range usually includes bankrupt companies, companies close to bankruptcy and companies in post-reorganization. Managers are not looking for a short-term return, knowing they will usually have to invest over the medium to long term to realize the hoped-for profits. By definition, distressed companies need time and much work to recover.

Investments can be made through various kinds of securities, typically including a form of debt or equities and warrants, or any combination of these.[25] When a distressed company is reorganized, the management team and the creditors look to decrease the balance sheet leverage of the company. Current debt is then exchanged into a combination of debt and equities; the new equities are essential as they enable the company to decrease its leverage and pay lower interest rates. The new debt is usually issued at a lower rate, that can be supported by the company. Managers take a position if they estimate that after the reorganization the company will go back into profit.

Managers base their decisions not only on a lower interest rate charge but also on a change of management[26] and on the hypothesis that capital will be reinvested. The recovery process implies several steps, each of which can represent an investment opportunity; managers will step in earlier or later depending on their liquidity needs, their risk tolerance and their involvement. The risk–return profile changes significantly from the day of the bankruptcy to six months later when the rescue plan is agreed; during the first phase of the reorganization, the uncertainty surrounding the future of the company is at its peak and this is also when the pressure of time is highest; the pressure on the management, shareholders and creditors is at its maximum. Some managers are early investors and consider investment at this point; such managers often tend to play an active role in the restructuring and they not only invest in securities but also become fully involved. It is not unusual for such a manager or one of their representatives to take a seat on the board or credit committee. This means, in some cases, an activist role. Their objective is to create value by facilitating the reorganization of the company.

Distressed investing requires not only a financial investment but also an investment of time. The role of managers can in some case include the search for potential co-investors; in most cases managers, given their access to inside information, will not be allowed to trade positions.

The securities of distressed companies tend to be traded at a price that is lower than what is perceived as fair value; this is justified by the negative news flows around the company and because of the limited liquidity. In addition most institutional investors tend to sell the shares in these companies, because they do not want to hold risky paper and they want to prevent any risk to their own reputation. Legal constraints and window dressing can also justify partial or total sales. All these put direct pressure on prices.

There are two ways to profit from an attractive distressed company; it can be done either in absolute terms or in relative terms. The absolute is based exclusively on the intrinsic value of the company, estimated by using a fundamental analysis. When the market value of a security is perceived as being significantly below its fundamental value, and managers estimate that the security will go back up to its fundamental value when the restructuring process has been completed, they take a position or increase an existing one. Relative positions, however, are taken by combining positions in securities perceived as relatively mispriced. During a restructuring it often happens that the price of some securities moves more than some others. The manager takes a relative position, buying the cheap securities and going short on the expensive. The short is not always easy to implement because of liquidity constraints – but bear in mind that distressed securities is not about smaller or mid-cap companies. Some of the biggest opportunities that emerged over the last decade were in large companies. Relative positioning is also called capital structure arbitrage. It is not specific to distressed investing as it is also used in other event driven strategies.

Managers investing in distressed companies have to find out every-thing about the company in question, but they should also have a deep understanding of the bankruptcy process; the two are equally impor-tant. Information on the company can be gathered directly from internal sources and also from industry contacts, legal advisors and consultants. The deep understanding of the legal framework is important because there may be unexpected legal limitations or implications; for example, under certain conditions part of a distressed company debt may be con-verted into equities.

The United States is the main market for distressed investing. The American legislator supports distressed companies. There is a specific part of the United States Bankruptcy Code, Chapter 11, which permits reorganization under the bankruptcy laws of the United States. Chapter 11 bankruptcy is available to every business and individual, although it is primarily used by corporate entities. This law exempts bankrupt or almost bankrupt companies from having to repay their creditors. It organizes in detail the restructuring of the debt, and defines strict communication rules, including forming a creditor committee; the objective is to avoid distressed companies falling into liquidation, as regulated by Chapter 7 of the same code. In continental Europe the mindset has for a long time been very different, even if things are evolving; bankruptcies have in most cases been seen more as the end of something rather than the start of something new. This is why the European distressed securities business is less well developed.

Figure 3.37 summarizes how distressed managers analyse the world. This will not be the case for every fund manager but it is a good illustra-tion. The top left part of the figure indicates that the companies con-sidered are distressed. The top right-hand side indicates that these fund managers look for companies with a bad balance sheet structure. The bottom left-hand side of the diagram confirms that the manager will consider only companies that have an interesting product or service to sell and can determine the quality of the management. The bottom-right hand side confirms that the potential markets is not limited to small and mid-caps but also includes larger companies.

Risk management is especially important in distressed investing, and there are various ways to proceed. Even if each investment seems par-ticularly risky on first sight, managers manage the risk of their portfolio by diversifying it across various companies, sectors and industries, and types of security, and by investing in companies at various stages of their recovery phase. Managers tend also to limit the proportion of the portfo-lio allocated to a single company or to a conglomerate. The objectives and time horizon have to be defined before any investment, and these will be

Figure 3.37   Analysis of the range by a distressed securities fund manager

constantly reviewed. At the same time, managers may use various hedging tools; equities may be hedged to balance any debt exposure, or sector or global hedges may also be taken through indices or put options.

8.3   Illustration

Callahan Nordrhein-Westfalen GmbH is a German company specializing in television cabling. The company went bankrupt in 2002 because of a high debt exposure and some operational issues. On this basis, the fund manager performed a deep analysis of the company, concluding that the core activity of the company, analogical transmission, was stable and performing well. In this case, our distressed manager negotiated a balance sheet restructure with the original banks. They also made changes in the management team, and negotiated a director's seat on the board representing smaller shareholders. The manager took a long position in the securitized first-lien bank debt at an average purchase price 40 per cent of the face value, based on the perception that the main activity of the company was performing well enough to support the interest payments. The restructuring became effective in the last quarter of 2002; the company performed above expectations in 2003 and 2004, and the manager closed its position close to face value in 2004. The return on capital invested surpassed 150 per cent over two years and a few months. Very attractive returns – but remember that at any moment between the restructure and the positive perception of the market they could have lost their money if they had had to sell.

8.4   Advantages and drawbacks

Distressed investing is an event driven strategy, meaning that it can provide interesting returns under any market conditions. These returns rely more heavily on the manager's skill than on market conditions. Even during recession or in period of high interest rates, distressed companies can offer attractive returns if the reorganization succeeds.

On another side, investments in distressed companies are not liquid. This means that this kind of fund cannot easily turn positions, and that the turnover tends to be very low. An important element of success in distressed securities investing is how often a manager can close a position. This is simplified if the asset base increases over time; this allows the manager to build a book of companies at different phases of their recovery process and in consequence to smooth the returns to some extent. The investment horizon will range from a few weeks for late distressed investors to several years for early ones. As a consequence these funds are not liquid; at best they offer quarterly redemptions, and at worst annual with 6 to 12 months' notice.

8.5   Performance

Hedge Fund Research describes distressed/restructuring strategies as:

> *strategies which employ an investment process focused on corporate fixed income instruments, primarily on corporate credit instruments of companies trading at significant discounts to their value at issuance or obliged (par value) at maturity as a result of either formal bankruptcy proceeding or financial market perception of near term proceedings. Managers are typically actively involved with the management of these companies, frequently involved on creditors' committees in negotiating the exchange of securities for alternative obligations, either swaps of debt, equity or hybrid securities. Managers employ fundamental credit processes focused on valuation and asset coverage of securities of distressed firms; in most cases portfolio exposures are concentrated in instruments which are publicly traded, in some cases actively and in others under reduced liquidity but in general for which a reasonable public market exists. In contrast to Special Situations, Distressed Strategies employ primarily debt (greater than 60%) but also may maintain related equity exposure.*

Figure 3.38 shows the evolution of US$100 invested in the HFRI ED: Distressed/ Restructuring index since January 1990 compared with other similar investments in the HFRI Fund Weighted Composite index, the equity market, represented by MSCI World, and the bond market, represented by the Barclays Aggregate Bond index. An investment of US$100

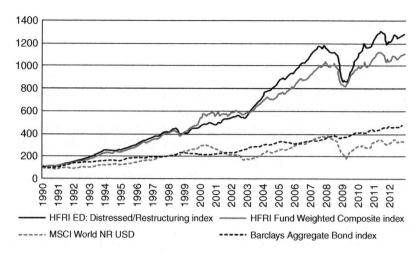

Figure 3.38   Evolution of US$100 invested in the HFRI ED: Distressed/Restructuring index

Source: Based on numbers obtained from Hedge Fund Research, Inc.

in the HFRI ED: Distressed/Restructuring index would have become US$1346 at the end of 2012. The same investment in the equity market, bond market or global hedge fund market would have become US$1105, US$352 or US$472 respectively.

The HFRI ED: Distressed/Restructuring index offered an average annual return of 12.6 per cent per year over the whole period, against 7.2 per cent for the equity market and 7.4 per cent for the bond market. More recently, it has offered 9.5 per cent per year on average over the last decade and 4.7 per cent per year on average over the last five years. The fall has been significant, and it can largely be explained by the very low performance of 2008; this strategy is illiquid by nature, and the liquidity crisis of 2008 directly impacted distressed managers.

Volatility has been relatively low over the whole period, at 6.6 per cent, and 6.8 per cent over the last decade but increasing to 7.9 per cent over the last five years. This is significantly lower than equities, which ranged between 15 and 20 per cent depending on the period in question. The strategy has offered volatility in line with that of the bond index, even if the last five years have been more volatile. The risk–return ratio over the whole period remains attractive.

Table 3.15 shows the yearly returns, the mean annual return, the standard deviation, the minimum annual return, the maximum annual return

Table 3.15 Performance statistics of the HFRI ED: Distressed/Restructuring index and comparative indices

	HFRI ED: Distressed/ Restructuring Index	HFRI Fund Weighted Composite Index	MSCI World NR USD	Barclays Aggregate Bond Index	Performance vs. HFRI	Performance vs. MSCI World
1990	6.4%	5.8%	-17.0%	12.7%	0.6%	23.5%
1991	35.7%	32.2%	18.3%	16.0%	3.5%	17.4%
1992	25.2%	21.2%	-5.2%	5.8%	4.0%	30.5%
1993	32.5%	30.9%	22.5%	11.1%	1.7%	10.0%
1994	3.8%	4.1%	5.1%	0.2%	-0.3%	-1.2%
1995	19.7%	21.5%	20.7%	19.7%	-1.8%	-1.0%
1996	20.8%	21.1%	13.5%	4.9%	-0.3%	7.3%
1997	15.4%	16.8%	15.8%	3.8%	-1.4%	-0.4%
1998	-4.2%	2.6%	24.3%	13.7%	-6.9%	-28.6%
1999	16.9%	31.3%	24.9%	-5.2%	-14.4%	-8.0%
2000	2.8%	5.0%	-13.2%	3.2%	-2.2%	16.0%
2001	13.3%	4.6%	-16.8%	1.6%	8.7%	30.1%
2002	5.3%	-1.5%	-19.9%	16.5%	6.7%	25.2%
2003	29.6%	19.5%	33.1%	12.5%	10.0%	-3.5%
2004	18.9%	9.0%	14.7%	9.3%	9.9%	4.2%
2005	2.6%	3.5%	4.5%	1.3%	-0.9%	-1.9%
2006	15.9%	12.9%	20.1%	6.6%	3.1%	-4.1%
2007	5.1%	10.0%	9.0%	9.5%	-4.9%	-4.0%
2008	-25.2%	-19.0%	-40.7%	4.8%	-6.2%	15.5%
2009	28.1%	20.0%	30.0%	6.9%	8.2%	-1.8%
2010	12.1%	10.2%	11.8%	5.5%	1.9%	0.4%
2011	-1.8%	-5.3%	-5.5%	5.6%	3.5%	3.7%
2012	10.1%	6.4%	15.8%	4.3%	3.8%	-5.7%
Mean annual return (whole period)	12.6%	11.4%	7.2%	7.4%	1.1%	5.4%
Volatility (whole period)	6.6%	7.0%	15.6%	5.5%	NA	NA
Meanannual return 2003–2012	9.5%	6.7%	9.3%	6.6%	2.8%	0.3%
Volatility 2003–2012	6.8%	6.5%	16.2%	6.1%	NA	NA
Meanaverage return 2007–2012	4.7%	2.5%	2.3%	5.4%	2.2%	2.4%
Volatility 2007–2012	7.9%	7.4%	19.4%	6.4%	NA	NA
Minimum annual return	-25.2%	-19.0%	-40.7%	-5.2%	-14.4%	-28.6%
Maximum annual return	35.7%	32.2%	33.1%	19.7%	10.0%	30.5%

Source: Based on data from Hedge Fund Research, Inc.

and the spread of the strategies relative to the comparative indices. It leads to the following remarks:

– Over the 23 years covered, the HFRI ED: Distressed/ Restructuring index was negative in two years: in 2008 (–5.4 per cent) and in 2002 (–0.9 per cent). 2008 was the most difficult year for the hedge fund industry as a whole. The equity index finished down in 7 years out of 23, including in the 2000–2002 bear market, 2008 and 2011. The bond index suffered negative returns for one year only, in 1999.
– The maximum annual returns of the HFRI ED: Distressed/ Restructuring index were achieved in 1991 (35.7 per cent), 1993 (32.5 per cent) and 2009 (28.1 per cent). These numbers are strong, particularly given the limited volatility of the monthly returns.
– The spread in returns between the HFRI ED: Distressed/ Restructuring index and the comparative indices has been volatile. The strategy has outperformed the global hedge fund index 13 times out of 23, the equity index 12 times and the bond index 16 times. The largest out-performance of the HFRI ED: Distressed/ Restructuring index relative to the equity index was 30.5 per cent, in 1992, while the largest under-performance was 28.6 per cent, in 1998. Relative to the bond index, the largest outperformance was achieved in 1999 at 22.1 per cent, and the largest underperformance was 30 per cent, in 2008.

9   PIPE funds

PIPE stands for Private Investment in Public Entities/Equities – that is com-panies that have all, or at least a portion, of their shares traded on a stock exchange. Such financing is done directly between a fund and a company. Such transactions had existed for more than a decade, but the market col-lapsed during the difficult years of 2000 to 2002. In the following years it came back to life and many of the investors used the hedge fund structure. The market of PIPE funds grew quite large before the liquidity crisis of 2008, but after that it lost the interest of investors, who prefer more liquid strategies. This strategy was created in 1982 in the United States as a result of a new Securities and Exchange Commission regulation that created cer-tain exemptions relating to the public sale of virtually bankrupt compa-nies; to avoid bankruptcy these companies could make a private offering rather a public one; PIPE funds are also called Regulation D funds.

9.1   Methodology

PIPE funds aim to play the role of investment banks for companies that no longer have access to the market. Limited access to the market may come from limited liquidity, difficult market conditions or for any other reason including operational issues. PIPE funds tend to work with small companies, with less than US$250 million market capitalization. This goes down to micro-cap (less than US$50 million) and nano cap (less than US$25 million market cap). Such companies are usually listed on the NASDAQ, AMEX, New York Stock Exchange or on local exchanges in the United States and on the Alternative Investment Market (AIM) in the United Kingdom. Deals have also been done in Canada, Poland and China. The role of PIPE funds in the life of companies is illustrated in Figure 3.39.

In a typical American PIPE transaction, the public company sells unregistered securities at a discount relative to their market value. As they are unregistered, these securities cannot be sold on the secondary market before being registered with the SEC. Such securities usually take the form of convertible bonds or preference convertible bonds; they are purely private and cannot be traded on any exchange during the waiting phase; also, they are usually created with an obligation for the company to register them with the SEC; the registration process takes usually 90 to 120 days.

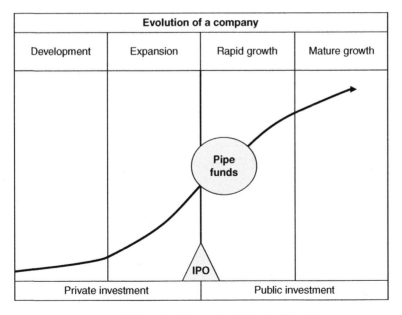

Figure 3.39 Illustration of the role of PIPE funds in the life of a company

The main advantages for the issuer getting additional capital from private markets are:

- **Rapidity**: a few weeks, as against a few months for public offerings.
- Direct negotiation: the offer is negotiated direct, so it can correspond closely to the company's needs.
- **Cheapness**: a private issue process is cheaper than a public one.
- **Postponed dilution**: a public issue leads to direct capital dilution, while with a private issue this is delayed.
- **Control**: the control of the company is maintained.
- **Market perception**: a public financing is riskier, as the market may not be receptive.
- **Availability**: public financing conditions are becoming more and more stringent and expensive, so smaller companies usually do not have the choice and have to go for private offers.
- **Discretion**: there is more discretion on the deal, as the securities issued are private before getting registered.

The interest for the investor is that they can access securities at a discount relative to their intrinsic value. Such transactions have three main environments that will determine the level of risk:

- The company is in, or has just emerged from, difficulties, and it is looking for capital to support its future development.
- The company is looking for short-term financing for a new project.
- The company is mature and it is looking to finance an acquisition or new projects.

The typical structure of a PIPE transaction is illustrated in Figure 3.40. It starts with an analysis of the financial health of the company; in an ideal world managers look to finance companies with strong numbers and projects, but in practice, the strength of the company is always balanced

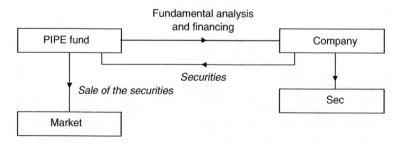

Figure 3.40 Typical structure of a PIPE transaction

by an interest rate that can be negotiated. A fund may finance a company if it estimates it to be strong enough to survive the next 12 to 18 months, without guarantee for longer term as long as the interest rate paid is sufficient; the crucial point is to avoid companies with a significant risk of bankruptcy. Several managers will usually work together on a single deal, as PIPE portfolios tend to be well diversified, limiting exposure to any single company. The transaction will be carried out in tranches, and the company must then register the security each time with the SEC. Once the securities are registered, the manager can get to work on realizing its investment and will sell the securities unless there is a section in the contract that specifies a minimum holding period. To realize the securities the manager has to convert the bonds into equities and then sell them while limiting the impact on the price of the securities; liquidity thus is an essential element in a PIPE transaction.

PIPE transactions also usually includes warrants aside of the convertibles. These are free long-term options to the manager.

The tranche structure can be illustrated with the following example. A company needs US$10 million. A PIPE manager agrees to finance 30 per cent of this on the following basis:

– a first tranche of US$1 million, to be paid on signature of the agreement
– a second tranche of US$1 million, to be paid when the company asks for the registration of the securities underlying the transaction
– a third tranche of US$1 million, to be paid when the securities are registered.

Companies looking for rapid financing are usually not liquid, and one of the difficulties in the process is to be able to liquidate the position without impacting the price of the stock.

There are two types of PIPE fund: traditional and structured.

• Traditional PIPE funds have a fixed conversion ratio in the convertible. This means that at conversion the fund will get a fixed number of stocks independently of the evolution of the stock price. The risk here is that the stock price may fall between the signature of the agreement and the registration.
• Structured PIPE deals includes specific characteristics such as a variable conversion ratio which means that investors do not get a fixed number of shares per convertible but a fixed value of shares. Also called toxic PIPE deals, such deals may be dangerous for companies, as if their stock price falls investors receive more shares; if it falls significantly investors may get a significant number of shares and can sometimes take the company over.

There have been cases where investors hedged their position in the convertible. This put pressure on the stock price, which started to fall. For stocks trading at a few dollars or even a few pence in some cases, the situation could rapidly become problematic. In the United States the regulators have changed the ruling to make such a state of affairs impossible in the future, but the situation has still to evolve in new markets like Poland and China.

The PIPE market increased significantly between 2002 and 2007; close to 1500 deals were reported by PlacementTracker.com. The growth in terms of assets has been even more important; PlacementTracker.com estimates that the value of PIPE transaction went from close to US$10 billion in 2003 to over US$100 billion in 2008. The liquidity crisis of 2008 had a strong impact on the strategy. The number of transactions fell – but more importantly the liquidity disappeared, meaning that most managers have not been able to realize their investments. Since then, investor interest has been more limited and liquidity did not come back.

9.2 Types of transaction

There are various ways to carry out private transactions. The classic way is to use unregistered convertible bonds. Table 3.16 reports various types of private transactions. For every kind of transaction we show the structure, the form of protection and the potential return. These include discounted equity transactions, preference senior convertibles, bridge notes, senior secured convertible notes, self-liquidating debentures and asset-backed loans. Each transaction will be have its own specific features, but there are certain characteristics common to them: the coupon usually ranges from 6 to 12 per cent; the manager negotiates a discount from the market value, and the transaction is secured by company's assets (in some case even by personal assets of the owner); the manager negotiates between 50 and 200 per cent hedge through five-year warrants that have an exercise price close to the price of the share when the transaction is signed; the conversion rate may be fixed, in which case the manager is exposed to a directional long exposure, or it can have a ratchet discount system.

For example, consider the case of a stock trading at US$1. The manager agrees with the company that the convertible will be converted at a minimum of US$0.90, a discount of 10 per cent of the stock price at conversion. If the stock price stays stable the manager gets a 10 per cent discount, and if the equity price increases the manager will still be able to convert at US$0.9 per share. If the price increases to US$2.50 per share, a conversion at US$0.90 per share means a discount of 64 per cent relative to the share price at conversion. If the stock price falls the conversion

Table 3.16 Types of private transaction

Style	Structure	Form of protection	Potential gain
Equity	– Buy a group of shares at a discounted price.	– Hedging through short selling. – Revaluation of the price paid on the basis of earnings or income.	– The maximum profit will depend on the discount. – Potential gain on stock price increase. – Negotiation of warrants.
Senior Convertible Preference	– Securities that pay a fixed interest with a (usually discounted) conversion rate.	– Hedging of the share price through equities when it is possible and allowed. – Negotiation of a physical guarantee (real estate, equipment and so on).	– Fixed interest constitutes the minimum return. – Potential gain on stock price increase. – Advantageous conversion rate.
Bridge Notes	– Debt securities with a coupon and an equity kicker between 50 and 100% of initial investment.	– Notes have a high seniority, and they are paid back in the case of secondary share offering.	– Fixed interest constitutes the minimum return. – Free share are issued when the debt securities are paid back.
Senior Secured Convertible Notes	– Debt instruments with fixed interest and a conversion of debt with a negotiated discount.	– Securitized notes by assets (real estate, equipment and so on). – Conversion rate redefined depending on market conditions.	– Fixed interest rate. – Potential increase of the share price over conversion. – The company agrees to buy back the notes at a premium relative to the principal if the security does not get registered or if the discount is not available.
Self-Liquidating Debentures	– Variable debt instrument that pays a fixed interest with a conversion rate defined and negotiated with a discount relative to movements of the underlying share.	– Notes with interest have to be repaid on a monthly basis with a floating discount to share price.	– Fixed interest rate and a discount relative to conversion. – Negotiation of warrants.
Asset-Backed Loans	– Credit product that pays a fixed interest rate and the principal at maturity.	– Loans guaranteed by assets that include real estate and equipment. – Negotiation of a share buyback in case of limited liquidity.	– Fixed interest rate. – Potential gain on stock price increase.

Figure 3.41 Illustration of a variable conversion rate PIPE transaction

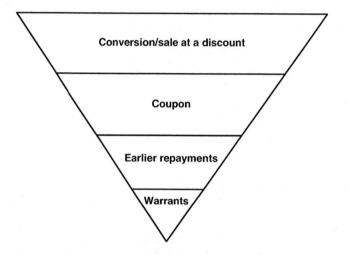

Figure 3.42 Sources of returns for PIPE funds

price would fall also, to keep the 10 per cent discount. Figure 3.41 illustrates variable conversion rate PIPE transactions.

Note also that manager tends to stay below 5 per cent of the value of the company at any time, avoiding the requirement to declare their holdings. In practice, to exit a position a manager will convert a small number of shares at a time and sell them before converting more. The sources of return in PIPE deals include discount conversion, the coupon, penalties in case of earlier repayment and warrants. Figure 3.42 reports these sources.

Table 3.17 shows the evolution of the number of PIPE and Reg S transactions and of the amount of money invested. The impact of the liquidity crisis that started in 2008 is clear and important.

9.3 Underlying risks

They are three main sources of risks relating to PIPE funds. The first is the credit risk; this includes the risk of default that is real in this part of

Table 3.17 Evolution of the number of PIPE and Reg S transactions and of the amount of money invested

	Number of transactions	Amounts (US$ millions)
2001	945	14,966
2002	858	13,049
2003	1,456	19,193
2004	1,998	21,658
2005	2,171	28,077
2006	1,623	31,272
2007	1,623	86,696
2008	1,154	123,897
2009	1,020	36,854
2010	1,149	38,544
2011	923	26,606
2012	821	32,797
	15,741	473,609

Source: PlacementTracker.com

the financial world. As managers are investing in companies looking for nedded sources of capital, the risk is high. The manager mitigates this risk with guarantees on real estate assets, inventories or equipment – but it would take time and cost money to realize any such asset, so a manager will usually prefer to negotiate a new deal with the company in case of issues. The second source of risk is the liquidity risk. PIPE deals are private deals, and by definition private deals are illiquid. In addition, once converted into equities the problem is still real, as stocks of companies doing PIPE transactions trade at a few dollars per share to a few cents, and they have very limited daily volumes. It usually takes weeks to months for a manager to go out of a transaction. The third source of risk is valuation. There is a debate on valuation; some managers will use the cost price for unregistered securities while others will discount the equity price. This debate is also applicable to warrants; when they are out-of-the-money they should be valued at zero, but things become more complicated when they are in-the-money. A rule applied by many is to use a discounted Black & Scholes pricing model, but the problem is that it is difficult to justify giving value to something that cannot be sold. In addition, the underlying stocks tend to be very volatile, meaning that their valuation in the portfolio may be volatile as well. From there, the problem is more about what discount to apply; some managers will take 30 or 40 per cent, while others will go up to 90 per cent. These valuation issues lead to difficulties when assessing the quality of a manager, and they should be analysed in detail before considering any investment.

9.4   Illustrations[27]

Private deals may have very different structures and specific characteristics; these examples may not be representative of what is applied by other managers.

9.4.1   Ascent Solar Technologies

This example is about a bridginge loan that was given to Ascent Solar Technologies quoted on NASDAQ small cap. Table 3.18 shows the characteristics of the transaction. The company negotiated this bridge loan before making a secondary offering; the loan had a coupon of 12 per cent, and the principal of the loan was to be paid back at the secondary offering, when the manager would get the same amount in equities.

During the second quarter of the following year the credit was paid back and 45,454 new ordinary shares were issued. At the same time 45,454 A Warrants were issued, with an exercise price of US$6.6 per share and 90,908 B Warrants were issued with an exercise price of US$11.2 per share. The 45,454 ordinary shares were sold by the manager in February 2007 at an average price of US$7 per share, for a total profit of US$318,000. A Warrants were sold at an average price of US$2.75 each, for a total of US$124,998.50 and; B Warrants were sold at a price of US$2.15 per unit, for a total profit of US$19,270.36. Total profits include the coupon paid, and the profits on the sale of the equity and the warrants.

9.4.2   Quest Minerals and Mining Corporation

Quest Minerals and Mining Corporation issued a private senior secured convertible. The characteristics of the deal are shown in Table 3.19. The deal relates to a convertible paying 8 per cent; this bond is convertible at a 30 per cent discount to equity market price. The deal is covered by two types of warrants and a coal mine.

At the time of the transaction the manager was able to short sell the stock at a price of US$1.2 per share and locked in a profit of US$300,000. From there the situation became more complicated, as the company was not able to pay its interest payments and defaulted. The manager started the recovery process. The company paid US$250,000 during the restructuring and US$450,000 in restructuring costs. The warrants were reset

Table 3.18   Ascent Solar Technologies bridge loan deal characteristics

Coupon:	12%
Investment date:	December 2005
Amount invested:	US$300,000
Principal:	Credit paid back at secondary offering
Protection:	100% hedged through secondary share offering

Table 3.19   Quest Minerals PIPE transaction in 2004

Coupon:	8%
Investment date:	October 2004
Capital invested:	US$500,000
Conversion:	30% discount to market price
Warrants:	200% through A warrants that do not need cash
	A minimum of 1/3 share per warrant
	200% through B warrants at 150% of initial conversion rate
Collateral:	Priority on a coal reserve with over US$100 million coal value

Table 3.20   Puda Coal convertible bond deal characteristics

Coupon:	0%
Investment date:	November 2005
Amount invested:	US$100,000
Conversion into:	Ordinary shares
Conversion rate:	US$0.5 per share
Warrant:	100% hedging through warrants at US$0.6 per share
Penalty:	1% per month in case of delay in the registration process

at a lower conversion rate negotiated at one third of their original price. During the first half of 2006 the manager was able to sell 4 million warrants for US$180,000. Over the following year, the manager continued to convert the convertible with a 30 per cent discount for a profit of US$450,000. The total profits came to around US$880,000.

9.4.3   Puda Coal Inc.

This example illustrates the fixed conversion rate convertible structure with warrants. Puda Coal Inc. agreed with a manager on a convertible with the characteristics reported in Table 3.20.

The manager hedged the position over the summer of 2006 by selling US$300,000 worth of shares for a profit of US$180,000. The transaction closed as follows:

- In November 2006, the manager sold 200,000 shares at a price of US$1.35 per share, for a profit of US$270,000
- The manager kept the warrant position from which he could profit in the case of a share price increase.

The profits on the position totalled US$180,000 on the short hedge and US$270,000 on the position closure – but this does not exclude the warrants that may go into the money over their lifetime.

9.5   Advantages and drawbacks

The PIPE strategy is interesting because it combines a series of small trans-actions within a diversified portfolio. The warrants enable the manager to keep some long-term options free in case some companies succeed or get bought over the years following the transaction. In addition, PIPE trans-actions finance a part of the market that is not of interest to other market players; this enables the strategy to offer stable and attractive returns over time. In normal market conditions, the number of defaults is limited and diversification is sufficient in order to manage short-term volatility.

The main drawback of the strategy is linked to its risks, the lack of liquidity remaining the most important. PIPE funds are constantly at the limit of the liquidity spectrum for open-ended funds; it is not con-ceivable to drop down further and to do less liquid deals within reason. Several managers manage this liquidity issue by refinancing the same companies over time. They look to identify high quality PIPE candi-dates, then they propose balanced deals where both the company and the fund can make money and work together over time. It is probably a good way to manage the risk, as managers that focus only on their benefits usually become rapidly unstuck. In practice, however, this pro-tection is not sufficient, as most investors – and institutional investors in particular – tend to avoid funds with a bad press. The liquidity of the micro and nano cap market is very limited, particularly during periods of stress when there is no liquidity at all in any of these stocks. The manager is also exposed to a legal risk, because any single element of the legal document that is unclear can cost the fund its investment. There is also the reputational risk; PIPE deals are private until they are registered. At registration everything becomes public, including the name of the participants as well as the details of the deal. Investors do not necessar-ily want any of their managers to be exposed to private deals, to avoid any reputational risk.

9.6   Performance

Hedge Fund Research describes Private Issue/Regulation D strategies that employ an investment process as:

> *primarily focused on opportunities in equity and equity related instruments of companies which are primarily private and illiquid in nature. These most frequently involve realizing an investment premium for holding private obli-gations or securities for which a reasonably liquid market does not readily exist until such time as a catalyst such as new security issuance or emer-gence from bankruptcy proceedings occurs. Managers employ fundamental*

valuation processes focused on asset coverage of securities of issuer firms, and would expect over a given market cycle to maintain greater than 50% of the portfolio in private securities, including Regulation D or PIPE transactions.

Figure 3.43 shows the evolution of US$100 invested in the HFRI ED: Private Issue/Regulation D index since January 1996 compared with other similar investments in the HFRI Fund Weighted Composite index, the equity market, represented by MSCI World, and the bond market, represented by the Barclays Aggregate Bond index. An investment of US$100 in the HFRI ED: Private Issue/Regulation D index would have become US$556 by the end of 2012. The same investment in the equity market, bond market or global hedge fund market would have become US$394, US$244 or US$256 respectively.

The HFRI ED: Private Issue/Regulation D index offered an average annual return of 11 per cent per year over the whole period, against 7.1 per cent for the equity market and 6.2 per cent for the bond market. More recently it has offered 4.9 per cent per year on average over the last decade and 0.9 per cent per year on average over the last five years. The fall has been significant and it can be largely explained by the very low performance of 2008; this strategy is illiquid by its very nature, and the liquidity crisis of 2008 directly impacted the strategy.

Volatility was relatively low over the whole period, at 7 per cent; it was 6.3 per cent over the last decade but increased to 5.7 per cent over the last five years. This is significantly lower than equities, which ranged between

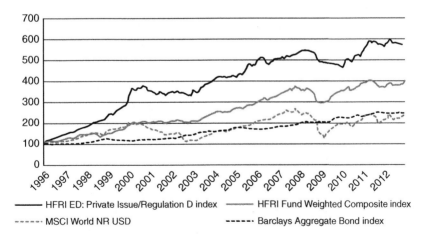

Figure 3.43   Evolution of US$100 invested in the HFRI ED: Private Issue/Regulation D index

Source: Based on numbers obtained from Hedge Fund Research, Inc.

15 per cent and 20 per cent depending on the period in question. The strategy offered a volatility in line with that of the bond index even if the last five years have been more volatile. The risk–return ratio over the whole period remains attractive.

Table 3.21 shows the yearly returns, the mean annual return, the standard deviation, the minimum annual return, the maximum annual return and the spread of the strategies relative to the comparative indices. It leads to the following remarks:

- Over the 17 years covered, the HFRI ED: Private Issue/Regulation D index was negative in four years: in 2012 (–1.3 per cent), in 2008 (–10.1 per cent), in 2002 (–5.5 per cent) and 2001 (–1.7 per cent). 2008 was the most difficult year for the hedge fund industry as a whole. 2002 was a very difficult year for equities. The equity index finished down 5 years out of 17, including the 2000–2002 bear market, 2008 and 2011. The bond index suffered negative returns for one year only, in 1999.
- The maximum annual returns of the HFRI ED: Private Issue/Regulation D index were achieved in 1996 (44.6 per cent), 1999 (34.9 per cent) and 1997 (26.9 per cent). These numbers are strong, particularly given the limited volatility of the monthly returns. More recent numbers have been lower; this can probably be explained by market conditions but also by constant evolution in the regulation surrounding PIPE deals, which has been becoming more and more stringent.
- The spread in returns between the HFRI ED: Private Issue/Regulation D index and the comparative indices has been volatile. The strategy has outperformed the global hedge fund index 10 times out of 17, the equity index 10 times and the bond index 12 times. The largest outperformance of the HFRI ED: Private Issue/Regulation D index relative to the equity index was 31.1 per cent, in 1996, while the largest underperformance was 33.4 per cent, in 2008. Relative to the bond index, the largest outperformance was achieved in 2003 at 33.1 per cent, and the largest underperformance was 40.7 per cent, in 2008.

10   Volatility Arbitrage

Volatility is a concept that is largely diffused in finance; the volatility of a security is the rate at which the price of a security varies on the upside and on the downside. Mathematically, it is estimated by the annualized standard deviation of the price of a security. Some managers specialize in investing in volatility; their aim is to profit from discrepancy between implied and realized volatility.

Table 3.21 Performance statistics of the HFRI ED: Private Issue/Regulation D index and comparative indices

	HFRI ED: Private Issue/Regulation D Index	HFRI Fund Weighted Composite Index	MSCI World NR USD	Barclays Aggregate Bond Index	Performance vs. HFRI	Performance vs. MSCI World	Performance vs. Barclays Aggregate
1996	44.6%	21.1%	13.5%	4.9%	23.5%	31.1%	13.5%
1997	26.9%	16.8%	15.8%	3.8%	10.1%	11.2%	15.8%
1998	26.3%	2.6%	24.3%	13.7%	23.7%	1.9%	24.3%
1999	34.1%	31.3%	24.9%	-5.2%	2.8%	9.2%	24.9%
2000	14.5%	5.0%	-13.2%	3.2%	9.5%	27.6%	-13.2%
2001	-1.7%	4.6%	-16.8%	1.6%	-6.3%	15.1%	-16.8%
2002	-5.5%	-1.5%	-19.9%	16.5%	-4.0%	14.4%	-19.9%
2003	20.5%	19.5%	33.1%	12.5%	1.0%	-12.6%	33.1%
2004	6.1%	9.0%	14.7%	9.3%	-3.0%	-8.7%	14.7%
2005	4.2%	3.5%	4.5%	1.3%	0.7%	-0.3%	4.5%
2006	6.8%	12.9%	20.1%	6.6%	-6.1%	-13.2%	20.1%
2007	6.6%	10.0%	9.0%	9.5%	-3.3%	-2.4%	9.0%
2008	-10.1%	-19.0%	-40.7%	4.8%	8.9%	30.6%	-40.7%
2009	-3.4%	20.0%	30.0%	6.9%	-23.4%	-33.4%	30.0%
2010	12.9%	10.2%	11.8%	5.5%	2.7%	1.2%	11.8%
2011	6.3%	-5.3%	-5.5%	5.6%	11.5%	11.8%	-5.5%
2012	-1.3%	6.4%	15.8%	4.3%	-7.7%	-9.5%	8.2%
Mean annual return (whole period)	11.0%	8.7%	7.1%	6.2%	2.4%	4.4%	6.7%
Volatility (whole period)	7.0%	7.4%	16.1%	5.7%	NA	NA	NA
Meanannual return 2003–2012	4.9%	6.7%	9.3%	6.6%	-1.9%	-3.6%	8.5%
Volatility 2003–2012	6.3%	6.5%	16.2%	6.1%	NA	NA	NA
Meanaverage return 2007–2012	0.9%	2.5%	2.3%	5.4%	-1.6%	0.1%	0.7%
Volatility 2007–2012	5.7%	7.4%	19.4%	6.4%	NA	NA	NA
Minimum annual return	-10.1%	-19.0%	-40.7%	-5.2%	-23.4%	-33.4%	-40.7%
Maximum annual return	44.6%	31.3%	33.1%	16.5%	23.7%	31.1%	33.1%

Source: Based on data from Hedge Fund Research, Inc.

10.1 Methodology

Volatility arbitrage is implemented by managers aiming to profit from changes in volatility. The can profit from an increase or from a decrease of volatility, by combining positions in call and put options. Many managers take only long positions and they sell their product as an insurance against volatility for a portfolio. An increase in volatility almost always corresponds with a decrease in the markets, markets always being more volatile on the downside than on the upside.

The manager may invest only in equity volatility, or can include commodities, rates and currencies. A manager focusing on equities will be focused either on the volatility of the S&P 500, or include other markets, the most typical being the Eurostoxx and the Nikkei. The underlying idea of in volatility is that there are numerous players in the financial markets, only a few of whom understand volatility movements and their underlying reasons. In addition, only a few players have the data and tools to be able to analyse volatility correctly, and the experience necessary to understand and implement complex option strategies. Most participants in the markets see options and other derivatives as hedging tools and use them almost exclusively for that without considering the other side of the position. In addition, most players in the option markets consider options in terms of premiums representing the cost of implementing a position rather than in terms of volatility.

Managers applying this strategy intend to profit from these elements as well as from the relations between the volatility of different markets and their evolution over time. Inherent within volatility arbitrage is the combination of long and short positions. These options can be differentiated by the underlying security, exercise price, maturity or type. Managers tend to use internal valuation models in order to determine the real price of an option or a set of options, just as an equity manager would do with a company. The price of an option is directly linked to the volatility of the underlying asset; the more volatile the underlying asset, the more expensive the option. The link between volatility and price of an option is positive because there is a higher chance that the exercise price will be attained for highly volatile options. In a typical case, the manager will take a long position in an option that they perceive as undervalued meaning that implied volatility is significantly lower than realized volatility. The option will then be hedged by selling or buying the corresponding underlying asset through another option. The hedging ratio is called the delta[28]; it is a measure of the sensitivity of the price variation of an option to the movement in the underlying asset. A long position in volatility is profitable if the price of the underlying asset moves rapidly, and it will lose money if the price is less volatile than expected – in which case the time value of the option decreases. Long positions in volatility are either traded aggressively in order to capture the daily volatility of the equity (if the underlying asset is an equity) if the manager anticipates that the share is likely to continue to trade within certain limits, or less aggressively if the equity is perceived to be following a trend.

An inverse position means that the manager sells volatility and options delta-neutral; in this case the objective is to sell options that have a high price relative to the volatility of the underlying asset in order to capture the time premium by adjusting the hedging. When a manager is long on volatility, every hedging adjustment should lead to a profit and when a manager is short on volatility every new hedge is likely to lead to a loss.

Starting from the classic strategy described above, each manager will diversify his/her portfolio using complementary investment techniques. Some managers also become involved in the volatility relations between the equity markets and the currency markets through variance swaps. Others take positions on relations between currencies and equities through exotic options, or between the volatility of the currency markets and commodities through surface modelling, or the volatility relation between the equity markets and the credit markets through correlation trading. These techniques are complex and we will not cover them in detail here.

Short positions are in this case called short volatility funds. The typical short volatility position consists of selling out-of-the-money put options.[29] Such a positioning offers a stable return through the premium of the option sold, though the price to be paid is a consequent loss potential in case of rapid downside market movements. In such a case, the value of the put option will grow rapidly, and the potential loss for the seller of the option can become significant. Options are the classic product used in order to take volatility positions; other securities typically used include convertibles, as they combine a bond with an option.

10.2 Illustrations

We show four volatility positions, put and call spreads, calendar spreads and strike spreads. There are numerous other ways to take positions in volatility, but they all tend to be based on the same principles.

In the context of the sale of out-of-the-money put spreads and call spreads, the manager takes position in options with the same underlyer, generally the S&P 500, and aims to profit from an increase in volatility. This means that the aim is to profit from a movement of the value of the underlying index outside the limits determined by the positioning. We consider four cases: bull put spreads, bear put spreads, bull call spreads and bear call spreads:

- A bull put spread is implemented by buying a put option and by selling at the same time a put option on the same underlyer, but at a higher exercise price. If the price of the underlying asset increases slightly, the option bought expires without value and the option sold would lead to a profit. If the movement is important the two options will have no value left. A fall in the two options will lead to a profit. The transaction is built on an initial profit, as the option sold has more value that the option bought. We illustrate a bull put spread in Figure 3.44.
- A bear put spread is the inverse of the bull put spread. The manager sells a put an buy another one on the same underlying but at a higher exercise price.

Identical positions can be taken through call options:

- A bull call spread is obtained by selling an out-of-the-money call option and by buying a call option with a higher exercise price. Such positions need a cash outflow at implementation as the option bought costs more than the option sold.
- A bear call spread is obtained by buying a call option and selling a call option with a lower exercise price. Such a positioning is interesting when the manager anticipates a limited decrease in the price of the underlying asset. These positions are illustrated in Figures 3.46 to 3.47.

A calendar spread is created by combining identical call or put options on the same underlying asset, with an identical exercise price but a different maturity. The manager sells the option with the shorter maturity

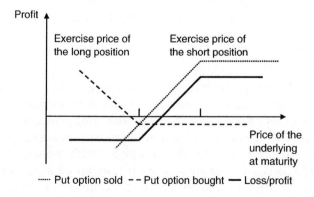

Figure 3.44 Bull put spread

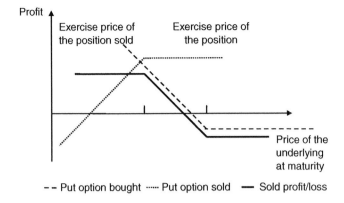

Figure 3.45 Bear put spread

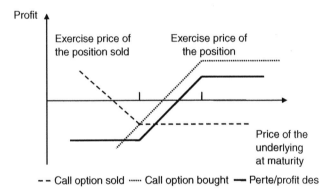

Figure 3.46 Bull call spread

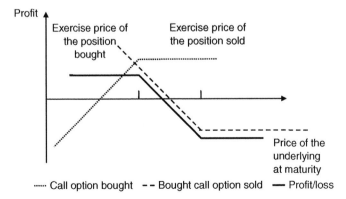

Figure 3.47 Bear call spread

at a higher price than has been paid to buy the option with the longer maturity. Calendar spread is illustrated in Figure 3.48. Such positions are initiated when the implicit volatility of options varies significantly from historical norms and when the manager anticipates a return to normality

Strike spread, also called ratio spread, is built by taking positions in identical call and put options. These options have the same underlyer and the same maturity, but a different exercise price, the difference between exercise prices being smaller than the difference in premium. Such a positioning is usually taken by selling more options than the number bought. Such a strategy is applied when the difference in volatility between the exercise prices has moved out of historical values; the manager buys the option with the exercise price that has the higher implicit volatility and sells the other. This strategy is implemented by manager when he or she anticipates low short-term volatility. The potential gains are limited while the potential loss is unlimited. A call ratio spread is illustrated in Figure 3.49; in our illustration two call options are sold and one is bought.

10.3   Advantages and drawbacks

Volatility arbitrage is interesting because the potential gains and losses are predetermined, depending on the evolution of the price of the underlying asset. The manager can precisely determine the level of risk taken. It is also of interest because the positioning can be rapidly adapted by buying or selling another option. On the other hand it is not easy for investors to understand the structure of the portfolio and the level of risk of some positions taken. While our examples are easy to understand, a complete portfolio is far more complex. In addition the interaction between positions can complicate the structure of the portfolio and make it incomprehensible. In addition it is worth bearing in mind that

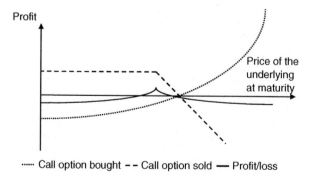

····· Call option bought - - Call option sold —— Profit/loss

Figure 3.48   Call calendar spread

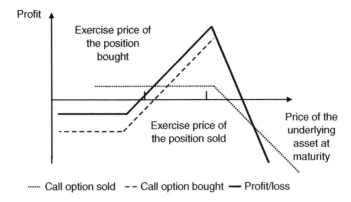

Figure 3.49 Call ratio spread

while the sale of a put option can have only a limited profit it has unlimited potential loss. This is not just a theoretical point; investors looking at option strategies need to be aware of the positioning taken by the managers to understand the risks taken. In addition, certain positions that bet on a decrease in volatility will also have a limited recurrent profit but an unlimited loss potential. Such strategies will usually offer very stable returns for some time (in some cases, years) before possibly facing a significant loss over just a month; timing is key when investing in such structures.

10.4 Performance

Hedge Fund Research, Inc. defines six sub-strategies within the relative value strategy. One of these is called Relative Value: Volatility strategies. There is, however, no published index for it, so we cannot carry out a performance analysis on it.

11 Multi-strategy

Unlike funds of funds, multi-strategy funds are not invested in funds managed by outside managers. They are products offered by single manager (usually a large one) offering a few individual funds to their clients and adding to their offering a diversified product that groups a few single strategies.

11.1 Methodology

Managers typically combine two to five investment strategies in order to offer a diversified product. Depending on the particular case, the company may offer individual funds and a multi-strategy fund or propose only a diversified portfolio. Each strategy is typically managed independently, but for close or linked strategies such as convertible arbitrage and volatility arbitrage that may be managed by the same team or manager. Like for fund of funds, capital is allocated between various managers in order to limit the exposure to manager and strategy risk. They will usually, however, be less diversified than funds of funds; only one fund or team per strategy will be combined. But as assets grow this may change – some very large players in the field combine more than 100 different management teams.

The strategy breakdown may be stable over time or be managed actively. When the strategy is managed in-house, the breakdown between strategies will tend to be stable or to evolve within bands. When external teams are used, the lead manager of the global portfolio usually retains the right to change the capital allocation over time. In this case rebalancing will usually be carried out monthly, quarterly or semi-annually. This does not mean that investors will not be able to redeem more often, but that the portfolio is actively managed.

11.2 Illustration

Multi-strategy funds can be of two types. Either a manager allocates assets between various funds or accounts managed by independent teams that will implement various investment strategies; in this case each sub-portfolio will be managed using a single strategy as presented here. The other type has a single team that includes several specialists, each managing a specific part of the assets. The portfolio is then a global portfolio managed in house. We illustrate this second case.

The various steps in the implementation of a multi-strategy fund are as shown in Figure 3.50. We consider a US$100 million fund; the manager will be investing in equities, government bonds and currencies. The process starts with the equity team deciding the allocation between long and short positions. It can for example decide to take a market neutral position, long on certain markets and short on others. Depending on the managers' strengths they will take positions in indices combine indices with stocks, or focus on individual stocks. A strategy like this will usually have a limited market exposure.

A second team manages a fixed income arbitrage book focused on developed government debt. It takes bets on market trends combined with bottom-up security selection. In this case the team anticipates a decrease in interest rates and it takes a long bias; the same team also takes positions on the curve. Another part of the team develops views on currencies

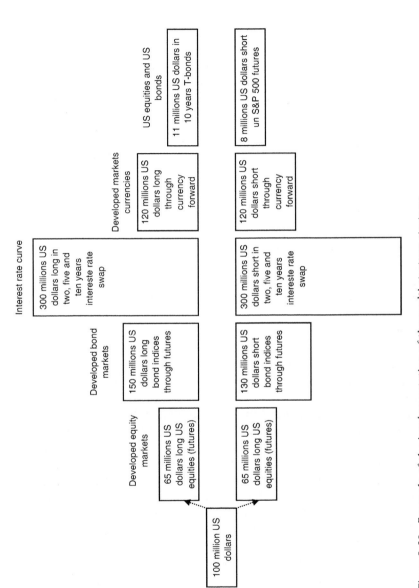

Figure 3.50 Example of the implementation of the multi-strategy strategy

through forwards. Finally there is a macro overlay, implemented by the strategist. At this point in time they decide to go slightly short in equities and long in government bonds.

11.3   Advantages and drawbacks

The first attraction of multi-strategy funds is that they offer a diversified exposure to hedge funds, as do funds of hedge funds. A multi-strategy fund gives investors access to a diversified exposure to hedge funds with a relatively low minimum. The liquidity provided is usually in line with the underlying strategies or may be more attractive in order to be of interest to investors. Like funds of funds, multi-strategy funds also offer a diversification of the risk of individual strategy. But a specific advantage of this strategy compared to funds of funds is that multi-strategy managers do not have to perform a due diligence on the underlying manager. This limits the costs compared to those of a fund of hedge fund team, which must constantly be on the lookout for the best managers in any specific strategy, so multi-strategy funds can offer a more attractive fee structure. Finally multi-strategy funds either rebalance monthly or quarterly or do this consistently based on market opportunity. In the last case there is a clear edge for multi-strategy funds over funds of funds, as those can only rebalance monthly or quarterly with a notice period and sometimes subject to a lockup period.

The main inconvenience of multi-strategy funds compared to funds of hedge funds is the lack of freedom in the choice of underlying manager. When a company offers five individual funds and a multi-strategy fund combining them, the multi-strategy fund will always be invested in these five strategies.

In addition multi-strategy funds tend to stick to the same manager even if performance is dissapointing. Yet while this argument is true for one part of the multi-strategy funds, we have to nuance it as there are a seires of large multi-strategy funds that work differently. Those funds are managed by independent teams that are in charge of a part of these assets of the fund and the assets under management depend on their performance. There may be changes in the team managing the assets.

Furthermore, multi-strategy managers do not always have the same level of transparency as do funds of funds. Another difference is that when the underlying funds are closed to new investments multi-strategy funds will usually also be closed to new investments while funds of funds tend to continue to look for assets.

A final element to mention in relation to multi-strategy funds is that many investors do not consider such funds because of their lack of visibility. Investors do not have much visibility on the positioning of multi-strategy funds and this prevents some of them from investing in the strategy.

11.4 Performance

Hedge Fund Research, Inc. defines multi-strategy funds for each of their strategies (equity hedge, macro, event driven and relative value), but in practice, it is only for the last of these that an index is published for. in this section, we use this HFRI RV: Multi-Strategy index; it

> *employs an investment thesis which is predicated on realization of a spread between related yield instruments in which one or multiple components of the spread contains a fixed income, derivative, equity, real estate, MLP or combination of these or other instruments. Strategies are typically quantitatively driven to measure the existing relationship between instruments and, in some cases, identify attractive positions in which the risk adjusted spread between these instruments represents an attractive opportunity for the investment manager. In many cases these strategies may exist as distinct strategies across which a vehicle which allocates directly, or may exist as related strategies over which a single individual or decision making process manages. Multi-strategy is not intended to provide broadest-based mass market investors appeal, but are most frequently distinguished from others arbitrage strategies in that they expect to maintain >30% of portfolio exposure in 2 or more strategies meaningfully distinct from each other that are expected to respond to diverse market influences.*

Figure 3.51 shows the evolution of US$100 invested in the HFRI RV: Multi-Strategy index since January 1996 compared with other similar investments in the HFRI Fund Weighted Composite index, the equity market, represented by MSCI World, and the bond market, represented by the Barclays Aggregate Bond index. An investment of US$100 in the HFRI RV: Multi-Strategy index would have become US$646 by the end of 2012. The same investment in the equity market, bond market or global hedge fund market would have become US$1105, US$352 or US$472 respectively.

The HFRI RV: Multi-Strategy index offered an average annual return of 8.7 per cent per year over the whole period, against 7.2 per cent for the equity market and 7.4 per cent for the bond market. More recently it has offered 5.5 per cent per year on average over the last decade and 4.7 per cent per year on average over the last five years. The fall has been significant, and it can be largely explained by the very low performance of 2008 and to a lesser extent in 2011.

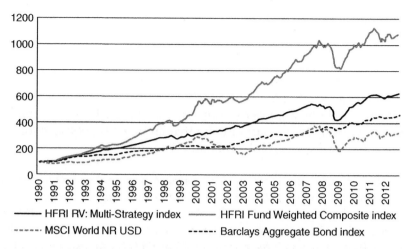

Figure 3.51   Evolution of US$100 invested in the HFRI RV: Multi-Strategy index
Source: Based on numbers obtained from Hedge Fund Research, Inc.

Volatility has been low over the whole period, at 4.4 per cent, and 5.1 per cent over the last decade but increasing to 6.4 per cent over the last five years. This is significantly lower than equities, which ranged between 15 per cent and 20 per cent depending on the period in question. The strategy offered a volatility in line with that of the bond index. The risk–return ratio over the whole period remains attractive.

Table 3.22 shows the yearly returns, the mean annual return, the standard deviation, the minimum annual return, the maximum annual return and the spread of the strategies relative to the comparative indices. It leads to the following remarks:

– Over the 23 years covered, the HFRI RV: Multi-Strategy index was negative in three years: in 2008 (–20.3 per cent), in 2011 (–2.4 per cent) and 1998 (–2 per cent). 2008 was the most difficult year for the hedge fund industry as a whole. The equity index finished down in 7 years out of 23, including the 2000–2002 bear market, 2008 and 2011. The bond index suffered negative returns for one year only, in 1999.
– The maximum annual returns of the HFRI RV: Multi-Strategy index were achieved in 1991 (27.4 per cent), 2009 (24.7 per cent) and 1992 (18.5 per cent). These numbers are strong, particularly given the limited volatility of the monthly returns.
– The spread in returns between the HFRI RV: Multi-Strategy index and the comparative indices has been volatile. The strategy has outperformed the global hedge fund index 8 times out of 23, the equity index

Table 3.22 Performance statistics of the HFRI RV: Multi-Strategy index and comparative indices

	HFRI RV: Multi-Strategy Index	HFRI Fund Weighted Composite Index	MSCI World NR USD	Barclays Aggregate Bond Index	Performance vs. HFRI	Performance vs. MSCI World	Performance vs. Barclays Aggregate
1990	6.5%	5.8%	-17.0%	12.7%	0.7%	23.5%	-6.2%
1991	27.4%	32.2%	18.3%	16.0%	-4.7%	9.2%	11.4%
1992	18.5%	21.2%	-5.2%	5.8%	-2.8%	23.7%	12.7%
1993	16.7%	30.9%	22.5%	11.1%	-14.2%	-5.8%	5.6%
1994	7.6%	4.1%	5.1%	0.2%	3.5%	2.5%	7.3%
1995	12.4%	21.5%	20.7%	19.7%	-9.1%	-8.3%	-7.2%
1996	14.8%	21.1%	13.5%	4.9%	-6.3%	1.3%	9.9%
1997	11.9%	16.8%	15.8%	3.8%	-4.9%	-3.9%	8.1%
1998	-2.0%	2.6%	24.3%	13.7%	-4.7%	-26.4%	-15.8%
1999	11.0%	31.3%	24.9%	-5.2%	-20.3%	-14.0%	16.1%
2000	3.4%	5.0%	-13.2%	3.2%	-1.6%	16.6%	0.2%
2001	10.4%	4.6%	-16.8%	1.6%	5.7%	27.2%	8.8%
2002	6.5%	-1.5%	-19.9%	16.5%	7.9%	26.4%	-10.0%
2003	11.5%	19.5%	33.1%	12.5%	-8.0%	-21.6%	-1.0%
2004	8.2%	9.0%	14.7%	9.3%	-0.8%	-6.5%	-1.1%
2005	1.0%	3.5%	4.5%	1.3%	-2.5%	-3.4%	-0.2%
2006	9.0%	12.9%	20.1%	6.6%	-3.9%	-11.1%	2.4%
2007	1.8%	10.0%	9.0%	9.5%	-8.2%	-7.2%	-7.7%
2008	-20.3%	-19.0%	-40.7%	4.8%	-1.3%	20.4%	-25.1%
2009	24.7%	20.0%	30.0%	6.9%	4.7%	-5.3%	17.7%
2010	13.2%	10.2%	11.8%	5.5%	2.9%	1.4%	7.6%
2011	-2.4%	-5.3%	-5.5%	5.6%	2.8%	3.1%	-8.1%
2012	8.2%	6.4%	15.8%	4.3%	1.8%	-7.6%	3.9%
Mean annual return (whole period)	8.7%	11.4%	7.2%	7.4%	-2.7%	1.5%	1.3%
Volatility (whole period)	4.4%	7.0%	15.6%	5.5%	NA	NA	NA
Meanannual return 2003–2012	5.5%	6.7%	9.3%	6.6%	-1.2%	-3.8%	-1.2%
Volatility 2003–2012	5.1%	6.5%	16.2%	6.1%	NA	NA	NA
Meanaverage return 2007–2012	4.7%	2.5%	2.3%	5.4%	2.2%	2.4%	-0.8%
Volatility 2007–2012	6.4%	7.4%	19.4%	6.4%	NA	NA	NA
Minimum annual return	-20.3%	-19.0%	-40.7%	-5.2%	-20.3%	-26.4%	-25.1%
Maximum annual return	27.4%	32.2%	33.1%	19.7%	7.9%	27.2%	17.7%

Source: Based on data from Hedge Fund Research, Inc.

11 times and the bond index 13 times. The largest outperformance of the HFRI RV: Multi-Strategy index relative to the equity index was 27.2 per cent, in 2001, while the largest underperformance was at 26.4 per cent, in 1998. Relative to the bond index, the largest outperformance was achieved in 2009 at 17.7 per cent, and the largest underperformance was 25.1 per cent, in 2008.

12   Asset-based lending

As the name suggests, asset-based lending means lending money on the basis of an asset used as collateral. This strategy emerged in the United States and is unique, and completely different from the others;. It is not about investing in equities, bonds or any other public securities but lending to companies for specific projects guaranteed by specific assets usually linked to the project or to the corresponding order. This strategy has no link with asset-based securities that are securities created by grouping debt securities such as corporate debt, consumer credit or mortgages in assets that are then split into tranches. Asset-based lending funds are not hedge funds *per se*, but as the industry grew many funds applying this strategy adopted the structure of hedge funds. Companies active in this market to be small, with less than US$100 million in revenues and that have no access to banks because of their size, low trading volume or because of an unconventional development model that is difficult to understand. The American Small Business Administration and the American Chamber of Commerce estimated that there are more than 275,000 American companies with revenues of between US$5 million and US$100 million in 2012.

12.1   Methodology

Managers of asset-based lending (ABL) funds issue loans guaranteed by specific assets of the company. The assets used as collateral can vary; examples include firm orders, real estate assets, equipment, a stock of cars for a car reseller, a harvest for a coffee producer, a future flow of cash or intellectual properties for companies in the entertainment sector. Even though real estate and movable assets remain amongst the favourites, almost anything goes. These transactions also usually include warrants.

The ABL strategy is based on two essential elements: the flow of transactions and the collateral. The first question regarding the flow of transactions is: How does the management team source its transactions? The answer to this question is essential, because without transaction flow there are no portfolio and no returns. In private loans there is no organized market. There are two main scenarios. In the first, transactions are sourced internally, in which case it is essential to understand the type of transaction, their creation process and what elements can affect the team's ability to create new positions. In the second scenario, the manager works with specialized agencies that propose transactions. Such agencies are usually paid by the number of transactions proposed rather than the number of transactions realized, meaning that the management team's main source of alpha would arise from selecting the good transactions from which to build a diversified portfolio rather than from negotiating the transactions. Many ABL funds lend for the short term only, so they constantly need to source ideas.

The flow of transactions underlying the strategy will depend on numerous factors including the relations established, the geographical environment and the competition in the manager's area of competence. When looking at a company, a manager must analyse a whole set of elements in order to confirm the capacity of the company to face its commitment, even though the collateral can serve as a tool of last resort if needed. The main elements that must be checked to limit as far as possible the risk of non-payment and the risk of fraud include:

– a check on the management team's reputation
– a company visit and formal discussion with the management team
– an analysis of the financial and operational strength of the company
– a formal valuation of the assets of the company
– the search for other potential commitments
– a discussion with the main clients, suppliers and other strategic relations
– an analysis of the industry and the company's competitiveness
– a deep analysis of the financial aspects
– potential positions in warrants or options.

The transaction is not done exclusively on the basis of the credit quality of the company, as there is a collateral available. Its value should be estimated when the transaction is entered into, but it should also be consistently monitored as its value will evolve over time.

There are several kinds of collateral. We have grouped them in three categories: intangible (a right, or a virtual asset), tangible (an object) and tangible fixed (real estate or the equivalent). The nature of the collaterals will require different forms of work; for example a future cash flow based on sales should be followed closely; if the payment is weekly a monthly check is necessary. In the case of movable assets such as commodities, planes, boats or equipment, the check on the collateral can be less frequent. In the case of real estate assets, the collateral cannot be moved; it is observable and insured, so the checks can be less frequent. The risk is that the manager can be exposed to a loss if there is a problem with the company and if the collateral is overstated. Figure 3.52 illustrates the functioning of the ABL strategy.

The collateral should then be secured. In this context the United States and the United Kingdom are particularly interesting, as the collateral can be registered. A collateral can then be guaranteed as first or second lien. In some cases there can be several collaterals for the same transaction, including not only assets as mentioned previously, but also personal guarantees by the owners of the businesses.

In case of default by the company the lender should be able to make use of the collateral. The fundamental element in case of litigation is the documentation at the basis of the transaction. In an ideal world managers prefer not to have to use the collateral as this takes time and can cost a lot of money in legal fees and opportunity cost – but they should be ready to do so if needed. So we want to emphasize that credit analysis remains key in this strategy even when there is a collateral. The use of the collateral should remain marginal, and a manager will not have to use it if the

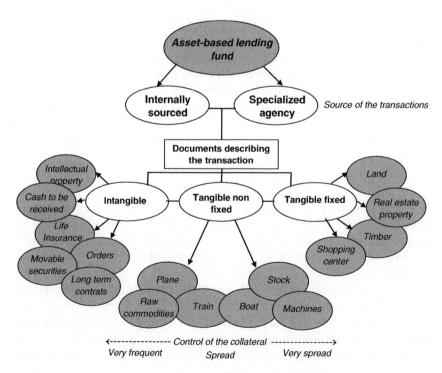

Figure 3.52   Illustration of the asset-based lending strategy

credit analysis has been performed correctly and if the company can pay back the loan according to the terms agreed.

A secured transaction is generally structured with a high security ratio. This means that the collateral covers not only the capital but also the interest owed. The duration of the loan is usually around a year, with a maximum duration of three to four years. Interest rates are around 15 to 20 per cent in normal market conditions. Typical characteristics of a deal are reported in Table 3.23.

In most cases the collateral is blocked and protected within a separate legal entity. The implementation of a position takes usually two to three months from the start of the due diligence, the negotiation and the structure. There is a series of sub-strategies, some of which we present below. In practice, some funds will focus on one or a series of sub-strategies or they will combine some of the strategies described below.

12.1.1 Stock financing

There is usually a gap between the production of a good and the payment for it by the client. The company must also, apart from other things, buy the equipment and pay the workers. Companies often look for short-term financial support at various stages of their growth, and funds applying this strategy will help the company finance its growth and cover the credit risk between delivery to clients and payments. Products or invoices are usually used as collateral. The security ratio is generally at two to three times for this kind of transactions. The fund finances the producer and receives the payment. Figure 3.53 illustrates stock financing.

Another version of the same strategy consists of financing the purchase of stock surpluses of an established reseller at a discount and selling them on to discount stores. This strategy works particularly well for electronic goods, which have a short life, and this strategy is possible because the intermediaries between the established resellers and the discount stores have no access to traditional sources of financing. This kind of financing is usually carried out over a short period of time (usually less than 180 days).

Table 3.23 Typical characteristics of an ABL transaction

Size:	US$1 to 50 million
Coupon:	10 to 20%
Maturity:	6 to 48 months
Structuring commission:	2 to 5%
Collateral:	Various
Hedge:	1 to 2 times the principal
Warrants:	1 to 5%
Personal guarantee:	If possible

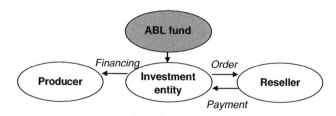

Figure 3.53   Stock financing illustration

It is also worth mentioning that a specific version of this strategy, called agricultural finance, has emerged in Brazil, an important producer of cattle, sugar and coffee. Producers there have historically been dependent on federal grants, but these decrease significantly during the 1990s, leading to the emergence of opportunities integrated within the ABL strategy.

12.1.2   Trade finance

The fund plays the role of intermediary between a producer or supplier, usually established in a developing country, and a client in a developed market. The fund assumes the credit risk of the supplier, generally an importer, merchant or distributor with a solid credit rating. The collateral is the goods, and the fund plays an intermediary role. The accompanying documents are important in this process.

This sub-strategy is illustrated in Figure 3.54; the producer wants to sell products rapidly. The fund plays the role of cushion, financing the goods presold to the final reseller and using the goods as collateral. It will organize the transport of the goods, and will usually deal with the other players such as the transporter and the customs. The goods used as collateral are usually not perishables.

12.1.3   Real estate financing

Real estate financing consists of short-term mortgage financing or refinancing. This includes, amongst other things, bridge financing before the long-term financing is carried out, the financing of a building, the acquisition of a mortgage, the financing of a rehabilitation, the resolution of a bankruptcy, the repurchase of a commercial good or a consolidation of debts. The security ratio of this kind of deal is between two and three, and the valuation of the property should be carried out independently by a third party. This sub-strategy is illustrated in Figure 3.55.

12.1.4   Corporate direct

In this sub-strategy, the fund gives a short-term loan (generally 6 to 24 months) to a company against a collateral. This definition is broad and mainly concerns companies that have no access to the traditional credit

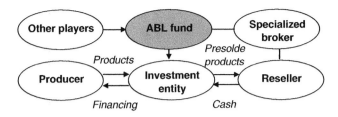

Figure 3.54   Trade finance illustration

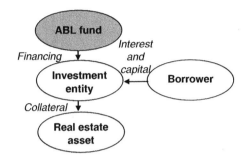

Figure 3.55   Real estate financing strategy

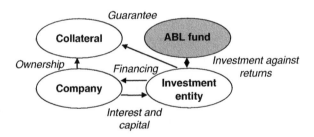

Figure 3.56   Illustration of the corporate direct sub-strategy

market. The strategy is simple: the fund finances a company through an investment entity in the exchange of an interest. The investment entity grants the loan to the fund against interest and capital reimbursement at maturity. The company retains the right to the collateral, which is the guarantee for the investment entity if it does not receive the interest and/ or the capital. Figure 3.56 illustrates the corporate direct sub-strategy.

12.1.5   Life insurance financing

in 1911, the Supreme Court of the United States protected the right of American citizens to sell one of their most valuable personal investments:

their life insurance policy. This historic ruling and subsequent US court rulings have protected US consumer rights to realize value and liquidity in their life insurance investment through transactions known as life settlements. The market has grown since then, and it started a new phase of growth in 1998. It represents more than US$400 billion nominal, and is of concern to nearly 40 million individuals over the age of 65. In the current context, loans are granted to individuals in order to finance their life insurance premium, with the amount due in case of death as a warranty. Creditors are usually wealthy elderly people who take out loans and use their life insurance as collateral in case of default. Such loans typically have a two-year horizon, are secured by the insurance policy and may have additional guarantees. In case of death, the loan is paid back by the life insurance company. In case of survival the insured person can either sell the insurance policy to pay back the credit or keep the insurance and pay back the credit from another source of capital. This kind of transaction will always be carried out with the approval of the insurer. There may be an intermediary that groups the policies. This sub-strategy is illustrated in the Figure 3.57. In other cases the fund may buy the life insurance back from the insured person.

12.1.6   Vehicle loans

Vehicle loans are based on the underlying idea that some funds buy personal credit granted to lower-quality borrowers, with their car as collateral. As the borrowers are of lower quality the offer of such credit is limited. This means that there is an important return difference between classical consumption credit and such credits. Such transactions cover typical loans from US$10,000 to US$15,000 and have a one- to four-year maturity. The interest rate is fixed, and ranges from 15 to 28 per cent. Funds have four sources of revenue:

– monthly interest paid on the credit
– a reduction on the price (20 per cent)
– potential early repayment by the borrower
– the possibility of reselling the loan to other players.

The structure of this sub-strategy is shown in Figure 3.58. Funds applying this sub-strategy tend to work in tandem with the companies granting the loan before they decide to lend the money. This enables them to precisely determine the characteristics required.

Two interesting features to mention about this kind of financing are that a fund will work with insured vehicles only, and that in some cases the lender will install a GPS system in the car in order to be sure of finding it if required.

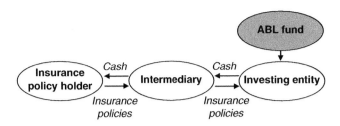

Figure 3.57 Illustration of life insurance financing

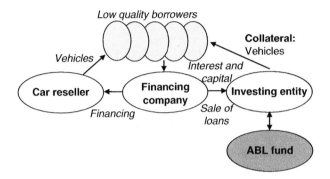

Figure 3.58 Typical structure of the car loans strategy

12.1.7 Other sub-strategies

Entertainment finance is the short- to medium-term financing of the production or distribution of films, music and electronic games against the cash generated. The collateral can be agreements on distribution or government grants. In the case of film or music catalogues, the collateral will be the asset itself. Aircraft leasing is the financing of planes for airlines with the planes themselves as guarantees. Green financing is the financing of ecological companies, including biomass, biodiesel and photovoltaic panels.

There are numerous ways to finance companies using their assets as collateral. We report a large set of ABL sub-strategies in Figure 3.59.

The main market for ABL funds is the United States, and California is the state with the highest concentration. Sectors in which the companies are more active are retail, metals and food and beverage. The Commercial Finance Association estimates that the ABL market increased from around US$50 billion in 1980 to US$300 billion in 2001/2002 – and to over US$500 billion in 2007. The 2008 liquidity crisis, however, directly impacted the market, which suffered and shrunk significantly. The ABL industry nevertheless plays a fundamental role in the economy. Companies that obtain financing through this system have access to capital that is not available to them in the traditional system; small loans

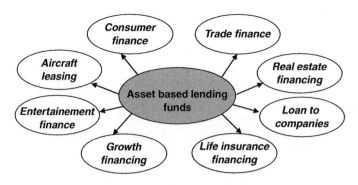

Figure 3.59   Main ABL sub-strategies

are not an interesting market for commercial banks. The lender can also make good profits, depending on the conditions they can negotiate.

12.2   The risks

The ABL strategy has very different risks from other alternative strategies – because with it we are not in the world of financial markets but in the real economy. There is no hedge in place, and no mathematical model. This strategy is about a loan with a collateral being granted to a counterparty.

The risks are linked to the transaction process. The first risk concerns the estimation of the value of the underlying asset. It can be deliberately wrong (which constitutes fraud) or become so because of an external event (for example, in the case of the arrival of a new competitive product that decreases the value of a stock used as collateral, or if there is a fall in related commodity prices). Then there is a legal risk; documents may be imprecise or unclear. A third source is the risk of collateral; in a case of default the manager may not be able to realize the collateral. Funds financing grain or coffee crops are directly exposed to this risk; bad weather can be insured against – but there's nothing if the grain or coffee is not harvested for some other reason. Then there is a risk on the security ratio; this must be sufficiently high to cover the loan with a safety margin.

Liquidity risk is highly relevant to the ABL strategy, as the underlying investments are not liquid. Loans tend to be granted in the short term only (from a few months to a few years), but we are a long way away from the liquidity available to developed market equities. The risk gets more severe in periods of economic slowdown. In this context, the value of the collateral will fall as the risk of default of the borrower increases. The only way to mitigate this risk is to diversify the portfolio; this diversification should be carried out not only on a geographical basis but also by type of transaction, time horizon and type of collateral used. It is also key that the liquidity of the fund should remain in line with the liquidity offered to investors in the fund – for a fund operating loans over 36 to 48 months, it is difficult to propose monthly liquidity with 30 days' notice.

Another important risk in the ABL strategy is that of fraud. This risk is fundamental, and several cases were discovered in 2008. Fraud will often be supported by the lender. It can take different forms, from "forgetting" to invoice, false inventory reports or the misappropriation of a collateral to the multiple use of non-existent collateral. In this context it is essential for managers not to use existing documents to check a guarantee for a new transaction, but to work from scratch in every single case. In addition, the collateral must be inspected. Several hedge funds were exposed to a fraud perpetrated by Petters, one of the largest agencies active in ABL. Petters produced documents that proved to investors that they were reselling goods such as flat screens to discount stores at a profit – but according to the FBI, the documents were false. Some hedge funds were exposed to this fraud because they had invested with Petters directly, while others were invested in funds that were working with Petters.

Similar to fraud risk is valuation risk, in that it is not only about estimating the correct price for something that may have no market, but also because managers have either intervened in the process or at least been part of the definition of the pricing process. This risk increases when market conditions are becoming more rigorous. The main risks of the strategy are given in Figure 3.60.

In terms of risk, it is also worth mentioning that in ABL funds the size of the assets under management is a very important factor. When assets under management grow, the management team has to make a difficult choice; either they increase the number of positions, or the size per position. In both cases this will lead to additional risk. In the first case there

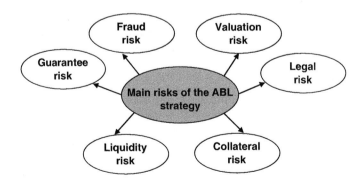

Figure 3.60 Main sources of risks in the ABL strategy

will be more positions to follow, so the team has to find more attractive ideas. In the second case, they will have to deal with larger companies, which may put them in a position where potential returns are lower.

Each sub-strategy has its specific risks. Life insurance financing has a relatively high legal risk as the legal environment may change. Strategies exposed to movable assets are dependent on the state of the global economy and usually also on technological developments. In period of slowdown the resale value of most goods will fall. A new product can also impact the value of a collateral, whose price may fall significantly. Because of this, when selecting ABL funds it is important to diversify the allocation – and to do this not only by sub-strategy but also by management style; managers creating their own transactions should be favoured, to avoid overexposure to large transactions. The type of collateral used should also be diversified. Finally geographical diversification is finally important, as managers tend to work with local companies.

12.3 Illustrations

In this section we illustrate a few specific sub-strategies, though in practice, each manager will develop their own strategy with its specific characteristics.

12.3.1 Trade finance

The first illustration is about a trade finance fund. The fund agrees to finance a company that sells sportswear. The sports company receives an order from a chain of supermarkets with 100 branches in the United States, for trainers made in Asia, but the Asian producer will only accept the order for payment in cash. The role of the fund is to finance the cash required by the order, using the trainers as collateral. In practice, the fund finances 85 per cent of the order as the remaining 15 per cent are financed by the sports company. The manager registers the collateral, issues a letter of credit to the sports brand and pays the Asian producer. It also finances the transport and complete the customs documents; they are repaid when the goods are received by the final reseller. This example is illustrated in Figure 3.61.

12.3.2 Real estate financing

Consider a real estate developer that wants to buy a US$5 million real estate property. The developer advances US$500,000 to secure the property. As banks usually require 120 days' notice to grant a loan, the developer gets a short-term loan from an asset-based lending fund. The fund lends the money between the point at which the agreement to buy is signed and the time when the bank grants the loan with the real estate as collateral.

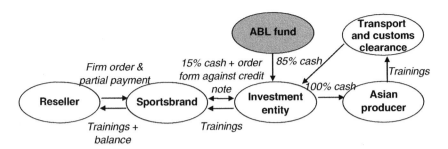

Figure 3.61   Illustration of the trade finance sub-strategy

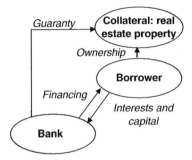

Figure 3.62   Initial position of the transaction

In another context, consider a fund that buys an underperforming commercial real estate for US$1.5 million from a bank in Florida in March 2006. The good is secured by another real estate property, located close to an interstate highway in Pompano in Florida. An estimation of its value based on recent transactions in the region indicates US$10–13 per square metre, giving the property a value of between US$4.2 million and US$5.5 million. The initial situation is shown in Figure 3.62.

At the outset, the bank finances the borrower for the payment of interest and the capital, with the real estate property as collateral. But if the borrower cannot afford the payments any more, the bank will typically sell its right on the collateral with a discount to its value to avoid to manage the whole process. The situation after the sale of the loan by the bank to the fund is shown in Figure 3.63. In the present case the fund recovers US$1.8 million within six months. This represents an annualized gross return around 38.5 per cent.

12.3.3   Legal proceedings financing

In March 2007, a fund granted a renewable US$10 million loan to a company specializing in lending money to plaintiffs that wants to go to the court. The principle is that the company advances the cash necessary to

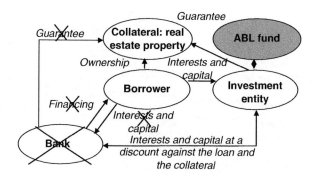

Figure 3.63   Position after the fund entered the transaction

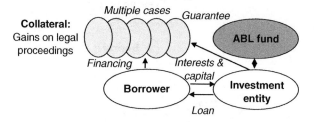

Figure 3.64   Legal proceedings financing

the plaintiff in trials in order to pay for the cost inherent to the procedure using the contingent benefit as collateral. In this context the fund paid 85 per cent of the costs of the plaintiffs. This amount represented only a fraction of the potential gains as every case has a 45 per cent potential return. This enabled the fund to support the losses on the lost cases. The essential element here is that the fund finances the company using the potential gains of the cases as collateral. This includes not only the current cases but also finished cases for which payments are expected. In addition, the company financed a maximum of 85 per cent of the cost in any case. This means that people always have to personally invest. In the practical case described here the fund got a 17.5 per cent interest on the loan. Figure 3.64 illustrates legal proceedings financing.

12.3.4   *Life insurance financing*

This practical case regards a 80-year-old man with a future life expectation of ten years. The face value of his life insurance is US$1 million. Premiums are at 3.5 per cent. The theoretical inflexion point is in 29 years, when the man would have 109 years. The transaction is the following:

– A 25 months loan for a value of US$70,000.

– The structuring commission perceived by the fund will be three per cent of the face value, US$30,000.
– The creation commission is US$2000.

The total loan is consequently US$102,000 (US$70,000 + US$30,000 + US$2000). The cash outflows is only US$70,000, as the commissions are paid to the fund. This means that for a US$102,000 loan the fund has to pay only US$70,000. The interest rate paid is 10 per cent. The value of the loan at the end of the 25-month period will be US$124,404 for an annualized return around 22 per cent.

Three outcomes are possible:

1. The insured person repays the loan: the return on investment is around 22 per cent.
2. The person insured defaults on the loan: the returns come from the realization of the collateral. The estimation of this based on an actuarial model is around US$191,000, for a total return close to 44 per cent.
3. The person insured dies during the loan: the returns come from an anticipated payment of the credit before maturity. This leads to a return of over 22 per cent thanks to penalties.

The main risks in this case are the risk of fraud by the insured person regarding the state of their health, or the risk of suicide not covered by the life insurance.

12.4   Advantages and drawbacks

The main advantages of the asset-based lending strategy are its low correlation with financial markets and its stability. In normal conditions the strategy offers very stable returns. In addition the strategy is close to the real economy and the concepts underlying its implementation are easy to understand. The main drawbacks of the strategy are, however, linked to its advantages. The fact that the strategy is close to the economy makes it vulnerable to the environment. When the economy is slowing down this will affect many companies at the same time; they will face difficulties and ABL funds will have a higher risk of facing defaults. Another element to consider is the lack of liquidity; this strategy is amongst the less liquid strategies available in the hedge fund world. It takes a long time – usually weeks or months – to realize a collateral in case of default.

In a nutshell, however, the lack of liquidity of the strategy combined with the cyclical nature of the strategy balances its stability and understandability.

13   Long/short equity

Also called "equity hedge," the name long/short arises from the origins of the strategy; long/short equity managers take both long and short positions in equities. This strategy is the closest to that implemented by Alfred W. Jones, the father of the hedge fund industry; the idea is to manage market risk by combining long and short positions within a long-biased portfolio. Returns have two sources, and these depend to a greater extent from the ability of the manager to select the right securities to buy and sell while keeping some exposure to the market, potentials adding leverage to enhance the returns.

13.1   Methodology

Specialists in this strategy analyse a large number of companies, usually based on fundamental analysis and on ratios such as price–earnings or the price-to-book ratios, and on the future perspective of the companies concerned. They use various valuation methodologies and compare the prices of the shares relative to their historical values and to the market as a whole. Managers look for cheap stocks to invest in, and for expensive stocks to short. Once these securities have been identified, they look for an entry point in order to make a maximum profit. Technical analysis may be used for that.

The construction of a portfolio is shown in Figure 3.65. The left triangle illustrates the long book; it is exposed to market risk, industry risk and stock or company-specific risk. The central triangle represents the short part of the portfolio, and the right triangle the portfolio as a whole. In this last triangle, part of the market and industry risk is balanced thanks

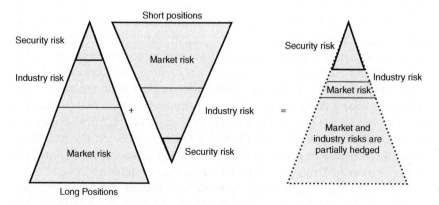

Figure 3.65   Building of a classic long/short position

to the combination of long and short positions; the main source of risk for the portfolio becomes stock-specific.[30]

All the funds follow the same logical pattern; they invest in undervalued securities and sell overvalued securities short while anticipating the direction of the market as a whole. As the strategy has grown, more and more funds have specialized in what have become sub-strategies, including sector-specific funds, growth- or value-oriented funds, and region- or country-specific funds. Other managers focus on smaller companies. The long/short strategy is based on the ability of specialists to identified under and overvalued securities; they take positions in the corresponding companies while keeping some exposure to the market as a whole.[31]

Some managers will implement pair trading positions; this is based on the idea of taking balanced positions in companies that have some sort of link; they can, for example, be part of the same group of companies or be in the same sector. In other cases, the manager will take stock-specific risks on the long side and hedge this with short positions in futures on indices or by using options; in this case, the shorts are there more to balance the risk of the portfolio than to create alpha.

There are no established rules regarding leverage, and each manager will have his/her own approach. Most managers will keep the gross exposure below 200 per cent. Regarding market exposure is typically kept at 40 to 60 per cent net long. Some managers will be active in their exposure management, ranging from market neutral (or even net short in some cases) to a fully exposed book. In bull market conditions, long/short managers will generally have over 75 per cent of their portfolio in long positions and 25 per cent of their portfolio in short, but in more difficult market conditions the trend is the opposite; longs tend to decrease, to 50 per cent, and shorts increase, to about the same percentage.

Table 3.24 and Figure 3.66 show the exposure of a fund over a 16-week period, illustrating how a manager positions his or her portfolio dependent on market conditions. During the first four weeks the manager has an important long book and an important short book. This means that although he/she can see many stock-specific opportunities, the market trend is unclear; his/her gross exposure is relatively high while their net exposure is close to zero. From week 5 to week 8 the short book increases and becomes bigger than the long book. The gross exposure decreases, but remains relatively high while the net exposure becomes negative. A positioning like this means that stock-specific opportunities remain important but that the manager is negative on the market. From week 9 to week 12, the long and short books decrease in size. The gross exposure drops below 100 per cent and the net remains low. The manager is uncertain of the market and cannot see any clear opportunities, so he/she cuts

Table 3.24   Long/short equity market exposure over time

Positioning	Time	Longs	Shorts	Gross exposure	Net exposure
Many longs and shorts	Week 1	85%	65%	150%	20%
	Week 2	83%	70%	153%	13%
	Week 3	80%	72%	152%	8%
	Week 4	78%	80%	158%	−2%
A few longs/ many shorts	Week 5	60%	75%	135%	−15%
	Week 6	50%	70%	120%	−20%
	Week 7	47%	60%	107%	−13%
	Week 8	40%	54%	94%	−14%
A few longs/a few shorts	Week 9	42%	40%	82%	2%
	Week 10	44%	30%	74%	14%
	Week 11	38%	26%	64%	12%
	Week 12	33%	20%	53%	13%
Many longs/a few shorts	Week 13	50%	18%	68%	32%
	Week 14	65%	15%	80%	50%
	Week 15	82%	16%	98%	66%
	Week 16	95%	9%	104%	86%

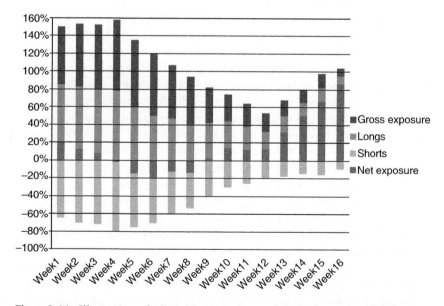

Figure 3.66   Illustration of a long/short equity market exposure over time

the overall level of risk of the portfolio. In the last four weeks the long book increases in size and the short book remains low. The gross exposure is in the median range, but the net exposure is high. The manager is positive on the market and finds many long opportunities.

13.2 Equity non-hedge

The concept of this strategy is similar to that of long/short equity funds, in that while Managers tend to use the same methodology on the long side, the main difference is that they take no, or very limited, hedging positions. This strategy differs from that of classic mutual funds as the manager can usually use leverage, but more importantly they tend to invest in less liquid securities. The equity non-hedge strategy is by definition a directional strategy. Such funds also differ from long/short equity funds through the exposure they have and their portfolio construction; while equity hedge funds tend to be diversified by sector and by number of positions, equity non-hedge funds will usually be concentrated on a few sectors and/or positions. They also tend to invest in the less liquid securities that cannot be hedged.

This strategy includes funds on the borderline between hedge funds and private equity and emerging market funds investing in smaller companies. The use of derivatives is not usual in this strategy, even though there are exceptions.

13.3 Long/short equity vs. equity market neutral

The long/short equity strategy is similar to the equity market neutral strategy in that they both combine long and short positions in equities. The main difference arises from the fact that long/short equity funds tend to have a long bias and to offer exposure to the equity market over time, while equity market neutral funds will always remain neutral. Long/short equity funds aim to offer a long exposure during market rallies and to be hedged against market risk during volatile market conditions. The manager will either look for securities that should outperform during market rallies and drop less than the market during falling markets, or actively manage the exposure to reach this objective. Equity market neutral funds play the relative price evolution between securities or basket of securities, focusing on the relation between the securities rather than their evolution relative to market movements. Another difference between long/short equity and equity market neutral funds is in the proportion of the portfolio allocated to long and short positions. Equity market neutral funds balance their portfolio between long and short positions to limit the exposure to the market and to be market neutral. Long/short equity managers, however, invest their assets in undervalued (long) and overvalued (short) companies while keeping some exposure to the market as a whole. Over a shorter time period they may become market neutral, net short or almost exclusively long – but in the long term they offer a limited but long exposure to the market.

A last element of differentiation resides in the number of lines. While specific funds may differ, most long/short managers tend to have 50 to 80 long positions and slightly fewer short positions. Equity market neutral funds tend to be much more diversified. It is not unusual for managers to have over 100 long and short positions. Quantitative strategies tend to be even more diversified. These differences are fundamental, and lie at the heart of the two strategies.

13.4   Illustration

There are numerous ways to apply the long/short equity strategy; we illustrate this here with two long examples, and give a short example in the short selling strategy section.

13.4.1   Clip Corporation

Clip Corporation is a company based in Nagoya, Japan. This company started with a focus on the training of young people. It diversified its activities, to coach football to kids of between four and ten years of age, and by the end of 2004 this activity alone represented 60 per cent of the profits. Parents were paying ¥5000 a month for a 90-minute training session each week. The manager went to visit the company during the second half of 2004. The management explained to the fund manager that they estimated that the football school could grow by 20 to 30 per cent annually for three years. They said that to manage this growth they were renting new fields in various cities and that they were instructors. The implementation costs remained low and the operational margin was over 20 per cent. The manager analysed the documents and the numbers and integrated other elements such as the fact that the stock was trading around eight to nine times the anticipated profits for next year. In addition, the company said that the high cash balance would be used either to make an acquisition or to increase the dividend. On this basis the manager estimated that the company was clearly underpriced and that the potential upside was over 80 per cent, so he took a position in January 2005 at an average price of ¥1120. The stock price started to rise, and then shot up when the company announced an increase in its dividends. Figure 3.67 shows the evolution of the Clip Corporation stock price over that period.

This is an example of a company that is not followed by classic long-only mutual funds because of a size issue. It illustrates the added value of hedge funds that can go down in the market capitalization range.

13.4.2   Barnes & Noble, Inc.

In June 2000, Barnes & Noble was the leader in book selling in the United States. Between June and November 2000 the share price stayed around US$19.5 per share, a historical low. At this time, the company was growing

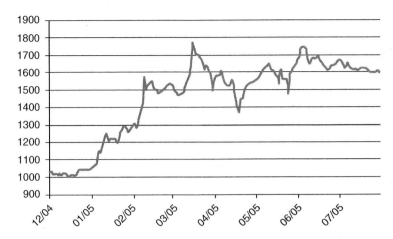

Figure 3.67 Evolution of the stock price of Clip Corporation between December 2004 and July 2005

rapidly mainly due to its internet sales, through www.barnesandnoble. com, owned at 40 per cent by Barnes & Noble. In addition, the company expected its growth to continue as a result of an increase in its range with an investment in video games and computer programs.

The company was of interest because:

– it was the leader in its industry
– it was exposed to the potential of the internet
– it was trading at a historical low.

The manager analysed the company and despite the slowdown in the economy he was convinced about the company's potential growth thanks to its new market. He took a first position in June 2000, reinforced in November, at an average price of US$19.50. The stock price first moved in November; from April 2001 on it rose steadily and in July 2001 reached US$35, a total increase of around 80 per cent. Although the stock was still trading below its historical peak of US$48, the manager closed the position between July and August at an average price of US$36.10, for a total gross return of 85 per cent, estimating that the future short-term potential was limited. The stock price evolution over the period is reported in Figure 3.68.

13.5 Advantages and drawbacks

The long/short equity investment strategy is widely applied because it has all the advantages of a classic long-only equity mutual fund plus others coming from the ability to short equities. The strategy is easy to

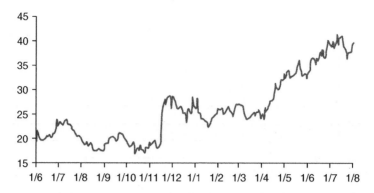

Figure 3.68 Evolution of the stock price of Barnes & Noble between June 2000 and July 2001

understand and should perform well if the manager is able to identify successful companies. It is liquid and easy to implement. In addition, the manager has the ability to hedge or cover market risk through short positions and can make money by identifying over-priced companies.

Another advantage is that the returns of long/short equity fund profit to some extent from the long-term returns of the equity market. The main drawback of the strategy is that it is applied by a lot of managers. There are more people chasing the same number of opportunities. In addition, the equity markets have been volatile over recent times and this has also impacted the strategy, which has as a result posted negative returns for two years out of five.

13.6   Performance

Hedge Fund Research describes equity hedge managers as:

> *managers who maintain positions both long and short in primarily equity and equity derivative securities. A wide variety of investment processes can be employed to arrive at an investment decision, including both quantitative and fundamental techniques; strategies can be broadly diversified or narrowly focused on specific sectors and can range broadly in terms of levels of net exposure, leverage employed, holding period, concentrations of market capitalizations and valuation ranges of typical portfolios. Equity Hedge managers would typically maintain at least 50%, and may in some cases be substantially entirely invested in equities, both long and short.*

Figure 3.69 shows the evolution of US$100 invested in the HFRI Equity Hedge (Total) index since January 1990 compared with other similar investments in the HFRI Fund Weighted Composite index, the equity

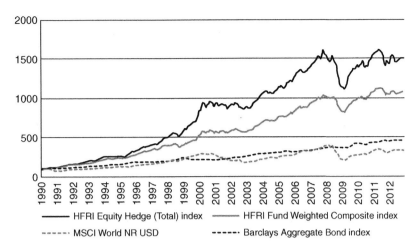

Figure 3.69 Evolution of US$100 invested in the HFRI Equity Hedge (Total) index

Source: Based on numbers obtained from Hedge Fund Research, Inc.

market, represented by MSCI World, and the bond market, represented by the Barclays Aggregate Bond index. An investment of US$100 in the HFRI Equity Hedge (Total) index would have become US$1545 by the end of 2012. The same investment in the equity market, bond market or global hedge fund market would have become US$1105, US$352 or US$472 respectively.

The HFRI Equity Hedge (Total) index offered an average annual return of 13.5 per cent per year over the whole period, against 7.2 per cent for the equity market and 7.4 per cent for the bond market. More recently it has offered 6.2 per cent per year on average over the last decade and 1.5 per cent per year on average over the last five years. The fall has been significant and it can be largely explained by the very low performance of 2008 (–26.7 per cent) and in 2011 (–8.4 per cent). This strategy is directional to some extent by its very nature, and very difficult periods in equities will impact the strategy even if some managers are positioned well.

Volatility was relatively high over the whole period, at 9.2 per cent, and 8.8 per cent over the last decade, and increasing to 10.2 per cent over the last five years. This remains lower than equities, which ranged between 15 and 20 per cent depending on the period in question. The strategy's volatility ranges between that of equities, and bonds that stayed around 6 per cent over the various periods covered. The risk–return ratio over the whole period remains reasonably attractive, even not much so as some other strategies over the very long term.

Table 3.25 shows the yearly returns, the mean annual return, the standard deviation, the minimum annual return, the maximum annual return and the spread of the strategies relative to the comparative indices. It leads to the following remarks:

- Over the 23 years covered, the HFRI Equity Hedge (Total) index was negative in three years: 2008 (−26.7 per cent), 2011 (−8.4 per cent) and 2002 (−4.7 per cent). 2008 was the most difficult year for the hedge fund industry as a whole. 2011 and 2002 were difficult years for equities. The equity index finished down in 7 years out of 23 including the 2000–2002 bear market, 2008 and 2011. The bond index suffered negative returns for one year only, in 1999.
- The maximum annual returns of the HFRI Equity Hedge (Total) index were achieved in 1999 (44.2 per cent), 1991 (40.1 per cent) and 1995 (31 per cent). These numbers are strong, and were always achieved in years that were also strong for equities. More recently, numbers have been lower.
- The spread in returns between the HFRI Equity Hedge (Total) index and the comparative indices has been volatile. The strategy has outperformed the global hedge fund index 15 times out of 23, the equity index 13 times and the bond index 18 times. The largest outperformance of the HFRI Equity Hedge (Total) index relative to the equity index was 31.4 per cent, in 1990, while the largest underperformance was 12.6 per cent, in 2003. Relative to the bond index, the largest outperformance was achieved in 1999 at 49.4 per cent, and the largest underperformance was 31.4 per cent, in 2008.

14 Emerging markets

Emerging markets represent more than 85 per cent of the world's population and more than 75 per cent of the earth's surface – but in the financial markets they still represent less than 10 per cent of listed shares and less than 15 per cent of tradable government debt. These numbers indicate the importance of the long-term development potential of these markets. Since the start of the 21st century the main emerging markets, such as Brazil, Russia, India and China, have become more important and have become considered as key players in the world economic system. Their importance will probably continue to grow in the years to come.

Emerging markets funds invest in emerging markets (previously called developing countries). For operational and analytical purposes, the World Bank's main criterion for classifying economies is gross national income (GNI) per capita.[32] Every economy is classified by its GNI per capita as

Table 3.25 Performance statistics of the HFRI Equity Hedge (Total) index and comparative indices

	HFRI Equity Hedge (Total) Index	HFRI Fund Weighted Composite Index	MSCI World NR USD	Barclays Aggregate Bond Index	Performance vs. HFRI	Performance vs. MSCI World	Performance vs. Barclays Aggregate
1990	14.4%	5.8%	-17.0%	12.7%	8.6%	31.4%	1.7%
1991	40.1%	32.2%	18.3%	16.0%	8.0%	21.9%	24.1%
1992	21.3%	21.2%	-5.2%	5.8%	0.1%	26.5%	15.5%
1993	27.9%	30.9%	22.5%	11.1%	-2.9%	5.4%	16.9%
1994	2.6%	4.1%	5.1%	0.2%	-1.5%	-2.5%	2.4%
1995	31.0%	21.5%	20.7%	19.7%	9.5%	10.3%	11.4%
1996	21.8%	21.1%	13.5%	4.9%	0.7%	8.3%	16.8%
1997	23.4%	16.8%	15.8%	3.8%	6.6%	7.6%	19.6%
1998	16.0%	2.6%	24.3%	13.7%	13.4%	-8.4%	2.3%
1999	44.2%	31.3%	24.9%	-5.2%	12.9%	19.3%	49.4%
2000	9.1%	5.0%	-13.2%	3.2%	4.1%	22.3%	5.9%
2001	0.4%	4.6%	-16.8%	1.6%	-4.2%	17.2%	-1.2%
2002	-4.7%	-1.5%	-19.9%	16.5%	-3.3%	15.2%	-21.2%
2003	20.5%	19.5%	33.1%	12.5%	1.0%	-12.6%	8.0%
2004	7.7%	9.0%	14.7%	9.3%	-1.4%	-7.0%	-1.6%
2005	4.0%	3.5%	4.5%	1.3%	0.5%	-0.5%	2.7%
2006	11.7%	12.9%	20.1%	6.6%	-1.2%	-8.4%	5.1%
2007	10.5%	10.0%	9.0%	9.5%	0.5%	1.4%	1.0%
2008	-26.7%	-19.0%	-40.7%	4.8%	-7.6%	14.1%	-31.4%
2009	24.6%	20.0%	30.0%	6.9%	4.6%	-5.4%	17.6%
2010	10.5%	10.2%	11.8%	5.5%	0.2%	-1.3%	4.9%
2011	-8.4%	-5.3%	-5.5%	5.6%	-3.1%	-2.8%	-14.0%
2012	7.4%	6.4%	15.8%	4.3%	1.0%	-8.4%	3.1%
Mean annual return (whole period)	13.5%	11.4%	7.2%	7.4%	2.0%	6.2%	6.0%
Volatility (whole period)	9.2%	7.0%	15.6%	5.5%	NA	NA	NA
Meanannual return 2003–2012	6.2%	6.7%	9.3%	6.6%	-0.5%	-3.1%	-0.5%
Volatility 2003–2012	8.8%	6.5%	16.2%	6.1%	NA	NA	NA
Meanaverage return 2007–2012	1.5%	2.5%	2.3%	5.4%	-1.0%	-0.8%	-4.0%
Volatility 2007–2012	10.2%	7.4%	19.4%	6.4%	NA	NA	NA
Minimum annual return	-26.7%	-19.0%	-40.7%	-5.2%	-7.6%	-12.6%	-31.4%
Maximum annual return	44.2%	32.2%	33.1%	19.7%	13.4%	31.4%	49.4%

Source: Based on data from Hedge Fund Research, Inc.

low (up to US$1005), lower middle (US$1006 to US$3975), upper middle (US$3976 to US$12,275), and high (over US$12,276). Classification by income does not necessarily reflect developmental status, but countries with low and lower middle incomes tend to be in Latin America, Africa, emerging Europe, the Middle East and Asia.

As with classic long only fund management, some hedge fund managers specialize in emerging markets. Managers applying these strategies mainly take long positions in securities issued by companies based in emerging markets or issued by emerging countries (bonds). These positions may be balanced with short positions, but they usually have a long bias.

14.1   Methodology

Emerging market managers invest in the equities, fixed income instruments and/or currencies of emerging markets. They are specialists, as the implementation of this type of strategy requires experience and specific knowledge, these markets being very different from developed ones. The rules governing companies and their communication may differ significantly from one jurisdiction to another, and more importantly the standards for corporate governance differ significantly. A local presence in, or at least regular visits to, the region, country and companies considered for investment is also necessary. On the positive side, emerging markets offer very good opportunities for those who know these markets well and for managers that can manage the volatility – which can be particularly high when global uncertainty reaches high levels.

As reported in Figure 3.70, the main attractions of emerging markets include their rapid growth, their continuous development that leads to growth in the opportunity set as more developing countries emerge. Other opportunities include the improvement in liquidity – even though

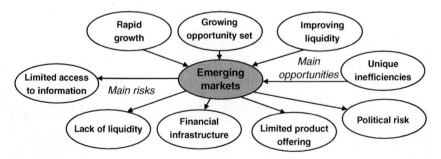

Figure 3.70   The main opportunities (arrow into emerging markets) and risks (arrow out of emerging markets) of emerging markets

emerging markets tend to remain less liquid than developed ones, particularly during periods of stress and as a result of their unique inefficiencies. These opportunities are balanced by the following risks, as shown at the bottom of Figure 3.70, which include limited access to information, a lack of liquidity, an underdeveloped financial infrastructure and product offering, and a high political risk.

There are various kinds of emerging markets, all of which are characterized by a higher presence of inefficiencies, which arise mainly from the lack of information regarding companies, and from their lack of robustness. This creates investment opportunities for the specialist investor who can identify underpriced securities. Emerging markets can also be characterized by their lack of financial infrastructure; only a few of them comply with international accounting standards, and in most cases the set of securities available is limited to equities, bonds and currencies.

Each part of the world has its own attraction:

- Emerging Europe: convergence towards the European Union and important commodities reserve, led by Russia.
- Asia: export-driven growth with internal consumption starting to grow and support growth
- Latin America: commodities remain key (mainly in Brazil and Venezuela) and the region remains exposed to the United States.
- Africa: at an early stage of development, where natural resources are key.

Emerging market equity managers base their equity investments on a fundamental analysis in order to identify the companies that will enable them to make their expected profits. This analysis includes a review of the accounting numbers as well as a comparison of the company with its competitors, with the idea of identifying a company trading at a market value below its intrinsic one. In order to make profits, the manager tries to get a complete overview of the company and to know as much as possible about it, so onsite visits are fundamental. In this context, company-specific news is important, but the entire environment – including local or national politicians, customers, suppliers and other market participants – must be integrated. Financial statements should also be analysed in order to determine the variability of the returns and the use of capital. In the end, the aim is to determine the growth potential of the company and its ability to create value while integrating the macroeconomic environment. The management team is particularly important. They should not only be competent but also be open to foreign investors and be willing to communicate.

On the fixed income side, managers will either invest in hard currency and/or in local currency. Whereas the hard currency market (typically US dollar bonds) is the historical market, the currency has gained much interest over the last 10 to 15 years and it is now the bigger of the two. When investing in US dollar denominated bonds, the manager gets a spread for the credit risk of emerging markets relative to Treasury bills; in local currencies, however, the manager gets not only the spread over Treasuries but also gets paid for the risk of inflation, and to make money on the currency. Currencies are the most volatile element to consider when investing in local currency emerging market debt, even if they tend to appreciate over time. An absolute return emerging market debt fund manager will typically actively divide the allocation between local and hard currencies; they may also consider corporate emerging market debt and/or have an allocation to inflation-linked emerging market securities. Fixed income investing in emerging markets is mainly about government bonds, and managers should have a deep knowledge of macroeconomics and the countries in addition to a deep knowledge of and experience in bond, and potentially currency, investing.

Emerging market managers either invest worldwide or focus on a particular region such as Asia, Asia ex-Japan, Latin America, or Eastern Europe. They may also specialize in a specific country, such as Russia, Brazil or India. In addition there are global funds that may invest in global emerging markets; such funds usually vary their exposure to any region or country depending on market conditions and on the evolution of the fundamentals of the countries or companies considered. Under the same logic, some emerging market managers allocate part of the assets to developed market companies, usually with a focus on companies that are directly exposed to the growth of emerging markets.

Shorting is usually difficult in emerging markets even though its availability has improved; it is now possible to implement short positions on the most liquid Asian, Eastern European and Latin American companies. To hedge their positions, managers tend to use American Depositary Receipts (ADRs), American securities representing participation in a foreign company. These can be shortened, enabling the manager to deal with the short-term volatility.

Macroeconomic risk is important in the case of emerging markets. Managers integrate the macroeconomic elements in their investment process by using specific economic models that enable them to diversify the portfolio their risk. In long/short strategies implemented in developed markets, managers hedge a long position in a security with a corresponding short in a linked security. Liquidity constraints lead most emerging managers to hedge their long book with regional, country or sector indices. This is also an interesting way to hedge the portfolio against rapid downside movements. Another way to do that is to consistently retain a bucket of out-of-the-money put options to protect the portfolio in case of any significant movement (usually 5 per cent or more). These options would pay if the index fells significantly.

Each investment management team will have its own investment process, and here we present a specific case to illustrate our purpose (see Figure 3.71). Firstly, the team looks to identify the market dynamic by integrating global factors, country factors and elements specific to the country.

- Global factors include the geopolitical context, risk aversion, investors' sentiment, growth potential, the currency, commodity prices, market liquidity and the level of interest rates.
- Country factors include elements such as growth, sentiment, liquidity and interest rates, to which should be added the balance of payments, the consensus both on the sellers' and buyers' side, local politics and specific technical factors.
- Company-specific factors include growth potential, the quality of management, the dividend policy, the return on investment, the quality of the balance sheet, technical factors, and the margins and their trend, as well as the consensus on the buyers' side and the sellers' side.

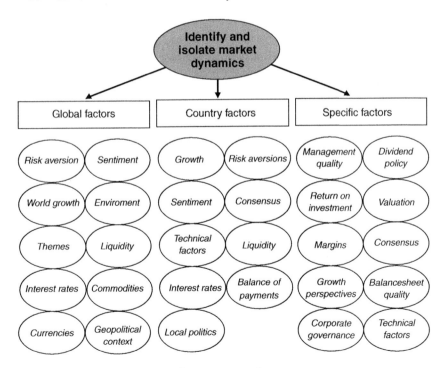

Figure 3.71   Market dynamics of emerging markets

When these market dynamics have been identified, the managers look for the scenarios induced by the markets. A complete analysis of the fixed income, currency and equity markets is required.

The aggregated information combined with a fundamental analysis of companies enables the manager to build a portfolio whose size and position will depend on the manager's conviction and the level of desired risk. Then, the manager will look to identify the scenarios implied by the markets, by integrating the information coming not only from the equity market but also the fixed income and currency elements.

The securities used by emerging market managers will depend on the profile of the manager and on the market conditions. For a long time the fixed income and currency markets were the more active, but over the last decade the situation has evolved, and now equities have become more liquid. In addition it has become possible to take a short position against almost any index. For stock-specific shorts the situation has improved, but the cost of borrowing the stocks tends to remain high, and their liquidity relatively limited apart from those in very large companies.

14.2   Illustrations

Emerging market managers are different from developed market managers by their they focus on developing markets and because they often invest in less well-known companies. Most managers apply a long/short equity strategy. We illustrate this using two examples, a long and a short.

14.2.1   Billabong

Billabong is a company that produces and distributes clothing and equipment for surfing and other extreme sports. Early in 2001, the company had a portfolio of attractive brands, was managed by a highly competent management team and was offering high and stable returns. The fund manager performed a fundamental analysis of the company and decided to take a long position. (We use the term fundamental as opposed to speculative. In the first case the manager analyses the company in detail and decides to invest because the company's future looks attractive. In the case of a speculative position, the manager takes a position because of a price evolution spread relative to the historical average or competitors, without explicitly considering the fundamentals of the company.) This manager applied a dynamic long/short equity strategy, partially adjusting the position after every important and unexpected price movement. In January 2001 he took a first position at 5 per cent, at a price of A$97. The price did not move much until August, when it rose rapidly. So He adjusted his position by selling 20 per cent of the securities in the portfolio at A$190, realizing a portion of his potential profit. Early in September the price of the stock fell, from A$190 to S$155. He decided to adjust the position and to buy 25 per cent more; then after a strong rally early in October he sold half of his position. Convinced of the opportunity in this stock, the manager maintained the position while being active in managing its exposure over time. Table 3.26 summarizes the evolution of the positions invested in Billabong over the corresponding period.

14.2.2 *Li & Fung*

The same manager analysed Li & Fung, a Hong Kong-based company that exports consumer goods such as clothes, fashion accessories, toys, craft items, sporting goods, stationery, shoes, travel goods and housewares. Early in May 2001 the manager estimated that the company was overvalued, both in absolute terms (relative to historical prices) and in relative terms (relative to other companies in the same sector). In addition, this company was heavily exposed to the world economic slowdown that was taking place. The publication of its decreasing earnings constituted the catalyst; the manager decided to take a 5 per cent short position at US$15. As in the previous example, he remained active in managing his exposure. In May, the stock price started to fall almost continuously. Early in August, when the stock price had fallen by more than 15 per cent, he closed 20 per cent of his position and at the end of September decided to close it completely when the stock price, having touched a US$7 floor, started to rebound. Figure 3.72 shows the evolution of the share on the period under review.

14.3 Advantages and drawbacks

Emerging markets offer numerous opportunities for experienced investors. They are characterized by a lack of information and accounting standards, unsophisticated local investors, and a higher political risk and a large number of non-specialized managers. One of the main risks specific to emerging markets is that factors external to companies can have

Table 3.26 Illustration of the emerging markets strategy using Billabong from January 2001 to December 2001

	Price	Share price movement	Adjustment
1 January	97	0.0%	0%
1 August	155	54.6%	0%
15 August	190	96.0%	–20%
1 September	155	–18.4%	+25%
15 October	205	32.0%	–50%
1 December	190	–7.3%	0

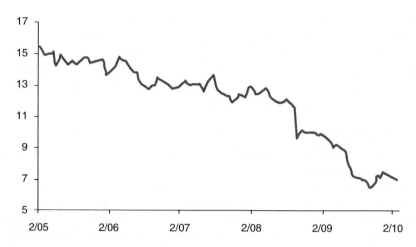

Figure 3.72   Evolution of the price of Li & Fung from May 2001 to October 2001

important short-term impacts. Such events include global macro uncertainty and flights to quality market conditions, uncertainties regarding elections and a world economic slowdown. Even though the long-term prospects of these markets are strong. These short-term elements put any investment at risk.

14.4   Performance

Hedge Fund Research defines emerging markets hedge funds as follows:[33] *The constituents of the HFRI Emerging Markets (Total) index are selected according to their regional investment focus. There are no investment strategy criteria for inclusion in these indices. Funds classified as Emerging Markets have a regional investment focus in one of the following geographic areas: Asia ex-Japan, Russia/Eastern Europe, Latin America, Africa and the Middle East; funds with no primary focus in any of those regions are classified as Global. At the current time, HFR does not publish separate indices for funds focused in the Africa and Middle East regions; however, these funds are represented in the HFRI Emerging Markets (Total) Index.*

Hedge Fund Research, Inc. sub-divides the emerging market strategy into five sub-strategies:

- HFRI Emerging Markets (Total) index: a fund weighted composite of all Emerging Markets funds.
- HFRI Emerging Markets: Asia ex-Japan index; primary focus on Asia, typically with up to 10 per cent exposure in Japan.
- HFRI Emerging Markets: Global index: no more than 50 per cent exposure in any single geographic region.

– HFRI Emerging Markets: Russia/Eastern Europe index: primary focus on these regions, with more than 50 per cent exposure in these markets.
– HFRI Emerging Markets: Latin America index: a primary focus on the countries of Latin America, with greater than 50 per cent exposure in these markets.

Figure 3.73 shows the evolution of US$100 invested in the HFRI Emerging Markets (Total) index since January 1990 compared to other similar investments in the HFRI Fund Weighted Composite index, the equity market, represented by MSCI World, and the bond market, represented by the Barclays Aggregate Bond index. An investment of US$100 in the HFRI Emerging Markets (Total) index would have become US$1489 by the end of 2012. The same investment in the equity market, bond market or global hedge fund market would have become US$1105, US$352 or US$472 respectively.

The HFRI Emerging Markets (Total) index offered an average annual return of 14.9 per cent per year over the whole period, as against 7.2 per cent for the equity market and 7.4 per cent for the bond market. More recently it has offered 12.4 per cent per year on average over the last decade and 2.2 per cent per year on average over the last five years. The fall has been significant and it can largely be explained by the very low performance of 2008 (–37.4 per cent) and 2011 (–14 per cent). This strategy

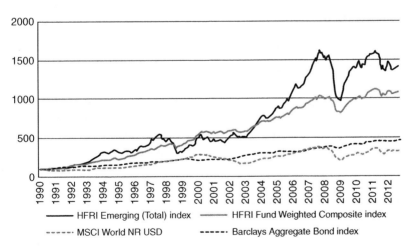

Figure 3.73 Evolution of US$100 invested in the HFRI Emerging Markets (Total) index

Source: Based on numbers obtained from Hedge Fund Research, Inc.

is directional by nature, as emerging market funds tend to have a limited short book.

Volatility has been high at 14.3 per cent over the whole period, and 12.1 per cent over the last decade but increasing again to 13.8 per cent over the last five years. This remains slightly lower than equities, which ranged between 15 per cent and 20 per cent depending on the period in question, but this is significantly higher than every other hedge fund strategy available. This volatility is significantly higher than bonds, which had a volatility close to 6 per cent over the whole period and over the sub-period considered. The risk–return ratio over the whole period remains attractive even though it is not as attractive as in some other strategies over the very long term.

Table 3.27 shows the yearly returns, the mean annual return, the standard deviation, the minimum annual return, the maximum annual return and the spread of the strategies relative to the comparative indices. It leads to the following remarks:

– Over the 23 years covered, the HFRI Emerging Markets (Total) index was negative in five years. The three most difficult years were 2008 (–37.3 per cent), 1998 (–33 per cent) and 2011 (–14 per cent). 2008 was the most difficult year for the hedge fund industry as a whole, 1998 was the year of the LTCM bailout, the end of the Asian crisis and the default by Russia. The equity index finished down in 7 years out of 23 including the 2000–2002 bear market, 2008 and 2011. The bond index suffered negative returns for one year only, in 1999.
– The maximum annual returns of the HFRI Emerging Markets (Total) index were achieved in 1991 (79.2 per cent), 1999 (55.9 per cent) and 1991 (45.4 per cent). These numbers are strong and always happened during strong years for equities. The main issue continues to be volatility on the downside.
– The spread in returns between the HFRI Emerging Markets (Total) index and the comparative indices has been volatile. The strategy has outperformed the global hedge fund index 15 times out of 23, the equity index 17 times and the bond index 16 times. The largest outperformance of the HFRI Emerging Markets (Total) index relative to the equity index was 56.7 per cent, in 1993, while the largest underperformance was 57.3 per cent, in 1998. Relative to the bond index the largest outperformance was achieved in 1993 at 68.3 per cent, and the largest underperformance was 46.7 per cent, in 1998 (Figure 3.74).

The difference in performance between the regional indices has been important. As an example, the HFRI Emerging Markets: Asia ex-Japan index was almost flat in 1996 while the HFRI Emerging Markets: Global index was up almost 37 per cent. In 2001, some indices were down while others finished the year up; the HFRI Emerging Markets: Russia/Eastern Europe Index was up almost 43 per cent.

Table 3.28 shows the performance of the HFRI emerging market indices during the 1997–1998 crises. To put it in context, Asian markets faced a financial crisis over the second half of 1997 that continued through early 1998; then at the end of August 1998 Russia defaulted on its debt. Table 3.28 shows the performance of the emerging market indices from August 1997 to September 1998. The index that suffered most over the period was the HFRI Emerging Markets: Russia/Eastern Europe Index, which lost 68 per cent at the worst point. The HFRI Emerging Markets: Latin America index and the HFRI Emerging Markets: Asia ex-Japan index both lost between 30 and 33 per cent. Table 3.28 is interesting because it indicates that emerging market have not all been impacted to the same extent by the crises; the Asian ex-Japan index fell continuously during the Asian crisis losing over 7 per cent every month. On the other hand, the Russian default led the Eastern European index to fall by almost 40 per cent over a single month. The global emerging market index lost 27.5 per cent and the total index 21 per cent.

15 Sector funds

Sector-specialized funds focus on a particular segment of the economy. The managers of such funds tend to have spent a significant part of their career analysing a specific sector and have developed a deep knowledge of it. In some cases they will only consider securities of companies that sell the same product or offer the same service and that are grouped within a certain sector. In other cases they will define their investable universe more broadly.

15.1 Methodology

Sector fund managers take long and short positions in the securities of companies within particular sectors or sub-sectors. They may invest in just one sector or may consider a few sectors that are similar or linked to one another. They tend to combine classic fundamental analysis with specific knowledge of the industry in question. They do not necessarily have a positive or long bias in this industry but may actively manage the exposure, or may be market neutral. In addition to fundamentally attractive companies, managers also look for a catalyst – an important event such as the launch of a new product, a restructuring or a change

Table 3.27 Performance statistics of the HFRI Emerging Markets (Total) index, the other HFRI regional emerging market indices and comparative indices

	HFRI Emerging Markets (Total) Index	HFRI Emerging Markets: Asia ex-Japan Index	HFRI Emerging Markets: Global Index	HFRI Emerging Markets: Latin America Index	HFRI Emerging Markets: Russia/ Eastern Europe Index	HFRI Fund Weighted Composite Index	MSCI World NR USD	Barclays Aggregate Bond Index	Performance (Total) vs. HFRI	Performance (Total) vs. MSCI World	Performance (Total) vs. Barclays Aggregate
1990	-3.4%	-3.4%	NA	NA	NA	5.8%	-17.0%	12.7%	-9.2%	13.7%	-16.1%
1991	45.4%	30.2%	NA	74.9%	NA	32.2%	18.3%	16.0%	13.2%	27.1%	29.4%
1992	24.4%	20.2%	30.9%	23.3%	NA	21.2%	-5.2%	5.8%	3.1%	29.6%	18.6%
1993	79.2%	80.1%	87.1%	74.9%	NA	30.9%	22.5%	11.1%	48.3%	56.7%	68.1%
1994	3.4%	-8.4%	7.6%	26.0%	25.0%	4.1%	5.1%	0.2%	-0.7%	-1.7%	3.1%
1995	0.7%	-2.4%	9.0%	-5.6%	0.6%	21.5%	20.7%	19.7%	-20.8%	-20.0%	-19.0%
1996	27.1%	3.3%	35.7%	29.8%	83.2%	21.1%	13.5%	4.9%	6.0%	13.7%	22.2%
1997	16.6%	-2.2%	19.9%	14.7%	59.5%	16.8%	15.8%	3.8%	-0.2%	0.8%	12.8%
1998	-33.0%	-11.9%	-36.4%	-19.2%	-63.9%	2.6%	24.3%	13.7%	-35.6%	-57.3%	-46.7%
1999	55.9%	60.3%	40.1%	56.3%	83.3%	31.3%	24.9%	-5.2%	24.6%	30.9%	61.0%
2000	-10.7%	-23.3%	-9.4%	-1.8%	1.6%	5.0%	-13.2%	3.2%	-15.7%	2.5%	-13.9%
2001	10.4%	-0.8%	11.5%	-5.7%	42.9%	4.6%	-16.8%	1.6%	5.7%	27.2%	8.8%
2002	3.7%	2.8%	0.0%	-12.9%	26.5%	-1.5%	-19.9%	16.5%	5.2%	23.6%	-12.8%
2003	39.4%	46.6%	32.4%	42.0%	41.7%	19.5%	33.1%	12.5%	19.8%	6.3%	26.9%
2004	18.4%	10.1%	15.7%	13.3%	32.0%	9.0%	14.7%	9.3%	9.4%	3.7%	9.1%
2005	5.8%	5.0%	5.2%	5.0%	8.5%	3.5%	4.5%	1.3%	2.3%	1.3%	4.5%
2006	24.3%	27.6%	18.2%	15.4%	38.7%	12.9%	20.1%	6.6%	11.4%	4.2%	17.6%
2007	24.9%	34.1%	20.4%	17.6%	24.8%	10.0%	9.0%	9.5%	15.0%	15.9%	15.4%
2008	-37.3%	-33.5%	-30.9%	-29.0%	-59.4%	-19.0%	-40.7%	4.8%	-18.2%	3.5%	-42.0%
2009	40.3%	37.5%	35.0%	47.1%	50.7%	20.0%	30.0%	6.9%	20.3%	10.3%	33.3%
2010	11.4%	10.8%	11.7%	7.8%	14.7%	10.2%	11.8%	5.5%	1.2%	-0.3%	5.9%
2011	-14.0%	-18.1%	-9.7%	-10.6%	-18.6%	-5.3%	-5.5%	5.6%	-8.8%	-8.5%	-19.6%
2012	10.4%	1.0%	1.4%	3.4%	-1.9%	6.4%	15.8%	4.3%	4.0%	-5.5%	6.1%

Mean annual return (whole period)	14.9%	11.6%	14.1%	16.7%	20.5%	11.4%	7.2%	7.4%	3.5%	7.7%	7.5%
Volatility (whole period)	14.3%	13.7%	13.4%	18.1%	27.5%	7.0%	15.6%	5.5%	NA	NA	NA
Mean annual return 2003–2012	12.4%	12.1%	9.9%	11.2%	13.1%	6.7%	9.3%	6.6%	5.6%	3.1%	5.7%
Volatility 2003–2012	12.1%	13.2%	10.0%	12.5%	19.9%	6.5%	16.2%	6.1%	NA	NA	NA
Mean average return 2007–2012	2.2%	-0.4%	1.5%	3.7%	-2.9%	2.5%	2.3%	5.4%	-0.3%	-0.1%	-3.3%
Volatility 2007–2012	13.8%	15.0%	11.6%	13.9%	22.5%	7.4%	19.4%	6.4%	NA	NA	NA
Minimum annual return	-37.3%	-33.5%	-36.4%	-29.0%	-63.9%	-19.0%	-40.7%	-5.2%	-35.6%	-57.3%	-46.7%
Maximum annual return	79.2%	80.1%	87.1%	74.9%	83.3%	32.2%	33.1%	19.7%	48.3%	56.7%	68.1%

Source: Based on data from Hedge Fund Research, Inc.

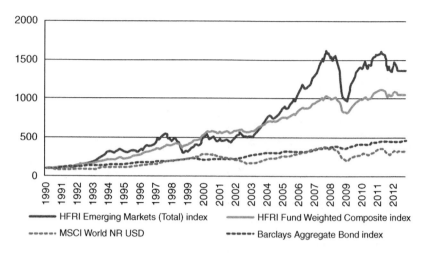

Figure 3.74 Performance statistics of the HFRI Emerging Markets (Total) index and comparative indices

in legislation – to take a position. The logic is the opposite for short positions; when they look for securities to short they look for undervalued securities and a negative catalyst. Managers must also pay particular attention to the global macroeconomic situation, and to monetary and cyclical elements that will impact not only the market as a whole but also, more importantly, the sector in which they invest.

Sector managers tend to have a deep knowledge of their sector and to have a defined list of stocks they know and which they will consider for investment. Managers will often take a long position in a stock for some time before going short, as either company-specific factors change or there is a change in the market environment. In consequence, sector managers tend to be familiar with the behaviour of the main players in their sector over long periods of time. They tend to meet the management of these companies regularly to put the check the numbers and to analyse in detail the strategies put in place. They may even talk to suppliers clients and employees.

When managers invest in several sectors, those sectors will usually be linked to each other. An example would be a fund specializing in the automotive sector that also considers tyre producers. In most cases, sector managers implement long/short strategies, and equity market neutral strategies, and to a lesser extent event driven strategies. A typical sector portfolio will consist of two parts: a longer term portfolio of companies in which the manager has a strong belief; and shorter-term positions, securities that are temporarily under- or overvalued. This second book is more opportunistic.

Table 3.28 Return of the HFRI Emerging Market indices during the Asian and the Russian crises

	HFRI Emerging Markets (Total) Index	HFRI Emerging Markets: Asia ex-Japan Index	HFRI Emerging Markets: Global Index	HFRI Emerging Markets: Latin America Index	HFRI Emerging Markets: Russia/ Eastern Europe Index	HFRI Fund Weighted Composite Index	MSCI World NR USD	Barclays Aggregate Bond Index
08/97	-2.1%	-2.8%	-0.2%	-5.8%	1.9%	0.3%	-6.7%	-0.2%
09/97	0.6%	-4.4%	2.7%	2.8%	2.6%	3.7%	5.4%	2.0%
10/97	-8.0%	-7.0%	-6.2%	-11.1%	-7.9%	-1.5%	-5.3%	1.8%
11/97	-3.9%	-2.7%	-5.0%	0.0%	-12.8%	-0.9%	1.8%	-0.5%
12/97	1.3%	-1.9%	1.3%	2.3%	6.5%	0.9%	1.2%	0.2%
01/98	-5.4%	-4.1%	-4.4%	-3.2%	-11.5%	-0.7%	2.8%	0.9%
02/98	4.0%	6.0%	3.4%	3.3%	3.2%	3.3%	6.7%	0.6%
03/98	2.9%	0.1%	2.8%	5.4%	3.9%	3.0%	4.2%	-0.3%
04/98	-0.6%	-1.8%	0.7%	-0.9%	-0.6%	1.0%	1.0%	1.2%
05/98	-9.3%	-5.5%	-8.1%	-8.0%	-17.1%	-2.1%	-1.3%	0.7%
06/98	-6.0%	-5.7%	-5.0%	-4.0%	-10.2%	-0.1%	2.4%	0.2%
07/98	-0.3%	-2.1%	0.5%	3.5%	-2.8%	-0.8%	-0.2%	0.6%
08/98	-21.0%	-6.6%	-27.5%	-15.6%	-38.6%	-8.7%	-13.4%	2.1%
09/98	-5.0%	-0.7%	-5.7%	-2.4%	-14.8%	0.7%	1.8%	4.7%
Performance	-43.4%	-33.2%	-43.0%	-30.7%	-68.1%	-2.6%	-1.5%	14.9%
Volatility	22.1%	11.6%	27.3%	21.1%	41.4%	10.5%	18.4%	4.7%

15.2   Illustrations

We give three examples.[34]

15.2.1   Pediatrix Medical Group (PDX)

Pediatrix Medical Group is one of the largest companies in the United States specializing in neo-natal and maternal-fetal services relating mainly to premature babies. By the middle of 2006, Pediatrix owned 25 per cent of the market share of its sector and the competition was limited. The share price was trading at historically low levels because the company was under investigation. This led to the company to delay the publication of its financial results despite an annual growth in earnings of 15 per cent per share. The consensus amongst analysts was that the investigation would have no important implications. Having analysed the company the manager decided to take a long position. The most important elements on the back of this decision were:

– rapid growth of earnings, around 15 per cent
– solid financial health (the company had financed several acquisitions on the basis of the cash generated by its activities)
– a share trading below eight times the ratio economic value to EBITDA
– an anticipated favourable issue regarding the current investigation.

The shares were trading at US$45.3 on 30 June 2006. The manager anticipated that the share should be trading at higher multipliers than its peers because it was generating plenty of cash and because it had only a small debt. Historically the ratio of its economic value to the EBITDA of comparable companies was trading around six to nine times, but the manager estimated Pediatrix to be able to reach ten to twelve times; accordingly, the price objective of the security was US$70 per share. In August 2007 the company published its financial statements and the price rallied, as expected. At the end of December 2007 the share was trading at US$68.15 per share, close to the US$70 estimated by the manager and 50 per cent higher than the original price paid. The manager decided to close the position. The evolution of the share price of Pediatrix over this period is reported in Figure 3.75.

15.2.2   Triad Hospitals, Inc. (TRI)

Triad Hospitals is an hospital operator based in Plano, Texas. It was founded in 1999, when the Pacific Group of hospitals spun off from the Hospital Corporation of America. The manager followed the stock for some time and took a small position. In the fourth quarter of 2006, the manager decided to increase her position in Triad Hospitals based on a fundamental analysis because:

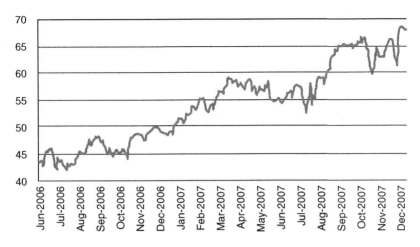

Figure 3.75 Share price of Pediatrix between 2006 and 2007

– its stock was trading at only approximately 6 times the 2007 EBITDA, while the market value of hospitals was close to 8.5 times EBITDA
– the company had recently published numbers below expectations, which had led to a rapid fall in the stock price.

The manager took a position at a discount estimated at 30 per cent relative to the private value of the company on the basis of the value per bed.[35] Over the following weeks the share price of the company rose rapidly because TPG-Axon Capital Management, a privately owned hedge fund sponsor, announced that they held more than 5 million shares of Triad Hospitals and they wanted the management of Triad Hospitals to improve the return on capital invested for shareholders. The fund manager estimated that the long-term potential for the share remained important. During the first quarter of 2007, the company announced a share buyback at US$50.25 per share, a 16 per cent premium relative to the market price, and a 33 per cent premium over the price paid by the manager. On 20 March 2007, Triad announced that another company, Community Health Systems, had proposed a cash merger for US$7.3 billion @ US$54. The offer was accepted, and the transaction was closed during the second semester of 2007; the manager made a total profit of 43 per cent. In this example, the sector-specific position became an event driven position.

15.2.3 Host Hotels and Resorts, Inc. (ticker HST)

Host Hotels and Resorts, Inc. is a real estate investment trust specialized in luxury housing. This industry was supported by a certain type of investor, who estimated that companies in that industry are interesting potential targets for private equity funds. The manager in our example analysed the sector and the company and concluded that at the time the sector was not fundamentally attractive to private equity managers because of its very limited liquidity. In addition, the lack of liquidity in the sector was exacerbated by a mismatch between the demand and the offer; the offer was still increasing while the demand was slowing down. Those characteristics were not clear in the numbers or in discussions with companies – but several hotels had started various projects whose development would be likely to accelerate in 2008 and 2009. PriceWaterhouseCoopers estimated that the offer – which increased from 4 per cent to 12 per cent early in 2007 – was overtaking the demand and that the situation could get worse. The manager's prediction was correct. The share price of the company peaked at around US$28 per share in February 2007. She took a position at US$26.04 per share. At that price level the ratio of economic value to EBITDA was around 13. The stock price fell to US$19; at that point the manager covered 25 per cent of her position, and closed it when the price dropped to US$18 per share. The share price evolution of Host Hotels and Resorts is reported in Figure 3.76.

15.3   Advantages and drawbacks

Sector specialists tend to have a good knowledge of the sectors they invest in, which probably explains why the sector index is one of the best performing strategies over time. From an investor's point of view, the classification of managers by sector encourages activity in the portfolio management and results in a clearer split between the strategies and exposures of the funds invested in the portfolios. However, there is a

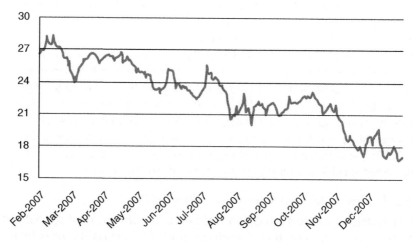

Figure 3.76   Share price of Host Hotels & Resorts, Inc. in 2007

risk inherent to sector investing that is also present in emerging market investing; managers may fall in love with their sectors or certain companies, and be unable to put them in a global context. In addition the investment range will be smaller, which may lead to a higher volatility, particularly in the short term.

15.4 Performance

Hedge Fund Research, Inc. defines two sector indices described below:[36]

Sector – Energy/Basic Materials: strategies which employ investment processes designed to identify opportunities in securities in specific niche areas of the market in which the Manager maintains a level of expertise which exceeds that of a market generalist in identifying companies engaged in the production and procurement of inputs to industrial processes, and implicitly sensitive to the direction of price trends as determined by shifts in supply and demand factors, and implicitly sensitive to the direction of broader economic trends. Energy/Basic Materials strategies typically maintain a primary focus in this area or expect to maintain in excess of 50% of portfolio exposure to these sectors over various market cycles.

Sector – Technology/Healthcare strategies employ investment processes designed to identify opportunities in securities in specific niche areas of the market in which the Manager maintains a level of expertise which exceeds that of a market generalist in identifying opportunities in companies engaged in all development, production and application of technology, biotechnology and as related to production of pharmaceuticals and healthcare industry. Though some diversity exists as a across [sic] sub-strategy, strategies implicitly exhibit some characteristic sensitivity to broader growth trends, or in the case of the latter, developments specific to the healthcare industry. Technology/Healthcare strategies typically maintain a primary focus in this area or expect to maintain in excess of 50% of portfolio exposure to these sectors over a various market cycles.

As the two indices do not start at the same moment we must perform two independent performance analyses.

Figure 3.77 shows the evolution of US$100 invested in the HFRI EH: Sector – Energy/Basic Materials index since January 1995 compared with other similar investments in the HFRI Fund Weighted Composite index, the equity market, represented by MSCI World, and the bond market, represented by the Barclays Aggregate Bond index.

An investment of US$100 in the HFRI EH: Sector – Energy/Basic Materials index in January 1995 would have become US$1320 by the end of 2012.

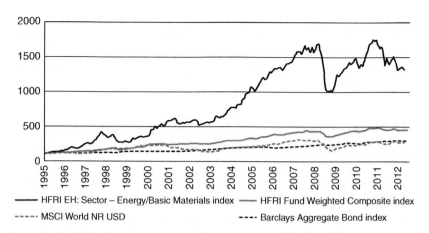

Figure 3.77 Evolution of US$100 invested in the HFRI EH: Sector – Energy/Basic Materials index

The same investment in the equity market, bond market or global hedge fund market would have become US$294, US$307 or US$478 respectively.

Table 3.29 shows the yearly returns, the mean annual return, the standard deviation, the minimum annual return, the maximum annual return and the spread of the strategies relative to the comparative indices. It leads to the following remarks:

– Over the 18 years covered, the HFRI EH: Sector – Energy/Basic Materials index was negative in five years. The three most difficult years were 2008 (–38.3 per cent), 1998 (–22.5 per cent) and 2011 (–16.7 per cent). 2008 was the most difficult year for the hedge fund industry as a whole, 1998 was the year of the LTCM bailout, the end of the Asian crisis and the Russian default. The equity index finished down in 5 years out of 18 including the 2000–2002 bear market, 2008 and 2011. The bond index suffered negative returns for one year only, in 1999.
– The maximum annual returns of the HFRI EH: Sector – Energy/Basic Materials index were achieved in 1995 (58.5 per cent), 1996 (58.4 per cent) and 1997 (47.5 per cent). These numbers are very strong.
– The spread in returns between the HFRI EH: Sector – Energy/Basic Materials index and the comparative indices has been volatile. The strategy has outperformed the global hedge fund index 11 times out of 18, the equity index 13 times and the bond index 12 times. The largest outperformance of the HFRI EH: Sector – Energy/Basic Materials index relative to the equity index was 71.5 per cent, in 2000, while the

Table 3.29   Performance statistics of the HFRI EH: Sector – Energy/Basic Materials index and comparative indices

	HFRI EH: Sector - Energy/Basic Materials Index	HFRI Fund Weighted Composite Index	MSCI World NR USD	Barclays Aggregate Bond Index	Performance vs. HFRI	Performance vs. MSCI World	Performance vs. Barclays
1995	58.5%	21.5%	20.7%	19.7%	36.9%	37.7%	38.8%
1996	58.4%	21.1%	13.5%	4.9%	37.3%	44.9%	53.5%
1997	47.5%	16.8%	15.8%	3.8%	30.7%	31.7%	43.7%
1998	-22.5%	2.6%	24.3%	13.7%	-25.1%	-46.9%	-36.2%
1999	25.5%	31.3%	24.9%	-5.2%	-5.8%	0.6%	30.7%
2000	58.4%	5.0%	-13.2%	3.2%	53.4%	71.5%	55.2%
2001	0.4%	4.6%	-16.8%	1.6%	-4.3%	17.2%	-1.2%
2002	-1.5%	-1.5%	-19.9%	16.5%	-0.04%	18.4%	-18.0%
2003	28.8%	19.5%	33.1%	12.5%	9.3%	-4.3%	16.3%
2004	34.9%	9.0%	14.7%	9.3%	25.9%	20.2%	25.6%
2005	6.4%	3.5%	4.5%	1.3%	2.9%	1.9%	5.1%
2006	16.1%	12.9%	20.1%	6.6%	3.2%	-3.9%	9.5%
2007	16.4%	10.0%	9.0%	9.5%	6.4%	7.4%	6.9%
2008	-38.3%	-19.0%	-40.7%	4.8%	-19.3%	2.4%	-43.1%
2009	41.8%	20.0%	30.0%	6.9%	21.8%	11.8%	34.9%
2010	17.4%	10.2%	11.8%	5.5%	7.2%	5.6%	11.9%
2011	-16.7%	-5.3%	-5.5%	5.6%	-11.4%	-11.1%	-22.3%
2012	-5.6%	6.4%	15.8%	4.3%	-12.0%	-21.5%	-9.9%
Mean annual return (whole period)	18.1%	9.4%	7.9%	6.9%	8.7%	10.2%	11.2%
Volatility (whole period)	18.3%	7.0%	15.6%	5.5%	NA	NA	NA
Meanannual return 2003–2012	10.1%	6.7%	9.3%	6.6%	3.4%	0.9%	3.5%
Volatility 2003–2012	15.3%	6.5%	16.2%	6.1%	NA	NA	NA
Meanaverage return 2007–2012	-0.3%	2.5%	2.3%	5.4%	-2.7%	-2.5%	-5.7%
Volatility 2007–2012	17.0%	7.4%	19.4%	6.4%	NA	NA	NA
Minimum annual return	-38.3%	-19.0%	-40.7%	-5.2%	-25.1%	-46.9%	-43.1%
Maximum annual return	58.5%	31.3%	33.1%	19.7%	53.4%	71.5%	55.2%

Source: Based on data from Hedge Fund Research, Inc.

largest underperformance was 46.9 per cent, in 1998. Relative to the bond index, the largest outperformance was achieved in 2000 at 55.2 per cent, and the largest underperformance was 43.1 per cent, in 2008.

Figure 3.78 shows the evolution of US$100 invested in the HFRI EH: Sector – Technology/Healthcare index since January 1991 compared with other similar investments in the HFRI Fund Weighted Composite index, the equity market, represented by MSCI World, and the bond market, represented by the Barclays Aggregate Bond index.

An investment of US$100 in the HFRI EH: Sector – Technology/ Healthcare index in January 1991 would have become US$1866 by the end of 2012. The same investment in the equity market, bond market or global hedge fund market would have become US$424, US$419 or US$1044 respectively.

The HFRI EH: Sector – Technology/Healthcare index offered an average annual return of 17.1 per cent per year over the whole period, against 8.3 per cent for the equity market and 7.2 per cent for the bond market. More recently, it has offered 9 per cent per year on average over the last decade and 5.1 per cent per year on average over the last five years. The fall has been significant, but it started from a high average return over the whole period, and recent years have been more difficult for the hedge fund industry.

Volatility has been high, at 16.4 per cent, over the whole period but it has decreased over the last decade to 8.6 per cent and has stayed at 8.6 per cent over the last five years. This remains lower than equities, which

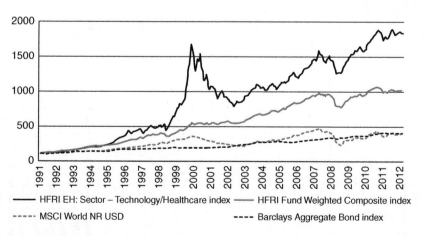

Figure 3.78   Evolution of US$100 invested in the HFRI EH: Sector – Technology/ Healthcare index

Source: Based on numbers obtained from Hedge Fund Research, Inc.

ranged between 15 and 20 per cent depending on the period in question, but higher than bonds, especially over the first part of the period under review. The risk–return ratio over the whole period remains particularly attractive.

Table 3.30 shows the yearly returns, the mean annual return, the standard deviation, the minimum annual return, the maximum annual return and the spread of the strategies relative to the comparative indices. It leads to the following remarks:

– Over the 22 years covered, the HFRI EH: Sector – Technology/Healthcare index was negative in three years: 2008 (–16.7 per cent), in 2000 (–15.3 per cent) and 2001 (–12.8 per cent). 2008 was the most difficult year for the hedge fund industry as a whole, 2000 was a turning point in equity markets and the start of a bear market, and 2001 was the second year of this three-year bear cycle. The equity index finished down in 6 years out of 22, including the 2000–2002 bear market, 2008 and 2011. The bond index suffered negative returns for one year only, in 1999.
– The maximum annual returns of the HFRI EH: Sector – Technology/Healthcare index were achieved in 1999 (124.3 per cent), 1992 (30.7 per cent) and 1993 and 1996 (30.6 per cent). These numbers are strong.
– The spread in returns between the HFRI EH: Sector – Technology/Healthcare index and the comparative indices has been volatile. The strategy outperformed the global hedge fund index 13 times out of 22, the equity index 14 times and the bond index 16 times. The largest outperformance of the HFRI EH: Sector – Technology/Healthcare index relative to the equity index was 99.3 per cent, in 1999, while the largest underperformance was 9.4 per cent, in 2004. Relative to the bond index, the largest outperformance was achieved in 1999 at 129.4 per cent, and the largest underperformance was 33.1 per cent, in 2002.

16   Credit/high yield

The high yield strategy groups funds that invest in the higher-risk part of the bond investment spectrum, but before any potential bankruptcy is envisaged. Such funds tend to be focused on corporate debt, but high yielding government debt may also be considered. Such funds tend to have a long bias.

16.1   Methodology

The high yield market can be split into several subsets that illustrate the importance of this market. The American corporate high yield market

Table 3.30 Performance statistics of the HFRI EH: Sector – Technology/Healthcare index and comparative indices

	HFRI EH: Sector – Technology/ Healthcare Index	HFRI Fund Weighted Composite Index	MSCI World NR USD	Barclays Aggregate Bond Index	Performance vs. HFRI	Performance vs. MSCI World	Performance vs. Barclays
1991	19.0%	32.2%	18.3%	16.0%	-13.2%	0.7%	2.9%
1992	30.7%	21.2%	-5.2%	5.8%	9.5%	36.0%	24.9%
1993	30.6%	30.9%	22.5%	11.1%	-0.3%	8.1%	19.5%
1994	10.0%	4.1%	5.1%	0.2%	5.9%	5.0%	9.8%
1995	50.9%	21.5%	20.7%	19.7%	29.4%	30.2%	31.2%
1996	30.6%	21.1%	13.5%	4.9%	9.5%	17.1%	25.7%
1997	6.9%	16.8%	15.8%	3.8%	-9.9%	-8.9%	3.1%
1998	28.5%	2.6%	24.3%	13.7%	25.8%	4.1%	14.8%
1999	124.3%	31.3%	24.9%	-5.2%	93.0%	99.3%	129.4%
2000	-15.3%	5.0%	-13.2%	3.2%	-20.3%	-2.1%	-18.5%
2001	-12.8%	4.6%	-16.8%	1.6%	-17.4%	4.0%	-14.4%
2002	-16.5%	-1.5%	-19.9%	16.5%	-15.1%	3.3%	-33.1%
2003	25.4%	19.5%	33.1%	12.5%	5.9%	-7.7%	12.9%
2004	5.4%	9.0%	14.7%	9.3%	-3.7%	-9.4%	-3.9%
2005	4.9%	3.5%	4.5%	1.3%	1.4%	0.4%	3.6%
2006	13.9%	12.9%	20.1%	6.6%	1.0%	-6.2%	7.2%
2007	14.8%	10.0%	9.0%	9.5%	4.8%	5.7%	5.3%
2008	-16.7%	-19.0%	-40.7%	4.8%	2.3%	24.0%	-21.5%
2009	25.8%	20.0%	30.0%	6.9%	5.8%	-4.2%	18.8%
2010	9.4%	10.2%	11.8%	5.5%	-0.9%	-2.4%	3.8%
2011	1.3%	-5.3%	-5.5%	5.6%	6.5%	6.8%	-4.4%
2012	5.6%	6.4%	15.8%	4.3%	-0.7%	-10.2%	1.3%
Mean annual return (whole period)	17.1%	11.7%	8.3%	7.2%	5.4%	8.8%	9.9%
Volatility (whole period)	16.4%	7.0%	15.6%	5.5%	NA	NA	NA
Meanannual return 2003–2012	9.0%	6.7%	9.3%	6.6%	2.2%	-0.3%	2.3%
Volatility 2003–2012	8.6%	6.5%	16.2%	6.1%	NA	NA	NA
Meanaverage return 2007–2012	5.1%	2.5%	2.3%	5.4%	2.6%	2.8%	-0.4%
Volatility 2007–2012	8.6%	7.4%	19.4%	6.4%	NA	NA	NA
Minimum annual return	-16.7%	-19.0%	-40.7%	-5.2%	-20.3%	-10.2%	-33.1%
Maximum annual return	124.3%	32.2%	33.1%	19.7%	93.0%	99.3%	129.4%

Source: Based on data from Hedge Fund Research, Inc.

is the largest, and this is where most funds are active; other funds may consider or be focused on European high yield bonds, emerging markets (both government and corporate), leveraged bank debt, crossover debt or distressed securities. Some fund managers will focus on markets, and some on the type of security, while others will be more opportunistic.

The high yield strategy applied to fixed income markets is based on the same principle as that of the long/short equity strategy. The idea is to identify fundamentally undervalued securities and to go long in those securities. At the same time, they look for expensive credit to go short on, and to hedge the global portfolio. Managers analyse companies and their capital structure in detail in order to determine their ability to repay the bond. The economic environment – including the level of interest rates, the default rate and the status of the economy in general – will have an important impact on the valuation of these securities. A complete credit analysis integrates many elements; the main ones are reported in Figure 3.79. They include capital flows, the borrower capacity, the management, operational efficiency, the capital structure, potential guarantees, controls or the profile of the company.

The high yield strategy focuses on bond issuers with a relatively high risk of default, so a complete credit analysis should integrate much information, enabling the management team to determine the ability of a creditor to pay its debt in due course. This explains why the quality of a fund manager resides completely in his or her ability to pick the right credits. In every case, portfolios will be diversified in a series of independent positions. According to the investment methodology, the manager may have an almost exclusively long book with some global hedges, or will combine long and short positions, integrating some relative value

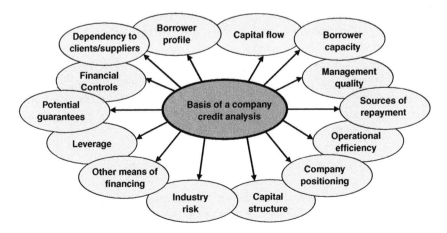

Figure 3.79 The main components of a credit analysis

or capital structure arbitrage positions. Short credit positions are usually taken through credit default swaps on individual securities or indices. In practice, managers will manage their exposure and integrate the market conditions; when these are favourable fund manager will typically be long and leverage will be used to demultiply the returns, but during periods of high volatility, funds managers tend to be under-invested and may increase the number of hedges in the portfolio. Sub-strategies such as capital structure arbitrage and pair trading may be applied.

16.2 Correlation trading

This technique was first developed in the United States but then spread to other markets. The strategy is not about the correlation between the securities but about the correlation of their risk of default and about the valuation of various credit instruments. Credit correlation products are used in a portfolio whose product price is a function of the correlation between the risk of default of the securities in the portfolio. A correlation of 1 means that the securities considered are perfectly correlated and a correlation of –1 means that the securities are perfectly negatively correlated. The managers determine the dependence between the probabilities that companies will default. They want to understand the joint probability that the situation will become unfavourable. What will happen if Intel and Microsoft both default?

The term "correlation trading" refers to investments or transactions that come from long or short positions to correlation products. There are two kinds of players in this market:

- Fundamental investors looking to buy cheap assets in order to increase their return. Such investors take long-term positions and get an interest rate higher that that they would obtain directly through a credit default swap, but with a lower liquidity.
- Traders that aim to take relative value positions, to buy the convexity of volatility or cheap correlation. These players generally combine various products in order to select the risks they want to take and to obtain the corresponding returns. These investors tend to be shorter term and include hedge fund managers.

The strategy is based on the use of collateralized debt obligation (CDO). Without going into the technical details, the underlying idea of these investment is that the issuer of the structured product groups a series of debt assets (such as corporate debt) to create a set. The assets are divided into various classes that pay investors with the cash generated. Each class has a different level of risk, a predefined seniority and a specific return that depends on the underlying risk. The interest for investor is that they will be able to buy one of the classes, also called tranches, depending on their profile and their appetite for risk; lower tranche will pay a higher coupon but will be exposed to a higher level of risk. The interest for issuers is that the level of risk of the portfolio can be hedged, reducing the capital requirement. The CDO market grew significantly in the year 2000; while in 1997 it had represented only US$64 million, by 2003 the total issuances were over US$400 million. As the market grew the products gained complexity, but the underlying idea remained the same. 2007 was the peak of this market – which has almost completely disappeared during the financial crisis.

The correlation of default represents the propensity for several issuers to default together within a specific period of time. As defaults are rare events, the probability of such simultaneous default is extremely low, and it is difficult to estimate because of a lack of historical data. The determination of such a probability is based on a complex numerical methodology called the copula functions. These functions offer an efficient way to link multiple one-dimensional survival curves to a unique multidimensional survival curve. The model can be used to price each individual tranche. The high number of credits in the portfolio significantly increases the number of default correlations to consider, making it very complex to determine the price of the securities considered. A simplified way to get an estimation is to use an identical survival rate for each tranche – but this is only an approximation. Depending on the underlying hypothesis the copula functions can be categorized as Gaussian, Student, Marshall-Olkin, Gumbel, each of which corresponds to a defined probability function. For example, a Gaussian probability function corresponds to a normal distribution, and the Gaussian copula system has, as a result of its simplicity, become standard in the industry. Pricing models are based on the following elements:

– the correlation of defaults
– the spreads between the elements in the portfolio
– the number of credits in the portfolio and their relative size
– the difference in rate within the tranches
– the maturity of the transaction
– the recovery rate on each credit
– the risk-free interest rate.

Using such model, managers are able to determine the implicit correlation of default and to determine if there is any arbitrage opportunity when they know the market premium for a tranche and when they have an estimation for each of the elements listed. This methodology uses the same underlying idea as the volatility arbitrage by using option valuation models like Black & Scholes. The only difference is that we are considering the correlation between the risk of default and not the implicit volatility of options.

The managers can take either a long or a short position in correlation. For every level of correlation, the equity tranche will be the first to be impacted in case of default. On the other side the senior tranche is less risky because it is covered by a set of subordinated tranches. Figure 3.80 illustrates the relation that exists between the tranches and the default correlation. There are three types: an equity tranche, an intermediary tranche and a senior tranche. The expected loss of a portfolio is independent of the correlation between the defaults, but it is a function of the probability of default and the recovery rate. The correlation determines how the expected losses are spread amongst the capital structure. At a low level of default correlation, the portfolio can be expected to have a high likelihood of only few defaults, so the loss probability on a senior tranche is low, confirming its low level of risk. The few defaults that will arise will be absorbed mainly by the equity tranche. However, at higher levels of default correlation the credits in portfolio will behave like a unique asset. In this case senior tranches become more risky.

In practice managers will be either long in correlation and take a long position in the equity tranche or they will take a short position in the senior tranche. Alternatively, they could take a short position in correlation, taking a short position in the equity tranche, or a long position in the senior tranche. This is illustrated in Table 3.31.

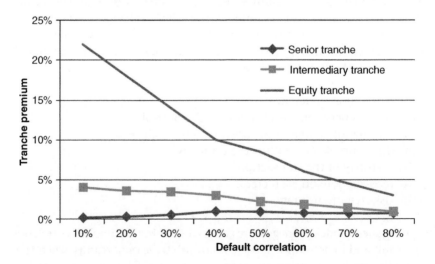

Figure 3.80   Relation between CDO tranches and the default correlation

Table 3.31 Positioning based on correlation views

	Exposition to the subordinated tranche	Exposition to the senior tranche
Long position in correlation	LONG	SHORT
Short position in correlation	SHORT	LONG

Finally, we can estimate a delta, a gamma, a theta and a rho[37] in the context of correlation trading. This delta measures the sensitivity of the tranche to a change in the credit of the company. As in the case of option trading, this delta can be adjusted to the level desired by the manager with the use of adequate products such as a credit default swap. In addition, the main risk of such a strategy, apart from the market risk, is that the model used may not be a reflection of reality, particularly in periods of stress. The underlying hypothesis of normality is not always verified in reality, and managers usually rely on that hypothesis when they perform their analyses.

16.3 Illustration

The following example comes from a management team that anticipated that the market was too bearish; the manager took a long position in a credit and hedged this position with a short position in a five-year credit default swap. In May 2005 the bonds of Interpublic Group, a marketing and advertising company, fell (that is, the spread relative to the risk-free rate increased) because of a negative news flow including the facts that:

– the company had not yet published its financial results for 2004 and the Securities and Exchange Commission was investigating a potential adjustment of previous results
– the credit conditions of the bonds required that the financial statements should be published before the end of June to avoid a default
– the bond conditions required the publishing of financial statements by the end of September, and
– the company announced that it had lost General Motors, an important client.

Under these conditions, the five-year credit default swap of the company widened in May from 89 basis points to 350 basis points. At that point, the manager decided to take a position; he felt sure that despite the recent issues the bond was cheap, particularly relative to the equity that had moved only a little. He combined two positions, selling protection because he anticipated the spread to decrease as soon as the financial

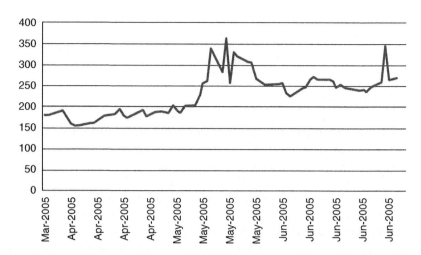

Figure 3.81 Evolution of the five-year credit default swap of Interpublic Group in 2005

statements were published. He combined this position with long positions in at-the-money put options that had been bought to limit the potential loss if the share should fall significantly. The manager closed the positions around 250 basis points. In Figure 3.81, we show the evolution of the spread of the five-year credit default swap.

16.4 Advantages and drawbacks

The high yield strategy aims to offer attractive returns for reasonable liquidity. The strategy tends to be less liquid than fixed income arbitrage funds, but more liquid than distressed securities. The expected returns are typically over 10 per cent net over a full cycle. Volatility may be an issue in the short term and during period of uncertainties, but these times also offer the greatest opportunities to managers. One of the main drawbacks of the strategy is that it is cyclical by nature; the sub-investment grade bond market will suffer as a whole during periods of uncertainty and spreads can widen rapidly, impacting returns even when portfolios have some hedges in place. It is, however, worth mentioning some funds have a net short bias; helping the portfolio during volatile periods.

16.5 Performance

There is no pure credit index published by Hedge Fund Research, Inc; the closest thing is the HFRI RV: Fixed Income – Corporate index. They define this index as follows:[38]

The HFRI RV: Fixed Income – Corporate index includes strategies in which the investment thesis is predicated on realization of a spread between related instruments in which one or multiple components of the spread is a corporate fixed income instrument. Strategies employ an investment process designed to isolate attractive opportunities between a variety of fixed income instruments, typically realizing an attractive spread between multiple corporate bonds or between a corporate and risk free government bond. Fixed Income – Corporate strategies differ from Event Driven: Credit Arbitrage in that the former more typically involve more general market hedges which may vary in the degree to which they limit fixed income market exposure, while the latter typically involve arbitrage positions with little or no net credit market exposure, but are predicated on specific, anticipated idiosyncratic developments. It is worth mentioning that there is an Event Driven Credit Arbitrage sub-strategy defined by no index published.

Figure 3.82 shows the evolution of US$100 invested in the HFRI RV: Fixed Income – Corporate index since January 1990 compared with other similar investments in the HFRI Fund Weighted Composite index, the equity market, represented by MSCI World, and the bond market, represented by the Barclays Aggregate Bond index.

An investment of US$100 in the HFRI RV: Fixed Income – Corporate index would have become US$586 by the end of 2012. The same investment in the equity market, bond market or global hedge fund market would have become US$1105, US$352 or US$472 respectively.

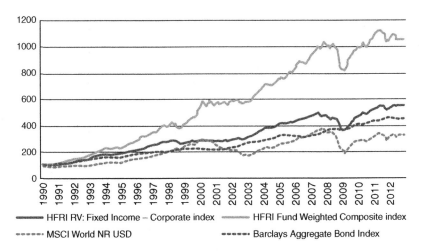

Figure 3.82 Evolution of US$100 invested in the HFRI RV: Fixed Income – Corporate index

Source: Based on numbers obtained from Hedge Fund Research, Inc.

The HFRI RV: Fixed Income – Corporate index offered an average annual return of 8.7 per cent per year over the whole period, against 7.2 per cent for the equity market and 7.4 per cent for the bond market. More recently it has offered 7.3 per cent per year on average over the last decade and 4.7 per cent per year on average over the last five years. These returns have fallen, but recent years have been more difficult for the hedge fund industry, and the strategy suffered in 2008.

Volatility has been relatively low over the whole period and over the last decade, at 6.6 and 6.4 per cent, and interestingly it has slightly decreased over the last five years, to 6 per cent. This remains significantly lower than equities, which ranged between 15 and 20 per cent depending on the period in question, and slightly higher than bonds over the whole period and the last 10 years, but lower than bonds more recently. The risk–return ratio over the whole period remains particularly attractive.

Table 3.32 shows the yearly returns, the mean annual return, the standard deviation, the minimum annual return, the maximum annual return and the spread of the strategies relative to the comparative indices. It leads to the following remarks:

– Over the 23 years covered, the HFRI RV: Fixed Income – Corporate index was negative in three years: 2008 (–24.2 per cent), in 1990 (–12.1 per cent) and 2000 (–3 per cent). 2008 was the most difficult year for the hedge fund industry. It is not, however, clear why the strategy underperformed in 1990, even though it was a difficult year for equities as a whole. The equity index finished down in 6 years out of 23, including the 2000–2002 bear market, 2008 and 2011. The bond index suffered negative returns for one year only, in 1999.
– The maximum annual returns of the HFRI RV: Fixed Income – Corporate index were achieved in 1991 (41.8 per cent), 2009 (30.7 per cent) and 1993 (22.7 per cent). These numbers are relatively strong, but high annual returns remains relatively rare for this strategy.
– The spread in returns between the HFRI RV: Fixed Income – Corporate index and the comparative indices has been volatile. The strategy outperformed the global hedge fund index 9 times out of 23, the equity index 12 times and the bond index 15 times. The largest outperformance of the HFRI RV: Fixed Income – Corporate index relative to the equity index was 25.7 per cent, in 1992, while the largest underperformance was 29.6 per cent, in 1998. Relative to the bond index, the largest outperformance was achieved in 1991 at 25.8 per cent, and the largest underperformance was 29 per cent, in 2008.

Table 3.32 Performance statistics of the HFRI RV: Fixed Income – Corporate index and comparative indices

	HFRI RV: Fixed Income – Corporate Index	HFRI Fund Weighted Composite Index	MSCI World NR USD	Barclays Aggregate Bond Index	Performance vs. HFRI	Performance vs. MSCI World	Performance vs. Barclays Aggregate
1990	-12.1%	5.8%	-17.0%	12.7%	-17.9%	4.9%	-24.8%
1991	41.8%	32.2%	18.3%	16.0%	9.6%	23.5%	25.8%
1992	18.5%	21.2%	-5.2%	5.8%	-2.7%	23.8%	12.7%
1993	22.7%	30.9%	22.5%	11.1%	-8.2%	0.2%	11.6%
1994	1.5%	4.1%	5.1%	0.2%	-2.6%	-3.6%	1.2%
1995	15.2%	21.5%	20.7%	19.7%	-6.3%	-5.5%	-4.5%
1996	16.2%	21.1%	13.5%	4.9%	-4.9%	2.76%	11.3%
1997	12.5%	16.8%	15.8%	3.8%	-4.3%	-3.2%	8.7%
1998	-5.3%	2.5%	24.3%	13.7%	-7.9%	-29.6%	-19.0%
1999	7.3%	31.3%	24.9%	-5.2%	-23.9%	-17.6%	12.5%
2000	-3.0%	5.0%	-13.2%	3.2%	-8.0%	10.1%	-6.2%
2001	5.4%	4.5%	-16.8%	1.6%	0.7%	22.2%	3.8%
2002	5.8%	-1.5%	-19.9%	16.5%	7.2%	25.7%	-10.7%
2003	21.3%	19.5%	33.1%	12.5%	1.8%	-11.8%	8.8%
2004	10.5%	9.0%	14.7%	9.3%	1.5%	-4.2%	1.2%
2005	1.4%	3.5%	4.5%	1.3%	-2.1%	-3.1%	0.1%
2006	10.8%	12.9%	20.1%	6.6%	-2.1%	-9.3%	4.1%
2007	-0.7%	10.0%	9.0%	9.5%	-10.7%	-9.8%	-10.2%
2008	-24.2%	-19.0%	-40.7%	4.8%	-5.2%	16.5%	-29.0%
2009	30.7%	20.0%	30.0%	6.9%	10.7%	0.7%	23.8%
2010	11.8%	10.2%	11.8%	5.5%	1.6%	0.0%	6.3%
2011	0.8%	-5.3%	-5.5%	5.6%	6.1%	6.4%	-4.8%
2012	11.0%	6.4%	15.8%	4.3%	4.6%	-4.8%	6.7%
Mean annual return (whole period)	8.7%	11.4%	7.2%	7.4%	-2.7%	1.5%	1.3%
Volatility (whole period)	6.6%	7.0%	15.6%	5.5%	NA	NA	NA
Meanannual return 2003–2012	7.3%	6.7%	9.3%	6.6%	0.6%	-1.9%	0.7%
Volatility 2003–2012	6.4%	6.5%	16.2%	6.1%	NA	NA	NA
Meanaverage return 2007–2012	6.0%	2.5%	2.3%	5.4%	3.6%	3.8%	0.6%
Volatility 2007–2012	7.9%	7.4%	19.4%	6.4%	NA	NA	NA
Minimum annual return	-24.2%	-19.0%	-40.7%	-5.2%	-23.9%	-29.6%	-29.0%
Maximum annual return	41.8%	32.2%	33.1%	19.7%	10.7%	25.7%	25.8%

Source: Based on data from Hedge Fund Research, Inc.

17   Short selling

The objective of the managers in implementing short strategies is to provide a hedge for diversified portfolios. This strategy is based on the search for overvalued securities or markets and selling them short. As explained in Chapter 2, short players do not own the stock they sell short but borrow them in order to sell them on the market. Then, they buy the stocks back later at a lower price, and return them to the lender.

17.1   Methodology

Most strategies presented in this chapter include a short component in their implementation. Short selling is used either as a portfolio hedge or as a source of profits. Just as some managers focus on long positions with no or marginal short positions, so do others focus on the short side; their objective is to offer returns by focusing on shorts hedged by some long positions to balance the portfolio. The idea is to profit from the falls in the market and in stock prices with the cushion coming from the interest rate received on the cash resulting from the implementation of the short positions. The global position will typically be net short. The strategy performs successfully as long as the price of the securities sold short decreases. The cash generated from the short positions will provide some returns from which the cost of borrowing should be deducted. Technically a short position does not require any initial investment, but merely a collateral as a guarantee, however the party borrowing the securities must pay any relevant dividend to the counterparty lending them; this means that it can be costly to borrow a security attracting a high yield. As the position becomes favourable to the borrower, they will be able to invest an increasing part of the money retained as collateral, but if the situation becomes less favourable to the investor, the collateral will have to be increased.

The implementation of short positions is, however, more complicated than it seems at first sight. The main potential obstacles are:

– **Prohibition and taxation**: in some markets short selling is banned, and in other places it is allowed but heavily taxed. In Australia, for example, the profits made through shorts are taxed while any loss realized on them cannot be deducted from tax.
– **Counterparty**: a lender of the securities must be found.
– **Analyst recommendations**: analysts publish many more recommendations for purchase than sale. This makes it more difficult for managers to find ideas, so they will have to rely much more on internally generated ideas.

– **Other elements**: there are psychological elements. Many investors prefer to buy a company they believe in rather than trying to make money by profiting from a company facing problems or difficulties.

17.2 Illustrations

We present two examples, Okamura and New Century Financial.

17.2.1 Okamura

Okamura's main activity is selling furniture in Japan. The company is the leader in the sector. At the end of 2004, the fund manager performed a complete analysis of the company, and estimated that the interesting profits published by the company over the last three years were mainly due to cost cutting combined with a significant increase in the number of new offices built thanks to fiscal stimulus. The manager estimated that the stock was overvalued by 30 per cent, as the fiscal stimulus was coming to an end and as the effect of the cost cutting had been integrated into the prices. A discussion with the management of the company confirmed that the company was facing some margin issues in its second business, the supply to smaller resellers. So the manager took a short position in January 2005 at an average price of ¥930. The price continued to move around this value until the company announced its financial results early in March, at which point, the shares dropped more than 10 per cent, and the manager closed his position a few days later. Figure 3.83 shows the evolution of the price of Okamura over that period.

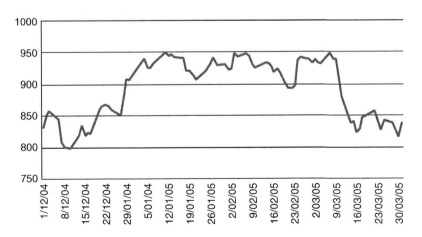

Figure 3.83 Evolution of the stock price of Okamura Corporation

17.2.2   New Century Financial

New Century Financial is a US real estate investment trust, a financing company that provides first and second lien real estate credit. The manager performed a complete fundamental analysis of the company, and she found that the development model of the company and the stability of its dividend depended on its capacity to continue increasing its issuing volumes independent of the environment. This is possible in a favourable credit environment, but it became more difficult in the third quarter of 2006. The manager, who had met the management of the company several times in the past, had observed that the company tended to be very aggressive in its forecasts and in its promotion. She met them again after the summer of 2006,. and this meeting convinced her that there was a serious risk that the company was looking for volume without paying enough attention to the quality of the credits. A presentation by the chief executive officer at a conference early in November 2006 enabled her to consolidate her view; he announced that the company would probably have to reduce the dividend in 2007. Even though the stock price did not move significantly after this announcement, she took a short position in the middle of December 2006. Then over the following months more and more borrowers started to default on their real estate mortgages; the company had been so lax that it was facing defaults not only on second lien mortgages but even on first lien. Under these conditions, those who had bought securities issued by New Century could activate a put option with the obligation to buy them back. The company lost its sources of finance, and early in April 2007 went bankrupt. The manager closed her positions at an average price of US$0.91, for an approximate gain of 99 per cent. Figure 3.84 shows the evolution of the stock price of New Century Financial over that period.

17.3   Advantages and drawbacks

Despite its intellectual interest, short selling remains an exception, and the objective of those fund managers that specialize in short selling is usually to propose a solution to diversify a multi-strategy portfolio rather than operating with the fundamental belief that money can be created by being net short over the long term. The strategy has the very interesting feature of being negatively correlated with all the other alternative strategies; its main feature is that its returns will be consistently negative in normal market conditions but that it will pay out very well during volatile periods. On the other side, while the potential losses are unlimited, the potential profits are limited to 100 per cent – and that happens only if the security goes bankrupt. On the other hand a stock can provide over

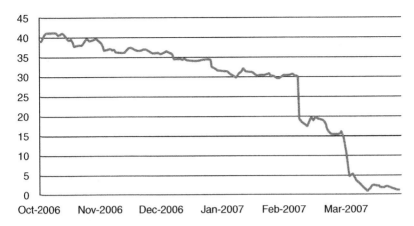

Figure 3.84 Evolution of the stock price of New Century Financial

100 per cent over a period of time, confirming that the potential loss from shorting is unlimited. Another problem of the strategy is that not all shares can be shorted easily, especially less liquid stocks. This reduces the opportunity set for the managers applying this strategy.

17.4 Performance

Hedge Fund Research, Inc. defines short bias funds as those:[39]

> *that employ analytical techniques in which the investment thesis is predicated on assessment of the valuation characteristics on the underlying companies with the goal of identifying overvalued companies. Short Biased strategies may vary the investment level or the level of short exposure over market cycles, but the primary distinguishing characteristic is that the manager maintains consistent short exposure and expects to outperform traditional equity managers in declining equity markets. Investment theses may be fundamental or technical and nature and manager has a particular focus, above that of a market generalist, on identification of overvalued companies and would expect to maintain a net short equity position over various market cycles.*

Figure 3.85 shows the evolution of US$100 invested in the HFRI EH: Short Bias index since January 1990 compared with other similar investments in the HFRI Fund Weighted Composite index, the equity market,

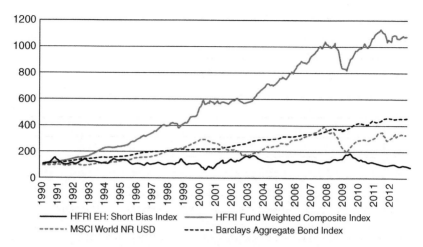

Figure 3.85 Evolution of US$100 invested in the HFRI EH: Short Bias Index
Source: Based on numbers obtained from Hedge Fund Research, Inc.

represented by MSCI World, and the bond market, represented by the Barclays Aggregate Bond index.

An investment of US$100 in the HFRI EH: Short Bias index would have become US$87.8 by the end of 2012. The same investment in the equity market, bond market or global hedge fund market would have become US$1105, US$352 or US$472 respectively.

The HFRI EH: Short Bias index offered an average annual return of 1.1 per cent per year over the whole period, against 7.2 per cent for the equity market and 7.4 per cent for the bond market. More recently, it has offered −5.5 per cent per year on average over the last decade, and −6.7 per cent per year on average over the last five years. These returns are the lowest of all the indices analysed, but it is important to keep in mind that the aim of the strategy is to offer protection against difficult equity markets and to offer uncorrelated returns. As we will see in the next chapter, the strategy has played its part. It is clear, however, that on a stand-alone basis, a short-biased fund is of less interest.

Volatility was high over the whole period, at 18.7 per cent. It has been lower over the last decade, at 11.4 per cent, and it has increased, back to 13.1 per cent, over the last five years. This is in line with equities, which ranged between 15 and 20 per cent depending on the period in question, and significantly higher than bonds over the entire period considered.

Table 3.33 shows the yearly returns, the mean annual return, the standard deviation, the minimum annual return, the maximum annual return

Table 3.33 Performance statistics of the HFRI EH: Short Bias index and comparative indices

	HFRI EH: Short Bias Index	HFRI Fund Weighted Composite Index	MSCI World NR USD	Barclays Aggregate Bond Index	Performance vs. HFRI	Performance vs. MSCI World	Performance vs. Barclays Aggregate
1990	36.2%	5.8%	-17.0%	12.7%	30.4%	53.2%	23.5%
1991	-17.0%	32.2%	18.3%	16.0%	-49.2%	-35.2%	-33.0%
1992	10.0%	21.2%	-5.2%	5.8%	-11.2%	15.3%	4.3%
1993	-7.5%	30.9%	22.5%	11.1%	-38.4%	-30.0%	-18.6%
1994	18.5%	4.1%	5.1%	0.2%	14.4%	13.5%	18.3%
1995	-17.1%	21.5%	20.7%	19.7%	-38.6%	-37.9%	-36.8%
1996	-4.0%	21.1%	13.5%	4.9%	-25.1%	-17.5%	-8.9%
1997	3.9%	16.8%	15.8%	3.8%	-12.9%	-11.9%	0.1%
1998	-0.5%	2.6%	24.3%	13.7%	-3.2%	-24.9%	-14.3%
1999	-24.4%	31.3%	24.9%	-5.2%	-55.7%	-49.3%	-19.2%
2000	34.6%	5.0%	-13.2%	3.2%	29.6%	47.8%	31.5%
2001	9.0%	4.6%	-16.8%	1.6%	4.4%	25.8%	7.4%
2002	29.2%	-1.5%	-19.9%	16.5%	30.6%	49.1%	12.6%
2003	-21.8%	19.5%	33.1%	12.5%	-41.3%	-54.9%	-34.3%
2004	-3.8%	9.0%	14.7%	9.3%	-12.9%	-18.5%	-13.1%
2005	-1.3%	3.5%	4.5%	1.3%	-4.8%	-5.8%	-2.6%
2006	-2.6%	12.9%	20.1%	6.6%	-15.5%	-22.7%	-9.3%
2007	4.7%	10.0%	9.0%	9.5%	-5.2%	-4.3%	-4.8%
2008	28.4%	-19.0%	-40.7%	4.8%	47.4%	69.1%	23.6%
2009	-24.0%	20.0%	30.0%	6.9%	-44.0%	-54.0%	-31.0%
2010	-18.0%	10.2%	11.8%	5.5%	-28.3%	-29.8%	-23.6%
2011	0.4%	-5.3%	-5.5%	5.6%	5.6%	5.9%	-5.3%
2012	-17.2%	6.4%	15.8%	4.3%	-23.6%	-33.1%	-21.6%
Mean annual return (whole period)	0.7%	11.4%	7.2%	7.4%	-10.8%	-6.5%	-6.7%
Volatility (whole period)	18.7%	7.0%	15.6%	5.5%	NA	NA	NA
Meanannual return 2003–2012	-5.5%	6.7%	9.3%	6.6%	-12.3%	-14.8%	-12.2%
Volatility 2003–2012	11.4%	6.5%	16.2%	6.1%	NA	NA	NA
Meanaverage return 2007–2012	-6.1%	2.5%	2.3%	5.4%	-8.6%	-8.4%	-11.5%
Volatility 2007–2012	13.1%	7.4%	19.4%	6.4%	NA	NA	NA
Minimum annual return	-24.4%	-19.0%	-40.7%	-5.2%	-55.7%	-54.9%	-36.8%
Maximum annual return	36.2%	32.2%	33.1%	19.7%	47.4%	69.1%	31.5%

Source: Based on data from Hedge Fund Research, Inc.

and the spread of the strategies relative to the comparative indices. It leads to the following remarks:

– Over the 23 years covered, the HFRI EH: Short Bias index was negative for 13 years. The most difficult years were 1999 (–24.4 per cent), 2009 (–24 per cent) and 2010 (–18 per cent). 1999 and 2009 were strong years for equities. 2010 was a correct year, but not excessively strong. The equity index finished down in 6 years out of 23 including the 2000–2002 bear market, 2008 and 2011. The bond index suffered negative returns for one year only, in 1999.
– The maximum annual returns of the HFRI EH: Short Bias index were achieved in 1990 (36.6 per cent), 2000 (34.6 per cent) and 2002 (29.2 per cent). These numbers are strong and, interestingly, were achieved during years that were difficult for equities.
– The spread in returns between the HFRI EH: Short Bias index and the comparative indices has been volatile. The strategy outperformed the global hedge fund index 7 times out of 23, and the equity and bond indices 8 times. The largest outperformance of the HFRI EH: Short Bias index relative to the equity index was 69.1 per cent, in 2008, while the largest underperformance was 54.9 per cent, in 2003. Relative to the bond index, the largest outperformance was achieved in 2000 at 31.5 per cent, and the largest underperformance was 36.8 per cent, in 1995.

18 Macro

This strategy was initiated by Julian Robertson in 1986, when he created the Jaguar fund. Unlike the other strategies described here, macro fund managers focus on macroenomonic factors. They are global or international managers who use an opportunistic approach, taking positions according to the changes they forecast in the economic global environment, as reflected in the price of equities, currencies, interest rates, inflation, commodities or the fiscal policy. For a long time, macro funds represented the bulk of the assets of the hedge fund universe. According to Hedge Fund Research, Inc., they represented over 70 per cent of the industry in 1990,[40] at which time the main macro hedge fund managers each had several billion US dollars in assets under management. The advertising made around these funds in the 1980s led to an increase in the number of macro funds. During the 1990s the investment strategies applied by these managers became more and more complex and diversified. It is difficult to estimate precisely the number and percentage of macro funds nowadays but various estimations give a number close to 20 per cent.

18.1 Principles

Macro managers develop a global view over the world markets and their interconnections in order to profit from any kind of opportunities whenever they appear. They analyse macroeconomic trends linked to government or monetary policies, economic cycles, new technologies and so on. In order to identify price spreads between the variables they apply a top-down strategy that aims to focus on the estimation of the impact that these events will have on the price of financial instruments. These managers can usually invests in a large number of markets and apply an investment policy that is determined on a case-by-case basis. Depending on the opportunities they gain exposure to one or several sectors or markets through diversified financial instruments they select on the basis of their objectives. They realize gains by correctly anticipating price movements in global markets and by keeping the flexibility to use any kind of approach that will enable them to profit from price distortion.

Macro investing is very different from the investment strategies applied by other hedge fund managers, as it is more an overall approach than a precise strategy. According to the opportunity set, managers decide whether or not to invest, their final objective being to profit from inefficiencies in the markets. They use fundamental and/or technical analysis to gain a global overview of a country and will in many cases use technical analysis in order to determine whether or not the long-term trends can be verified on the short term. Macro managers are often described as speculators in a series of markets including equities, fixed income, currencies and commodities. While many hedge fund strategies need a particular economic environment to perform, the characteristics of their strategy enable macro managers to perform over time whenever the opportunity emerges.

18.2 Methodology

Macro managers look for unusual price fluctuations that are far from their equilibrium. In such conditions, the perception of market participants deviates from actual levels, creating an opportunity. The managers make a profit by identifying where the risk premium is the furthest from the equilibrium situation and by investing accordingly. Then they determine when the extraordinary conditions that led to the specific situation are likely to change or when they will be counterbalanced by a new trend that goes in another direction. Hence, timing is one of the key elements of the strategy.

As a theoretical illustration, consider difficult market conditions. Macro managers tend to consider that most price fluctuations in financial markets tend to stay within one standard deviation around the mean, categorizing this level of volatility as normal. When price fluctuations exceed that, opportunities emerge, and over two standard deviations the opportunity is exceptional – such opportunities emerge only a few times per decade. Arbitrage opportunities emerge when movements are significant, and macro investors make profits by either positioning their fund to profit from a return to the mean or by anticipating further movements. Examples of such movements include those in the eurodollar bond market in 1994, the Asian crisis in 1997–1998, the subprime crisis in 2007 and the financial crisis that followed it, in 2008.

Macro fund investment starts with a phase in which the macroeconomic trend merges with a bias from dominant investors in such a way that both are reinforcing each other. For example, consider the accelerated macroeconomic growth supported by important investment that happened in the years leading up to 2000; market price increased rapidly and significantly until the values of the securities had moved so far from reality that new opportunities appeared. At that point, the market was not supported by market participants any more, and this lack of confidence led to a reversal in the trend. During crisis, this turning point can be identified by important political changes that push markets into uncertainty and that aim to push the trend back to normality. The art of macro investing resides in the ability of the managers to identify the approach of a turning point and to take a position accordingly.

18.3 Illustrations

We present three examples that illustrate the principle of macro investing. We start with the loosening of Turkish monetary conditions. The second example is a bet on the evolution of the exchange rate of US dollars against Japanese yen. Then we describe a position taken by a manager in German financial companies in 2000.

18.3.1 Loosening of monetary conditions[41]

The top-down rationale is that in mid-2012 the European Monetary Union balance sheets were becoming increasingly stressed whilst the policy response had until then been inadequate. The ramifications of this were a deteriorating regional and global economic activity outlook at the same time as an increased likelihood of an acceleration of global monetary easing. This in turn both supported inflows into emerging markets and an easing of its monetary policy to the extent to which global economic activity was slowing, whilst EMU currencies were stronger than they otherwise would have been, given easily developed market policy. The bottom-up rationale was based on an analysis of the reaction by Turkey's central bank that suggested a mixed-growth outlook coupled with an improvement in the underlying inflation picture, meaning that they would preside over a loosening of monetary conditions (defined as the degree of openness of the weighted change in interest and exchange rates). In the case of Turkey, the fund manager expected them to ease monetary conditions through allowing the weighted cost of bank funding to fall, at the same time being slightly more tolerant of any exchange rate weakness.

The trade was a long in 2016 maturity Turkish government bonds in Turkish lira funded locally, versus a short in Turkish lira with a 50/50 EUR/USD basket, with a ratio of three to one in notional terms. The manager entered the position on 4 July 2012. Figure 3.86 shows the weighted average cost of Central Bank of Turkey (CBT) funding. The weighted average cost of funding represents Turkey's banking sector cost of funding from the CBT; it is a weighted average across all the CBT's liquidity provision facilities with the amount of funding providing at each rate a discretionary decision on behalf of the CBT according to the extent they would like to tighten/loosen policy on any given day.

The easing position of Turkish monetary conditions is a good example of a discretionary macro trade, given that:

- it is supported both by top-down and bottom-up fundamentals
- it has policymakers in its favour (that is, it is correct to work on the assumption that policymakers would like to preside over looser monetary conditions)

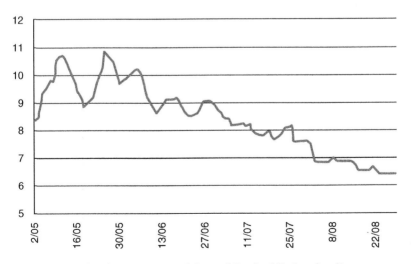

Figure 3.86   Weighted average cost of Central Bank of Turkey funding

- it has a well defined tail risk, especially in the scenario that the bearish FX exposure would offset losses on the constructive bond exposure.

Position scaling, stop-losses and take-profit targets were a function of the underlying return distribution of the monetary conditions trade. During July, the rapid easing of monetary conditions which occurred (front-loaded in the longer-dated bonds) meant that the take-profit target which had been set with a one-month time horizon in mind was achieved within a shorter period of time. The position was closed in July 12. Figure 3.87 shows the monetary conditions index; it is calculated as a weighted average of changes in Turkey's interest and exchange rates, which is then made into an index. The weight is a function of Turkey's export/GDP and a lower index represents more stimulating conditions for the economy.

18.3.2 *Yen–dollar carry trade*

One of the strategies widely used by macro funds is called a "carry trade"; its aim is to profit from an interest rate differential between two currencies. The basic principle is to borrow money in the currency with the lower interest rate and to invest these assets in another currency with a higher interest rate. There are two sources of profit in a carry trade position:

– the return from the spread in the interest rates of the corresponding currencies
– the return from the appreciation of the currency with the higher interest rate.

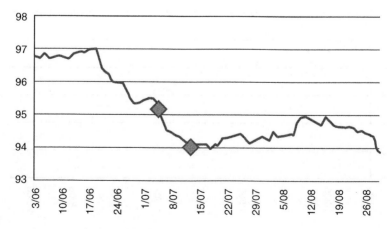

Figure 3.87   The Monetary Condition index

Currencies typically paired in carry trades include: the Japanese yen against the pound sterling, the Australian dollar, the euro, the Canadian dollar, or the US dollar; or the pound sterling against the Swiss franc. The yen is widely used in carry trades because the Bank of Japan kept its interest rates close to zero for several years. This particular case took place in November 2001; the Japanese economy was in a desperate situation and the set of reforms expected for some time were not happening. At the same time, the United States started to recover and regain the confidence lost on 11 September 2001, and its Federal Reserve was working on re-establishing confidence in financial markets. The transaction consisted of taking a position intended to profit from a yen weakening against the US dollar, achieved with a put option on the yen against the dollar. The exercise price of such options was around ¥127 on the market while the exchange rate on the market was slightly over ¥120. The manager took a position. Figure 3.88 illustrates the evolution of the exchange rate from November to December 2001; it shows that the exchange rate started changing significantly during the second half of December, passing the ¥127 level and leading to an attractive gain on the option.

18.3.3 Sector consolidation

The German government announced at the end of 1999 that there was a project to cut taxes on the sale of cross-shareholding. This political decision created a consolidation opportunity for German financial institutions. The transaction consisted of taking a long volatility position in equities of various German institutions working on the hypothesis that volatility would increase. Our manager, focusing on Deutsche Bank,

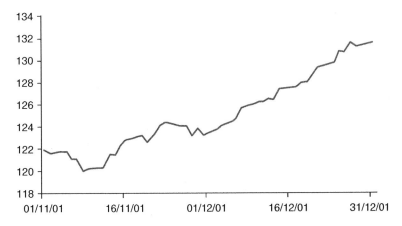

Figure 3.88 Evolution of the JPY–USD exchange rate between November 2001 and December 2001

Allianz AG, Dresdner Bank and Commerzbank, took a position through options. The objective of the positions was not to anticipate any increase or decrease in price terms but to profit from higher volatility in the price of the securities.

In March, Allianz announced that it was selling its holding in Dresdner Bank to Deutsche Bank in exchange for a part of its retail network. On the day of the merger announcement, the share price of Allianz rose rapidly, while the prices of Deutsche Bank and Dresdner Bank increased rapidly as well, but then fell. The merger was cancelled in April, leading to a fall in the share price of Allianz and an increase in the share prices of Deutsche Bank and Dresdner Bank. Figure 3.89 shows the corresponding share price movements.

The interest in this example lies in the fact that the position was not taken in order to profit from an increase or decrease in the security prices, but on an increase in volatility in a German sector due to a political decision.

18.4 Advantages and drawbacks

The main advantage of macro investing is that the strategy does not focus on one particular market or one type of security based on a formalized investment process. Managers have much freedom, enabling them to invest in any set of opportunities and/or tendencies that emerge. This is of particular importance in the case of macro funds. In addition, macro funds are easy to understand, as the bulk of their portfolio is made of a

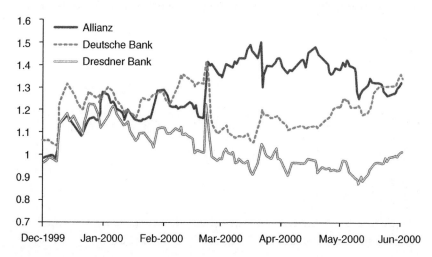

Figure 3.89 Evolution of the share price of Allianz, Deutsche Bank and Dresdner Bank in 2000

few bets on equities, interest rates, currencies or commodities. Finally, during volatile market conditions this strategy tends to perform well, as managers will invest in securities other than equities, or may even go short in equities.

However, macro funds are usually seen a particularly risky because of the difficulty in timing investments in them. This image is reinforced by the large profits or losses that some funds faced over very short periods of time. Many press articles waxed lyrical about the large gains made by the Soros Quantum fund or the Robertson Tiger fund during their period of glory – only to focus on their impressive losses a few years later. In addition, macro managers tend to use leverage extensively. This, combined with the concentration of ideas, explains the relative high volatility of the strategy. Every potential investor should be aware of the fact that they can make significant returns over a short period of time by investing in macro funds, but that they can also lose 10, 30 or even 50 per cent within a few months when the market is unfavourable to the managers they invest with.

18.5   Performance

Hedge Fund Research, Inc. defines macro managers as:[42]

> *investment managers which trade a broad range of strategies in which the investment process is predicated on movements in underlying economic variables and the impact these have on equity, fixed income, hard currency and commodity markets. Managers employ a variety of techniques, both discretionary and systematic analysis, combinations of top down and bottom up theses, quantitative and fundamental approaches and long and short term holding periods. Although some strategies employ RV techniques, Macro strategies are distinct from RV strategies in that the primary investment thesis is predicated on predicted or future movements in the underlying instruments, rather than realization of a valuation discrepancy between securities. In a similar way, while both Macro and equity hedge managers may hold equity securities, the overriding investment thesis is predicated on the impact movements in underlying macroeconomic variables may have on security prices, as opposed to EH, in which the fundamental characteristics of the company are the most significant and integral to investment thesis.*

Figure 3.90 shows the evolution of US$100 invested in the HFRI Macro (Total) index since January 1990 compared with other similar investments in the HFRI Fund Weighted Composite index, the equity market, represented by MSCI World, and the bond market, represented by the Barclays Aggregate Bond index.

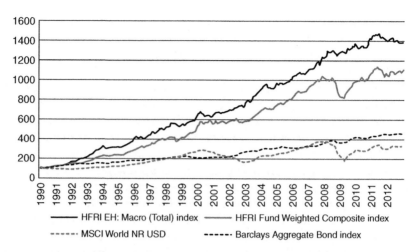

Figure 3.90   Evolution of US$100 invested in the HFRI EH: Macro (Total) index
Source: Based on numbers obtained from Hedge Fund Research, Inc.

An investment of US$100 in the HFRI Macro (Total) index would have become US$1390 by the end of 2012. The same investment in the equity market, bond market or global hedge fund market would have become US$1059, US$322 or US$453 respectively.

The HFRI Macro (Total) index offered an average annual return of 12.7 per cent per year over the whole period, as against 6.8 per cent for the equity market and 7.2 per cent for the bond market. More recently, it has offered 6 per cent per year on average over the last decade and 2.5 per cent per year on average over the last five years. These returns have fallen significantly over recent times – interestingly, though, not because of a difficult 2008 this time, but because several years were slightly positive and more recent years have been negative.

Volatility has been relatively low, at 7.6 per cent. It has been lower over the last decade and the last five years, at 5.3 per cent. This is significantly lower than equities, which ranged between 15 and 20 per cent depending on the period in question, and in line with or lower than bonds depending on the period covered.

Table 3.34 shows the yearly returns, the mean annual return, the standard deviation, the minimum annual return, the maximum annual return and the spread of the strategies relative to the comparative indices. It leads to the following remarks:

– Over the 23 years covered, the HFRI Macro (Total) index was negative for three years over the period: 1994 (–4.3 per cent), 2011 (–4.2 per

Table 3.34 Performance statistics of the HFRI Macro (Total) index and comparative indices

	HFRI Macro (Total) Index	HFRI Fund Weighted Composite Index	MSCI World NR USD	Barclays Aggregate Bond Index	Performance vs. HFRI	Performance vs. MSCI World	Performance vs. Barclays Aggregate
1990	12.6%	5.8%	−17.0%	12.7%	6.8%	29.6%	−0.2%
1991	46.7%	32.2%	18.3%	16.0%	14.5%	28.4%	30.6%
1992	27.2%	21.2%	−5.2%	5.8%	6.0%	32.4%	21.4%
1993	53.3%	30.9%	22.5%	11.1%	22.4%	30.8%	42.2%
1994	−4.3%	4.1%	5.1%	0.2%	−8.4%	−9.4%	−4.5%
1995	29.3%	21.5%	20.7%	19.7%	7.8%	8.6%	9.7%
1996	9.3%	21.1%	13.5%	4.9%	−11.8%	−4.2%	4.4%
1997	18.8%	16.8%	15.8%	3.8%	2.0%	3.1%	15.0%
1998	6.2%	2.6%	24.3%	13.7%	3.6%	−18.1%	−7.5%
1999	17.6%	31.3%	24.9%	−5.2%	−13.7%	−7.3%	22.8%
2000	2.0%	5.0%	−13.2%	3.2%	−3.0%	15.1%	−1.2%
2001	6.9%	4.6%	−16.8%	1.6%	2.2%	23.7%	5.3%
2002	7.4%	−1.5%	−19.9%	16.5%	8.9%	27.3%	−9.1%
2003	21.4%	19.5%	33.1%	12.5%	1.9%	−11.7%	8.9%
2004	4.6%	9.0%	14.7%	9.3%	−4.4%	−10.1%	−4.6%
2005	2.4%	3.5%	4.5%	1.3%	−1.1%	−2.1%	1.1%
2006	8.2%	12.9%	20.1%	6.6%	−4.7%	−11.9%	1.5%
2007	11.1%	10.0%	9.0%	9.5%	1.1%	2.1%	1.6%
2008	4.8%	−19.0%	−40.7%	4.8%	23.9%	45.5%	0.0%
2009	4.3%	20.0%	30.0%	6.9%	−15.6%	−25.6%	−2.6%
2010	8.1%	10.2%	11.8%	5.5%	−2.2%	−3.7%	2.5%
2011	−4.2%	−5.3%	−5.5%	5.6%	1.1%	1.4%	−9.8%
2012	−0.1%	6.4%	15.8%	4.3%	−6.4%	−15.9%	−4.4%
Mean annual return (whole period)	12.8%	11.4%	7.2%	7.4%	1.3%	5.6%	5.4%
Volatility (whole period)	7.6%	7.0%	15.6%	5.5%	NA	NA	NA
Meanannual return 2003–2012	6.1%	6.7%	9.3%	6.6%	−0.7%	−3.2%	−0.6%
Volatility 2003–2012	5.3%	6.5%	16.2%	6.1%	NA	NA	NA
Meanaverage return 2007–2012	2.6%	2.5%	2.3%	5.4%	0.1%	0.3%	−2.8%
Volatility 2007–2012	5.3%	7.4%	19.4%	6.4%	NA	NA	NA
Minimum annual return	−4.3%	−19.0%	−40.7%	−5.2%	−15.6%	−25.6%	−9.8%
Maximum annual return	53.3%	32.2%	33.1%	19.7%	23.9%	45.5%	42.2%

Source: Based on data from Hedge Fund Research, Inc.

cent) and 2012 (–0.5 per cent). The equity index finished down in 6 years out of 23 including the 2000–2002 bear market, 2008 and 2011. The bond index suffered negative returns for one year only, in 1999.
- The maximum annual returns of the HFRI Macro (Total) index were achieved in 1993 (53.3 per cent), 1991 (46.7 per cent) and 1995 (29.3 per cent). Although these numbers are strong, most of the strong annual returns were achieved during the first half of the period under review.
- The spread in returns between the HFRI Macro (Total) index and the comparative indices has been volatile. The strategy outperformed the global hedge fund index times 13 out of 23, the equity index 12 times and the bond index 8 times. The largest outperformance of the HFRI Macro (Total) index relative to the equity index was 45.5 per cent, in 2008, while the largest underperformance was 25.6 per cent, in 2009. Relative to the bond index, the largest outperformance was achieved in 1993 at 42.2 per cent, and the largest underperformance was 9.8 per cent, in 2011.

19 Commodity trading advisors

Commonly called CTA or managed futures, such funds invest exclusively in futures. These funds are not always classified as hedge funds by industry professionals, but most academic studies include CTA and hedge funds in their analysis.[43] CTA managers take a position by applying advanced technical analysis tools. They look for a trend in the market and take a position through futures aiming to profit from the trend continuing. They usually invest in futures on financial instruments with a focus on commodities.

This strategy emerged in the 1970s. At the outset, the management techniques used were basic and the moving average was the starting point. The industry grew rapidly in the early 1980s when two well-known commodity traders, Richard Dennis and William Eckhardt, decided to determine whether traders' abilities were inherent, genetically inherited, or could be learned. Eckhardt was convinced that everything was a question of innate ability, while Dennis thought that anybody could be trained. This is what they did:

- They hired 23 people out of a set of 1000, and trained them to become a trader in two weeks.
- The strategy was based exclusively on chart analysis, and the traders were to buy when the price rose past certain limits and sell on historical lows being reached.
- Over the following weeks the traders earned on average over 80 per cent annualized and generated profits of over US$100 million.

This experience proved that mechanical/technical tools can create systematic returns as long as the rules are applied consistently. Since then the techniques have evolved, and in the early 1990s a true revolution happened with the emergence of an analysis program that automatically generated basic indicators. Since then, developments have accelerated and the largest CTAs now have over 20 to 30 PhDs improving the models.

19.1 Methodology

CTAs are funds managed quantitatively, using complex mathematical models implemented automatically by very powerful computers. The multi-model approach usually integrates trend-following models, models based on fundamental and econometric data, and in some cases models based on behavioural finance. For a few years, the orders have been carried out automatically by the machines without human intervention; on a day-to-day basis, staff are in place mainly to check that everything is running as expected and to update the current models in order to improve performance. The largest teams include dozens of researchers that continuously look for new ways to automatically and systematically make money on the futures markets, potentially including new data, new models or new investment horizons.

At the start, the specialists look for a trend. This can be done either on a discretionary (less common, and using mainly qualitative data) or a systematic basis (which focuses on quantitative data). Whichever technique they favour, the managers have the same objective: to identify future market trends.

Examples of well-known techniques include:[44]

- *Autocorrelation*: the correlation of a variable with itself over time. This technique enables the model to determine to what extent previous prices can help to predict future prices.
- *Bets on volatility spreads*: when price movements of an asset exceed a certain value.
- *Positions scale in integrating volatility*: to gauge the size of a position on the basis of volatility, reducing it in periods of high volatility and vice versa.
- *Conditional execution*: signals are placed in the market with predefined conditions such as *buy if the volatility is below X and the price over 100*.
- *Carry trade*: an analysis of the difference in interest rate and implementation of a position in the currency market.
- *Back-to-the-mean*: an anticipation strategy that aims to identify significant market reversals.

- *Probability signals – position weight*: if the probability of a directional change is favourable, the size of the position is increased.
- *Algorithm management/high frequency trading*: traders are replaced by computers that carry out transactions automatically, usually at a high frequency.
- *Non-parametrical approach*: reduction of dependence on a temporal horizon, to offer more stable returns.
- *Dynamic sector allocation*: allocation to various market sectors such as commodities or currencies, adjusted on the basis of the opportunity and/or the trends.
- *Behavioural finance*: a strategy based on identifying recurrent errors in the markets generated by human behaviour.
- *Fundamental methodology*: econometric models that value some markets relative to the economic cycle.

In the CTA world there are various sub-strategies, the main ones being trend-following, trend reversals and contrarian funds. The first aim to profit from medium- to long-term trends in various markets, and look for opportunities within various time horizons; short-term positions are usually taken for three to five days – even within a single day in some cases – or they can extend to a few weeks. Trend reversal funds aim to profit from turning points in the market. Contrarian funds aim to sell at the peak of the market and buy at the bottom. As illustrated in Figure 3.91, various sub-strategies intervene at different moments.

A special feature of this strategy is that in some cases the positions will be implemented for a few weeks or months while in other cases they will be changed several times in a single day. In practice it is key to analyse

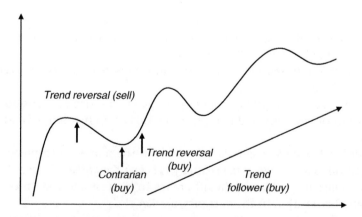

Figure 3.91   Timing of the main sub-strategies

each CTA on a case-by-case basis because there can be significant differences between funds available.

In terms of risk management, each fund will also have its volatility budget. Some teams pay particular attention to limiting the downside risk through automatic sales or by not entering into positions seen as risky – but in most cases the aim is to identify trends and, when a trend is identified, to profit from it. This means that positions, and the risk allocation to them, tend to be relatively important. The next step is to take a position by buying or selling futures. Funds tend to be diversified in the futures market; the positions will be identified by the model, and the management team will have a more passive role, merely checking that the positions taken are in line with the objective and the profile of the fund. In the relatively rare case of discretionary management, the role of the manager is more important. Some managers will consider the whole spectrum of futures available – from crops to interest rates – while others will be more focused.

Managers tend to take long and short positions in futures on indices, and they define the maximum level of loss they intend to support. When this level is reached, the whole portfolio is usually closed down. Managed futures funds have a high leverage built into them, because futures are traded on a margin – unlike with cash equities, it is only the margin, ranging from less than 1 per cent to 5 per cent of the notional value of the future, that is paid to the broker.

19.2 Short-term traders

Some managed futures funds apply a strategy commonly called "short-term traders." This strategy is similar to that of the CTA because it is systematic – but it does not always invest only in futures but in some case also invests in equities, liquid exchange-traded funds and indices. Opportunities are identified systematically, and they are filtered by a technical system to estimate the potential of each opportunity. When short-term opportunities are interesting, the cash is invested. But these kinds of funds are not always invested. Short-term traders frequently remain in cash for a few days or weeks in a month, so the level of risk of the strategy is limited to the time period when the fund is invested.

As an illustration consider a fund that combines three strategies in order to capture short-term market movements.

– **Strategy 1**: based on the S&P500 and very liquid exchange-traded funds. It builds a portfolio of oversold shares at predefined buy and sell levels. This strategy increases exposure to equities when markets fall over the short term, and sells positions short when they recover a predefined portion of their losses. Positions are usually maintained for three to four days.

- **Strategy 2**: follows 2000 liquid shares and liquid exchange-traded funds. The strategy buys shares that start the day as normal but fall rapidly during the day; the aim is to profit from intraday V-shape movements.
- **Strategy 3**: aims to hedge the portfolio. It maintains a portfolio hedge in case of an important market fall without any recovery.

19.3   Illustrations

We give three examples. We start with a basic trend-following strategy that aims to illustrate the concept. The second example presents a moving-average strategy. The final example is based on a more complex two-entry model.

19.3.1   Trend-following strategy

Commodity trading advisors are managed quantitatively; the models identify trends in the markets and managers take positions based on these trends. We present a typical trend-following strategy, with two segments. The first looks for medium-term trends (from a few weeks to a few months) while the second looks for shorter-term movements (from a few days to a few weeks). It covers various indices and takes position through trackers.[45] The core principle of the strategy is that market volatility is higher than its average return.

Early in July 2002, the model predicted a decrease in the Russell 2000.[46] Companies grouped in the Russell 2000 represented about 8 per cent of the capitalization of the Russell 3000. The manager took a short position in the Russell 2000 ishares tracker on 1 July.[47] By 3 July the value of the tracker had fallen by one standard deviation, and the model recommended to partially close the positions because a reversal was possible. The reversal started but a new downside trend started a few days later. The model recommended increasing the short position on 16 July. On 23 July a new floor at two standard deviations below the average monthly price was reached, and the model recommended another partial hedge. The manager closed the position on 31 July. The chronology of the events is reported in Figure 3.92 while the evolution of the Russell 2000 ishares is reported in Figure 3.93.

Bear in mind that this position in the Russell 2000 is a part of a more global book that usually combines shorter-term models like the one presented here with longer-term trend-following models.

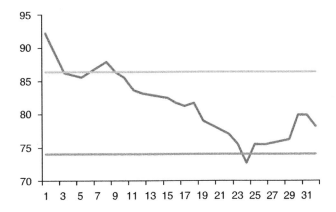

Figure 3.92 CTA strategy illustration

Figure 3.93 Evolution of Russell 2000 ishares in July 2002

19.3.2 Moving-average strategy[48]

Trend-following systems come in many different forms, depending on the manager's beliefs on how to successfully capture price trends in futures contracts. However, the common factor is that the systematic trend followers use past and present price data to decide whether they should go long, go short, or stay out of a market. The most commonly mentioned indicators for trend followers are moving-average systems, breakout systems and Bollinger bands. Here we focus on one version of the most intuitive system, using moving averages. Figure 3.94 shows the price of the sugar future contract, a fast-moving average (for each day, the past 25-day average price of the sugar futures contract) and a slow-moving average (the past 100-day average price of the sugar futures contract). When the fast-moving average rises above the slow-moving average, the system generates a buy signal and when the fast-moving average drops below the slow-moving average the system generates a sell signal. This is of course a very simplified picture of how trend-followers work; however, the basic principles are similar. Figure 3.94 shows the position resulting from a system with a number of different moving averages. When the model examines the graph, it sees that when a trend develops the system starts

Figure 3.94 Evolution of the price of a sugar futures contract, a slow- and a fast-moving average

participating in the market and when a reversal occurs, the system also reverses to an opposite position.

19.3.3   Two-entry model[49]

As presented in the heart of the section, the underlying hypothesis of trend-following strategies is that on average past trends tend to persist, so they can be used as a predictor of future returns. The converse scenario, perfect for this strategy, is a mean-reverting market that oscillates in a period that is the double of the window used to detect the trend. In practice, the fundamental question is the choice of time window used to measure past trends; a long term-return indicator (one year or more), medium-term (two to three months) or a shorter-term (weeks, days or intraday). By using a shorter window one can expect to capture the actual trend in the market more accurately and to detect changes in market regimes (rally, turnarounds) early enough. However, the shorter the window, the more volatile the indicator, so the higher the chance of being exposed to false signals. This will also lead to an increase in the turnover of the strategy, which will more quickly lose a mean-reverting market.

   The model presented analyses 50 futures markets, selected because of their liquidity and diversification benefits. It includes:

– equity indices
– futures short-term interest rates
– futures in 2–30 years sovereign debt

– futures in metals (copper, aluminium, gold and so on)
– currency futures
– futures in agricultural commodities (cotton, sugar, soybean, corn, wheat and so on)
– futures in energy (gas, oil and so on).

This model detects trends from quantitative signals, and it aims to detect the direction of each trend (bullish, bearish or neutral) as well as its intensity. From there the allocation module and the risk control aggregate those signals to create a definitive portfolio. Regarding risk control and allocation, the exposure to a contract can be expressed in nominal to the net asset value. To enable risk comparison between positions on such differentiated asset classes, two complementary measures are used:

– the margin of equity of the position, expressed as a proportion of the net asset value of the fund
– the volatility of the profit and loss on the position, expressed as a proportion of the net asset value of the fund.

The total risk budget of the fund is distributed between the contracts. The main objective is to profit from a diversification effect, and to control the volatility of the fund in order for it to stay close to the target – around 14 per cent in this case. The portfolio is adjusted daily depending on the movements of the signals and the risk indicators.

As an illustration, we consider the positions taken in gold during the year 2011, as shown in Figure 3.95. The positions are taken on futures in 100 troy ounces of gold (equivalent to three kilograms) listed on the COMEX,[50] whose price is normalized at 100 at the start of the year. Figure 3.95 shows the future price, the volatility and the trend over the same period. Figure 3.96 shows the exposure, risk and profit and loss of the fund on the transactions.

A significant trend is detected during the month of March. On this basis, the model takes a moderate exposure representing close to 1 per cent of the fund assets in nominal terms and ten basis points in volatility. This position is increased between June and July, representing up to 10 per cent of the nominal exposure and 1.2 per cent contribution to the volatility of the fund. From August onward, the volatility increased significantly at the same time as the trend signal decreased strongly. For a similar and constant level of risk, the model started to reduce its exposure.

This significant decrease in exposure enabled the risk of loss to be limited when the markets turned, as they did in October. The following

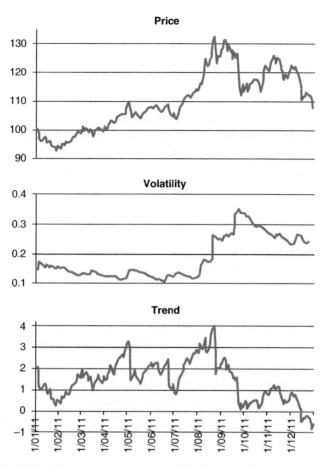

Figure 3.95   Gold, 100 troy ounce price in 2011

movements led to smaller positions in more volatile market conditions for the rest of the year. Tables 3.35 and 3.36 show the exposure taken over the year (normalized for the level of risk) and the profit and loss over the second half of the year; they include not only the gold position but a series of other future markets (shown in the first column). They indicate how complicated such a portfolio can be. The strategy aims to keep its level of risk stable but, as shown in Table 3.35, the exposure can vary considerably over time. From August onward, the level of risk taken decreased to compensate for the increase in the correlation between assets and the increase in volatility. The performance was worst from mid-September to mid-November; this period corresponded to a volatile market without any visible trends.

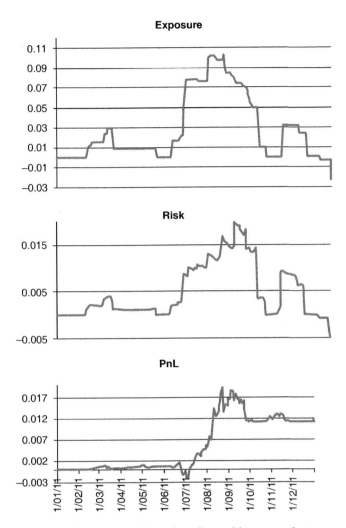

Figure 3.96   The fund exposure, risk and profits and losses on the transaction

19.4 Advantages and drawbacks

CTA are amongst the most liquid vehicles available, enabling them to move rapidly and at a limited cost. In addition such funds are highly regulated. Another advantage is that there is no problem at all in the implementation of short selling and in some markets there are even certain tax advantages related to investing in futures. On the performance side, some authors stress the ability of these funds to be positively correlated with equities during up markets and negatively correlated during

Table 3.35 Profit and loss over the year (29 July 2011–30 December 2011)

	Expo	Expo Vol.	Vol. Contrib.	Cum.	30-12	16-12	02-12	18-11	04-11	21-10	07-10	23-09	09-09	26-08	12-08	29-07	15-07	01-07	17-06	03-06	20-05	06-05	22-04	08-04	25-03	11-03	25-02	11-02	28-01	14-01
pnls.per	501.59	5.38	12.32	141	113	277	15	135	-165	-67	-394	-427	1	225	171	491	298	-115	-186	268	29	-226	284	16	-451	-34	49	155	-214	-106
LONG.GILT.FUTURE.1	43.99	3.35	0.59	853	27	92	-25	18	71	-22	-80	26	83	14	220	138	222	-112	59	33	20	64	74	-52	-1	-2	0	-1	-3	-11
US.10YR.NOTE.FUT.1	27.56	1.54	0.24	409	3	21	7	0	11	-11	-28	1	22	6	85	28	137	-93	28	91	22	68	45	-23	-15	14	22	-29	2	3
US.5YR.NOTE..CBT..1	128.37	3.36	0.69	378	6	31	7	-5	25	4	-24	-7	14	4	63	35	112	-64	29	74	23	45	20	-8	-12	11	17	-29	4	6
NATURAL.GAS.FUTR.1	-12.18	-3.73	2.55	356	68	155	-39	142	-9	-47	103	2	-13	23	4	38	-21	2	10	0	0	-28	-104	123	-194	41	-26	113	34	-20
US.LONG.BOND.CBT..1	1.03	0.14	0.02	254	0	2	-1	1	3	-19	-27	28	39	13	63	21	69	-66	13	35	11	53	39	-27	-1	3	27	-22	4	-6
EURO.BOBL.FUTURE.1	15.99	0.75	0.11	152	4	17	-5	-9	27	-3	-19	-3	35	22	75	27	40	-16	0	0	-1	0	-1	0	0	1	0	-2	-20	-23
EURO.BUND.FUTURE.1	14.4	1.29	0.18	122	10	11	-5	-5	12	-5	-13	–	28	14	58	26	39	-9	4	0	0	0	2	3	0	0	0	-1	-31	-11
GOLD.100.OZ.FUTR.1	-2.31	-0.55	-0.1	111	-1	0	-5	-6	12	0	-2	-64	25	29	68	23	54	-29	2	0	1	-1	0	0	-2	1	5	-1	0	0
CAC40.10.EURO.FUT.1	0	0	0	93	-10	66	108	146	-64	22	-5	4	3	-19	13	3	-22	9	-1	-2	3	3	7	-65	-68	-75	45	19	3	33
COCOA.FUTURE.1	-7.41	-2.49	0.15	93	0	0	-8	-12	10	1	-3	51	0	1	-2	0	0	-63	-6	0	3	-79	50	36	4	32	22	-1	0	0
SILVER.FUTURE.1	-0.01	0	0	51	0	-5	0	10	20	-3	0	0	0	-5	20	0	0	0	0	0	-13	-74	-6	43	0	34	17	0	-1	-1
WTI.CRUDE.FUTURE.1	0	0	0	43	0	0	0	0	0	0	-2	-8	2	14	40	-4	-17	0	0	0	0	1	0	0	-4	-3	-3	3	0	2
DAX.INDEX.FUTURE.1	0	0	0	34	0	0	0	0	0	0	0	0	9	0	20	-2	-36	18	5	-11	5	0	0	0	0	0	-9	3	-1	25
EURO.STOXX.50.1	-0.02	-0.01	0	20	0	0	0	0	0	0	0	0	0	0	-70	-35	-6	14	-1	-6	-11	0	0	0	0	0	0	14	7	22
DJIA.MINI.e.CBOT.1	5.85	1.3	0.45	18	14	-4	0	0	0	0	0	0	0	0	1	48	43	56	-12	-36	-31	14	11	17	18	-5	-14	55	9	0
JPN.YEN.CURR.FUT.1	53.93	3.56	0.77	9	58	11	-71	57	-175	59	-11	11	-15	1	0	0	-13	-22	-36	5	-11	35	81	-91	-23	2	0	0	0	-25
JPN.10Y.BOND.TSE..1	0	0	0	3	0	1	-19	10	9	-11	-1	5	10	-3	0	0	0	-19	5	34	-31	53	60	-62	4	2	0	0	0	0
BP.CURRENCY.FUT.1	0	0	0	-1	-1	0	0	0	0	0	0	3	10	1	-5	-5	-27	0	25	17	-2	-8	11	9	-4	0	0	-38	-6	0
FTSE.100.IDX.FUT.1	0	0	0	-10	0	0	0	0	0	0	0	0	-4	1	6	36	30	0	17	4	35	-7	-10	0	-3	-2	-1	0	-1	1
SUGAR..11..WORLD..1	-5.89	-1.71	0.23	-11	3	0	2	-24	-10	17	-12	-8	-25	21	-59	-1	-25	54	-21	-16	0	-51	4	-23	-30	4	2	3	32	-13
HANG.SENG.IDX.FUT.1	-10.01	-2.69	0.72	-15	-12	41	-33	51	-67	2	-6	44	-25	59	-1	4	-11	34	-16	16	0	0	2	8	-9	16	8	-43	-30	48
MEXICAN.PESO.FUT.1	0	0	0	-16	0	0	0	0	0	-3	-6	44	-6	-1	-77	-8	10	0	-27	-1	3	-3	13	17	-3	8	8	-30	-11	44
SOYBEAN.OIL.FUTR.1	-4.58	-0.94	0.01	-22	-22	6	8	5	-3	-4	-5	3	0	0	-7	-9	-3	27	23	5	7	-12	-8	15	5	-9	-13	7	19	-3
COFFEE..C..FUTURE.1	0	0	0	-25	10	-9	-22	17	-41	44	8	-3	5	8	-1	0	0	-5	-21	19	-95	-21	27	9	-18	11	22	8	19	-11
LME.PRI.ALUM.FUTR.1	-7.17	-1.34	-0.17	-25	-10	-4	0	0	-13	5	-2	-72	-20	117	0	0	-15	15	-15	0	-21	-33	8	15	12	-5	1	15	2	0
X90DAY.EURO..FUTR.1	0	0	0	-32	0	0	0	-54	4	12	-25	0	0	0	-12	8	-59	11	-25	-2	2	3	-1	17	-4	3	6	0	2	2
IBEX.35.INDX.FUTR.1	0	0	0	-33	0	0	0	0	0	0	-3	0	0	0	-14	10	6	23	0	4	-13	0	0	0	0	-9	0	3	15	0
COPPER.FUTURE.1	-0.66	-0.22	-0.03	-33	-1	0	0	-1	0	0	0	-17	-5	4	-3	0	0	10	-12	1	2	-45	-10	8	18	0	0	2	15	0

Instrument	Expo	Expo Vol.	Vol. Contrib.	Cum.																										
PALLADIUM.FUTURE.1	0	0	0	-36	0	4	6	-38	1	-4	6	-7	-4	0	0	0	0	0	0	0	0	0	0	0	0	0	0
EURO.SCHATZ.FUT.1	5,25	0,07	0,01	-39	0	1	1	0	4	0	-10	-3	24	4	72	6	7	-10	0	0	-3	0	-8	2	0	-16	-5	-2	-38	-65
X90DAY.EURO..FUTR.3	0	0	0	-41	0	0	0	-85	35	16	-84	1	-11	-16	27	15	-24	4	-17	16	22	12	24	13	-16	13	38	-20	12	-1
SOYBEAN.FUTURE.1	-9,14	-1,83	0,23	-45	-53	5	18	16	0	-1	0	-12	0	17	-6	-8	39	-11	-37	14	1	-25	-5	13	9	-16	-28	9	-11	9
CHF.CURRENCY.FUT.1	-0,9	-0,12	0	-52	0	-16	1	-5	-4	-13	8	-7	-92	-60	48	51	17	0	-6	19	21	2	5	0	0	0	0	0	0	0
COTTON.NO.2.FUTR.1	-8,46	-2,21	0,13	-56	-52	63	12	37	4	-33	2	-63	35	4	-3	3	-37	-13	-34	12	0	-43	-15	-3	-3	15	-1	20	22	-3
C..CURRENCY.FUT.1	0	0	0	-61	0	0	0	0	-1	0	0	0	0	0	-54	-6	0	1	0	0	36	-1	0	0	0	0	0	0	0	0
CORN.FUTURE.1	-3,42	-0,82	0,03	-67	-47	13	16	4	-2	-1	-2	-25	-2	3	3	-1	17	-36	-13	-3	0	-33	-2	6	2	-5	0	3	0	0
GASOLINE.RBOB.FUT.1	17,84	5,11	1,81	-71	115	-78	81	-93	-1	0	8	-33	-1	9	-76	-4	3	1	-1	0	6	0	0	0	-9	3	12	-1	-19	12
X90DAY.EURO..FUTR.2	0	0	0	-91	0	0	31	-14	0	0	-67	10	-15	-5	-14	14	-42	15	-29	2	6	6	0	24	-11	18	16	-3	7	-1
LIVE.CATTLE.FUTR.1	1	0,16	-0,02	-94	-1	-50	0	-68	16	16	82	-35	11	-111	26	13	-17	3	0	0	1	-41	-25	-12	22	16	52	-1	-19	12
PLATINUM.FUTURE.1	-0,1	-0,03	0	-102	0	0	0	0	0	-1	-20	-70	1	-12	1	19	0	0	0	0	0	0	0	0	0	0	0	0	0	0
USD.ZAR.CURR.FUT.1	0	0	0	-105	0	0	0	0	-1	-9	0	-28	-8	11	-52	0	-15	3	-2	8	-2	0	0	0	0	0	0	0	-5	-16
NIKKEI.225..SGX..1	-7,79	-1,41	0,26	-114	-4	20	-26	41	-11	-10	-30	31	4	11	2	-24	0	-1	0	-3	1	0	0	-8	-74	-44	-21	9	-6	4
S.P500.EMINI.FUT.1	12,45	3,05	1,05	-141	23	-9	0	2	0	0	-2	0	-11	-11	-164	-17	57	-20	-24	-24	-5	3	6	9	6	-8	-6	41	-14	29
EURO.FX.CURR.FUT.1	0	0	0	-142	0	0	0	0	-2	0	-3	-16	-69	23	2	0	0	0	0	0	-5	-9	6	4	0	0	0	0	0	-72
A..CURRENCY.FUT.1	0	0	0	-144	0	0	0	0	-5	0	-6	-82	-10	28	-108	-12	0	0	-3	0	0	0	0	0	0	0	0	0	0	0
WHEAT.FUTURE.CBT..1	-5,69	-1,7	0,3	-151	-64	36	-8	26	-5	-57	7	-8	-6	5	1	0	16	-38	-32	-13	10	0	0	0	0	0	0	2	0	0
X3MO.EURO.EURIBOR.1	20,7	0,13	0,01	-187	1	-1	3	-3	2	-1	-35	0	38	-15	51	5	16	0	0	-15	-3	-4	-8	6	0	-75	-53	25	-22	-85
HEATING.OIL..FUTR.1	19,36	4,06	1,44	-188	30	-123	-24	-23	15	23	-31	-86	-2	7	10	2	2	0	0	0	0	0	0	0	-3	3	9	0	2	4
NASDAQ.100.E.MINI.1	10,57	2,46	0,83	-215	14	-20	1	-3	-8	-4	-48	-27	-12	-7	-162	1	1	50	-26	-18	-9	-1	18	6	5	-13	-13	46	-24	44
EURO.JPY.FUTURE.1	0	0	0	-229	0	0	0	0	0	-3	13	18	7	0	-14	-7	-40	19	-19	10	4	-26	-17	2	-33	0	-2	-17	-70	-55
EURO.GBP.FUTURE.1	-37,55	-2,61	-0,15	-268	4	0	0	0	-23	-6	-16	-7	-44	10	10	-10	-106	49	-15	4	7	-43	-1	0	0	0	-14	-1	-53	-2

Expo = exposure, Expo Vol. = exposure volatility, Vol. Contrib. = volatility contribution and Cum. = cumulative contribution.

Table 3.36 Risk (29 July 2011–30 December 2011)

volx.per	P&L	Mean	30-12	16-12	02-12	18-11	04-11	21-10	07-10	23-09	09-09	26-08	12-08	29-07	15-07	01-07	17-06	03-06	20-05	06-05	22-04	08-04	25-03	11-03	25-02	11-02	28-01	14-01
volx.per	141	27.38	4.1	4.8	9	18	17	18	19	18	22	30	34	36	39	49	49	42	37	33	32	33	29	28	27	25	23	22
GASOLINE.RBOB.FUT.1	-71	1.21	5.4	4.8	4.6	0.7	1.9	3.8	0.4	1.1	1	1.3	2.5	1.2	0.3	0.1	0.1	0	2.5	2.6	2.1	1.8	1.6	0.2	0.3	0.3	0.7	1.1
LONG.GILT.FUTURE.1	853	2.88	3.6	3.9	4.1	3.8	4.3	4.5	3.3	3.3	3.4	3.7	5.1	5.7	5.3	4.1	3.1	2.4	2.5	2.6	2.4	1.8	1.6	0.2	0	0	0.2	0.5
JPN.YEN.CURR.FUT.1	9	2.11	3.5	4.1	4.4	5	4.6	3.9	3.8	2.1	1.5	1.3	1.6	1.3	1.4	1.5	1.7	1.7	1.9	2.2	2.4	2.5	2.1	0.1	0	0	0	0.5
HEATING.OIL.FUTR.1	-188	0.99	3.4	3.6	3.4	0.7	2.2	3.9	3.8	2.4	0.8	0.8	0.6	0.6	0.8	0.7	0.1	0	0	0	0	0	0	0.1	0.3	0.2	0.2	0.2
US.5YR.NOTE.CBT..1	378	1.49	3.1	2.2	1.1	1.2	1.3	0.7	1	0.9	0.9	1.1	1.6	1.7	3.2	2.7	2.3	2.2	2	1.3	1.3	0.9	0.9	0.8	0.7	0.8	1	1
S.P500.EMINI.FUT.1	-141	1.01	2.7	0.9	0	0.1	0.1	0.1	0	1.5	1.5	0.7	1.2	1.7	1.6	1.5	1.4	1.2	1	1	1.3	1.3	1.3	0.9	0.9	1	1.1	1.1
NASDAQ.100.E.MINI..1	-215	1.13	2.3	1.5	0.3	0.5	0.9	0.5	2	1.3	1.3	0.2	1.2	1.8	1.5	1.1	0.9	1	1	1.1	1.2	1.3	1.2	1.1	1.1	1.1	1.2	1.2
US.10YR.NOTE.FUT.1	409	1.61	1.4	1	0.6	0.6	0.7	0.6	1.2	1.2	1.2	1.3	1.5	1.8	3.7	3.3	2.8	2.5	2.4	1.9	1.9	2	2.1	1.5	1.5	1	1	0.9
DJIA.MINI.e.CBOT.1	18	0.93	1.3	0.5	0.1	0	0	0	0	0.1	0.8	0	0.5	1.6	1.5	1.5	1.4	1.5	1.4	1.5	1.5	1.7	1.8	1.5	1.2	1	1.4	1.2
EURO.BUND.FUTURE.1	122	0.59	0.9	0.5	0.6	0.4	0.6	0.4	0.6	1	0.8	0.7	1.5	1.9	1.5	1.2	0.4	0.2	0	0	0	0	0	0	0	0	0	1.2
EURO.BOBL.FUTURE.1	152	0.71	0.8	0.8	0.8	0.8	0.9	0.8	1	1.2	0.8	1.4	2.1	2.5	1.3	0.7	0.1	0.1	0	0	0.5	0.6	0	0	0	0.1	0.6	1.1
COFFEE...C..FUTURE.1	-25	1.43	0.6	0.3	1.1	2.4	2.2	2.4	0	1.5	1.3	3.9	0.5	0.6	3.8	0.9	1	0.9	2.7	2.2	1.6	0.6	0.5	1.3	1.2	1.3	1.3	1.4
US.LONG.BOND.CBT..1	254	1.24	0.1	0.1	0.2	0.2	0.2	0.2	1.9	1.8	1.8	1.8	1.1	1.3	1.8	2	2.3	1.8	1.9	1.6	1.6	1.7	1.9	1.5	1.1	1.1	1.3	1.4
X3MO.EURO.EURIBOR.1	-187	0.45	0.2	0.2	0.2	0.2	0.1	0.1	0.8	0.8	1.1	1.2	1.1	0.5	1.1	0	0	0	-0	-1	-1	-1	-0	0.4	0.4	0.5	2.1	0.4
EURO.SCHATZ.FUT.1	-39	0.5	0.1	0.1	0.1	0.2	0.1	0.1	0.4	0.4	0.4	1.1	1.4	1.4	0.4	0.3	0	0	-0	-0	-0	-0	-0	0.2	0.2	1.3	1.6	1.7
LIVE.CATTLE.FUTR.1	-94	1.78	0.1	0.5	2.5	2.7	3.1	3.6	4.4	3.1	1.2	2.9	1.6	1	0.9	0.9	0	0	0	0	0	0	0	0.2	1.3	1.6	1.6	1.6
USD.ZAR.CURR.FUT.1	-105	-0.28	0.1	0	0	-0	-0	-0	-1	-1	-1	-1	-1	0	-1	0.4	0.3	-0	-0	-0	-0	-0	0	0.2	0	0	-0	-0
JPN.10Y.BOND.TSE..1	3	1.15	0.3	0	0.3	0.8	0.7	0.9	1	1.7	0.8	0.2	1.5	0	0.3	2.9	2.6	2	1.9	0.9	2.2	2.4	2.2	0.1	1	1.1	2.4	2.6
X90DAY.EURO..FUTR.3	-41	1.17	0	0	0	1.4	2	1.9	2	1.2	1.3	1.5	1.5	0	1.4	1.2	1.1	1.1	1.1	1.9	1.1	1	1.1	1.1	1	1.1	1.3	1.4
X90DAY.EURO..FUTR.1	-32	0.53	0	0	0	1	1.2	1.2	1.3	1.1	0.6	0.7	0.8	1.5	0.6	0.6	0.3	0.3	0.3	0.3	0.3	0.3	0.3	0.3	0.4	0.4	0.5	0.6
X90DAY.EURO..FUTR.2	-91	0.86	0	0	0	0.3	0.2	0.1	2	2	1.5	1.7	1.8	1.5	1.4	1.2	0.8	0.8	0.7	0.6	0.7	0.6	0.6	0.7	0.6	0.6	0.9	1
C..CURRENCY.FUT.1	-61	0.05	0	0	0	0.1	0.1	0	0	0	0	0	0.6	0.3	0	0	0	0	0	0	0	0	0	0	0	0	0.9	0
BP.CURRENCY.FUT.1	-1	0.15	0.2	0.2	0.8	0	0	0	0	0.1	0.4	0.8	0.5	0.8	0	0	0.2	0.5	0.5	0.6	0.7	0.4	0.2	0.1	0	0	0	0
WTI.CRUDE.FUTURE.1	43	0.64	0	0	0	1.2	1.2	0.4	0	0.3	0.6	0.6	0.4	0	0	0	0	0	1.3	1.3	1.7	1.7	2.1	1.1	3.2	1.1	0	0.1
A..CURRENCY.FUT.1	-144	0.45	0	0	0	0.1	0.1	0	0.1	1.5	1.8	2.1	2.3	1.3	1	1	0.5	0	0	0	0	0	0	0	0	0	0	0.1
DAX.INDEX.FUTURE.1	34	0.12	0	0	0	0	0	-0	-0	-0	-1	-1	-1	0.6	0.6	0.9	0.8	0.8	0.7	0.1	0	0	0	0.1	0.1	0.1	0.1	0.1
EURO.JPY.FUTURE.1	-229	0.02	0	0	0	0	0	-1	-1	-0	-0	-0	0.6	1	1.1	1	0.8	1.1	1.2	1	0.9	0.3	-0	-0	0.1	0.1	-2	-3
EURO.FX.CURR.FUT.1	-142	0.19	0	0	0	0	0	0.2	0.2	1.1	1.3	1.5	1	0.2	0	0	0	0.2	0.2	0.6	0.5	0.2	0	0	0	0	0	-2

CAC40.10.EURO.FUT.1	93	0.16	0	0	0	0	0	0	0	0	-0	-0	-0	-0	-1	0.1	0.5	0.3	0.2	0.2	0	0	0	0	0	0	0	0.5	0.9	1.1	1.2	1.3
PALLADIUM.FUTURE.1	-36	0.14	0	0.4	1	1.6	0.7	0	-0	0.2	0.1	0	0	0.1	0	0	0.9	0.8	0.8	0.9	0.8	0.8	0.7	0.7	0.6	0.6	0.5	0	0	0	0	0
MEXICAN.PESO.FUT.1	-16	0.39	0	0	0	0	0	0	-1	-0	0	0	0.7	0	0	0.9	0.9	1	1	0.9	1	0.8	0.7	0.6	0.6	0.5	0	0	0.1	0.1	1	1.2
IBEX.35.INDX.FUTR.1	-33	0.38	0	0	0	0	0	0	-0	-0	-0	-0	0	1.4	1.3	1.3	1	1.5	1.5	1	0.6	0.7	0.2	0	0	0.2	0.7	0.8	0.7	1	0.9
FTSE.100.IDX.FUT.1	-10	0.17	0	0	0	0	0	0	-0	-1	-1	-2	-1	0	1.2	1.6	1.6	1.5	1.2	1.2	1.4	1.1	1	0.1	0.1	0.1	0.2	0.1	0.1	0.1	0.1
SILVER.FUTURE.1	51	0.43	0	0	0.4	1.2	1.2	0.7	0.2	0	0	0.4	0.4	0.4	0.4	0	0	0	0.5	1	1	1	1.1	1.4	1.3	0.7	0.7	0.2	0.1	0.2	0.1
EURO.STOXX.50.1	20	0.27	-0	0	0	0	0	0	0	0	0	0	0.9	0.9	1	0.7	0.7	0.5	0.5	0.5	0.3	0	0	0	0	0	0.6	0.6	0.9	1	0.9
PLATINUM.FUTURE.1	-102	0.13	-0	-0	0	0	0	0	0.3	1.1	1.2	0.5	0.2	0.1	0.5	0.2	0.4	0.5	0.5	0	0	0	0	0	0	0	0	0	0	0	0
CHF.CURRENCY.FUT.1	-52	0.53	-0	0.7	0.7	0	0.3	0	-1	0.6	2.3	3.6	2.9	0.1	0.4	0.4	0.4	0.4	0.4	0.4	0.4	0.3	0	0	0	0	0	0	0	0	0
COPPER.FUTURE.1	-33	0.32	-0	0	0	0	0.2	0	0	0.5	0.4	0.5	0.1	0.2	0.5	0.5	0.6	0.6	0.6	0.5	1	1	0.9	0.1	0.1	0.1	0	0	0	0	0
GOLD.100.OZ.FUTR.1	111	0.48	-0	-0	0.3	0.8	0.8	0	0.2	1.3	1.8	1.6	1.4	1.2	0.4	1	0.5	0.3	0.1	0.1	0.1	0.6	0.8	0.8	0.8	0.2	0.3	0.2	0.1	0.1	0
SOYBEAN.OIL.FUTR.1	-22	0.19	-1	-1	-1	-0	-0	-0	-0	0.1	0.3	0.3	0.3	0.4	0.5	0.5	0.5	0.6	0.5	0.5	0.8	0.8	0.8	0.8	0.8	0.7	0.8	0.7	0.3	0.7
CORN.FUTURE.1	-67	0.17	-1	-2	-2	-0	-0	-0	0.2	0.5	0.1	0.1	0.2	0.2	1.1	1.4	1.3	1.3	1.1	1.3	1.2	0.2	0.2	0.2	0.2	0.2	0.2	0.1	0.1	0.1
SUGAR..11.WORLD..1	-11	1.58	-1	-0	1.3	1.3	1.2	0.6	1.7	2.2	3.2	2.7	3.9	3.5	1.8	1	1.5	1.3	1.4	1.3	1.2	1.6	-1	1.6	2.6	2.7	2.6	2.2	1.8	1.9
NIKKEI.226.SGX..1	-114	-0.63	-1	-2	-2	-2	-2	-3	-3	-2	-0	-2	0	0	0	-1	-1	-0	-0	0	0	-1	1.8	1.5	0.6	-1	-0	0.4	0.5	0.4	0.2
WHEAT.FUTURE.CBT..1	-151	-0.06	-2	-2	-1	-1	-1	-1	-1	0.2	0.2	0.3	0.2	0.4	0.7	0.8	1.2	1.2	1.3	1.1	1	0	0	0.7	0.5	0.4	0.4	0.5	0	0
LME.PRI.ALUM.FUTR.1	-25	0.05	-2	-0	0	0	-0	-0	-1	0	0	0	0.5	0.4	0	0	0	1	1.2	1.1	1.3	0.8	0.7	0.7	0.8	0.6	0.5	0.1	0.6	0.4	0
SOYBEAN.FUTU.RE.1	-45	0.54	-2	-2	-2	-1	-1	-0	-0	0.1	0.6	0.4	0.6	0.5	1	0.7	1.3	1.2	1.4	1.3	1.3	1.6	1.5	1.5	1.4	1.5	1.5	1.4	1.4	1.5	1.6
COTTON.NO.2.FUTR.1	-56	0.35	-3	-3	-3	-0	-2	1.6	0.8	1.7	1.9	1	1.7	0.6	0.6	1.2	1.3	1.2	0.4	0.6	0.5	0.5	0.4	0.6	0.6	0.6	0.6	0.6	0.6	0.6	0.6
EURO.GBP.FUTURE.1	-268	0.49	-2	-0	0.3	0.8	0.3	0.4	0.6	0.3	1	1.7	2.5	3	3.1	2.2	1.8	0.2	1	1	1	1	0.1	0.2	0.2	0	0	0	0	-1	-1
HANG.SENG.IDX.FUT.1	-15	-0.41	-3	-3	-2	-1	-1	-1	-1	-1	0.3	1	0.7	0.2	0.8	0.1	0	-0	-0	0	0.6	1.1	1.3	1.3	1.4	1.3	1.3	1.4	1.6
COCOA.FUTURE.1	93	-0.57	-4	-3	-4	-2	-2	-1	-1	-1	-0	-0	-1	-0	-1	-1	-2	0.6	1.3	3	2.9	1.7	0.2	1.3	0.6	0.4	0.6	0.6	0	0
NATURAL.GAS..FUTR.1	356	-2.85	-4	-4	-3	-3	-3	-0	-3	-2	-3	-2	-3	-1	-2	-1	-1	-2	-1	0	1	0.7	2.5	3	3.1	2.2	1.8	0.2	1	0.6

market difficulties. While this is probably true for relatively long periods of bear or bull market conditions, this result is not so clear in sideways market conditions.

The other advantage of CTA is that these funds are managed quantitatively, whereas most hedge fund strategies are managed by a manager or a team of managers who take the decisions. In this case, however, everything is automatic and there are advantages to systematic investing. Firstly, a computer can process a huge amount of data and integrate every new element or piece of information within a few seconds. Secondly it can combine basic relations with more complex ones in a global and diversified portfolio. Thirdly, CTA programs are more flexible than humans and have no behavioural bias. Another advantage of the strategy is that the statistical distribution of the profits achieved by the trend-following strategy is asymmetric; the strategy tends to lead to frequent but limited losses, but to be exposed to larger, though less frequent, gains. In contrast to most alternative strategies, the trend-following strategy has a return distribution with a positive skew – an advantage on a risk management front, but may be an issue for investors as the risk measured by volatility appears to be much higher.

The main drawback of the strategy is the historical volatility of the returns; losses of 5, 10 or even 15 per cent within a single month are relatively frequent, even though they tend to be followed by a few strong months. In addition the minimum investment for the largest funds tend to be high.

19.5 Performance

Hedge Fund Research, Inc. includes CTA within the HFRI Macro: Systematic Diversified index. These are defined as follows:[51]

> *Systematic: Diversified strategies have investment processes typically as a function of mathematical, algorithmic and technical models, with little or no influence of individuals over the portfolio positioning. Strategies employ an investment process designed to identify opportunities in markets exhibiting trending or momentum characteristics across individual instruments or asset classes. Strategies typically employ quantitative process [sic] which focus on statistically robust or technical patterns in the return series of the asset, and typically focus on highly liquid instruments and maintain shorter holding periods than either discretionary or mean reverting strategies. Although some strategies seek to employ counter trend models, strategies benefit most from an environment characterized by persistent, discernible trending behaviour. Systematic Diversified strategies typically would expect to have no greater than 35% of portfolio in either dedicated currency or commodity exposures over a given market cycle.*

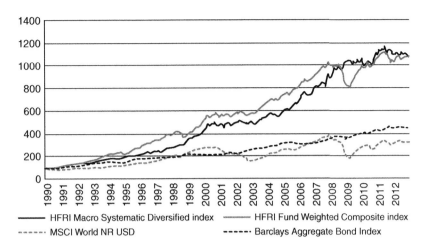

Figure 3.97 Evolution of US$100 invested in the HFRI EH: Short Bias index
Source: Based on numbers obtained from Hedge Fund Research, Inc.

Figure 3.97 shows the evolution of US$100 invested in the HFRI Macro: Systematic Diversified index since January 1990 compared with other similar investments in the HFRI Fund Weighted Composite index, the equity market, represented by MSCI World, and the bond market, represented by the Barclays Aggregate Bond index.

An investment of US$100 in the HFRI Macro: Systematic Diversified index would have become US$1080 by the end of 2012. The same investment in the equity market, bond market or global hedge fund market would have become US$1105, US$352 or US$472 respectively.

The HFRI Macro: Systematic Diversified index offered an average annual return of 10.9 per cent per year over the whole period, against 7.2 per cent for the equity market and 7.4 per cent for the bond market. More recently, it has offered 7.5 per cent per year on average over the last decade and 4 per cent per year on average over the last five years. These returns have fallen significantly over recent times. Interestingly, this is not because of a difficult 2008 but because three years out of the last four have been negative.

Volatility has been relatively low, at 7.5 per cent. It has, however, increased over the last decade, to 8.1 per cent, and to 8.8 per cent over the last five years. This is significantly lower than equities, which ranged between 15 and 20 per cent depending on the period in question, and slightly higher than bonds.

Table 3.37 shows the yearly returns, the mean annual return, the standard deviation, the minimum annual return, the maximum annual return

Table 3.37 Performance statistics of the HFRI Macro: Systematic Diversified index and comparative indices

	HFRI Macro: Systematic Diversified Index	HFRI Fund Weighted Composite Index	MSCI World NR USD	Barclays Aggregate Bond Index	Performance vs. HFRI	Performance vs. MSCI World	Performance vs. Barclays Aggregate
1990	13.5%	5.8%	-17.0%	12.7%	7.7%	30.5%	0.8%
1991	23.1%	32.2%	18.3%	16.0%	-9.0%	4.9%	7.1%
1992	7.7%	21.2%	-5.2%	5.8%	-13.5%	13.0%	1.9%
1993	24.2%	30.9%	22.5%	11.1%	-6.7%	1.7%	13.1%
1994	3.5%	4.1%	5.1%	0.2%	-0.6%	-1.6%	3.3%
1995	12.6%	21.5%	20.7%	19.7%	-8.9%	-8.1%	-7.1%
1996	13.5%	21.1%	13.5%	4.9%	-7.6%	-0.01%	8.6%
1997	13.6%	16.8%	15.8%	3.8%	-3.2%	-2.2%	9.8%
1998	24.8%	2.6%	24.3%	13.7%	22.2%	0.5%	11.1%
1999	26.2%	31.3%	24.9%	-5.2%	-5.1%	1.2%	31.3%
2000	11.8%	5.0%	-13.2%	3.2%	6.8%	25.0%	8.6%
2001	4.1%	4.6%	-16.8%	1.6%	-0.5%	20.9%	2.5%
2002	-3.3%	-1.5%	-19.9%	16.5%	-1.8%	16.6%	-19.8%
2003	15.4%	19.5%	33.1%	12.5%	-4.2%	-17.8%	2.8%
2004	6.4%	9.0%	14.7%	9.3%	-2.6%	-8.3%	-2.8%
2005	6.1%	3.5%	4.5%	1.3%	2.6%	1.6%	4.8%
2006	16.8%	12.9%	20.1%	6.6%	3.9%	-3.2%	10.2%
2007	10.3%	10.0%	9.0%	9.5%	0.4%	1.3%	0.9%
2008	18.1%	-19.0%	-40.7%	4.8%	37.1%	58.8%	13.3%
2009	-1.7%	20.0%	30.0%	6.9%	-21.7%	-31.7%	-8.6%
2010	9.8%	10.2%	11.8%	5.5%	-0.5%	-2.0%	4.2%
2011	-3.5%	-5.3%	-5.5%	5.6%	1.7%	2.0%	-9.2%
2012	-2.5%	6.4%	15.8%	4.3%	-8.9%	-18.3%	-6.8%
Mean annual return (whole period)	10.9%	11.4%	7.2%	7.4%	-0.5%	3.7%	3.5%
Volatility (whole period)	7.5%	7.0%	15.6%	5.5%	NA	NA	NA
Meanannual return 2003–2012	7.5%	6.7%	9.3%	6.6%	0.8%	-1.8%	0.9%
Volatility 2003–2012	8.1%	6.5%	16.2%	6.1%	NA	NA	NA
Meanaverage return 2007–2012	4.0%	2.5%	2.3%	5.4%	1.6%	1.8%	-1.4%
Volatility 2007–2012	8.8%	7.4%	19.4%	6.4%	NA	NA	NA
Minimum annual return	-3.5%	-19.0%	-40.7%	-5.2%	-21.7%	-31.7%	-19.8%
Maximum annual return	26.2%	32.2%	33.1%	19.7%	37.1%	58.8%	31.3%

Source: Based on data from Hedge Fund Research, Inc.

and the spread of the strategies relative to the comparative indices. It leads to the following remarks:

– Over the 23 years covered, the HFRI Macro: Systematic Diversified index was negative for five years over the period. The three most difficult years were 2011 (–3.5 per cent), 2002 (–3.3 per cent) and 2012 (–2.5 per cent). The equity index finished down 6 years out of 23 including the 2000–2002 bear market, 2008 and 2011. The bond index suffered negative returns for one year only, in 1999.
– The maximum annual returns of the HFRI Macro: Systematic Diversified index were achieved in 1999 (26.2 per cent), 1993 (24.2 per cent) and 1991 (23.1 per cent). These numbers are relatively strong, but not as strong as many other strategies – probably not truly representative of the reality of the main players in the strategy, which have been more volatile but have performed much more strongly.
– The spread in returns between the HFRI Macro: Systematic Diversified index and the comparative indices has been volatile. The strategy outperformed the global hedge fund index 8 times out of 23, the equity index 13 times and the bond index 17 times. The largest outperformance of the HFRI Macro: Systematic Diversified index relative to the equity index was 58.8 per cent, in 2008, while the largest underperformance was 31.7 per cent, in 2009. Relative to the bond index, the largest outperformance was achieved in 1999 at 31.3 per cent, and the largest underperformance was 19.8 per cent, in 2002.

20 Fund of funds

Funds of funds invest in other funds. This is not about applying various alternative strategies within a portfolio, as do relative value arbitrage or multi-strategy funds, but selecting external fund managers and building a diversified portfolio. Diversification will be obtained in terms of strategies, asset managers and liquidity profiles. The funds combined have no link between them outside of the strategy implemented, in some cases. The objective of such a strategy is to obtain a diversified product by investing in a single product that is fully diversified.

20.1 Why funds of funds?

Most hedge funds are domiciled in tax havens and are managed from all around the world. Potential investors have limited access to information regarding these funds, and they cannot consider investing in any of them unless they spend a significant amount of time and money in order to perform a complete due diligence. Even when they have access to the investment team, managers tend to remain discreet about their strategy. In addition, few investors know enough about the hedge fund market to distinguish funds by other elements than their performance or the main principles of their strategy. Finally, most funds require high minimum investments, usually at a minimum of US$1 million, so only investors of very high net worth can create a diversified portfolio. It is usually recommended that 5 to 20 per cent of a portfolio should be allocated to alternative strategies; in order to allocate 20 per cent of a portfolio to a single hedge fund with a US$1 million minimum investment, a minimum of US$5 million is required. To go the 5 funds it is US$25 million.

These stringent criteria created a demand for a product enabling investors to obtain a diversified portfolio of hedge funds built by fund selection specialists with a deep knowledge of the industry. This was the start of the fund of hedge funds industry. Figure 3.98 illustrates a typical fund of funds structure.

Individual strategies tend to be risky, so funds of funds have the main objective of diversifying the risks. They do this in various ways, as illustrated in Figure 3.99:

– by the number of funds in which they invest
– by combining various investment strategies
– by investing across the globe
– by combining funds with different levels of risk
– by combining fund profiles (quantitatively and qualitatively managed funds)
– by combining different liquidity profiles
– by combining funds with different levels of market exposure.

Table 3.38 illustrates diversification by number of funds and investment strategies. The fund of funds is diversified across six investment strategies, and several funds are considered per investment strategy. Over time, each strategy faces challenging moments and at least one negative year; the fund of funds is, however, positive every year thanks to its diversification, balancing the losses and enabling the strategy sub-portfolio to face a limited downside. The fund of funds offers a relatively stable and attractive gross return for a lower level of risk than do individual strategies.

In addition to their diversification benefits, funds of funds are appreciated because they require minimum investments that are much lower than for individual funds; usually below US$50,000.

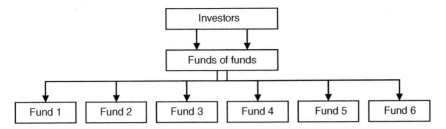

Figure 3.98   A typical fund of funds structure

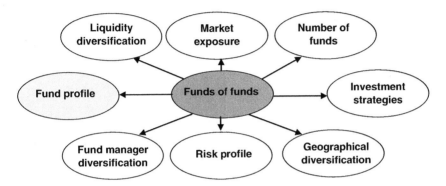

Figure 3.99   Fund of funds diversification

Table 3.38   Diversification benefit of a fund of funds

	Long/ short (6 funds)	Fixed-income arbitrage (4 funds)	Convertible arbitrage (4 funds)	Short selling (2 funds)	Event driven (3 funds)	Macro (3 funds)	Funds of funds (22 funds)
Year 1	18%	13%	−16%	−12%	25%	31%	12.3%
Year 2	37%	17%	16%	−21%	32%	27%	23.5%
Year 3	5%	4%	19%	18%	28%	−12%	9.1%
Year 4	19%	−8%	25%	1%	37%	19%	16.8%
Year 5	−16%	13%	3%	22%	8%	15%	4.0%
Year 6	28%	9%	5%	5%	−25%	38%	12.0%
Allocation	25%	19%	18%	6%	16%	16%	100%
Average annual return	15%	8%	9%	2%	18%	20%	13%
Standard deviation	19%	9%	15%	17%	23%	18%	7%

20.2 Methodology

The first step in the management of a fund of funds is the search for investment ideas. Hedge funds are generally private funds, and there is no single source of information that provides a list of all the funds available. The main sources of ideas are shown in Figure 3.100. Specialized databases represent the first source of ideas, followed by independent fund marketers, the press, conferences and other fund managers. Prime brokers offer a capital introduction service, and they organize events during which they present the funds they work with. This has become an essential source of information. Consultants and the competition – other fund of funds – are final sources of ideas.

When funds of funds managers select a fund, they use both qualitative and quantitative criteria and they perform a complete due diligence[52] – mandatory before any investment can be considered. The Securities and Exchange Commission (2007) recommends a series of minimal checks that should be performed before investing in any hedge fund:

– read the memorandum and other legal documents carefully
– understand how assets are valued
– check the commissions
– analyse the potential limitations in liquidity
– perform research on the past experience of the manager
– do not be afraid to ask questions.

Those criteria are essential, but probably not sufficient in a world as complex as the world of hedge funds. The main qualitative criteria we recommend checking also include:

1. The asset manager
   • General information (address, phone, fax, email)

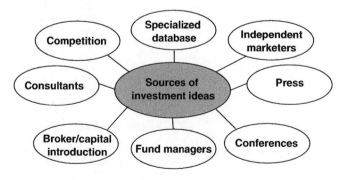

Figure 3.100   Sources of ideas

- Number and type of contacts
- Source of the idea
- History of the asset management company
- Legal structure
- Organization of third parties
- Registration with any regulatory body
- Other activities of the principals[53]
- Potential investments of the principals in the products
- Information on the entire set of products managed by the asset manager
- AUM (in total and per product, plus their evolution over time)
- Client base
- Service providers.

2. The team
- The biographies and experience of the manager(s)
- Information on the complete investment team
- The integrity and reputation of the investment team
- The stability of the team over time
- Potential personal investment of the manager
- Potential conflicts of interest.

3. Compliance
- Biography and experience of the person in charge of compliance and ethics
- Detailed procedure regarding personal transactions
- Side letters
- Retrocessions.

4. Performance
- Complete series of net past performance
- Comparison of the performance of the fund against any account or other fund based on the same strategy.

5. Investment process
- The fund objective in terms of return and the risk budget
- Strategy classification
- Description of the strategy and the investment philosophy
- Detailed presentation of the strategy
- Illustration of the strategy
- Cash policy
- Computer program used
- Presentation of typical favourable and unfavourable environments
- Risk factors
- Presentation of the decision process
- Consistency and discipline of the process.

6. Portfolio
   - Policy in terms of exposure and hedging
   - Types of securities used and their typical percentages
   - Geographical exposure and historical variations
   - Sector exposure and historical variations
   - Turnover
   - Concentration
   - Liquidity and limits
   - Valuation policy
   - Portfolio construction
   - How positions are followed.
7. Risk management
   - Risk tolerance
   - Risk management policy (instructions, risk assessment, liquidity, counterparties)
   - Operational risk management policy
   - Stop-loss procedures
   - Programs used in the context of risk management
   - External controls
   - Reasons behind significant past losses
   - Details about assets transfer
   - Presentation of every risk specific to the strategy.
8. Fund
   - General information (including the name as specified in the memorandum, country of domiciliation, legal structure, potential quotation on an exchange, date of creation, currency)
   - Fees and commissions (management fee, performance fee, potential entry and exit fees, setup costs and any other expenses)
   - Liquidity elements (including minimum investment, consequent investment, frequency of subscriptions and redemptions, notice period, delay before cash is paid back, potential holdback, policy regarding payments in kind, potential gate, lockup)
   - Board of directors, with the biographies of the directors.
9. Information
   - Analysis of financial statements
   - Auditors' conclusion
   - Launch price of the shares
   - Current price of the shares
   - Details about the information diffused and its periodicity
   - External sources of performance (Bloomberg, Morningstar, database)
   - Level of transparency

- Net asset value estimation process (equalization, new class)
- End of fiscal year.

10. External parties
    - Administrator
    - Auditors
    - Prime broker
    - Legal advisers.

11. Perspectives
    - Current and future perspective of the manager(s)
    - Robustness of the strategy applied
    - Future of the strategy.

12. References
    - Previous employer
    - Previous colleague
    - Previous counterparty
    - Current counterparty
    - Others.

The categories of elements to analyse during the due diligence process are reported in Figure 3.101.

The quantitative analysis is not limited to looking at the returns, comparing them with competitive funds and considering the risk of the fund; a complete and detailed analysis of tools specific to the return characteristics offered by the industry should be performed. Such tools include the complete return distribution, various ratios, liquidity risk measures[54] and regression techniques to explain previous returns. The two aspects of the analysis (qualitative and quantitative) are both necessary and are

Figure 3.101 Qualitative aspects to consider before investing in a fund

linked to one another; quantitative analysis on a stand-alone basis does not integrate many aspects of past performance. On the other hand, performance is probably the most important element in the end; even if all the qualitative aspects of a fund attract the interest of potential investors, bad numbers may steer them away.

During the process it is necessary to double-check that past performance has been audited, that it can be attributed to the current manager and that there has not been any significant change in the management team. The risk management policy is also very important. Hedge funds are free in their management processes, and most funds tend to invest in derivative products and use leverage. So it is necessary that every fund has a rigorous risk management process, enabling the team to follow individual positions, sectors and country exposures and any other aspect of a portfolio that could help the manager limit the losses in case of adverse market movement. Most fund of funds managers visit company managers on site, so they can check most of the elements covered during the due diligence process. Each fund of funds manager determines the criteria that are mandatory in considering a fund for investment; there is usually an initial screening that can be either qualitative or quantitative.

Fund of funds managers tend to invest in a minimum of 20 funds and do not systematically use leverage. They have a performance objective of 5 to 10 per cent, with a volatility budget below 10 and more often around 5 to 6 per cent. The hedge fund industry relies heavily on people because of its relative opaqueness; this aspect is present in the fund selection process and in the management of funds of funds. For most fund of funds managers, the personality of the manager is key in the selection process. Over the last few years, however, the due diligence process has focused not only on the asset manager and the product but more and more on operational risk management and portfolio management risk analysis. The aspects covered during this process include:

1. The net asset value estimation process
   - Frequency of portfolio valuation
   - Source of positioning
   - Potential instructions
   - Sources of information on cash movement
   - Rules governing transactions
   - Independency of the valuation process
   - Externalization of the process
   - Sources of prices
   - Sources of prices for complex products
   - Potential interventions by the manager in the past

- check for the net asset value
- Audit and frequency.
2. Accounting systems
   - Potential accounting management
   - Potential limitation on access to the account at the prime broker.
3. Transfer of assets
   - Precise description of the asset transfer process.
4. Compliance
   - Compliance process regarding restrictions and limits
   - Minimum investment
   - Leverage
   - Size of the positions
   - Other restrictions.
5. Money laundering
   - Implementation of anti-money-laundering procedures.

20.3   The choice of a fund of funds

The choice of a fund of funds is different from that of an individual fund. Investors using such diversified products tend to invest in a limited number of them, as a fund of funds enables them to obtain direct diversification of the portion of their portfolio allocated to hedge funds. The main element to focus on for fund of funds investors is to understand the approach used by the fund of funds and how this approach is put into practice.

Most fund of funds managers aim to offer stable returns; to obtain these they tend to focus on non-directional low-risk strategies. Their typical objective is to offer 5 to 8 per cent a year with a volatility of around 6 per cent. Other funds try to obtain an average performance of over 10 per cent. typically by reducing the number of funds and by considering more aggressive directional funds. Such funds will also be more opportunistic in the market chosen. In other cases, managers will allocate a significant portion of their portfolio to a single strategy such as macro, short selling or event driven funds, or even suggest a thematic portfolio to profit from a specific opportunity; such funds will be actively managed, and the managers will rotate more actively the exposure over time. Figure 3.102 shows four typical fund of funds structures, from a concentrated single-strategy dynamic fund of funds to a diversified multi-strategy fund of funds.

Some funds of funds focus on a specific portion of the hedge fund world; an interesting example of an emerging market fund of funds is reported in Figure 3.103; it combines long/short equity, long-only leveraged and equity market neutral funds within a single portfolio.

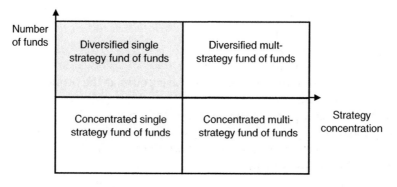

Figure 3.102   Main fund of funds offerings

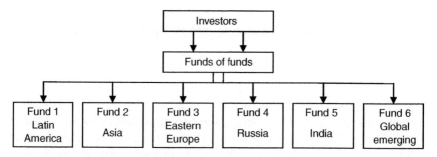

Figure 3.103   Example of an emerging market fund of funds

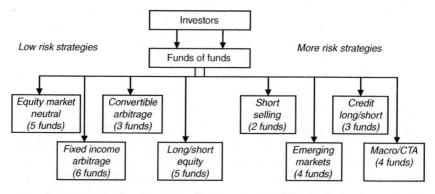

Figure 3.104   Example of a multi-strategy fund of funds

Finally, a typical multi-strategy structure is shown in Figure 3.104. Such funds tend to have a relatively high number of funds within their portfolio. A typical minimum is around 20, but it is not unusual to see portfolios with 30 to 40 names.

20.4 Advantages and drawbacks

The main advantage of funds of funds is that they enable investors to invest, albeit indirectly, in funds that they would not have had access to individually. In addition, such a product enables the manager to diversify the risk of the portfolio. Another element is that as professional investors, fund of funds manager obtain a better transparency into the funds, not only regarding the strategy but usually on the underlying positions. On the liquidity side, funds of funds correspond to a real need in final investors. They usually offer monthly, to quarterly liquidity, while the underlying individual funds usually offer monthly, quarterly and in some case semi-annual or annual liquidity. Funds of funds tend to keep some cash or to have access to a line of credit in case of large redemptions.

Funds of funds are usually the only way to invest in funds closed to new subscriptions, as funds of funds can be invested in a fund closed to new investors. In addition, fund of funds manager can usually add to positions in a fund that is soft closed (closed to new investors but open to existing investors). This is the same as holding a call option on the future performance of a manager. In addition, the growth of the hedge fund industry has made it more difficult for investors to identify the best managers, but fund of funds investors can delegate this choice to professional investors, who are likely to be better informed and have access to more information thanks to the size of their investment; they should be able to form a better judgement because they work full-time in the field. Fund of funds managers perform a thorough due diligence before making any investment, and they continuously follow the positions they have in portfolio while constantly keeping a lookout for new opportunities; they are fully dedicated to fund-picking and portfolio construction.

The main inconvenience of a fund of funds is the double fee structure. Funds of funds usually charge lower fees than individual funds, but these costs come in addition to the underlying fund fees. Fund of funds fees tend to be between 0.5 and 2 per cent management fees, with an average around 1.4 per cent, plus an performance fee within a range of 0 to 20 per cent, averaging 10 per cent. These levels tend to be standard, but there are usually high-water mark systems and potentially a hurdle rate in place.

Another inconvenience is the risk of diversifying the best ideas; although investment in a fund of funds enables the investor to limit the global risk of their portfolio by diversifying individual fund risk, a fund of funds manager will not always be able to discover enough top-notch managers to spread the portfolio between managers of an equally high quality. More weight should be given to the best ideas, but their performance will be nevertheless be diversified. A fund of funds portfolio will typically underperform its top ten positions. In risk-adjusted terms the situation may be different, and this can explain why funds of funds tend to be over-diversified.

The third drawback of funds of funds is that by definition the hedge fund industry is relatively opaque. While funds of funds have better access to much information that individual clients cannot access, we have not yet attained the same standard as the mutual fund industry. The situation improved significantly after the 2008 liquidity crisis, and the largest hedge fund houses have become institutionalized – but there is still room for improvement.

20.5 Performance

Hedge Fund Research, Inc. defines fund of funds as follows:[55]

> *funds that invest with multiple managers through funds or managed accounts. The strategy designs a diversified portfolio of managers with the objective of significantly lowering the risk (volatility) of investing with an individual manager. The Fund of Funds manager has discretion in choosing which strategies to invest in for the portfolio. A manager may allocate funds to numerous managers within a single strategy, or with numerous managers in multiple strategies. The minimum investment in a Fund of Funds may be lower than an investment in an individual hedge fund or managed account. The investor has the advantage of diversification among managers and styles with significantly less capital than investing with separate managers.*

The strategy is sub-divided into four sub-strategies:

– **Fund of Funds – Conservative**: such a fund will, according to Hedge Fund Research, Inc., exhibit one or more of the following characteristics:

seeks consistent returns by primarily investing in funds that generally engage in more "conservative" strategies, such as Equity Market Neutral, Fixed Income Arbitrage, and Convertible Arbitrage; exhibits a lower historical annual standard deviation than the HFRI Fund of Funds Composite Index. A fund in the HFRI FOF Conservative Index shows generally consistent performance regardless of market conditions.

– **Fund of Funds – Diversified**: such a fund will exhibit one or more of the following characteristics:

invests in a variety of strategies among multiple managers; historical annual return and/or a standard deviation generally similar to the HFRI Fund of Fund Composite index; demonstrates generally close performance and returns distribution correlation to the HFRI Fund of Fund Composite Index. A fund in the HFRI FOF Diversified Index tends to show minimal loss in down markets while achieving superior returns in up markets.

– **Fund of Funds – Market Defensive**: such a fund will exhibit one or more of the following characteristics:

invests in funds that generally engage in short-biased strategies such as short selling and managed futures; shows a negative correlation to the general market benchmarks (S&P). A fund in the FOF Market Defensive Index exhibits higher returns during down markets than during up markets.

– **Fund of Funds – Strategic**: such a fund will exhibit one or more of the following characteristics:

seeks superior returns by primarily investing in funds that generally engage in more opportunistic strategies such as Emerging Markets, Sector specific, and Equity Hedge; exhibits a greater dispersion of returns and higher volatility compared to the HFRI Fund of Funds Composite Index. A fund in the HFRI FOF Strategic Index tends to outperform the HFRI Fund of Fund Composite Index in up markets and underperform the index in down markets.

Figure 3.105 shows the evolution of US$100 invested in the HFRI Fund of Funds Composite index since January 1990 compared with other similar investments in the HFRI Fund Weighted Composite index, the equity

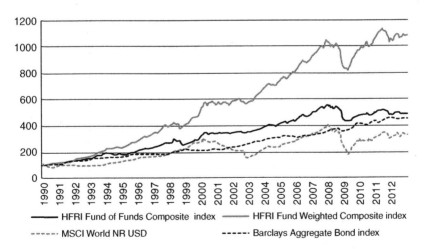

Figure 3.105   Evolution of US$100 invested in the HFRI Fund of Funds Composite index

Source: Based on numbers obtained from Hedge Fund Research, Inc.

market, represented by MSCI World, and the bond market, represented by the Barclays Aggregate Bond index.

An investment of US$100 in the HFRI Fund of Funds Composite index would have become US$504 by the end of 2012. The same investment in the equity market, bond market or global hedge fund market would have become US$1105, US$352 or US$472 respectively.

The HFRI Fund of Funds Composite index offered an average annual return of 7.6 per cent per year over the whole period, against 7.2 per cent for the equity market and 7.4 per cent for the bond market. More recently, it has offered 3.7 per cent per year on average over the last decade, and has been negative –1 per cent per year on average over the last five years. These returns have fallen significantly over recent times mainly because of the difficult returns of 2008 and to a lesser extent 2011.

Volatility has been relatively low, at 5.8 per cent over the whole period and 5.5 per cent over the last ten years. It has increased to 6.3 per cent over the last five years. This is significantly lower than equities, which ranged between 15 and 20 per cent depending on the period in question, and in line with the volatility of the bond index.

Table 3.39 shows the yearly returns, the mean annual return, the standard deviation, the minimum annual return, the maximum annual return and the spread of the strategies relative to the comparative indices. It leads to the following remarks:

– Over the 23 years covered the HFRI Fund of Funds Composite index was negative in three years: 2008 (–21.4 per cent), 2011 (–5.7) and 1998 (–5.1 per cent). The equity index finished down 6 years out of 23, including the 2000–2002 bear market, 2008 and 2011. The bond index suffered negative returns for one year only, in 1999.
– The maximum annual returns of the HFRI Fund of Funds Composite index were achieved in 1999 (26.5 per cent), 1993 (26.3 per cent) and 1990 (17.5 per cent). These numbers are relatively strong.
– The spread in returns between the HFRI Fund of Funds Composite index and the comparative indices has been volatile. The strategy has outperformed the global hedge fund index 3 times out of 23, the equity index 11 times and the bond index 14 times. The largest outperformance of the HFRI Fund of Funds Composite index relative to the equity index was 11.7 per cent, in 1990, while the largest underperformance was 17.7 per cent, in 1991. Relative to the bond index, the largest outperformance was achieved in 1999 at 31.6 per cent, and the largest underperformance was 26.4 per cent, in 2008.

The fund of funds sub-indices show similar performances for years of low volatility, but there are greater differences in volatile periods such as 2008 where defensive strategies have outperformed.

Figure 3.106 shows the evolution of US$100 invested in the five fund of funds indices over the whole period.

21   Other investment strategies

We have described the main investment strategies within the hedge fund industry, but not all existing funds enter into the classifications we have used. While many of these funds with unclear or specific strategies tend to enter into the classification closest to them, we have observed new and informal sub-strategies, and these do not have any comparative index. In order to go into detail further, we present a few of them in this section.

The hedge fund industry, like the rest of the world, is in constant evolution. So it is possible that a strategy currently described as rare or specific may become more common over the next few years.

21.1   Closed-end fund arbitrage

Closed-end fund arbitrage is rare on a stand-alone basis, tending to be applied within multi-strategy funds and certain event driven funds. It combines long positions in listed funds combined with shorts in the underlying securities, or a proxy to hedge, partially or fully, the market risk. In some cases the manager can become activism, for instance when the opportunity is huge and the manager wins the support of other investors. Closed-end fund arbitrage is an original strategy that aims to profit from an arbitrage opportunity arising between the listed value of a fund and the value of the underlying securities. Closed-end funds gained much interest over the 2005 to 2007 period; it was of interest to managers that wanted to invest in less liquid securities with stable assets over time. These funds are closed-end. but tend to be listed on exchanges like the AIM (Alternative Investment Market) in London. The trading price is driven purely by the balance between supply and demand.

Closed-end fund arbitrage managers take positions in listed closed-end funds that are trading at a significant discount relative to their net asset value, with the objective of closing their position at net asset value or closer to it, at least. These kinds of funds are generally invested in equities, bonds, real estate and/or private equity. When the manager identifies a fund trading at an attractive discount to its net asset value he/she considers it for an investment. The issue is usually to find a way to hedge the market risk, at least in part. The choice of hedging tools will depend on the fund and on the historical correlations – but hedging is not always possible. Take the case of a Chinese direct real estate fund; this cannot be hedged through equities or through credit products. The final objective of the manager is to sell the fund close to its net asset value and for positions that have been partially or fully hedged, to close

Table 3.39 Performance statistics of the HFRI Fund of Funds Composite index and comparative indices

	HFRI Fund of Funds Composite Index	HFRI FOF: Conservative Index	HFRI FOF: Diversified Index	HFRI FOF: Market Defensive Index	HFRI FOF: Strategic Index	HFRI Fund Weighted Composite Index	MSCI World NR USD	Barclays Aggregate Bond Index	Performance (composite) vs. HFRI	Performance (composite) vs. MSCI World	Performance (composite) vs. Barclays Aggregate
1990	17.5%	14.2%	17.0%	26.3%	33.0%	5.8%	-17.0%	12.7%	11.7%	34.5%	4.8%
1991	14.5%	11.8%	13.8%	8.4%	23.7%	32.2%	18.3%	16.0%	-17.7%	-3.8%	-1.5%
1992	12.3%	7.3%	10.3%	2.6%	25.2%	21.2%	-5.2%	5.8%	-8.9%	17.6%	6.5%
1993	26.3%	16.3%	25.4%	19.0%	37.3%	30.9%	22.5%	11.1%	-4.6%	3.8%	15.2%
1994	-3.5%	-1.2%	-3.1%	1.3%	-7.6%	4.1%	5.1%	0.2%	-7.6%	-8.6%	-3.7%
1995	11.1%	13.1%	7.8%	9.9%	16.9%	21.5%	20.7%	19.7%	-10.4%	-9.6%	-8.6%
1996	14.4%	13.7%	12.8%	16.8%	16.1%	21.1%	13.5%	4.9%	-6.7%	0.9%	9.5%
1997	16.2%	15.0%	13.7%	16.1%	22.8%	16.8%	15.8%	3.8%	-0.6%	0.4%	12.4%
1998	-5.1%	-1.6%	-5.5%	-4.1%	-9.8%	2.6%	24.3%	13.7%	-7.7%	-29.5%	-18.8%
1999	26.5%	18.9%	28.5%	13.8%	38.5%	31.3%	24.9%	-5.2%	-4.8%	1.5%	31.6%
2000	4.1%	5.8%	2.5%	15.4%	-0.6%	5.0%	-13.2%	3.2%	-0.9%	17.3%	0.9%
2001	2.8%	3.1%	2.8%	7.3%	1.2%	4.6%	-16.8%	1.6%	-1.8%	19.6%	1.2%
2002	1.0%	3.6%	1.2%	8.2%	-4.0%	-1.5%	-19.9%	16.5%	2.5%	20.9%	-15.5%
2003	11.6%	9.0%	11.4%	8.5%	15.8%	19.5%	33.1%	12.5%	-7.9%	-21.5%	-0.9%
2004	6.9%	5.8%	7.2%	3.3%	8.3%	9.0%	14.7%	9.3%	-2.2%	-7.9%	-2.4%
2005	2.9%	2.1%	2.8%	2.9%	3.6%	3.5%	4.5%	1.3%	-0.6%	-1.6%	1.6%
2006	10.4%	9.2%	10.2%	9.0%	11.8%	12.9%	20.1%	6.6%	-2.5%	-9.7%	3.8%
2007	10.3%	7.7%	9.7%	10.8%	12.8%	10.0%	9.0%	9.5%	0.3%	1.2%	0.8%
2008	-21.4%	-19.9%	-20.9%	6.0%	-25.2%	-19.0%	-40.7%	4.8%	-2.3%	19.3%	-26.2%
2009	11.5%	9.6%	11.5%	3.4%	13.2%	20.0%	30.0%	6.9%	-8.5%	-18.5%	4.5%
2010	5.7%	5.1%	5.5%	5.0%	6.3%	10.2%	11.8%	5.5%	-4.5%	-6.1%	0.2%
2011	-5.7%	-3.6%	-5.0%	-6.7%	-7.3%	-5.3%	-5.5%	5.6%	-0.5%	-0.2%	-11.4%
2012	4.8%	4.2%	4.8%	-1.7%	5.8%	6.4%	15.8%	4.3%	-1.6%	-11.0%	0.5%

Mean annual return (whole period)	7.6%	6.5%	7.1%	7.9%	10.3%	11.4%	7.2%	7.4%	-3.8%	0.4%	0.2%
Volatility (whole period)	5.8%	4.0%	6.0%	5.9%	8.7%	7.0%	15.6%	5.5%	NA	NA	NA
Mean annual return 2003–2012	3.7%	2.9%	3.7%	4.0%	4.5%	6.7%	9.3%	6.6%	-3.0%	-5.6%	-3.0%
Volatility 2003–2012	5.5%	4.4%	5.3%	5.4%	7.0%	6.5%	16.2%	6.1%	NA	NA	NA
Mean average return 2007–2012	-1.0%	-0.9%	-0.8%	1.2%	-1.4%	2.5%	2.3%	5.4%	-3.5%	-3.3%	-6.5%
Volatility 2007–2012	6.3%	5.2%	6.0%	5.8%	7.8%	7.4%	19.4%	6.4%	NA	NA	NA
Minimum annual return	-21.4%	-19.9%	-20.9%	-6.7%	-25.2%	-19.0%	-40.7%	-5.2%	-17.7%	-29.5%	-26.2%
Maximum annual return	26.5%	18.9%	28.5%	26.3%	38.5%	32.2%	33.1%	19.7%	11.7%	34.5%	31.6%

Source: Based on data from Hedge Fund Research, Inc.

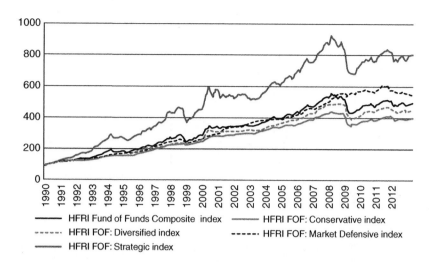

Figure 3.106 Evolution of US$100 invested in the HFRI Fund of funds indices
Source: Based on numbers obtained from Hedge Fund Research, Inc.

the hedging at the same time. The manager will usually work with other shareholders to unlock the value of the fund, and will often get a seat on the board. Another way to reduce the discount for listed funds with cash available is to buy back shares at net asset value from shareholders, and in extreme cases the process can go up to the realization of the asset. If the majority of the shareholders decide to liquidate, the fund assets can be realized. This particular scenario is not always attractive, as many listed closed-end funds tend to be invested in less liquid securities. A closed-end arbitrage fund usually has around 10 to 15 positions which will have been accumulated over time, and only a few of which are active at the same time.

21.1.1 Illustration – Gartmore European Investment Trust (GEO)[56]

Gartmore European Investment Trust is a fund established in the United Kingdom; it invests in Continental Europe and focuses on large companies. Between 2005 and 2006 the manager accumulated positions in the fund with an initial discount of 15 per cent. The average discount of these positions turned out to be 7.12 per cent relative to the net asset value. The fund announced in July 2006 that there was to be an analysis of the discount control system with a view to offering alternatives to the shareholders, and as a result a share buyback at 3.5 per cent discount was offered to the shareholders. The closed-end fund arbitrage manager refused this offer, as he believed that the quality of the manager was such that this discount was overlarge. He suggested that new and experienced directors should be sought. This proposal was refused, and the board of the fund simultaneously proposed an exit through a public offering, which was accepted. The position was kept for one and a half years, and the gross return over LIBOR was around 9.4 per cent gross. The evolution of the share price of the Gartmore European Investment Trust is given in Figure 3.107.

21.1.2   Illustration – JPM Fleming Overseas (JMO)

JPM Fleming Overseas is a closed-end fund investing in high quality world equities, which is listed on the London stock exchange. The manager initiated his position in the fund early in 2005, and it took him eight months to build the position he wanted. He was able to build this position with an average discount on a net asset value of 8.6 per cent, and after the eight months he held 22 per cent of the fund. From there he was able to negotiate an exit with the board, which agreed to make a public offering on the fund manager's holding at a 3.5 per cent discount on the net asset value. The annualized return of the position was 7.5 per cent over LIBOR. The evolution of the share price of JPM Fleming Overseas is reported in Figure 3.108.

21.1.3   Advantages and drawbacks

Closed-end fund arbitrage is attractive because it is an original strategy that aims to profit from a spread between a relatively illiquid product (a closed-end fund) and the securities that form it. Under normal market conditions any unjustified discount should disappear at some stage. The role of the manager is to build a portfolio combining various positions, and to become active if necessary.

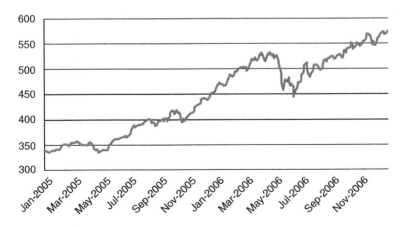

Figure 3.107   Evolution of the share price of Gartmore European Investment Trust

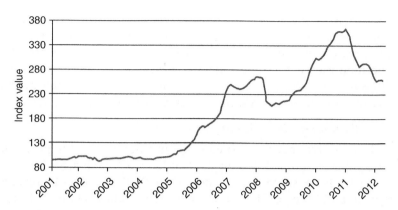

Figure 3.108 Evolution of the share price of JPM Fleming Overseas Investment

The main risk of this strategy is liquidity. During periods of crisis, investors desperately look for liquidity and the discounts of listed funds relative to their net asset value tend to increase significantly. Fund managers that were not fully invested at the start of the crisis have been able to profit from the opportunity, but if they were fully invested they will have faced liquidity issues.

A second important risk is the hedging risk. It is possible to correctly hedge funds invested in liquid securities, but this becomes more complicated when the fund is invested in small capitalization, emerging markets, real estate or private securities. For this reason closed-end funds specialists will keep a balanced position between funds invested in liquid securities that can be hedged and funds invested in less liquid securities that cannot be hedged easily. Managers will consider funds invested in less liquid securities, because these funds usually represent the best opportunities.

21.2 Electricity trading

A few funds are dedicated to this market and a few multi-strategy funds allocate part of their assets to this asset class. Electricity trading is about investing in electricity and its derivatives. New investment products have emerged over the last few years, and standardized contracts trade in multiple forms. The volume traded, the volatility and new development are affected by the general development of the energy market, the state of the economy as a whole, the level of liberalization of the markets, the integration of borders and political decisions such as restrictions on CO_2 emissions. The underlying idea is to profit from the seasonal aspect of the production of electricity that leads to relatively high volatility in prices as well as from the development of the relations between countries. In the context of the development and the liberalization of the electricity market, Figure 3.109 illustrates the levels of development of the electricity market in the United States, the United Kingdom and Germany as well as the level of maturity of the (more advanced) Nordic markets, where it is possible to do some trading in electricity derivatives.

While the physical transactions of commodities such as electricity trading are limited to producers and distributors, as physical delivery is involved, the financial markets are widely used for hedging purposes and for risk management. Various elements are involved in the determination of market prices, including the prices of coal, gas and petrol as well as average temperatures.

The financial products available include listed and quoted weekly futures, monthly, quarterly and annual forward contracts, options on quarterly or annual forwards, 1000+ tons of CO^2 emission allowances from the European Union (on dioxins and other greenhouse gases) and certificates supporting the production of renewable energy.

The funds present on these markets use some or all of these products and aim to profit from evolutions in their price relations. To achieve this, the managers make a fundamental analysis of the market, price trends, and macroeconomic and politic development. They use internally developed valuation models combined with meteorological data in order to predict the weather as precisely as possible, and then buy or sell the corresponding products when they believe the time is right. Such portfolios generally combine transactions in a position aiming to bet on long-term price variations integrating the price of CO_2, oil and transport costs by sea or otherwise, as well as the price on various markets. Then the manager will take relative positions. International markets remain underdeveloped, however, and so the opportunities to profit from price spreads between countries are still limited; however, the situation will probably evolve. The presence of options on this market enables managers to take positions in the underlying volatility of the market and to play shorter-, medium- and long-term trends. Finally, an analysis of historical price relations will also create the opportunity of using technical analysis. An example of an investment product of a fund invested in electricity is shown in Figure 3.110.

21.3 Option arbitrage

Option arbitrage groups several strategies that rely on informational inefficiencies. They are all based on mathematical models, rapidity

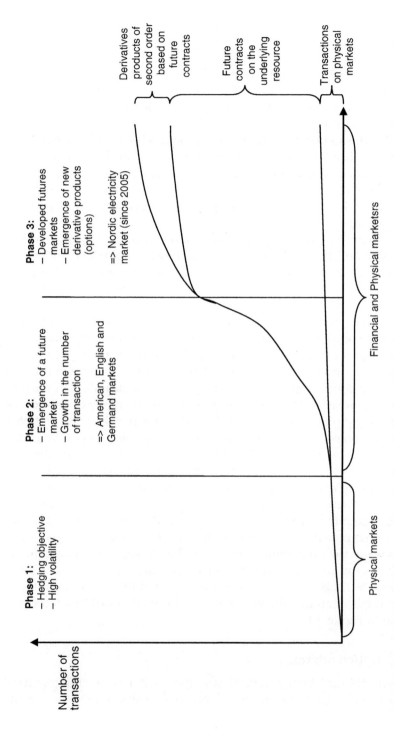

Figure 3.109 The liberalization and development of the electricity market

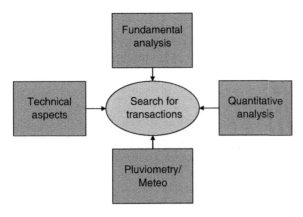

Figure 3.110 Standard investment procedure in an electricity trading fund

of execution, low transaction costs and cheap access to leverage. Few funds apply this strategy, but it has nevertheless gained interest. It is carried out using internally developed option pricing models that can be adapted to various scenarios, volatility conditions and other effects such as asymmetry or flattening. Positions are generally taken by a synthetic option-replication strategy, which usually relies on listed options – but over-the-counter options may be used. The investment process is relatively straightforward; the manager defines a set of relations to be checked and will then take a position as soon an opportunity is identified. The profit per position tends to be small, but leverage will usually be used quite extensively to create attractive returns. The strategy is a function of the number of positions taken and of the level of leverage used. Some funds rely on this strategy on a stand-alone basis, while others combine it with other strategies such as convertible arbitrage. One of the techniques applied by the managers of such funds is to take long positions in equities and either to sell futures short, or to hedge their positions by using options.

Option arbitrage usually means volatility trading and balanced positions. The option market offers opportunities because options are difficult to price, because they offer the opportunity to lever the positions taken, and because the option market tends to be directly impacted by unbalanced supply and demand, particularly in period of stress.

Funds specializing in option arbitrage generally have a low correlation with classic indices. This means that, like short selling funds, they are mainly used for diversification purposes.

21.4 Weather funds

The world of financial instruments evolves continuously. Catastrophe bonds and climate derivatives have gained interest and both of them represent billions of US dollars in notional.[57] Catastrophe bonds have the objective of covering extremely rare events, that occur only once or twice a century. Such events are caused by natural forces, and include earthquakes, hurricanes and serious floods. Such bonds are made of a principal and coupons, both of which are linked to the event. The coupon is defined in advance, and investors should post the notional amount of the bond on an account that pays the risk-free rate. Catastrophe bonds are issued with a spread over the risk-free rate. The spread, which constitutes the risk premium is typically 4 to 7 per cent.

Climate derivatives protect companies in the energy, agriculture, food and construction sectors against climate issues such as snow, rain or temperature changes. These are financial products in which two parties agree on an exchange of cash determined by reference to official weather data. They can also be used as hedging tools by companies whose activities are directly impacted by climate, and they usually take the form of options, swaps or other more complex and specific structures such as collars (see next paragraph). The underlying asset of these products is usually the temperature; examples include the number of summer days with a minimum temperature and the number of winter days with a predetermined maximum temperature, the average temperature over a certain period such as a festival, the levels of precipitation or sunshine, or the wind speed.

A multitude of players use derivative products, including gas companies, electricity providers, cattle producers, builders and drink producers; all of these can be heavily impacted by the weather. The products give a buyer the right to receive, in exchange for payment of a premium, a predefined amount per unit of temperature over a predefined exercise price, with an overall maximum limit. A swap enables a buyer to receive a fixed amount per unit of time in excess of the exercise price, with a predefined maximum amount. The difference is that for a swap there is no premium because the buyer has no particular right, but is simply counter-balancing the risk of the seller. A collar is almost identical to a swap, the only difference being that the exercise prices are fixed at different levels within a spread, and no payment is made. Depending on the exercise price a premium may or may not be paid. By their very nature, climate derivatives are close to the money, and they have been created in order to protect buyers from extreme, or at least adverse, events.

Such products are used by multi-strategy funds and by a few specialized managers. Some managers combine these products into a single portfolio, which will be diversified geographically and by underlying risk. Geographical diversification usually means a limitation of the exposure of the fund per region (Europe; US East Coast, West Coast, Mid-west and South; Asia; Australasia; Rest of the World). The underlying risk diversification usually means a portfolio diversification between the products linked to winter temperatures, summer temperatures, rain, snow and so on. Long and short exposures can be combined. Managers of such funds aim to offer exposure to an asset class offering returns that are not correlated with classic markets. It should be obvious that such securities are not correlated with the financial markets; it is only important events that can have a long-lasting effect on interest rates or on the equity market. But apart from those, there is no formal link between the average Paris summer temperature, or the amount of rain during the Munich Oktoberfest, and the evolution of the S&P 500. Managers aim to manage these products by arbitrating their spread as shown in Formula 3.19:

$$CDS = TP + RP + CP \qquad (3.19)$$

where:
CDS = climate derivative spread
TP = technical premium
RP = risk premium
CP = commercial premium.

The technical premium is the expected value of loss; it is calculated from the historical cost distribution, reshaped to include new information such as changes in the risk and the environment. The risk premium corresponds to the profit the investor expects to make as a result of taking the risk, and integrates the investor's risk aversion as well as its utility function. The commercial premium comes from other factors such as the limited liquidity and the pricing risk. A manager can be a seller of an option indexed on the potential realization of a catastrophe, and may hedge certain factors. The aim is to evaluate a derivative product on the basis of its three price parameters and to make a profit by arbitraging any mismatch.

21.5 Wine investing

Anglo-Saxons have for many years seen wine as an investment, and various forms of wine funds have existed for decades. Such funds usually take the form of closed-end funds with the underlying idea of selecting the best wines and keeping them for 10 or 15 years. Figure 3.111 shows the evolution of the Liv-ex Fine Wine Index that groups the market price of the 100 best châteaux in top vintages, according to Robert Parker. A

Figure 3.111   Evolution of the Liv-Ex 100 Fine Wine index
Source: Liv-ex Fine Wine Index.

US$100 investment in this portfolio in January 2004 could have become US$360 by 2011, and US$260 by November 2012.

An analysis performed by Beck in 2008 shows that an investment in wine since 1950 would have offered an annual average gross return of close to 15 per cent. Between 1987 and 2007 the five-year rolling average return was around 27 per cent, with no negative period.

More recently a few open-ended structures have been created, due to an increased liquidity in the market. Such funds tend to apply a more elaborate strategy than buy and hold; Figure 3.112 illustrates some of the techniques applied, such as relative value, future investing, discovery of new talent and the scarcity effect.

– *Relative value*: investing in wine includes buying wines that appear to be undervalued and selling wines that look overvalued. Relative positioning can be taken in a certain wine to favour one vintage over another, or by favouring one château over another for the same vintage. A manager aims to create a multi-dimensionally diversified portfolio of wines. Elements to include are the producers, the vintages, the ratings of the wines and the length of time they can be stored. A deep analysis will enable the manager to identify which wines are under- or over-priced, and to take relative value positions – which in this context means not combining long and short positions but selling positions in wines that are over-priced and buying those that are underpriced.
– *Future investing*: this implies buying wines, whether from wine merchants or direct from a château, before they are actually available and bottled;

Figure 3.112   Typical investment strategies in a wine fund

this market was created to improve the cash flow for the producers. It can offer great opportunities to the investor, too, because the price of the wines tends to increase over the first few years of life of a new vintage, when the product is not quite ready. Access to future investment in wines is, however, relatively closed, and in order to obtain allocations it is important to have well established relations with the main wine merchants in Bordeaux.

– *Discovery of new talents*: in the world of wine, the discovery of new talents is the equivalent of fundamental analysis in equities. Its objective is to identify which wines are undervalued and hence represent the best opportunities. The wine market is led by a few well-known wine critics, who have a strong impact on the price of the wines. It often happens, however, that they revise their notes, thus creating opportunities for the manager that has identified a good product at the right price. The new talents can also offer opportunities because they are less well known and so can represent attractive opportunities if they achieve a good rating.

– *Rarity effect*: a final strategy consists of taking important positions in relatively rare wines. Those can be older wines close to maturity and whose world stock is very limited, or younger wines that are produced in limited quantity.

Figure 3.113 was published by a company specializing in wine investing, and it illustrates the inefficiency of the wine market. It gives the minimum and maximum prices asked by the largest Bordeaux wine merchant for certain wines, and the results clearly indicate the opportunity open to anyone who can estimate the true value of these wines; for Lafite Rothschild 1998, for example, the prices range from €420 to 550 per bottle.

To put these prices into context, the wines considered here are traded between professionals and kept in bonded warehouses whose temperature and humidity is precisely controlled; wines do not physically move until sold to the end client. In addition, every case coming in or going out of the warehouse is photographed and insured. In practice, the manager will have a list of wines that he or she looks for with the corresponding

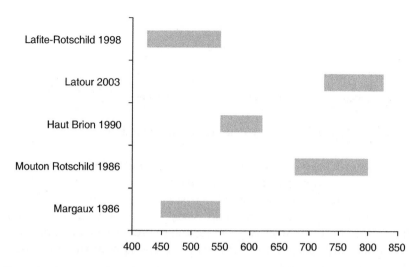

Figure 3.113   Examples of inefficiencies in the wine market
Source: OWC asset management.

price, like an equity manager, plus a list of wines he is ready to sell with the corresponding price. He or she will be in constant contact with counterparties and will trade when target prices are attained. For wines on sale a fund manager may also work with private clients or restaurants, or may sell some wines in auctions.

The risk management process is similar to that of a classic risk management process, but with certain limits and diversification rules. Such funds will by definition be biased towards Bordeaux, which is by far the most liquid market; and most funds will not invest before 1982, when bonded warehouse were created. The quality of older vintages is difficult to check.

In terms of valuation there are various methodologies – which all, however, rely on the catalogues of the main Bordeaux wine merchants and auction houses. As there is no organized wine market as such, the best way to value a case is by using the market price. Generally, valuation methodologies will be based on the lowest catalogue price or on an average of a few prices in order to get a price that is the closest to the market price, that is the price at which the manager should be able to sell his or her position.

21.6   MLP

Master Limited Partnerships (MLPs) are to energy what real estate investment trusts (REITS) are to the real estate market; public companies that have to comply with the same rules as listed companies whose securities are exchangeable. The special feature of MLPs is that their structure benefits from a favourable fiscal status; their investors are partners that own shares and receive a deductible cash flow, a kind of tax-free high-yielding share. MLPs are generally Small/Medium Enterprises (SME) that manage the exploration, development, search, production, processing, refining, transport, storage and marketing of natural products and minerals such as oil, gas and refined products.

Specialized managers usually take long positions based on attractive fundamentals, and they integrate the tax advantages. Managers try to differentiate themselves from one another in their market analysis, management team and analysis of projects. These funds fall into the hedge fund category because of their private structure, their fee structure and their limited liquidity, but positions are not easily hedged, mainly in the case of uncertainties. The market was heavily impacted by the liquidity issues of the second half of 2007.

22 Summary

This chapter has focused on the various investment strategies applied by hedge fund managers. We started by classifying these strategies into categories, strategies and sub-strategies, enabling us to differentiate between directional and non-directional strategies that have a significantly different profile and will be used differently by investors. Then we analysed the main investment strategies one by one in detail. We presented the special features of each of them, discussed their advantages and drawbacks, illustrated each of them with practical examples and reviewed their historical performance. This analysis has enabled us to understand the fundamental and specific differences that exist between the funds that are all known as hedge funds but which apply different strategies. We also discussed the opportunities and risks.

The world of hedge funds is constantly evolving, so some of the strategies given priority here will lose some interest and some marginal ones may become more important. This chapter is the heart of this book and, putting into context as it does what some of the best investors in the world are doing, is probably the most interesting part of it, where your learning curve should have been the steepest.

Appendix A: Bond rating

A bond rating is a measure of quality, and is given by a rating agency, the main three being Moody's, Standard & Poor's and Fitch. They all work in a similar way; first they define nine levels of quality within simplified

Table 3A.1   Bond ratings

Standard & Poor's	Moody's	
AAA	Aaa	*Investment grade*
AA	Aa	
A	A	
BBB	Baa	
BB	Ba	*High yield*
B	B	
CCC	Caa	*Distressed*
CC	Ca	
C	C	

scales, rating the issues rather than the issuer as one bond issue from any one issuer may be more risky than another. Rating defines the risk of loss in case of default; it combines the probability of default and the probability of recovery. It is not a quantitative measure, but a classification of a measure of the quality of the risk. Table A.1 compares the ratings from two of the main agencies. The top part shows the low-risk issues, the central part shows bonds considered as high yielding with a higher level of risk, and the bottom part shows the distressed part of the markets. For more information please read Bessis (2000) Chapter 8.

Appendix B: Convertibles basics

A convertible is a security that gives its holder the right to exchange it for a predetermined number of shares at any point between the dates of its issuance and its maturity. It can be exchangeable against ordinary or preference shares, depending on the characteristics defined on issuance. Convertibles are, however, issued as subordinated debt; the conversion right is a call option usually held by the investor that can decide whether or not to proceed to the conversion depending on the opportunity and on personal preference. If the investor decides not to convert the convertible into equities they will receive the coupons over the life of the bond and the principal will be paid back at maturity. In some cases the issuer keeps the right to proceed to a total or partial anticipated reimbursement; if so, the bond is said to be callable, whereas a bond is puttable if this right is in the hands of the buyer. In the first case the issuer can decide to repay the bond earlier if this is considered to be it is a prudent choice, and this right is often exercised in order to force conversion. This optionality is paid by the issuer. In the case of optionality in the hands of the holder, part of, or the whole, bond could be sold by the buyer to the issuer at a predetermined price, enabling the latter to gain protection against unwanted events such as dilution of the shareholders or premium contraction. In most cases convertibles are protected against share split or share dividend.

In addition to the classical characteristics such as issuer, coupon, maturity, notional and others, convertibles are defined by specific characteristics fixed on issuance. Those factors include the investment premium, conversion ratio, conversion price, conversion premium, conversion value and parity. For more information please see Capocci (2003b) or Lummer & Riepe (1993).

Exchangeables are classified within the same category as convertibles; they are convertible securities that can be converted into shares of a company different from the issuer. In the current book we use the term "convertibles" as a generic term to embrace not only convertibles but exchangeables as well.

Appendix C: Duration, modified duration and convexity

Duration, also called Macaulay Duration, is a measure of the sensitivity of the price of a bond to a change in interest rates. It is a measure of the average maturity of a bond or, more generally, of a claim, independently of the characteristics relative to the payments of the coupon.

The idea consists of estimating the average life of the various cash flows while taking as weighting coefficient the current value of each payment relative to the price of the bond.

For each maturity, going from 1 to n and for the successive payments C, C, C,...., C+F, the duration formula is as follows:

$$D = \sum_{i=1}^{n} w_i \times i$$

with $w_i = \dfrac{C \times (1+y)^{-i}}{P}$ $\qquad (i = 1, 2, ..., n-1)$

and $w_i = \dfrac{(C+F) \times (1+y)^{-n}}{P}$ $\qquad (i = n)$

where:
D = Macaulay duration
C = coupon rate
Y = yield at maturity
P = price of the bond

F = notional payment at maturity

n = number of years over which the bond pays a coupon.

If a bond has, say, a duration of three years the price of the bond will decrease by 3 per cent for any 1 per cent increase in interest rates, and vice versa; the price of the bond will increase by 3 per cent for every 1 per cent decrease in interest rates. Such a bond is less risky that another bond with a duration of six years whose price moves by 6 per cent for every variation of 1 per cent in interest rates; the bond with a longer maturity will be more impacted by a change in interest rates because that change will impact it over a longer period of time.

Modified duration is a direct measure of the impact of a change in interest rate and a change in the price of a bond. It is defined as follows:

$$MD = (-\frac{1}{P}) \times \frac{\Delta P}{\Delta y} = \frac{1}{(1+y)} * D$$

where:

MD = modified duration.

Duration is an interesting but incomplete measure of the impact of movements in interest rates on a bond. It is correct for marginal moves only, and for more important moves convexity should also be considered.

Convexity completes the duration measure because the latter does not capture precisely the true relation that exists between the price of a bond and interest rates. The mathematical measure of convexity is as follows:

$$CV = \frac{1}{P} \times \frac{\Delta^2 P}{(\Delta y)^2}$$

The right-hand side of the formula is the second derived function of the price relative to maturity. In practice, the formula used to quantify convexity is the following:

$$CV = \frac{1}{P} \times \frac{\Delta^2 P}{(\Delta y)^2} = \frac{1}{(1+y)^2} \times \sum_{t=1}^{T} t(t+1) \times \frac{C_t / (1+y)^t}{P}$$

Modified duration and convexity are usually combined in order to arrive at a correct estimation of the impact of an interest rate variation on the price, using the following formula:

$$\% \,Price = (-DM) \times \Delta y + \frac{1}{2} \times C \times (\Delta y)^2$$

Appendix D: Hedge Fund Research Indices construction

The HFRI Monthly Indices (HFRI) are equally-weighted performance indexes. The HFRI are divided into four main strategies, each with multiple sub-strategies. All single-manager HFRI Index constituents are included in the HFRI Fund Weighted Composite, which accounts for over 2200 funds listed on the internal HFR Database. Funds included in the HFRI Monthly Indices must:

– report monthly returns
– report net returns
– report assets in US dollars
– have at least US$50 million under management, or have been actively trading for at least 12 months.

Notes on indices:

– Funds are eligible for inclusion in the HFRI the month after their addition to HFR Database. For instance, a fund added to the HFR Database in June is eligible for inclusion in the indices upon reporting its July performance.
– The HFRI are updated three times a month: Flash Update (fifth business day of the month), Mid Update (15th of the month – or the following business day), and End Update (the first business day of the following month)
– If a fund liquidates/closes, the performance of that fund will be included in the HFRI as at that fund's last reported performance update.
– The HFRI Fund of Funds index is not included in the HFRI Fund Weighted Composite index.
– Both domestic and offshore funds are included in the HFRI. In cases where a manager lists mirror-performance funds, only the fund with the larger asset size is included in the HFRI.[58]

Appendix E: The Greeks

Certain Greek character indicate measures of the sensitivity of a portfolio or of an option to movements in the underlying factors such as maturity, time, interest rates and volatility. These can also be estimated for securities with implied option features, like convertibles. The most widely used Greeks are delta, gamma, theta, vega, and rho:

- Delta is the sensitivity of an option to change in the price of the underlying asset. In other words, everything else being equal, the value of an option will change by the delta following any movement in the underlying price. The closer delta is to zero, the less sensitive is the portfolio to any move in the underlying security, and a delta-neutral portfolio means that the portfolio is not exposed to movement in the underlying price. To obtain the overall delta of a portfolio, the value of the delta of each individual position should be multiplied by its size; the delta of the portfolio is the sum of these numbers. The value of this parameter tells us the quantity of underlyer that should be bought or sold in order to immunize the portfolio against movements in the price of the underlyer. Delta is estimated using the following formula

$$Delta = \frac{\delta P}{\delta S} = N(d_1)$$

where:
∂P = variation of the price of the portfolio or the option
∂S = variation of the price of the underlyer.

- The gamma of a portfolio is the secondary derivative function of the portfolio relative to the underlyer. It is a measure of the sensitivity of the delta to movements in the price of the underlyer, so is a measure of volatility. The gamma of an option is always positive; a gamma close to zero means that the portfolio is neutral against larger movements in the underlyer. It can be estimated using the following formula:

$$Gamma = \frac{\delta^2 P}{\delta S^2} = \frac{1}{S\sigma\sqrt{T}} N'(d_1)$$

- Theta gives information on the impact of the passage of time on the portfolio. The theta of an option is negative, and the value of an option decreases when maturity approaches. Theta can be estimated using the following formula:

$$Theta = \frac{\delta C}{\delta t} = \frac{S\sigma}{2\sqrt{T}} N'(d_1) + Kre^{-rt}N(d_2)$$

- The vega of a portfolio is the change in its value relative to an increase or decrease in the volatility of the underlyer by 1 point. A vega-neutral portfolio is immune against changes in the volatility of the underlyer. Vega can be estimated using the following formula:

$$Vega = \frac{\delta C}{\delta \sigma} = S\sqrt{T}N'(d_1)$$

- Rho measures the sensitivity of an option or a portfolio to changes in interest rates. This value can be either positive or negative. Rho can be estimated using the following formula:

$$Rho = \frac{\delta C}{\delta r} = TKre^{-rt}N(d_2)$$

4
Hedge Fund Performance Over Time

This chapter analyses the historical performance of hedge funds and their relations with traditional markets. We will not present complex quantitative tools but if you are interested in these, we recommend you have a look at Capocci (2007),[1] which focuses on decomposing hedge fund returns and on the effect of integrating hedge funds into a classical portfolio.

We start this chapter with a section giving the specific features of hedge fund data. We focus the second section on the historical performance of the industry before, in Section 3, analysing historical performance per investment strategy. The fourth section analyses the performance of hedge funds during extreme market movements and the fifth presents the results of the main academic studies on the topic. We round this chapter off with an analysis of the correlation between hedge fund strategies and between hedge funds and traditional markets, including equities, bonds and commodities.

1 Data

1.1 Specific features of hedge fund data

There is no official database of hedge funds so, although many funds have provided a considerable amount of information to one or more private databases, access to data and its reliability remains an issue. There are various databases that group information on hedge funds, but most of them have existed for only 10 to 20 years.[2] The academic world expended much time and energy on the analysis of hedge fund databases in order to determine the overlaps between them, and the overall results indicate that a limited number of funds report to several different databases. Some results are of even greater concern; Liang (2000) identified significant differences in similar funds within different databases. These differences appeared in terms of returns, assets under management, launch date and

382

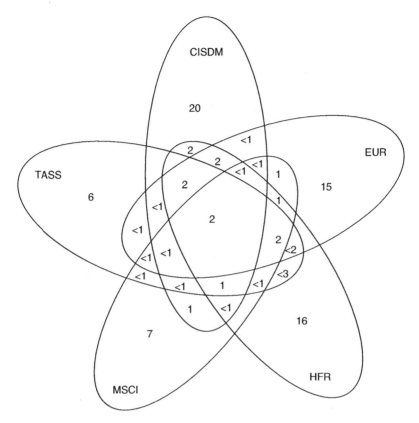

Figure 4.1 Comparison of the main hedge fund databases
Source: Fung and Hsieh (2006).

fee structure, but in some cases funds were even not classified in the same investment strategy.

Figure 4.1 gives a comparison of these databases using a Venn diagram. The database analysed includes Hedge Fund Research, Dow Jones Credit Suisse, EurekaHedge, BarclayHedge and the Morningstar CISDM database. This figure divides the hedge fund industry up as if it was made of just the funds in these databases. The numbers reported are given as a percentage. The results are clear: only 2 per cent of the funds are represented in all five databases. This means that the results of any analysis obtained using one database may be different on using a different database, as the funds in the databases are different. In addition, the results obtained using a single database may not be valid for the industry as a whole, because the database in question represents only a portion of the whole industry.

The quality of the data reported by hedge fund databases has also been often criticized, because the data is reported on only a voluntary basis and because the performance reported in the database comes directly from the management companies; performance is usually either inserted into the system directly by the asset manager or sent via email. So the risk of handling error is real, explaining why databases tend to mention that the last three months of data are not final. One way to mitigate this issue is to use data coming directly from the administrators – but this leads to extra work.

1.2 Biases

Problems related to databases lead to potential biases in those databases. Such biases have been largely studied by academic researchers. The first arises from the fact that the information available through database providers is reported exclusively on a voluntary basis. It is the fund managers who decide whether or not they will report information on their fund to a database, what information they choose to report, and which database providers they will work with. This explains why these databases are incomplete. This bias is known as an auto-reporting bias; it cannot be quantified and it is present in every database by default, as they acquire information exclusively on a voluntary basis. Although most database providers mention that they do the necessary checks on the information they get, they tend not to clarify how these checks are implemented.

The second important bias is the survivorship bias.[3] This is present in a database when it includes only those funds that have existed throughout the whole period under review. A fund can cease reporting its performance to a database for various reasons; bad performance explains half of the cases but academic studies based on various sources report other factors, such as fund mergers, in 10 per cent of cases. The remaining 40 per cent tend to be funds that stop reporting but continue to exist;[4] these do have, however, a tendency to underperform the hedge fund industry as a whole. In the academic world, survivorship bias is defined as the difference in performance between existing funds that have survived over the whole period analysed and the performance of the entire database (including "dissolved funds,") which includes both the former and the funds that were dissolved before the end of the period under review.[5] A significant difference in performance indicates that dissolved funds underperformed the funds that survived throughout the period. This means that a database that does not include the dissolved funds is biased and the returns will be overestimated. The estimations of this bias range fro m 1 to 3 per cent,[6] meaning that a fund that existed throughout the period offers a performance that is 1 to 3 per cent higher than the whole set of funds in that database.

Table 4.1 gives an estimate of the survivorship bias in a published academic study. It shows the annual performance year on year, and separates dissolved and surviving funds. The difference in performance between surviving and dissolved funds is positive every single year, and in volatile In this specific case, our estimate of the survivorship bias is 1.51 per cent for the whole period, rising to 2.61 per cent during the second half when the data was more reliable.

Table 4.1   Estimate of survivorship bias

Panel A: Annual Performance

Year	All funds			Surviving funds			Dissolved funds		
	Return	Std. dev.	Obs.	Return	Std. dev.	Obs.	Return	Std. dev.	Obs.
1994	1.81%	1.59%	8601	2.97%	1.38%	3419	1.03%	1.79%	5182
1995	18.64%	0.97%	10641	19.89%	1.02%	4630	17.65%	0.96%	6011
1996	21.29%	1.44%	13049	23.57%	1.29%	6200	19.25%	1.57%	6849
1997	20.40%	2.04%	15860	22.39%	1.89%	8136	18.32%	2.21%	7724
1998	3.59%	3.18%	17872	4.42%	3.03%	9954	2.58%	3.38%	7918
1999	33.46%	2.45%	18798	33.79%	2.21%	12052	33.29%	2.93%	6746
2000	9.62%	2.91%	20221	14.42%	2.34%	14395	−2.28%	4.34%	5826
2001	5.71%	1.62%	20591	8.00%	1.39%	16706	−3.17%	2.59%	3885
2002	0.43%	1.26%	20771	1.17%	1.21%	18899	−4.89%	1.99%	1872
Mean 94–99	0.17	1.95%	14137	0.18	1.80%	7399	0.15	2.14%	6738
Mean 00–02	0.05	1.93%	20528	0.08	1.65%	16667	−0.03	2.97%	3861
Mean 94–02	0.13	1.94%	16267	0.15	1.75%	10488	0.09	2.42 %	5779

Panel B: Surviving funds – All funds

Year	Return	
1994	0.01	
1995	0.01	
1996	0.02	
1997	0.02	
1998	0.01	
1999	0.00	
2000	0.05	
2001	0.02	
2002	0.01	
Bias 1/94–3/00	0.09	Per month
	1.03	Per year
Bias 4/00–12/02	0.22	Per month
	2.61	Per year
Bias 1/94–12/02	0.13	Per month
	1.51	Per year

Source: Capocci (2007).

We are convinced that in practice the impact of survivorship bias remains limited, as it can be counterbalanced by various elements; first, some managers stop reporting to database when they close their funds to new investors. Secondly, funds that have performed well in the past and are still open to investors will have a clear incentive to report their performance to databases.

The addition of high quality funds and their track records into a database may lead to another bias called instant history bias,[7] which is estimated by comparing two series of returns. The first includes the whole set of funds included in the database from Month 1 until the last data point available; the second includes the same information, except that for every fund the first few months of data – 12, 24 or 36 months – are removed. A comparison of the returns of the two series indicates whether or not this bias is present. The differences in performance shown in Table 4.2 oscillate between 1.3 per cent and 2.3 per cent. Those numbers mean that the funds analysed offered on average 1.3 per cent of additional returns over the first 12 months of existence. It is interesting to note that the difference in performance gets larger between 24 and 36 months. This is a clear indication of the presence of instant history bias.

A final issue with hedge fund data is the high attrition rate of the industry analyzed into details in the Section 14.2.1 of Chapter 2.

1.3   The indices

There are a multitude of hedge fund indices that aim to represent the performance of the hedge fund industry, and part of the academic literature has focused on these indices.[8] Table 4.3 shows the main hedge fund data providers and their main characteristics.

Table 4.2   Estimate of the instant return history bias

1994–2002	Average monthly return	Monthly difference	Annual difference	Average number of funds
All funds	0.99%	NA	NA	1356
Less than 12 months	0.88%	0.11%	1.32%	1174
Less than 24 months	0.84%	0.15%	1.80%	999
Less than 36 months	0.81%	0.18%	2.16%	837
Less than 48 months	0.81%	0.18%	2.16%	694
Less than 60 months	0.80%	0.19%	2.28%	570

Source: Capocci (2007).

Table 4.3 Comparison of hedge fund indices

	Index launch	Database creation	Weighting	Funds in the database	Funds in the index	Rebalancing
Altvest	2000	1993	Equ.w.	+3200	+2200	Monthly
Barclay Group	2003	1997	Equ.w.	4460	4400	Monthly
CISDM	1994	1990	Median	7600	3892	Monthly
CSFB/Tremont	1999	1994	Asset.w.	4500	413	Quarterly
EACM	1996	1996	Equ.w.	100	100	Annual
EDHEC	2003	1997	MCA	ND	ND	Quarterly
Hennessee	1987	1987	Equ.w.	+3000	900	Annual
HF net	1998	1995	Equ.w.	+5000	+3600	Monthly
HFR	1994	1990	Equ.w.	2300	+1600	Monthly
MSCI	2002	2002	Equ.w. & Asset.w.	+2000	+2000	Quarterly
Van Hedge	1994	1988	Multi-factor	6700	+2000	Monthly

Equ.w. = equally weighted. Asset.w. = asset weighted. MCA = main component analysis.

Source: Amenc and Martellini (2003).

The literature on the subject reports five main potential problems in these indices:

1. the quality of the data used to build the indices
2. the representativeness of the indices, which do not include non-reporting funds
3. the construction of the indices, which can either be equally-weighted or asset-weighted
4. repartition by strategy that can differ significantly
5. significant performance differences for identical strategies in indices built by different providers.[9]

2 Performance of the hedge fund industry

Figure 4.2 reports the evolution of US$100 invested in the HFRI Fund Weighted Composite index since January 1990 compared with other similar investments in the equity market, represented by the MSCI World, and the bond market, represented by the Barclays Aggregate Bond index. An investment of US$100 in the HFRI Fund Weighted Composite index would have become US$1105 by the end of December 2012. The same investment in the equity market or bond market would have become US$352 or US$472 respectively. This good relative performance can be

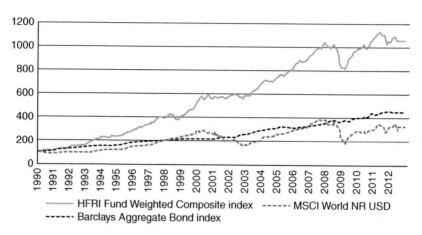

Figure 4.2   Evolution of US$100 invested in the HFRI Fund Weighted Composite index

Source: Based on numbers obtained from Hedge Fund Research, Inc.

explained by the fact that the index is highly diversified both in terms of strategies and by markets.

The HFRI Fund Weighted Composite index offered an average annual return of 11.4 per cent per year over the whole period, against 7.2 per cent for the equity market and 7.4 per cent for the bond market. The annual performance has been strong, ranging between –19 per cent and +32.2 per cent. Over the last decade the average performance has been around 6.7 per cent, but over the last five years it fell to 2.5 per cent on average. This decrease can be explained by the difficult performance of 2008 at –19 per cent and to a lesser extent in 2011, when the industry lost 5.3 per cent.

Volatility has been around 7 per cent over the whole period. It has been slightly lower over the last decade, at 6.5 per cent, but has increase to 7.4 per cent over the last five years. This is significantly lower than equities, which ranged between 15 and 20 per cent depending on the period considered. The strategy has been slightly more volatile than the bond index, which had a volatility close to 6 per cent over the various sub-periods.

Table 4.4 reports the yearly returns, the mean annual return, the standard deviation, the minimum annual return, the maximum annual return and the spread of the strategies relative to the comparative indices. It leads to the following remarks:

– Over the 23 years covered, the HFRI Fund Weighted Composite index was negative for two years only, in 2008 (–19 per cent) and 2011 (–5.3 per cent). 2008 was a very difficult year for equities, and the lack of

Table 4.4 Annual return of the Hedge Fund Composite index compared to that of equities and bonds

	HFRI Fund Weighted Composite index	MSCI World NR USD	Barclays Aggregate Bond index	Performance vs. MSCI World	Performance vs. Barclays
1990	5.8%	−17.0%	12.7%	22.8%	−6.9%
1991	32.2%	18.3%	16.0%	13.9%	16.1%
1992	21.2%	−5.2%	5.8%	26.4%	15.4%
1993	30.9%	22.5%	11.1%	8.4%	19.8%
1994	4.1%	5.1%	0.2%	−1.0%	3.9%
1995	21.5%	20.7%	19.7%	0.8%	1.8%
1996	21.1%	13.5%	4.9%	7.6%	16.2%
1997	16.8%	15.8%	3.8%	1.0%	13.0%
1998	2.6%	24.3%	13.7%	−21.7%	−11.1%
1999	31.3%	24.9%	−5.2%	6.4%	36.5%
2000	5.0%	−13.2%	3.2%	18.2%	1.8%
2001	4.6%	−16.8%	1.6%	21.4%	3.0%
2002	−1.5%	−19.9%	16.5%	18.4%	−18.0%
2003	19.5%	33.1%	12.5%	−13.6%	7.0%
2004	9.0%	14.7%	9.3%	−5.7%	−0.2%
2005	3.5%	4.5%	1.3%	−1.0%	2.2%
2006	12.9%	20.1%	6.6%	−7.2%	6.3%
2007	10.0%	9.0%	9.5%	0.9%	0.5%
2008	−19.0%	−40.7%	4.8%	21.7%	−23.8%
2009	20.0%	30.0%	6.9%	−10.0%	13.1%
2010	10.2%	11.8%	5.5%	−1.5%	4.7%
2011	−5.3%	−5.5%	5.6%	0.3%	−10.9%
2012*	6.4%	15.8%	4.3%	−9.5%	2.0%
Mean annual return (whole period)	11.4%	7.2%	7.4%	4.2%	4.0%
Volatility (whole period)	7.0%	15.6%	5.5%	NA	NA
Mean annual return 2003–2012	6.7%	9.3%	6.6%	-2.5%	0.1%
Volatility 2003–2012	6.5%	16.2%	6.1%	NA	NA
Mean average return 2007–2012	2.5%	2.3%	5.4%	0.2%	−3.0%
Volatility 2007–2012	7.4%	19.4%	6.4%	NA	NA
Minimum annual return	−19.0%	−40.7%	−5.2%	−21.7%	−23.8%
Maximum annual return	32.2%	33.1%	19.7%	26.4%	36.5%

Source: Based on data from Hedge Fund Research, Inc.

liquidity directly impacted hedge fund return. 2011 was another negative year for equities. The numbers reported are not as bad as they
were in 2008, but volatility was high and the market conditions were
not favourable for absolute return strategies. The equity index finished
down in 7 years out of 23 including the 2000–2002 bear market, in
2008 and 2011, and the bond index offered negative returns for one
year only, in 1999.
– The maximum annual returns of the HFRI Fund Weighted Composite
index were achieved in 1991 (32.2 per cent), 1999 (31.3 per cent) and
1993 (30.9 per cent), and the best return offered over the last 10 years
(20 per cent) was achieved in 2009.
– The spread in returns between the HFRI Fund Weighted Composite
index and the comparative indices varies widely over time, but tends to
be positive, meaning that hedge funds as a whole tend to outperform
the equity market and the bond market. The largest outperformance of
the HFRI Fund Weighted Composite index relative to equities was 26.4
per cent in 1992, while the largest underperformance was 21.7 per cent,
in 1998. Relative to the bond index, the largest outperformance was
achieved in 1999 at 36.5 per cent, and the largest underperformance
was 23.8 per cent, in 2008.

Figure 4.3 reports the spread in annual returns between these indices.
It indicates the presence of a certain degree of cyclicality in the numbers
reported, particularly in relation to the equity market.

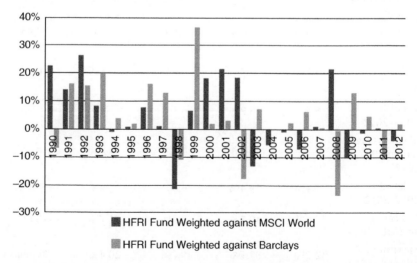

Figure 4.3 Relative performance of hedge funds with the MSCI World and the
Barclays Global Bond index

Source: Based on numbers obtained from Hedge Fund Research, Inc.

Hedge funds outperformed the equity index over the first few years; then they underperformed it between 1995 and 1998, before outperforming again until 2002, when dropping again, to underperform until 2009. More recently, however, the trend has not been so clear.

Hedge funds lagged bonds in 1990 but outperformed between 1991 and 1997. They lagged significantly in 1998 before largely outperforming bonds in 1999. Between 2000 and 2008 the spread in the returns was low, with the exception of 2002 when hedge funds underperformed significantly. In 2008 and to a lesser extent in 2011, hedge funds suffered, dropping below the bond index.

Such a general overview with an exclusive focus on performance is of only limited interest, as risk aspects should also be taken into consideration – but it nevertheless gives an interesting general context and helps give a better idea of the profile of the hedge fund industry.

3   Hedge fund performance and volatility by strategy

This section analyses the performance and the volatility of hedge funds, and compares these factors to equity and bond indices.

3.1   Statistical analysis

Table 4.5 compares the strategies analysed in Chapter 3, using basic statistics such as mean annual return, annual volatility, minimum annual return, maximum annualized return, and the percentage of positive or negative years. It is interesting because it indicates that over the long and medium term hedge funds as a whole have offered attractive returns. We should mention, however, that the 11.4 per cent annualized returns over the long term is probably rather high, as financial markets were not as well developed at the start of the period covered; the 6.7 per cent offered over the medium term is probably more in line with what we could expect from absolute return strategies throughout a full cycle. This is slightly below the long-term returns of bonds and equities. The lower short-term returns, at 2.5 per cent, since 2007 should also be balanced, as this period includes not only several crises but also the most difficult year that the hedge fund industry has faced for decades. Volatility is more stable over time; it stays between 6.5 and 7.4 per cent depending on the market conditions – slightly higher than bonds, but significantly lower than equities. While this is true at an industry level, it is important to remember that it will be somewhat different at a strategy level and may be completely different at an individual fund level, as some funds will look for enhanced returns and will take directional bets that will lead to a high volatility.

Table 4.7 Comparison between the indices (January 1990-December 2012)

	Mean annual return (whole period)	Volatility (whole period)	Sharpe score	Mean annual return 2003-2012	Volatility 2003-2012	Sharpe score	Mean average return 2007-2012	Volatility 2007-2012	Sharpe score	Minimum	Maximum	> 0	< 0
HFRI Fund Weighted Composite Index	11.4%	7.0%	1.63	6.7%	6.5%	1.04	2.5%	7.4%	0.33	-19.0%	32.2%	87.0%	13.0%
MSCI World NR USD	7.2%	15.6%	0.46	9.3%	16.2%	0.57	2.3%	19.4%	0.12	-40.7%	33.1%	69.6%	30.4%
Barclays Aggregate Bond Index	7.4%	5.5%	1.35	6.6%	6.1%	1.09	5.4%	6.4%	0.85	-5.2%	19.7%	95.7%	4.3%
HFRI EH: Equity Market Neutral Index	0.9%	3.3%	0.28	0.2%	2.8%	0.07	-0.1%	3.3%	-0.03	-2.6%	3.6%	91.3%	8.7%
HFRI EH: Quantitative Directional	2.6%	13.0%	0.20	1.9%	10.0%	0.19	1.1%	9.9%	0.11	-2.4%	10.7%	91.3%	8.7%
HFRI Relative Value (Total) Index	10.5%	4.4%	2.38	6.9%	4.9%	1.40	6.0%	6.1%	0.98	-18.0%	27.1%	95.7%	4.3%
HFRI RV: Fixed Income – Convertible Arbitrage Index	9.9%	6.7%	1.47	7.4%	9.3%	0.80	8.6%	11.7%	0.74	-33.7%	60.2%	87.0%	13.0%
HFRI Macro: Systematic Diversified Index	10.9%	7.5%	1.46	7.5%	8.1%	0.92	4.0%	8.8%	0.45	-3.5%	26.2%	82.6%	17.4%
HFRI ED: Distressed/Restructuring Index	12.6%	6.6%	1.90	9.5%	6.8%	1.40	4.7%	7.9%	0.59	-25.2%	35.7%	87.0%	13.0%
HFRI Emerging Markets (Total) Index	14.9%	14.3%	1.05	12.4%	12.1%	1.02	2.2%	13.8%	0.16	-37.3%	79.2%	78.3%	21.7%
HFRI Emerging Markets: Asia ex-Japan Index	11.6%	13.7%	0.84	12.1%	13.2%	0.92	-0.4%	15.0%	-0.03	-33.5%	80.1%	60.9%	39.1%
HFRI Emerging Markets: Global Index	14.1%	13.4%	1.05	9.9%	10.0%	0.99	1.5%	11.6%	0.13	-36.4%	87.1%	76.2%	23.8%
HFRI Emerging Markets: Latin America Index	16.7%	18.1%	0.92	11.2%	12.5%	0.90	3.7%	13.9%	0.27	-29.0%	74.9%	68.2%	31.8%
HFRI Emerging Markets: Russia/Eastern Europe Index	20.5%	27.5%	0.75	13.1%	19.9%	0.66	-2.9%	22.5%	-0.13	-63.9%	83.3%	78.9%	21.1%

Index													
HFRI Equity Hedge (Total) Index	13.1%	9.2%	1.42	6.2%	8.8%	0.70	1.5%	10.2%	0.15	-26.7%	44.2%	87.0%	13.0%
HFRI Event Driven (Total) Index	12.1%	6.9%	1.75	8.6%	6.8%	1.26	4.1%	7.7%	0.53	-21.8%	28.2%	82.6%	17.4%
HFRI RV: Fixed Income – Asset Backed	9.7%	4.1%	2.36	8.7%	3.1%	2.82	11.3%	3.8%	2.97	-9.2%	23.9%	85.0%	15.0%
HFRI Fund of Funds Composite Index	7.6%	5.8%	1.31	3.7%	5.5%	0.67	-1.0%	6.3%	-0.16	-21.4%	26.5%	82.6%	17.4%
HFRI FOF: Conservative Index	6.5%	4.0%	1.64	2.9%	4.4%	0.66	-0.9%	5.2%	-0.17	-19.9%	18.9%	82.6%	17.4%
HFRI FOF: Diversified Index	7.1%	6.0%	1.19	3.7%	5.3%	0.70	-0.8%	6.0%	-0.14	-20.9%	28.5%	82.6%	17.4%
HFRI FOF: Market Defensive Index	7.9%	5.9%	1.34	4.0%	5.4%	0.75	1.2%	5.8%	0.21	-6.7%	26.3%	87.0%	13.0%
HFRI FOF: Strategic Index	10.3%	8.7%	1.19	4.5%	7.0%	0.65	-1.4%	7.8%	-0.18	-25.2%	38.5%	73.9%	26.1%
HFRI Macro (Total) Index	12.8%	7.6%	1.68	6.1%	5.3%	1.15	2.6%	5.3%	0.49	-4.3%	53.3%	87.0%	13.0%
HFRI ED: Merger Arbitrage Index	8.6%	4.1%	2.09	5.1%	3.3%	1.54	3.0%	3.3%	0.91	-5.4%	20.2%	91.3%	8.7%
HFRI RV: Multi-Strategy Index	8.7%	4.4%	1.98	5.5%	5.1%	1.08	4.7%	6.4%	0.73	-20.3%	27.4%	87.0%	13.0%
HFRI ED: Private Issue/ Regulation D Index	11.0%	7.0%	1.57	4.9%	6.3%	0.77	0.9%	5.7%	0.15	-10.1%	44.6%	70.6%	29.4%
HFRI RV: Fixed Income – Corporate Index	8.7%	6.6%	1.32	7.3%	7.4%	0.99	6.0%	6.9%	0.87	-24.2%	41.8%	78.3%	21.7%
HFRI EH: Sector – Energy/Basic Materials Index	17.1%	16.4%	1.05	9.0%	8.6%	1.05	5.1%	8.6%	0.59	-16.7%	124.3%	81.8%	18.2%
HFRI EH: Sector – Technology/Healthcare Index	11.7%	7.0%	1.67	6.7%	6.5%	1.04	2.5%	7.4%	0.33	-19.0%	32.2%	86.4%	13.6%
HFRI EH: Short Bias Index	0.7%	18.7%	0.04	-5.5%	11.4%	-0.49	-6.1%	13.1%	-0.47	-24.4%	36.2%	43.5%	56.5%

Source: Based on data from Hedge Fund Research, Inc.

A closer look at the strategy numbers indicates that 15 strategy indices offered an annualized return of over 10 per cent over the long term, while 12 of them offered an annualized return of less than 10 per cent over that period. 19 indices had a volatility of less than 10 per cent over the long term, and 8 over that level. Over 10 years, only 4 strategies offered an annualized return over 10 per cent, and only 6 had had a volatility of under 10 per cent. Almost half of them offered more than 7 per cent annualized. The volatility profile over 10 years is not significantly different from the long-term profile, the only noticeable difference being that the convertible arbitrage volatility increased significantly over the period while that of emerging market funds and the sector technology and healthcare index decreased significantly. Over shorter term, 8 strategies posted negative returns while 19 were positive – but only 5 of them at over 5 per cent.

The most rewarding strategy over the long term has been the emerging market Russia/Eastern Europe index, with an impressive 20.5 per cent annualized. This does involve, however, high volatility – over 25 per cent. In addition the worst year of the strategy was down almost 64 per cent. Other strategies that performed well over the long term include the other emerging market indices, sector funds, equity hedge funds, macro and CTAs. On the other hand, equity market neutral funds and short-biased funds did not perform well, and their mean annualized return was close to zero.

The emerging market strategies have also been the best performing over the medium term, at 13.1 per cent for the Russia/Eastern Europe index. The sector index follows that, with distressed managers and event driven specialists. Equity hedge funds fell below the average. Equity market neutral funds continued to offer a return close to zero, and short-biased funds lost 4.5 per cent on average over the period covered. Over shorter term fixed income strategies took the lead in a environment difficult for equities. Fixed-income asset-backed funds offered on average 11.3 per cent, followed by convertible arbitrages at 8.6 per cent. Surprisingly, short-biased funds continued to offer the lowest returns, at a –6.1 per cent on average.

The columns reporting the minimum and maximum returns give a clear differentiation between directional and non-directional strategies. In their worst year, non-directional strategies dropped below 10 per cent, while the directional ones tended to lose more than 20 per cent in their worst year; the exceptions are macro funds and CTAs. This year was 2008 in most cases. This is also true on the positive side; it is clear that directional strategies, which lost heavily in their worst years, have achieved even higher numbers in absolute terms in their best. On the other hand, some non-directional strategies, such as fixed-income asset-backed or merger arbitrage, have been able to post over 20 per cent in their best year without suffering so much, showing a very attractive asymmetric risk profile.

The last two columns show the percentage of positive and negative years, confirming the absolute return nature of the industry. Most of the strategies had less than 20 per cent negative years, the exceptions being directional strategies such as emerging markets, sector specialists and a few others. The equity market neutral index and the merger arbitrage index have even been able to post positive returns in over 90 per cent of the years covered. Although this is not as good as the bond index, at 4 per cent of negative years, it is significantly better than the equity index, with 30 per cent of negative years.

The Sharpe score columns balance the risks and rewards (or said differently return and volatility). Unlike the Sharpe ratio, it does not integrate the risk-free returns – but in a comparison context this element has no impact. Sharpe ratios range from 0 to 2.4, with both a mean and a median at around 1.3. The most attractive strategies in terms of risk–return profile over the long term are relative value, fixed-income asset-backed, merger arbitrage and distressed securities. On the other hand, short-biased funds are less attractive in risk–return terms, followed by quantitative directional market neutral funds and equity market neutral funds. The MSCI World has a Sharpe score of 0.46 just above the three worst hedge fund indices. The bond index has a Sharpe score over the long term of 1.35, close to the average hedge fund score, and lower than that of the hedge fund composite index, at 1.63.

Over the medium term, the Sharpe scores range from –0.5 to 2.8, with a mean and a median of around 0.9. The most attractive strategies in terms of risk–return trade-off are fixed-income asset-backed, followed by merger arbitrage and distressed securities. Short-biased funds, market neutral quantitative directional and equity market neutral funds remain less attractive. The MSCI World has a Sharpe score of around 0.6 which is in the lower range of that of the hedge fund indices. The bond index score, at 1.1, is close to that of the composite hedge fund index; this is in the higher range of that of hedge fund indices.

Over the short term, the range of Sharpe scores remains the same as over the medium term, varying between –0.5 and +3. The mean and the median are lower, at 0.37 and 0.2 respectively. The Sharpe score of the fixed-income asset-backed funds remains high, at 2.97, but the second highest, the merger arbitrage index, is only at 0.9. Short-biased funds continue to offer a less attractive risk–return profile, followed by fund of funds indices and emerging market Russia, all with negative Sharpe scores.

All-in-all composite hedge fund numbers are attractive over the long term. Shorter-term numbers have not been so good, but the industry as a whole has been able to offer absolute returns not only over the long and medium term but even in the shorter term. On a year-on-year basis, 2008 was very difficult for the industry, but when put into a three-to-five year context it remains correct. The industry offers a risk–return profile that is more attractive than equities and in line with bonds.

On a strategy-by-strategy basis, low-volatility strategies tend to have offered more attractive risk–return profiles, but those with the lowest volatility, such as equity market neutral funds, have not been able to offer attractive returns over the long term. Highly volatile strategies, in contrast, while having been able to offer attractive returns over the long term, may disappoint over the shorter term. The abiding interest of the industry lies in the fact that its returns tend to offer a return with a relative limited correlation to with traditional assets.

3.2   Graphical analysis

This section analyses hedge fund statistics in greater detail. We start with an analysis of the beta of the industry as a whole and of individual strategies over time, before looking at the risk–return trade-off. We focus not only on the return–standard deviation balance but also on the return–maximal losses and an extended Sharpe ratio that integrates higher moments. Then we analyse omega,[10] normality triangles, autocorrelation and the return distribution.

3.2.1   Beta

Beta is a measure of the systemic risk of an investment. It is a coefficient that establishes to what extend the return of a security follows that of an index. It is a measure of relative riskiness. Its formula is shown below:

$$\beta_a = \frac{Cov(r_a, r_p)}{Var(r_p)} \tag{4.1}$$

where:
r_a = the rate of return of the asset
r_p = the rate of return of the portfolio
$Cov(r_a, r_p)$ = the covariance between the rates of return and
$Var(r_p)$ = the variance of the portfolio.

Table 4.6 shows the beta of a series of classic and hedge fund indices over several periods of time. Over the long term the beta of the directional strategies to equities tends to be around 0.6, while the beta of non-directional strategies is usually close to 0.2. This is in line with expectations.

In addition, the estimated beta of short-biased funds is significantly negative, at –0.8, and that of the equity market neutral fund is close to zero. The numbers given remain consistent over the medium and shorter terms even when the mean and median correlations increase slightly. The largest change in correlation between the long and the medium terms is the increase in the beta of short-biased funds, from –0.8 to –0.6, and the decrease in the beta of the sector technology/healthcare index, from 0.65 to 0.42. The largest changes in beta between the long and shorter terms are the increase in the beta of convertible arbitrage funds, from 0.22 to 0.45, and the decrease in the beta of the sector technology/healthcare index, from 0.65 to 0.37.

The betas of hedge fund indices to bond indices over the long term are much lower; almost all of them are below 0.4. The only exception is in sector energy/basic material; close to 0.7. Over the medium term the increase in the beta is, however, more pronounced, for instance the mean and median beta to bonds increases from around 0.1 to 0.3. Interestingly, the main increases were in the emerging market indices. Over the short term, this pattern is even more important. We can explain this by the facts that correlation between markets increased during the recent crisis, and that the emerging market currencies have played an important role not only for emerging market bond funds but also for emerging market equity funds. Another element may be that there is a diversification effect, as the fixed income benchmark used is quite large, and because we are comparing it to hedge fund indices that tend to have funds with different profiles even when grouped within the same strategy.

The evolution of the three-year rolling beta of the composite index to the MSCI World is given in Figure 4.4. It shows some interesting patterns; firstly, the beta was not stable over time, ranging from 0.1 to 0.5, with a mean and a median close to 0.35. This is in line with the active management profile of hedge funds. Secondly, it peaked first at the end of 1999, which interestingly includes the Asian crisis, the Russian default, LTCM and the 1999 dotcom bubble. Then it slowly decreased until the middle of 2005, confirming the fact that hedge funds were able to lower their exposure to equities during the 2000–2002 bear markets. From there it increased again, to reach a second peak early in 2007, and it stayed high for a year; this corresponds to the 2005–2007 bull markets. From there it decreased slowly, to go back to 0.35 more recently. Figure 4.4 clearly shows that there is a certain amount of cyclicality in hedge fund equity beta.

Figure 4.5 shows the beta related to the bond index; here the cyclicality is less obvious. The beta started at zero and ranged between –0.4 and 0.4, but stayed between –0.2 and 0.2 for most of the time. Since 2009, it has, however, risen, and it peaked at over 0.5 early in 2012.

Table 4.6 Beta of hedge funds relative to traditional indices (January 1990 - June 2012)

	Beta to equities (whole period)	Beta to equities 2003–2012	Beta to equities 2007–2012	Beta to bonds (whole period)	Beta to bonds 2003–2012	Beta to bonds 2007–2012
HFRI Fund Weighted Composite index	0.34	0.35	0.33	0.17	0.34	0.45
MSCI World NR USD	1.00	1.00	1.00	0.84	1.06	1.50
Barclays Aggregate Bond index	0.10	0.15	0.15	1.00	1.00	1.00
HFRI ED: Distressed/Restructuring index	0.22	0.32	0.31	0.06	0.24	0.27
HFRI ED: Merger Arbitrage index	0.13	0.15	0.13	0.06	0.13	0.18
HFRI ED: Private Issue/Regulation D index	0.16	0.15	0.14	-0.06	0.08	0.11
HFRI EH: Equity Market Neutral index	0.05	0.09	0.09	0.08	0.04	0.05
HFRI EH: Quantitative Directional index	0.63	0.54	0.45	0.24	0.43	0.54
HFRI EH: Sector – Energy/Basic Materials index	0.63	0.74	0.72	0.69	0.85	0.99
HFRI EH: Sector – Technology/Healthcare index	0.65	0.42	0.37	0.09	0.27	0.33
HFRI EH: Short Bias index	-0.81	-0.60	-0.58	-0.17	-0.32	-0.49
HFRI Emerging Markets (Total) index	0.22	0.32	0.31	0.06	0.24	0.27
HFRI Emerging Markets: Asia ex-Japan index	0.64	0.63	0.61	0.29	0.73	0.91
HFRI Emerging Markets: Global index	0.59	0.63	0.59	0.36	0.70	0.94
HFRI Emerging Markets: Latin America index	0.54	0.51	0.49	0.07	0.57	0.72

HFRI Emerging Markets: Russia/Eastern Europe index	0.67	0.59	0.56	0.32	0.71	0.88
HFRI Equity Hedge (Total) index	0.43	0.49	0.48	0.23	0.40	0.58
HFRI Event Driven (Total) index	0.31	0.36	0.34	0.11	0.29	0.36
HFRI Fund of Funds Composite index	0.21	0.26	0.24	0.10	0.23	0.27
HFRI FOF: Conservative index	0.14	0.19	0.18	0.08	0.14	0.15
HFRI FOF: Diversified index	0.21	0.24	0.22	0.07	0.19	0.22
HFRI FOF: Market Defensive index	0.05	0.10	0.05	0.18	0.30	0.27
HFRI FOF: Strategic index	0.31	0.35	0.32	0.13	0.31	0.40
HFRI Macro (Total) index	0.18	0.11	0.06	0.33	0.35	0.31
HFRI Macro: Systematic Diversified index	0.20	0.09	-0.04	0.20	0.30	0.36
HFRI Relative Value (Total) index	0.15	0.23	0.24	0.09	0.19	0.27
HFRI RV: Fixed Income-Asset Backed	0.05	0.08	0.09	0.00	0.04	0.04
HFRI RV: Fixed Income – Convertible Arbitrage index	0.22	0.39	0.45	0.25	0.46	0.67
HFRI RV: Fixed Income – Corporate index	0.23	0.29	0.30	0.10	0.20	0.27
HFRI RV: Multi-Strategy index	0.16	0.23	0.24	0.13	0.23	0.29

Source: Based on data from Hedge Fund Research, Inc.

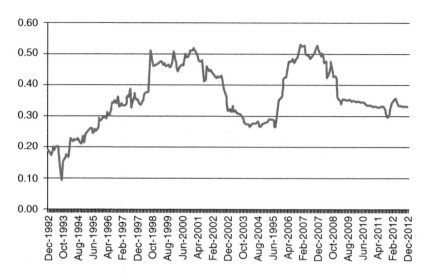

Figure 4.4 Evolution of the three-year rolling beta of the HFRI Fund Weighted Composite index as against the MSCI World

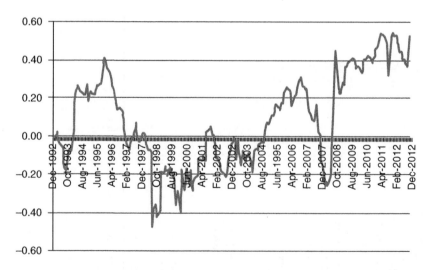

Figure 4.5 Evolution of the three-year rolling beta of the HFRI Fund Weighted Composite index as against the Barclays Global Bond index

3.2.2 Risk–return trade-off

Figures 4.6 to 4.8 report the risk–return trade-off between traditional markets and hedge fund strategies. They are interesting because they put the relative risk level of hedge fund strategies into context and enable us to identify the strategies offering the best risk–return trade-off over the various periods under review. We use standard deviation as the measure of risk. Figure 4.6 focuses on the long term. The more dynamic strategies were sector funds, emerging market funds and short-biased funds. These indices had a volatility profile in line with that of the equity market, represented by the MSCI World. Their long-term annualized volatility ranged between 15 and 20 per cent. Quantitative directional funds were not far behind, but their long-term annualized volatility was below 15 per cent. Then they were followed by many strategies with a long-term volatility of between 5 and 10 per cent.

The bond market, represented by the Barclays Aggregate Bond index, has a long-term volatility of around 5.5 per cent, meaning that strategies on the left-hand side of the range have a profile in line with bonds over the long term. Such indices include convertible arbitrage, event driven, distressed securities, Regulation D, fixed income corporate and funds of hedge funds. It may seem astonishing that event driven funds have a risk profile identical to bonds over the long term; but this can be explained by the fact that there are so many ways in which to implement this strategy

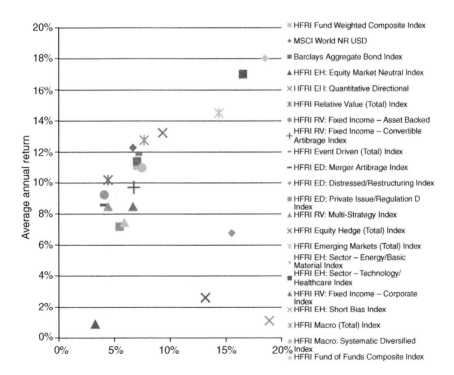

Figure 4.6 Risk–return profile of hedge fund strategies over the long term (inception–30 June 2012)

that the diversification effect is very strong at index level. Our experience tells us that individual event driven funds tend to have a volatility level on the right-hand side of the 5-to-10-per-cent range rather than on the left of it. The same could arise regarding distressed securities funds, but here the answer is different; while the strategy is not a liquid one, this does not mean that it is volatile; in practice, the liquidity risk in the strategy leads to an autocorrelation of returns and a relatively low-volatility profile. On the higher scale of low-volatility strategies – that is strategies with a long-term volatility of between 7.5 per cent and 10 per cent – we find the macro index, the CTA index and the equity hedge index. This result is in line with expectations. On the far left-hand side of the volatility range we find strategies with a long-term volatility of below 5 per cent.

The lowest risk strategy of the entire range is the equity market neutral index, followed by the merger arbitrage index and the fixed income asset-backed index. The relative value and the multi-strategy indices have a slightly higher volatility, closer to that of the bond index.

In terms of performance, the higher-risk strategies have, in most cases, provided the highest returns. Out of 19 strategies reported in the graph, 15 have a return profile in line with their level of risk. The three exceptions are the equity market neutral index, which offered an average performance close to zero over the period, but which was achieved with the lowest level of volatility; the quantitative directional index, which offered less than 3 per cent annual average return for a volatility relatively close to that of the equity index; and the short bias index, which had a volatility higher than the equity index, for an average return around 1 per cent. This last result is in line with the profile of the strategy and with the returns offered by equities over the period covered.

Figure 4.7 gives the same information for the last decade, during which time the volatility of the traditional indices has increased slightly. The profile of the strategies in terms of risk was broadly the same as over the long term; for most strategies the change in volatility has been limited, the notable exception on the upside being the convertible arbitrage index, whose volatility increased from 6.5 per cent over the whole period to 9.5 per cent over the last ten years. This can be explained by the extremely difficult year for the strategy in 2008, when the index was down over 33 per cent overall, with a very volatile September. In this higher-risk environment a few strategies posted stable returns; the fixed-income asset-backed index's volatility lost 1 per cent of volatility, at 4.1 per cent, and the emerging market index lost 2 points of volatility, at 14.4 per cent. This can probably be mainly explained by the larger opportunity set and the greater ability to short in emerging markets, which were volatile. Sector

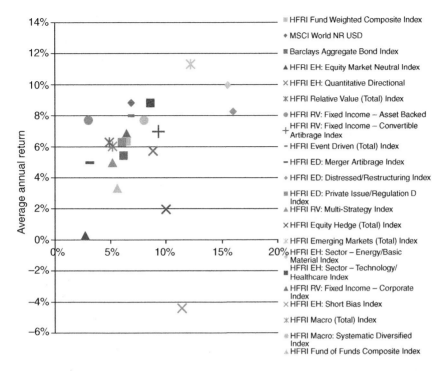

Figure 4.7 Risk–return profile of hedge fund strategies over the medium term (January 2003–30 June 2012)

hedge fund strategies also lost a few points of volatility, but they kept a similar risk–return profile. Short-biased funds and macro managers were also significantly less volatile.

In risk–return terms, the same pattern can be found even if the out-performance for every strategy is not as obvious as before; while all but three indices overtook the MSCI World in absolute terms over the whole period, only four indices did so over the last decade. Nevertheless, most indices offered slightly lower average annual returns for significantly less volatility. As illustrated by the Hedge Fund Weighted Composite index, in most cases the returns remained relatively high for a significantly lower volatility level – but the supremacy of hedge fund can be challenged. The profile of four hedge fund indices was unattractive, in that the equity market neutral index provided lower returns for a very low volatility; the fund of funds index offered on average less than a 4 per cent return for a volatility level of over 5 per cent; the quantitative directional index was only slightly positive on average over the last decade, with a volatility

404   The Complete Guide to Hedge Funds and Hedge Fund Strategies

level of over 10 per cent; finally for the first time a single strategy, short-biased funds, produced a negative return on average over the last decade. This can be explained by the fact that the over the last decade equity index performance was strong, despite peaks in volatility.

Figure 4.8 shows the same information over the last five years. The situation continues to deteriorate – but let me put these numbers into perspective. First of all, this period includes only five years, one of which is 2008. That was the year when equities fell by more than 40 per cent, and it was the year of the liquidity crisis that affected hedge funds more than any other crisis previously. It has also led to changes at the heart of the industry. I am not saying that this cannot happen again, but that if a similar situation would happen, many managers that faced liquidity issues that year should be able to handle things better. Secondly, as with any crisis that affects an entire industry, there were exceptions that were able to post correct returns over that period. The hedge fund composite index offered a slightly positive average return of close to 2 per cent over this period. Several indices, including the relative value index, the technology/healthcare sector index, the fixed-income corporate index and

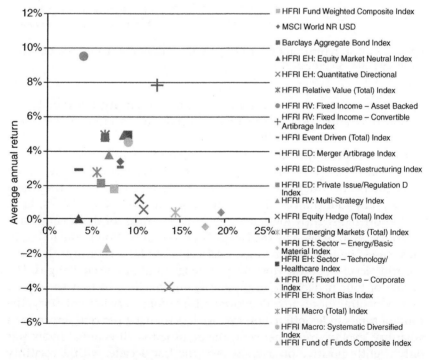

Figure 4.8 Risk–return profile of hedge fund strategies over the shorter term (January 2007–30 June 2012)

the macro/CTA index posted positive average returns of close to 5 per cent. A few exceptions, such as fixed income asset-backed or fixed income convertible arbitrage offered an average return of over 7.5 per cent. The MSCI World was flat, and the Barclays Aggregate Bond index offered an average annual return of just below 5 per cent. In this context, most volatile equity strategies did badly; out of the 19 hedge fund indices, 4 had a negative average annual return: the equity market neutral (almost flat), the fund of funds, the short bias and the energy/basic material sector. This last element shows that even when hedge funds did not offer attractive returns over this period, most of them at least managed to protect capital. This is the aim of absolute return strategies.

Another risk measure that might be of interest in the case of absolute return strategies is the maximum annual loss. Many investors integrate hedge funds within their portfolios because of their potential for diversification and their limited volatility. The first objective of these investors is to limit the maximum potential loss. Figure 4.9 displays this statistic for the whole period under review; for a shorter period of time we should use a monthly or quarterly maximum loss. Investor wants to avoid indices at

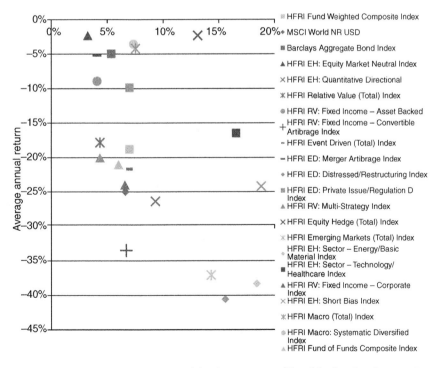

Figure 4.9 Risk (maximum annual loss)–return profile of hedge fund strategies over the long term (inception–30 June 2012)

the bottom, and for strategies at the top to be further left. No single strategy was able to offer positive returns for the 20+ years covered, but the good news is that most of them posted negative returns for only one or two years. All the low-volatility strategies faced maximum annual losses of lower than 10 per cent. Dynamic directional strategies, such as the sector index and the emerging market index, suffered the biggest fall, but none of them underperformed the MSCI World.

A few numbers have to be pointed out. Firstly, the convertible arbitrage index lost over 35 per cent in a single year despite having been a low-volatility strategy throughout the period. This is explained by the fact that the strategy was hit very hard by the 2008 liquidity issues. The same can be said for the multi-strategy index; over the long term, the index was less volatile than bond, but it dropped by 20 per cent in 2008. The bad numbers posted by multi-strategy funds can be explained by the fact that such funds tend to have been exposed to convertible arbitrage at that time, but the other numbers are in line with expectations and long-term volatility. The maximum drop in the composite hedge fund index was 19 per cent, in 2008.

3.2.3 Extended risk measure

Several studies have stressed the limitations of traditional performance measures based on standard deviation as a risk measure. Jagannathan and Korajczyk (1986) demonstrated that fund managers could build portfolios with apparently strong abilities to outperform the markets, which turned out not to be the case in practice. More recently, Goetzmann et al. (2006) proved that it is relatively easy to get attractive statistics based on classic measures like the alpha of Jensen by using a simple rebalancing technique. To integrate these issues Capocci, Duquenne and Hübner (2007) developed an extended risk measure that integrates the specific features of alternative strategies. If you are interested in the technical details regarding construction of this measure, please read the original paper. The extended risk measure is calculated as follows:

$$R_x = \frac{1}{2}V_x - \frac{1}{6}CS_x + \frac{1}{24}C^2K_x \tag{4.2}$$

where:
R_x = extended risk
V_x = variance of the series
C = risk appetite, which is estimated at 10 for a dynamic investor and 60 for a very defensive one
S_x = skewness of the series[11]
K_x = kurtosis of the series[12]

We estimated the value of R_x for the set of strategies for the two levels of risk appetite based on monthly data. The results are reported in Table 4.7 and illustrated in Figures 4.10 and 4.11.

Table 4.7 shows that in many cases the results obtained using the extended measure are in line with those obtained using standard deviation. This is particularly true for the bond index, the private issue/regulation D index and the fund of funds market defensive index. There are however some notable exceptions. Firstly, some strategies with negative skewness and positive kurtosis that were seen as relatively safe using standard deviation alone are now found amongst the higher-risk strategies: these include merger arbitrage funds, the fund of funds conservative

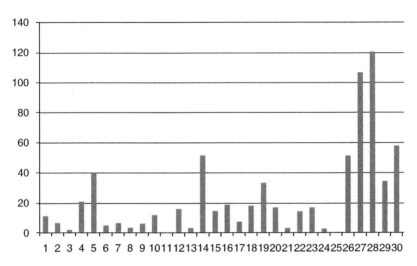

Figure 4.10 Measure of risk of hedge funds using an extended risk measure (C = 10)
1 = HFRI Fund Weighted Composite Index, 2 = MSCI World NR USD, 3 = Barclays Aggregate Bond Index, 4 = HFRI ED: Distressed/Restructuring Index, 5 = HFRI ED: Merger Arbitrage Index, 6 = HFRI ED: Private Issue/Regulation D Index, 7 = HFRI EH: Equity Market Neutral Index, 8 = HFRI EH: Quantitative Directional, 9 = HFRI EH: Sector - Energy/Basic Materials Index, 10 = HFRI EH: Sector - Technology/ Healthcare, 11 = HFRI EH: Short Bias Index, 12 = HFRI Emerging Markets (Total) Index, 13 = HFRI Emerging Markets: Asia ex-Japan Index, 14 = HFRI Emerging Markets: Global Index, 15 = HFRI Emerging Markets: Latin America Index, 16 = HFRI Emerging Markets: Russia/Eastern Europe Index, 17 = HFRI Equity Hedge (Total) Index, 18 = HFRI Event Driven (Total) Index, 19 = HFRI FOF: Conservative Index, 20 = HFRI FOF: Diversified Index, 21 = HFRI FOF: Market Defensive Index, 22 = HFRI FOF: Strategic Index, 23 = HFRI Fund of Funds Composite Index, 24 = HFRI Macro (Total) Index, 25 = HFRI Macro: Systematic Diversified Index, 26 = HFRI Relative Value (Total) Index, 27 = HFRI RV: Fixed Income-Asset Backed, 28 = HFRI RV: Fixed Income-Convertible Arbitrage Index, 29 = HFRI RV: Fixed Income-Corporate Index, 30 = HFRI RV: Multi-Strategy Index.

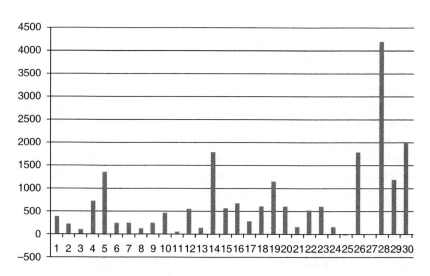

Figure 4.11   Measure of risk of hedge funds using an extended risk measure (C = 60)
1 = HFRI Fund Weighted Composite Index, 2 = MSCI World NR USD, 3 = Barclays
Aggregate Bond Index, 4 = HFRI ED: Distressed/Restructuring Index, 5 = HFRI ED:
Merger Arbitrage Index, 6 = HFRI ED: Private Issue/Regulation D Index, 7 =HFRI
EH: Equity Market Neutral Index, 8 = HFRI EH: Quantitative Directional, 9 =HFRI
EH: Sector - Energy/Basic Materials Index, 10 = HFRI EH: Sector - Technology/
Healthcare, 11 = HFRI EH: Short Bias Index, 12 = HFRI Emerging Markets (Total)
Index, 13 = HFRI Emerging Markets: Asia ex-Japan Index, 14 = HFRI Emerging
Markets: Global Index, 15 = HFRI Emerging Markets: Latin America Index, 16 =
HFRI Emerging Markets: Russia/Eastern Europe Index, 17 = HFRI Equity Hedge
(Total) Index, 18 = HFRI Event Driven (Total) Index, 19 = HFRI FOF: Conservative
Index, 20 = HFRI FOF: Diversified Index, 21 = HFRI FOF: Market Defensive Index,
22 = HFRI FOF: Strategic Index, 23 = HFRI Fund of Funds Composite Index, 24 =
HFRI Macro (Total) Index, 25 = HFRI Macro: Systematic Diversified Index, 26 =
HFRI Relative Value (Total) Index, 27 = HFRI RV: Fixed Income-Asset Backed, 28 =
HFRI RV: Fixed Income-Convertible Arbitrage Index, 29 = HFRI RV: Fixed Income-
Corporate Index, 30 = HFRI RV: Multi-Strategy Index.

index, the fixed income convertible arbitrage index and fixed income
asset-backed index. The rank of each of these strategies has moved by
more than 15, meaning that they are much riskier when the asymmetry
of the return distribution and the risk of fat tails are integrated.[13] The
same is true to a lesser extent for distressed securities managers, equity
market neutral funds, event driven funds, fund of funds (diversified and
composite indices), relative-value funds and multi-strategy funds. On the
other hand, short-biased funds, emerging market Asia ex-Japan funds, sector energy/basic materials funds and the MSCI World index are ranked as
significantly less risky when the higher moments are taken into account.
The same is true to a lesser extent for quantitative directional funds, sector

Table 4.7 Estimation of the extended risk measure

					Risk measure	
	Std. Dev.	Variance	Skewness	Kurtosis	C = 10	C = 60
HFRI Fund Weighted Composite index	2	4.1%	-0.7	2.4	11.2	367.0
MSCI World NR USD	4.5	20.1%	-0.6	1.3	6.5	201.1
Barclays Aggregate Bond index	1.6	2.5%	0.0	0.5	2.1	75.0
HFRI ED: Distressed/Restructuring index	1.9	3.7%	-1.0	4.7	21.3	715.0
HFRI ED: Merger Arbitrage index	1.2	1.4%	-2.1	8.8	40.2	1341.0
HFRI ED: Private Issue/Regulation D index	2	4.1%	0.6	1.5	5.3	219.0
HFRI EH: Equity Market Neutral index	1	0.9%	-0.3	1.5	6.8	228.0
HFRI EH: Quantitative Directional	3.8	14.3%	-0.4	0.7	3.7	109.1
HFRI EH: Sector – Energy/Basic Materials index	5.4	28.7%	0.0	1.5	6.4	225.1
HFRI EH: Sector – Technology/Healthcare index	4.8	22.8%	0.4	3.0	11.9	446.1
HFRI EH: Short Bias index	5.5	29.7%	0.2	0.2	0.6	27.8
HFRI Emerging Markets (Total) index	4.2	17.3%	-0.8	3.5	16.0	533.1
HFRI Emerging Markets: Asia ex-Japan index	3.9	15.6%	-0.1	0.8	3.6	121.1
HFRI Emerging Markets: Global index	3.9	14.9%	-1.7	11.7	51.7	1772.1
HFRI Emerging Markets: Latin America index	5.2	27.3%	0.4	3.7	14.9	551.1
HFRI Emerging Markets: Russia/Eastern Europe index	7.9	62.9%	-0.3	4.4	19.1	663.3
HFRI Equity Hedge (Total) index	2.7	7.2%	-0.3	1.7	7.6	258.0
HFRI Event Driven (Total) index	2	4.0%	-1.3	3.8	18.1	587.5
HFRI FOF: Conservative index	1.2	1.3%	-1.7	7.4	33.7	1127.0
HFRI FOF: Diversified index	1.7	3.0%	-0.4	3.9	16.9	589.0
HFRI FOF: Market Defensive index	1.7	2.9%	0.2	0.9	3.4	133.0
HFRI FOF: Strategic index	2.5	6.4%	-0.5	3.3	14.6	500.0
HFRI Fund of Funds Composite index	1.7	2.9%	-0.7	3.8	17.0	577.0
HFRI Macro (Total) index	2	4.2%	0.5	0.9	3.0	132.5
HFRI Macro: Systematic Diversified index	2.1	4.3%	0.1	-0.3	0.7	-45.4
HFRI Relative Value (Total) index	2.1	4.3%	-1.7	11.7	51.5	1768.5
HFRI RV: Fixed Income – Asset Backed	2.1	4.3%	-3.5	24.2	107.0	3672.6
HFRI RV: Fixed Income – Convertible Arbitrage index	2	4.2%	-3.0	27.8	120.7	4192.7
HFRI RV: Fixed Income – Corporate index	2.2	4.8%	-1.3	7.7	34.5	1175.2
HFRI RV: Multi-Strategy index	2.2	4.7%	-2.1	13.1	57.9	1981.4

Source: Based on data from Hedge Fund Research, Inc.

technology/healthcare funds, emerging markets Latin America funds and systematic macro managers.

In terms of ranking, there are no significant differences between very defensive and dynamic investors; the difference is mainly in terms of scale.

Figures 4.12 and 4.13 show the estimate of the extended risk measure for each strategy over the whole period. In both cases the fixed income convertible arbitrage and the fixed income asset-backed indices have a significantly higher level of risk than the other strategies. On the other hand, macro systematic, short-biased funds and, interestingly, emerging market Asia funds have a lower risk profile. This result is worthy of note, because this extended measure does not take into account just the volatility of returns but also the asymmetry in the distribution of returns and the risk of fat tails. Indices classified as lower risk may have a relatively high volatility, but this is only a part of the risk as positively skewed series or returns with limited fat tail risk are attractive for investors and will be seen as safer.

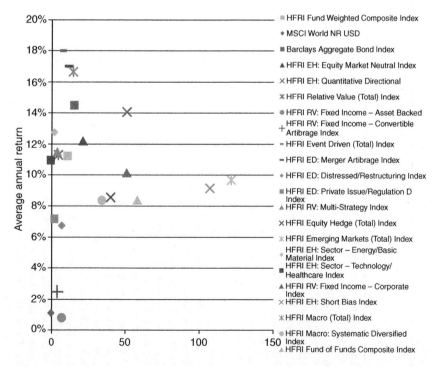

Figure 4.12 Risk (extended risk measure)–return profile of hedge fund strategies over the long term (inception–30 June 2012) for a very defensive investor

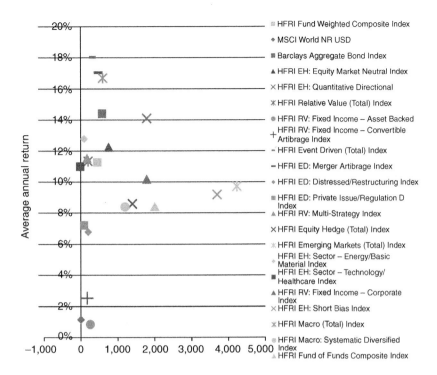

Figure 4.13   Risk (extended risk measure)–return profile of hedge fund strategies over the long term (inception–30 June 2012) for a dynamic investor

3.2.4   Omega

Traditional measures aiming to compare a series of risk-adjusted returns, such as the Sharpe ratio, Treynor ratio and information ratio, have been questioned by academics and practitioners as to their effectiveness in turbulent markets. This section introduces the omega, an advanced measure developed by Keating and Shadwick (2002). It is the ratio of the average realized return in excess of a given target return, to the average realized loss relative to that same target return. It is like a return distribution that includes higher moments and gives a risk–reward measure whose returns are weighted by their probability. The approach is based upon newer insights and developments in mathematical techniques that facilitate the analysis of returns distributions. It involves partitioning returns into profit and loss above and below a specific return threshold, then looking at the probability-weighted ratio of the returns above and below the partition.

$$\Omega(r) = \frac{I_2(r)}{I_1(r)} \tag{4.3}$$

where: $I_1(r) = \int_a^r F(x)dx$ and $I_2(r) = \int_r^b (1 - F(x))dx$

F = the cumulative distribution function of the asset returns defined on the interval [a,b]
r = the return level regarded as a loss threshold.

For any investor, returns below their specific loss threshold are considered as losses and returns above the threshold as gains. A higher omega value is always preferred to a lower value; in other words, the value of the omega function at r is the ratio of probability-weighted gains relative to r, to probability-weighted losses relative to r. Figure 4.14 illustrates the concept: $I_1(r)$ is the light-grey area on the bottom left and $I_2(r)$ is black on the top right.

By considering this omega ratio at all values of the returns threshold, we obtain a function that is characteristic of the specific asset or portfolio. The main advantages of omega are that it makes no assumption about preference or utility, works directly with the returns series, and is as statistically significant as the returns. In addition, it does not require estimation of moments, and it captures all the risk–reward characteristics. Figure 4.15 reports the omega of the HFRI Fund Weighted Hedge Fund index and the MSCI World based on the period January 1990–June 2012; it enables us to compare the profile of the two series of returns. Consider two extreme cases: for an expected return of 20 per cent (a strong bullish environment), the hedge fund value of omega is at 19.7, as against 9.2

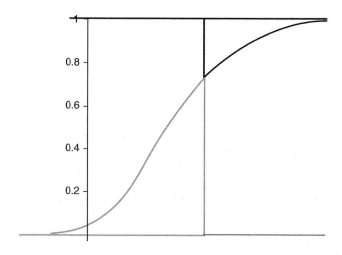

Figure 4.14   Omega

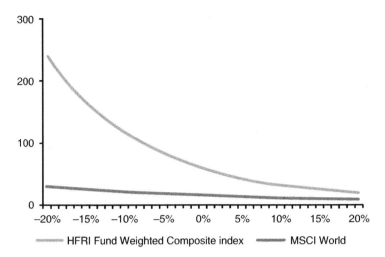

Figure 4.15   Omega of the HFRI Fund Weighted Hedge Fund index and the MSCI World

for the MSCI World, indicating that hedge funds have a more attractive profile. On the other hand, consider a very bearish market environment where the expected return is –20 per cent. The value of omega for the hedge fund index is 239, as against 30 for the MSCI World; the difference is very high. All in all, hedge funds are superior to equities for any value between –20 per cent and + 20 per cent; when the complete distribution of returns is taken into consideration, hedge funds as an industry have a more attractive profile than that of equities according to the omega measure.

Figure 4.16 compares the hedge fund index with the Barclays Aggregate Bond index. Whereas for negative expected returns, the bond index is much more attractive, over 2 per cent hedge funds become more interesting. At 20 per cent, the omega of hedge funds is at 20 compared to a value of 15 for the bond index. This result is in line with our expectations, as bonds remain the safer asset class.

We performed the same analysis for the various strategy indices, and the results we obtained at an individual strategy level tended to be in line with those obtained overall. On the downside, market neutral strategies tend to be much more attractive than the equity index; compared with the bond index, the main change takes place at the level at which hedge funds start to become more interesting than the bond index. The main exception is the HFRI EH: Short Bias index, which never attains an omega higher than the equity and bond indices. As an illustration, in Figures 4.17 and 4.18 we show the HFRI ED: Merger Arbitrage index compared to the MSCI World and the Barclays Aggregate Bond index.

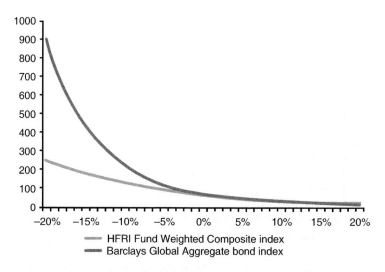

Figure 4.16 Omega of the HFRI Fund Weighted Hedge Fund index and the Barclays Aggregate Bond index

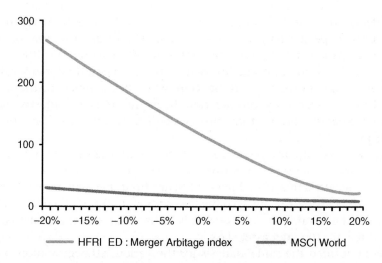

Figure 4.17 Omega of the HFRI ED: Merger Arbitrage index and the MSCI World

3.2.5 *Normality triangles*

Normality triangles summarize the main descriptive statistics and enable us to compare series of returns. Figure 4.19 gives the Sharpe score, skewness and kurtosis for the composite hedge fund index and traditional indices. It shows that the indices are not differentiated in terms of Sharpe score, but that they are in terms of the third and fourth moments. The hedge fund index has a higher skewness and a higher kurtosis than both

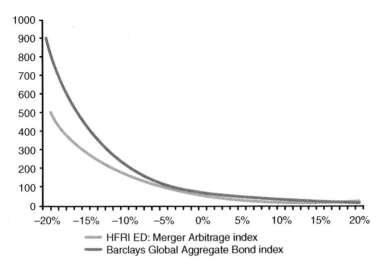

Figure 4.18 Omega of the HFRI ED: Merger Arbitrage index and the Barclays Aggregate Bond index

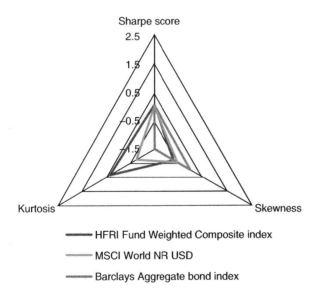

Figure 4.19 Normality triangle for the composite Hedge Fund index and the reference indices over the long term (inception–30 June 2012)

of the traditional indices. The higher skewness is attractive, as this means that the distribution of returns has a positive skew. The higher kurtosis, on the other hand, indicates that hedge funds tend to have a higher risk of fat tails. This is not attractive.

Figure 4.20 gives the same information but for the merger arbitrage index. The Sharpe score is in line with the other indices, but the strategy has a lower skewness and a significantly higher kurtosis, meaning a significant higher risk of fat tails.

3.2.6 Probability return distribution

The probability distribution of a series of returns is a statistical function that describes all the possible values and likelihoods, within a given range, that a variable can take. This range will be between the minimum and maximum statistically possible values, but the precise location where the possible value is likely to be plotted on the probability distribution depends on a number of factors, including the distributions mean, standard deviation, skewness and kurtosis. Figure 4.21 gives the probability distributions of the HFRI Fund Weighted Hedge Fund index and the MSCI World. That of the hedge fund index indicates that hedge funds tend to offer positive returns close to 80 per cent of the time, and that two times out of three those returns will be between zero and 2 per cent. This distribution of returns is concentrated even if there is a small chance of losing or gaining more than 3 per cent. On the other hand, the distribution of the MSCI World indicates that returns tend to be spread and that the risk of losing more than 5 per cent is almost as important as the chance of gaining more than 5 per cent. These distributions indicate that it is luck

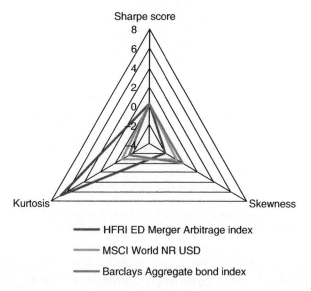

Figure 4.20 Normality triangle for the merger arbitrage index and the reference indices over the long term (inception–30 June 2012)

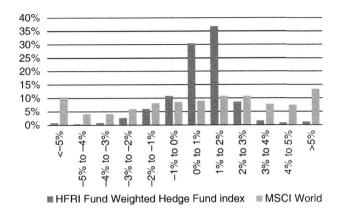

Figure 4.21 Probability return distribution of the HFRI Fund Weighted Hedge Fund index and the MSCI World over the long term (1 January 1990–30 June 2012)

more than anything else that governs the likelihood of making money; none of them is similar to the normal distribution, which constitutes the hypothesis underlying many tools such as the Sharpe ratio, which is based on the underlying hypothesis of normality because it uses standard deviation alone to characterize the distribution of returns. That is adequate in the case of a normal distribution, but not in the two cases presented here where the asymmetry (skewness) and the presence of fat tails (kurtosis) have to be integrated.

Figure 4.22 shows the same return distribution in hedge funds and the Barclays Global Aggregate Bond index. The distribution of the bond index is completely different from that of the equity index; it is more concentrated than the equity index but less so than the hedge fund index. All the returns are between −4 and +5 per cent. The hedge fund index is superior because there is only a 10 per cent chance of making a small loss (zero to −1), as against 20 per cent for the bond index – but on the other hand, with bonds the risk of a big loss (and a big profit) is non-existent.

In order to perform the same analysis for the individual strategies, we show four of them, illustrating the special features of certain strategies. Figure 4.23 shows the HFRI EH: Equity Market Neutral index, whose distribution is even more concentrated than that of the global hedge fund index. Almost half the returns over the 20+ year period are between zero and 1 per cent. In addition, all of them stay between −3 and +4. Those characteristics are in line with the profile of the strategy.

In Figure 4.24, we give the probability return distribution of the HFRI Emerging Markets (Total) index and the MSCI World. This is a directional strategy; its distribution is much closer to that of the MSCI World and

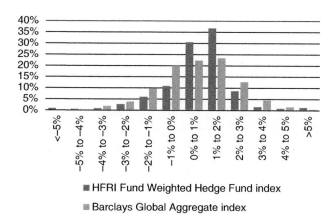

Figure 4.22 Probability return distribution of the HFRI Fund Weighted Hedge Fund index and the Barclays Global Aggregate Bond index (inception–30 June 2012)

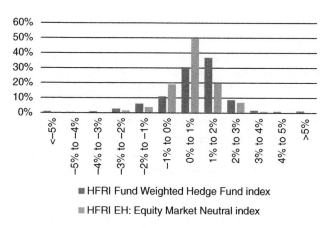

Figure 4.23 Probability return distribution of the HFRI Fund Weighted Hedge Fund index and the HFRI EH: Equity Market Neutral index (inception–30 June 2012)

in fact, it does not seem much more attractive than equities. Its slightly greater attraction arises from the fact that the emerging hedge fund index is negative only 34 per cent of the time, against 41.1 per cent for the MSCI World. In addition the percentage of returns below –5 per cent is 7.4 per cent for emerging hedge funds, as against 10.4 per cent for the MSCI World. On the other hand, the additional percentage of positive returns are spread between +1 and +4. Emerging hedge funds may fail to take advantage of the strongest rallies, but this is normal as such rallies tend to be led by liquidity. Emerging hedge funds have a profile in line with

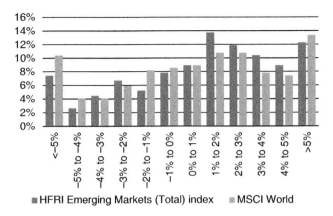

Figure 4.24 Probability return distribution of the HFRI Emerging Markets (Total) index and the MSCI World (inception–30 June 2012)

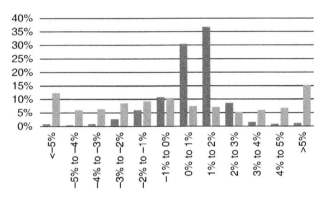

Figure 4.25 Probability return distribution of the HFRI Fund Weighted Hedge Fund index and HFRI EH: Short Bias index (inception–30 June 2012)

equities, but they provide better protection than do long-only diversified equities.

The return distribution of the HFRI ED: Short Bias index is given in Figure 4.25. We have included it because it is very different from that of most other strategies. This strategy exists only to diversify portfolios and Figure 4.25 shows that the risk of fat tail is very important in this case, 27.3 per cent of the returns being either below –5 per cent or over +5 per cent, and over 52 per cent of the returns being below –3 or over +3.

Finally, we report the distribution of returns of the HFRI Macro index in Figure 4.26. Macro managers are opportunistic; the return distribution indicates that the strategy has a higher chance of making small losses – an

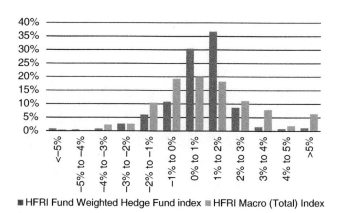

Figure 4.26 Probability return distribution of the HFRI Fund Weighted Hedge Fund index and the HFRI Macro index (inception–30 June 2012)

almost 30 per cent probability of zero to –2 per cent – but it also offers a greater chance of making big profits. The strategy offers more than 2 per cent per month in more than one month out of four. On the other hand, it loses more than 2 per cent only 5 per cent of the time.

Our return distribution analysis leads to three interesting conclusions. Firstly, hedge funds as a whole offer over the long term distribution that is much more attractive than that of equities; hedge funds will lag during strong rallies, but will tend to offer stable returns and to protect on the downside. Secondly, hedge funds offer less protection than do bonds during times of turmoil, but they tend to offer positive returns more often and have small losses less often. The third conclusion is that every hedge fund strategy will have a specific return distribution and that the profile of the strategy will usually be reflected in that return distribution. This aspect is very important in a portfolio context, and we illustrate it with a few selected strategies.

4 Performance during extreme market conditions

Hedge funds aim to offer positive absolute returns in any market environment, but we know that in practice this is impossible. It is however interesting to quantify the success of hedge fund managers in doing so. In order to do this we have identified the MSCI World's worst 25 months between January 1990 and June 2012, and in Figure 4.27 we give the performance of the hedge fund composite index over that time. The same analysis, compared to the Barclays Global Aggregate's worst 25 months is given in Figure 4.28.

Figure 4.27 indicates that on three occasions over the 25 selected months the hedge fund composite index finished up, while the bond index was

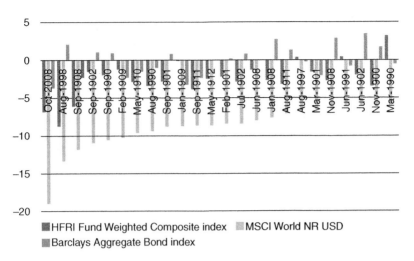

Figure 4.27 Performance during volatile equity markets (January 1990–June 2012)

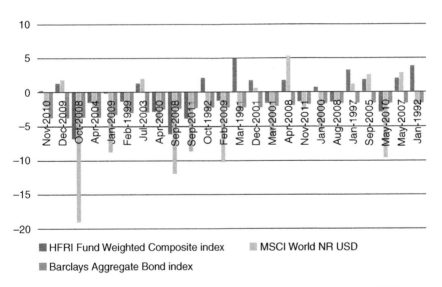

Figure 4.28 Performance during volatile bond markets (January 1990–June 2012)

positive almost half of the times. It lost less than 2.5 per cent half of the times, and lost more than 5 per cent four times. The average loss for the hedge fund index was around 2.5 per cent, while the equity index lost close to 9 per cent on average, against a bond index performance of close to zero. An unlucky investment of US$100 during these 25 specific months would have lost 90 per cent of its value had it been invested in equities, but only 45 per cent in hedge funds and a few per cent in bonds. This result indicates the ability of hedge funds to deliver absolute returns during volatile equity markets.

The same information estimated during difficult periods for the bond market is given in Figure 4.28; the equity index finished up seven times, and the hedge fund index was up almost half of the times. The equity index lost less than 2.5 per cent almost half of the times while the hedge fund index did so 19 times out of 25. The equity index lost more than 5 per cent nine times compared to the hedge fund index's three times. On average, the bond index fell by 2.3 per cent, against marginal losses for hedge funds and 3.6 per cent for the equity index. An unlucky investment of US$100 over these difficult months would have lost 60 per cent in equities and close to 45 per cent in bonds – but less than 8 per cent in hedge funds. This result indicates that volatile times for the bond market tends not to directly impact hedge funds.

These results suggest that the absolute nature of hedge funds work better when bonds are facing downturns than when equities do. This result is, however, not totally correct; Figure 4.29 reports the percentage of positive months for hedge funds, equities and bonds as well as the percentage of months over –1, 2, 3, 4 and 5 per cent. Hedge funds have offered more positive months than bonds and equities over the 20+ years covered;

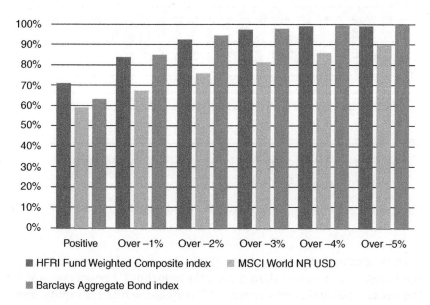

Figure 4.29 Performance during volatile equity markets (January 1990–June 2012)

hedge fund returns were positive 71 per cent of the time, against 63 per cent for bonds and 59 per cent for equities. In addition this number increases more rapidly than the corresponding equity number when we are not focusing on positive returns only, but are also taking small losses into consideration. Losses of over 3 per cent took place less than 3 per cent of the time in hedge funds and bonds, compared to close to 20 per cent of the time in equities. This result confirms that while hedge funds may face losses, such losses tend to be very limited.

The same analysis covering difficult months for the hedge fund composite index is shown in Figure 4.30; it indicates that the equity market has never been positive when hedge funds faced significant drawdowns. The bond index was positive slightly more than half of the times. Hedge funds lost less than 2.5 per cent half of the times, while equities lost less than 2.5 per cent four times and bonds hardly ever lost more than 2.5 per cent. In three cases only hedge funds lost more than 5 per cent, while equities lost more than 5 per cent 16 times out of 25, and bonds only twice lost more than 5 per cent. The average loss for hedge funds was below 3 per cent, as against almost 7 per cent for equities and a slightly positive performance for bonds. An unlucky investment of US$100 in hedge funds would have lost slightly more than 50 per cent, against 84 per cent in equities and a positive return of 10 per cent in bonds. These results indicate that hedge funds and bonds are probably a good complement for one another. It is worth mentioning that – at the time of writing – the three worst months ever for hedge funds since 1990 were from August to October 2008. In addition, 6 out of the 17 worst ever months

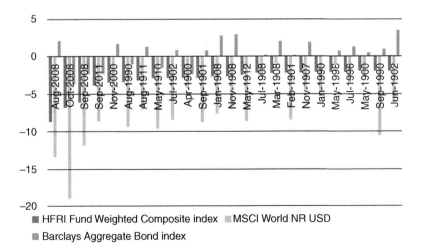

Figure 4.30 Performance during volatile times for hedge funds (January 1990–June 2012)

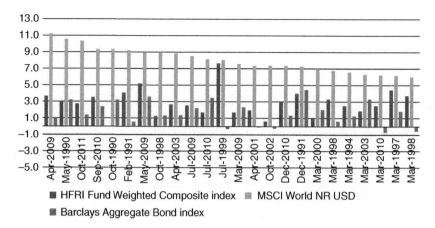

Figure 4.31 Performance during strong equity markets (January 1990–June 2012)

were in 2008; this confirms the importance of the impact of 2008 on the industry.

A similar analysis of the best 25 months for the MSCI World index indicates that hedge funds offered positive returns almost every time equities rallied (there is one exception, but on that occasion the return posted by the hedge fund index was almost flat), while bonds finished down almost 25 per cent of the time. The average gain for equities is 8 per cent against 2.8 per cent for hedge funds and 1.5 per cent for bonds. A lucky investment of US$100 in equities over these 25 months would have ended up with US$640, as against US$195 in hedge funds and US$145 in bonds (Figure 4.31).

The performance of the indices during strong bond markets is reported in Figure 4.32. Hedge funds and equities were positive three times out of four; This ratio increases to nine times out of ten for hedge funds for losses under 2.5 per cent. The average gain for bonds is 3.4 per cent, against 1.2 per cent for hedge funds and 2.3 per cent for equities. A lucky investment of US$100 over these periods would have ended up with US$226 in bonds, US$133 in hedge funds and US$163 in equities.

Equities rallied almost 90 per cent of the time when hedge funds posted strong returns. Bonds finished positive slightly more than 50 per cent of the time . The average gain for hedge funds is 4.2 per cent, against 4.4 per cent for equities and 0.7 per cent for bonds. A lucky investment of US$100 during these months would have ended up with US$268 in hedge funds, US$305 in equities and US$118 in bonds (Figure 4.33).

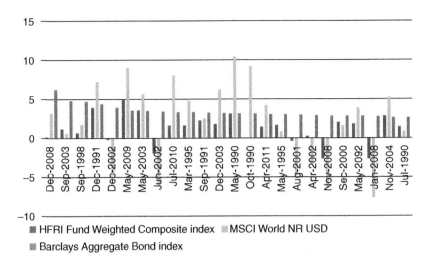

Figure 4.32 Performance during strong bond markets (January 1990–June 2012)

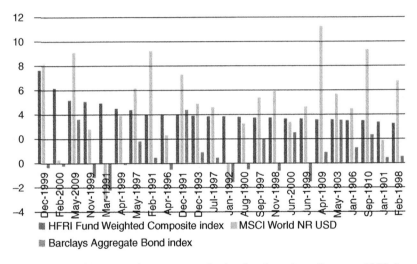

Figure 4.33 Performance during strong hedge fund markets (January 1990–June 2012)

Table 4.8 summarizes our analysis. The numbers suggest that hedge funds offer an attractive return profile; in difficult equity markets, they protect the downside to some extent, and also catch most of the upside, the scale of the loss remaining limited in most cases. When bonds are turbulent, the statistics are even more attractive. During volatile market conditions the average loss in hedge funds remains limited in most cases;

Table 4.8 Relative performance of the indices under various market conditions

Bear equity market

	HFRI Fund Weighted Composite index	MSCI World NR USD	Barclays Aggregate Bond index
Average return	-2.5	-8.9	-0.1
Positive return	12%	0%	48%
Return > -2.5%	48%	0%	88%
US$100 investment	54	11	98

Bull equity market

	HFRI Fund Weighted Composite index	MSCI World NR USD	Barclays Aggregate Bond index
Average return	2.8	8.0	1.5
Positive return	96%	100%	76%
Return > -2.5%	100%	100%	100%
US$100 investment	199	677	144

Bear bond market

	HFRI Fund Weighted Composite index	MSCI World NR USD	Barclays Aggregate Bond index
Average return	-0.3	-3.6	-2.3
Positive return	44%	28%	0%
Return > -2.5%	76%	48%	72%
US$100 investment	92	39	55

Bull bond market

	HFRI Fund Weighted Composite index	MSCI World NR USD	Barclays Aggregate Bond index
Average return	1.2	2.3	3.4
Positive return	76%	76%	100%
Return > -2.5%	92%	76%	100%
US$100 investment	135	170	232

Bear hedge fund market

	HFRI Fund Weighted Composite index	MSCI World NR USD	Barclays Aggregate Bond index
Average return	-2.9	-6.8	0.3
Positive return	0%	0%	60%
Return > -2.5%	48%	16%	88%
US$100 investment	45	16	109

Bull hedge fund market

	HFRI Fund Weighted Composite index	MSCI World NR USD	Barclays Aggregate Bond index
Average return	4.2	4.4	0.7
Positive return	100%	88%	56%
Return > -2.5%	100%	92%	100%
US$100 investment	277	287	117

in bull market conditions the capture ratio is correct and in line with the volatility of the industry.

5   Academic research[14]

There have been many studies on hedge funds, covering many aspects of the industry. This section aims to provide an overall literature review on hedge fund studies. As illustrated in Table 4.9, hedge fund academic studies can be classified in four categories:

1. Hedge fund performance
2. Hedge fund investment style
3. Correlation analysis and diversification power
4. Other studies.

1. The first category includes studies focused on hedge fund performance, and includes three fields.
- The first includes studies comparing the performance of hedge funds with equity and other indices (see for example Ackermann, McEnally and Ravenscraft, 1999; Brown, Goetzmann and Ibbotson, 1999; Liang, 1999; Amin and Kat, 2003; Liang, 2001; Barès, Gibson and Gyger, 2003; Liang, 2003; Agarwal and Naik, 2004). The results of such studies are mixed; some authors (Brown et al., 1999; Liang, 1999; Capocci et al., 2005) conclude that hedge funds have been able to outperform traditional indices, while others (Ackermann et al., 1999; Agarwal and Naik, 2004) are more cautious in their conclusions. Hübner and Papageorgiou (2006), meanwhile, find that there are three kinds of persistence in hedge fund returns:
  - Firstly, statistical evidence of positive persistence based on alphas for non-directional portfolios in the bullish period.
  - Secondly, statistical evidence of negative persistence for directional portfolios in both the bullish and the bearish periods.
  - Finally, statistical evidence of progressive positive persistence based on alphas for funds of funds in both the bullish and the bearish periods.
- The second field of hedge fund performance analysis compares the performance of hedge funds with mutual funds. In this context, Ackermann et al. (1999) and Liang (1999) find that hedge funds consistently achieve better performance than mutual funds, although they are lower and more volatile than the reference market indices considered.
- As mentioned in Capocci (2007), the third field of hedge fund performance analysis includes the study of the persistence of hedge fund

returns. Persistence is particularly important in the case of hedge funds because, as suggested by Brown et al. (1999) and Liang (2000, 2001), the hedge fund industry has a higher attrition rate than is the case in mutual funds (see Brown et al., 1999). They prove that offshore hedge funds have positive risk-adjusted returns, but they attribute this result to style effect and conclude that there is no proof of any particular alpha-generating capacity in fund managers. Agarwal and Naik (2000) analyse the presence of persistence in hedge fund returns using a one-year moving average period. They find that there is proof of persistence in hedge fund performance, particularly for poorly performing funds that continue to underperform (Table 4.9).

The vast majority of performance studies on hedge funds have not focused solely on their behaviour under different market conditions. The periods under review do not favour this exercise, as between 1994 and March 2000 the periods of downward-trending stock markets were rare and discontinuous. For the period 1990–1998, Edwards and Caglayan (2001) found that only three types of hedge fund strategies (market neutral, event driven and macro) provided protection to investors when stock markets decline. More recently, Ennis and Sebastian (2003) contended that in general hedge funds did not provide investor protection after the market downturn of March 2000; rather, their superior performance was mostly due to the good market timing of their managers.

2. The second global category of hedge fund academic studies includes authors that try to analyse and describe hedge fund investment styles and who explain these features with style models (see for example, Fung and Hsieh, 1997; Brown, Goetzmann and Park, 1998; Brealy and Kaplanis, 2001; Brown et al., 2001; Liang 2001; Ben Dor and Jagannathan, 2003 and Liang 2003). In this context, Fung and Hsieh (1997) apply Sharpe's style analysis (see Sharpe, 1992) to a large sample of hedge funds and commodity trading advisors (CTAs). They assume that fund returns are linearly related to the returns through a number of factors, and they measure those factors through eight mimicking portfolios. They find that the regressions had little explanatory power and consequently suggest that the resulting low adjusted r-square is due to the funds' trading strategy. Ben Dor and Jagannathan (2002) stress the importance of selecting the correct style benchmarks, and emphasize how the use of inappropriate style benchmarks may lead to the wrong conclusion.

A particular aspect that has been taken into account more recently is the style drift in hedge fund returns. This effect arises from the fact that hedge fund managers are opportunity-driven and therefore change their

Table 4.9 Four global categories of hedge fund academic studies

Hedge Fund Performance	Hedge Fund Investment Style	Correlation Analysis and Diversification Power	Other Studies
– Comparison with classical markets (Ackermann et al., 1999; Brown et al., 1999; Liang, 1999; Amin & Kat, 2001; Liang, 2001; Barès et al., 2002; Liang, 2003; Agarwal & Naik, 2004).	– Sharpe-style analysis (Fung & Hsieh, 1997; Brown et al., 1998; Brealy & Kaplanis, 2001; Brown & Goetzmann, 2001; Liang 2001; Ben Dor & Jagannathan, 2002; Liang 2003).	– Correlation analysis (Fung & Hsieh, 1997; Schneeweis & Spurgin, 1997; Liang, 1999; Agarwal & Naik, 1999).	– Risks (Schneeweis & Spurgin, 1999; Jorion, 2000; Amenc et al., 2002a, 2002b; Berényi, 2002).
			– Bias analysis (Liang, 2000; Fung & Hsieh, 2000).
– Comparison with mutual funds (Ackermann et al., 1999 and Liang 1999).	– Rolling regression (McGuire, Remolona and Tsatsaronis, 2005).		– Hedge fund indices (Brooks and Kat, 2001; Amenc and Martellini, 2002; Fung and Hsieh, 2002b).
– Persistence in performance (Agarwal and Naik, 2000; Brown et al, 1999; Hübner and Papageorgiou, 2006; Liang 2001; Liang, 2000).	– Dynamic model (Swinkels and Van der Sluis, 2001; Posthuma and Van der Sluis).	– Diversification power (Amin and Kat, 2001; Amenc and Martellini, 2002).	– CTAs (see for example Edwards and Park, 1996; Fung and Hsieh, 2001; Gregoriou and Rouah, 2003; Liang, 2003; Spurgin and Georgiev, 2001).

Source: Capocci (2007).

style over time. Brown et al. (1998) analysed hedge fund returns during the 1997–98 Asian crisis, using rolling regression to take style drift into account. Their methodology consists in realizing a set of linear regressions and moving the estimation period of each of them by a single observation. This simple technique enables the style variation of a manager over time to be observed. It does, however, have one major drawback: the choice of number of observations used for the estimation. McGuire, Remolona and Tsatsaronis (2005) apply the same methodology. To handle this issue, Posthuma and Van der Sluis (2005) propose using a dynamic style model, in which beta can vary over time, developed by Swinkels and Van der Sluis (2001). This technique is adaptive, in the sense that changes in the style exposures are picked up automatically from the data. Unlike the ad hoc rolling regression approach, the time variation in the exposures is explicitly modelled. No restrictions are imposed on the betas. As stressed by Posthuma and Van der Sluis, this model is a state–space model and can be estimated by using standard Kalman filter techniques. No window size or ad hoc chosen length need be used; the Kalman filter procedure chooses the optimal weighting scheme directly from the data. The filter is an adaptive system based on the measurement and updating equations.

3. The third global category of hedge fund academic studies focuses on the correlation of hedge funds with other investment products, and analyses the power of the diversification properties of hedge funds. Fung and Hsieh (1997) and Schneeweis and Spurgin (1998) prove that the insertion of hedge funds into a portfolio can significantly improve its risk–return profile, thanks to the weak correlation to the funds with other financial securities. This low correlation is also emphasized by Liang (1999) as well as by Agarwal and Naik (2004). Meanwhile, Amin and Kat (2001) find that stand-alone investment hedge funds do not offer a superior risk–return profile, but that a great majority of funds classified as inefficient on a stand-alone basis are able to produce an efficient payoff profile when mixed with the S&P 500. They obtained the best results when 10–20 per cent of the portfolio value was invested in hedge funds. Next, Kooli (2007) analyses the power of hedge funds as an efficient frontier enhancer. He finds that hedge funds as an asset class improve the mean-variance frontier of sets of benchmarks portfolios. A mean-variance frontier of a given set of assets is the boundary of the set of means and variances of returns on all portfolios of the given assets that can be achieved, but that investors who already hold a diversified portfolio do not improve their statistics by using hedge funds. Kooli (2007) finds, however, that funds of hedge funds do bring diversification for mean-variance investors.

Taking all these results into consideration, hedge funds are seen as good investment tool. Amenc and Martellini (2002) prove on the basis of ex-post estimations that the inclusion of hedge funds in a portfolio can lead to a significant decrease in the volatility of the portfolio without leading to a significant change in the returns. This implies that a stronger risk control does not necessarily correspond to a decrease in return.

4. In the fourth global category of hedge fund academic studies, "Other studies", certain authors have analysed various other aspects of the hedge fund industry. Schneeweis and Spurgin (2000), Jorion (2000), Amenc, Curtis and Martellini (2002), Amenc, Martellini and Vaissié (2002) and Berényi (2002) study the risks involved in hedge fund investments. Schneeweis and Spurgin (1999) and Amenc, Martellini and Vaissié (2002) prove that hedge fund returns are not only exposed to the market risk, but that other risks, such as volatility risk, default risk or liquidity risk, have to be considered. Liang (2000) analyse the presence of survivorship bias in hedge fund data, and Fung and Hsieh (2000) include other biases in their analysis. Ackermann et al. (1998) emphasize that stricter legal limitations on mutual funds rather than on hedge funds hinder their performance.

Some authors also studied hedge fund indices (see Brooks and Kat, 2001; Amenc and Martellini, 2003). There are many different hedge fund index providers, such as EACM, HFR, CSFB/Tremont, Zurich Capital, Van Hedge, the Hennessee Group, Hedgefund.net, LJH Global Investment, Mar, Altvest and Magnum. Fung and Hsieh (2002b) looked at the natural biases present in hedge fund indices.

Commodity trading advisors (CTAs) form a specific category in the hedge fund world. Hedge funds, first appeared an academic journal in 1997, but CTAs have been studied for a longer period of time. Several studies were published in the late 1980s and in the early 1990s (see for example, Lintner, 1983; Bessembinder, 2002). Since 1997, some authors have considered CTAs as part of the hedge fund world (Fung and Hsieh, 1997; Schneeweis and Spurgin, 2000), whereas others have studied them either by separating them from hedge funds (Liang, 2003) or on a completely stand-alone basis (Fung and Hsieh, 2001; Gregoriou and Rouah, 2003 and Capocci, 2004b).

Research into CTAs is very sparse, however, and it is difficult to present a complete literature review. Billingsley and Chance (1996) and Edwards and Park (1996) demonstrate that CTAs can add diversification to stocks and bonds in a mean-variance framework. Schneeweis, Savanayana and McCarthy (1991) and Schneeweis (1996) state that the benefits of CTAs are similar to those of hedge funds, in that they improve upon and can offer a superior risk-adjusted return trade-off to stock and bond indices while acting as diversifiers in investment portfolios. Fung and Hsieh (1997) prove that a constructed CTA style factor has a persistently positive return when the S&P 500 has a negative return. According to Schneeweis, Spurgin and Georgiev (2001), CTAs are well known in short stock markets. Fung and Hsieh (2001) analyse CTAs and conclude that they are similar to look-back calls and look-back puts.[15]

Gregoriou and Rouah (2003) examine whether the percentage changes in the NAVs of CTAs follow random walks, and prove that all classifications (except the diversified sub-index) do indeed behave like a random walk. The effectiveness of CTAs in enhancing the risk–return characteristics of portfolios could be compromised when pure random-walk behaviour is identified. Kat (2002) finds that an allocation to managed futures allows investors to achieve a very substantial degree of overall risk reduction at limited cost. Managed futures appear to be more efficient diversifiers than hedge funds.

Regarding performance, the results are mitigated even though Edwards and Caglayan (2001) conclude that during bear markets CTAs provide greater downside protection than do hedge funds, and also produce higher returns along with a negative correlation with stock returns. Schneeweis and Georgiev (2002) conclude that careful inclusion of CTA managers in an investment portfolio can enhance its return characteristics, especially during severe bear markets. Schneeweis, Spurgin and McCarthy (1996) observe that performance persistence is virtually non-existent between 1987 and 1995. But there is little information on the long-term diligence of these funds (Irwin, Zulauf and Ward, 1994, Kazemi, 1996). In his book *Managed Trading: Myths and Truths*, Jack Schwager reviews the literature on whether CTAs exhibit performance persistence, and conducts his own analysis; he concludes that there is little evidence that the top-performing funds can be predicted. According to Worthington (2001), between 1990 and 1998 the correlation of managed futures to the S&P 500 during its best 30 months was 0.33, and during the worst 30 months it was −0.25. Georgiev (2001) underlines, however, that one of the drawbacks of CTAs is that during bull markets their performance is generally inferior to that of hedge funds. Brorsen and Townsend (2002) have shown that a minimal amount of performance persistence is found in CTAs, and that some advantages might exist in selecting CTAs based on past performance when a long time series of data is available and accurate methods are used. Finally, Capocci (2004b) proves that there is persistence in CTA returns for the badly performing funds that tend to continue to significantly underperform their peers.

6 Return decomposition

The purpose of my PhD thesis, *An Analysis of Hedge Fund Strategies*, was to understand hedge fund managers and to explain how they create alpha over time. This involved developing, testing and improving a performance analysis model in order to understand hedge fund performance on the one hand, while on the other hand developing and adapting a methodology to determine whether or not there is any persistence in hedge fund returns. We achieved this objective by means of three complementary studies.

The first aimed at answering the question What factors might explain hedge fund returns? We based our multi-factor performance decomposition model on models that have been used in the mutual fund literature for years: Fama and French (1993) and Carhart (1997). The Capital Asset Pricing Model (CAPM) from Sharpe (1966) uses a single factor, beta, to compare a portfolio with the market as a whole. But more generally, you can add factors to a regression model to give a better *r*-squared fit. Fama and French (1993) started with the observation that two classes of stocks have tended to do better than the market as a whole: small caps and stocks with a high book-value-to-price ratio (usually called value stocks; the inverse are growth stocks). They then added two factors to CAPM to reflect a portfolio's exposure to these two classes. Carhart (1997) identified that there was momentum in the market, and added a fourth factor to take that momentum into account.

Even if hedge funds differ from mutual funds in not just the strategy they apply but also the securities they use and the freedom they have in their management, they are still investment funds. As such, we judged that a model coming from the mutual fund literature would be a good basis on which to build a new performance decomposition model specific to hedge funds. We added a few factors to take into account the fact that, in addition to US equities, hedge funds invest in non-US equities and in bonds (government bonds, corporate bonds, high yield and a default measure), as well as a commodity index. Our model evolved over time for several reasons. Firstly, some factors that did not help explain hedge fund performance were removed. Secondly, in some cases, the correlation between factors increased, leading to a risk of multicolinearity, so we had to remove them. Finally, certain factors that seemed to help decomposing the performance were added. The various models that developed over time are described in Table 4.10.

As shown in Table 4.10, the first model had 11 factors, the second 10 and the one used in the last part of the analysis had two versions, with 10 and 14 factors. In model 2, we readjusted the factor used in model 1 to

Table 4.10 Multi-factor performance decomposition model

	Model 1 *Capocci and Hübner (2004)*	Model 2 *Capocci, Corhay and Hübner (2005)*	Model 3 *Capocci (2006) – 1*	Model 4 *Capocci (2006) – 2*
Alpha	X	X	X	X
US stock market	X	X	X	X
Size	X	X	X	X
Style	X	X	X	X
International style	X	n/a	n/a	n/a
Momentum	X	X	X	X
Non-US stock market	X	X	X	X
US Bond	X	n/a	n/a	n/a
Wd Gov bond	X	X	X	X
EMBI	X	X	X	X
Lehman BAA	X	n/a	n/a	n/a
High yield	n/a	X	X	X
Mortgage	n/a	X	n/a	n/a
GSCI	X	X	X	X
Currency	n/a	n/a	X	X
Option factors	n/a	n/a	n/a	X
Number of factors	11	10	10	14

This table compares the multi-factor performance models used in the thesis. Size = the size market risk premium of Fama and French (1993), style = the style market risk premium of Fama and French (1993), international style = the international style market risk premium of Fama and French (1996), momentum = Carhart's (1997) "momentum" factor, non-US stock market = MSCI World excluding US, US bonds = the Lehman Aggregate US Bond index, Wd Gov Bond = JPMorgan world government bond index, EMBI = JP Morgan Emerging Market Bond index, Lehman BAA = the Lehman BAA Corporate Bond index, High yield = Lehman High Yield Bond index, Mortgage = Lehman Mortgage-Backed Securities index, Salomon World Government Bond index, GSCI = Goldman Sach Commodity index, Currency = the Federal Reserve Bank Trade Weighted Dollar index, Option factors = Agarwal and Naik (2004) at-the-money (ATMC), out-of-the money (OTMC) European call option factors, and at-the-money (ATMP) and out-of-the money (OTMP) European put option factors.

integrate a high yield factor and a mortgage-backed securities factor, in order to take into consideration the significant increase in the number of funds exposed to the high yield market and to determine the degree of the exposure of fixed income funds to the mortgage; it turned out that the high yield factor helped with this, but the mortgage factor did not. The third model we developed was more powerfully accurate; it had a relatively low number of factors but they covered almost all the aspects of hedge fund investing, enabling us to reach very high R^2, the measure typically used to determine the quality of a model.

Over the three studies on the persistence in hedge fund performance, the objective was to explain long-term hedge fund performance in order to determine whether any hedge fund strategies significantly outperformed traditional markets over time. The results indicated that most hedge fund strategies did indeed offer significant alpha over a long period of time. These results were not due to the lack of power of the model since, in all cases, the adjusted *r*-squared figures were very high. The next logical step was to perform the same analysis under various market conditions, and this was done in the second study; we analysed hedge fund performance and persistence in performance in bull market conditions, in bear market conditions and throughout a full cycle. Results indicate that hedge funds tend to outperform during bull market conditions but that under bear market conditions outperformance, if any, is not significant; the only strategy that is able to outperform in both market conditions market neutral – and these needed further analysis, to be carried out in dedicated research.

Once we had confirmed that hedge fund strategies do significantly outperform traditional markets over time, we analysed the persistence of this performance. In other words, we looked at whether there was a repetitive way to isolate the outperformance over time. At this level, we reached the second important basic concept used in the second study: the decile classification of Carhart (1997). As we state in the study:

> Active hedge fund selection strategies could increase the expected return on a portfolio if hedge fund performance is predictable. The hypothesis that hedge funds with a superior average return in this period will also have a superior average return in the next period is called the hypothesis of persistence in performance.

Carhart's methodology is relatively easy to understand: each year, all funds are, based on their previous year's return, ranked into ten equally-weighted portfolios, which are held until the following January and then rebalanced. The combination of the multi-factor model with this methodology enabled us to determine whether there is persistence in hedge fund returns.

Results indicate that there is some proof of persistence for low-volatility funds that tend to be neither the best performers nor the worst, but that offer relatively consistent returns over time. This result was the first important conclusion. It needed deeper analysis over a shorter period of time, which was carried out in the second study. Persistence analysis indicated that superior performance was predominantly predictable in bull market conditions (prior to March 2000). Our results confirmed previous studies that found that persistence, if any, is mostly located among medium performers, whereas in bear market conditions, only negative persistence could be found among the past losers, suggesting that bad performance had probably been the decisive factor in hedge fund mortality.

In both studies, it was low-volatility funds that provided significant alpha. The only issue is that these funds tend to be classified in the middle decile portfolios; this led us to the conclusion that we needed another way of classifying hedge funds in the persistence analysis in order to be able to clearly identify the funds that significantly and consistently outperformed. So this was precisely what we did in our third study; in it, we tested several ways of classifying funds on the basis of their past statistics: returns, volatility, Sharpe ratio, alpha, beta, skewness and kurtosis. Our results clearly indicated that measures incorporating volatility are very good at helping investors create alpha and consistently and significantly outperform traditional indices. We checked the robustness of our results by performing the same analysis over sub-periods, during both bull and bear market conditions (defined as the up and down months of the S&P 500 and the consecutive bull and bear market periods) and by changing the month of classification (to June instead of January). We found a consistent, systematic way of creating pure alpha using a simple classification methodology based on basic statistics: risk–return trade-off measures (Sharpe score), pure volatility measures (standard deviation), and to a lesser extent beta exposure; this classification appears to a be better and more stable way of classifying hedge funds in order to detect persistency in returns. Funds providing stable returns with limited volatility and/or with limited exposure to the equity market consistently and significantly outperformed equity and bond markets. We give the specific features and main conclusions of these studies in Table 4.11.

7   Inserting hedge funds into a classical portfolio

The third part of my thesis focused on the impact of inserting hedge funds into a classical portfolio of stock and bond mutual funds. The very fact that hedge funds exhibit abnormal returns is the fundamental reason why traditional tools like the mean-variance efficient frontier analysis should not be used for their analysis. In this study we developed the idea of an adapted capital market line in an extended risk–return framework that included not only volatility as a measure of risk but also higher moments.

Our methodology is based on Taylor's expansion of the Linex utility function developed by Bell (1988).[16] We decomposed this function and took into account the mean returns, the volatility, the asymmetry of the return distribution (skewness) and the presence of fat tails (kurtosis). This

Table 4.11 Objectives and main conclusion of the performance decomposition studies

	Objective 1	Conclusion 1	Objective 2	Conclusion 2
An Analysis of Hedge Fund Performance	– Determine if hedge fund strategies significantly outperform traditional markets	– Most hedge fund strategies do offer significant alpha over the long term despite a high R^2	– Determine if hedge fund strategies significantly and persistently outperform traditional markets	– There is no proof of persistence in hedge funds, except in low volatile funds that tend to be neither the best performers nor the worst
Hedge Fund Performance and Persistence in Bull and Bear Markets	– Determine if hedge fund strategies significantly outperform traditional markets in bull and/or bear market conditions	– Hedge funds tend to outperform during bull market conditions (not significantly in bear markets)	– Determine if hedge fund strategies significantly and persistently outperform traditional markets in bull and/or bear market conditions	– No significant outperformance in bear market conditions, except in market neutral funds
The Sustainability of Hedge Fund Performance	– Determine if hedge fund strategies significantly outperform traditional markets using several risk-adjusted measures	– Most hedge fund strategies do offer significant alpha over the long term despite a high R^2	– Find a systematic way of buying hedge funds in order to significantly and persistently outperform traditional markets	– Systematic outperformance of hedge fund portfolios invested in previous year's low volatile funds (measured by Sharpe score, standard deviation)

This Table shows the specific features, objectives and conclusion of the studies grouped in Part 1: Persistence in Hedge Fund Performance. Part 1 contains three studies ("An Analysis of Hedge Fund Performance," "Hedge Fund Performance and Persistence in Bull and Bear Markets" and "The Sustainability of Hedge Fund Performance: new insights"). For each study we have shown its main specific features along with its primary and secondary objectives and conclusions.

decomposition enabled us to define a new and extended risk measure that we used in a classical risk–return framework, the only difference being that the risk factor was no longer defined only by the standard deviation of the returns. This new tool had the same underlying idea as the classical efficient frontier and could be illustrated in the same way while taking into account more sophisticated statistics.

Our results indicate that directional hedge funds should be considered separately from non-directional hedge funds and funds of hedge funds. Adding a small allocation to directional hedge funds does not significantly change the risk–return profile offered by the global portfolio. However, when more than 20 per cent was allocated to directional hedge funds, there is a significant improvement for diversified portfolios (with 20 to 80 per cent allocated to the risky asset). An allocation of more than 50 per cent to directional hedge funds provides significantly more attractive returns in every case.

However, adding non-directional hedge funds or fund of funds to a classical portfolio enables investors to attain higher levels of returns for low- and medium-risk levels, for allocations to hedge funds of as little as 10 per cent. But with high allocations to the risky asset, non-directional strategies do not help in diversifying and reaching higher return levels. Our results confirmed that non-directional strategies and funds of funds helped diversify low-risk profile investments, and should be used for this purpose.

The newly adapted and efficient frontier opens new doors for asset allocators. Based on the clients' objective and the market conditions, it determines whether or not hedge funds should be added to the existing portfolio. Moreover, it helps to determine which hedge fund strategy should be favoured. We show the specific features, objectives and main conclusions of this research in Table 4.12.

8   Correlation analysis

Hedge funds aim to help investors diversify their investment portfolio. This section focuses on historical correlations[17] between hedge funds and classical indices as well as on the correlation between hedge fund strategies. We start with monthly data and progress to daily data.

8.1   Correlation between hedge funds and classical markets

The correlation between hedge funds and traditional markets has been widely studied in academic research. Fung and Hsieh (1997) and Schneeweis and Spurgin (1997) proved that the insertion of hedge funds

Table 4.12 Objectives and main conclusions of the study analysing the impact of inserting hedge funds into a classical portfolio

	Objective 1	Conclusion 1	Objective 2	Conclusion 2
Diversifying using hedge funds	*– Develop a methodology to determine if a portfolio can be diversified with securities displaying abnormal return distribution characteristics*	*– Taylor's expansion of Bell's utility function enables us to take skewness and kurtosis into account – the adapted Capital Market Line and new efficient frontier complete the development*	*– Determine if bond and/ or equity investors should include hedge funds in their portfolio*	*– High allocation of directional hedge funds do significantly improve the profile – adding a small allocation of non-directional hedge funds and funds of hedge funds significantly improves the profile*

This Table gives the specific features, objectives and conclusions of the study of Part 3: Hedge Funds as Diversification Tools. Part 3 contains one study (Diversifying using Hedge Funds: a utility-based approach). We show the main specific features of the study, its first and second objective and its conclusions.

into a portfolio could, because of their weak correlation with other financial securities, significantly improve its risk–return profile. This low correlation is also emphasized by Liang (1999), Agarwal and Naik (1999) and Capocci and Hübner (2004). Amin and Kat (2001) found that stand-alone investment hedge funds do not offer a superior risk–return profile, but that a great majority of funds classified as inefficient on a stand-alone basis are able to produce an efficient payoff profile when combined with the S&P500; best results are obtained when 10–20 per cent of the portfolio value is invested in hedge funds.

Taking all these results into account, hedge funds are attractive investment products. Amenc and Martellini (2002) proved on the basis of ex-post estimations that the inclusion of hedge funds in a portfolio can lead to a significant decrease in the volatility of a portfolio without leading to a significant change in returns. This means that stronger risk control does not necessarily correspond with a decrease in returns.

We updated the results previously obtained by analysing the performance between hedge fund indices and traditional indices. For this, we used the indices from the individual strategies in Chapter 3: the MSCI World and the Barclays Aggregate Bond index.[18] We then added the MSCI Emerging Markets index,[19] the Barclays Global High Yield index[20] and the S&P GSCI index.[21]

We performed the analysis over three periods: long-term, from the launch of the HFRI indices; medium term, from January 2003; and short-term, from January 2008.

Table 4.13 displays the correlation between hedge fund indices and traditional indices over the entire period. Analysis of this table provides the following information:

1. **Correlation with the MSCI World**: The correlation between hedge funds and global equity markets, as measured by the MSCI World, is relatively high. It ranges from −0.67 to 0.75, but only one correlation coefficient is negative. The average and median correlation coefficients are close to 0.5. In addition, 75 per cent of the strategies have a correlation with the MSCI World over 0.5. This means that over the long term, hedge funds have been correlated with equities overall. Directional strategies tend to have a higher correlation with the MSCI World; the highest coefficient reported is the correlation between the HFRI EH: Quantitative Directional, closely followed by the HFRI Fund Weighted Composite index and the HFRI Equity Hedge (Total) index. This is in line with expectations. Some non-directional strategies, such as the HFRI EH: Equity Market Neutral index and the HFRI RV: Fixed Income-Asset Backed, have a lower correlation with equities, while others, such as the HFRI Relative Value (Total) index, have a correlation with the MSCI World over 0.5. This is less intuitive as market neutral or relative value strategies should have a long-term correlation of lower than 0.3 or, at the worst, 0.5.

2. **Correlation with MSCI Emerging Market Equity index**: The correlation between hedge funds and emerging market equity as measured by the MSCI Emerging Market Equity index is also relatively high. It ranges from −0.60 to 0.88, but only one correlation coefficient is negative. The mean and median correlation coefficients reported are close to 0.55. In addition 71 per cent of the strategies have a correlation with emerging markets over 0.5. This means that over the long term, hedge funds have been correlated overall with emerging market equities, though the numbers reported are slightly higher than those obtained for the MSCI World. Directional strategies tend to have a high correlation with emerging markets. The highest coefficient reported is, as expected, the correlation of the emerging strategies. The HFRI Fund Weighted Composite index is not far behind, at 0.8. This suggests that over the long term hedge funds have profited from a high exposure to the emerging markets that performed well over the period under review. Some non-directional strategies, such as the HFRI EH: Equity Market Neutral index and the HFRI RV: Fixed Income-Asset Backed, have a lower correlation with equities, while others, such as the HFRI

Table 4.13   Correlation between hedge funds and classical indices[22] (January 1990–June 2012)

	MSCI World NR USD	MSCI Emerging Market Equity index	Barclays Aggregate Bond index	Barclays Global High Yield index	S&P GSCI
HFRI Fund Weighted Composite index	0.75	0.80	0.13	0.72	0.32
HFRI EH: Equity Market Neutral index	0.26	0.18	0.13	0.18	0.30
HFRI EH: Quantitative Directional	0.75	0.73	0.10	0.64	0.19
HFRI Relative Value (Total) index	0.54	0.56	0.11	0.70	0.34
HFRI RV: Fixed Income-Asset Backed	0.18	0.19	0.00	0.32	0.13
HFRI RV: Fixed Income-Convertible Arbitrage index	0.51	0.52	0.20	0.71	0.34
HFRI Event Driven (Total) index	0.69	0.70	0.09	0.76	0.27
HFRI ED: Merger Arbitrage index	0.51	0.49	0.09	0.56	0.14
HFRI ED: Distressed/Restructuring index	0.53	0.60	0.05	0.72	0.28
HFRI ED: Private Issue/Regulation D index	0.37	0.31	-0.05	0.26	0.27
HFRI RV: Multi-Strategy index	0.57	0.61	0.16	0.74	0.29
HFRI Equity Hedge (Total) index	0.73	0.71	0.14	0.63	0.36
HFRI Emerging Markets (Total) index	0.70	0.88	0.11	0.70	0.23
HFRI Emerging Markets: Asia ex-Japan index	0.67	0.84	0.14	0.60	0.22
HFRI Emerging Markets: Global index	0.61	0.82	0.03	0.70	0.29
HFRI Emerging Markets: Latin America index	0.57	0.74	0.10	0.62	0.20
HFRI Emerging Markets: Russia/East. Europe index	0.53	0.70	0.01	0.55	0.28
HFRI EH: Sector – Energy/Basic Materials index	0.54	0.53	0.21	0.49	0.52
HFRI EH: Sector – Technology/Healthcare index	0.60	0.59	0.03	0.46	0.22
HFRI RV: Fixed Income-Corporate index	0.54	0.57	0.09	0.80	0.20
HFRI EH: Short Bias index	-0.67	-0.60	-0.05	-0.53	-0.11
HFRI Macro (Total) index	0.36	0.44	0.24	0.38	0.17
HFRI Macro: Systematic Diversified index	0.42	0.41	0.15	0.20	0.11
HFRI Fund of Funds Composite index	0.56	0.67	0.09	0.57	0.38
Mean	0.49	0.54	0.10	0.52	0.25
Median	0.54	0.60	0.10	0.61	0.27
Minimum	-0.67	-0.60	-0.05	-0.53	-0.11
Maximum	0.75	0.88	0.24	0.80	0.52
Correlation > 0.5	75%	71%	0%	67%	4%
Correlation < 0.5 & > 0	21%	25%	87%	29%	91%
Correlation < 0	4%	4%	13%	4%	4%

Relative Value (Total) index, have a correlation with the MSCI World over 0.5. This is less intuitive.

3. **Correlation with the Barclays Aggregate Bond index:** The correlation coefficients with the Barclays Aggregate Bond index are much lower, usually close to 0. Overall, 87 per cent of the coefficients are between 0 and 0.5, showing that over the long term the exposure of hedge funds to the bond market has been relatively limited. The highest numbers are reported for the HFRI Macro (Total) index, the HFRI EH: Sector – Energy/Basic Materials index and the HFRI RV: Fixed Income-Convertible Arbitrage index. While this is understandable for macro funds and fixed-income convertible arbitrage, it is more difficult to understand why sector-specific equity funds can be correlated with this asset class.

4. **Correlation with the Barclays Global High Yield index:** The correlation coefficients reported for this index are much higher, in line with those obtained for equity indices. The main difference is the repartition of the coefficients, as these are typically not the same strategies that were highly correlated with the equity indices that are in turn highly correlated with the high yield index. Coefficients range from −0.53 to 0.8, but only one correlation coefficient is negative; the average and median correlation coefficients are close to 0.55. In addition, 67 per cent of the strategies have a correlation with the Barclays Global High Yield index of over 0.5; this means that over the long term, hedge funds have been correlated overall with high yield. Fixed-income and event driven strategies tend to have a higher correlation with high yield. The highest coefficient reported is the correlation with the HFRI RV: Fixed Income-Corporate index, the HFRI Event Driven (Total) index and the HFRI RV: Multi-Strategy index. Typical non-directional strategies, such as the HFRI EH: Equity Market Neutral index and the HFRI RV: Fixed Income-Asset Backed index, have a low correlation with high yield, while others, such as the HFRI Relative Value (Total) index, have a correlation with the index of over 0.5. The HFRI Fund Weighted Composite index has a correlation with the high yield index of over 0.7, confirming that high yield has played an important role for hedge fund strategies in the past.

5. **Correlation with the S&P GSCI index:** The correlation coefficients reported are lower, ranging from −0.11 to 0.52. In all, 91 per cent of the coefficients are between 0 and 0.5; this means that over the long term the exposure of hedge funds to the commodities has been limited, at least for hedge funds as an industry. The HFRI Fund Weighted Composite index has a correlation with the commodity index of 0.3. Finally, as expected, the highest correlation reported is with HFRI EH: Sector – Energy/Basic Materials index, at 0.52.

Table 4.14 gives the same information, but starting in January 2003. There is one important element to stress: the numbers tend to be higher. In practice, 91 per cent of the coefficients reported in this table are higher than those reported in the previous table. Coefficients increase on average by 0.14. The largest increases are in the correlation of equity market neutral funds with the equity indices. The biggest decrease is in the correlation of systematic macro funds with equity indices. This is in line with the fact that recent years have been volatile and that trend-following is one of the few strategies that tend to go net short during bear market conditions.

Table 4.15 gives the same information, but starting in January 2008. The correlation coefficients have increased again. in practice, 89 per cent of the coefficients in this table are higher than the ones in the previous table. Coefficients increase on average by 0.2 (in addition to the 0.14 in the previous paragraph). This time, while the largest increases take place in the commodity index, the biggest decrease is again in systematic macro funds, for the reason mentioned above. In all, 64 per cent of the coefficients reported are over 0.5, and 49 per cent of these are over 0.75. These numbers are particularly high, but they should be put into context to some extent as this period includes 2008, when hedge funds suffered along with the traditional markets, and 2009, when the hedge fund industry profited from the market rebound.

Figure 4.34 reports the average correlation of the hedge fund indices with the reference indices. The increasing correlation trend is clear, even in the Barclays Aggregate Bond index, which is less correlated overall.

8.2 Correlation between hedge fund strategies

8.2.1 *Monthly data*

Table 4.16 displays the correlation between hedge fund strategies over the whole period. The numbers are higher than those that would be expected given the fact that most strategies are not investing in the same markets. The HFRI Fund Weighted Composite index has a mean correlation with the sub-indices at 0.66 and a median at 0.72; it is negatively correlated with short-biased funds and has a low correlation with relative-value funds, at 0.28. Of the correlation coefficients, 85 per cent are over 0.5.

At a strategy level, the three strategies that have the lower average correlation with the other strategies over the long term are short-biased funds (−0.45), fixed-income asset-backed (0.26) and the macro systematic diversified index (0.30). On the other hand, the fund of funds composite index (0.63), event driven funds (0.61) and equity hedge indices (0.6) are relatively highly correlated with the other strategies. This is logical, as funds of funds are made up of other funds, and as event driven and equity hedge funds tend to feature strongly in both databases and portfolios.

Table 4.14   Correlation between hedge funds and traditional indices (January 2003–June 2012)

	MSCI World NR USD	MSCI Emerging Market Equity index	Barclays Aggregate Bond index	Barclays Global High Yield index	S&P GSCI
HFRI Fund Weighted Composite index	0.89	0.92	0.32	0.77	0.60
HFRI EH: Equity Market Neutral index	0.55	0.58	0.08	0.35	0.53
HFRI EH: Quantitative Directional	0.88	0.88	0.26	0.67	0.46
HFRI Relative Value (Total) index	0.75	0.77	0.24	0.86	0.53
HFRI RV: Fixed Income-Asset Backed	0.42	0.36	0.08	0.60	0.31
HFRI RV: Fixed Income-Convertible Arbitrage index	0.69	0.71	0.30	0.85	0.47
HFRI Event Driven (Total) index	0.86	0.84	0.26	0.79	0.53
HFRI ED: Merger Arbitrage index	0.74	0.76	0.25	0.62	0.39
HFRI ED: Distressed/Restructuring index	0.76	0.72	0.21	0.76	0.53
HFRI ED: Private Issue/Regulation D index	0.40	0.36	0.08	0.32	0.39
HFRI RV: Multi-Strategy index	0.72	0.71	0.27	0.84	0.52
HFRI Equity Hedge (Total) index	0.91	0.93	0.28	0.77	0.59
HFRI Emerging Markets (Total) index	0.85	0.95	0.36	0.77	0.58
HFRI Emerging Markets: Asia ex-Japan index	0.80	0.92	0.33	0.67	0.50
HFRI Emerging Markets: Global index	0.85	0.94	0.35	0.79	0.59
HFRI Emerging Markets: Latin America index	0.78	0.85	0.35	0.78	0.44
HFRI Emerging Markets: Russia/East. Europe index	0.77	0.83	0.32	0.70	0.63
HFRI EH: Sector – Energy/Basic Materials index	0.78	0.82	0.33	0.70	0.70
HFRI EH: Sector – Technology/Healthcare index	0.80	0.81	0.19	0.64	0.39
HFRI RV: Fixed Income-Corporate index	0.74	0.69	0.19	0.84	0.50
HFRI EH: Short Bias index	-0.86	-0.75	-0.17	-0.69	-0.31
HFRI Macro (Total) index	0.35	0.48	0.41	0.21	0.43
HFRI Macro: Systematic Diversified index	0.18	0.27	0.23	-0.02	0.16
HFRI Fund of Funds Composite index	0.77	0.83	0.25	0.68	0.60
Mean	0.64	0.67	0.24	0.59	0.46
Median	0.76	0.79	0.26	0.70	0.51
Minimum	-0.86	-0.75	-0.17	-0.69	-0.31
Maximum	0.91	0.95	0.41	0.86	0.70
Correlation > 0.5	75%	75%	0%	80%	45%
Correlation < 0.5 & > 0	20%	20%	95%	10%	50%
Correlation < 0	5%	5%	5%	10%	5%

Table 4.15 Correlation between hedge funds and classical indices (January 2008–June 2012)

	MSCI World NR USD	MSCI Emerging Market Equity index	Barclays Aggregate Bond index	Barclays Global High Yield index	S&P GSCI
HFRI Fund Weighted Composite index	0.90	0.93	0.38	0.85	0.77
HFRI EH: Equity Market Neutral index	0.55	0.55	0.10	0.39	0.67
HFRI EH: Quantitative Directional	0.95	0.93	0.36	0.82	0.71
HFRI Relative Value (Total) index	0.77	0.81	0.27	0.90	0.67
HFRI RV: Fixed Income – Asset Backed	0.49	0.48	0.06	0.65	0.42
HFRI RV: Fixed Income – Convertible Arbitrage index	0.74	0.81	0.35	0.89	0.62
HFRI Event Driven (Total) index	0.88	0.87	0.30	0.87	0.75
HFRI ED: Merger Arbitrage index	0.83	0.85	0.37	0.79	0.58
HFRI ED: Distressed/Restructuring index	0.77	0.76	0.21	0.81	0.73
HFRI ED: Private Issue/Regulation D index	0.50	0.40	0.12	0.40	0.54
HFRI RV: Multi-Strategy index	0.74	0.77	0.28	0.85	0.65
HFRI Equity Hedge (Total) index	0.93	0.95	0.36	0.86	0.76
HFRI Emerging Markets (Total) index	0.89	0.96	0.42	0.87	0.75
HFRI Emerging Markets: Asia ex-Japan index	0.85	0.95	0.44	0.82	0.63
HFRI Emerging Markets: Global index	0.87	0.94	0.41	0.89	0.77
HFRI Emerging Markets: Latin America index	0.82	0.92	0.41	0.86	0.73
HFRI Emerging Markets: Russia/Eastern Europe index	0.84	0.87	0.36	0.80	0.79
HFRI EH: Sector – Energy/Basic Materials index	0.83	0.88	0.36	0.80	0.80
HFRI EH: Sector – Technology/Healthcare index	0.90	0.88	0.26	0.82	0.63
HFRI RV: Fixed Income-Corporate index	0.76	0.77	0.22	0.87	0.68
HFRI EH: Short Bias index	-0.90	-0.83	-0.24	-0.75	-0.52
HFRI Macro (Total) index	0.25	0.31	0.41	0.15	0.39
HFRI Macro: Systematic Diversified index	-0.10	-0.07	0.30	-0.20	0.07
HFRI Fund of Funds Composite index	0.79	0.83	0.29	0.78	0.77
Mean	0.66	0.69	0.28	0.66	0.60
Median	0.81	0.84	0.33	0.82	0.68
Minimum	-0.90	-0.83	-0.24	-0.75	-0.52
Maximum	0.95	0.96	0.44	0.90	0.80
Correlation > 0.5	75%	75%	0%	80%	80%
Correlation < 0.5 & > 0	15%	15%	95%	10%	15%
Correlation < 0	10%	10%	5%	10%	5%

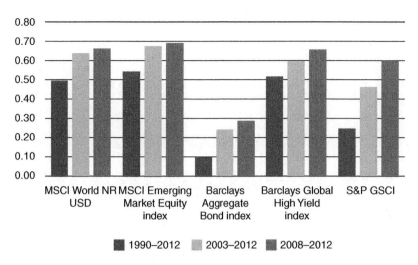

Figure 4.34 Mean correlation between hedge fund indices and the traditional indices

A similar analysis covering the January 2003 to June 2012 period (not reported for the sake of brevity) gives a higher mean correlation between the composite index and the strategies, at 0.75, and a median at 0.86. Individual correlations range from −0.77 (short-biased) to 0.99 (multi-strategy funds). For the period starting in January 2008, the mean correlation between the composite index and individual strategies increases to 0.76, and the median to 0.9; this is clearly due to the 2008 liquidity crisis, which impacted the entire industry. Figure 4.35 gives the average correlation of the global hedge fund strategies over the long, medium and shorter term; the increase in numbers is clearly visible.

While the increase in correlation between hedge funds is obvious, this result should be balanced with the fact that the estimation of correlation is based only on the correlation between indices, not between individual funds. Capocci and Mahieu (2003) carried out a similar analysis using indices set against the individual funds used to build these indices; the conclusion drawn from the analysis was that there is a significantly higher correlation between hedge fund indices than within individual hedge funds.

Figure 4.36 gives the mean, median, minimum and maximum correlations between individual funds within strategies (all the individual funds used to build the indices) and in a series of It shows how disparate individual correlations can be. For example, consider event driven funds; the minimum correlation with individual hedge funds applying other strategies is, at −0.06, slightly negative, whereas the mean is at 0.41, the median at 0.55 and the maximum at 0.7.

Table 4.16 Correlation between hedge fund strategies (January 1990–June 2012)

	1	2	3	4	5	6	7	8	9	10	11	12	13	14	15	16	17	18	19
1 HFRI Fund Weighted Composite index	1.00																		
2 HFRI EH: Equity Market Neutral index	0.45	1.00																	
3 HFRI EH: Quantitative Directional	0.92	0.32	1.00																
4 HFRI Relative Value (Total) index	0.72	0.41	0.56	1.00															
5 HFRI RV: Fixed Income – Asset Backed	0.28	0.19	0.40	0.40	1.00														
6 HFRI RV: Fixed Income – Convertible Arbitrage index	0.62	0.31	0.80	0.37	0.37	1.00													
7 HFRI Event Driven (Total) index	0.90	0.40	0.76	0.35	0.66	0.66	1.00												
8 HFRI ED: Merger Arbitrage index	0.65	0.34	0.55	0.14	0.48	0.48	0.75	1.00											
9 HFRI ED: Distressed/Restructuring index	0.79	0.39	0.79	0.43	0.66	0.66	0.86	0.57	1.00										
10 HFRI ED: Private Issue/Regulation D index	0.52	0.34	0.36	0.06	0.28	0.28	0.49	0.38	0.42	1.00									
11 HFRI RV: Multi-Strategy index	0.74	0.37	0.80	0.62	0.78	0.78	0.75	0.48	0.77	0.34	1.00								
12 HFRI Equity Hedge (Total) index	0.95	0.50	0.68	0.22	0.60	0.60	0.84	0.59	0.70	0.54	0.67	1.00							
13 HFRI Emerging Markets (Total) index	0.86	0.26	0.61	0.28	0.53	0.53	0.76	0.52	0.70	0.38	0.67	0.74	1.00						
14 HFRI EH: Sector – Energy/Basic Materials index	0.64	0.44	0.58	0.15	0.52	0.52	0.61	0.51	0.55	0.27	0.55	0.64	0.54	1.00					
15 HFRI EH: Sector – Technology/Healthcare index	0.79	0.27	0.44	0.12	0.33	0.33	0.65	0.45	0.48	0.49	0.44	0.80	0.58	0.34	1.00				
16 HFRI RV: Fixed Income-Corporate index	0.69	0.26	0.70	0.51	0.67	0.67	0.77	0.56	0.82	0.32	0.81	0.58	0.63	0.49	0.38	1.00			
17 HFRI EH: Short Bias index	-0.74	-0.14	-0.40	-0.11	-0.33	-0.33	-0.62	-0.41	-0.48	-0.38	-0.44	-0.74	-0.58	-0.35	-0.81	-0.45	1.00		
18 HFRI Macro (Total) index	0.64	0.33	0.34	0.18	0.25	0.25	0.51	0.34	0.43	0.31	0.43	0.56	0.57	0.39	0.43	0.38	-0.35	1.00	
19 HFRI Macro: Systematic Diversified index	0.56	0.24	0.16	-0.11	0.07	0.07	0.39	0.29	0.26	0.33	0.19	0.51	0.41	0.34	0.55	0.17	-0.50	0.58	1.00
20 HFRI Fund of Funds Composite index	0.87	0.50	0.67	0.35	0.60	0.60	0.76	0.51	0.71	0.51	0.68	0.82	0.79	0.60	0.64	0.54	-0.50	0.67	0.46

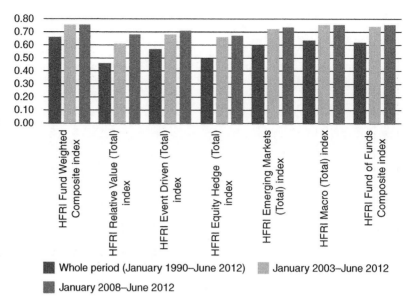

Figure 4.35 Average correlation between hedge fund strategies and the HFR Global Hedge Fund index

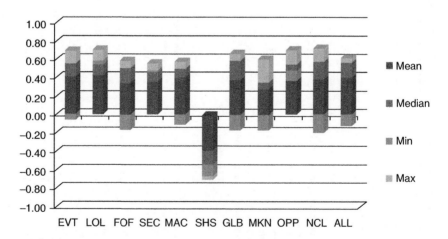

Figure 4.36 Average correlation between hedge fund strategies

Source: Capocci and Mahieu (2003) based on the MAR database. EVT = Event driven, LOL = Long Only Leveraged, FoF = Funds of Funds, SEC = Sectors , MAC = Global Macro, SHS = Short Sellers, GLB = Global, MKN = Market Neutral, OPP = US Opportunistics, NCL = Non Classified, ALL = All Funds.

8.2.2 Daily data

Hedge Fund Research, Inc. started publishing daily estimation of hedge fund returns a few years ago and they built indices starting in January 2003 and 2004. We carried out a study on these data.[23] In it we analysed hedge fund strategy indices,[24] the HFRX Global index, which groups all the funds used to build the strategy indices using their assets as weighting tool, the HFRX Equally-weighted index, the HFRX Absolute Return index, which includes funds aiming to offer absolute returns, and the HFRX Market Directional index, which integrates the directional funds. Table 4.17 has two parts, the first giving the correlation between the daily hedge fund returns, and the second the correlation between the hedge fund indices and a series of traditional indices.

The first part of Table 4.17 indicates that the directional strategies, including equity hedge, event driven and market directional, are highly correlated with one another. Pure non-directional strategies, such as distressed securities, equity market neutral and convertible arbitrage, are not much correlated with the other strategies and the indices. Part 2 of Table 4.19 indicates that the correlation between the directional strategies, the global indices and the equities indices is high, particularly so for the American equity indices and for the emerging market equity indices that performed well during the period analysed.

For arbitrage strategies, particularly for convertible arbitrage, distressed securities and equity market neutral funds, the values are low to very low. These results are in line with most publications on the subject.

Table 4.18 gives the annual correlations within the daily indices. It is interesting because its correlation coefficients tend to increase over time; the correlation of the hedge global index with the other indices tended to increase from 0.4 in 2003 to 0.65 in 2007, and the same trend exists between the hedge global index and the equity indices. The second part of the table indicates that the result is different for the convertible arbitrage strategy, as its correlation with the other indices has remained relatively stable. For equity market neutral funds, the correlation remained stable until 2006, but increased in 2007. Equity hedge funds had a historical correlation with the other hedge fund indices of around 0.5 until 2006, subsequently increasing slightly, as did the correlation of this index with equity indices.

Table 4.17 Correlation between daily hedge fund indices and reference indices

A: Correlation between daily hedge funds indices (4 January 2003–28 December 2007)

	1	2	3	4	5	6	7	8	9	10	11	12
1 Hedge Global Index	1											
2 Hedge Equally-Weighted		1										
3 Hedge Absolute Return	0.6	0.68	1									
4 Hedge Market Directional			0.48	1								
5 Convertible Arbitrage	0.1	0.25	0.33	0.01	1							
6 Distressed Securities	0.25	0.32	0.36	0.19	0.13	1						
7 Equity Hedge	0.29		0.46		−0.0	0.17	1					
8 Equity Market Neutral		0.43	0.45	0.26	0.07	0.08	0.21	1				
9 Event Driven			0.47	0.73	0.02	0.24		0.2	1			
10 Macro	0.71	0.74	0.49		0.12	0.13	0.49	0.2	0.44	1		
11 Merger Arbitrage	0.5	0.56	0.28	0.52	−0.0	0.05	0.5	0.14	0.53	0.22	1	
12 Volatility	0.5	0.55	0.53	0.44	0.16	0.15	0.34	0.2	0.33	0.3	0.23	1

B: Correlation between daily hedge fund indices and reference indices (4 January 2003–28 December 2007)

	1	2	3	4	5	6	7	8	9	10	11	12
13 S&P 500	0.66	0.53	0.2	0.72	-0.2	0.04	0.75	0.06	0.68	0.21	0.45	0.21
14 Eurostoxx 50	0.63	0.59	0.45	0.65	0.03	0.19	0.6	0.17	0.57	0.44	0.31	0.25
15 Nasdaq	0.57	0.44	0.15	0.65	-0.1	0.05	0.67	0	0.6	0.16	0.37	0.16
16 Russel 3000	0.68	0.55	0.21	0.74	-0.2	0.05	0.62	0.07	0.7	0.23	0.46	0.22
17 MSCI Europe	0.67	0.64	0.48	0.67	0.06	0.19	0.62	0.2	0.59	0.5	0.32	0.28
18 MSCI EM BRIC USD	0.06	0.64	0.01	0.19	0.01	0.26	0.8	0.73	0.52	0.44	0.72	0.65
19 MSCI Glob. Emerging Mkt	0.71	0.67	0.51	0.67	0.12	0.18	0.66	0.22	0.55	0.58	0.26	0.28
20 MSCI EM Latin American	0.73	0.64	0.37	0.73	-0.1	0.11	0.71	0.16	0.66	0.42	0.4	0.25
21 MSCI Eastern Europe	0.49	0.48	0.39	0.51	0.07	0.14	0.45	0.16	0.39	0.42	0.2	0.2
22 MSCI Asia	0.42	0.4	0.4	0.32	0.15	0.13	0.38	0.14	0.25	0.4	0.07	0.18
23 MSCI China	0.43	0.42	0.35	0.38	0.12	0.11	0.38	0.15	0.29	0.39	0.13	0.22
24 NIKKEI	0.3	0.28	0.32	0.19	0.1	0.11	0.28	0.11	0.16	0.28	0.03	0.11

Correlation coefficients > 0.75 are in black, coefficients < 0.75 and > 0.5 are in dark grey, coefficients < 0.5 and > 0.25 are in light grey and coefficients < 0 are in white.

Table 4.18 Annual correlation coefficients between daily hedge funds indices and references indices

Hedge Global index

	2003	2004	2005	2006	2007
Hedge Equally–Weighted	0.9	0.94	0.93	0.96	0.96
Hedge Absolute Return	NA	NA	0.53	0.72	0.62
Hedge Market Directional	NA	NA	0.92	0.95	0.98
Convertible Arbitrage	0.04	0.12	0	-0.1	0.25
Distressed Securities	0.16	0.34	0.25	0.49	0.13
Equity Hedge	0.89	0.91	0.94	0.97	0.94
Equity Market Neutral	-0.1	0.18	0.22	0.51	0.31
Event Driven	0.61	0.78	0.89	0.91	0.89
Macro	0.47	0.51	0.53	0.71	0.83
Merger Arbitrage	0.27	0.41	0.51	0.46	0.58
Volatility	0.37	0.39	0.39	0.42	0.71
Mean	0.4	0.51	0.56	0.63	0.65
S&P 500	0.55	0.63	0.7	0.72	0.7
Eurostoxx 50	0.48	0.59	0.54	0.71	0.76
Russel 3000	0.59	0.66	0.73	0.75	0.72
MSCI China	0.26	0.41	0.34	0.5	0.49
MSCI GEM	0.42	0.68	0.65	0.77	0.79
MSCI LatAm	0.5	0.69	0.69	0.8	0.79
MSCI EE	0.23	0.35	0.49	0.61	0.67
MSCI FE x–J	0.29	0.52	0.41	0.54	0.57
MSCI Asia	0.4	0.53	0.42	0.51	0.39
NIKKEI Japan	0.38	0.48	0.37	0.46	0.09
MSCI BRIC	NA	NA	NA	0.78	0.77
Mean	0.43	0.55	0.54	0.65	0.6

Convertible Arbitrage

	2003	2004	2005	2006	2007
Hedge Global index	0.04	0.12	0	-0.1	0.25
Hedge Equally-weighted	0.29	0.27	0.23	0.05	0.35
Hedge absolute return	NA	NA	0.42	0.11	0.34
Hedge market directional	NA	NA	-0.1	-0.2	0.16
Distressed securities	0.2	0.18	0.21	-0.1	0.09
Equity hedge	-0.1	0.0	-0.1	-0.2	0.13
Equity market neutral	0.14	0.08	-0.1	0.0	0.14
Event driven	-0.1	-0.1	-0.1	-0.2	0.2
Macro	0.01	0.09	0.03	0	0.25
Merger arbitrage	0.04	-0.1	0.0	-0.2	0.01
Volatility	0.09	0.26	0	0.2	0.25
Mean	0.07	0.08	0.05	-0.1	0.2
S&P 500	-0.2	-0.2	-0.1	-0.3	-0.06
Eurostoxx 50	0.0	-0.01	0.03	-0.2	0.24
Russel 3000	-0.2	-0.2	-0.1	-0.3	-0.07
MSCI China	0.0	0	-0.01	0.06	0.35
MSCI GEM	0.0	0.04	0	0.05	0.37
MSCI LatAm	-0.1	-0.1	-0.1	-0.21	0.02
MSCI EE	0.0	0.1	0.03	-0.01	0.25
MSCI FE x–J	0.0	0.05	0.02	0.17	0.42
MSCI Asia	0	0.09	0.06	0.15	0.37
NIKKEI Japan	0.03	0.09	0.07	0.08	0.23
MSCI BRIC	NA	NA	NA	-0.02	0.31
Mean	-0.08	-0.03	-0.02	-0.08	0.19

Equity Market Neutral

	2003	2004	2005	2006	2007
Hedge Global index	-0.1	0.18	0.22	0.51	0.31
Hedge Equally-Weighted	0.16	0.33	0.34	0.6	0.46
Hedge Absolute Return	NA	NA	0.08	0.58	0.59
Hedge Market Directional	NA	NA	0.19	0.43	0.25
Convertible Arbitrage	0.14	0.08	-0.1	0.0	0.14
Distressed Securities	0.14	0.11	0.0	0.22	0.05
Equity Hedge	-0.2	0.12	0.23	0.48	0.23
Event Driven	-0.1	0.11	0.21	0.4	0.23
Macro	0.04	0.08	0.01	0.37	0.25
Merger Arbitrage	-0.1	0.04	0.28	0.14	0.15
Volatility	0.05	0.1	0.03	0.25	0.32
Mean	0	0.13	0.14	0.36	0.27
S&P 500	-0.3	0.03	0.17	0.27	0.09
Eurostoxx 50	-0.3	0.13	0.07	0.42	0.3
Russel 3000	-0.3	0.03	0.19	0.29	0.09
MSCI China	-0.1	0.15	0.0	0.29	0.22
MSCI GEM	-0.3	0.17	0.13	0.46	0.28
MSCI LatAm	-0.3	0.13	0.26	0.4	0.15
MSCI EE	-0.1	0.11	0.09	0.39	0.21
MSCI FE x-J	-0.2	0.16	0.01	0.36	0.25
MSCI Asia	-0.1	0.12	0.0	0.42	0.2
NIKKEI Japan	-0.1	0.09	0.0	0.42	0.12
MSCI BRIC	NA	NA	NA	0.45	0.27
Mean	-0.2	0.09	0.08	0.37	0.18

Equity Hedge

	2003	2004	2005	2006	2007
Hedge Global index	0.89	0.91	0.94	0.97	0.94
Hedge Equally-Weighted	0.64	0.75	0.8	0.89	0.85
Hedge Absolute Return	NA	NA	0.35	0.64	0.49
Hedge Market Directional	NA	NA	0.86	0.91	0.95
Convertible Arbitrage	-0.1	0.0	-0.1	-0.2	0.13
Distressed Securities	0.04	0.23	0.18	0.39	0.04
Hedge Market Directional	-0.2	0.12	0.23	0.48	0.23
Event Driven	0.53	0.72	0.86	0.88	0.85
Macro	0.21	0.24	0.28	0.55	0.65
Merger Arbitrage	0.29	0.4	0.53	0.47	0.58
Volatility	0.08	0.21	0.28	0.3	0.59
Mean	0.26	0.4	0.47	0.57	0.57
S&P 500	0.66	0.73	0.8	0.79	0.8
Eurostoxx 50	0.53	0.55	0.48	0.68	0.69
Russel 3000	0.69	0.77	0.84	0.82	0.82
MSCI China	0.26	0.35	0.24	0.45	0.45
MSCI GEM	0.44	0.6	0.53	0.73	0.74
MSCI LatAm	0.57	0.71	0.69	0.83	0.85
MSCI EE	0.23	0.27	0.37	0.57	0.61
MSCI FE x-J	0.3	0.44	0.31	0.48	0.51
MSCI Asia	0.39	0.44	0.29	0.47	0.34
NIKKEI Japan	0.38	0.4	0.26	0.43	0.07
MSCI BRIC	NA	NA	NA	0.76	0.74
Mean	0.47	0.54	0.5	0.64	0.6

These results are shown graphically in Figures 4.37 and 4.38; the first focuses on the correlation coefficients between the hedge global index and the other daily hedge fund indices. The second gives the annual correlation between this index and the reference indices.

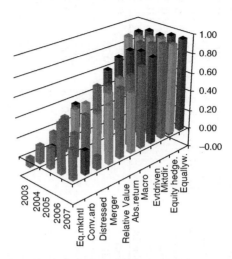

Figure 4.37 Annual correlation between the hedge global index and the other daily hedge fund indices Eq. mkt ntl = equity market neutal, Conv.arb. = convertible arbitrage, Distressed = distressed securities, Merger = merger arbitrage, Abs. return = absolute return, Mk. dir. = market directional, Equally w. = equally-weighted global index.

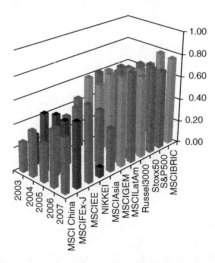

Figure 4.38 Annual correlation between the hedge global index and reference indices. MSCIF Ex-J = MSCI Free ex-Japan index, MSCI EE = MSCI Eastern Europe index, MSCI GEM = MSCI Global Emerging Markets index, MSCI LatAM = MSCI Latin America, Stoxx50 = Eurostoxx 50 index, MSCI BRIC = MSCI Brazil, Russia, India, China index.

9 Summary

In this chapter we analysed the historical performance of the hedge fund industry. We started by describing the potential issues with hedge fund data, including the survivorship bias. Then we analysed and compared the performance of hedge funds – globally and per strategy – against traditional indices. This enabled us to put numbers on theory and, more importantly, to differentiate between strategies. From there we carried out an analysis of hedge funds by integrating new measures such as the extended Sharpe ratio and omega. We also compared the return distribution of hedge funds and a few hedge fund strategies against traditional markets. We then analysed extreme market conditions. Finally, we performed an overview of the main academic research on the subject before analysing in detail various aspects of correlation over the short, medium and long term.

5
Hedge Funds, LTCM and Recent Crises

This chapter provides an analysis first of the bailout of Long-Term Capital Management in 1998, then of the role of hedge funds in the worst financial crises of recent times. This chapter will thus describe another side of the hedge fund industry; hedge funds have faced difficulties and have also been impacted by crisis periods; in some cases, they have even had an impact on the financial industry as a whole.

1 Long-term capital management

Long-Term Capital Portfolio LP. is probably one of the most famous hedge funds in the world. Unfortunately, this fund is notorious mainly because of the significant difficulties it faced in 1998. This section aims to describe the progress of this fund from its creation in 1994 to its bailout at the end of 1998. We start by describing the market context in September 1998. We then present the fund. Finally we analyse how and why the fund was saved. Let's start with a sentence on this topic by Alan Greenspan, President of the American Federal Reserve at the time of the bailout:

> Had the failure of LTCM triggered the seizing up of markets, substantial damage could have been inflicted on many market participants, including some not directly involved with the firm, and could have potentially impaired the economies of many nations, including our own.[1]

1.1 The situation in September 1998

Before focusing on the Long-Term Capital Portfolio fund itself, we would like to describe the atmosphere in the financial markets during the early days of the second half of 2008. This description puts the facts into their difficult context.

1.1.1 The losses of Soros et al.

For a few months, there were rumours according which a few large hedge funds had made wrong bets and had had to support losses. On Wednesday 26 August 1998, Stanley Druckenmiller, the manager of George Soros' well-known Quantum fund announced on television that one of the largest investors on earth, George Soros and his colleagues, had made some mistakes and that Soros' funds, including the Quantum fund, had lost over US$2 billion since the start of the Russian debt crisis a few weeks earlier. They had invested large amounts in Russia, and the situation had evolved against them. In addition, liquidity disappeared when the securities were down, and there was nothing to be done other than keep those securities that had almost no remaining value left. Despite those losses, Druckenmiller confirmed that the year-to-date return of the Quantum fund was nevertheless positive overall, close to 19 per cent. From this point, there changes were made by Soros that included the closure of one of the funds that had lost over 30 per cent in total. In fact, this announcement turned out to be the first of a series – it was merely the tip of the iceberg, as many other hedge funds were suffering. It also signalled the start of two important changes:

– A greater openness in general
– A greater transparency regarding losses.

In the next few days a series of other fund managers made similar announcements, including one that announced a loss of close to 85 per cent; its AUM moved from over US$300 million to US$25 million over a few weeks. Over that period, losses of 10 to 20 per cent were common. Until the middle of September, the funds managed by Tiger Management, Julian Robertson's asset management company, remained an exception. In a statement on 16 September 1998, however, Robertson announced that his funds had lost US$2.1 billion overall, approximately 10 per cent of their value, arising mainly from a short position that had been taken in the Japanese yen against the US dollar.[2] Like the Soros funds, Robertson's funds were still positive overall for the year. But the situation became more complicated over the following weeks, and during October 1998 Robertson's funds lost US$3.4 billion in value. This brought the year-to-date performance down close to zero. They finished the year down, losing a significant proportion of their assets between performance and redemptions.

1.1.2 Fixed-income arbitrage

Fixed-income arbitrage funds apply investment strategies based on complex quantitative models.[3] These models rely on underlying hypotheses such as the normality of the distribution of returns, that is, that the function of distribution of returns has a skew and an excess kurtosis insignificantly different from zero.[4] This hypothesis is however not true in reality as distributions tend to have fat tails. This means that losses higher than those anticipated by the models may be made. Most of the events that happened during this period had never happened before, and the models had been built on the underlying hypothesis that there was a 95 to 99 per cent chance that this would not happen.

Early in August 1998, the fixed-income arbitrage strategy was operating in a blaze of glory; there had never been more funds applying the strategy and more assets invested in it. So the spreads on which the strategy was being implemented were minimal, and leverage was largely being used in order to offer attractive returns. Then on 17 August Russia announced a default of US$40 billion on its debt; this announcement led to a liquidity crisis in financial markets and a flight to quality. Credit spreads widened significantly, and attained historical highs.

Over that period several fixed-income securities whose prices were not linked during normal market conditions evolved in parallel, and the models used no longer worked. The search for quality over the short term was such that the American interest rate curve became inverse. In normal market conditions this would have meant that the country was going into recession. It was a technical move, and the Federal Reserve announced two consecutive cuts in interest rate to stabilize the situation. Many funds lost money over that period, and the trend was strongly negative.

1.2 Long-term capital management

Long-Term Capital Management, LP. (LTCM) is an asset management company founded in 1994 and based in Greenwich, Connecticut, USA. It's main portfolio was called Long-Term Capital Portfolio, LP. The founder of LTCM was John W. Meriwether; he had been a well-known bond trader at Salomon Brothers. Meriwether rose to become the head of the domestic fixed-income arbitrage desk in the early 1980s. In 1991 he left the company after one of his team heads – Paul Mozer – was caught up in a Treasury securities trading scandal; he had been cheating on Treasuries auctions by putting in more orders than the company could afford. The Treasury threatened Salomon Brothers, potentially forbidding the company from participating in future auctions. Certain investors then started putting pressure on company bonds and it started facing difficulties, at which point Warren Buffet became president. Meriwether was ordered to pay a US$50,000 fine by the Securities and Exchange Commission.

In 1993 he started to raise assets in order to create a new fund. From the start, LTCM was an ambitious project. His first objective was to recreate Salomon Brothers' bond desk, inviting various well-known individuals to become partners of the management company. He successfully persuaded, amongst others, two men who were to become Nobel prizewinners: Merton Miller, famous American professor, originator of Continuous Time Finance, and Myron Scholes, one of the founders of Option Theory. Another participant was David Mullins, a former vice-president of the Federal Reserve. At the launch, the partners invested a total of US$150 million.

The fund was difficult to access and offered little liquidity. Fees were high even for the hedge fund world; management fees were at 2 per cent and performance fees at 25 per cent of the profits. Finally, there was a three year lockup, and the minimum investment was US$3 million. The fund was the archetypal fixed-income arbitrage hedge fund, active on many markets and in many countries. Its main strategy was to profit from spreads in prices of similar assets; typical positions included convergence trades in European countries or dynamic hedging positions, trading classic bonds, convertible bonds, mortgage bonds, high yield bonds and equities. The fund was also active in the merger and acquisitions market, in emerging markets and in the catastrophe bond market.

While the fund was diversified geographically, it was not very diversified in terms of risks. The fund was broadly positioned to profit from a liquidity spread tightening and a credit spread tightening, and/or to profit from volatility moves. In normal market conditions even if one of the constituents did not evolve in the desired direction, there was a geographical and a market diversification that helped to mitigate any exposure and potential loss.

By 24 February 1994, the day LTCM began trading, the company had amassed just over US$1 billion in capital. From the start, LTCM had a prominent position in the hedge fund community thanks to the reputation of its partners and because of the huge amount of capital they managed. It was also because of the reputation of the individuals most deeply involved that the management team was able to keep silent about the investment strategy implemented, the relative size of the positions taken and the total exposure of the fund.

In the first year, while most fixed-income arbirage funds were losing money, the fund offered a net performance of 2 per cent. In October, while it was clear that the fund would be finishing the year with a good performance, Meriwether wrote a letter to investors reminding them that they could lose money in the short term; a document was attached to this letter written by Merton and Scholes analysing the risk inherent within the fund, concluding that it would lose at least 5 per cent of its assets 12 per cent of the time and making similar estimates relating to 15 and 20 per cent losses. At that time the notion of risk was not associated with leverage but with fund volatility. This measure was consistently followed and adjusted in order to stay within the defined range. At the end of 1995, the fund was up 43 per cent net of fees due, amongst other things, to positions in Italian bonds. Over its first 24 months of existence the fund had only once faced a loss of more than 1 per cent.

In spring 1996 the fund had US$ several billion in assets, and more than 100 employees. By the end of that year, the fund was up by a strong 41 per cent net; this performance could be explained mainly by the positions taken in the Japanese convertible market, in highly speculative bonds, in interest rate swaps and, again, in Italian bonds. But the problem was that as time went by it became more and more difficult for the management team to identify enough opportunities to diversify the portfolio correctly; in order to make a decent profit, the fund needed to take highly-leveraged positions as the arbitrage opportunities were tiny, especially in the convergence trades. By the end of 1997, the fund was up by 17 per cent. The manager decided to increase the balance sheet leverage by reducing its capital, by roughly 36 per cent, to approximately to US$4.8 billion, and early investors received US$1.82 for every US$1 invested while retaining a similar investment in the fund.

The investment portfolio of LTCM was 80 per cent invested in government bonds of the G7 (United States, Canada, France, Italy, Japan, Germany and United Kingdom). The portfolio was also heavily invested in other markets, including equities, futures and over the counter derivatives. The fund was taking long and short positions in government bonds, corporate and mortgage bonds as well as in equities; it was active on more than 10 futures markets, the positions being mainly concentrated in interest rate futures. In addition, the fund was exposed to over-the-counter derivatives such as swaps or options with a dozen counterparties. The fund was also active in the currency market, mainly to hedge unwanted risks.

Early in 1998 the fund was invested for a value of US$140 billion, nearly 30 times its equity of just below US$5 billion. LTCM was the hedge fund with the highest level of leverage of all the hedge funds reporting to the Commodity Futures and Trading Commission.[5] This situation continued until August. The main feature of the fund was the scale of its activities; it was taking long and short positions of over US$50 billion.

1.3 History of the bailout

The fund started to lose money in spring 1998; Asia was slowly recovering from its financial crisis, while Russia was facing issues, and interest rate spreads were very low. The fund faced its first important losses in May and June 1998, when the mortgage bond market was suffering; the fund lost 6.42 per cent and 10.14 per cent, reducing LTCM's capital by US$461 million. So at this point the fund was already having a difficult year – but the year had not yet come to an end; on 17 August 1998, Russia unexpectedly announced a default on its debt and the concomitant high volatility deepened the fund's losses. Most bond spreads widened significantly while the fund was trying to profit from an interest rate tightening in converging Europe; in a nutshell, spreads widened, uncorrelated markets became correlated and liquidity spreads increased rapidly and significantly. In addition the fund's had a significant position in a relative value trade between to Royal Dutch and Shell. The spread between the companies moved against the fund. The size of its positions and the high leverage of the fund made the portfolio vulnerable to the exceptional market conditions that prevailed over those few months.

While it has been estimated that until then the fund had never lost more than US$35 million of its assets in a single day, on Friday 21 August it lost more than US$553 million. The leverage increased from 28 to 51. At that point, the partners were actively looking for assets, but were unable to find enough money. Friday 28 August was the second most difficult day for the fund, with US$277 million lost. At the end of August 1998, the fund was engaged in forward contracts for a notional gross amount of over US$500 billion. It was committed to swaps of over US$750 billion and in options and other over-the-counter derivative products of more than US$15 billion. At the same time, panicking investors sold Japanese and European bonds to buy US Treasury bonds. The convergence play went against the fund, which faced huge losses as the values of the bonds diverged. By the end of August, the fund had lost US$1.85 billion in capital. As a result of these losses, LTCM had to liquidate a number of its positions at a highly unfavourable moment, suffering further losses. In addition, the management company faced liquidity issues as it was invested into the fund; it owed US$165 million to a group of banks that were asking to be repaid. The partners decided to pay nobody, nor to favour any player. When three hedge funds out of four were losing money, LTCM lost US$1.9 billion, 45 per cent of its assets.

The fund had a high number of counterparties – for example, the government bond trading team was working with 75 counterparties – which explains how it had become possible to reach such a high level of leverage. It is also because there were so many counterparties that the liquidity issues were not discovered earlier. Another serious issue was that there were so many elements to integrate that the true level of risk inherent within the portfolio was unclear; no single counterparty had access to the whole portfolio, and nobody was aware of what was happening.

During the first two weeks of September, the fund faced new losses, leading to issues regarding lines of credit. On Friday 18 September, downside pressures combined with recent losses led to fears about the ability of the fund to face its obligations. On 21 September, Bear Stearns, one of the main brokers of LTCM, asked the fund to secure its exposures, and reduced the liquidity it had provided to the fund. Others counterparties rapidly followed suit, and these tensions increased the risk that LTCM might go bankrupt. That day alone, the fund lost US$553 million. At that point the leverage had increased to over 100 – meaning that any 1 per cent lost would lead to the bankruptcy.

LTCM was so important in notional exposures that a default would probably have led to a cascade of bankruptcies. So in Tuesday 22, the four main counterparties of LTCM looked for alternatives to avoid any default. At first, no solutions could be found, but eventually came up with the consortium; the Federal Reserve Bank of New York organized a bailout of US$3625 million by the major creditors to avoid a wider collapse in the financial markets. The contributions from the various institutions were as follows:[6]

- $300 million: Bankers Trust, Barclays, Chase, Credit Suisse First Boston, Deutsche Bank, Goldman Sachs, Merrill Lynch, J.P. Morgan, Morgan Stanley, Salomon Smith Barney, UBS;
- $125 million: Société Générale;
- $100 million: Lehman Brothers, Paribas;
  Bear Stearns declined to participate.

The idea was that the main counterparties of the fund would recapitalize it. In return, the participating banks were to get a 90 per cent share in the fund and a promise that a supervisory board would be established. LTCM's partners received a 10 per cent stake – still worth about US$400 million – but this money was completely consumed by the debt. On 23 September, the net asset of LTCM was reduced to US$600 million, balanced by commitments of US$100 billion for a total leverage of over 160, and the investors lost 92 per cent of their investments. Out of the US$4.4 billion lost, US$1.9 billion had come from the partners, US$700 million from Swiss banks, and US$1.8 billion from other investors.[7] The consortium created on 23 September was called Oversight Partners, LLC, and it took over operational control. Meriwether and his partners continued to manage the fund, but they had to report to a bankers' committee sitting with them; any important decision had to be taken in conjunction with this committee.

Table 5.1 reports the breakdown of the loss of the fund; it is clear that it was the swap positions and the volatility exposures cost the majority of

Table 5.1 Losses of LTCM by market

Market	Loss in US$ millions
Swaps	1600
Equity volatility	1300
Russia and other emerging markets	430
Directional trades in developed markets	371
Equity pairs	286
Yield curve arbitrage	215
S&P 500 stocks	203
Junk bond arbitrage	100
TOTAL	3704

Source: Lowenstein (2000).

the losses. All the other elements together represented US$1.6 billion, and these alone would have been manageable. But The positions on the swap market and on volatility were too large. LTCM failed because the team was not able to measure, control and manage its risk. Most transactions were not diversified.

1.4 Why was the fund saved?

As mentioned in the previous section, the main feature of this fund was the scale of the positions taken and the extent of the leverage implemented. Hundreds of other managers implementing the same strategy could also have taken wrong positions – but none of those would have impacted the largest players in Wall Street or indeed the entire system.

If the fund had become insolvent this would have led to a crisis; counterparties would have had to close positions and realize large losses. They would also have had to liquidate collaterals. This would have led to unforeseeable and potentially important adverse price movements. Lowenstein (2000) estimated that in case of bankruptcy the main 17 counterparties would have lost up to US$500 million each, totalling between US$3 billion and US$5 billion. The Federal Reserve intervened for one reason: creditors and counterparties would have lost so much money that some of them would have faced the risk of bankruptcy, putting others into issues. Shortly said, this could have put the whole financial system into problems.

1.5 The effects and the questions still open

The problems encountered by LTCM have had a very serious impact on the hedge fund world and leading to numerous questions. This section focuses on the effects and the questions that arose in the aftermath of the bailout.

1.5.1   The effects

There were four direct effects that impacted the hedge fund industry. Firstly, several funds lost assets and were liquidated; this was particularly the case for funds applying fixed-income arbitrage strategies. Secondly, the concept of leverage began to frighten investors. The highly leveraged strategies that survived had to adapt their strategy, reducing the level of leverage they were using in the implementation of their strategy. Thirdly, at that time transparency was still taboo in the hedge fund industry. This bailout was a catalyst; institutional investors were the first to start requesting for more of transparency. At that point the industry was still far from current standards, but there was a definite and necessary change in mentality from then on. Finally, more and more investors started to diversify their portfolio across funds and strategies; while most investors remained relatively concentrated until then.

1.5.2   Questions still open

The first question is to find out how it might be possible to improve transparency in the hedge fund world, particularly regarding data relative to positioning and leverage. It is worth asking whether LCTM's investors and counterparties were aware of the nature and the size of the exposure of the fund and the level of risks that it had been accumulating. Regarding investors, this was clearly not the case, as the information disseminated by the team was very limited. Regarding creditors and counterparties the position is not completely clear, but they were unlikely to have been aware. It is clear that even if any single counterparty knew that the positions that the fund had taken on their behalf represented only a part of the funds' total notional exposure, none could have imagined the scale of the combined positions.

The leverage question has been mentioned in many papers and debated across the industry. Nothing formal or legal has, however, been published. The industry would have to continue to be self-regulated. Fifteen years later the leverage issue has not become a regular problem; there was the 2008 liquidity crisis, which we will discuss later in this chapter, but this was more a leverage issue in the financial world and a lack of liquidity rather than an issue with the high level of leverage across hedge funds. The increase in interest from institutional investors has probably helped the self-regulation of the industry.

The second important element that emerged from this bailout relates to measures relating to risk management. How can rare events be measured? There are measures such as Value at Risk, which gives a measure of the percentage of the time when more than a certain amount or percentage might be lost – but they do not give any precise idea of the scale of any potential loss. In the case of LTCM, the existing models underestimated the probability of important loss. Since then, the tools available have improved and risk management has become a more important part of any investment process. The tools currently available tools have not, however, yet proved that they are sufficient, and this remains an important potential source of risk.

1.6   Subsequent developments

Over the few weeks that followed the creation of the consortium, the fund continued to lose money. Then in the fourth quarter of 1998, it started to make new profits. One year after the bailout, the fund was up 10 per cent and was able to pay back the money invested by the consortium. Early in 2000 the fund was liquidated.

After the unwinding of LTCM, Meriwether launched JMW Partners with the majority of his previous team. By December 1999, they had raised US$250 million for a fund that would continue most of LTCM's strategies but with a lower level of leverage. Their flagship fund was called Relative Value Opportunity Fund II. The prospectus limited the leverage for this fund to 15. In 2008, after a few good years, the fund lost 31 per cent, and on 7 July 2009 it was announced that the fund would be closed after suffering a loss of 44 per cent in the main fund between September 2007 and February 2009.

2   Hedge funds and financial crisis

Hedge funds have often been censured by politicians during periods of financial turmoil. This happened in 1992 during the exchange rate mechanism crisis, in 1994 during the bond market turmoil and the Mexican economic crisis, during the 1997 Asian crisis and, more recently, during the 2007 subprime crisis. In each case, hedge fund managers were found to be at fault through having taken significant positions in the markets affected. In this section we analyse the role that hedge funds played during these periods of financial stress.

2.1   The exchange rate mechanism crisis of 1992

This crisis is generally the first one associated with hedge funds.[8] To understand what happened it is necessary to go back to 1987. The European Exchange Rate Mechanism (ERM) was a system that had been introduced by the European Community in March 1979 as part of the European Monetary System (EMS); its purpose was to reduce exchange rate variability and achieve monetary stability in Europe in preparation for the Economic and Monetary Union and the introduction of a single currency, the euro, on 1 January 1999. Between 1987 and 1991 there were important capital flows within the European Community between countries with lower and higher interest rates, and many hedge funds in international markets seized this opportunity. The simple strategy consisted of borrowing the currency of countries paying low interest rates, such as Germany, and investing this money in the countries paying a higher interest rate, such as Italy, Spain and Greece. The currency risk was limited by the ERM system; the currencies were linked to one another and they could not move up or down by more than 2.25 per cent. This strategy, applied by most macro funds and fixed-income arbitrage funds, was called the convergence play. But while more and more players were trying to profit from this situation, problems began to arise; the unit cost for labour in Italy increased by almost 20 per cent over the four years preceding the crisis, and fears of an over-valued Italian lira were exacerbated by the deterioration of Italy's current account and by weakness in the profitability of the exchanges.

The situation was identical in the United Kingdom. The pound sterling rose strongly in the period preceding its entry into the European Exchange Rate Mechanism (ERM) in 1990.[9] This led to fears of over-valuation that were reinforced by the widening of the current account. In addition, Finland and Sweden both suffered from a sharp decrease in their exchange with Russia while, following a referendum, Denmark rejected the Maastricht treaty in June 1992.[10] In this context, some countries faced difficulties in financing their current account deficit with external capital, and this put pressures on exchange rates.

Two events led to the collapse of the system. Firstly, between March and September 1992 the Deutsche mark gained close to 20 per cent against the US dollar. This had a direct impact on the competitiveness of European companies. Secondly, the increase in the German interest rate on the 16 July 1992 increased the cost of financing.

Macro managers were the first to discover the opportunity and take advantage of this change in trend by taking a position. While a number of them played the convergence trade, most of them went short against the expensive currencies through forwards.[11] While the trade was common across hedge fund managers, they were not the only ones to take such positions; bank proprietary dealing desks, specialized mutual funds and even institutional investors also did so.

To illustrate this strategy, consider a manager who enters into a forward contract on the pound sterling on 1 August 1992 with an exchange rate of US$1.40 to £1 sterling. The manager, expecting a fall in the exchange rate, sells £10 million sterling forward for 1 October, at a rate of 1.38. This

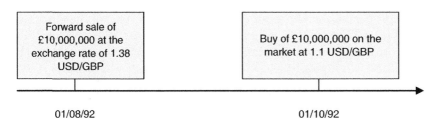

Forward sale of
£10,000,000 at the
exchange rate of 1.38
USD/GBP

Buy of £10,000,000 on the
market at 1.1 USD/GBP

01/08/92   01/10/92

Figure 5.1 Illustration of a position of a hedge fund in the pound sterling

date marks the start of the second phase of the transaction; at this point, the manager sells £10 million at the current selling rate of US$1.38 per £1, but not actually having these funds in stock, has to buy them on the cash market. The current purchase rate being only US$1.1 per £1 sterling the manager can buy the dollars at a much lower price. Figure 5.1 illustrates this process.

The manager buys £10 million at US$1.1 per £1 sterling, and sells them at US$1.38 per £1 sterling. This enables him or her to make a profit of (1.38 – 1.1) × 10 million: US$2,800,000. The trade described remains theoretical but the process is correct. In addition, even when we know that the position was typical at that time, we cannot tell how many managers have implemented it and the size of the positions taken. The International Monetary Fund reported in 1993 that a large macro fund very active in the currency market took a US$10 billion position on that transaction. The name of George Soros is often associated with this. Some macro funds also benefited from short positions taken relative to the Italian lira, while others lost money when the Spanish peseta was devalued.

We believe that certain macro funds played an important role in the 1992 crisis. These funds played the role of leader; their positioning was perceived as a signal that led other players to either take the same positions to make money or avoid to taking a position against it. Both led to the same results; although the hedge fund industry is small, the difference is that the macro strategy was the one best represented by far in terms of assets – and this strategy is usually leveraged.

2.2   The bond market turbulence of 1994

Hedge funds have also been accused of playing an important role in the turbulence that took place in the bond market in 1994.

In the second quarter of 1993, the AUM of the hedge fund industry had grown, and a large part of the industry was invested in European government bonds, which were offering attractive yields. The markets were relatively calm after the crisis of 1992. The widening of the exchange rate spreads between European currencies that were part of the European Monetary Union, from 2 to 15 per cent in August 1993, offered new opportunities to investors. Markets were expecting interest rates to fall significantly to support the economy. A typical trade was to use Japanese yen to finance a position in European bonds in order to profit from the low Japanese interest rates. An interest rate differential that was favouring more and more bonds in US dollars led many managers to buy US dollars against the Japanese yen and the Deutsche mark.

Against all expectations, in February two 25 basis points increases were announced in the United States, while Japanese interest rates remained stable and the German Bundesbank lowered its interest rates. On this basis many players sold large quantities of forwards on government debt. These transactions had the consequence of lowering the price of the underlying bonds and increasing their yield on developed markets bonds from 50 basis points early in February to 150 basis points at the end of March. The shock wave propagated rapidly to other government bond markets, and interest rates increased rapidly. This stopped growth expectations; over the next two months the S&P 500 and the MSCI World lost 9 per cent and 6 per cent respectively. The US dollar weakened against the Japanese yen, dropping from ¥110 to ¥100.

In this case it is not clear that "hedge funds" as an industry made large profits on these market movements. The typical position was to expect a decrease in European interest rates. But in fact, in 1994 most players lost money. Well-known hedge fund managers such as George Soros and Michael Steinhardt lost a great deal of money; on 14 February Soros lost more than US$500 million, while in early April Steinhardt reported a loss of close to US$1 billion, representing 25 per cent of his AUM.[12]

2.3   The Tequila crisis of 1994–95

The Mexican crisis, usually called the Tequila crisis, started with a deep recession that hit the country at the end of 1994. These difficulties led first to a devaluation of 15 per cent of the Mexican peso, on 20 December. The situation worsened over the next few days, and the peso went down by another 30 per cent. At the same time, equities fell rapidly, and local interest rates increased just as rapidly. Following the issuers he gross domestic product fell by 6.2 per cent in 1995; over the year and short-term interest rates increased to 71.5 per cent in April 1995 and the annual rate of inflation increased to 52 per cent.

The role of hedge funds in this crisis has not been established. Various studies on the subject have concluded that this crisis happened mainly because of local players and that the role of international investors was limited.[13] There are various reasons for this, the first being the size of the

Mexican market. Emerging markets in general, the Mexican market in particular, were very small in global financial markets and not attractive to large players. While it was possible to take a position on the currency through derivatives it was not always easy to go out of them, and it was not always smart to rely on the solubility of the local counterparty. Secondly, local players were the first to gain access to the information and in case of potential stress on the Mexican peso would always have been the first to move their money into US dollars. This situation was exacerbated by the deregulation of the domestic financial market and international transactions. Finally, while the role of hedge funds in a few other crises has been researched and recognized, and while large players have profited from them, this is not the case for the Mexican issues.

2.4 The Asian crisis of 1997–98

The Asian crisis was probably one of the most important crises of the 1990s because it impacted an entire continent. So, first the facts, then a look at the role of hedge funds by using the arguments in two of the main theories, one that there were fundamental issues and the other that this was an investor-led crisis.

2.4.1 The facts

Until 1997, almost half of the total world capital going into developing countries had flowed into Asia. The economies of South-East Asia in particular maintained high interest rates attractive to foreign investors looking for a high rate of return. As a result, the region's economies had received large inflows of assets, whose prices rose dramatically in consequence. At the same time, in the late 1980s and early 1990s, the regional economies of Thailand, Malaysia, Indonesia, Singapore, and South Korea experienced high growth rates in GDP, often of over 10 per cent a year. This achievement was widely acclaimed by financial institutions, including the International Monetary Fund (IMF) and the World Bank, as part of the "Asian economic miracle."

It is important to note that the capital flows had been very strong for years and that the ratio of private debt to GDP had also increased significantly; in 1996, this had reached 58 per cent in Thailand, 31 per cent in Malaysia and 151 per cent in the Philippines. In addition, the structure of the debt evolved unfavourably; at the end of 1996, the proportion of debt maturing over a maximum of one year rose to 50 per cent on average, reaching 67 per cent in South Korea, 61 per cent in Indonesia and 65 per cent in Thailand.

The early signs of the crisis appeared in January 1997 when various Asian companies defaulted on their debt. Some even went bankrupt. The first large company to go bankrupt, at the end of January 1997, was the Korean group Hanbo Steel, the country's second largest steel company. Then a strengthening of the US dollar against the Japanese yen led to a decrease in the competitiveness of the Asian economies that were closely linked to the US dollar. In addition, an increase in interest rates in a few developed markets made investing in Asia less attractive than in these markets.

In May, other signs appeared; on 14 and 15 May, in an unstable political environment, the Thai baht was attacked by investors. On 30 June 1997, Prime Minister Chavalit Yongchaiyudh said that he would not devalue the baht – and this was the start of the real problems, as the Thai government failed to defend the baht, which was pegged to the basket of currencies in which the US dollar was the main component, against international speculators. On 2 July, Thailand had to let the baht float, and it lost 20 per cent against the US dollar.

Meanwhile, in June 1997, Indonesia was still far from crisis; it had low inflation, a trade surplus of more than US$900 million, huge foreign exchange reserves of more than US$20 billion and a good banking sector. But a large number of Indonesian corporations had borrowed in US dollars. This practice had worked well for years as the Indonesian rupiah had strengthened against the dollar. As the value of their local currency rose, their effective levels of debt and financing costs decreased. In July 1997, when Thailand floated the baht, Indonesia's monetary authorities widened the rupiah currency trading band. On 11 August 1997, the IMF unveiled a rescue package for Thailand of more than US$17 billion. The rupiah suddenly came under severe attack; on 14 August, the managed floating exchange regime was replaced by a free-floating exchange rate arrangement. The rupiah dropped further. The IMF came forward with a rescue package of US$23 billion, but the rupiah was sinking further. In September, the rupiah and the Jakarta Stock Exchange touched a historic low. In January 1998, the International Monetary Fund suspended its help to Indonesia, and this continued until President Suharto resigned in May. A few weeks later, Singapore and then Hong Kong were hit.

South Korea's stock market suffered also during this period, and on 4 December 1997 the IMF agreed on a US$55 billion rescue package.

2.4.2   The role of hedge fund in the crisis

The Japanese finance minister maintained that hedge funds played a role in the Asian crisis. He also maintained that the information was not correctly incorporated in the market risk.[14] It is true that rating agencies such as Standard & Poor's and Moody's kept relatively high ratings for the Asian countries and large Asian corporations until the start of the crisis.

According to Mahathir bin Mohamed, Prime Minister of Malaysia from July 1981 to October 2003, Soros – as the instigator of the hedge fund Quantum – may have been partially responsible for the 1997 economic crash in the South-East Asian markets. According to Mahathir, in the three years leading up to the crash, Soros had invested in short-term speculative investments in South-East Asian stock markets and real estate, then divested himself rapidly of these at the first signs of currency devaluation. Soros' response was that Mahathir was using him "as a scapegoat for his own mistakes," that Mahathir's threats (hastily retracted by Malaysian finance officials) to ban currency trading were "a recipe for disaster" and that Mahathir was "a menace to his own country."[15]

Two hypotheses emerged from the crisis. According to the first, it is the sudden changes in market expectations and confidence that were the main source of the financial tumult and its spread. While the macroeconomic performance of some countries deteriorated around the middle of the 1990s, the strength and depth of the 1997–98 Asian crisis arose not so much from fundamental issues as from the fears of local and international investors, reinforced by the political responses by the IMF and the international financial community. According to this hypothesis, hedge funds were at least partially responsible for the crisis. The second theory sustains that, the crisis was a consequence of political and structural distortions in the countries in the region. It was fundamental disequilibrium that led to the financial and monetary crisis even though, once it had started, market reactions amplified or at least accelerated the process.

For years the two theories have been in opposition with one another. Various studies have been published on the role of hedge funds during this crisis. Two early studies of interest, one published by an IMF team and the other by university professors,[16] both concluded that hedge funds did not play a significant role in the crisis. The first based their arguments on the fact that while some hedge funds were big in absolute terms they remained small relative to large institutional investors such as the banks, pension funds and mutual funds that could also have played a part. In addition – unlike in 1992 when it was clear that some hedge funds had taken up their positions early – in 1997 there were no proof. Many hedge funds had taken short positions against the Thai baht, but most had not taken any positions in other Asian currencies. The second study empirically analysed the role of hedge funds during the Asian crisis. They tested the hypothesis that hedge funds were responsible for the fall in Asian currencies[17] both globally and individually. They based their analysis on the positioning of the ten largest macro funds invested mainly in currencies, and proved that the positions taken by the different funds were correlated but that these funds could neither have led to the movements in the markets nor, more importantly, have influenced them even if there had been a wish to do so. In sum, the authors concluded that neither the exposure nor the realized profits of these main funds were abnormal over the crisis period. There is no empirical evidence to indicate that Soros or any other hedge fund manager was responsible for the Asian crisis. The analyses into whether these funds could have led to the crisis concluded that although the long and short positions in the currencies fluctuated considerably over the period covered, these movements were not associated with any significant move in the exchange rate and that they could not have influenced the exchange rates.

2.4.3 The fundamentals

The economic fundamentals of the region had been deteriorating for some time. This included structural and political distortions in the countries of the region. The current accounts of many countries were negative for several years.[18] Large current account deficits could be supported as long as growth was strong, which was indeed the case for the majority of the countries until 1996. But when the growth slowed, the situation became unsustainable.

The monetary policy of these countries was also a potential issue. The exchange rate policies of most Asian countries were closely linked to the US dollar. While this policy enabled them to profit from stability in their nominal exchange rate relative to the US dollar, this also meant that a change in the nominal and real value of the US dollar relative to the yen and to European currencies could create imbalances. After the summer of 1995, the US dollar started to appreciate against most other currencies. Asian currencies pegged to the US dollar were also strengthened indirectly; so imports of Asian products to Europe and Japan became more expensive and less attractive.

Finally, the opacity and weakness of the Asian financial sector is the last strong and fundamental argument that led to the crisis. In almost every country in the region hit by the crisis, the standards of the banks and other financial institutions were low; they tend to be badly managed, not transparent and close to large companies and conglomerates. They clearly played a role in the start and the spread of the crisis. Insufficiently controlled and not subject to the competition of large international competitors, they borrowed heavily abroad and usually in local currencies without a correct credit risk assessment. In addition, they were usually linked to local politics, so were limited by prudent controls.

2.4.4 Conclusion

Our analysis leads us to conclude that while it is likely that some investors profited from the Asian crisis and that some hedge funds were part of that group, the roots of the Asian crisis were probably more fundamental than speculative. Hedge funds have been accused of deserting the sinking ship as the problems appeared, but this cannot be seen as a reason for a crisis. We believe that given the way the situation was evolving through 1996 and early 1997, a crisis was unavoidable. Global institutional investors as a whole can be seen as partially responsible for the scale of the crisis but not for it as a whole. To conclude, it is interesting to mention that in 2006, during a visit by Soros to Malaysia on a book tour of the region, he met the previous Malaysian Prime Minister Mahathir for the first time. Mahathir conceded that in the end, he did not view Soros as responsible for the financial crisis.

2.5   The subprime crisis of 2007

2007 will remain in the annals as the year of the American real estate crisis. This crisis was followed by an unprecedented liquidity crisis that hit the whole financial system in 2008.

2.5.1   The basis

Many preliminary factors added up to the creation of an unsustainable situation. The first was the fact that between 2001 and 2004 the American Federal Reserve dropped its interest rates heavily to support the American economy, which had been showing signs of weakness since the attacks of 11 September, 2001. These low rates enabled many Americans to buy a house or an apartment, as the cost of financing was low, leading to an increase in demand for real estate and a consequent increase in real estate prices. This was particularly important mainly in California. The issue arising from that was that many borrowers including low-income households were able to negotiate new mortgages on the reevaluation of their real estate asset with credit institutions that were not very demanding on guarantees. Such mortgages had a structure such that the monthly payments were lower during the first few years, the payments often being limited to the payment of the deductible interest. The repayment of capital was postponed until the envisaged sale of the property at a higher price a few years later. Such loans were usually given with fixed interest for two years before becoming variable. The average price of American houses has been multiplied by five between 2000 and 2005.

Mortgages to low-income households are labelled subprime; in 2006, they represented 24 per cent of the new mortgages given in the United States. At the end of that year they represented close to 13 per cent of the total existing mortgages in the United States, at US$10,200 billion in value, whereas in 2001 they were at 8.5 per cent. Figure 5.2 shows the evolution of the subprime market. It shows the ratio of the value of the

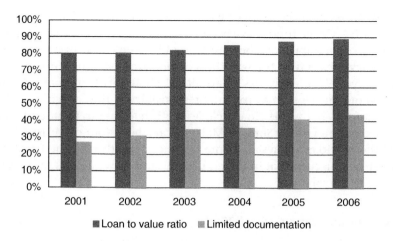

Figure 5.2 Evolution of the loan to value ratio and the ratio of mortgage requests with limited documentation

credit relative to the value of the goods bought, and this ratio increased from just under 80 per cent in 2001 to nearly 90 per cent in 2006. The personal investment required decreased, confirming that access to credit had been facilitated during that period. The percentage of cases with limited information also increased significantly, from 27 per cent in 2001 to 44 per cent in confirming that lending companies became less stringent.

Figure 5.3 juxtaposes the ratio of 100 per cent financed mortgages with the percentage of 100 per cent financed mortgages with limited documentation. Unfortunately, the two statistics also evolved in the wrong way.

The variable interest rate system, with its inherent risk of increase, was a source of solvency risk to these households. Because of the fragility of their financial situation, these households could only refinance an increase in their interest repayment through a favourable reevaluation of the value of their property.

This means that the foundations of the crisis were already in place in 2006, when the Federal Reserve increased its interest rate (see Figure 5.4). This led to an increasing pressure on the creditors that had mortgages with variable interest rates. In addition, the sales of real estate started to slow, putting pressure on real estate prices and leading to a decrease of the richness effect in the households. The combination of these two factors led to an increase in the default rate. The consequent mortgage repayment issues led to issues for specialized mortgage originators focusing on the lower end of this business, because of the combination of a decrease in real estate price in 2006 and an increase in the interest rates

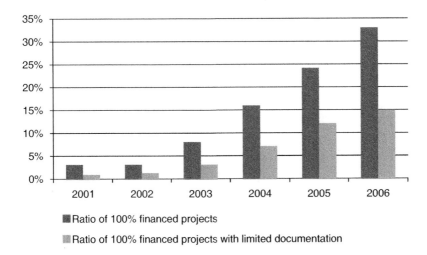

Figure 5.3 Evolution of the ratios of a 100 per cent financed real estate project and evolution of the ratio of 100 per cent financed real estate projects with limited documentation

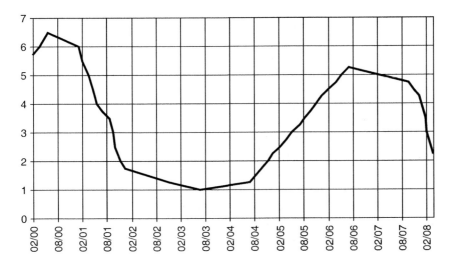

Figure 5.4 Evolution of the key interest rate of the Federal Reserve

This put some players in that market into bankruptcy as the price of the house or apartment fell below the value of the guarantee. The evolution of American real estate price is given in Figure 5.5.

Up till now, we have described a typical real estate bubble. There is however one major difference between the American real estate market

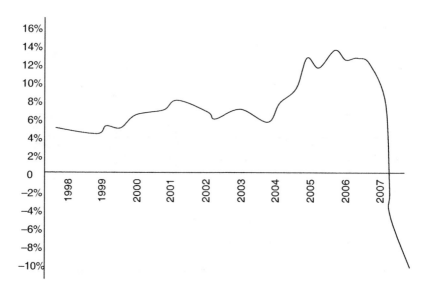

Figure 5.5 Estimation of the evolution of the price of American real estate

and others, such as the European market: securitization vehicles. This is a financial technique that consists of aggregating the risk and then transferring it to third parties. This process can transform illiquid assets in financial securities tradable on financial markets. The idea is to group a set of securities such as mortgages and to create a product that groups these securities. This collateralized product will be divided into tranches, each with a varying level of risk associated with it. These securities and the associated risks can be bought or through a structured product to third parties. Subprime mortgages represent the assets with the higher level of risk in this case. The securitization process is shown in Figure 5.6.

Collateralized debt obligations (CDOs) are bonds collateralized with other debt, such as residential mortgage-backed securities (RMBS) or commercial mortgage-backed securities (CMBS). The capital structure of a CDO consists of several tranches, labelled AAA or BBB plus the equity tranches, and the typical leverage in a RMBS CDO is 20:1. The manager of the CDO structures the CDO and buys the equity tranche, usually charging a relatively high commission to manage the structure. In addition, investment banks are paid commissions, and rating agencies are paid for the rating.

In the mid-2000s over 85 per cent of the CDOs received a rating of AAA or AA even when the collateral in almost every case was BBB or BBB-.

The difference between the traditional model and the subprime model is illustrated in Figure 5.7. Traditionally, banks financed mortgages with

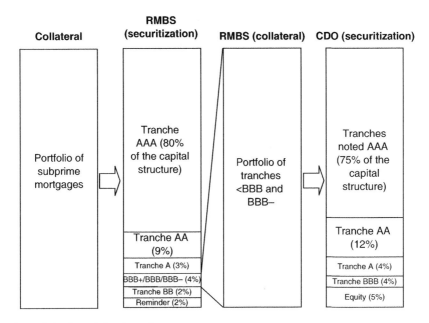

Figure 5.6 Securitization of mortgages

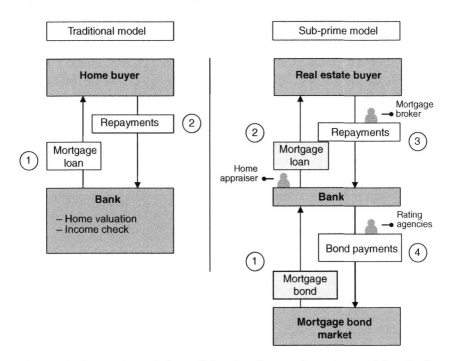

Figure 5.7 Comparison of the traditional real estate financing model and sub-prime model

guarantees given by their customers (on the left of the figure), limiting the amount that could be lent. Recently, the model applied by banks evolved towards a new structure in which mortgages were sold on the debt market. This evolution increased the liquidity of the market and made mortgages easier to obtain. It also led to abuse as mortgage originators did not have the same incentive to select the people they financed so carefully, because the mortgage risk would be handed on. The right-hand side of Figure 5.7 illustrates this process; the originator was still present but was only an intermediary between the buyer of the real estate and the mortgage-backed securities market.

New players came into play: mortgage brokers, home appraisers and rating agencies. Mortgage brokers are intermediaries; they search out mortgages for individuals or companies, and as the real estate market grew, these brokers gained in importance. Home appraisers put a value on a property. And as with any other bond, rating agencies gave a rating aiming to quantify the default risk on the mortgage.

The process moved from a bank that lends money to customers buying properties to a more complex structure in which the bank was selling a mortgage product. The bank provided the mortgage against repayment by the borrowers and payment to the holder of the mortgage-backed securities sold by the bank. This business was highly profitable for banks, which charged a commission for every credit sold, and this pushed mortgage brokers to sell more and more of these products.

The American mortgage market became biased towards subprime mortgages between 2004 and 2006. It has been estimated that by the end of 2006 the subprime market represented 20 per cent of the American mortgage market. In total more than US$1200 billion worth of subprime credit was issued between 2005 and 2006. Table 5.2 shows the breakdown of the American real estate industry over the summer of 2007. The low-risk part of the market is the government-backed part of it, close to 60 per cent of the total. The subprime mortgage market represented 19 per cent of the market, followed by the Jumbo market[19] at 13 per cent and the Alt-A[20] at

Table 5.2 Size and breakdown of the American real estate industry at the end of the second semester of 2007

	Size	Breakdown (%)
Government-backed	$4t	59
Subprime	$1.3t	19
Alt-A	$0.6t	9
Jumbo	$0.9t	13
Total	$6.8t	100

Source: Federal Reserve, Bank of England, SIFMA.

9 per cent. Subprimes, Alt-A and Jumbo together can be seen as the distressed part of the American real estate market.

The problems in the American real estate market put a great deal of pressure on other securitized markets built on the same principles, including investment funds linked to these markets and the banking system as a whole, which was heavily exposed to these kind of products. On a global level, the crisis that started over the summer of 2007 was a crisis of confidence in the financial system. It led to increased volatility in the markets and to a high level of risk aversion towards any form of credit risk. The whole credit market had been heavily impacted as fears of default increased. The interbank market froze completely, largely due to prevailing fears of the unknown amidst banks. There was a lack of liquidity in the markets, and the central banks had to intervene to inject liquidity into the system. In addition, the Federal Reserve lowered its interest rate. On Thursday 9 August 2007, the Federal Reserve's Open Market Trading Desk (the desk) injected US$24 billion into the American banking system. This was carried in two operations of equal size. On the following day, the desk was in the market again three times, putting in a total of US$38 billion.[21] The Federal Reserve's operations followed hard on the heels of two even larger injections, by the European Central Bank (ECB) in Frankfurt. Over the same period, the ECB had put nearly €95 billion into European financial institutions. This was followed by the somewhat smaller transactions of €61 billion, €47.7 billion and then, in two separate transactions shortly afterwards, €25 billion. Taking into account the intervention of other central banks, more than US$330 billion were injected into the markets.

Table 5.3 reports the estimation of the potential losses of the main players around the globe due to the subprime crisis. The numbers reported are in US$ millions. While these numbers are only estimates they give us an idea of the scale of the problem. For example, Citigroup provisioned US$6 billion for potential losses over the third quarter of 2007 and US$10 billion for the last quarter of the year.

Figure 5.8 confirms the magnitude of the damage, giving an estimate of the total exposure of the main financial institutions to the subprime crisis and its consequences. Citibank had the highest exposure to the crisis with losses of around US$80 billion. In Europe, UBS Investment Bank faced losses of more than US$ 40 million. Globally, the losses were from around US$220 billion to US$480 billion, depending on the source.[22]

2.5.2   The role of hedge funds

The French President Nicolas Sarkozy distinguished himself in 2007 by blaming hedge funds, and speculators in general, for the emerging subprime crisis. While this is an easy answer to a complicated problem, he

Table 5.3 Subprime exposure of the main financial institutions

	Writedowns – 3Q07	Guidance – 4Q07	Remaining subprime exposures
Citigroup	6056	10,000	72,000
Merrill Lynch	8900		21,500
Bank of America	1841	3900	19,000
JP Morgan	2450		18,800
Bear Stearns	850	1200	12,884
Morgan Stanley	1200	3700	6000
Goldman Sachs	2400		4700
Lehman Brothers	1600		1800
UBS	5069	1724	35,100
SocGen	476		6292
Commerzbank	428		1801
Deutsche Postbank	90		1176
KBC	57		1044
Credit Suisse	1897		
HSBC	4325		

Source: Company reports, Deutsche Bank estimates.

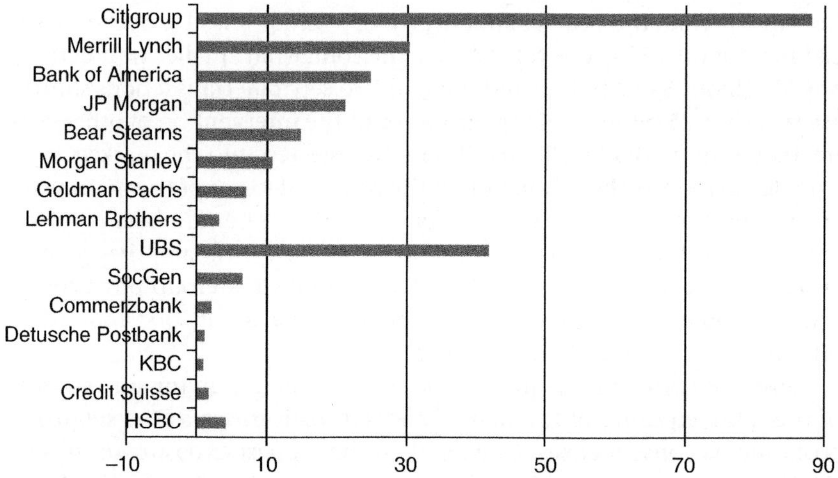

Figure 5.8 Estimation of the total exposure to the subprime crisis by the principal global financial institutions
Source: Deutsche Bank estimates.

was not the only person that believed that the role of hedge funds was predominant. There have been various studies on the role of hedge funds during the subprime crisis; we will focus on two of them and summarize their main conclusions.

Firstly, two arguments stated by Amenc (2007) on the role of hedge funds in the subprime crisis. First, he concluded that hedge funds were not responsible for the crisis. The sharp fall in value and the temporary illiquidity of asset-backed securities, commercial paper secured against high-risk mortgages supplied by subprime lenders, sparked a crisis of confidence that quickly spread to the credit market as a whole, going so far as to affect the market of investment-grade corporate bonds. Investment in hedge funds made up less than 5 per cent of total institutional investment, and strategies with high exposure to credit risk accounted for 20 per cent or less of the assets invested in hedge funds. It is hard to believe that all the transfers of credit risk could have been carried out with hedge funds alone as counterparties. In 2006, the US market alone represented US$4.6 trillion worth of issues of securitized debt, derivatives, claim transfers on secondary markets and other debt instruments. The problem was that banks were affected by excessive investment in asset-backed securities and in structured credit products that turned out to be illiquid, and those banks thus appeared insolvent to their counterparties in the money market. So it was the most heavily regulated institutions in the world that required the intervention of central banks on a massive scale.

Secondly, the use of credit derivatives has since 2003 been subject to codes of conduct as well as to both domestic and international regulation. So the funds that symbolized the subprime crisis in France, and continental Europe more generally, are those that respected the rules on the use of credit derivatives that were in place. The crisis of confidence in the financial information reported by lenders was caused by the unexpected halt by a few major banks in the valuation, subscription, and redemption of so-called dynamic cash funds. It was not caused by unregulated parties or by forbidden practices, but by regulation that failed to take into account the major risk of illiquidity that goes along with the default risk traditionally associated with credit instruments.

An interesting study by the International Monetary Fund[23] published in 2008 confirmed that the causes of the crisis in subprime mortgages were clear. They began with poor underwriting practices, which became legion. But damage was propagated at each stage of the complicated process in which a risky home loan was originated, then became an asset-backed security, that then formed part of a collateralized debt obligation (CDO) that was rated and sold to investors. The study mainly examined how the losses spread to other parts of the global financial system, mentioning ten developments that caused the subprime crisis to erupt. None of these related directly to hedge funds:[24]

1. The dismal quality of subprime and Alt-A lending standards in 2006–07.

2. The extent and speed of rating downgrades of asset-backed securities.
3. The panic in money market funds in August 2007.
4. The "hidden" banking system.
5. The extent of the banks' liquidity commitments.
6. The speed of bank liquidity runs.
7. The concentration of subprime credit risk in bond insurers.
8. The collapse of the municipal bond and student loan markets.
9. The dependence of the US mortgage market on state-sponsored entities in the crisis.
10. The scale of the banks' forced deleveraging.

From there the author suggested various ways of managing such issues in the future, but only one that could impact hedge funds directly: to moderate leverage. Key parts of modern financial markets involve so much leverage that they are vulnerable to large price movements and market illiquidity; unwinding that leverage exacerbates credit tightness, and distressed trading generates excessive price movements. Policymakers should tighten prudent restraints on leverage, perhaps through higher capital or collateralization requirements.

It is true that certain hedge funds, such as the two sponsored by the Wall Street firm Bear Stearns, faced issues in liquidating large positions in those securities. But it was not until the French bank BNP Paribas announced in August that it was suspending withdrawals from some money market funds that the wider interbank market turmoil began. Fearing strong customer demand for cash withdrawals, money market funds defensively shifted their portfolios from medium- and long-term bank deposits and commercial paper to overnight and very short maturities. This provoked a strong demand for short-term liquidity and a collapse in the market for asset-backed commercial paper. Short-term paper were used to fund off-balance-sheet investments in long-term assets. That made it difficult for banks in Europe and North America to borrow for much longer than overnight. Even though there were few bank solvency concerns at this stage, the rewards for lending at longer maturities were insufficient to compensate for the risk of lending to a counterparty that might be in trouble.

On the other hand, it is true that several hedge fund managers have been able to anticipate the crisis and to take a position accordingly. The most famous cases are John Paulson, the CEO of Paulson and Co., and Philip Falcone, manager of Harbinger. In the last part of this section we explain how fund managers were able to make fortune by anticipating such a crisis.

The first challenge for a manager aware of a bubble in the mortgage-backed securities market is to find a way of profiting from an increase in the failure rate of mortgages. The easiest way to do this is by taking short positions in debt products that include subprime mortgages as underlyers, such as collateralized debt obligations (CDO), commercial mortgage-backed securities (CMBS), asset-based securities (ABS) and credit default swaps (CDS). CDOs are tailor-made structured products created by banks, that group 100 to 250 assets such as residential mortgage-backed securities, asset-backed securities and bonds. In this case, we are referring to CDOs on mortgage-backed securities. This kind of product is built on implicit leverage, and it is the strong appetite of banks for these products that enabled managers to continue to take positions despite the weak fundamentals. This sustained the spreads on subprime RMBS over several months, even while the number of sales and the prices were starting to decrease, and it clearly amplified the crisis once it had started. Once the position was initiated, a fall in the price of property and an increase in the default rate were sufficient to lead directly to the crisis.

February 2007 was the true start of the crisis. The delinquency rate of subprime mortgages increased by close to 90 per cent over a 12-month period,[25] the spreads of the low quality tranches widened and the volume of new issuances fell rapidly. The average price of a BBB initiated in 2006 fell from 96 at the end of 2006 to just 20 at the end of 2007. In addition, while some funds took positions as early as July 2006, rating agencies waited until July 2007 to review the rating of many mortgage-backed securities exposed to subprime mortgages. Only a few hedge fund managers were able to identify the crisis and find a way of playing this opportunity.

2.6   The liquidity crisis that followed the subprime crisis

The subprime crisis was the visible part of the iceberg. It started in the second half of 2006 in the United States, with the increase in the default in higher-risk mortgages. It became public in July 2007, when periodical adjudications did not get enough interest. It became impossible to put a value on those securities that had to be provisioned at a value close to zero. At the same time, the owners were unable to liquidate their positions. Investors became suspicious of securitized securities that included an exposure to subprime mortgages. Then the crisis spread to the banking system, and even more problematic the inter-banking market. The defiance in the liquidity of the collaterals and the uncertainty on the real exposures of counterparties led to a progressive slowdown in the inter-banking market that put many banks around the world into difficulty. The authorities first believed that it was a banking liquidity crisis, and central banks injected massive liquidities into the inter-banking market until the first bankruptcy happened. Then, in September 2008, it hit well-known banks.

The liquidity crisis arose from the same basis as the subprime crisis. Nevertheless, this was not about a portion of the American population that is over-indebted, but an issue relating to the entire financial system. Financial leverage has been present in our economies for many years, but it has increased as a result of the creation of new investment products that have become more and more complex. To some extent the two crises can be put in parallel. The subprime market worked as long as the value of real estate properties increased and as long as the cost of financing remained low; the increase in leverage in the financial system enabled capital flows to increase, and the cost of finance to decrease. But the increase became overwhelming, and banks and other financial institutions faced such liquidity needs that they could no longer meet them. Banks facing these liquidity needs saw, in many cases, a sizeable number of their customers leaving with their assets. Other banks stopped providing finance to the inter-banking market. All of this amplified the issues. The catalyst was the bankruptcy of Lehman Brothers, one of the main American players. The bank faced very important liquidity issues, and it was unable to honour its commitments. This decision led banks to take urgency measures. To gain access to the Federal Reserve support, banks had to implement important changes. Others, such as Bear Stearns, Merrill Lynch, Washington Mutual and Wachovia, were bought.

From the summer of 2007 onwards, banks all over the world had to enact in their accounts a depreciation of the values of any assets that had a link to subprime mortgages, and in particular ABS and CDO. From the summer of 2007 to the summer of 2008, these depreciations amounted to US$500 billion. These directly impacted banks' capital structure. Some of them were able to balance these losses by issuing new shares to increase their capital. In other cases they had to ask their local government to support their liquidity. Over the spring of 2008, the British government nationalized Northern Rock that had became a victim of a run on its deposits. But this was only the start, and many other institutions faced difficulties in autumn. On 8 September 2008, the American mortgage agencies Freddy Mac and Fannie Mae were placed into conservatorship by the U.S. Treasury. On 15 September, Lehman Brothers went bankrupt, and the next day, the United States Federal Reserve Bank created a US$85 billion credit facility to enable the AIG to meet increased collateral obligations consequent on a credit rating downgrade, in exchange for the issuance of a stock warrant to the Federal Reserve Bank for almost 80 per cent of the equity of AIG. In continental Europe, Fortis was the first large bank to become nationalized on 29 September. In the United Kingdom on 8 October three out of the four main banks accepted the principle of a recapitalization imposed by the then prime minister, Gordon Brown. On

11 October, France and Germany announced that they might also have to recapitalize some banks, but without giving any names.

In the United States, one of the first measures to be suggested, which arose from a law proposed by the Treasury Secretary Henry Paulson and by the President of the Federal Reserve Ben Bernanke, was the Troubled Asset Relief Program (TARP). Initially, this plan was for a buyback of US$700 billion of toxic assets (mainly mortgage-backed securities). On 11 November, Henry Paulson radically changed the approach, and from that point the government took capital participation in the weaker financial institutions in order to support their liquidity. In Europe, the various national plans announced around the second weekend of October amounted to €1700 billion; they integrated refinancing guarantees as well as recapitalization and nationalization plans that were presented in the United Kingdom at the end of the month. In the preceding week, all the equity markets had lost more than 20 per cent. Fears of a global and sustainable undercapitalization of the banking system led into a solvability crisis followed by a stock market crash. To put this into context, during the week of 6 October the French main index, the CAC 40, lost 22 per cent of its value.

2.7 Conclusion

These last three sections focus on the subprime crisis and the liquidity crisis that followed. We started by presenting the weaknesses and the fundamentals of the American real estate market. Then we described the way the issues were linked as well as their impact on the American and world financial markets. We examined how some players in the hedge fund world positioned themselves to profit from this opportunity. As with other crises, we believe that the real estate market was already unbalanced, and that while some hedge funds profited from the opportunity, none of them were the catalyst.

3 Summary

In this chapter we have covered two periods during which interest in hedge funds strongly increased. The analysis of Long-Term Capital Management enabled us to understand the context in which the company was created, its development, and the basics of its investment strategy as well as the reasons behind its bankruptcy and the reasons leading to a consortium of banks refinancing the fund.

The second part of the chapter focused on the role of hedge funds during the main financial crisis in the last 20 years. This analysis has enabled us to understand how hedge funds could potentially have played a significant role in the start or the development of these crises. While in some cases there are more elements supporting an active role by hedge fund managers, in most cases their intervention seems to have been more opportunistic than playing any catalyst role. All in all, there are always people making money when others are losing. The main point is that during crisis most investors tend to lose a lot of money, and they cannot accept the fact that some other may have the right trade in their portfolio and these investors continue to perform well.

6
Hedge Funds, Regulation and Mutual Funds

This chapter starts by focusing on hedge fund regulation. While we aim to be complete, we will remain general on regulations. This part of the book should be seen as an introduction on the topic. In addition, by combining historical rules with more recent ones, we aim to give you a broad overview of the problems. Before incorporating any of the elements in this book into your plans, however, we strongly recommend that you take legal advice. The rules and regulations do evolve very rapidly.

In the second part of the chapter we compare hedge funds and mutual funds, by which we mean traditional mutual funds available in European countries and in the United States. This comparison is interesting even though the boundary between the two has to some extent disappeared since it has been possible to implement some hedge fund strategies under UCITS structures. It is also necessary because although both worlds are identical in principle, the implementation of the strategy is different. They are identical in that hedge funds and mutual funds are investment portfolios managed by professionals, so the basic principles are identical – but the reality is often very different, and it is crucially important to distinguish the two products as they tend not to have the same objectives and more importantly they do not have the same tools and techniques available to them to reach their objectives.

The first objective of a hedge fund manager when creating a fund is to profit from a degree of freedom not available to mutual fund managers. This is usually combined with an absolute return performance objective. In contrast, the first objective of a mutual fund is typically to beat a reference index. Inherent within their structure, such funds are intended to be distributed to the widest audience through retail and institutional investors, in order to get the highest asset base. Such characteristics are general and probably reductive. It does not mean that every hedge fund has an absolute return objective and that every mutual fund aims to outperform a classic equity or bond index, but it has been true of most of them for the last few decades. In the case of hedge funds, the idea of liberty implies a degree of freedom in the choice of securities and tools and techniques used. In the case of a mutual fund, the objective to sell a product to retail investors means an increased level of legal constraints, and strict limitations in the management of the fund; these constraints also apply to liquidity, the fee structure and communication with investors.

The main differences between hedge funds and mutual funds arise from the rules and regulations they have to comply with. This explains why we have started this chapter with a general section on hedge fund regulation. In the second section, we compare hedge funds and mutual funds using their regulation frameworks. In this context the US provides a perfect illustration of the historical differences, as the hedge fund market originated in that country. The third section focuses on the other main differences that exist between hedge funds and mutual funds. The fourth section summarizes our analysis, and the last section compares hedge funds and mutual funds in terms of diversification power and performance.

1   Hedge fund regulation

This section introduces the laws and regulations that regulate the advertising and implementation of hedge funds. As mentioned in the introduction, regulations are in constant evolution, and in the world of alternative investments, more than anywhere else, regulations are constantly reviewed. In this context it is entirely possible that in a few months from publication the regulatory framework presented here will not be fully up to date.

1.1   The principles

Historically, hedge funds have been implemented in the US with an offshore mirror structure, with hedge fund managers using offshore vehicles for non-US investors and for US non-taxable investors, and onshore funds for US-taxable investors. Such funds had a private structure and usually took the structure of a limited partnership. With the emergence of new regulation in Europe it has become possible to create onshore hedge funds in Europe. Depending on the structure chosen, such funds have gained a greater or lesser degree of freedom in the implementation of their strategy, and they may or may not qualify for a passport enabling them to be sold Europe-wide. Private onshore funds such as Qualified Investment Funds in Ireland or Specialized Investment Funds in Luxembourg[1] do not qualify for the passport and require a high minimum investment, but their managers profit from a higher level of freedom in their management. In contrast, funds under a UCITS structure have to comply with stricter rules but they can be more easily sold to a greater number of potential investors. The structure of a fund will not only impact the freedom of the manager but also the kind of investors that can invest in the fund. Investors tend to have formal constraints regarding offshore funds. Retail investors may consider only funds within the UCITS structure for direct investments.

Hedge fund regulation is also of interest because every country has its own rules. These have evolved in Europe with the implementation of the UCITS III Directive for retail and is it on the way to evolve further with the harmonized regulation of European private funds under the Alternative Investment Fund Management Directive (AIFMD).

In both Europe and the United States the term "hedge fund" has not been legally defined. In Europe there was nothing to define alternative strategies until alternative UCITS were allowed. This regulation followed the European Directive of 20 December 1985[2] that regulates mutual funds and allows European funds respecting certain constraints to receive agreement from the jurisdiction of the country of their implementation to be sold in the other countries of the European Union. To be saleable abroad, a fund should comply with strict constraints including investing only in transferable securities.

Regulation is one of the hottest topics in the hedge fund industry, particularly since the liquidity crisis of 2008. The debate arose because several cases of fraud were reported.[3] One school of thought is that hedge fund should be highly regulated, and another is that the industry can be self-regulated. The industry believes that an excessive trust in the efficiency of public policies and the pertinence of financial regulation is by no means a perfect solution, and most arguments in favour of increased regulation are essentially based on such trust. The bankruptcy of large hedge funds such as Amaranth[4] probably justifies the opposing point of view; it demonstrates that the risks of investing in hedge funds, such as the lack of liquidity or the risk of concentration, are balanced by the orderly management of a bailout. The liquidity crisis of 2008 spurred regulators into action, and both American and European regulators adapted the existing legal frameworks. Retail investors had access to the industry through funds of funds and they were hit by the liquidity crisis.

1.2 North America

We start by focusing on the original market for hedge funds, the United States, before presenting the regulatory framework of its North American neighbour, Canada.

1.2.1 The United States

For decades, hedge funds have had the opportunity of remaining unregulated in many aspects. The entire industry has generally operated under special exemptions in the Securities Act of 1933 and the Investment Advisers and Investment Company Acts of 1940, the idea being that hedge funds were available to only a small segment of highly sophisticated investors who did not need regulatory protection. However, as the hedge fund industry grew and turned into a multi-trillion business, its impact on the financial system spread far beyond these sophisticated investors. The Securities and Exchange Commission has attempted to regulate hedge funds on more than one occasion, but never successfully. Only when the Dodd–Frank Wall Street Reform and Consumer Protection Act was signed by President Obama on 21 July 2010 did Congress grant their authority – but the SEC has yet to implement some of the Act's recommendations.

The vast majority of hedge funds take the structure of a limited partnership. This structure has two main advantages: advantageous fiscal treatment, as returns are not taxed at fund level but only at investor level, and a limited liability. The second legal form that can be taken is the limited liability company structure. Funds established in the United States have to comply with the requirements of the SEC and the Commodity Futures Trading Commission when they trade derivatives.

The basis of hedge fund regulation is the Securities Act of 1933, which requires every security offered to be registered with the SEC. There are exceptions, however, and the main exemption is that private offers need not be registered. So most hedge funds remain private – they can thus remain exempted from this requirement. By taking limited partnership or limited liability companies, hedge funds fall under the Investment Company Act. Because of this they can only accept investments from accredited investors without advertising publicly.

By law, investing in hedge funds is limited by regulation. For instance:

- the number of investors should not go over 100, including at least 65 that that should be accredited investors
- the number of investors should stay below 500 as long as all the investors are qualified clients.

Accredited investors were defined under the Rule 501 of Regulation D of the Securities Act of 1933. The passage of the Dodd–Frank Act resulted in a revised definition of the term "accredited investor," which since 1982 has meant an investor with either a total net worth of at least US$1 million or an annual income of at least US$200,000 (or US$300,000 joint with spouse). The new definition also excludes an investor's primary residence from the US$1 million net worth standard, effectively raising the threshold for new hedge fund investors. Existing investors affected by the change in definition could, however, stay invested in their funds. The SEC estimated that the number of accredited investor households shrank from 10.5 million to 7.6 million people, a 28 per cent drop. In addition the Dodd–Frank Act requires the SEC to increase the US$1 million net worth threshold after four years to a level deemed appropriate by the SEC threshold. The SEC must review the definition of "accredited investor" at least once every four years. Qualified clients defined in Rule 205–3 are those who satisfy one or both of the following criteria, among others:

- natural persons or companies that have at least US$750,000 under the management of an adviser
- natural persons or companies that have a net worth of more than US$1.5 million at the time the advisory contract is entered into.

On 19 September, 2011, the AUM threshold increased to US$1 million and the net worth threshold increased from US$1.5 million to US$2 million. In addition, it was decided that each of the thresholds would be adjusted by the SEC for inflation at least once every five years, and furthermore, that if a fund accepts investment from non-accredited investors, it should reasonably believe that every investor has enough knowledge and experience to understand the risks underlying the fund.

To retain freedom in their management, funds should keep their structure private. In this context they have to limit the number of investors. In addition, they may not make any public offering and may not advertise the fund in any format (journal, magazine, television, radio, direct mail or internet for example). They should also write a confidential investment memorandum that should amongst other things include the structure of the entity, details about the manager, the liquidity constraints and the fee structure, as well as giving a detailed presentation of the investment strategy. Those descriptions may remain general in order to enable the manager to have some flexibility in day-to-day management. Section 205(a)(1) of the Advisers Act generally prohibits a registered investment adviser from entering into any advisory contract that provides for compensation based on a share of the capital gains or capital appreciation of a client's account or any portion thereof (that is, a performance fee). Rule 205–3 under the Advisers Act provides an exemption from this performance fee prohibition, permitting a registered investment adviser to enter into performance fee arrangements with qualified clients.

Until recently Section 203(b)(3) of the Investment Advisers Act of 1940 enabled many managers to avoid registration with the SEC if it had fewer than 15 clients, did not present itself to the public as an investment adviser and did not serve as an investment adviser to a registered investment company or business development company. Title IV of the Dodd–Frank Act eliminated the private adviser exemption. But from 30 March 2012, all private fund advisors with more than US$150 million in AUM had to register with the SEC, regardless of the number of underlying clients. Private advisers, including advisers to hedge funds, are now subject to the same registration, regulatory oversight and other requirements. Those include examination applied to other SEC regulated investment advisers. Norm Champ, deputy director, Office of Compliance Inspections and Examinations of the US Securities and Exchange Commission, wrote in May 2012 that based on available information he believed that 48 of the 50 largest hedge fund advisers in the world had registered with the Commission as of May 2012.[5] There are, however, a number of new exemptions from registration for investment advisers, including the following:

- **Foreign private adviser exemption:** The Dodd–Frank Act includes a narrow registration exemption for any foreign private adviser, defined as any investment adviser who has no place of business in the United States and who has fewer than 15 clients and investors in the US in private funds. In addition, the adviser should have aggregate AUM attributable to clients in the United States and investors in the United States in private funds advised by the adviser of less than US$25 million (or a higher amount that the SEC may, by rule, deem appropriate). It should not hold itself out generally to the US public as an investment adviser, act as an investment adviser to any registered investment company under the Investment Company Act of 1940 (the Investment Company Act) or act as a business development company under Section 54 of the Investment Company Act.
- **Private fund and mid-sized private fund adviser exemptions:** The Dodd–Frank Act directs the SEC to create a specific exemption from registration for investment advisers who advise private funds only and who have assets of less than US$150 million under management in the United States. Under the Dodd–Frank Act, a private fund is defined as a fund that would be an investment company but for Section 3(c)(1) or 3(c)(7) of the Investment Company Act. The Dodd–Frank Act further

requires the SEC to establish exemptions for investment advisers of mid-sized private funds, although this term is not defined. The SEC is required to take into account the size, governance and investment strategy of these funds when creating these exemptions for advisers to mid-sized funds, and to establish registration and examination procedures that reflect the level of systemic risk posed by such funds.

- **Advisers to venture capital funds**: The Dodd–Frank Act directs the SEC to provide an exemption from registration for investment advisers who solely act as advisers to one or more venture capital funds.
- **Advisers to family offices**: Family offices are exempt from registration because they are excluded from the definition of investment adviser under the Dodd–Frank Act.

With the new rule, all but the very smallest advisers will be subject to regulatory scrutiny. The new registration regime calls for hedge funds to establish a basic compliance programme, make more public disclosure of critical items to investors (such as conflicts of interest, key service providers, and custody matters), as well as being subjected to the possibility of examination by regulators.

The federal government has left a substantial portion of the burden of registration to the states, as it has raised the AUM minimum for registration with the SEC to over US$100 million in most cases, but it is the states that are required to register the funds with AUM of between US$ 25 million and US$100 million.

There are approximately 3990 investment advisers that manage one or more private funds registered with the SEC, of which 34 per cent had registered since the date the Dodd–Frank Act took effect, 21 July 2011. Of those 3990 registered private fund advisers, 7 per cent are domiciled in a country outside the US, most of them being domiciled in the United Kingdom. Registered private fund advisers have reported to the SEC that they advise 30,617 private funds with total assets of US$8 trillion. The SEC estimated that hedge funds represent 53 per cent of the gross assets of private funds.[6]

Another element covered by the Dodd–Frank Act regards disclosure. Registration means compulsory disclosure. In October 2011, the SEC passed rules requiring all private fund advisors to fill out a Form PF. Prior to this ruling, advisors had only been required to file an annual Form ADV There is a minimum asset requirement of $US25 million to file Form ADV. Part 1 of that form is publicly available and contains basic operational information; Part 2 contains more in-depth disclosures, such as the ownership of the firm, the services offered, the AUM, fees and compensation, conflicts of interest, investment strategies and risks, disciplinary history, financial affiliations and brokerage practices. Part 2 is not publicly available, but advisors must distribute it to their clients. The newly introduced Form PF goes further than Form ADV, collecting more detailed investment and strategy information. Section 1 of Form PF, to be submitted by all private funds, requires a declaration of gross and net assets, total fund borrowings, monthly performance, trading and clearing mechanisms, and counterparty credit risk. Section 2, which is mandatory for hedge funds managing at least US$1.5 billion, requires more detailed disclosure, including aggregate long and short exposures by type of security (including derivatives), liquidity of the portfolio, collateral postings, Value at Risk and risk-sensitivity estimates. Large funds are now not only required to meet these more stringent disclosure rules, but also have to file Form PF on a quarterly basis, while smaller funds need only do this annually. It is worth noting that among all the information required, detailed data relating to the portfolio holding is not included. Hedge funds are required to keep records of their trading and investment positions, which are subject only to SEC inspection, but they do not need to report this data in any forms filed with the SEC.

Hedge funds are also likely to see a reduced number of eligible institutional investors, thanks to a part of the Dodd–Frank Act proposed by former Federal Reserve Chairman Paul Volcker. If a private fund qualifies as a systemically important non-bank entity it will be subject to significant new regulations. Historically, banks have provided seed money for many internal and external hedge funds, but the Volcker Rule bars banking entities from engaging in proprietary trading and prohibits them from investing in or sponsoring hedge funds and private equity funds. The Volcker Rule could also stop other institutional investors from investing in hedge funds, as the definition of "banking entity" is not clear. The Preqin 2011 Global Investor Report on Hedge Funds states that strictly defined banks represent only 3 per cent of institutional hedge fund investors, but that institutional investors represent 61 per cent of these assets.

The Dodd–Frank Act extends regulation to another previously unregulated area, the over-the-counter derivatives markets in which hedge funds are large players. The Act broadly defines the term "swap" to mean most OTC financial contracts and gives authority to the US Commodity Futures Trading Commission and the SEC to provide a better description. The Dodd–Frank Act also mandates that swap dealers and major swap participants, which could be defined by the SEC and the CFTC to include hedge funds, will be subject to record keeping, reporting, margin, capital, and business conduct requirements. While the implications of this swap regulation could be vast, the implementation has hit a road block. By the middle of 2011, both the CFTC and the SEC voted to delay progress on swap regulation (and could do so indefinitely) because they cannot clearly define the key terms.

1.2.2 Canada

Regulation of the hedge fund industry in Canada has undergone significant reform with the introduction of National Instrument 31–103 – Registration Requirements and Exemptions. With this reform, which became effective on 28 September 2009, direct regulation of the industry now applies at two levels; the activity level of the market participant (fund manager/dealer/advisor), and secondly at the product level. Hedge funds which offer their securities in Canada or to Canadian residents must comply with these regulations.

Market participants' registration requirements are driven by the nature (called the business trigger) of their business activities. Business triggers may include whether a firm is paid for its activities, whether the firm is acting as intermediary and whether the firms' employees actively solicit clients. There are no business trigger considerations for the investment fund manager category. Firms that act as fund manager must register. This is expected to include general partners of hedge funds organized as limited partnerships. Portfolio managers or adviser firms who manage hedge fund portfolios, and dealer firms who sell hedge fund securities, must both be registered, and in most cases multiple registrations are required. Hedge fund managers are required to be registered as exempt market dealers (formerly, limited market dealer) in all provinces where they wish to market and sell their funds. Key employees of registrants must also register, and in all registration categories minimum individual registrations are required. The requirement to register with securities regulatory authorities to provide portfolio management services involves demonstrating significant previous experience to securities regulators as well as developing and maintaining a comprehensive compliance program for the money management firm. As a money manager registered with a provincial securities commission, a hedge fund manager is subject to a compliance audit by securities regulators. All registrants must meet minimum capital and insurance requirements. They must also establish and document a system of internal controls to ensure regulatory compliance and manage business risks. Fund Managers must disclose, on a quarterly basis, NAV errors of the funds. In addition, all registration categories must file audited financial statements with the regulators.

Direct regulation of hedge fund products in Canada is dependent upon whether the fund is distributed under a prospectus, under exemptions in securities regulation that allow the fund to be sold without a prospectus, or through a linked product such as a principal protected note (PPN).

Hedge funds sold pursuant to a prospectus comprise a small portion of the overall hedge fund market in Canada, the majority falling into the other categories. Retail investors have begun to constitute a larger source of investors for Canadian hedge funds and Canadian distributors due to the advent of various structured products that are either exempted from the application of the prospectus rules or are offered by way of a prospectus. Hedge funds sold under a prospectus and hedge funds sold under the prospectus exemptions are both subject to a range of general securities legislation requirements. Hedge funds sold under exemptions from prospectus requirements may only be sold to accredited investors who meet certain net income or financial asset tests, certain types of investors such as a Canadian pension fund, or to investors who can make a minimum purchase in the hedge fund of 150,000 Canadian dollars. This is the most common method to distribute hedge fund in Canada. While these funds are not required to provide a prospectus they do generally provide an offering memorandum and are typically required to provide certain continuous disclosures, such as annual financial statements, to investors.

Disclosure requirements apply, depending on how the hedge fund is sold. Hedge funds sold pursuant to a prospectus are subject to continuous disclosure requirements, which include specified disclosures in the prospectus and annual and semi-annual filing of financial statements and management reports on fund performance. Prospectus-exempt funds are required to deliver annual audited financial statements. Annual financial statements are required to be filed or delivered within 90 days of the fund's year-end. PPNs, which may give retail investors access to alternative investments through market-linked notes issued by deposit-taking institutions, are currently largely outside the scope of securities regulations in Canada. Instead federal PPN regulations specify requirements for the content, manner and timing of disclosure for PPNs issued by federal financial institutions. However the securities regulatory regime does impose suitability and know-your-client obligations on dealer registrants who distribute these products.

Aside from securities regulations, Canadian hedge fund managers are also required to comply with provincial and federal privacy legislation in connection with the collection, use, disclosure and disposal of personal information about their investors. It should be noted that hedge funds are also subject to certain reporting requirements under Canadian anti-money laundering and anti-terrorist financing legislation. There are also restrictions on the advertising and promotional strategies that Canadian hedge funds can employ. For instance, securities legislation generally prohibits the promotion of privately offered investments in securities on radio or television. Subject to strict guidelines, in certain Canadian province, hedge funds are permitted to advertise an offering of securities to accredited investors in newspapers and other print media.

1.3   Europe

There is an existing vehicle that can be sold throughout Europe: the Undertakings Collective Investment Transferable Securities (UCITS). This structure was originally created for traditional funds investing in liquid markets such as bonds and/or equities, but with the implementation of UCITS III in 2003 the rule evolved, and several alternative strategies can now be implemented, with limitations, under the UCITS structure. We will explain the UCITS rules, then introduce the new Alternative Investment Fund Management Directive (AIFMD). Then, we present the specific features of the private offers in selected European countries.

1.3.1   Alternative UCITS

A UCITS is a mutual fund based in the European Union. UCITS funds can be sold to any investor within the European Union under a harmonized regulatory regime. They have a strong brand identity across Europe, Asia and South America, and are distributed for sale in over fifty countries. The original Directive introducing the concept of a standard fund structure, UCITS I, was adopted in 1985. However, due to differing cross-border marketing restrictions in member states and the restricted range of asset classes permitted, the original Directive prevented UCITS from benefiting from the increasing range of investments that were available in the market. A second draft directive, UCITS II, was developed to rectify these issues, but extended political argument between EU countries caused it to be abandoned.

It was not until 2003 that the UCITS directive was amended by a new Directive, UCITS III, which was itself made up of two directives: the Product Directive and the Management Directive. The Product Directive expanded the type and range of investments that could be held within a UCITS. The Management Directive sought to give a European passport to management companies of a UCITS fund to enable them to operate throughout the European Union as well as tightening up risk management frameworks and increasing managers' capitalization requirements. It is this combined UCITS III Directive that fund managers now refer to when they mention UCITS III-compliant or newcits funds. In general, they mean that the fund is taking advantage of the wider investment potential. One of the key benefits of the UCITS III Product Directive was the broadening of the investment potential available to mutual funds, including derivatives for specific investment purposes. The Management Directive, meanwhile, developed the existing concept of the product passport. Under the passport, a UCITS fund in one member state can be freely marketed to investors in another EU country, subject to a processing period. The Management Directive also introduced new prospectus requirements as well as demanding that all UCITS funds use a simplified prospectus as a marketing document throughout the European Economic Area (EEA). Permissions to allow managers to operate funds domiciled in other countries (the management passport) were not, however, a complete success and the new UCITS IV Directive that came into force in 2012 aimed in part to rectify this.

A UCITS can only invest in eligible assets. The original UCITS directive was restrictive in scope and effectively allowed only equity and bond funds. UCITS III then expanded the range of available investments to include derivatives for investment purposes, other UCITS and cash; this dramatically increased investor choice, allowing for cash funds, funds of fund, mixed asset funds and alternative UCITS. UCITS must operate on a principle of risk spreading, which means that restrictions apply limiting the spread of investments, leverage and exposure. UCITS III, however, re-defined how derivative exposure can be measured. A UCITS must be open-ended, that is, shares or units in the fund may be redeemed on demand by investors. A UCITS must be liquid, that is, its underlying investments must be liquid enough to support redemptions in the fund on at least a fortnightly basis. In practice, the vast majority of UCITS funds are daily dealing. Assets must be entrusted to an independent custodian or depositary and held in a ring-fenced account on behalf of investors.

As part of UCITS III then, the Product Directive expanded the type of investments available to allow a UCITS to invest in derivatives not only for efficient portfolio management (EPM) or hedging purposes but for investment purposes as well. This has allowed a number of hedge fund strategies to be accommodated within the UCITS format such as equity long/short, convertible arbitrage, merger arbitrage, macro or relative value. Some strategies, however, will not easily fit within a UCITS framework because the underlying asset class (such as individual commodities or bank loans) is not permissible or because of the lack of liquidity (for example, distressed debt). The eligible assets that a UCITS can invest in include the following:

- **Transferable securities**: Publicly traded equities or bonds, listed on mainstream stock exchanges. Broadly, this was the range of assets allowed under UCITS I.

- **Deposits and Money Market instruments (MMIs)**: Cash deposits with credit institutions can be held as investment assets, together with MMIs. These might include treasury and local authority bills, certificates of deposit or commercial paper. In addition, pure cash funds can now be UCITS.
- **Other mutual funds**: UCITS were always able to invest in other funds, although this was restricted. UCITS III relaxed that restriction, providing a further ability to invest in other open-ended mutual funds where those are other UCITS or non-UCITS funds with UCITS-like cons traits.
- **Financial Derivative Instruments**: Under UCITS I, derivatives could only be used for hedging and EPM, to reduce risk or cost, or to replicate a position that could otherwise be achieved through investing directly in the asset. Under UCITS III, UCITS funds are able to use derivatives for investment purposes, an to use exchange traded or over-the-counter instruments, with certain limitations. The underlyer of a derivative must be an eligible asset of the type mentioned above (interest rates, foreign exchange rates and currencies or financial indices).

Physical short selling is not permitted. However, the same economic effect can be achieved, and is allowed, through the use of derivatives such as Contracts for Difference (CFDs). Firms must have systems and controls in place that can measure the derivative risk and provide an appropriate level of cover, which can mean that on the opposite side of the exposure there must be cash, a similar asset or balancing derivative giving a balancing exposure to a similar underlying asset, covering the original derivative exposure. It can also mean that some UCITS III funds may have high levels of gross exposure. Certain assets remain out of scope and are ineligible; these include real estate, bank loans, physical metals such as gold (although certain securities based on metals are permitted) and commodities.

A UCITS must be properly diversified. There are a number of different limits, all of them in place since UCITS I, but the best known is the 5/10/40 Rule. This states that a UCITS may not invest more than 5 per cent of its assets in securities issued by a single issuer. However, this limit can be increased up to 10 per cent provided that where the 5 per cent limit is exceeded the exposure to these issuers, added together, does not exceed 40 per cent of the fund's assets. There are also rules around the proportion of a company that a UCITS may hold in that it might gain significant influence over the company's management. Rules exist, too, regarding the amount of a company's debt or non-voting shares that can be held.

Whether funds use derivatives for investment purposes or for EPM, the exposure to such contracts has to be constantly reviewed. UCITS III more formally introduced the concept of having appropriate risk monitoring of the overall exposure created by derivatives, although the Directive itself goes into less detail than might be expected.

A UCITS must have risk management systems in place which are explained in the risk management process (RMP), which sets out how the risks of a UCITS positions (including risks arising out of its use of derivatives) will be measured and monitored. Long-only funds with EPM, or UCITS funds making a simplistic use of derivatives, are considered to be non-sophisticated and may use the Commitment Approach to establish risk levels; in essence this takes the gross exposure of the fund into consideration. The Commitment Approach basically aggregates the underlying notional value of stock and derivatives to determine the degree of gross exposure, called "global exposure" by the Directive. Under this measure, the leverage limit generated by using financial derivatives is limited to 100 per cent of the UCITS net asset value. With the 10 per cent short-term overdraft facility permitted to all funds, this means the total gross exposure of the fund cannot exceed 210 per cent of the net asset value of the fund. Sophisticated funds that use derivatives in a more complex way have to use Value at Risk (VaR) to estimate risk. Gross exposures may go beyond the 210 per cent limit of the commitment approach. The VaR approach estimates the potential for loss that is likely to be experienced in a given time period. For UCITS purposes, it is calculated on a monthly basis to a confidence interval of 99 per cent. So if a UCITS has a monthly 99 per cent VaR of say 8 per cent, we would expect, 99 times in 100, the NAV to fall no more than 8 per cent in any single month. Absolute return funds must stay within the limit of 20 per cent; this is high, and most funds will have lower VaR limits set by the prospectus.

The passporting of funds cross-border within Europe took a massive step forward with UCITS III but there are still some difficulties; so UCITS IV is intended to aid consumer choice further by making passporting easier and encouraging further cross-border distribution of strong and imaginative products. On the assets side, EurekaHedge estimates that the assets of European UCITS III hedge funds were over US$400 billion at the end of June 2012, coming from US$300 billion in assets early in 2010. UCITS funds represented around 50 per cent of the launches since 2010.

1.3.2 AIF & AIFM

The Alternative Investment Fund Managers Directive (AIFMD) is a European Union law that will put hedge funds and private equity funds under the supervision of an EU regulatory body. These funds have not been subject to the same rules protecting the investing public as have mutual and pension funds, and it is lack of financial regulation that is widely seen to have contributed to the severity of the global financial crisis. The European Parliament voted through a final text of the Directive on 11 November 2010. The proposals have to be written into national statute books by 22 July 2013, and will be effective thenceforth. At the time of writing this chapter, we can share some elements with you.

An AIF is defined, in summary, as a collective investment undertaking (other than a UCITS fund) that raises capital from a number of investors and invests in accordance with a defined investment policy, for the benefit of those investors. The Directive will apply to all EU AIFMs that manage one or more AIF, irrespective of where the AIFs are domiciled. The Directive will also apply to all non-EU AIFMs that manage one or more AIFs domiciled in the EU or market one or more AIFs in the EU. An AIF that is self-managed will itself be considered as the AIFM. The Directive has different effects, depending on whether the AIF or the AIFM is established within or outside the EU. The broad scope of the Directive is designed to ensure a level playing field and, according to the European Commission, to help minimize the risks of regulatory arbitrage. The Directive provides for a lighter regime for an AIFM where the cumulative AIFs under management fall below a threshold of €100 million. If the AIF is not leveraged and has a lock-in period of five years or more, this threshold is raised to €500 million.

AIFMs will be required to be authorized under the Directive by the competent regulatory authority of their home state. Conditions for authorization include a minimum initial capital (a self-managed AIF must have at least €300,000 in capital, and AIFMs managing one or more AIFs must have at least €125,000 in capital). Where the value of the portfolios of the AIF managed by the AIFM exceeds €250 million, additional own funds are required. The persons conducting the business of the AIFM must be of sufficiently good reputation and sufficiently experienced in relation to the investment strategies pursued by each AIF.

An authorized AIFM will be required on an ongoing basis to:

- employ effectively the resources and procedures that are necessary for the proper performance of its business activities
- take all reasonable steps to avoid conflicts of interests and to identify and manage any conflicts of interest to prevent them
- comply with all applicable regulatory requirements so as to promote the best interests of each AIF, its investors and the integrity of the market

- have sound remuneration policies and practices in place that are consistent with and promote sound and effective risk management
- implement adequate systems to identify, measure, manage and monitor all risks relevant to each AIF investment strategy
- set a maximum level of leverage which the AIFM may employ on behalf of each AIF it manages; and to employ an appropriate liquidity management system for each AIF.

One of the cornerstones of the Directive is the introduction of a single market framework to regulate the offer or placing of shares or units in an AIF. It introduces a European passport under which authorized AIFMs can market EU AIFs to professional investors throughout the EU, subject to a notification procedure. The Directive as adopted will enable non-EU AIFMs to market to investors across the EU without first having to seek permission from each Member State and comply with different national laws. Non-EU AIFMs will only obtain a passport if the non-EU country in which they are located meets minimum regulatory standards and has agreements in place with Member States to allow information sharing. There will be at least a two-year time lag before a passport is available for non-EU AIFMs marketing any AIF or for EU AIFMs marketing non-EU AIFs in Europe, as this is dependent on the European Securities and Markets Authority (ESMA) issuing positive advice in this regard.

1.3.3   United Kingdom

The United Kingdom, and London in particular, remains one of the favourite centres for hedge fund managers even though other jurisdictions are increasing their share. Nowadays, close to 50 per cent of the European hedge funds are based in London. While this number remains high in absolute terms, it has decreased over the last few years. The funds tend to be offshore; this means that the hedge fund manager will be directly regulated but that the underlying fund is not.

Authorised Investment Funds (AIFs) are collective investment schemes authorized and regulated by the Financial Conduct Authority[7] (FCA) under the terms of the Financial Services and Markets Act 2000 (FSMA). The rules dealing with the constitution and investment powers of AIFs are set out in the FCA's COLL handbook. Hedge fund strategies can be set up under two different legal forms, and they fall into one of three categories defined by the FCA.

- **UCITS funds, as described above**: These schemes can be marketed to retail investors within any European Union member state.

- **Non-UCITS retail funds**: Non-UCITS retail funds (often referred to as NURS funds) are any AIF which, whilst not being UCITS schemes, are not Qualified Investor Schemes. Their investment potential is less restricted than that of UCITS schemes. They can be marketed to retail investors.
- **Qualified Investor Schemes (QIS)**: QIS funds are AIFs with wider investment and borrowing potential than either UCITS funds or NURS funds, and can be marketed only to qualified investors. These funds can take short positions, use leverage and invest in derivatives. Qualified investors are individuals that meet at least two of the following three criteria:
  - they must have carried out transactions of a significant size (at least £1000) on securities markets at an average frequency of at least 10 per quarter over the last four quarters
  - their security portfolio must exceeds £500,000
  - they work, or have worked for at least one year, in the financial sector in a professional position which requires knowledge of securities investment.

AIFs can have two different legal forms:

- **Authorised Unit Trusts (AUTs)**: An AUT is a unit trust scheme that has been authorized by the Financial Services Authority. It must meet certain conditions concerning its management structure and the type of investments it can hold. Only authorized schemes can be sold to the general public (the retail market).
- **Open-ended Investment Companies (OEICs)**: An OEIC is a collective investment scheme structured as a company with variable capital and which satisfies the property and investment condition in FSMA Section 236. Once authorized by the FCA, it must be incorporated as a company under the Open-Ended Investment Companies Regulations 2001. There are also limitations regarding its distribution and advertising.

1.3.4 Germany

German regulation was modified in January 2004 by an Investment Act (*Investmentgesetz*) and an Investment Tax Act (*Investmentsteuergesetz*). These laws introduced a new regime covering single hedge funds and funds of hedge funds; whereas individual hedge funds do not face any restriction regarding their investment strategy, funds of hedge funds, which can be distributed to any kind of investor, even through a public offer, have to comply with strict rules. In Germany, hedge funds are called

Sondervermögen mit zusätzlichen Risiken (investment funds with additional risks). In December 2007, a number of legal amendments to the acts concerning hedge funds came into force.

Domestic and foreign individual hedge funds may not be publicly distributed to retail investors. According to the amendments to the Investment Act of December 2007, not only German individual hedge funds but also foreign ones – which are distributed separately for private placement – fall under the scope of the Act if the foreign investment vehicle generally qualifies as a foreign investment fund according to the Investment Act and the respective circular of the German regulator, the *Bundesanstalt für Finanzdienstleistungsaufsicht* (usually called BaFin). No public offer is allowed for individual hedge funds. Before 2004, access to hedge funds was enabled through certificates that were usually linked to listed products with capital guarantee that could use leverage. One of the key amendments of December 2007 to the Investment Act in relation to hedge funds is the setting of formal legal rules for prime brokers referring to individual hedge funds. Before that, prime brokers had been regulated only by some decrees subsequent to the Investment Act.

There are a few specific rules that are worth mentioning. First of all, German hedge funds can invest in any kind of security except directly in real estate. Other constraints are that the funds have to be diversified, and a maximum of 30 per cent of any fund can be invested in unlisted securities. There are no wealth constraints regarding potential investors but they should be able to redeem on at least a quarterly basis. All the documents used in Germany have to be translated into German. The mandatory documents and information are the same as those required for mutual funds; for example, the prospectus should contain a general advertisement as well as precise information on the investment strategy, the fee structure and the liquidity features. Annual and semi-annual financial statements have to be published respectively four and two months after the end of the corresponding period. In addition the asset management company should be registered with the BaFin, and it should obtain a special licence.

German and foreign funds of funds that aim to offer their product to the German market also have to respect specific rules. They cannot, for example, invest in individual funds that are based in jurisdictions that do not cooperate in terms of money laundering in the context of international agreements. There are also investment limits, including the fact that any position is limited to 20 per cent maximum. In addition a fund of funds may not invest in more than two funds from the same issuer, and a fund of funds of funds is prohibited. Other constraints include the fact that fund of hedge funds cannot use leverage and cannot take short positions.

As a professional investor, a fund of funds management company should also prove that it possesses the minimum information required for every fund. This includes the last annual and semi-annual financial statements, official documents such as the prospectus, a complete due diligence as well as any information on the investment restrictions, including the liquidity, leverage and the position regarding short selling. Most of the constraints relating to individual funds remain in place for funds of funds; the main difference between individual funds and funds of hedge funds is that while the latter may be marketed publicly under some constraints, this is never the case for individual funds. Foreign individual funds and funds of hedge funds can only be distributed in Germany if they are supervised within their jurisdiction of origin by an authority that cooperates with the German regulator; in addition any foreign fund should use the services of both a local intermediary and a German transfer agent. A foreign fund should also comply with the same rules as local funds and work with a depositary offering the same guarantee as a German one. Foreign funds are taxed at the same level as German funds, the level depending on the classification: transparent, semi-transparent and non-transparent. For a fund to be classified as transparent, its manager should disseminate a lot of information in the portfolio in German.

1.3.5   Luxembourg

Until December 2002, investment restrictions applicable to funds adopting alternative investment strategies in Luxembourg were analysed on a case-by-case basis by the local regulator, the Commission de Surveillance du Secteur Financier (CSSF), making the registration procedure lengthy and complicated. In 2002, the Luxembourg authority published a circular on alternative investments, facilitating the creation of regulated alternative products. Since then, Luxembourg hedge funds have been able to short sell, and use leverage and derivative products, but they still have to comply with serious restrictions. The introduction of an adapted private form of funds, Specialized Investment Funds (SIF), in 2007 created a new legal framework that supported the growth of the Luxembourg hedge fund industry. The rules have been clarified and simplified. SIFs can be sold to professional investors and to individual investors that are classified as well-informed investors and that either invest a minimum of €125,000 per fund or are certified by a credit institution, an investment company or an asset management company as knowledgeable and capable to invest. There is no obligation on the manager or promoter to register, but for the fund directors to be accepted by the regulator they have to prove their capability and their knowledge in the corresponding field. The auditors also have to be approved by the CSSF. An original feature of this legal structure is that the product may be launched before being accepted. The demand should be filled over the month following the launch of the product. A prospectus should be written but there is no minimum information to provide. The annual report should be published within six months of the end of the year. There is no obligation to publish semi-annual financial statements or to publish a net asset value. The constraints are on the valuation of the assets of the fund should be estimated on an equitable basis and on the the risks that should be diversified. Finally, the assets should reach a minimum of €1,250,000 one year after the launch.

1.3.6 Italy

Italy was one of the first countries of the European Union to regulate hedge funds, in May 1999. This law authorized a new type of asset management company, called Società di Gestione del Rispiarmio (Sgr) Speculative.

In line with the norms dictated by the Bank of Italy, those companies were permitted to make private offers to individuals and companies alternative products (no public offers were permitted). The specific features of the Italian hedge funds include that fact that they can invest in any kind of assets available. There is also no limit on investment amounts, minimum diversification or liquidity. A fund can have up to 200 investors, and it should provide the same documentations as do mutual funds, apart from the prospectus, which is not mandatory. The financial statements should be produced within four months of the end of the exercise and the semi-annual statement within two months. Foreign funds can only be sold in Italy after having been accepted by the Bank of Italy; the constraints to comply with regarding structure, controls and manager capabilities are quite stringent.

1.3.7 Switzerland

Swiss laws distinguish three kinds of fund: real estate funds, value funds and the others with special risks funds. Hedge funds form part of the third category. Swiss hedge funds can invest in any assets apart from physical commodities; they can use leverage, take short positions and invest in derivatives, but their use has to be defined and limited in the fund rules. There is no constraint on type of investor or minimum investment (which must nevertheless be discussed with the regulator) and no general rule regarding liquidity. Any investor should sign a document stating that he/she understands the risks of investing in hedge funds. The documentation required is the same as that required for mutual funds; the prospectus should clearly define the investment strategy as well as giving a precise description of the risk and a glossary. Direct advertising is permitted, but this is limited to 20 potential investors, and the text must include a long warning on the underlying risks. Everyone selling or distributing foreign funds professionally in Switzerland should in most cases possess a licence given by the local regulator, the Commission Bancaire Fédérale (CBF). A fund will be classified as a fund of hedge funds if it invests more than 49 per cent in other funds, the limit per position being 20 per cent; the other rules are in line with those applicable to individual funds. The main difference is that for funds of hedge funds public advertising is permitted. Foreign funds can be proposed on the Swiss market if they respect the same rules as Swiss funds.

1.3.8 France

Since 2004, there have been no significant changes in the regulation applicable to hedge-fund-like products in France. Pursuant to the 2003 Financial Security Act, the Autorité des Marchés Financiers (AMF) authorized in 2004 the creation of two new types of funds that share a number of characteristics similar to those of hedge funds and, in particular, permit the use of leverage. These structures are ARIA funds and contractual funds.

There are three types of ARIA funds. The first consists of simple funds. Such funds are subject to certain rules relating to diversification of holdings, and may use leverage up to two times the net assets. Potential investors with a minimum net worth of €1 million or a minimum of one year of relevant work experience are subject to a minimum investment threshold of €10,000; other individual investors are required to make a minimum investment of €125,000. Certain qualified investors are, however, not subject to any minimum investment thresholds. The second type of ARIA funds include leveraged funds. These are subject to rules regarding diversification and minimum investment thresholds identical to those applying to simple funds, but may leverage up to four times their net assets. On the other side, the asset manager behind the product should get a specific approval to manage such products. The third type includes funds of alternative funds. They may leverage up to 200 per cent of net assets and they are required to invest in a minimum of nine underlying funds. The minimum investment in these is €10,000 except for capital guaranteed products, and again certain qualified investors are not subject to any minimum investment threshold. The maximum notification period is 35 days.

Contractual funds benefit from more freedom than ARIA funds. They are not subject to rules regarding diversification of holdings or limits on the amount of leverage they may employ – but the investment rules, the securities used and the limits should be detailed in the prospectus. Individual investors with a minimum net worth of €1 million or individual investors with a minimum of one year of relevant work experience are subject to a minimum investment threshold of €30,000. Other individual investors are required to make a minimum investment of €250,000, and yet again certain qualified investors are not subject to any minimum investment. From 24 October 2008, contractual funds have also been permitted to invest in assets other than securities or financial instruments, such as aircraft, ships, works of art and real estate, provided they comply with specific requirements set out by regulations. Semi-annual and annual financial statements should be published within four and two months of the end of the period. The net asset value should be published at least once a quarter. Contractual funds may be approved after their launch as long as the management company is approved by the regulator.

Futures funds are also allowed in France. They may invest in the futures markets and in commodities, and are not subject to a leverage cap. Anyone can invest in futures funds with a minimum investment of €10,000.

In order to create and manage an ARIA leveraged fund, a contractual fund or a futures fund, the investment management company must obtain specific approval from the AMF, though no specific approval is required for a simple ARIA fund. In fact all investment management companies in France are registered with and regulated by the AMF; no foreign fund can be offered to any French investor unless it has been approved by the AMF.

1.3.9 Ireland

Ireland and Luxembourg have been competing for years to become leader of the mutual fund and private fund markets. The Irish regulator is called the Irish Financial Services Regulatory Authority. Three different fund structures are available for hedge funds in Ireland: Qualifying Investor Funds (QIF), Professional Investor Funds (PIF) and retail funds of hedge funds. Created in February 2007, the QIF is the most popular structure for the establishment of regulated individual funds and fund of hedge funds, mainly because such funds have no restrictions on investment strategy or gearing and because they can be authorized by the Irish Financial Regulator within 24 hours of the submission of relevant documentation to the Financial Regulator. This is comparable with the SIF structure in Luxembourg.

Such funds can be sold to qualified individual investors with assets of a minimum of €1,250,000 (without including their principal private residence into account) or to institutions that invest a minimum of €25 million on a discretionary basis. These funds require a minimum investment of €250,000. A complete prospectus should be produced, precisely describing the objective of the fund and its investment policy. It should also cover other elements, such as the leverage policy and its potential use over time, as well as information on proposed investments. Other restrictions include the fact that funds should respect the principle of risk repartition. In addition, semi-annual and annual financial statements have to be sent to the regulator and should be available to investors. Monthly returns as well as the gross and net asset value must also be sent to the regulator. Other specific features include the fact that the name of the fund should not be confusing and the fact that funds offering limited liquidity (less than quarterly) should specify this on the first page of the prospectus. Since 2007, a fast-track approval process has been available to the promoters of Irish funds; this process is available to firms that are regulated as investment firms under the Markets in Financial Instruments Directive (MiFID), in a Member State of the European Economic Area (EEA) (European Union Member States plus Norway, Iceland and Liechtenstein). On provision of the necessary information set out in the financial regulator's application checklist, and subject to certain criteria, the Financial Regulator will accept the entity as a promoter for an Irish fund within one week of receipt of the application. This fast-track process is highly attractive to those seeking speed to market and timely fund launch.

In December 2009, Ireland introduced new company law changes to facilitate greater efficiency for funds (incorporated as investment companies) redomiciling into Ireland. The new legislation provides an effective and straightforward migration of corporate funds to Ireland by allowing a non-Irish corporate funds to reregister as an Irish company and continue in existence as a UCITS or non-UCITS fund authorized by the Irish Financial Regulator. As the process does not require the setting up of a new legal entity, this provides an opportunity for the non-Irish fund company to move to an EU/OECD[8] regulated jurisdiction and enjoy the benefits of retaining its company structure.

1.3.10 Malta

The Malta regulator is the Malta Finance Service Authority (MFSA). Collective Investment Schemes are regulated under a framework regime incorporated in the Investment Services Act and are based on the level of sophistication and the level of protection required by the target investor. The principal categories of collective investment schemes that can be set up include retail investment schemes (UCITS or non-UCITS) and professional investment funds (PIF). PIF cannot be sold retail, but are limited to qualified investors (typically with more than €750k in assets; minimum investment is €75,000), experienced investors (people with expertise in or specific knowledge of financial markets; minimum investments €10,000) or extraordinary investors (the main constraint being that they manage over 7.5 million in assets, minimum investment is €750k). There are no limits regarding the investment strategy implemented by a PIF, but there are some regarding leverage, especially when the fund is sold to qualified or experienced investors. Every fund must be approved by the MFSA before being sold in Malta. The asset manager does not have to be domiciled in Malta, but should be established within a regulated jurisdiction of the EU or the OECD (plus a few exceptions). Furthermore, although hedge funds are typically established as PIF, it is also possible for a fund established overseas to transfer its domicile to Malta and apply to be registered as a PIF. It is also possible to change funds domiciled offshore to Malta under the Companies Act, Continuation of Companies Regulations of 2002. The MFSA published guidelines giving a simple, one-step procedure to be followed by funds intending to change their domicile to Malta. The guidelines specify the documentation required from fund promoters and outline the way the process is handled by the Authorisation Unit and the Registry of Companies at the MFSA.

1.3.11   Spain

The Comisión Nacional del Mercado de Valores (CNMV) is the regulator in charge of supervising and inspecting the Spanish stock market and the activities of all participants in those markets. Until 2005, there was no legal framework that enabled the implementation of hedge funds in Spain; in addition, it was very difficult for local investors to invest in offshore funds. The current Spanish regulatory framework that defines Collective Investment Schemes (CIS) for single hedge funds and funds of hedge funds is based on a law and a Royal Decree that were adopted in November 2005 (followed by a Ministerial Order and some circulars published between 2006 and 2008) and that provide a basic framework for launching and distributing domestic individual hedge funds and funds of hedge funds in Spain. The framework covers, amongst other things, the distribution of domestic hedge fund products to institutional and retail investors, and specific requirements for hedge fund managers regarding authorization and ongoing requirements covering organizational matters, internal control and risk management matters, as well as controls over outsourcing and operational risk.

The marketing of single manager hedge funds is limited to approaching qualified investors only. However, access to retail investors is not prevented on the basis of unsolicited marketing, provided that the retail investor acknowledges in writing that he/she understands the level of risk connected with investment in such products. The MiFID rules also impose higher transparency. Marketing of foreign hedge fund products remains subject to prior authorization by the CNMV. It seems likely, however, that authorization may be granted in cases where foreign hedge fund products are subject to similar regulatory requirements as those applicable to domestic funds. The CNMV pays particular attention to investor protection matters in determining whether or not authorization will be granted.

Hedge funds are set up as free collective investment schemes (Inversión Colectiva de Inversión Libre). Such funds can invest in any kind of financial assets, with certain constraints regarding liquidity, diversification and transparency. Leverage excluding derivatives is limited to five times, and hedge funds may not invest in raw materials. Any hedge fund should have a minimum of 25 clients by its first anniversary. Net asset values should usually be published quarterly, and redemptions have to be paid within two liquidity dates and maximum nine months of the request. The minimum investment is a strict €50,000 and the rules regarding documentation are the same as those relating to UCITS funds. There are also a few, relatively complex, constraints regarding the use of securities and prime brokers.

Funds of hedge funds can be sold to retail, but they have to invest minimum 60 per cent of their assets in funds. Those assets should be invested in domestic or foreign funds as long these funds are domiciled in a country of the OECD or the asset management company is overseen by an OECD jurisdiction. Any single position is limited to 10 per cent. Minimal due diligence rules are defined. Most other rules are in line with the ones applicable to single hedge funds.

Finally it is worth mentioning that every investor must sign a document stipulating that they are aware of the specific risks underlying investment in hedge funds. In addition, a complete prospectus covering the investment strategy, the risks and risk profile of the fund, the investment methodology, any liquidity constraints and the fee structure should be published. Foreign funds may register as long as they comply with all the rules applicable to local players. This stringent law has encouraged many international players to become associated with Spanish institutions in order to offer their hedge fund products on the Spanish market.

1.4 Australia

In Australia, there is currently no regulation specific to hedge funds. Hedge funds along with other forms of collective investment, are primarily regulated by the Corporations Act 2001. Both hedge funds and their managers domiciled in Australia, as well as those domiciled offshore and managing funds sold in Australia, need to meet the regulatory requirements of the Corporations Act. The Australian regulatory requirements applying to hedge funds depend largely on the type of entity used. Unit trusts (in Australia, known as *managed investment schemes*) are the predominant investment vehicle in that country.

Managed investment schemes typically involve a company being appointed to act as trustee (*responsible entity*), although that company may then delegate the investment management function. Hedge fund trustees and managers are subject to the Australian financial services (AFS) licensing regime, and need to either hold a licence or fall within one of the relevant exemptions. The licensing requirement can be triggered not only by an entity acting as investment manager but also by offshore entities marketing to Australian investors (although some allowances have been made when the investment manager is authorised in certain foreign jurisdictions if the manager acts for sophisticated or professional investor clients only). Hedge funds are generally required to register as managed investment schemes with the Australian Securities and Investments Commission (ASIC) unless they are offered only to wholesale clients. For registered schemes, the Corporations Act and ASIC impose various requirements, including the scheme's trust deed (*constitution*), compliance and governance arrangements. Nevertheless, registration carries with it advantages from a distribution perspective within Australia, since institutional investors such as superannuation funds may prefer to invest in funds which are subject to the compliance and integrity requirements associated with registration.

From a disclosure perspective, hedge funds offered to retail clients must prepare a product disclosure statement (PDS) in connection with the offer. While a PDS is only required for funds offered to wholesale clients, it is usual industry practice to issue an additional information memorandum or private placement memorandum. There is further regulation covering marketing materials issued in connection with a fund.

Finally, the investment activities of hedge fund managers are regulated by the conduct provisions of the Corporations Act, which imposes prohibitions on insider trading, naked short selling and engaging in misleading and deceptive conduct. There is also a range of administrative obligations imposed on hedge funds due to the AFS licensing scheme check regarding anti-money laundering and counter-terrorism financing requirements, in addition to obligation to produce audited financial statements for the manager and the fund, and requirements as to how to accept and deal with retail investor moneys.

1.5   Offshore jurisdictions

Hedge funds have historically been created in two versions, the US version and its offshore counterpart. There are several reasons for this. Firstly, the US versions were created to offer hedge funds to American investors; remember that typical hedge fund investors have for decades been high net worth American investors. Offshore funds were created for two kinds of investors; non-American investors, and tax-exempt American investors such as pension funds. Offshore jurisdictions have also attracted interest because of their low level of tax, because funds can be created quickly and cheaply, and because the constraints regarding the implementation of the investment strategy are usually very low limited. While offshore investing has for decades been the most common way to invest for non-US and US tax-exempt investors, the implementation of new laws enabling the creation of regulated hedge fund structures such as UCITS for retail clients and private high net worth structures like QIF or SIF is changing the situation, at least for non-US investors. In addition the recently created AIFM structure will probably push the trend forward. The only investors that will probably not change their way of investing are US tax-exempt investors.

When choosing where to domicile a fund, several factors have to be taken into account: cost, the level of freedom in the implementation of the investment strategy, time needed to create the fund, the confidentiality (even though the importance of this element has decreased), the level of regulation, investors' protection and the investors' perception. Even if every offshore jurisdiction offers advantages in comparison with the developed and heavily regulated markets, each of them has its specific features, and not every offshore jurisdiction offers a full set of advantages. These are the most common ones:

- *Fiscal advantage*: most jurisdictions do not charge capital gains taxes.
- *Set-up costs*: the set-up cost to implement a fund in offshore jurisdictions is significantly lower than in regulated markets. The exact amount is determined on a case-by-case basis.
- *Flexibility*: fund managers have a lot of freedom in the implementation of their investment strategy. As we have already mentioned, things have been improving regarding regulation, particularly in Europe, but in most cases there may nevertheless be constraints regarding leverage and the securities that can be used.
- *Rapidity*: it is possible to create and register a fund offshore within a few days or weeks, whereas this tends to take up to several months in onshore regulated countries. The situation has however changed in certain places, such as Ireland, Luxembourg and Malta, where this can

be achieved in a few days and where in some cases the fund can even be launched before filling it with the local regulator.

- *Local infrastructure*: some recognized offshore jurisdictions such as the Cayman Islands offer a complete infrastructure ready to set up funds, including high quality administrators, custodians and legal advisers.
- *Investors and minimum investments*: the rules governing investors are less strict than those normally in place in regulated centres, in terms of both net worth and numbers. The legal minimum investment tends to be around US$100,000, against US$ million in the United States and €250,000 in Ireland.
- *Local representation:* offshore centres generally request that the fund have a local address and, in some cases, a local administrator. In regulated centres, the company must usually be represented locally and, in some cases the management must be carried out within the country, which can increase costs significantly.

There are numerous offshore centres around the world. As shown in Figure 6.1, hedge funds tend to be represented mainly in the Cayman Islands, the British Virgin Islands, Bermuda and the Bahamas (BVI).[9] While some of those are extra-territorial British centres they are responsible for their own governance, and the United Kingdom remains responsible solely for external affairs, defence and the courts. Other offshore centres include Andorra, Angola, Barbados, Belize, Gibraltar,

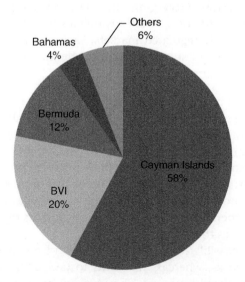

Figure 6.1   Breakdown of the domicile of offshore hedge funds
Source: ECB.

Guernsey, the Isle of Man, Jersey, Liberia, Mauritius and the Turks and Caicos Islands.

The United States also has local offshore centres, the best known being the state of Delaware. Delaware is the smallest state of the Union, and it is located close to Washington. It offers several fiscal and legal advantages as long as the activities of the manager are based offshore, that is outside the United States. Delaware state only charges an annual tax to companies, a fixed amount of just US$200 for a limited liability company. The local laws have been conceived to enable foreign investors to create their own offshore company in a clear legal framework with the necessary flexibility. The only real constraint for a non-resident to open a company in Delaware is to use the services of an agent registered with the local authorities. The company should as a consequence be domiciled with the agent. The fact that a fund is domiciled in Delaware does not mean that the asset manager or management team have to be based in the same jurisdiction as the fund; the managers are generally based in recognized financial centres such as London, Hong Kong and New York. The local registration relates only to the fund; this is what defines the rules and constraints regarding the fund as well as the court competent in case of litigation.

1.5.1 Cayman Islands

The local regulator is the Cayman Islands Monetary Authority (CIMA). Cayman-based funds are required to register under the mutual fund law with the CIMA and they are required to file certain extracts from the offering memorandum. Hedge funds tend to take the form of an exempted limited partnership. The minimum legal investment is US$100,000. There are two main forms of local funds: private, sold only to professional investors or high net worth individuals, and public. Hedge funds have to be set up under the private fund structure. While for decades the constraints were relatively limited, they have increased over recent years. However, the centre remains of interest due to its rapidity, its advantageous fiscal laws, its cost advantages, the quality of its local service providers and its flexibility in the definitions of investment strategy and investment structure.

1.5.2 British Virgin Islands

The Investment Services Division of the British Virgin Islands Financial Services Commission (FSC) is responsible for the regulation and supervision of all mutual funds operating within and from the territory. The British Virgin Islands is a British Overseas Territory, hence legislation is based on the British legal system and English Common Law. Since the introduction of the International Business Companies Act of 1984 and its successor, the Business Companies Act of 2004 (BCA), the territory has made significant progress and has become a leading international financial service centre. New legislation concerning mutual funds, called the Security and Investment Business Act, has been enacted recently. As at the date of writing it has not yet been fully applied, so we will describe the current environment and recommend you get legal advice for more up-to-date information.

Hedge funds can be of three types. Firstly, private; typically a fund that is offered to a maximum of 50 investors or that will be offered to potential investors only on a private basis. Secondly, professional; these are funds that will be offered to professional investors only, for a minimum investment of US$100,000. Professional investors can be defined in two ways: either their main activity consists of buying or selling securities equivalent to those traded by the fund; or they are an individual who has signed a document confirming that they (singly or jointly with spouse) has over US$1 million and who accepts being considered as a professional investor. Thirdly, the public funds that have to comply with strict rules, including amongst other things providing a complete and detailed prospectus that has to be approved by the director of the investment business and by the fund directors, local representation and financial statements. There are no restrictions regarding investment, whether the fund be private, professional or public. Changes include the possibility of: an increased audit requirement for private and professional funds, who may be required to appoint an auditor to prepare annual audited financial statements; stricter constraints regarding minimum investment; the potential requirement to have a minimum of two directors; and the requirement for all BVI funds to appoint an authorized representative resident in the BVI unless they already have a significant management presence there.

2   Hedge funds vs. mutual funds

Laws and regulation constantly evolve, but the basic principles remain stable over time. The main change is that even though mutual funds must continue to comply with stricter regulations than hedge funds, mutual funds are tending to gain more and more freedom in their management. In contrast, while offshore hedge funds tend to continue to enjoy the greater levels of freedom in their structure and management, more and more fund managers have decided to create regulated funds. Such funds will be either fully regulated retail funds, usually sold as UCITS structures or private funds that retain a considerable degree of freedom in their management even though the rules they have to comply with maybe more restrictive than those relating to funds in the offshore world.

Mutual fund managers have to comply with much stricter rules not only regarding their investment strategy but also in their communication and even in their fee structure. The aim of this section is explain the typical differences that exist between hedge funds and mutual funds. We will not consider alternative UCITS funds that are regulated and that tend at this stage to be more an exception than the rule. We will focus our attention on private hedge funds and fully regulated mutual funds, and we will base the bulk of this analysis on the US market as this is the market where hedge funds legal structures and mutual funds have co-existed for the longest time.

The main legal constraints that are worth presenting relate to the prospectus, short selling, liquidity, the use of leverage, the kind of securities that can be bought, fees and communication. Then, there are also the differences between typical investors, registration of the asset management company and oversight by the regulator. The American laws regulating mutual funds are the Securities Act of 1933, Securities Exchange Act of 1934, Investment Company Act of 1940 and Investment Advisers Act. The Internal Revenue Code regulates the additional rules regarding portfolio diversification and the distribution of profits, and the National Association of Securities Dealers, Inc. determines the rules regarding advertising and communication. The differences presented are not exhaustive and may not be valid in some markets, but they should help us to achieve our objective.

2.1 Management – prospectus, short selling, leverage, liquidity and securities used

Every investor in mutual funds should receive a copy of the investment prospectus, which should contain information relating to the management of the fund, its positioning and the fees charged. In the case of hedge funds, the prospectus is also an essential document. The mandatory information is, however, not always so precisely defined. As hedge funds are typically sold as private investments, the prospectus is seen as an agreement between the parties, and its private character means that it might be less precise. A second constraint on the management relates to information on historical transactions. In the case of a mutual fund, every transaction and the positioning of the fund should be recorded. But in the case of hedge funds this constraint is not present unless the fund is registered with local regulator[10], in which case the products differ in their use of leverage and short selling. The law does not always prevent mutual funds from short selling or leveraging the portfolio through derivatives; such positions are, however, not always easy to implement, and in any case the use of leverage by mutual funds tends to be more exceptions than the rule. In the case of hedge funds, short selling and leverage are very common, limits are not always formally defined by law but in most cases they are defined by the prospectus.

On the liquidity side, mutual funds usually have to be traded daily. Some funds may be weekly or in some cases bi-weekly, but even under the UCITS rule, bi-weekly is a formal limit. However, there are no formal limits for offshore hedge funds; there may be limits for private onshore funds but in the worst case, the minimum limit is quarterly. Offshore funds tend to offer monthly or quarterly liquidity after a notice period of, usually, one to three months, and many funds have lockup periods that tend to be a year. In many cases, redemptions are only possible at specific liquidity dates and the percentage of assets that can be redeemed at a single date – the gate – is typically limited to 10 per cent. Exit fees may also be charged.

Regarding pricing, market prices should be used. If they are not available, the prices should be determined by the board of directors. To offshore funds, the manager sometimes has to give his/her input in the pricing process to price less liquid securities but the process tends to be defined in the prospectus. Mutual funds have to be precise in the prospectus on the kind of securities that can be used by the manager. Hedge funds will naturally also report the kind of securities used – but they tend to be less detailed, in order to retain a greater level of freedom and disctretion.

2.2   Associated costs – fees and others

In the United States, mutual funds have to comply with strict federal laws that set clear limits on management fees. Distribution fees and other commissions are also limited. In addition, the fees have to be clearly indicated on the first page of the memorandum. Hedge funds do not, however, have formal limitations regarding the structure of the fees received, and as private entities hedge funds tend not to be regulated on this aspect; they tend to charge management fees, performance fees and in some cases entry and/ or exit fees. In some European countries their fees are, however, regulated.

2.3   Communication

Mutual funds can be publicly sold, and they are not limited in the way this is done. They can, for example, use newspapers, radio, public seminars, television or the internet. But the private character of hedge funds forbids hedge funds to perform any public advertising in any form. This naturally includes newspapers, television and radio – but also seminars for which invitations are widely disseminated. In addition access to information on the internet should be managed, and limited to high net worth investors. In practice, this is usually monitored by asking the internet use to tick a box to confirm that they fall under the conditions to get access to the required information. This constraint is the main reason explaining why hedge funds have remained discreet and comparatively unknown for decades.

2.4 Typical investors

Mutual funds can accept as many investors as they like. In addition, those investors do not have to respect any specific rules; the only constraint to respect in order to be able to invest in a mutual fund is to possess the amount corresponding to the minimum investment. This is typically a US$1000 or less. American hedge funds typically have to limit the number of investors to 99 or 499. In addition those investors have to be accredited or qualified, and their minimum investment must typically be US$1 million for US funds, or for offshore funds usually US$100,000. This is not the same for funds of funds, which are in most cases widely available and can be sold to retail investors. In regulated European countries the constraints are of the same order, but the minimum investments tend to be significantly lower, at €125,000 or €250,000.

2.5 Asset manager registration

Asset managers of mutual funds have to comply with strict rules. They have to register as investment adviser with the Securities and Exchange Commission, compelling them to publish a large amount of information. This includes information about the fund that will be publicly available to everyone (through the Form ADV available via the SEC website) and more delicate information that has to be sent directly to the SEC. In addition, the SEC can perform an audit at any point in order and on any registered company to check that any published information is true. The SEC also has the power to refuse or cancel any registration. In addition, registered companies have to name a compliance officer, they have to develop policies to protect non-public information, to ensure that the client interest is maintained, and to implement a code of ethics.

In contrast, hedge fund managers did not until recently have to register with the SEC, enabling them to avoid complying with the elements mentioned here. This changed in 2012, and American hedge fund managers now have to be registered with the SEC. In fact, it was already the case in regulated European jurisdictions and most reputable managers were already registered in the US also. Nevertheless, this is an important move for the industry, which is becoming more institutionalized.

2.6   Audit

Mutual funds must maintain their performance track records and have them audited for accuracy, ensuring that investors can trust the fund's stated returns. There are no formal rules for hedge funds, however, even when almost all the funds available are audited. Some funds investing in less liquid strategies tend to perform additional audits, typically semi-annually or even quarterly.

2.7   Directors

Directors are important for both mutual funds and hedge funds. In broad terms, the role of the board is to oversee the management and operations of the fund on behalf of its shareholders. Directors also have significant and specific responsibilities under the federal securities laws. Among other things, they oversee the performance of the fund, approve the fees paid to the investment adviser for its services, and oversee the fund's compliance program. A director's role is to provide oversight and not to be involved in day-to-day management. In the United States, the rules governing directors of mutual funds are strict; the federal securities laws impose significant responsibilities on mutual fund directors, and on independent directors in particular. One of the board's most important statutory responsibilities is to annually evaluate and approve the fund's contract with the adviser. Directors also must approve certain distribution plans. The federal securities laws also specifically require directors to oversee, among other things, fair valuation determinations for certain securities held by the fund, voting of proxies for the fund's portfolio securities, the compliance function, which includes approving written policies and procedures, and the hiring and compensation of the fund's chief compliance officer. In addition they have to oversee the process by which fund disclosure (including prospectuses) is prepared, reviewed, revised, and updated. As part of its general oversight responsibilities, the board monitors various fund matters, including investment performance, risk management, custody of assets, and shareholder services.

While board sizes vary, the 1940 Act requires that in the US at least 40 per cent of the directors on a board of a mutual fund must be independent; which means they have no link with the asset management company. In practice, independent directors hold an overwhelming majority (75 per cent) of board seats in nearly 90 per cent of the mutual funds. But as hedge funds tend to be private, they do not have to comply with the same rule. In practice, the industry has evolved and nowadays every hedge fund board has to include independent directors in order to attract investors.

3   Hedge funds vs. mutual funds: the other main differences

Hedge funds differ from mutual funds in elements apart from the legal ones. The main differences include personal investment, objectives, securities in the portfolio, investment strategies and size of the industries.

3.1   Personal investment

The first difference between mutual and hedge fund managers is the fact that hedge fund managers tend to invest a significant part of their personal wealth in their own fund. In addition they are typically the owner, or at least partner, in the asset management company. Hedge fund management companies were historically created by one or more managers from successful long-only mutual fund houses, that moved into the hedge fund industry once they had acquired sufficient experience and usually when they had got the support of a series of investors. This has changed to some extent, as more and more alternative managers have now spent their entire career in the alternative world. While there is no legal constraint, many investors – particularly the institutional ones – require hedge fund managers to invest in the fund they manage. In the mutual fund industry this can also happen but it is not typical and not a prerequisite for investors.

3.2   Objectives

Mutual funds have by definition the objective of beating a reference benchmark. They typically invest in an investment range that is represented by this benchmark, and tend to take mainly relative bets in order to outperform this benchmark. When they anticipate that a constituent of the benchmark should outperform, they will increase their exposure to it and when they estimate that a constituent of the index should underperform, they will decrease their exposure; this is the rule, but there are, naturally, exceptions. But in hedge funds the objective is typically to offer absolute performance. This means that hedge funds as an industry aim to offer positive returns independent of the evolution of the market as a whole. Depending on the strategy, this objective will be determined on an annual basis or over a longer cycle. Typically, more volatile strategies will try to offer an absolute return over a three-to-five-year cycle, while less volatile strategies such as market neutral will typically try to offer positive returns over a year.

There are two main ways of comparing hedge fund performance. The first is to compare the fund to hedge fund indices such as those of Hedge

Fund Research, mentioned in Chapter 3. Either a general hedge fund index can be used, or a specific strategy index. This enables the potential investor to fix a point of comparison. Another way is to compare the hedge fund with its objective. Managers typically define the medium- to long-term performance objective either in absolute terms (for example the fund aims to offer an annualized gross return of 10 per cent per year over a three-to-five-year cycle) or by adding a performance target to a risk-free benchmark (for example the fund aims to offer Libor plus 3 per cent net over a twelve-month period). A comparison of the performance against this objective over time will enable the potential investor to gain a better idea of the profile of the fund. In practice, both comparisons should be made, and seen as a minimum.

Then there is another category of hedge funds, with a higher beta. These include emerging market equity funds, long-biased long/short equity funds, short-biased funds, sector funds or long-only leveraged funds in equities, and long-biased credit funds on the fixed-income side. Such funds should also be compared to their respective long-only index.

3.3 Securities used

Hedge funds are providing less liquidity than mutual funds. This means that hedge funds benefit from a greater stability in their asset base. In practice, while the assets of mutual funds tend to remain relatively stable over time, in the case of hedge funds it is a given as the number of exit dates is limited. Thanks to this characteristic, hedge funds are less dependent on asset flows, can take longer-term positions and can invest in less liquid securities. It is not a rule throughout the industry, but it is often the case and, more importantly, it can be the case during market stress. This is what happened during the second half of 2008 when markets came under pressure and liquidity disappeared. The most liquid strategies were able to pay on time, but a significant number of funds investing in less liquid strategies suspended redemptions for a few to several month.

3.4 Investment strategies

The investment strategies implemented by mutual fund managers tend to be defined by objective and not by market. Mutual funds typically have the objective of beating a benchmark, hence my contention that mutual funds are defined by objective. In the case of hedge funds, however, it is the market on which the fund operates that is predominant. For example, the convertible arbitrage strategy invests in convertibles, long/short equity funds are invested in equities, and fixed-income arbitrage funds focus on the fixed-income market. For hedge funds, the objective cannot be the most important criterion, as funds applying completely different strategies may have the same absolute return objective and a similar volatility profile. Several academic studies[11] have shown empirically that the strategies implemented by hedge fund managers are different from those implemented by mutual fund managers, being considerably more dynamic, and with frequent modifications tending to be made to the portfolio.

3.5 Size of the industries

There is another significant difference between the hedge and the mutual industries: the size of the industry. While the hedge fund industry has grown significantly, over the last ten to fifteen years, it nevertheless remains very small relative to the mutual fund industry. As a point of comparison, the American mutual fund industry had around US$11.6 trillion in assets at the end of 2011[12] while our estimate of the size of the hedge fund industry as a whole in that country was around US$2 trillion. Around the world, assets in mutual funds are estimated to be at US$23 trillion.[13] In addition, there is a significant difference regarding the size of the players; the largest mutual fund in the United States has over US$250 billion in assets[14] while the largest hedge fund has around US$77 billion.[15] As shown in Table 6.1, the tenth largest mutual fund has around US$68 billion in assets, against US$25 billion in the tenth largest hedge fund house. Note that these numbers include both passive and active mutual funds. In addition while the numbers reported for mutual funds are for specific vehicles, for hedge funds we consider the whole assets of the company made up of a series of individual product. The totals at the bottom indicate that the ten largest mutual funds reached a total over a US$1 trillion, half the size of the entire hedge fund industry.

3.6 Comparative summary

We summarize the main differences between hedge funds and mutual funds in Table 6.2. In the first part of the table, we show the main legal differences, while the second part of the table lists the other elements of differentiation.

4 Portfolio diversification

Capocci and Hübner (2001) carried out an analysis of the impact of inserting hedge funds and mutual funds into a portfolio made of bonds and equities. They concluded that hedge funds and mutual funds both help diversify the portfolio in risk–return terms but that hedge funds brought

Table 6.1   The ten largest hedge fund groups and the ten largest mutual funds in 2012

	Hedge fund managers			mutual funds	
	NAME	ASSETS (US$ billion)	STRATEGY	NAME	ASSETS (US$ billion)
1	Bridgewater Associates	77.6	Macro	Pimco Total Return	263
2	Man Group	64.5	Multiple strategies	Vanguard Total Stock Market Index Fund	190
3	JP Morgan Asset Management	46.6	Multiple strategies	American Funds Growth Fund of America	115
4	Brevan Howard Asset Management	36.6	Macro	Vanguard 500 Index Investor Fund	111
5	Och-Ziff Capital Management Group	28.5	Multiple strategies	Vanguard Total Bond Market Index	111
6	Paulson & Co.	28	Multiple strategies	American Funds EuroPacific Growth	94
7	BlackRock Advisors	27.7	Multi-strategy	Fidelity Contrafund	81
8	Winton Capital Management	27	CTA	American Funds Capital Income Builder	76
9	Highbridge Capital Management	26.1	Multiple strategies	American Funds Income Fund of America	72
10	BlueCrest Capital Management	25	Multi-strategy	Vanguard Total International Stock Index	68
	Total	106.1		Total	1181

significant diversification in a greater number of cases. In addition, the insertion of hedge funds into a diversified portfolio made up of bonds, equities and mutual funds will have a significant positive impact in most cases, while the addition of mutual funds to a portfolio made of bonds, equities and hedge funds is interesting in only rare cases.

Capocci, Duquenne and Hübner (2007) developed an original tool to determine the impact of the insertion of hedge funds on a portfolio made up of mutual funds invested in bonds and equities. They concluded that hedge funds offer attractive risk–return profiles when the measure of risk

Table 6.2 Differentiation factors between hedge funds and mutual funds

Hedge funds	Mutual funds
Private funds	Public funds
For high net worth investors	For any kind of investor
Mandatory information very limited	Mandatory information is important
Unconstrained short selling	Short selling very limited
Limited constraints on leverage	Very limited use of leverage
Unconstrained use of derivatives	Very limited use of derivatives
Free fee structure	Highly regulated fee structure
Limited number of investors	Unlimited number of investors
Limited obligations regarding audit	Independent audit is mandatory
Limited guarantee regarding directors' independence	Strict rule regarding independent directors
Liquidity defined by the manager	Daily to bi-weekly liquidity
Advertising is forbidden	Advertising is authorized but regulated
Significant investment by the manager is an informal industry rule	Significant investment by the manager is an exception
Management and performance fees	Only management fees
Absolute performance objective	Relative performance is offered
Monthly to quarterly liquidity	Liquidity typically daily
High minimum investments	Very low minimum investments
Small, growing industry	Large, mature industry
Investment strategies defined by market	Investment strategies defined by objective

used is the volatility, but their results are more muted when an extended risk measure is used Endnote: See Section 3.2.3 of Chapter 4 for a definition of the extended risk measure. A risk measure that integrates the asymmetry of the distribution and the presence of fat tails indicates that directional strategies and non-directional strategies have to be separated. The authors considered a range of risk profiles, their choice depending on the allocation to the risky asset Endnote: In this context, the risky asset includes equities and hedge funds investments (directional and non-directional)., known as lambda; for example, a portfolio with a lambda of 20 per cent has allocated 20 per cent of its assets to the risky asset. The addition of directional hedge funds into an initial portfolio made up of 50 per cent bond mutual funds and 50 per cent equity mutual funds does not add any value if less than 20 per cent of the portfolio is allocated to directional hedge funds. But when 50 per cent of the portfolio is allocated to directional hedge funds, the new profile is more attractive for every risk profile.

These results are illustrated in Figure 6.2. This figure shows the variations of the expected return of a portfolio when the proportion allocated

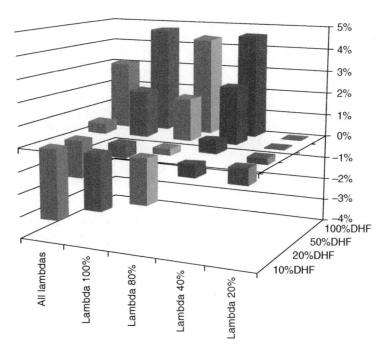

Figure 6.2 Inserting directional hedge funds in a portfolio made up of mutual funds

Note: DHF stands for directional hedge funds and lambda is the percentage of allocation to the risky asset.

Source: Capocci et al. (2007).

to directional hedge funds (DHF) goes from zero to 100 per cent for various levels of allocation to the risk-free asset (from 20 to 100 per cent). The expected return is significantly higher for higher allocation to directional hedge funds; for example, it is 4 per cent higher for a 40 per cent allocation to the risky asset that is represented by a full allocation to directional hedge funds.

The results regarding non-directional hedge funds and funds of hedge funds have been categorized as "non-directional hedge funds" (UHF) because they offer similar risk profiles. The addition of such non-directional hedge funds into an original portfolio made up of bonds and equities enables the investor to achieve higher returns very rapidly. Even at allocation levels to hedge funds of as low as 10 per cent, the impact may be statistically significant. For high allocations to the risky asset, however, non-directional hedge funds do not add value. Those results are illustrated in Figure 6.3.

The results obtained for directional funds are in contrast to those obtained for non-directional funds. This element indicates another point

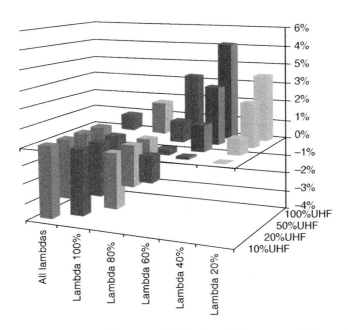

Figure 6.3 Inserting non-directional hedge funds into a portfolio made up of mutual funds

Note: UHF stands for non-directional hedge funds and lambda is the percentage of allocation to the risky asset.

Source: Capocci et al. (2007).

at which any general conclusions on the hedge fund industry as a whole should be made with particular care. It emphasizes the fact that directional strategies should be clearly differentiated from non-directional strategies; they do not offer the same profile, and should not be used by the same kind of investors. Broadly speaking, directional funds have to be used to gain additional returns and can replace or complete an exposure to equities, while non-directional funds help diversify a portfolio.

The study also analyses the impact of inserting mutual funds into a portfolio made up of hedge funds. The results indicate that mutual funds never help to diversify a portfolio made up of hedge funds, and this result is the same whether it is directional or non-directional hedge funds that are considered.

5 Summary

The final chapter focuses on three elements. We started by presenting the regulatory framework in which hedge funds are implemented with a particular focus on the United States, Europe and offshore jurisdictions. Our analysis indicates that there are still many different ways in which hedge funds can be set up, but that the legal framwork to implement hedge funds is improving. An important move was the implementation of UCITS III funds in Europe, which enabled managers to create public hedge funds. Another significant improvement will be the implementation of the AIFM Directive in 2013. While some countries such as Luxembourg provide a large degree of freedom to managers who set up private funds, others have implemented stricter rules. Our comparative analysis has helped us show that the main tend to be similar, even though each jurisdiction will have its own specific features.

While the creation of a hedge fund is quite common in the United States, the process can be longer and more complicated in some European countries than in others. This explains why European-based hedge funds tend to be set up mainly in Luxembourg and Ireland that have a favourable regulatory environment. The analysis of the rules governing offshore centres helped us to understand why the hedge funds have historically been based there.

The second part of this chapter focused on the main differences between hedge funds and mutual funds. We outlined the main legal differences first, using the American example. This analysis indicates that hedge fund managers have more freedom in the set up and management of their fund, whereas mutual funds have to comply with many constraints that aim to protect retail investors. Then, we enlarged the scope of our analysis to identify nearly 20 elements of differentiation.

The third part of this chapter covered the added value of hedge funds in a portfolio context. We reported the results of an academic study that analysed the added value of hedge funds within classical portfolios. This study, interestingly, used an extended risk measure that integrated the asymmetry of the distribution of returns and fat tail risk, which are important elements to integrate when analysing hedge funds. The results clearly also stressed that directional hedge funds should be seen as an improved proxy to equities while non-directional hedge funds and funds of hedge funds help investors diversify their portfolio. The results indicate that hedge funds offer characteristics totally different from those of mutual funds, and that the two types of investment product should probably be seen as complements to one another, rather than as competitors. Hedge funds tend to outperform mutual funds during difficult markets but most funds will lag long-only products during market rallies. All in all, diversification remains key.

Conclusion

Hedge funds form part of the investment universe of numerous investors, but the secretiveness surrounding these funds left them vulnerable to a bad press for a long time, and more recent events have led to a fear of these investment products. There have been some fraud cases, of which Madoff was the apotheosis, and there has of course been the liquidity issues that directly affected the industry late in 2008. While cases of fraud have undeniably existed, they have remained marginal in an industry that at that time included over 10,000 funds. With regard to liquidity, we do have to concede that, unlike in 2002, the vast majority of hedge funds were not able to offer attractive returns in 2008. But is that a sufficient reason not to invest or to consider such products? Certainly not!

We have described the hedge fund industry since its infancy. We spent time on the cornerstone of this industry before focusing on its development and its worldwide presence nowadays. Hedge funds have always offered something different from traditional mutual funds. Our illustrated detailed analysis of every investment strategy available shows that this industry has reached a phase of maturity, and that almost any investor should be able to find a product suited to their needs.

To reap most advantage from the system, it is however necessary either to undergo continuous training or to use competent specialized advisors, as the range is broad and the opportunity set very large; it is not the same as buying into equities, bonds, a mutual fund or an alternative fund. Structures tend to be smaller, the information flows less frequent and the liquidity constrained. More importantly, the investment strategy applied by hedge fund managers are complex and, in every single case, personallized. Each manager will manage his/her fund using his/her own investment process and his/her own rules and style. It is clear that there will be more similarities between two fund managers applying the same strategy than between two applying different ones, but each fund manager will apply his or her own strategy and investment process; they will build a portfolio specific to their profile in terms of risk and return. A series of elements such as diversification (geographical, sectorial, in terms of market capitalization or bond ratings for example), the number of positions, the concentration of the portfolio, the potential hedging of some risks, the decision as whether or not to be present in certain markets and many other factors will impact the profile and will be specific to the manager under review. To consider an investment into hedge funds, an investor should know and understand each strategy in detail, individualizing each fund in order to differentiate each manager from the others and to pick the desired fund; this way they can take an informed decision, not merely on the basis of past performance or thanks to a contact perceived as good.

This leads us to a new debate that has been raging in the industry. Can we offer hedge fund-like return with the use of a series of betas and not by searching for alpha? An increasing number of players of the industry today propose investable indices that aim to offer a beta exposure to the hedge fund industry and/or a particular investment strategy. Is this the future of alternative investments?

The answer is no. Such products have a market and will be of interest to certain clients or in some contexts to investors who want to rapidly move their exposure to hedge funds or to a strategy without having to perform long and costly due diligences – but this market will remain peripheral to the hedge fund industry. I position myself on the side of the search for alpha. Over the long term it is much more interesting to work to identify the managers that are building the hedge fund industry of tomorrow by their success rather than investing in a beta product that aims to replicate an average manager.

The industry lost as much as 20 per cent in 2008 – but it recovered slightly more than half of that in 2009 and close to a quarter of the funds were able to hit their high-water mark within 12 to 18 months of the crisis. This proves that the hedge fund industry is still alive and kicking. A good due diligence should enable investors to pick funds from amongst the 50 per cent best ones, even from the best 25 per cent – and this way a manager should be able to offer alpha rather than beta to their clients.

The third chapter of the book is particularly interesting because in it there are details of each investment strategy. Those examples illustrate the difficulty in understanding the subtleties of each investment strategy. Any investor can understand the principles of an alternative strategy from a few lines of description, but the practical examples compound the challenges. These examples demand more reflection, but they illustrate more precisely the opportunity and potential risks of each strategy. Every direct investor into hedge funds should be able to explain each strategy and to illustrate this with practical example; if they cannot do this, they should probably focus on mutual funds or funds of funds, or hire an adviser.

The last three chapters complete the picture. They put the hedge fund industry into overall perspective. Performance and statistics are analysed first, then the bailout of Long-Term Capital Management and the role of hedge funds during crisis have been covered in detail. Finally, hedge funds have to respect the laws and regulations that are continuously evolving; for better or for worse they have been involved in financial crises and they are different from mutual funds. The regulation element is particularly important as there have already been important changes regarding public funds, through the UCITS regulation that has enabled the implementation of several hedge fund strategies into retail products, and as we are facing the implementation of the AIFM Directive that will fundamentally change the state of play for non-UCITS funds sold into Europe.

We would like to finish this book by stressing how much pleasure it has been to analyse hedge funds – or alternative funds as they can also be called – for almost fifteen year. The managers in these funds have the opportunity to do almost anything and everything to make money and, in the vast majority of the cases, have done this ethically, in a world where you can perform over the long term only if they work in a win–win situation not only with their clients but also with the companies you invest in. The hedge fund industry was already interesting a few years ago when I published my first French book. Since then it has evolved a lot, but even though it is completely different today it is still exciting.

So, where do we go from here? The industry will continue its development but also its consolidation where the largest and best players will continue to gain more and more interest. Its evolution will probably continue to accelerate. It is not clear whether retail investors will be able to gain access to the whole spectrum of hedge funds, but it is clear that the investors who continue to analyse the industry in detail – those who work hard to understand the investment strategies, their evolution and their place in today's world and in investment portfolios – should be able to profit from this development and should be getting strong positive absolute returns over time.

Appendix: The CAIA association

Below, I introduce the association of the alternative industry that includes hedge funds, real estate, private equity and commodity trading advisors. It provides an interesting platform for those who would like to go further in the development of their knowledge of alternative investments in general and hedge funds in particular.

The Chartered Alternative Investment Analyst Association® is the global benchmark for alternative investment education. It administers the CAIA designation and exams; sponsors research and publications; connects alternative investment experts around the world, and advocates the highest standards in professional conduct. The CAIA Association has more than 5700 members in 80 countries, and 15 affiliated chapters in the following locations: San Francisco, Los Angeles, New York, Boston, Chicago, Canada, London, Switzerland, Luxembourg, Spain, France, Germany, Hong Kong, Singapore and Korea.

More information about the Association can be found at: www.caia.org.

Notes

Preface

1. In July 1995, Barron published a list of statistics of individual funds from the MAR database, one of the main databases provider at this time. The Securities and Exchange Commission announced that any future publication containing this kind of information could lead to a stricter regulation for the funds mentioned. Since then, the rules have been clarified and, as private vehicles, hedge funds may remain discreet regarding disclosure of information.

1 What is a Hedge Fund?

1. Source: https://thehfa.org/aboutus
2. Source: Nicholas (1999, p. 24).
3. Source: http://www.investopedia.com/terms/h/hedgefund.asp#axzz1sKoZomIX
4. See p. 4 of the glossary of http://www.sec.gov/rules/final/2011/ia-3308-formpf.pdf
5. We describe short selling in Section 8 of Chapter 2.
6. We define leverage in Section 9 of Chapter 2.
7. We define alternative investment strategies in Chapter 3.
8. Source: Loomis (1966).
9. Source: Loomis(1970).
10. Source: Securities and Exchange Commission (1969).
11. Source: Tremont Partners Inc. and TASS Investment Research (1999)
12. We analyse the correlation between hedge funds and classic investment products in Section 5 of Chapter 4.
13. We present the hedge fund academic literature in Section 3 of Chapter 4.
14. We define alternative investment strategies in Chapter 3.
15. See Chapter 6 for more information on this topic.
16. Source: Fiford (2004).
17. Our estimations of 46% of hedge fund assets in offshore jurisdictions is probably on the lower end of the estimation range. The AIMA, for example, estimates that 60% of hedge funds assets are in offshore centres.
18. We define "attrition rate" as the ratio of dissolved funds divided by the global number of existing funds.
19. We define alternative investment strategies in Chapter 3.
20. The AIMA estimates that there are approximately 850 European hedge funds, 500 managers for assets around $350 billions.
21. Source: www.mondoalternative.com
22. This estimation is probably on the higher end as the AIMA for example estimates that there are 750 Asian hedge funds managing $140 billion in assets.
23. As a point of reference, we estimated that long/short equity funds represented around 60 per cent of the Asian industry in 2008.
24. Source: Australian Trade Commission (2011).
25. The estimated number of funds in an industry varies from a provider to another.
26. This number does not take into account the double-counting of individual funds that may also be in funds of funds.

27. 'Emerging Europe' includes Turkey, while "Eastern Europe" does not.
28. Source: Soros (2000).
29. See Section 7.2 of Chapter 2 for a definition of the term "high-water mark."
30. Source: money.cnn.com/2000/03/30/mutualfunds/q_funds_tiger/
31. Source: Moody Subramanian (1995).
32. Source: Strom (1995).
33. Source: *FIN Alternatives* (2011) and *Institutional Investor* (2011).

2   Hedge Fund Characteristics

1. Unless stated differently, all the numbers reported in this section come from the websites of the respective database providers as of the end of 2012.
2. These numbers are from the websites of the corresponding companies.
3. Other database providers not analyzed here include Hedge Fund Intelligence and Bloomberg.
4. See http://alternativeinvestments.morningstar.com/pandora/docs/factsheets/Mstar-MSCI-Indexes.pdf for more information.
5. More and more data providers group funds by investment strategy while providing an additional classification by investment region or country. In our analysis we focus only on comparison by strategy.
6. Commodity Trading Advisers.
7. See Capocci, D. *An Analysis of Hedge Fund Strategies*, PhD thesis, Université de Liège, 2007, freely available on www.ssrn.com.
8. For more information on that topic, please seeEurohedge (1999).
9. In investment, alpha denotes the perception of a measure of the active return. It is risk-adjusted, meaning it is the return less a sum compensating for risk.
10. For more information on the investment strategies listed, please see Chapter 3.
11. In September 2002, two mortgage-backed securities funds managed by Beacon Hill Asset Management suffered from this. The managers did not trust the quantitative model, which led to the funds losing 10 per cent unlevered. The funds lost more than 50 per cent in total, as the funds were levered five times.
12. Source: Deloitte Research (2007).
13. Source: Technical Committee of the International Organization of Securities Commissions (2007).
14. We illustrate this risk in the first part of Chapter 5, presenting the bailout of Long-Term Capital Management.
15. Two elements ta balance this liquidity risk is that hedge fund liquidity terms have improved since the liquidity crisis and that this liquidity risk is more present in some strategies like distressed securities.
16. Source: The Bank of New York and Amber Partners (2006).
17. Source: Capco (2003).
18. Legal constraints are presented in Section 1 Chapter 6: the regulatory environment.
19. We define this term in Section 1.2 of Chapter 6 in the case of United States and Canada.
20. Funds applying equity market neutral and long/short strategies do not ask for a lockup period any more, and they tend to offer monthly liquidity with a 30-day notice period.
21. We estimate that this investor is the only one to redeem at the end of December.
22. If the fund stops accepting new investment but re-opens to existing investors after significant outflows, this should be seen as a European option.
23. Source: Casar and Gerakos (2008).

24. Source: Prequin (2009).
25. Source: Prequin (2009).
26. They make a profit as long as the sum of the cash gained from the sale plus the interest posted as collateral less the commission paid to borrow the securities is worth more than the securities bought. If they make a loss they will have to pay cash before being able to close the positions.
27. A repo, also called repurchase agreement, is an agreement by which one counter-party sells a security agreeing to buy it again later at a slightly higher price.
28. As an example we can consider a manager investing in Asian equities who decided during the first few volatile months of 2008 to take a long position through futures while hedging the risk of the portfolio by using individual stocks. This positioning would enable him/her to reposition the fund rapidly in case of rapid growth by using futures while trying to extract alpha on its stock selection capabilities on the short side.
29. Bertelli (2007).
30. See Gregoriou (2002) for an interesting paper on the subject.
31. We refer to the possibility of hedge funding market risk through futures for UCITS III funds.
32. Source: Russell Research (2012).
33. On this topic see, for example, Fung and Hsieh (1997), Ackermann et al. (1999), Liang (1999), Agarwal and Naik (1999), Capocci and Hübner (2003), Capocci and Mahieu (2003). We analyse the correlation between hedge funds and classic investment products in Chapter 4, Section 8: Correlation.
34. For more information see Capocci (2007).
35. See for example Jaeger and Wagner (2005).
36. Some academic authors are specialists on this topic.
37. An ETF (also called a tracker) is a financial product that can be traded on the main exchanges. It offers the performance of an index or a set of shares (sector, country or region) and can be traded like an equity.
38. In investment, "beta" denotes the perceived overall market risk; it is a measure of the extent to which the returns on a given stock have moved with the stock market. For full information, see Section 3.2.1.

3 Investment Strategies

1. In our performance analysis we have used the Barclays Aggregate Bond index as an approximation of the bond market, and the MSCI World Total Return for equities. The HFRI Global Fund Weighted index is used for comparison.
2. Those criticisms are true of all the hedge fund indices available. We chose the Hedge Fund Research indices because firstly they have become standard and secondly most other indices tend to have more serious biases.
3. Source: www.hedgefundresearch.com.
4. We describe these events in more detail in Section 1 of Chapter 5: *Long-Term Capital Management*.
5. We present some basic principles of duration and convexity in Appendix C.
6. Please note that this is true for a limited movement of interest rates only and that it is necessary to perform a deeper analysis and to introduce the concept of convexity for this relation to remain stable for large rate spreads.
7. If we do not consider the option premium, the manager invested US$10m in the bonds for six months, ending up with a US$2.3m profit and a return of around 23 per cent over six months.
8. Source: www.hedgefundresearch.com

9. See for example F. Fabozzi (2005).

10. This example comes from Andrew Bonita from Bonita Capital Management.

11. Preferred shares are a class of ownership in a corporation with a higher claim on the assets and earnings than has common stock. Preferred shares generally has a dividend that must be paid out before dividends to common stockholders but preference shares do not usually have voting rights.

12. We present convertibles in more detail in Appendix B.

13. The delta is a measure of the movement of the price of the convertible against a marginal move in the price of the underlying asset, see Appendix 3, The Greeks.

14. This delta-neutral position does not mean that the whole portfolio is hedged against moves in the price of the underlying security, but that the manager hedges his or her global position relative to a variation in the price of the underlying security while keeping an exposure to other factors such as gamma or theta. We define these in Appendix E.

15. If you are interested in the precise analysis of the impact of the underlying hypothesis of correlation in the case of convertible arbitrage, we recommend you read Capocci (2003b). In this study we analyse the real impact of the correlation on the performance of a portfolio made of convertibles and equities sold short.

16. Delta is a measure of the impact of a marginal movement of the price of the underlying asset on the price of the convertible. This measure is correct for marginal price movements only. Gamma is a measure of the sensitivity of the delta to variations in the price of the underlying security. It is a measure of volatility. For full information on these, plus on theta and vega, please see Appendix E, The Greeks.

17. In practice we distinguish historical volatility based on past prices of the underlying asset from implicit volatility based on model estimation.

18. We thank Andrej Rojek from Lydian Asset Management for providing the BRE Properties and Reva Pharmaceuticals examples.

19. A callable bond is a bond that can be redeemed by the issuer. A premium is paid to the bond owner when the bond is called.

20. A puttable bond is a bond that allows the holder to redeem the bond at a predetermined price at specified future dates without obligation.

21. See Section 6.3 for more information on activism and Section 9 for PIPE funds.

22. In most jurisdicitions, every shareholder that holds more than 5 per cent of a company has to make this information public.

23. We would like to thank Guilherme Carvalho and Nick Walker from York Asset Management Limited (Rio de Janeiro and New York) for having provided examples 2, 3 and 4 on the cash deal, the stock-for-stock deal and the unsuccessful deal.

24. The rating system is presented in Appendix A.

25. Market capitalization represents the consensus on the value of a company's equity. It is defined as the share price multiplied by the number of shares.
    Traditionally, companies are divided into large-cap (over US$10 billion, mid-cap between US$2 and 10 billion), and small-cap (below USUS2 billion).

26. A warrant is a security that gives to its holder the right to buy the shares of a company at a fixed price over a defined period.

27. During significant difficulties, management teams are often changed. Depending on the specific case, the fund manager will be active or passive in this process.

28. We thank Professional Traders Management, LLC for providing these examples.

29. The size of the top right part of the right triangle will be a function of the price of the securities held on the long side and the holding on the short side.

30. When managers aim to have a totally market neutral global position, the strategy is different. In this case we are talking about equity market neutral funds.

31. See Appendix E for a definition of delta.

32. An option is the right to buy a security at a certain moment for a certain price. Put options represent a right to sell a security. An out-of-the-money put option is

an option with a strike price that is lower than the market price of the underlying security. An out-of-the-money option has no intrinsic value but only possesses time value.

33. Source: www.hedgefundresearch.com
34. Source: http://data.worldbank.org/about/country-classifications
35. Thanks to Jamie Handwerker, manager of the CRM Windridge fund at CRM, LLC for giving me these three examples.
36. Source: www.hedgefundresearch.com
37. This is a measure commonly used to determine the value of a hospital.
38. Source: www.hedgefundresearch.com
39. Source: www.hedgefundresearch.com
40. For more information on rho, see Appendix E, The Greeks.
41. Source: Nicholas (1999), President of Hedge Fund Research, Inc.
42. Source: www.hedgefundresearch.com
43. Thanks to Martin Blum portfolio manager at Ithuba Capital for providing me with this example.
44. See for example Fung and Hsieh (1997, 2000), Schneeweis and Spurgin (1998), Edwards and Liew (1999) and Brown et al. (2001).
45. For more details see, for example, Della Cas et al. (2007).
46. Trackers, also called exchange-traded funds or ETFs, are financial products negotiable on the main world exchange. They offer the performance of an index or a set of shares, such as a sector, a country or a region, and they can, like equities, be traded intraday.
47. The Russell 2000 ishares is an American equity index that measures the performance of the smallest two thousand companies included in the Russell 3000. The Russell 3000 measures the performance of the three thousands smallest American companies as measured by their market capitalisation.
48. Thanks to Fredrik Huhtamäki from Estlander & Partners for providing this example.
49. Thanks to Guillaume Jamet from Lyxor Asset Management for providing this example.
50. COMEX is the primary market for trading metals such as gold, silver, copper and aluminium. Formerly known as the Commodity Exchange Inc., the COMEX merged with the New York Mercantile exchange in 1994, and became the division responsible for metal trading.
51. Source: www.hedgefundresearch.com
52. Due diligence is a process that includes a quantitative and qualitative analysis of a fund manager, a fund or an administrator. During this process, every aspect of the fund and the fund management company is analysed in detail. It also commonly includes one or more meetings with the management team. It is normally performed by an institutional investor before considering any investment.
53. The principals usually include the fund managers, but this is not always the case.
54. My PhD. thesis is a good introduction to the tools available: see Capocci, D. *An Analysis of Hedge Fund Strategies*, August 2007, University of Liège, freely available on www.ssrn.com.
55. Source: www.hedgefundresearch.com
56. Thanks to Bruno Sanglé-Ferrière of Carrousel Capital for providing the two examples cited.
57. Notional is the issuance amount of a bond, or the amount contracted for a derivative product.
58. These are separate legal entities that proposed access to the same strategy and portfolio to various investors. Strategies are usually proposed in onshore US version to US investors and offshore for non-US and US tax-exempt investors.

4   Hedge Fund Performance Over Time

1. D. Capocci, *An Analysis of Hedge Fund Strategies*, August 2007, University of Liège (Belgium), available on www.ssrn.com.
2. We outlined the main characteristics of hedge fund database providers in Section 1 of Chapter 2.
3. For more information on the subject, please see Fung and Hsieh (2000), Liang (2000) and Capocci and Hübner (2003).
4. See Gregoriou (2002) for a complete analysis.
5. Source: Capocci (2007).
6. See Fung and Hsieh (2000), Liang (2000) and Capocci and Hübner (2003).
7. This bias comes from the fact that when new funds are added into a database, historical returns are backfilled. This may overstate the industry performance as managers will only report past performance if it is attractive.
8. See for example Brooks and Kat (2001), Liew (2003) and Amenc and Martellini (2003).
9. Amenc and Martellini (2003) analysed the differences in performance of the various hedge fund indices that approximate the same investment strategies. They estimated differences of up to 22 per cent in a single month for similar strategies.
10. For full information about omega, see Section 3.2.4.
11. The skewness is the third central moment. It is a measure of the symmetry of a distribution of returns. A positively skewed return distribution is desirable and it has a median higher than its mean while a negatively skewed return distribution is not desirable and has a median lower than its mean.
12. The kurtosis is the fourth central moment. It is a measure of the flatness of a distribution of returns and of the presence of fat tails. A positive excess kurtosis indicates a return distribution with larger fat tails than the normal distribution and a greater chance to face important losses or gains.
13. A return distribution with fat tails is a probability distribution of an assets that has a greater chance of giving largerly positive or negative outcomes compared to a normal distribution. The tails of the distribution are fatter than the ones of a normal distribution.
14. This whole section is based on a review of the litterature performed in Capocci (2007).
15. Look-back options are exotic option. The payoff depends on the optimal (maximum or minimum) underlying asset's price occurring over the life of the option. The option allows the holder to "look-back" over time to determine the final payoff.
16. A linex is a specific utility function and it is made of a linear plus an exponential one. Such a function has some desirable additional properties including decreasing absolute risk aversion. See Bell (1988) for more information.
17. Correlation is defined as a standardized statistical measure of the interdependence of two variables. It is a measure of the correlation coefficient, that is the ratio of the covariance between the two series and the product of the respective standard deviations. The value of this coefficient will always be between −1 and +1; the closer the coefficient to +1, the higher the relation between the two series.
18. The Barclays Capital Aggregate Bond index, previously the Lehman Aggregate Bond index, is a broad-base index which has been maintained by Barclays Capital since it took over the index business of the now defunct Lehman Brothers, and it is often used to represent investment grade bonds traded in United States.
19. The MSCI Emerging Markets index is a free float-adjusted market capitalization index designed to measure equity market performance in the global emerging markets.

20. This is an unmanaged index considered to be representative of the fixed-rate, non-investment-grade debt of companies in the US, developed markets and emerging markets.
21. This is an unmanaged world production-weighted index composed of the principal physical commodities in active liquid futures markets.
22. Correlation coefficients are estimated throughout the January 1999 to September 2009 period. The exceptions are the HIFR Fixed Income-Asset Backed index, created in January 1993, the HFRI Private Issue/Regulation D, created in January 1996, the HFRI Sector – Energy/Basic Materials, created in January 1995, and the HFRI Sector – Technology/Healthcare index, created in January 1991.
23. See Capocci (2009).
24. The strategies defined are convertible arbitrage, distressed securities, equity hedge, equity market neutral, event driven, macro, merger arbitrage, relative value arbitrage and volatility.

5 Hedge Funds, LTCM and Recent Crises

1. Source: Greenspan (1998).
2. Wall Street Journal (1998).
3. See Section 11 of Chapter 3 for a detailed analysis of the fixed-income arbitrage strategy.
4. The skew or skewness measures the asymmetry of the probability density function. Qualitatively, a negative skewness indicates that the tail on the left side of the function is longer than that on the right side, and the bulk of the values, including the median, lie to the right of the mean. A positive skewness indicates that the tail on the right side is longer than that on the left, and the bulk of the values lie to the left of the mean. A zero value indicates that the values are relatively evenly distributed on both sides of the mean, typically implying a symmetric distribution. Kurtosis is any measure of the presence of fat tails in a probability density function. A positive excess kurtosis indicates a higher propensity to undergo infrequent extreme deviations rather than frequent modest-size deviations.
5. Congress created the Commodity Futures Trading Commission (CFTC) in 1974 as an independent agency with the mandate to regulate commodity futures and option markets in the United States.
6. Source: Lowenstein (2000).
7. Source: Jorion (2000).
8. See for example International Monetary Fund (1993) or Eichengreen et al. (1998).
9. The UK's entry into the ERM was intended as a precursor for its full integration into Europe's single currency, the Eurozone. However, the 1992 crash forced the UK's withdrawal from the ERM.
10. The rejection created doubt on the importance that European countries were giving to stability in the currency exchange rate.
11. To hedge their exposures, banks sold an equal amount of currencies on the cash market and entered a currency swap of the same maturity in the forward contract.
12. Source: Brown (2000).
13. See for example Frankel et al. (1996) or the International Monetary Fund (1995).
14. Source: Chapman, Spira and Carson (1999).
15. See for example Chapter 10 of Hoogvelt (2001), or Farley (1997).
16. See for example Eichengreen et al. (1998) and Brown et al. (1998).
17. Those currencies include the Philippine peso, the Taiwanese dollar, the Japanese yen, the Malaysian ringgit, the Singapore dollar and the Indonesian rupee.

18. The role of current account deficits as a source of tensions in financial markets has been stressed several times in the literature. On this subject, see between others Dornbusch et al. (1995), Ferretti et al. (1996a and b), Mishkin (1996), Kaminsky et al. (1998) and Roubini and Wachtel (1998).
19. A Jumbo mortgage is a credit given for an amount above the limits defined by the American government-backed agencies such as Freddie Mac and Fannie Mae.
20. The Alt-A category of mortgage is a categorization of credit and of borrowers for incomplete credit files and for files that are not standard in terms of real estate property, borrowing rate or anything regarding the documentation.
21. All the details can be found on the Federal Reserve Bank of New York's website, starting at http://www.newyorkfed.org. Every transaction is posted shortly after it is completed.
22. As an example, Deutsche Bank estimate that the total losses linked to the sub-prime crisis total between US$300 and US$400 billion, while UBS estimate those losses amount to US$480 billion.
23. See Dodd and Mills (2008).
24. For more details on each of these developments, please see Dodd and Mills (2008).
25. This delinquency rate rose past 100 per cent as early as April 2007.

6 Hedge Funds, Regulation and Mutual Funds

1. We will present those structures in detail later in the chapter.
2. European Directive 85/611/EU
3. See Danielsson and Zigrand (2007) for an in-depth analysis of the subject. Most of my arguments in this section come from this book.
4. For more information on the Amaranth story, see Thill (2006)
5. Source: Chapman and Cutler (2012)
6. Source: Securities and Exchange Commission (2012)
7. The Financial Conduct Authority (FCA) replaced the Financial Services Authority (FSA) in 2013 to become the new regulator in the United Kingdom.
8. Organisation for Economic Co-operation and Development
9. Langston Sibblies, Deputy Managing Director – General Council of the Cayman Islands Monetary Authority reported at the annual AIMA Conference in January 2007 that 7500 mutual funds had at least one of the characteristics of hedge funds.
10. See for example Fung and Hsieh (1997)
11. Recent regulations changes may balance this argument more in the future.
12. Source: Investment Company Institute (2012)
13. Source: Investment Company Institute (2012)
14. Source: Erne (2012).
15. Source: Burton et al. (2012)

Bibliography

Ackermann, C. and D. Ravenscraft, "The Impact of Regulatory Restrictions on Fund Performance: a Comparative Study of Hedge Funds and Mutual Funds", Working paper, University of Notre-Dame, 1998.

Ackermann, C., R. McEnally and D. Ravenscraft, "The Performance of Hedge Funds: Risk, Return, and Incentives," *Journal of Finance*, 54, 1999, 833–74.

Agarwal, V. and N. Naik, "Multi-Period Performance Persistence Analysis of Hedge Funds," *Journal of Financial and Quantitative Analysis*, 35, 2000, 327–42.

Agarwal, V. and N. Naik, "Risk and Portfolio Decisions involving Hedge Funds," *Review of Financial Studies*, 17, 1, spring 2004, 63–98.

Agarwal, V., "Intertemporal Variation in the Performance of Hedge Funds Employing a Contingent-Claim-Based Benchmark", Working paper, London Business School, 2001.

Alternative Investment Management Association, *Guide to Sound Practices for European Hedge Fund Managers*, AIMA Special Report, 2002.

Alternative Investment Management Association and ASSIRT, *Hedge Fund Booklet*, AIMA Special Report, 2002.

Aley, J., "Wall Street's King Quant," *Fortune*, 5 February 1996.

Amenc, N., *Three Early Lessons from theSubprime Lending Crisis:A French Answer to President Sarkozy*, August 2007.

Amenc, N., S. El Biedand and L. Martellini, "Predictability in Hedge Fund Returns," *Financial Analysts Journal*, 59, 5, 2003, 32–46.

Amenc, N., L. Martellini and M. Vaissié, *Benefits and Risks of Alternative Investment Strategies*, Working paper, MISYS/EDHEC multi-style/multi-class research program, 2002.

Amenc, N., Curtis S. and L. Martellini, *The Alpha and Omega of Hedge Fund Performance Measurement*, Working Paper, Edhec Risk and Asset Management Research Centre, 2002.

Amenc N., S. El Bied and L. Martellini, "Predictability in Hedge Fund Returns," *Financial Analysts Journal*, 59, 5, 2002, 32–46.

Amenc N. and L. Martellini, *The Brave New World of Hedge Funds Indices*, EDHEC Risk & Asset Management Research Centre, Working paper, 2003.

Amin, G and H. Kat, *Welcome to the Dark Side - Hedge Fund Attrition and Survivorship Bias over the period 1994–2001*, ICMA Centre Discussion Papers in Finance , Henley Business School, Reading University, 2001.

Amin, G. S. and H. M. Kat, "Hedge Fund Performance 1990–2000: Do the 'Money Machine' really add Value?," *Journal of Financial and Quantitative Analysis*, 38, 2, 2003a, 251–74.

Amin, G. S. and H. M. Kat, "Stocks, Bonds, and Hedge Funds," *Journal of Portfolio Management,* 29, 4, 2003b, 113–120.

Anjilvel, S. I., B. E. Boudreau, B. J. Johmann, M. l. W. Perskinand and M. S. Urias, "Hedge Funds – Strategy and Portfolio Insight," *Global Equity and Derivatives Markets, Morgan Stanley Quantitative Strategies*, XI, 12, December 2001, 1–16.

Anonymous, Barron, 10 July 1995, p.15.

541

Anonymous, BusinessWeek, "What's Bigger Than Cisco, Coke, Or McDonald's? Steve Feinberg's Cerberus, a Vast Hedge Fund that's Snapping up Companies – Lots of Them," 10 March 2005.

Assness, C, Krail, R. and J. Liew, "Do Hedge Funds Hedge," *Journal of Portfolio Management*, 28, 1, 2001, 6–19.

Australian Broadcasting Corporation, *Malaysian ex-premier Mahathir and billionaire Soros end feud*, 15 December 2006.

Australian Trade Commission, *Australian Hedge Funds*, August 2011 Australian Government, August 2011, http://www.austrade.gov.au

Bams, D. and R. Otten, "European Mutual Fund Performance," *European Financial Management*, 8, 1, 2002, 75–101.

Bank of International Settlements, *A Review of Financial Market Events in Autumn 1998*, Committee on the Global Financial System, Publication no 12, 1999.

Banking Technology, *European Hedge Fund*, Banking Technology Report, Informa Business, 1999.

Basilico P., *Il settore degli hedge funds in Italia*, Derivatives Expo de FOW, Milan, 22 May 2002.

Barham S. and C. Bonnett, *Starting a Hedge Fund – European Perspective*, ISI Publications, July 2005, 236p.

Barès, P-A, R. Gibson and S. Gyger, "Performance in the Hedge Fund Industry: An Analysis of Short and Long Term Persistence," *The Journal of Alternative Investments*, 6, 3, 2003, 25–41.

BBC News, *The US Sub-Prime Crisis in Graphics*, 21 November 2007, http://news.bbc.co.uk/2/hi/business/7073131.stm

Bear Sterns, *Starting a Hedge Fund*, Bear Sterns Seminars, 2000.

Bell, D. E, "One-Switch Utility Functions and a Measure of Risk," *Management Science*, 34, 12, 1988, 1416–24.

Beziz, P. and G. Petit, *The Mexican Crisis: were Signals Inadequate?*, Organisation pour la Coopération and le Développement Économique, May 1997.

Bekier, M., *Marketing of Hedge Funds*, PhD thesis in marketing, St. Gallen University, Switzerland, 1996.

Bessis, J., *Risk Management in Banking*, John Wiley and Sons, 2000.

Bessembinder, H., "Systematic Risk, Hedging Pressure, and Risk Premiums in Futures Markets," *Review of Financial Studies*, 5, 4, 2002, 637.

Berenyi, Z., "Measuring Hedge Fund Risk with Multi-moment Risk Measures," *Working Paper Series*, April 2002, available at SSRN: http://ssrn.com/abstract=309699

Bertelli, R., *Financial Leverage: Risks and Performance in Hedge Fund Strategies*, Working Paper, Department of Economic Law, University of Siena Italy, January 2007, 13p.

Billingsley, R. S. and D. M. Chance, "The Benefits and Limits of Diversification Among Commodity Trading Advisors," *Journal of Portfolio Management*, 23, 1, Fall 1996, 65–80.

Black Rock, *The Rise of UCITS III*, 2011.

Bollen N. and R. Whaley, "Hedge Fund Risk Dynamics: Implications for Performance Appraisal," *Journal of Finance*, 64, 2009, 987–1037.

Bourguinat H., *Finance Internationale*, 4th edition, Thémis Économie, 1999.

Brealy, R. A and E. Kaplanis, "Hedge Funds and Financial Stability: An Analysis of their Factor Exposures, *International Finance*, 4, 2001, 161–87.

Brorsen, B.W., and J. P. Townsend,, "Performance Persistence for Managed Futures," *Journal of Alternative Investments*, 4, 2002, 57–61.

Brown, S. J., Goetzmann, W. N. and R. G. Ibbotson, "Offshore Hedge Funds: Survival and Performance 1989–1995," *Journal of Business*, 72, 1, 1999, 91–118.

Brown, S. J., Goetzmann, W. N. and B. Liang, "Fees on Fees in Funds-on-Funds," *Journal of Investment Management*, 2, 4, 2002, 39–56.

Brown, S. J., Goetzmann, W. N. and J. Park, "Careers and Survival: Competition and Risk in the Hedge Fund and CTA Industry," *Journal of Finance*, 56, 5, 2001, 1869–86.

Brooks, C. and H. Kat, "The Statistical Properties of Hedge Fund Index Returns and their Implications for Investors," *Journal of Alternative Investment*, 5, 2, 2002, 26–44.

Brown W., *Convertible Arbitrage: Opportunity and Risk*, Tremont White Paper, November 2000.

Brittain, B., "Hedge Funds and the Institutional Investor," *Journal of International Financial Management and Accounting*, 12, 2, Summer 2001, 225–34.

Brooks, C. and H. Kat, *The Statistical Properties of Hedge Fund Index Returns and their Implication for Investors*, Working paper, The University of Reading, ISMA Center, 2001.

Brown, S., W. Goetzmann and R. Ibbotson, "Offshore Hedge Funds: Survival and Performance 1989–1995," *Journal of Business*, 72, 1999, 91–118.

Brown S, W. Goetzmann, B. Liang and C. Schwarz, Trust and Delegation, *Journal of Financial Economics*, volume 103, 2, February 2012, 221–234.

Brown S., T. Fraser and B. Liang, Hedge Fund Due Diligence: A source of Alpha in a Hedge Fund Portfolio Strategy, *Journal of Investment Management* 6(4), 2008, 23–33.

Brown S., G. Gregoriou and R. Pascalau, Review of Asset Pricing Studies, 2012, available at SSRN: http://ssrn.com/abstract=1436468.

Brown, S., W. Goetzmann, B. Liang, and C. Schwarz, Mandatory discosule and operational risk: Ebidend from hedge fund registration, *The Journal of Finance* 63, 2008a, 2785–2815.

Brown, S., W. Goetzmann, B. Liang, and C. Schwarz, Estimating operational risk for hedge funds: the omega-score, *Financial Analysts Journal* 65, 2008b, 43–33.

Brown, S., W. Goetzmann and J. Park, *Hedge Funds and the Asian Currency Crisis of 1997*, Working paper, National Bureau of Economic Research, May 1998.

Brown, S., W. Goetzmann and J. Park, "Conditions for Survival: Changing Risk and the Performance of Hedge Fund Managers and CTA," *Journal of Finance*, 56, 5, 2001, 1869–86.

Burton, K., A. Effinger and A. Levy, *Top Hedge Fund Returning 45% Under Julian Robertson's 36-Year-Old Disciple*, Bloomberg Magazine, January 2012.

Butler, D., G. Swart and W. Keunen, "Automation, Specialisation and Consolidation," *Risk and Reward*, October 2001, 28–31.

Caldwell T., "Introduction: The Model for Superior Performance," in *Hedge Funds: Investment and Portfolio Strategies for the Institutional Investor*, Jess Lederman and Robert A. Klein, McGraw-Hill: New York, 1995.

Capco, *Understanding and Mitigating Operational Risk in Hedge Fund Investments*, Research and Working Paper, 2002, 13p.

Capocci D., "Hedge Fund Daily Returns: A Prelaminary Analysis," in Finance and valeur(s): Liber Amicorum and Discipulorum, Les Editions de l'Université de Liège, 2009, 255p.

Capocci, D., F. Duquenne and G. Hübner, "Diversifying Using Hedge Funds: A Utility-Based Approach," University of Liège, Working paper, 2007.

Capocci, D. and G. Hübner, *Funds of Hedge Funds: Bias and Persistence in Returns,* in *Fund of Hedge Funds: Performance, Assessment, Diversification and Statistical Properties,* 2006, Elsevier Press.

Capocci, D. and V. Nevolo, "Funds of Hedge Funds versus Portfolios of Hedge Funds, in Hedge Funds: Insights in Performance Measurement," *Risk Analysis, and Portfolio Allocation,* John Wiley & Sons: New York, 2005.

Capocci, D. and G. Hübner, "The Hedge Fund Industry: Une Perspective Comparative," Revue Bancaire et Financière, July 2001, 281–92.

Capocci, D. and G. Hübner, "The hedge fund industry: une Perspective Empirique," Revue Bancaire et Financière, September 2001, 361–70.

Capocci, D. and G. Hübner, "An Analysis of Hedge Fund Performance," *Journal of Empirical Finance,* 11, 1, January 2004, 55–89.

Capocci, D. and R. Mahieu, "La corrélation entre les hedge funds et les produits d'investissement classiques," *La Revue du Financier,* 143, 2003, 4–25.

Capocci, D., *Les hedgefunds, un outil d'optimalisation de la performance du porte-feuille,* mémoire universitaire en vue de l'obtention de la licence en sciences de gestion, Université de Liège, 2000.

Capocci, D., *Hedgefunds, fonds communs and diversification du portefeuille,* Écho (Belgique), 14 December 2000, 18.

Capocci, D., *Les hedgefundsand performance du portefeuille,* AGEFI (Luxembourg), March 2001, 26–27.

Capocci, D., *Hedge Fund Performance,* Risk and Reward (UK), February 2002, 40–43.

Capocci, D., *La performance des hedge funds sous la loupe d'un expert,* AGEFI (Suisse), le 5 April 2002, 37.

Capocci, D., *Classer les Investment Strategies Alternatives,* Haute Finance (Suisse), November 2002, 110–112.

Capocci, D., *Les hedgefunds sont-ils réellement des fonds de couverture?,* Écho (Belgique), 24 May 2002, 18.

Capocci, D., *Caution trumps Risk,* Hedgenews.com, 4 April, 2003.

Capocci, D., *Les bases des hedge funds,* Le Jeudi (Luxembourg), 28 May 2003, 15.

Capocci, D., *Le développement des fonds alternatifs en Europe,* Banque Magazine, 2003a, 62–4.

Capocci, D., "La stratégie d'investissement convertible arbitrage: importance de l'hypothèse de corrélation," *Revue Bancaire and Financière,* 2003b, 166–78.

Capocci, D., "Étude comparative de la performance des hedgefunds: une approche multi-facteurs," *Banque and Marchés,* 60, 2003c, 22–31.

Capocci, D., "Inserting Convertible Arbitrage Funds in a Classical Portfolio: an Empirical Assessment," in Gregoriou, Karavas and Rouah (éd.), *Performance Evaluation of Hedge Funds: A Quantitative Approach,* Beard Books, Washington DC, 2004a.

Capocci, D., "CTA Performance and Survivorship Bias," in Gregoriou, Karavas and Rouah (éd.), *CTA Performance,* Beard Books, Washington, 2004b.

Capocci, D. *An Analysis of Hedge Fund Strategies,* Ph.D. Thesis, Université de Liège, 2007, freely available on www.ssrn.com.

Capocci, D., "Le développement des hedgefunds en 2007," *Revue Bancaire and Financière,* 2008, 55–64.

Carhart, M., *Survivor Bias and Mutual Funds Performance,* Ph.D. Dissertation, School of Business Administration, University of Southern California, 1995.

Carhart, M., "On Persistence in Mutual Fund Performance," *Journal of Finance,* 52, 1, 1997, 57–82.

Carhart, M., J. N. Carpenter, A. W. Lynch,and D.K. Musto, "Mutual Fund Survivorship," *Review of Financial Studies*,15, 5, 2002, 1439–63.

Cassar, G. and Gerakos, J., *Determinants of Hedge Fund Internal Controls and Fees. Chicago Booth Initiative on Global Markets*, The University of Chicago, Working Paper No. 46, June 2009.

Chapman and Cutler, "Dodd-Frank: Impact on Asset Management," information for investment advisers, broker-dealers and investment funds, January 1, 2012

Chapman, Spira and Carson, *Hedge Funds and their Effect on the Pacific Rim Crisis*, Chapman, Spira, and Carson Report, May 1999.

Chen, Y. and B. Liang, "Do Market Timing Hedge Funds Time the Market?," *Journal of Financial and Quantitative Analysis*, 40, 1, 2005, 493–517.

Commission de Surveillance du Secteur Financier Luxembourg, *Circulaire CSSF 20/80*, 5 December 2002.

Corsetti, G., P. Pesenti and N. Roubini, *What Caused the Asian Currency and Financial Crisis? Part I: A Macroeconomic Overview*, Working paper, National Bureau of Economic Research, 1998a.

Corsetti, G., P. Pesenti and N. Roubini, "What Caused the Asian Currency and Financial Crisis? Part II: The policy debate," Working paper, National Bureau of Economic Research, 1998b.

Cottier, P., *Hedge Funds and Managed Futures*, Université de St. Gallen, Paul Haupt (éd.), Bern, 1997.

Cullen, I., *AIMA Special Report: Marketing Hedge Funds*, Simmons and Simmons report, 1999.

Cutler, H., *Hedge Fund Risk: Perception and Reality*, Barclays Global Investors, September 2002.

Danielsson, J. and J.P. Zigrand, Regulating hedge funds, *Financial stability review*, 10 (Spec.), 2007, 29–36.

Davies, R., H. Kat and S. Lu, "Single Strategy Fund of Hedge Funds: How Many Funds?," in *Fund of Hedge Funds: Performance, Assessment, Diversification and Statistical Properties*, (ed.) Greg N. Gregoriou, Elsevier, 2006, pp. 203–10.

Davis, Polk and Wardwell, L. L. P., *Impact of the Dodd-Frank Act on Private Equity Funds, Hedge Funds and their Investment Advisers*, Private Equity Newsletter.

Deloitte, *Precautions that Pays Off: Risk Management and Valuation Practices in the Global Hedge Fund Industry*, Deloitte Research Study, 2007, 20p.

Deutsche Bank, *Deutsche Bank Alternative Investment Survey Identifies Investor Expectations for 2013*, Research Report, February 2013, 115p.

Di Gioia, G. *Funds of Hedge Funds: The Importance of Manager Selection*, Rasiniand Co, Special Report, 2001.

Diez de los Rios A. and R. Garcia, *Assessing and Valuing the Non-Linear Structure of Hedge Fund Returns*, Working Papers 06-31, Bank of Canada, 2006.

Dodd, R and M. Paul, *Outbreak: US Suprime Contagion*, Finance and Development, Vol 45, N. 2, June 2008.

Dodd, R., "Subprime: Tentacles of a Crisis," *Finance & Development*, 44, December 2007, 15–19.

Douglas, P., "Asian Markets Shows Its Maturity," Hedgeweek, April 2007, 8–11.

Dornbusch, R., I. Goldfajnand and R. Valdes, "Currency Crisis and Collapses," Brookings *Papers on Economic Activity*, 1, 1995, 219–70.

Douglas, G., R. Barnett and R. D. Lewis, "Merger Arbitrage in the 1990s," *Journal of Hedge Fund Research*, 3, 3, 1996.

Dunbar, N., "Meriwether's Meltdown," *Risk*, October 1998, 32–6.

Edwards, F. R., "Hedge Funds and the Collapse of Long-Term Capital Management," *Journal of Economic Perspectives*, 2, 13, 1999, 189–210.

Edwards, F. R. and M. O. Caglayan, "Hedge Fund and Commodity Fund Investments in Bull and Bear Markets," *Journal of Portfolio Management*, 27, 4, 2001, 97–108.

Edwards, F. R. and J. Liew, "Hedge Funds Versus Manager Futures as Asset Classes," *Journal of Derivatives*, 6, 1999, 45–64.

Eichengreen, B. and D. Mathieson (Avec, B. Chadha, A. Jansen, L. Kodres and S. Sharma), "Hedge Funds and Financial Market Dynamics," *International Monetary Fund*, Occasional Paper, 1998.

Elton, E., M. Gruber, S. Das and C. Blake, "The Persistence of Risk-adjusted Mutual Fund Performance," *Journal of Business*, 69, 2, 1996, 133–57.

Elton, E., M. Gruber, S. Das and M. Hlavka, "Efficiency with Costly Information: A Re-interpretation of Evidence from Managed Portfolios," *Review of Financial Studies* 6, 1, 1993, 1–21.

Ennis, R. M. and M. D. Sebastian, "A Critical Look at the Case for Hedge Funds," *Journal of Portfolio Management*, 29, 4, 2003, 103–12.

Erne, B., "The 10 Biggest Mutual Funds: Are They Really Worth Your Money?," *Forbes*, August 8 2012.

Eurekahedge, *Key Trends in European Hedge Funds*, White Paper, www.eurekahedge. com, August 2007.

Eurekahedge, *Key Trends in American Hedge Funds*, White Paper, www.eurekahedge. com, October 2007.

Eurekahedge, *Key Trends in Asian Hedge Funds*, White Paper, www.eurekahedge. com, March 2007.

Eurekahedge, *The Eurekahedge Report*, Research Report, August 2012 (2012a).

Eurekahedge, *The Eurekahedge Report*, Research Report, September 2012 (2012b).

Eurekahedge, *The Eurekahedge Report*, Research Report, October 2012 (2012c).

Eurohedge, *How to Start a European Hedge Fund*, Special Report, Benhill, 1999.

Fabozzi F., *Handbook of Mortgage Backed Securities*, fifth edition, McGraw-Hill, 2001.

Fama, E. and K. French, "Common Risk Factors in the Returns on Stocks and Bonds," *Journal of Financial Economics*, 33, 1, 1993, 3–56.

Farley, M., *Malaysian Leaders*, Soros Trade Barbs, Los Angeles Times, September 22, 1997.

Ferretti M., M. Gian and A. Razin, *Sustainability of Persistent Current Account Deficits*, Working paper, National Bureau of Economic Research, 1996a.

Ferretti M., M. Gian and A. Razin, *Current Account Sustainability : Selected East Asian and Latin American Experiences*, Working paper, National Bureau of Economic Research, 1996b.

Fiford, C., "South African Hedge Fund Industry Grows by Stealth," *AIMA Journal*, February 2004.

FIN Alternatives, *Soros, Paulson Post Biggest Returns Since Inception*, 13 September 2010.

International Monetary Fund, *International Capital Markets: PartI. Exchange Rate Management and International Capital Flows and Part II: Systemic Issues in International Finance*, World Economic and Financial Surveys, 1993.

International Monetary Fund, *Capital Markets: Developments, Prospects and Key Policy Issues*, World Economic and Financial Surveys, 1995.

International Monetary Fund, *1998 Annual Report of the International Monetary Fund*.

Fothergill, M. and C. Coke, *Funds of Hedge Funds: An Introduction to Multi-Manager Funds*, Europe Alternative Investment, Deutsche Bank Report, August 2000.

Frankel, J. and S. Schmukler, "Country Fund Discounts and the Mexican Crisis of December 1994: Did Local Residents Turn Pessimistic before International Investors?," *Open Economic Review*, 7, supplement 1, 1996, 511–34.

Freed, S., *An Overview of Long/short Equity Investing*, Working paper, William Mercer Investment Consulting, November 1999.

Fung, W. and D. Hsieh, "Hedge Fund Replication Strategies: Implications for Investors and Regulators," *Banque de France*, Financial Stability Review, Special issue on hedge funds, 2007.

Fung, W. and D. Hsieh, "Empirical Characteristics of Dynamic Trading Strategies: The Case of Hedge Funds," *Review of Financial Studies*, 10, 1997, 275–302.

Fung, W. and D. Hsieh, "Performance Characteristics of Hedge Funds and Commodity Funds: Natural vs Spurious Biases," *Journal of Quantitative and Financial Analysis*, 35, 2000, 291–307.

Fung, W. and D. Hsieh, "The Risk in Hedge Fund Strategies: Theory and Evidence from Trend Followers," *Review of Financial Studies*, 14, 2, 2001, 313–41.

Fung, W. and D. Hsieh, *A Risk Neutral Approach to Valuing Trend Following Trading Strategies*, Working Paper. Duke University, Durham, NC, 1998.

Fung, W. and D. Hsieh, "Is Mean-Variance Analysis applicable to Hedge Funds?," *Economics Letters*, 62, 1, 1999, 53–8.

Fung, W. and D. Hsieh, "The Risks in Fixed Income Hedge Fund Styles," *Journal of Fixed Income*, 12, 2, 2002a, 6–27.

Fung, W. and D. Hsieh, "Benchmarks of Hedge Fund Performance: Information Content and Measurement Biases," *Financial Analyst Journal*, 58, 2002b, 22–34.

Fung, W. and D. Hsieh, "Hedge Funds: An Industry in Its Adolescence," *Economic Review*, 91, 4, 2006, 81–91.

Furfine, C., *The Costs and Benefits of Moral Suasion: Evidence from the Rescue of Long-Term Capital Management*, Bank for International Settlements, 2001.

Gopalan S., *Survey Reveals over US$3.4 Billion under Management in Asia*, www.hedgeworld.com, 3 July 2001.

Gray, S., *Foreign Investors Embrace the Latin Hedge Fund Boom*, Hedgeweek, October 2006, 3–6.

Greenlaw, David, Jan Hatzius, Anil K. Kashyap and Hyun Song Shin, "Leveraged Losses: Lessons from the Mortgage Market Meltdown," paper presented at the U.S. Monetary Policy Forum Conference, 29 February 2008.

Greenspan, A., *Remarks before the 34th Annual Conference on Bank Structure and Competition*, Federal Reserve Bank of Chicago, May 1998.

Greenspan, A., *Private Sector Refinancing of the Large Hedge Fund, Long-Term Capital Management*, Testimony before the Committee on Banking and Financial Services, US Congress, Washington, October 1998.

Gregoriou, G., "Hedge Fund Survival Lifetimes," *Journal of Asset Management*, 3, 3, 2000, 237–52.

Georgiev, G., "Benefits of Commodity Investments," *Journal of Alternative Investments*, 4, 2001, 40-48.

Gregoriou, G. and F. Rouah, "Random Walk Behavior of CTAs Returns," *Journal of Alternative Investments*, 6, 2, 2003, 51–6.

Gregoriou, G.N., G. Hubner, N. Papageorgiou and F. Rouah. "Dominating Funds of Funds with Simple Hedge Fund Strategies." In *Fund of Hedge Funds: Performance, Assessment, Diversification and Statistical Properties*, Gregoriou, G.N. (ed.), Elsevier, 2006.

Guide to Structured Products, SG Corporate and Investment Banking.

Haden-Guest, A., "Top Billionaire Art Collectors," site internet du magazine *Forbes*, 8 March 2005.

Harcourt, "Hedge Funds and their Risks," Harcourt Investment Consulting Report.

Holt, A., "Regulating Hedge Funds won't work," *Portfolio International*, October 1998.

Hoogvelt, A., Chapter 10 *The Developmental States of East Asia" in "Globalization and the Postcolonial World: The New Political Economy of Development*, Johns Hopkins Press, 2001.

Hubner, G. and N. Papageorgiou, "Optional and Conditional Components in Hedge Fund Returns," *Working Paper Series*, October 2006, available at SSRN: http://ssrn.com/abstract=891425

Institutional Investor, *Hedge Funds: Who Is the Best of the Best ?*, 25 May 2011.

International Monetary Fund, *Global Financial Stability Report*, April 2008 (Washington).

International Committee of the fourth international, *More Questions than Answers on Hedge Fund Collapse*, October 1998.

Investment Company Institute, *2012 Investment Company Fact Book*, 52nd Edition.

Irwin, S., C. R. Zulaf and B. Ward, "The Predictability of Managed Futures Returns," *Journal of Derivatives*, Winter 1994, 20–27.

Jaeger, L. and C. Wagner, "Factor Modelling and Benchmarking of Hedge Funds: Can Passive Investments in Hedge Fund Strategies Deliver?" *Journal of Alternative Investments*, Winter 2005, 9–36.

Jagannathan, Ravi and Robert Korajczyk. "Assessing the Market Timing Performance of Managed Portfolios," *Journal of Business*, 59, 2, 1986, 217–235.

Jorion, P., "Risk Management Lessons from Long-Term Capital Management," *European Financial Management*, 6, September 2000, 277–300.

Kaiser, D. and F. Haberfelner, *Hedge Fund Biases After the Financial Crisis*, Research Paper, Centre for Practical Quantitative Finance, Frankfurt School of Finance, 2011, 27p.

Kaminsky, G., S. Lizondo and C. Reinhart, "Leading Indicators of Currency Crisis," *IMF Staff Papers*, March 1998.

Kat, H., *In Search of the Optimal Fund of Hedge Funds*, Cass Business School Research Paper, October 2002.

Kat, H and H. Palaro, "Hedge Fund Returns: You Can Make Them Yourself!" *Journal of Wealth Management*, 8, 2005, 62–68.

Kat, H. M. and H. P. Palaro, *Who Needs Hedge Funds? A Copula-Based Approach to Hedge Fund Return Replication*, Alternative Investment Research Centre Working Paper No. 27, November 2005.

Kat, H. M. and G. S. Amin, "Stocks, Bonds, and Hedge Funds," *Journal of Portfolio Management*, 29, 4, 2003, 113–20.

Kat, H. M. and J. Miffre, *Hedge Fund Performance: The Role of Non-Normality Risks and Conditional Asset Allocation*, Working paper WP-FF-21–2005, Cass Business School, 2005.

Kazemi, H., "The Stability of Variance and Return Forecasts: A Monte Carlo Simulation," *CISDM Working Paper*, University of Massachusetts, 1996.

Keating, C. and W. Shadwick. "A Universal Performance Measure," *Journal of Performance Measurement*, Spring 2002, 59–84.

Kooli, M., "The diversification benefits of hedge funds and funds of hedge funds," Derivatives Use, *Trading & Regulation*, 12, 4, 2007, 290–300.

Krugman, P., *What Happened to Asia*, mimeo, MIT, 1998.

Lederman, S., *Financial Products Fundamentals*, Clifford E. Kirsch (ed.), Practising Law Institute Press, 2001.

Lejonvarn, J. and C. Lekander, *Part 1: The Case for Market Neutral*, Barra report, 1999.

Lhabitant, F.-S, "Assessing Market Risk for Hedge Fund and Hedge Funds Portfolio," *Journal of Risk Finance*, 2, 4, 2001, 16 – 32.

Lewis, M., "How the Eggheads Cracked," *New York Times*, 24 January 1999.

Liang, B., "On the Performance of Hedge Funds," *Financial Analysts Journal*, 1999, 72–85.

Liang, B., "Hedge Funds: The Living and the Dead," *Journal of Financial and Quantitative Analysis*, 35, 2000, 309–25.

Liang, B., "Hedge Funds Performance: 1990–1999," *Financial Analysts Journal*, January/February 2001, 11–18.

Liang, B., *On the Performance of Alternative Investments: CTAs, Hedge Funds, and Funds-of-Funds*, Working Paper, Case Western Reserve University, Cleveland, 2003.

Liew, J., "Hedge Fund Index Investing Examined," *Journal of Portfolio Management*, 29, 2, 2003, 113–23.

Lintner, J., *The Potential Role of Managed Commodity-Financial Futures Accounts in Portfolios of Stocks and Bonds*. Annual Conference of the Financial Analysts Federation, Toronto, Canada, 1983.

Lo, A., "Risk Management for Hedge Funds: Introduction and Overview," *Financial Analyst Journal*, 57, 6, 2001, 16–33.

Loomis, C., "The Jones Nobody Keeps up with," *Fortune*, April 1966, 237–47.

Loomis, C., "Hard Times Come to the Hedge Funds," *Fortune*, January 1970, pp. 100–103 and 134–38.

Lowenstein, R., The Rise and Fall of Long-Term Capital Management: When Genius Failed, Random House Edition, 2000.

Lummer, S. and M. Riepe, "Convertible Bonds as an Asset Class: 1957–1992," *Journal of Fixed Income*, 3, 2, 1993, 47–57.

Mahathi, M., "Highwaymen of the Global Economy," *Wall Street Journal*, 23 September 1997.

Malkiel, B. and A. Saha, "Hedge Funds: Risk and Return," *Financial Analyst Journal*, 61, 6, 2005, 80–8.

Markowitz, H., "Portfolio Selection," *Journal of Finance*, 7, 1952, 77–91.

McCarthy D, T. Schneeweis and R. Spurgin, "Investments through CTS: An Alternative Managed Futures Investment," *Journal of Derivatives*, 3, 4, Summer 1996, 36–47.

McGovern, J., Chairman AIMA Canada, "Hedge Fund Industry in Canada," 2004.

McGuire, P., E. Remolona and K. Tsatsaronis, "Time-Varying Exposures and Leverage in Hedge Funds," *BIS Quarterly Review*, 2005, 59–72.

Mediratta, M., "European Hedge Funds: An Outlook for 2002," *Journal of Wealth Management*, 5, 1, 2002, 39–46.

Mishkin, F., "Understanding Financial Crises: A Developing Country Perspective," Working paper No. 5 600, National Bureau of Economic Research, May 1996.

Mitchell, M. and T. Pulvino, "Characteristics of Risk and Return in Risk Arbitrage," *Journal of Finance*, 56, 6, 2001, 2135–75.

Navone, M., *Diversifying Market Risk through Market Neutral Strategies*, Working paper, IEIF Bocconi University, 2001.

Nicholas, J., *Investing in Hedge Funds: Strategies for the New Marketplace*, Bloomberg Press, Princeton, 1999.

Nicholas, J., *Market Neutral Investing: Long/Short Hedge Fund Strategies*, Bloomberg Press, Princeton, 2000.

Oberuc, R. E., *Performance of Hedge Funds Relative to Traditional Investments*, Working paper, LaPorte Asset Allocation System.

Osborn, S., "Is there Enough Depth in the Talent Pool?," *International Fund Investment*, 10, October 2001, 23–6.

Osborn, S., "Why the Choice of Offshore Domicile Matters?," *International Fund Investment*, 11, April 2002, 49–55.

Park, J., *Managed Futures as an Investment Set*, Ph.D. Dissertation, Columbia University, 1995.

Peltz, L. *Life Cycle of a Hedge Fund : a Qualitative and Quantitative Look at how long a Fund stays in Existence*, Hedge MAR no 68, August 1999.

Perez M., "Capitalist Tools; Jiang Zemin; George Soros," *The New Republic*, Cambridge Diarist, 24 November 1997.

Posthuma, N., and P. J. Van der Sluis, *Analyzing Style Drift in Hedge Funds*, in Hedge Funds, G. Gregoriou, G. Hübner, N. Papageorgiou and F. Rouah (ed.) Wiley, 2005.

Posthuma, N. and P. J. Van der Sluis, *A Reality Check on Hedge Fund Returns*, Working paper ABP Investments, 2003.

Preqin, Does *"2 and 20" Still Exist? Results of Preqin's Hedge Fund Terms & Conditions Survey – Fees Special Report*, Research Report, July 2009, 6p.

President's Working Group on Financial Markets, *Hedge Funds, Leverage, and the Lessons of Long Term Capital Management*, April 1999.

Pricewaterhouse Coopers, *A Second Wind: The Regulation, Taxation and Distribution of Hedge Funds around the Globe*, Hedge Fund Whitepaper, 2010.

Rao, R. and J. Szilagyi, *The Coming Évolution of Hedge Fund Industry: a Case for Growth and Restructuring*, LLP/RR Capital Management Corp, March 1998.

Robertson, W., "Hedge Funds Miseries," *Fortune*, May 1971, 269.

Robinson, E., "The Outsiders : Short-sellers Profit from Wall Street's Pain," *Bloomberg Markets*, June 2003, 23–32.

Robson, R., "Starting an Alternative Investment Fund: a Practical Guide," *Robson Rhodes Special Report*, May 2001.

Rosner, J., "Stopping the Subprime Crisis," *NY Times*, 25 July 2007.

Roubini, N. and P. Wachtel, "Current Account Sustainability in Transition Economies," Working paper No. 6468, National Bureau of Economic Research, March 1998.

Russell Research, *Russell Investments Global Survey: Alternatives become mainstream*, Russell Research, 2007.

Russell Research, *Russell Investments 2010 Global Survey on Alternative Investing*, Russell Research, 2010, 16p.

Russell Research, *Russell Investments 2012 Global Survey on Alternative Investing*, Russell Research, 2012, 20p.

Rzepczynski, M and F. Neubauer, *Managed Futures in a Funds-of-Funds: there is Value with Style Diversification*, John W. Henry and Company, Information Series.

Securities and Exchange Commission, *Dodd-Frank Act Changes to Investment Adviser Registration Requirements – Preliminary Results*, 12 October 2012.

Securities and Exchange Commission, *35th Annual Report for the Fiscal Year ended June 30th*, Washington: Government Printing Office, 1969.

Schneeweis, T., "The Benefits of Managed Futures," *AIMA working paper*, 1996.

Schneeweis, T., "Dealing with Myths of Hedge Fund Investment," *Journal of Alternative Investments*, hiver 1998, 9–17.

Schneeweis, T. and R. Spurgin,. *Managed Futures, Hedge Funds and Mutual Fund Return Estimation: A Multi-Factor Approach*, Working paper, CISDM, University of Armhest, 1997.

Schneeweiss, T. & Georgiev, "The Benefits of Managed Futures," *Working Paper*, CISDM, University of Massachusets, 2002.

Schneeweis, T. and R. Spurgin, "Multi-Factor Analysis of Hedge Funds, Managed Futures and Mutual Fund Return and Risk Characteristics," *Journal of Alternative Investment*, 1, 1998, 1–24.

Schneeweis, T. and R. Spurgin, *Multi-Factor Models in Managed Futures, Hedge Funds and Mutual Fund Estimation,"* Working paper, CISDM, University of Armhest, 1999.

Schneeweis, T., H. Kazemi and G. Martin, *Understanding Hedge Fund Performance*, Research Paper, Lehman Brother, 2001.

Schneeweis, T. and R. Spurgin, "Quantitative Analysis of Hedge Funds and Managed Futures Return and Risks Characteristics," in *Evaluating and Implementing Hedge Fund Strategies*, Third Edition: The Experience of Managers and Investors, Institutional Investor Publishing, 2003.

Sharpe, W. F., "Capital Asset Prices: A Theory of Market Equilibrium under Conditions of Risk," *Journal of Finance*, 19, 3, 1964, 425–42.

Sharpe, W. F., "Mutual Fund Performance," *Journal of Business*, January 1966, 119–138.

Sharpe, W. F., "Asset Allocation: Management Style and Performance Measurement," *Journal of Portfolio Management*, 18, 2, 1992, 7–19.

Soros, G., *Letter to Shareholder from Soros Fund Management*, HedgeFund.net, 28 April 2000.

Sribala, S., *Selection of the Reader's Digest*, February 1996.

Strachman, D., *Getting Started in Hedge Funds*, John Wiley and Sons, 2000.

Strom, S., "Top Manager To Close Shop On Hedge Funds," *New York Times*, 12 October 1995, p. D1.

Subramannian, S., "A Farewell to Hedges," *Time Magazine*, 23 October 1995.

Suduk, K., "Currency Crisis in Korea –When and Why It Happened," *Asia-Pacific Financial Markets*, 7, 2000, 11–30.

Swinkels, L. and P. Van Der Sluis, "Return-based Style Analysis with Time-varying Exposures, Computing in Economics and Finance", *Society for Computational Economics*, 125, 2001.

Temple, P., "Long/short Equity – The Original Hedge Fund," *International Fund Investment*, 9, November 2001, 36–41.

Temple, P., "Institutions Waking up to Hedge Funds," *International Fund Investment*, 10, December 2001, 29–32.

Thill, H., *EDHEC Comments on the Amaranth Case*, Working paper, September 2006, 23p.

Tian, T., *Is the Dodd-Frank Act a Game Changer for Hedge Funds? Why this Mammoth Legislation will have a Profound Impact on Hedge Funds*, Morningstar Advisor, February 2, 2012.

Tremont Partners Inc. and TASS Investment Research: The Case for Hedge Funds, *The Journal of Alternative Investments*, Winter 1999, 71–72.

Tremont TASS Investment Research Limited, *The Case for Hedge Funds*, 2ème édition, April 2001.

Vickers, M., *The Most Powerful Trader on Wall Street You've Never Heard Of* cover story, Business Week, July, 2003.

Wall Street Journal, "Tiger Fund has September Loss of $2.1 Billion," *Wall Street Journal*, 17 September, 1998, p. C1.

Weisman, A., "Informationless Investing and Hedge Fund Performance Measurement Bias," *Journal of Portfolio Management*, 28, 4, 2002, 80–91.

Worthington, R.L., *Alternative Investments and the Semi-afluent Investor*, Research Report, Undiscovered Managers, Dallas, Texas, 2001.

Yoder, J., *Endowment Management: A Practical Guide*, Association of Governing Boards of Universities and College, Washington DC, 2004.

Zeba, A. and C. Grünig, *The European Hedge Fund Industry: An Overview,"* SwissHedge, Harcourt AG, 3ème trimestre 2002, pp. 8–12.

Index

Printed by Printforce, the Netherlands